CULTURAL HERITAGE LAW AND POLICY

Series Editors

PROFESSOR FRANCESCO FRANCIONI

Professor of International Law and Human Rights and Co-Director of the Academy of European Law at the European University Institute in Florence

PROFESSOR ANA VRDOLJAK

Associate Dean (Research) and Professor of Law, University of Technology, Sydney

State Succession in Cultural Property

CULTURAL HERITAGE LAW AND POLICY

The aim of this series is to publish significant and original research on and scholarly analysis of all aspects of cultural heritage law through the lens of international law, private international law, and comparative law. The series is wide in scope, traversing disciplines, regions, and viewpoints. Topics given particular prominence are those which, while of interest to academic lawyers, have significant bearing on policy making and current public discourse on the interaction between art, heritage, and the law.

State Succession in Cultural Property

ANDRZEJ JAKUBOWSKI

OXFORD
UNIVERSITY PRESS

OXFORD
UNIVERSITY PRESS

Great Clarendon Street, Oxford, OX2 6DP,
United Kingdom

Oxford University Press is a department of the University of Oxford. It furthers the University's objective of excellence in research, scholarship, and education by publishing worldwide. Oxford is a registered trade mark of Oxford University Press in the UK and in certain other countries

First Edition published in 2015

Published in the United States of America by Oxford University Press
198 Madison Avenue, New York, NY 10016, United States of America

British Library Cataloguing in Publication Data
Data available

Library of Congress Control Number: 2015941227

ISBN 978–0–19–873806–0

Series Editors' Preface

At a time when the understandings of states and their role in international law is being fundamentally challenged, Andrzej Jakubowski's book on state succession in cultural property squarely addresses these transformations and provides them with a much needed historical context. In so doing, it embodies an important aim of this book series, to place issues concerning the protection of cultural heritage squarely within the field of international law, broadly understood.

The break-up of federations after the Cold War and emergence of new states in recent years has reignited interest among international lawyers in state succession once again. While it is a recurring theme in the development of international law in the modern era, its application to cultural property has not been examined in a coherent and dedicated fashion. This book fills this gap by critically examining the principles and practices relating to state succession with respect to tangible cultural property, including succession in related rights and obligations under treaty and customary international law. This alone is an important contribution. However, as the author himself flags, this work is not confined to a positivist reading of the current law.

International law and related state practice is often in a state of flux and indeterminacy. Accordingly, the longer term contribution of this book is the author's recognition of the precariousness of the state in present day international law and international relations – despite (or perhaps because) of its centrality to his topic. He does this by engaging fully with developments in international human rights law, humanitarian law and cultural heritage law, and explaining their pertinence to a fuller, more cogent understanding of state succession in cultural property and as complementary considerations to the traditional criterion of territoriality in the event of a redrawing of national boundaries. This approach provides a sound rationale and a valuable source of innovative criteria for the future evolution of the law.

Francesco Francioni and Ana Filipa Vrdoljak

Preface

The allocation of cultural treasures in cases of state succession has always stimulated heated disputes and attracted public attention. Conflicts have been exacerbated and legal solutions hindered because of the strong emotions attached to cultural heritage and the rancour that sometimes flows from bitter memories. Having been born and raised in Poland, the country which in the past 100 years drastically changed its territorial boundaries and ethnic composition, I am accustomed to the overwhelming nature of the discourse on identity, lost heritage, and restitution. Assessments of past attitudes to history and contradictions between present uniform national identity and past multicultural traditions have always been an important element of public life in Poland, especially since 1989. In fact, following the political breakthrough almost every country of the former Eastern bloc initiated the long-awaited discussion regarding rights to cultural heritage hindered by the post-Second World War Potsdam agreements and Cold War ideological considerations. Observation of this explosion of previously suppressed national sentiments led me to focus my legal studies on international heritage law in search of universal answers to local problems.

The topic of state succession in cultural property is not new to international practice and scholarship. Indeed, attempts to provide a legal framework for the cultural aspects of state succession have been undertaken in international practice and legal scholarship since at least the mid-nineteenth century. These were strictly bound to the origin of the European nation-state, determining its territorial boundaries according to ethnic and cultural divisions. However, the set of principles applied to the allocation and distribution of cultural material did not take a form of any legally binding international instrument. In fact, the issue was neglected by international lawyers and scholars for several years following the era of decolonization, marked by the failure of colonized peoples and indigenous communities to recover their cultural patrimony from former colonial powers. The major doctrinal efforts were focused on the topic of self-determination of peoples and economic aspects of state succession—core questions for international legal order and political stability during the Cold War and decolonization. In this context, the cultural heritage dimension of state succession was perceived as a secondary issue.

The fall of the Berlin Wall and the subsequent dissolution of the Cold War political and territorial system, followed by the Balkan and now the Ukrainian crises, have once again put the issue on the table. Yet the doctrinal response to the current international practice seems unsatisfactory. As exemplified in the 2001 Resolution of the Institute of International Law (IIL), entitled *State Succession in Matters of Property and Debts,* the majority of legal scholarship focuses on the allocation of tangible cultural heritage based on two paramount criteria: territorial provenance and major cultural significance for a given state. Such an approach also provides for the solutions largely based on the mechanical application of the territoriality principle, *uti possidetis*, and exclusive territorial competence with regard to cultural property.

This book arises from the criticism of the existing traditional legal constructions, as they arguably do not recognize the important evolution from the narrowly defined 'cultural property' towards a broader, more human-oriented idea of 'cultural heritage'. Such a conceptual shift has occurred in the last 50 years, marked by the gradual recognition of the fundamental role performed by cultural manifestations in the preservation of human dignity and the continuous development of all mankind. I endeavour to analyse to what extent the practice and the theory of state succession reflect this evolution, by reconstructing the principles regulating interstate arrangements with regard to such matters in a broad historical and geographical framework. I attempt to identify the peculiarity of cultural heritage in its relation with the human communities, groups, and individuals who have created, maintained and enjoyed such a heritage. These, therefore, have a definite interest in staking their claim to the inherent link with their natural cultural heritage and not seeing it disappear by virtue of territorial vicissitudes and political changes involved in state succession. This observation leads the analysis towards the topic of international cultural heritage obligations and their content, sources, and status in state succession. Indeed, the very essence of the international heritage law is grounded in the conviction that cultural heritage concerns go beyond state sovereignty and thus touch upon the area of human rights. Moreover, these interests and values are also perceived as being vested in the international community as a whole. In fact, the recent international practice of state succession in cultural property seems to be moving towards international cultural cooperation, and beyond mere restitution and distribution considerations.

Thus, the core objective of this book is to offer a new doctrinal approach, based both on the principles of international cultural heritage law and human rights law. This implies the limitation of the contractual freedom of states in the matter of cultural agreements, in favour of the continuity of international cultural heritage obligations in cases of state succession. According to such a lens, the book also proposes a list of guiding principles relating to the succession of states in respect of tangible cultural heritage, which may contribute to the further development of both academic debate and international practice.

Andrzej Jakubowski

Acknowledgements

Like most scholarly efforts, this one is heavily indebted to many institutions and individuals. It is a pleasure to thank them now in print. Research for this book has been possible by a Polish national doctoral grant at the Law Department of the European University Institute, which provided me with excellent institutional support. I would also like to acknowledge the assistance of the Max-Planck Institute for Comparative and Private International Law in Hamburg, and the Max-Planck Institute for Comparative Public Law and International Law in Heidelberg.

I am very fortunate to have been able to receive guidance from my supervisor, Francesco Francioni, who constantly encouraged me in my research and showed me the true meaning of academic excellence and professionalism. I thank him for his patience, support, and enthusiasm wholeheartedly. I have also greatly benefited from the constant exchange of ideas and information with Ana Filipa Vrdoljak, whose work, *International Law, Museums and the Return of Cultural Objects* (2006), has always provided inspiration for my research.

The actual choice of the topic of this book owes a lot to Kurt Siehr, to whom I am extremely grateful. For suggestions, advice, and useful clarifications at different moments of my research, I should thank Lyndell V. Prott, Nawojka Cieślińska-Lobkowicz, Kerstin Odendahl, Wojciech Kowalski, Cynthia Scott, and Władysław Czapliński. This study also benefited from the comments of participants in the three consecutive sessions of the international annual seminar 'Kunst und Recht' (Art and Law), organized in 2008–2010 in Berlin, Vienna, and Munich, where I presented parts of my work in draft form. Special thanks for stimulating discussions and feedback go to the members of the Working Group on Cultural Heritage at the European University Institute: Adriana Bessa Da Costa Antunes Rodrigues, Alessandro Chechi, Lucas Lixinski, Jeanne-Marie Panayotopoulos, Robert Peters, Valentina Vadi, and Amy Strecker to whom I am also very grateful for her much appreciated linguistic revision of vast sections of this book.

An important part of my research is based on fact-finding and case-study analysis which would never have been possible without the generosity and professional assistance of many people. In particular, I would like to acknowledge Mečislav Borák, Silesian Land's Museum, Opava, Czech Republic; Esko Häkli, Helsinki University Library, University of Helsinki, Finland; Miha Pogačnik, Faculty of Law, University of Nova Gorica, Slovenia; Piotr Kosiewski, the Batory Foundation, Warsaw; Serhij Kot, Institute of History of Ukraine in Kyiv, National Academy of Science of Ukraine; Michał Michalski, Ministry of Culture and National Heritage, Poland; Solvita Zvidriņa, Ministry of Culture, Latvia; Majda Širca and Silvester Gaberščcek, Ministry of Culture, Slovenia; Ljubica Stefanovska, Ministry of Culture, Republic of Macedonia; Dino Zulumović, Commission to

Preserve National Monuments, Bosnia–Herzegovina; and Jovita Mikalkėnaitė, Ministry of Foreign Affairs, Lithuania.

I would like also to thank Emma Endean, and the staff at Oxford University Press for making the production of this book a pleasant process.

Last but not least, I wish to thank my family for their unfailing encouragement, patience, and optimism which gave me the strength in the last miles of this journey.

Contents

II. CONSOLIDATION AND CODIFICATION OF THE LAW (1940–1989)

III. BUILDING A NEW CONSENSUS ON CULTURAL HERITAGE: STATE SUCCESSION AFTER 1989

Table of Cases

COUNCIL OF THE LEAGUE NATIONS

EUROPEAN COURT OF HUMAN RIGHTS

GREECE

INTER-ALLIED REPARATIONS COMMISSION (1919–1921)

INTERNATIONAL COURT OF JUSTICE

INTERNATIONAL CRIMINAL COURT FOR THE FORMER YUGOSLAVIA

ITALY

PERMANENT COURT OF INTERNATIONAL JUSTICE

UNITED STATES

Table of Instruments

INTERNATIONAL

NATIONAL

MISCELLANEOUS

List of Abbreviations

AAL	*Art Antiquity and Law*
AAS	*Acta Apostolicae Sedis*
AFDI	*Annuaire Français de Droit International*
AJIL	*American Journal of International Law*
AVR	*Archiv des Völkerrechts*
BYIL	*British Yearbook of International Law*
CanYIL	*Canadian Yearbook of International Law*
Cd, Cmd, Cmnd	*UK Command Papers*
CETS	*Council of Europe Treaty Series*
CITRA	International Conference of the Round Table on Archives
CoE	Council of Europe
Corps universel diplomatique	Jean Dumont (Baron de Carlscroon), Jean Rousset de Missy, Jean Barbeyrac, *Corps universel diplomatique du droit des gens: contenant un recueil des traites d'alliance, de paix, de trêve, de neutralité, de commerce, d'échange de neutralité, de commerce, d'échange, de protection & de garantie, de toutes les conventions, transactions, pactes, concordats, & autres contrats, qui ont été faits en Europe, depuis le règne de l'Empereur Charlemagne jusques à présent* (P. Brunel, R., and G. Wetstein, les Janssons Waesberge, et L'Honoré et Chatelain, 1726–1731)
CSCE	Conference on Security and Co-operation in Europe
CUP	Cambridge University Press
D&H	Duncker & Humblot
EEC	European Economic Community
EJIL	*European Journal of International Law*
EPC	European Political Cooperation
ETS	*European Treaty Series*
EU	European Union
GU	*Gazzetta Ufficiale della Repubblica Italiana* (Official Gazette of the Italian Republic)
GYIL	*German Yearbook of International Law*
HILJ	*Harvard International Law Journal*
ICA	International Council on Archives
ICCPR	International Covenant on Civil and Political Rights
ICESCR	International Covenant on Economic, Social and Cultural Rights
ICOM	International Council of Museums
ICJ	International Court of Justice
ICJ Reports	*International Court of Justice Reports of Judgments, Advisory Opinions and Orders*
ICLQ	*International and Comparative Law Quarterly*
ICTY	International Criminal Tribunal for the former Yugoslavia
IDI/IIL	Institut de Droit International/Institute of International Law
IJCP	*International Journal of Cultural Property*
IJHR	*International Journal of Human Rights*

ILA	International Law Association
ILC	International Law Commission
ILM	*International Legal Materials*
ILO	International Labour Organization
IYIL	*Italian Yearbook of International Law*
KFOR	Kosovo Force
LN	League of Nations
LNOJ	*League of Nations Official Journal*
LNTS	*League of Nations Treaty Series*
Martens NRGT	*Nouveau recueil général de traités et autres actes relatifs aux rapports de droit international: continuation du grand recueil de G. Fr. de Martens* (2e série, 1876–1908, 3e série, 1909–1944/69)
Martens RMPT	*Recueil manuel et pratique de traités, conventions et autres actes diplomatiques sur lesquels sont établis les relations et les rapports existants aujourd'hui entre les divers états souverains du globe, depuis l'année 1760 j'usqu'à l'époque actuelle* (2e série, 1857–88)
NATO	North Atlantic Treaty Organization
Nijhoff	Martinus Nijhoff Publishers
NILR	*Netherlands International Law Review*
OECD	Organization for Economic Co-operation and Development
OSCE	Organization for Security and Co-operation in Europe
OUP	Oxford University Press
Parry's CTS	*Parry's Consolidated Treaty Series*
PCA	Permanent Court of Arbitration
PCIJ	Permanent Court of International Justice
PCIJ ser.A/B	*Permanent Court of International Justice, Collection of Judgments, Orders and Advisory Opinions* (1931–40)
PYIL	*Polish Yearbook of International Law*
RBDI	*Revue Belge de Droit International*
RCADI	*Recueil des Cours de l'Académie de la Haye (Collected Courses of the Hague Academy of International Law)*
RGDIP	*Revue Générale de Droit International Public*
SRSG	Special Representative of the Secretary-General of the United Nations
UK	United Kingdom of Great Britain and Northern Ireland
UKTS	*United Kingdom Treaty Series*
UN	United Nations
UNESCO	The United Nations Educational, Scientific and Cultural Organization
UNGA	United Nations General Assembly
UNGA Res.	United Nations General Assembly Resolution
UNHRC	United Nations Human Rights Council
Unidroit	International Institute for the Unification of Private Law
UNMIK	United Nations Interim Administration Mission in Kosovo
UNTS	*United Nations Treaty Series*
WH	World Heritage
WHC	World Heritage Committee
WHL	World Heritage List
YBUN	*Yearbook of United Nations*
YILC	*Yearbook of International Law Commission*

Introduction

> The point about the relationship between 'identity' and 'heritage' is that they are contingent upon one another: no identity without an act of remembrance of some origin(s) and that, which is remembered as origin(s), is constructed into the identity's heritage. This makes 'history' not into an objective, independent force, but identifies 'history' as a narrative. And as all narratives, it is a created and therefore chosen one, chosen, that is, by and for particular criteria tied to fundamental decisions about human life (the existential dimension); decisions which are themselves, in turn reflections of their place and time (the social dimension)... As a modern endeavour, the question of identity found its answer in the idea of the nation and in the national state as its political, social, economic, and cultural expression.[1]

'State succession' and 'cultural heritage' are profoundly interconnected and reflective of each other. In fact, they both derive from the universal idea of 'inheritance' and express the continuity between the past and the present. Cultural heritage is a powerful repository resource of wisdom intended to be preserved, enjoyed, and enriched by the creations of present generations and handed down to future ones.[2] It is a vehicle and key provider of collective memory and identity—the factors conditioning processes of creation, dismemberment, and extinction of states, to which legal and doctrinal frameworks are provided by the theory of state succession. The latter employs the conception of succession of legal persons and applies it to different scenarios of replacement of states with regard to international obligations of territory. These also involve the legal situation of individuals and groups and their rights to cultural heritage.

Paradoxically, the historic and semantic affinities between the concepts of cultural heritage and state succession do not alleviate their reciprocal relations. Indeed, the role of cultural heritage as an assertion of one's rights and legitimacy to control a determined area may foster hostile attitudes and cause violent solutions

[1] Peter Wagner, 'From Monuments to Human Rights: Redefining "Heritage" in the Work of the Council of Europe', in *Forward Planning: The Function of Cultural Heritage in Changing Europe* (Council of Europe, 2001), 9–28, at 17, available at <http://www.coe.int/t/dg4/cultureheritage/heritage/resources/Publications/ECC-PAT%282001%29161_EN.pdf>, accessed on 15 January 2015.

[2] Lyndell V. Prott and Patrick O'Keefe, 'Cultural Heritage or Cultural Property?', *IJCP* 1(1992)2, 307–20, at 311.

to territorial disputes. Therefore, cultural heritage has often been exposed to intentional destruction, suppression, and plunder—weapons which affect human communities dramatically.[3] The history of humankind is marked by an infinite number of examples of systematic cultural cleansing performed in the name of ethnic, national, and, more precisely, cultural 'purity', driven by ideological foundations of power and statehood. In parallel, the symbolic meanings of cultural heritage often lead to opposite tendencies aimed at restoring and/or (re)constructing national identities and collective memories through physical 'repatriation' of cultural treasures, despoiled or disparaged in the past.

The control, preservation, and enjoyment of cultural heritage do not however constitute the sole concern of state sovereignty. Indeed, the protection of cultural heritage has been subject to an extensive process of legislative internationalization, motivated by the recognition of the fundamental role performed by cultural manifestations in the preservation of human dignity and the continuous development of all mankind. This book focuses on the legal effects of state succession on tangible cultural heritage and explores the principles regulating interstate arrangements with regard to such material. It does not consider the mechanisms for the creation of states as regulated under international law nor the cultural reasons for their dissolution or extinction. Neither is it about the removal and restitution of cultural assets. The central problem that the book attempts to tackle is to what extent the principles and practice of state succession reflect the evolution of the concept of cultural heritage in international law. With this aim, the book reconstructs iterations of international practice and legal doctrine of state succession to tangible cultural heritage since the formation of European nation-states in the nineteenth century, through the experience of decolonization, to the post-Cold War dissolution of multinational states. It intends to identify shortcomings, problems, contradictions, possible common trends and standards, and discusses what principles may be brought to bear on international practice in terms of normative developments.

1. The Meaning and Relevance of Cultural Heritage

Intuitively, the general meaning of the concept 'cultural heritage' does not pose any particular difficulties. For the purposes of the analysis conducted by this book, however, its legal meaning requires some clarification.[4] The term 'cultural heritage'

[3] Janet Blake, 'On Defining the Cultural Heritage', *ICLQ* 49(2000)1, 61–85, at 84.

[4] For a doctrinal reconstruction of the evolution of the concept of cultural heritage in international law, see Francesco Francioni, 'A Dynamic Evolution of Concept and Scope: From Cultural Property to Cultural Heritage', in Abdulqawi A. Yusuf (ed), *Standard-Setting in UNESCO. Normative Action in Education, Science and Culture: Essays in Commemoration of the Sixtieth Anniversary of UNESCO*, Vol. 1 (UNESCO, 2007), 221–36; for the analysis of the importance of cultural roles and narratives in shaping heritage, see Derek Gillman, *The Idea of Cultural Heritage* (2nd edn, CUP, 2010).

can be found in international legal instruments since the 1950s. It was used for the first time by the 1954 Hague Convention,[5] adopted by the United Nations Educational, Scientific and Cultural Organization (UNESCO) in response to the immense destruction and plunder of monuments and works of art during the Second World War. The Convention expresses a common understanding of the international community that the introduction of uniform measures for protection of cultural heritage in time of war constitutes the interest of 'all peoples of the world'. Under Article 1, it defines the material object of protection—cultural property as 'movable or immovable property of great importance to the cultural heritage of every people'. As the protection refers to certain tangible property, the concept of cultural heritage thus has much broader connotations. In its ordinary meaning, it consists in the sum of movable and immovable property considered significant due to its historic, artistic, or religious interest.[6] The formulation 'great importance to the cultural heritage of every people' indicates, however, the fundamental axiological dimension of cultural heritage. In this sense, it may be defined as a reservoir of all the values and interests embodied by such material evidence.[7]

Over time, the legal notion of 'cultural heritage' evolved into a more human-oriented concept, comprising both tangible as well as intangible manifestations of human intellectual and spiritual achievements. In the vast legal literature on the topic, the systematization proposed by Lyndell V. Prott deserves special attention. Prott accurately summarizes the complexity of different legal aspects of cultural heritage and lists its five main constitutive elements: 1) human-made environments which include not only immovable property, such as buildings, parks, monuments, and the like, but also 'natural sites held by human beings to be of special significance'; 2) movables encompassing 'artworks of every kind', 'objects of historic importance', archaeological objects, human and animal remains, objects of 'scientific importance', etc; 3) 'the ideas on which new skills, techniques and knowledge are built', including the ideas covered by the concept of intellectual property; 4) 'patterns of behavior and knowledge' embodied by traditional rituals, skills, ceremonies, music, theatre, etc; 5) information on all the other constitutive elements of cultural heritage, for example how music was performed, on what occasions, etc.[8] Obviously, it may be argued that this list is not exhaustive as every society has different and constantly developing means of transmitting knowledge, yet it indicates the main dimensions constituting the concept of 'cultural heritage', though each element is differently regulated by international law.

The meaning and relevance of cultural heritage is also determined by national, universal, collective, and individual interests relating to its protection and

[5] Convention for the Protection of Cultural Property in the Event of Armed Conflict, adopted on 14 May 1955, entered into force on 7 August 1956, 249 UNTS 240.

[6] See Marie Cornu, *Le droit culturel des biens. l'intérêt culturel juridiquement protégé* (Bruylant, 1996), 48–56, 121–25, 30–37; Roger O'Keefe, 'The Meaning of "Cultural Property" under the 1954 Hague Convention', *NILR* 46(1999)1, 26–56, at 34.

[7] See Francioni, 'A Dynamic Evolution' (n 4) 228–33.

[8] Lyndell V. Prott, 'Problems of Private International Law for the Protection of the Cultural Heritage', *RCADI* 217(1989)5, 215–317, at 222–24.

safeguarding.[9] As mentioned with reference to the 1954 Hague Convention, the first main rationale for the protection of cultural heritage arises from the recognition of the right of every state to identify, physically control, and protect its tangible cultural heritage against destruction and plunder in time of war. A similar state-oriented definition of cultural heritage is applied under the second rationale for international protection, which consists in prohibiting and preventing the illicit movement of cultural property in peacetime. In relation to this, the international system established by the 1970 UNESCO Convention on the Means of Prohibiting and Preventing the Illicit Import, Export and Transfer of Ownership of Cultural Property[10] implies the procedural principle of international cooperation between states in order to protect their respective national heritage.

The third rationale goes beyond the state's interest in the protection of its national cultural heritage and addresses the idea of the general interest of all mankind in the protection of world heritage of exceptional interest. This concept, introduced at the universal level by the 1972 World Heritage Convention,[11] recognizes that certain cultural and natural sites are of outstanding universal value, important for all peoples. Thus, the duty of conservation and protection of world heritage is of a general interest and rests on the international community as a whole. A similar concern is also addressed by the regime of the 2001 UNESCO Convention on the Protection of the Underwater Cultural Heritage,[12] according to which underwater cultural heritage shall be considered as a key to the study of the history of man and civilizations. Therefore, such heritage shall enjoy special status under international law for the benefit of all mankind.

The fourth rationale arises from the conviction that protection of the variety of living cultures and the promotion of diversity of their expressions lie in the general interest of all humanity. Accordingly, this rationale regards the intangible aspects of cultural heritage protected at the universal level by the 2003 UNESCO Convention for the Safeguarding of the Intangible Cultural Heritage[13] and the 2005 UNESCO Convention on the Protection and Promotion of the Diversity of Cultural Expressions.[14]

The last rationale relates to the relationship between material and non-material cultural heritage and human rights.[15] This interplay may refer both to individual rights and collective rights.[16] It appears, however, that the fundamental

[9] Frank G. Fechner, 'The Fundamental Aims of Cultural Property Law', *IJCP* 7(1998)2, 376–94, at 382–88, John H. Merryman, 'The Public Interest in Cultural Property', *California Law Review* 77(1989)3, 339–64.

[10] Adopted on 14 November 1970, entered in force 24 April 1972, 823 UNTS 231.

[11] Convention Concerning the Protection of World Natural and Cultural Heritage, adopted on 16 November 1972, entered into force on 17 December 1975, 1037 UNTS 151.

[12] Adopted on 2 November 2001, entered into force on 2 January 2009, UNESCO Doc.31C/RES.24, (2002) 41 ILM 37.

[13] Adopted on 7 October 2003, entered into force on 20 April 2006, 2368 UNTS 3.

[14] Adopted on 20 October 2005, entered into force on 18 March 2007, 2440 UNTS 311.

[15] See Suzanne L. Schairer, 'The Intersection of Human Rights and Cultural Property Issues under International Law', *IYIL* 11(2001), 59–99.

[16] Ana Filipa Vrdoljak, 'Liberty, Equality, Diversity: States, Cultures and International Law', in Ana Filipa Vrdoljak (ed), *The Cultural Dimension of Human Rights* (OUP, 2013), 26–70; Janet Blake,

significance of cultural heritage for the creation and assertion of cultural identity places the issue within the context of group and collective rights of people.[17] In particular, this interplay concerns the rights of ethnic, linguistic, and religious minorities as well as indigenous peoples to enjoy their own culture in its material and non-material dimensions. Therefore, the protection of cultural heritage is nowadays more often perceived as an important element of the human rights system.

Arguably, state succession in cultural property involves all these problems and considerations owing to the very complex meaning of cultural heritage. A change of state sovereignty over a territory affects tangible and intangible cultural heritage as well as the rights and obligations related to it. This book focuses on tangible cultural heritage as the material aspect has been the main concern of well-documented international practice and doctrine of international law. Accordingly, it refers to state succession in respect of monuments of art, archaeology, and architecture, objects and sites of science, of religious worship (*res sacrae*), and of national or a group's memory. It also concerns historic archives and libraries of major cultural and historical significance, other than mere administrative or judicial records. This work does not deal with the question of human remains, as they are not goods or materials. They are parts of the human body and can seldom be treated in terms of succession. In practice, there is a limited group of human remains which may be considered as state property (eg mummified remains of extinct civilizations preserved in state-owned museums or scientific institutions).

Generally speaking, international legal texts on state succession do not pay much attention to the fate of tangible cultural heritage. They almost exclusively deal with the question of allocation of movable state cultural property, assuming that immovable property, including cultural sites, simply shares the destiny of the territory. In fact, state succession to movable cultural property is perceived as a certain exemption from general rules on the distribution of state property and archives, and is regulated by a set of non-binding principles (guidelines), applied on a case-by-case basis. Moreover, the status of cultural heritage obligations and the relevance of cultural cooperation in state succession has not been the subject of more profound doctrinal examination.

On the other hand, the allocation and distribution of cultural assets in cases of state succession has been extensively addressed in legal literature dealing with general concepts of restitution and repatriation of cultural property. The first fundamental legal texts on this topic published by Charles de Visscher, on the occasion of the post-First World War dismantling of multinational empires,[18] systemized

'Taking a Human Rights Approach to Cultural Heritage Protection', *Heritage & Society* 4(2011)2, 199–238.

[17] Blake, 'On Defining the Cultural Heritage' (n 3) 79.

[18] Charles De Visscher, *International Protection of Works of Art and Historic Monuments* (The Department of State Publications, 1949); Charles De Visscher, 'Les monuments historique et les oevres d'art en temps de guerre et dans les traités de paix', *La protection des monuments et oevres d'art en tempes de guerre. Manuel technique et juridique* (Office International des Musées, 1939).

developments in international practice, and doctrinally distinguished the situations of restitution of cultural property displaced in armed conflicts from those referring to the allocation of such assets as a result of territorial reconfigurations. In particular, Visscher recalled the case of the dissolution of Austria–Hungary and the legal reasoning applied by an international arbitration committee deciding on the distribution of the Habsburg collections. Importantly, he reaffirmed the emergence of new principles in international law, consisting in 'unity of art and collections',[19] and 'reconstruction of artistic and historic patrimony'.[20] He also classified different bonds associating a work of art with a given territory as 'the nationality or birthplace of the artist, the bond between the work and the nation's history, the artistic tradition inspiring it... and its allocation to a certain place or for a given use.' However, these considerations were only perceived on a non-binding basis for voluntary negotiations between sovereign states. Thus, they could not be treated as customary rules of international law, although their systematization and application was recommended.[21] Moreover, he also observed that in state practice territorial and national considerations were often challenged by the principle of 'inviolability of collections forming an organic whole, the completeness of which is in itself of world-wide value'.[22]

In the post-Second World War practice of reconstruction of dispersed cultural patrimonies, the allocation of cultural assets played an important role in cases of territorial transfers. In particular, the 1947 Peace Treaty with Italy contained a very complex set of provisions on the repatriation of cultural property to Yugoslavia, based on purely territorial considerations.[23] Thus, the territorial factor conditioned the inclusion of cultural aspects of state succession in the broader discourse on restitution. In light of this, the legal literature on this topic, including widely cited works by István Vásárhelyi[24] and Wojciech Kowalski,[25] generally put forward the principle of territorial provenance to govern the situation of cultural property removed in armed conflict and territorial transfers alike. Accordingly, a successor state may have a claim based on customary international law to recover all movable cultural heritage (not only state property) removed from the territory to which succession related.

The process of decolonization modified these considerations. The representatives of newly (post-colonial) independent states developed the cultural dimension of the principle of self-determination by defining the right of every independent people to regain, enjoy, and enrich their cultural heritage. The recognition of the collective identity of a people and its sovereignty over the territory has been perceived as implying the recognition of cultural autonomy and sovereignty over

[19] Visscher, *International Protection* (n 18) 836–37. [20] Ibid. 837. [21] Ibid.

[22] Ibid. 836.

[23] Treaty of Peace with Italy, signed on 10 February 1947, entered into force on 15 September 1947, 49 UNTS 3.

[24] István Vásárhelyi, *Restitution in International Law* (Akad. Kiadó, 1964).

[25] Wojciech Kowalski, 'Repatriation of Cultural Property Following a Cession of Territory or Dissolution of Multinational States', *AAL* 6(2001)2, 139–66, Wojciech Kowalski, 'Restitution of Works of Art Pursuant to Private and Public International Law', *RCADI* 288(2001), 9–244.

cultural resources, including those dispersed in the past. Thus, a clear theoretical link between independence, cultural development, and the physical restoration of cultural material has been established, though rarely accepted by former colonial powers, reluctant to share their collections with their former colonies. Due to these controversies, the principles on state succession to material cultural heritage have never been codified. The International Law Commission (ILC) decided that state cultural property would be covered by a general regime on state succession to state property. Other objects, not forming state property, were excluded from the final text of the 1983 Vienna Convention. Obviously, such a solution was unfavourable for newly independent states since a great part of cultural material displaced or pillaged under colonial occupation could hardly be classified as state property at the date of state succession. In fact, many objects and collections were passed to different non-state entities or private collectors. Therefore, the International Law Commission proposed that the complex post-colonial claims would be determined by a specialist UNESCO Committee. It appears that the majority of legal scholarship followed this view and separated the allocation of cultural property in 'classic' scenarios of succession of states, in particular in the European context, from those concerning decolonization.[26] The first group of cases would be settled in the framework of the formula of 'repatriation' applicable in particular to cession and dissolution of a multinational state. For instance, Wojciech Kowalski argues that 'their separate treatment is predetermined by the specific nature of these changes in the legal status and by the adopted systems of legal regulation.' Accordingly, 'as a result of the cession of territory the lands are usually restored to their original state organism, in the case of dissolution, the emerging states regain their previously lost independence.' He claims that these types of state succession usually concern 'old and clearly shaped national traditions and the corresponding cultural heritage tied to these traditions and expressing a certain national character. Thus, the necessity of regulating questions of cultural heritage seems obvious and natural and should as such be treated as an element of the general succession scheme.'[27]

Inversely, the fate of cultural property removed during colonialism should be governed under the rather vague *ex gratia* regime of 'return', based more on moral considerations—adequate for cases where objects left their countries of origin prior to the crystallization of national and international law on the protection of cultural property.[28] This particularly refers to relations between new states and third-party states, as many colonial removals of cultural items were performed by third-party states and their institutions. Therefore, it was argued that special rules for cases in which such states 'had profited from the colonial occupation' needed to be established. It was argued that the rules on the restitution of

[26] Kowalski, 'Repatriation of Cultural Property' (n 25) 162–63. [27] Ibid. 162–65.

[28] See UNESCO Doc. 20C/Resolutions and Corr. 4/7.6/5 (1978); UNESCO Doc. CC-86/WS/3 (1986).

cultural property removed in the event of war and under military duress could be extrapolated to cases of colonial occupation.[29]

The legitimacy of such a division has been partially questioned by a few representatives of legal scholarship. In particular, Ana F. Vrdoljak, in her monograph on the restitution of cultural objects under international law,[30] criticizes the solutions applied by the ILC. She explains that differences in substance between post-colonial and 'classic' scenarios of state succession in respect of cultural heritage do not convincingly justify the separate treatment of these situations. Vrdoljak recalls the controversies on the allocation of cultural property at the time of the post-First World War dismantling of multinational states and argues that the considerations advanced by former empires and newly independent states after 1918 are analogous to those used in decolonization by colonial powers and their former colonies. She explains that before the era of cultural heritage law, restitution began to emerge as 'an early marker of the transition within the international community from policies promoting cultural Darwinism to cultural pluralism.'[31] Accordingly, the physical control over the tangible aspects of cultural heritage is not merely linked to territorial or title considerations, but its role is crucial in protecting human dignity, of which cultural identity is one of the fundamental components. In this light, different legal frameworks providing the restoration of cultural heritage to the places and peoples who created them, including the principles of state succession to cultural property, reflect more general human-oriented rationales for restitution.[32]

The new wave of state succession processes in Central Eastern Europe after 1989 re-opened the broad discussion on the fate of cultural property. Again, the issues of restitution of cultural objects removed in the event of armed conflict were discussed together with those concerning the allocation of such material in cases of state succession. In fact, the interstate negotiations often jointly addressed these two different issues. Legal doctrine remained rather cautious on this topic, usually reaffirming the duty on parties to state succession to settle the controversies with regard to displaced cultural property. Yet at the level of principles relating to the allocation of such assets in state succession, the doctrine of international law has not generally advocated any new developments. As in the case of the 2001 IIL Resolution adopted by the Institute of International Law (IIL), entitled *State Succession in Matters of Property and Debts*,[33] it followed the view that the interstate arrangements in these matters shall be based on two paramount criteria: 1) territorial provenance, and 2) major significance to the cultural heritage of a successor state. The implementation of the content of these principles was left to the states concerned. Furthermore, it also appears that actual state practice in

[29] In particular see UNGA Res. 3187 (XXVIII) of 18 December 1973 'Restitution of Works of Art to Countries Victims of Expropriation', UN Doc. A/Res/3187(XXVIII).

[30] Ana F. Vrdoljak, *International Law, Museums and the Return of Cultural Objects* (CUP, 2006).

[31] Ibid. 3. [32] Ibid. 299–304.

[33] Available at: <http://www.idi-iil.org/idiE/resolutionsE/2001_van_01_en.PDF>, accessed on 15 January 2015.

this field has been scarcely studied, which is surprising given the volume of legal literature dealing with different aspects of state succession. There are, however, some important exemptions such as the excellent studies conducted by Patricia Kennedy Grimsted on the situation of historical archives in the case of the dissolution of the Soviet Union. Her monograph, *Trophies of War and Empire* (2001),[34] is the best source of information on this topic ever published.

Nonetheless, the post-Cold War dissolution of multinational states led to a critical revision of the existing theories on state succession to cultural property. Such a synthesizing approach can be observed particularly in German and Swiss literature.[35] Of special interest is the recent monograph on this topic by Yves Huguenin-Bergenat.[36] The author distinguishes four major non-binding principles applicable to the allocation of movable cultural property.[37] These are based on the settlements on the matter of the allocation of cultural property in the case of the post-First World War dissolution of Austria–Hungary, combined with some current tendencies in international law. Accordingly, the first rudimentary principle is defined as territorial provenance (origin) of cultural assets,[38] which is combined with the second principle—the preservation of cultural heritage. The link between these two principles is crucial because the protection of cultural property in its original historical, geographical, and cultural context constitutes one of the major fundamentals of international cultural heritage law. Therefore, the significance of certain objects for the cultural heritage of a successor state needs to be balanced by the local or regional value of a given object.[39] The applicability of these two principles can, however, be challenged by the principle of the integrity of internationally ranked collections. Finally, the distribution of state cultural property may simply follow the principle of equity. This essentially consists in the equitable apportionment of property of the predecessor states between its successors.[40] Thus, the findings of Huguenin-Bergenat for the first time explicitly combined the principles applicable to the allocation of state movable cultural property in state succession with generally recognized principles on the protection of cultural heritage. Yet his analysis primarily focused on technical principles on allocation and distribution of movable cultural property, avoiding a broader discussion on state succession in respect of international cultural heritage obligations and international responsibility.

[34] Patricia Kennedy Grimsted, *Trophies of War and Empire: The Archival Heritage of Ukraine, World War II and International Politics of Restitution* (Ukrainian Research Institute of Harvard University, 2004).

[35] Kerstin Odendahl, *Kulturgüterschutz* (Mohr Siebeck, 2005), 151–61, Sabine von Schorlemer, *Internationaler Kulturgüterschutz* (D&H, 1992), at 313 ff., Stefan Turner, 'Die Zuornung beweglicher Kulturgüter im Völkerrecht', in Wilfried Fiedler (ed), *Internationaler Kulturgüterschutz und deutsche Frage* (Mann Verlag, 1991), 19–108, at 74 ff.

[36] Yves Huguenin-Bergenat, Kulturgüter bei Staatensukzession: *Die internationalen Verträge Österreichs nach dem Zerfall der österreichisch-ungarischen Monarchie im Spiegel des aktuellen Völkerrechts* (De Gruyter, 2010).

[37] Ibid. 246–60. [38] Ibid. 246–50. [39] Ibid. 251–56. [40] Ibid. 256–60.

Apparently, the topic of state succession in cultural property has never been subject of a profound comprehensive legal investigation. Despite extensive scholarly contributions in the area of state succession and that of cultural heritage law, the analysis of the peculiarities of cultural property as an object of state succession is timely and needed. This is particular true in relation to ongoing processes of state succession in different parts of the globe (eg Kosovo, Palestine, Crimea), or possible future territorial and cultural transfigurations in the Middle East and North Africa. Thus, the old questions require new answers in the light of the growing complexity of cultural heritage obligations in international law.

As regards the consistency of use of certain terms throughout the book, it is important to explain that the term 'tangible cultural heritage', as applied to material cultural manifestations (movable and immovable evidences of human spiritual achievements), is often used with two other synonymous expressions: 'cultural patrimony' and 'cultural property'. The first of these expressions is usually applied in respect of developments of international law and practice prior to the Second World War, whereas 'cultural property' indicates the economic value of material cultural manifestations. The terms 'cultural objects', 'cultural material', and 'cultural items', regarding the movable aspect of tangible cultural heritage, are used interchangeably in this book.

2. Legal Effects of State Succession on Tangible Cultural Heritage

Although state succession lies at the heart of international law, at least since the mid-nineteenth century, its unanimously accepted definition has been never formulated. In the traditional doctrinal approach, as defined by Patrick D. O'Connell, the term 'state succession' referred to 'the factual situation which arises when one state is substituted for another in sovereignty over a given territory.'[41] More recent definitions focus on legal consequences of such a substitution. According to the definition adopted by the ILC, state succession means 'the replacement of one state by another in the responsibility for the international relations of territory.'[42] This wording is repeated by two conventions codifying the international law on state succession: the 1978 Vienna Convention on Succession of States in Respect of Treaties (1978 Vienna Convention),[43] and the 1983 Vienna Convention on Succession of states in Respect of state Property, Archives and Debts (1983 Vienna Convention).[44] Arguably, such an approach has also been shared by the prevailing international practice and legal

[41] Daniel Patrick O'Connell, *State Succession in Municipal Law and International Law*, Vol. 1 (CUP, 1967), 3.

[42] UN Doc. A/9610/Rev.1, para. 3 of the commentary to Art. 2 of the draft articles on succession of states in respect of treaties.

[43] Adopted on 23 August 1978, entered into force on 6 November 1996, 1946 UNTS 3.

[44] Adopted on 8 April 1983, not in force, UN Doc. A/CONF.117/14 (1983).

doctrine.[45] Similarly, the distinction between the succession of states, concerning the relationship between at least two state actors—predecessor and successor—and the succession of governments, referring to the change of government within one state, is widely recognized. However, the classifications of political events that may give rise to succession of states as well as the evaluation of their prerequisites and legal consequences remain disputable, due to the fact that state succession has to deal with complex political dynamics of power. Thus, the opinion that there are no general rules on state succession,[46] which primarily follow political considerations rather than legal principles,[47] is not uncommon in the literature.

For the purposes of methodological clarity, it seems necessary to follow the distinction between the territorial and legal aspects of state succession. In other words, state succession has a double nature, which consists in the transfer of sovereignty over a given territory, on the one hand, and succession in rights and obligations—pre-existing legal situations related to the territory, on the other. Accordingly, territorial succession constitutes 'title'—the cause for succession in other matters such as treaty obligations or other existing legal interstate situations and engagements, debts, administration, nationality of inhabitants, state property, state archives, etc.[48] State succession in this second instance also relates to the fate of material elements of cultural heritage and international obligations related to them.[49]

2.1 Title (cause) of state succession

Territorial succession manifests factual and political aspects of succession of states—it concerns cases in which the sovereignty of one state over a given territory passes to another state. With reference to this, international law sets out prerequisites of legality for such a replacement according to the widely accepted catalogue of categories (types) of state succession. The doctrine of international law has elaborated a variety of systematizations of such categories, reflecting the changing perception of the phenomena of statehood, mobility of frontiers, and acquisition of territorial sovereignty. In this regard, it is possible to indicate three main groups of considerations that need to be addressed.

[45] Malcolm N. Shaw, 'State Succession Revisited', *Finish Yearbook of International Law* 5(1994), 34–98, at 41, Rein Müllerson, *International Law, Rights and Politics: Developments in Eastern Europe and the CIS* (Routledge, 1994), 137, Alfred Verdross and Bruno Simma, *Universelles Völkerrecht* (3rd edn, D&H, 1984), 608.

[46] See Patrick Dumberry, *State Succession to International Responsibility* (Nijhoff, 2007) at 3–4, Vladimir D. Degan, 'Création et disparition de l'Etat (à la lumière du démembrement de trois fédérations multiethniques en Europe)', *RCADI* 279(1999), 195–375, at 247 ff.

[47] Daniel Patrick O'Connell, 'Recent Problems of State Succession in Relation to New States', *RCADI* 130(1970-II), 95–206, at 117–18, Daniel Patrick O'Connell, *The Law of State Succession* (CUP, 1956), 272.

[48] See an excellent introduction to the work of Jan H. W. Verzijl, *State Succession* (Sijthoff, 1974), 7 *International Law in Historical Perspective*, at 3.

[49] Ibid. 36, 105–8.

The first refers to the means by which territorial succession comes about by a treaty or by force. For centuries, the right to conquest was fully recognized in international law. Forced territorial annexation, partition, or conquest produced the same effects, in terms of territorial succession, as contractual cession based on a treaty.[50] In this context, a special formula concerned the situation of complete defeat of a party to a conflict, the extinction of a state—'*debellatio*' or 'subjugation'. In such circumstances, the victorious party was entitled to assume sovereign powers over the subjugated territory in the absence of any peace treaty.[51] Clearly, the 'title' of state succession based on the use of force is nowadays no longer legitimate under international law, at least since the formal prohibition of aggressive war by the UN Charter.[52] Precisely, this implies an obligation on all member states to 'refrain in their international relations from the threat or use of force against the territorial integrity or political independence of any state' (Article 2.4), and to settle international disputes by peaceful means (Article 33). In accordance with these provisions, both Vienna Conventions codifying the law on state succession explicitly provide that their application is limited 'only to the effects of a succession of states occurring in conformity with international law and, in particular, the principles of international law embodied in the Charter of the United Nations'.[53] Therefore, the military occupation of a state does not result in state succession, but it may lead to the *de facto* replacement of one state by another. The legal effects of such a replacement are highly disputable, particularly with reference to the legality of sovereign acts of states undertaken in respect of the territories acquired by forceful annexations and conquest prior to the adoption of the UN Charter. This controversy also involves the question of sovereign rights to the free disposal of cultural objects, in particular those removed from colonized territories.

The second consideration concerns the 'extent' of territorial succession. In other words, it refers to partial and universal territorial succession. This distinction appears crucial for the assessment of continuity and identity of states at the date of succession. Generally speaking, partial succession consists in the change of sovereignty over a part of the territory of the predecessor and does not involve a rupture in the continuity and identity of the predecessor state. A much more complex situation is universal territorial succession since the total dismemberment (*dismembratio*) of a predecessor state may lead to the emergence of completely

[50] Arthur B. Keith, *The Theory of State Succession with Special Reference to English and Colonial Law* (Waterlow and Sons, 1907), 1 ff.

[51] See Yutaka Arai-Takahashi, *The Law of Occupation Continuity and Change of International Humanitarian Law, and Its Interaction with International Human Rights Law* (Brill, 2009), 30–39, Eyāl Benveništî, *The International Law of Occupation* (2nd edn, Princeton University Press, 2004), 91–96, Gerhard Von Glahn, *The Occupation of Enemy Territory: A Commentary on the Law and Practice of Belligerent Occupation* (University of Minnesota Press, 1957), 273–86.

[52] Charter of the United Nations, signed on 26 June 1945, entered into force on 24 October 1945, 1 UNTS XVI, amended in 1963 (557 UNTS 143), in 1965 (638 UNTS 308), and in 1971 (892 UNTS 119).

[53] Art. 6 of the 1978 Vienna Convention and Art. 3 of the 1983 Vienna Convention.

new states that are different from the predecessor state. However, some new states may be considered identical with the predecessor and may continue its legal personality. Such situations are not uncommon in international practice. This was the case of the 1918 dissolution of Austria–Hungary, where both Austria and Hungary recognized themselves as identical with their predecessors, the Empire of Austria and the Kingdom of Hungary, respectively. Similar considerations were *inter alia* applied with reference to the Republic of Turkey after the complete dissolution of the Ottoman Empire (1923), and more recently in respect of the Russian Federation in the case of the dismemberment of the Soviet Union (1991). Moreover, the latter case showed other particularities. Accordingly, Baltic States were not recognized as successors of the Soviet Union, but the continuations of the independent states of Latvia, Estonia, and Lithuania which had been annexed by the Soviet Union in 1940 (principle of *postliminium*).[54] Such difficulties in the assessment of state identity and continuity may lead to profound controversies in respect of cultural heritage matters. For instance, are the 'completely' new independent states bound by the commitments contracted prior to the date of state succession; for example, an obligation to return a certain set of cultural items?

The third consideration concerns the classification of different scenarios of territorial succession. From the time of the first efforts to systemize these complex phenomena by Max Hüber[55] and Arthur B. Keith,[56] different typologies of territorial succession have evolved.[57] During the work on the codification of international law on state succession, the ILC reduced them to four basic categories (types), generally accepted by legal doctrine. First, the most frequent and traditional type of succession—cession—arises from the territorial transfers between existing states. This is understood as the contractual transfer of territory between states by an international treaty (eg cession of Alaska by Russia to the United States in 1867), or by adjudication based on the decision of an international court or arbitration board (eg the 1921 Council of League Nations' decision on the division of Upper Silesia between Germany and Poland). The second category refers to separation of part(s) of a state and dissolution of a state. Basically, it involves cases when succession takes place as a result of separatist movements aimed at secession (emancipation, gaining independence) of a given territory(ies) or complete dismemberment of a state. Secession usually implies the use of force, which may take the form of rebellion against the central state government. As it involves disintegration of state territory and an important rupture in international relations, the right to secede constitutes one of the most controversial issues of international law (eg secession of Chechnya from the Russian Federation in 1991,

[54] Ineta Ziemele, 'Is the Distinction between State Continuity and Sate Succession Reality or Fiction?' *Baltic Yearbook of International Law* 1(2001), 191–222.

[55] Max Huber, *Die Staatensuccession. Völkerrechtliche und staatsrechtliche Praxis im XIX. Jahrhundert* (D&H, 1898).

[56] Keith, *The Theory of State Succession* (n 50).

[57] For instance, see Brigitte Stern 'La succession d'États', *RCADI* 262(1996), 176–424, at 104–16; Annie Gruber, *Le droit international de la succession d'États* (Bruylant, 1986), 17–18.

secession of Kosovo from Serbia in 2008).[58] From the doctrinal point of view it is, however, important to make a distinction between secession and dissolution. Accordingly, secession usually refers to the situation where a portion of a given territory, being part of a state, forms a state in itself. Although such an entity secedes, the rest of the state retains its structure. Inversely, dissolution involves the extinction of the predecessor state, whose territories form two or more successor states (eg the dissolution of Czechoslovakia in 1992). The third category of state succession, identified by the ILC, concerns uniting (union, unification) of two or more states in one state. It seems that under this category the ILC also classifies the incorporation of a territory which, however, manifests certain significant differences. While unification involves a case where two or more states jointly form another state (eg Tanganyika and Zanzibar became Tanzania in 1964), incorporation refers to the situation where one state is absorbed by another, usually a bigger state (eg the incorporation of Hawaii into the United States in 1898, and more recently the case of unification of Germany through the incorporation of the German Democratic Republic (GDR) by the Federal Republic of Germany in 1990). The last category regards succession of states in the post-colonial context; that is, the gaining of independence by the former colonial (dependent) territories. The ILC noted that the colonial context of state succession was unique as it embodied both 'continuity and rupture'.[59]

In this catalogue of different types of territorial succession, it appears that only the case of uniting of states does not pose any particular controversies in terms of tangible cultural heritage. The other remaining categories usually require complex negotiations and arrangements between the states concerned.

2.2 Succession to pre-existing legal situations

Legal effects of territorial succession may include a wide range of pre-existing legal situations involving the fate of tangible cultural heritage. This refers first and foremost to the allocation and distribution of state movable property, the situation of immovable property, and the division of state property situated abroad. The second question regards the continuity and succession in international obligations concerning tangible cultural heritage. Apart from these, one may also recall other pre-existing legal situations relating to material cultural heritage which might be at stake in the case of state succession. In particular, the question may arise as to the principles regulating state succession in rights and obligations arising from internationally wrongful acts (delicts) against cultural heritage.

[58] See *inter alia* the articles by Christian Tomuschat, 'Secession and Self-determination', Andreas Zimmermann, 'Secession and the Law of State Succession', Photini Pazartzis, 'Secession and International Law: The European Dimension' in Marcelo G. Kohen (ed), *Secession. International Law Perspectives* (CUP, 2006), 23–45, 209–30, 355–73.

[59] UN Doc. A/7209/Rev.1, para. 64.

2.2.1 *State property*

State succession to tangible cultural heritage belongs to the second sphere of succession—that is, succession in pre-existing legal situations—as it regards assets situated or originated from a territory to which succession relates. More precisely, the material aspect determines the inclusion of tangible cultural heritage in the broader legal framework of state succession in matters of state property. Therefore, some general clarifications need to be addressed.

Under customary international law, the property of the predecessor state passes *ipso jure* to the successor. No internal acts by the successor are required for the validity of such a transfer. Moreover, the passing of state property takes place without compensation. The controversy arises, however, in respect of the notion of state property: whether it refers only to state property destined for public service or whether it also covers private state property destined for non-public use. Under the 1983 Vienna Convention, the term is defined as 'property, rights and interests which, at the date of the succession of states, were, according to the internal law of the predecessor State, owned by that State' (Article 8). Such an approach seems very practical as the exact content of this term needs to be constructed within a given territorial context of each specific case of state succession. In fact, it is a complex issue to find a common denominator that could serve as a basis for the various definitions of the term under the internal laws of all predecessor states.

International practice has not, however, been consistent in this matter and has usually privileged the solutions accorded by states. These may often concern not only state property *sensu stricto*—that is, property directly owned by a state—but also so-called para-state property, which includes property operated by different entities owned by a state, public, and local institutions, publicly owned companies and associations, as well as property of reigning dynasties.[60] Sometimes the interstate agreements can be more precise on defining state property, providing a complete list of state-owned assets which shall pass to the successor state. In any case, following the principle *nemo plus iuris in alium transferre potest quam ipse habet*, more rights than those vested in the predecessor cannot be transferred to the successor state. Therefore, state succession does not affect private property of individuals, non-state entities, and the property of third states.[61] It appears that the only broadly recognized derogation from this general rule consists in the 'principle of the permanent sovereignty of every people over its wealth and natural resources' introduced by the 1983 Vienna Convention in respect of post-colonial territories (Article 15.4), aiming to protect the sovereign rights of

[60] P. K. Menon, *The Succession of States in Respect to Treaties, State Property, Archives, and Debts* (Mellen, 1991), 77 ff., Verzijl, *State Succession* (n 48) 28–31, O'Connell, *The Law of State Succession* (n 47) 288.

[61] Carten Stahn, *The Law and Practice of International Territorial Administration: Versailles to Iraq and Beyond* (CUP, 2008), 492–96; Hersch Lauterpacht, 'Succession of States with Respect to Private Law Obligations', in Elihu Lauterpacht (ed), *International Law Collected Papers of Hersch Lauterpacht* (CUP, 1977), 121–39, O'Connell, *State Succession* (n 41) 237.

newly independent states against the property disposals and economic concessions made prior to independence.

Broadly speaking, the legal regime on the passing of state property is conditioned by the category of state succession. However, some general principles are applicable to all cases. As a general rule, upon succeeding to the territory of the predecessor state, the successor state succeeds to all state property of that prior state, wherever it may be located. Accordingly, real (immovable) property of the predecessor situated in the territory to which succession relates, shares the destiny of that territory and passes to the successor state. The regime on state succession to movable state property is more complex as it is driven by the consideration that such a category of property is not distributed merely on the basis of fortuitous location at the date of state succession.[62] Hence the paramount criterion for the distribution of state movable property is the connection with the activity of the predecessor state in respect of the territory to which the succession of states relates. In cases of dissolution of a multinational state, the principle of 'equity' is generally applicable. This provides the division of movable property in 'equitable proportions'.[63]

At first sight, the inclusion of material cultural heritage in the legal regime on state succession to state property may seem understandable and logical. However, the objectives driving the passing of state property from the predecessor to the successor state profoundly differ from those referring to succession in cultural heritage assets. In the first instance, the paramount consideration is to provide the successor state with all the tools indispensible for the efficient exercise of territorial sovereignty. Inversely, the control of material cultural heritage does not constitute a necessary factor for exercising state administrative power. It primarily regards the linkage between the territory, its human communities, and collective cultural identity, though some properties may also have strong symbolic connotations, embodying sovereign legitimacy to a given territory, for example, royal regalia. In addition, material cultural heritage is not always of state property and may belong to a variety of local and religious entities, private individuals, etc. Notwithstanding the principle providing that state succession shall not affect the private property of non-state entities, it often happens that private rights, such as the freedom of disposal of cultural property, are restricted by national legislation.[64]

Moreover, it is noticeable that the consistent application of the regime on state succession to movable cultural items raises some other doubts. Kurt Siehr rightly stresses that the provisions on equitable partition are not adequate for the distribution of cultural property. Furthermore, the principle of connection with the activity of the predecessor state may hardly be applicable. In particular, this refers

[62] Kurt Siehr, 'International Art Trade and Law', *RCADI* 243(1993)6, 9–292, at 126.

[63] See Władysław Czapliński, 'Equity and Equitable Principles in the Law of State Succession', in Mojmir Mrak (ed), *Succession of States* (Nijhoff 1999), 61–73.

[64] Władysław Czapliński, *Zmiany terytorialne w Europie Środkowej i Wschodniej i ich skutki międzynarodowo prawne* (Scholar, 1998), 150–53.

to historical objects and works of art of universal value. Such objects create serious problems since 'there are no clear-cut criteria in cultural property law as to their home State, domicile or nationality'.[65] Therefore, the evaluation of their local or territorial pertinence and connection with the activity of the predecessor state is questionable and hardly possible to determine.[66]

For these reasons, legal scholarship generally accepts the need for a certain derogation of the general regime on state succession to state property, justified by cultural considerations. Thus, international practice and legal doctrine recognize two reasons for such a 'derogation' in respect of movable cultural heritage. The first consists in the correlation of the rudimentary principle of territorial provenance of cultural assets and the principle of major significance to the cultural heritage of a successor state.[67] The second reason arises from the principle of self-determination of peoples in its 'external' meaning—referring to situations where a people breaks free from an existing state and forms its own state by means of secession or decolonization. In such an event, it may have a claim to recover its cultural identity by repatriation of cultural objects lost and removed in the past.

International practice, however, manifests a certain reluctance of states in applying legal argumentation in respect of the allocation of cultural property in state succession. In a number of recent cases, the actual returns have been made on the basis of moral considerations or *ex gratia* gestures in the framework of friendly relations between states. Such gestures constitute a highly convenient diplomatic instrument for predecessor states. Through the voluntary return of the most claimed objects, they manifest their 'good faith' and may often avoid long-lasting legal disputes and political controversies on the status of all cultural property removed from the territory to which succession of state relates. In addition, the increasing incidence of international cultural heritage law for interstate relations may affect the solutions accorded between states in respect of the allocation of cultural property. In particular, the role of the general procedural principle of cooperation in the sphere of cultural heritage cannot be underestimated. This principle, introduced at the universal level by the 1945 UNESCO Constitution[68] and the subsequent 1966 UNESCO Declaration of Principles of International Cultural Co-operation,[69] is driven by the common concern of the entire international community in the protection of cultural heritage in its local, national, and global dimensions. Moreover, it is also recognized that cultural cooperation and

[65] Kurt Siehr, 'International Art Trade and Law' (n 62) 126–7.

[66] Compare Erik Jayme, 'Die Nationalität des Kunstwerkes als Rechtsfrage', in Reinhard Mußgnug (ed), *Aktuelle Fragen des Kulturgüterschutzes: Beiträge zur Reform des deutschen Kulturgutschutzgesetzes 1955 und seiner Angleichung an den europäischen Kulturgüterschutz* (Müller, 1998), 7–29.

[67] See Ludwig Engstler, *Die territoriale Bindung von Kulturgütern im Rahmen des Völkerrechts* (C. Heymann, 1964).

[68] Constitution of the United Nations Educational, Scientific and Cultural Organization, adopted on 16 November 1945, entered into force on 4 November 1946, 4 UNTS 275.

[69] UNESCO Declaration of Principles of International Cultural Co-Operation, Paris, 4 November 1966, UNESCO Doc. 14C/Resolutions, 86–89.

the protection of cultural heritage serve as efficient tools in post-conflict reconciliation and stabilization of states and their boundaries.[70] Current state practice shows that actual agreements in respect of the fate of tangible cultural property may find a wide range of solutions based on international cultural cooperation, far beyond mere allocation and distribution considerations.

2.2.2 State archives

The fate of state archives in cases of territorial reconfigurations is one of the oldest objects of treaty regulation (since the Middle Ages). In the practice of European states, the majority of cession treaties have contained provisions on the transfer of archives.[71] The allocation of such material has been strictly conditioned by their content. In practice, administrative and judicial archives which entirely relate to a given territory pass to the successor state. Other documents or those partially or incidentally related to the transferred territory may be equitably divided or kept in their integrity by the predecessor, which shall grant the right of free access. These considerations closely reflect two general rules governing the administration of archives: territorial provenance and functional pertinence. Agreements between states may, however, reduce the extent of their application, by invoking the principle of the preservation of the integrity of archival fonds of the predecessor state and the principle of exclusion of secret and political archives from succession mechanisms.

The general regime on succession of state archives does not deal with the question of historic archives or libraries, which may constitute a rudimentary source of information about past development and traditions of human communities living in a given territory. Thus, the main considerations on the distribution of historic archives shall refer to the historical and cultural significance of such materials, not to their administrative function. This issue has been constantly approached in international practice. The need for certain derogations of general rules on state succession to archives has been addressed, but no consistent set of principles has been constructed. In particular, the question of distribution of archives of major cultural value became of special interest during the process of decolonization and the following codification of international law on state succession. As a result of the efforts of newly independent states, the 1983 Vienna Convention recognized the right of formerly colonized peoples 'to development, to information about their history, and to their cultural heritage' embodied in state archives which shall not

[70] Kerstin Odendahl and Mayte Peters, 'The Significance of Cultural Heritage for State Stability and Its Protection by International Law', in Julia Raue and Patrick Sutter (eds), *Facets and Practices of State Building* (Nijhoff, 2009), 263–79.

[71] Jean-Pierre Wallot, 'Les grands principes internationale concernant la migration des archives', *Archives* 28(1996–1997), 3–18; Ernest Posner, 'Effects of Changes of Sovereignty on Archives', in Ken Munden (ed), *Archives and the Public Interest: Selected Essays by Ernst Posner* (Public Affairs Press, 1967), 168–81; Eugenio Casanova, 'Gli archivi nei trattati internazionali', *Gli Archivi Italiani* 5(1918), 179–201.

be infringed by the succession arrangements with former colonial powers (Article 28.7). It remains questionable, however, as to how such a principle shall be implemented, and whether it may also be extrapolated to other categories of state succession beyond the colonial context.

2.2.3 State succession to international obligations

The increasing complexity of international conventional law on the protection of cultural heritage raises a question as to the nature and status of such obligations in state succession. Indeed, not only does state succession regard the relationships between the predecessor state and the successor but it may also greatly affect other members of the international community. Therefore, the continuity and rupture of international relations and commitments binding the predecessor has always been one of the major concerns of legal scholarship.

The core of doctrinal controversy consists in state succession to rights and obligations arising from international treaties. With reference to this, two general theories have been constructed: 'continuity' and 'clean slate' (*tabula rasa*). The first provides that a successor state is bound by international obligations undertaken by a predecessor state in respect of a territory to which succession of states relates. The second adopts a non-succession rule, which enables the successor state to decide which international engagements it will continue.[72] The application of one of these doctrines is, however, conditioned by the category of territorial succession. Accordingly, it is widely accepted that in the case of cession, the treaties of the predecessor state expire with regard to the ceded territory, while the treaties of the successor automatically take effect (the principle of mobility of treaty borders).[73] Arguably, incorporation of a state may have similar effects on the treaty engagements of the predecessor. Inversely, there is a common recognition of the continuity of non-political international treaties of the predecessor state in cases of states uniting. In respect of the secession and dissolution of a multinational state, the 'clean slate' rule has often been taken into consideration, though not consistently. Importantly, the ILC opted for the general continuity of obligations arising from the treaties of the predecessor state and such codified principles were adopted by the 1978 Vienna Convention (Articles 34–38). In the ILC's view, the 'clean slate' rule would only apply to newly independent states who were entitled to continue or reject the treaties contracted prior to independence (Article 16). However, international practice shows that the provisions of the convention on the continuity of treaties of the predecessor state in cases of secession and dissolution did reflect the rules of customary law at the time of their adoption. Moreover, the principle of continuity of treaties has never evolved into international custom

[72] See Matthew Craven, 'The Problem of State Succession and the Identity of States under International Law', *EJIL* 9(1998)1, 142–62, at 146–51.

[73] Tullio Treves, *Diritto internazionale: problemi fondamentali* (Giuffrè, 2005), 89, Marcelo G. Kohen, 'Le problème des frontières en cas de dissolution et de séparation d'États', *RBDI* 31(1998)1, 129–60.

in respect of these two categories of succession. In fact, successor states tend to maintain their sovereign capacity to 'pick and choose' the treaties adhered to by a predecessor state.[74] It appears that the principle of continuity is followed only with regard to state boundaries and other territorial regimes established by a treaty.[75]

In this context, the theory of so-called automatic succession to human rights treaties also needs to be discussed. In the current doctrine of international law, there is strong support for the concept claiming that human rights treaties continue to apply within the territory of a predecessor state, irrespective of the succession of states.[76] This is driven by the reasoning that the inhabitants of a territory cannot be deprived of the rights granted to them by a human rights treaty just because of state succession. Therefore, the obligations arising from such international instruments shall automatically bind the successor state, irrespective of the category of territorial succession. However, the existence of such a customary rule of international law does not seem to be confirmed by consistent international practice and *opinio iuris*,[77] though one may observe a certain mild tendency towards the continuity of such obligations.

Broadly speaking, international cultural heritage obligations are primarily established by multilateral treaties at the universal and regional levels. As they do not regulate state boundaries or other territorial regimes, it may seem that a successor state is free to decide whether it will accede to a cultural heritage treaty to which a predecessor state was a party. Such an approach may, however, be disputable with regard to the obligations towards tangible cultural heritage of outstanding universal value, whose preservation is of general interest to the international community, for example, cultural sites inscribed on the World Heritage List by a motion of the predecessor state. In this regard, one may argue that the obligations under the World Heritage Convention shall continue, irrespective of succession, as they do not constitute the mere concern of domestic jurisdiction.[78] Similarly, the

[74] ILA, 'Aspects of the Law on State Succession', Resolution No 3/2008, the 73rd ILA Conference, Rio De Janeiro, Brazil, 17–21 August, 2008, available at <http://www.ila-hq.org/en/committees/index.cfm/cid/11> accessed on 26 January 2015, paras. 4–13; compare Menno T. Kamminga, 'Human Rights Treaties and State Succession', in CoE European Commission for Democracy through Law (Venice Commission) (ed), *The Status of International Treaties on Human Rights* (Council of Europe Publ., 2006), 31–42; Menno T. Kamminga, 'Impact on State Succession in Respect of Treaties', in Menno T. Kamminga and Martin Scheinin (eds), *The Impact of Human Rights Law on General International Law* (OUP, 2009), 99–110; Akbar Rasulov, 'Revisiting State Succession to Humanitarian Treaties: Is There a Case for Automaticity?', *EJIL* 14(2003)1, 141–70.

[75] ILA, 'Aspects of the Law on State Succession', Resolution No 3/2008 (n 74) para. 9.

[76] See Shaw, 'State Succession Revisited' (n 45) 84; Menno T. Kamminga, 'State Succession of Human Rights Treaties', *EJIL* 7(1996)4, 469–84; Photini Pazartzis, 'State Succession to Multilateral Treaties: Recent Developments', *Austrian Review of International and European Law* 3(1998)3, 397–415, at 414; Isabelle Poupart, 'Succession aux traités et droits de l'homme: vers la reconnaissance d'une protection ininterrompue des individus', in Pierre Michel Eisemann and Martti Koskenniemi (eds), *La succession d'Etats: la codification á l'épreuve des faits/State Succession: Codification Tested against the Facts* (Nijhoff, 2000), 465–90.

[77] See Rasulov, 'Revisiting State Succession' (n 74) 169–70, ILA, 'Aspects of the Law on State Succession', Resolution No 3/2008 (n 74) para. 11.

[78] Compare Francesco Francioni, 'Culture, Heritage and Human Rights: An Introduction', in Francesco Francioni and Martin Scheinin (eds), *Cultural Human Rights* (Nijhoff, 2008), 1–16, at 10–11.

question of international obligations towards minorities and groups living within the territory to which succession of states relates, including the protection of their cultural rights, does not constitute the mere issue of state sovereignty. Indeed, in order to provide international stability and peaceful coexistence of ethnic and religious minorities, successor states have usually been bound to grant certain rights to such communities, which also included the right to enjoy their culture, heritage and traditions. The observance of these obligations has been guaranteed by the international community since at least the end of the First World War.

Another question regards the continuity of international cultural heritage obligations arising from sources other than a treaty. Indeed, from the moment of their emergence, successor states are bound not only by the obligations to which they expressly contracted or to which they succeeded but also by customary international law or general principles.[79] Therefore, the fact of state succession does not cease the obligations binding under general international law. Nevertheless the existence of such obligations in respect of cultural heritage is disputable.[80] Furthermore, it must be stressed that the continuity of international obligations arising from peremptory norms of international law does not regard the issue of state succession as such. These obligations are not contracted by a predecessor state in its sovereign capacity and they are not the subject of succession.

Apart from these considerations, recent international practice has unveiled certain new tendencies with regard to the protection of tangible cultural heritage of ethnic and national minorities which do not easily fit within a general regime on state succession. Accordingly, the obligation to protect cultural heritage constitutes a part of the broader enforcement of human rights standards perceived as requirements for the conditional recognition of newly independent states, in particular Bosnia–Herzegovina and Kosovo. Although these new states accepted a complex set of cultural heritage obligations, this was not exactly a case concerning the continuity of pre-existing international engagements contracted by the predecessor states, the Socialist Federal Republic of Yugoslavia (SFRY) and Serbia, respectively. It is also disputable as to whether adherence to this cultural heritage framework could be treated in terms of the enforcement of binding principles of general international law, since the volume of such obligations went beyond widely recognized international standards. Therefore, the link between cultural heritage obligations and human rights and minority protection needs further investigation.

[79] Martti Koskenniemi, 'Report of the Director of Studies of the English-Speaking Section of the Centre', in Pierre Michel Eisemann and Martti Koskenniemi (eds), *La succession d'États: la codification à l'épreuve des faits/State Succession: Codification Tested Against the Facts* (Nijhoff, 2000), 65–132, at 108.

[80] Compare Francesco Francioni, 'Au-delà des traités: l'émergence d'un noveau droit coutimier pour la protection du patrimoine culturel', *RGDIP* 11(2007)1, 19–42.

2.2.4 *State succession in matters of international responsibility*

Although it seems that the issue of international responsibility does not consider the fate of tangible cultural heritage in state succession as such, it may concern situations closely related to this topic such as restitution of cultural property and reparation for cultural loss. Moreover, it may also involve the issue of state succession to consequences of grave violations of cultural obligations affecting the international community as a whole, committed prior to the date of state succession. Hence, the analysis of this question requires more detailed investigation and commentary.

In this regard, it is necessary to distinguish the situations involving the continuity of international personality and identity of pre-succession states from that of new states. In fact, a continuing (or continuator) state retains its pre-existing rights and obligations arising from internationally wrongful acts, irrespective of the fact of state succession. Inversely, the situation of successor state is much more complex. In fact, international delicts have long been considered as being of 'personal' nature and thus they could only be attributed to the state responsible for their commitment, but not to its successor.[81] Consequently, the passing of international responsibility from the predecessor to the successor state has been excluded. In particular, successor states have tended to argue that they could not be bound to assume the responsibility of the predecessor state, when the act attributed to the latter constituted an 'odious' act; that is, serving against the vital interests of the successor state or its population. Therefore, the obligations arising from the commitment of such act were claimed as being non-transmissible and non-enforceable.

The developments of post-Cold War state practice and legal doctrine have, however, challenged non-succession theories. The first comprehensive research in the field, undertaken by Patick Dumberry,[82] revealed certain common patterns in assuming or rejecting succession to state responsibility depending on the types of succession of states and the 'specific situations and circumstances'.[83] Dumberry advocated that those practices could amount to the emergence of new rules of customary international law.[84] Yet the existence of already well-established rules of international law in this is area is still debatable.[85] It rather seems that each particular situation is solved according to its given factual situations, in conformity with the principles of equity, justice, and good relations between states. In this context, it is necessary to recall the initiative of the Institute of International Law (IIL), which within the framework of the works of its 14th Commission has drafted a catalogue of operational guiding principles on succession in consequences of internationally wrongful acts applicable to distinct categories of state

[81] James Crawford, *State Responsibility: The General Part* (CUP, 2013), at 441.
[82] Patrick Dumberry, *State Succession to International Responsibility* (Nijhoff, 2007).
[83] Ibid. 420–30. [84] Ibid. [85] Crawford, *State Responsibility* (n 81) at 455.

succession.[86] As these provide for equitable principle of 'intrinsically direct link of the consequences of the wrongful act with the territory or the population concerned', they may potentially serve as an important doctrinal indication for future instances of state succession.

Considering such new developments, this book addresses the issue of state succession in obligations and rights that may have their source in a breach of international law in respect of tangible cultural heritage. In particular, the book explores the issue in light of the gravity of such violations; that is, when a given act amounts to a violation of obligations *erga omnes* and rules of *jus cogens*.

3. Methodology and Structure

The relationship between the development of international cultural heritage law and the practice of state succession determines the methodological foundations of this book. Accordingly, the predominant perspective adopted throughout the book is that of international legal positivism. This approach may appear fully justified as the topic of state succession essentially concerned the legal relations between states as the original subjects of international law. In fact, the majority of the book deals with technical principles adopted by states in relation to the variety of pre-existing legal situations involving the status of state cultural property in state succession. In other words, it explores distinct contractual arrangements concluded and enforced by states.

On the other hand, this book argues that the volume of positive rules of international law in the areas of human rights and cultural heritage seems to override such an exclusive role of states in the creation of international legal rules of state succession. Therefore, it departs from 'classical' variants of positivism in legal scholarship, focusing on states and their exclusive role in international law-making.[87] It does not, however, intend to engage with current debates concerning the criticism or even condemnation of classical positivism, nor does it attempt to define what international legal positivism means nowadays. Rather it assumes that international law in a current post-modern constellation arises from a plurality of sources, and thus law-making processes may be much more complex and include different actors.[88] These not only comprise states, but also various groups of non-state actors, and the international community as a whole.

[86] Marcelo G. Kohen, Rapporteur, 'State Succession in Matters of State Responsibility'. Draft Resolution, IIL, 9 August 2013, 14th Commission, Tokyo Session, 2013, <http://www.idi-iil.org/idiE/navig_ann_2013.html>, accessed on 15 January 2015.

[87] See for instance Jochen von Bernstorff, *The Public International Law Theory of Hans Kelsen: Believing in Universal Law* (CUP, 2010), at 28–30.

[88] Jean d'Aspremont, *Formalism and the Sources of International Law: A Theory of the Ascertainment of Legal Rules* (OUP, 2011); Jean d'Aspremont (ed), *Participants in the International Legal System. Multiple Perspectives on Non-State Actors in International Law* (Routledge, 2011).

The overview of the literature of international law shows that the positivist approach, aimed at detecting legal norms and exploring their past and present content, constitutes the major methodological perspective applied by legal scholarship dealing with the phenomenon of state succession. Yet, there are also concepts voicing more 'pragmatic'[89] or 'policy-oriented'[90] approaches to state succession, beyond doctrinal formalism, in terms of solving real problems via various available techniques and considerations. According to these theories, solutions shall be achieved through negotiated settlements considering actual circumstances (including political, strategic, and diplomatic necessities) on the one hand, and respecting the objectives of global order, justice, and equity, on the other. In fact, such a perspective may seem extremely tempting for the purposes of analysing practices of state succession in matters of cultural property, since the majority of legal instruments treat these issues as the exemption from general regimes. As such, they are subject to negotiations between the parties concerned, who usually invoke and sometimes apply a range of non-judicially relevant arguments and criteria. Moreover, the actual practice of states in terms of cultural heritage disputes is often marked by resort to fluid notions of ethics, morality, and reconciliation.[91] However, such a perspective would arguably convert the entire analysis into a casuistic description of practices and techniques used. Therefore, this book, although acknowledging that the principles applicable to state succession in tangible cultural heritage are dynamic and often inconsistent, analyses the available state practice, *opinio juris* as well as doctrinal responses of the legal scholarship in order to detect their commonalities, which would serve to formulate more concrete normative conclusions. Through such a lens, this book attempts to reconstruct the international legal framework on state succession to tangible cultural heritage and to advocate postulates regarding desirable future developments, based on axiological considerations.

In regard to the sources consulted, the book is based on a range of international instruments, official documents of international organizations, and selected case

[89] For the concept of 'pragmatism' in relation to the law of state succession, see Konrad G. Bühler, *State Succession and Membership in International Organizations: Legal Theories versus Political Pragmatism* (Kluwer Law International, 2001); Dieter Papenfuß, 'The Fate of the International Treaties of the GDR within the Framework of German Unification', *AJIL* 92(1998)3, 469–90, at 470; Gerhard Hafner and Elisabeth Kornfeind, 'The Recent Austrian Practice of State Succession: Does the Clean Slate Rule Still Exist?', *Austrian Review of International and European Law* 1(1996)1, 1–49, at 22–26; Oscar Schachter, 'State Succession: The Once and Future Law', *Vanderbilt Journal of Transnational Law* 33(1993)2, 253–60;

[90] Tai-Heng Cheng, *State Succession to Commercial Obligations* (Transnational Publishers, 2006).

[91] Robert Peters, '"Remedying Historical Injustice": Ethical and Historical Considerations in Returning Cultural Materials', in Silvia Borelli and Federico Lenzerini (eds), *Cultural Heritage, Cultural Rights, Cultural Diversity. New Developments in International Law* (Nijhoff, 2012), 141–56, at 150–54; Marie Cornu and Marc-André Renold, 'New Developments in the Restitution of Cultural Property: Alternative Means of Dispute Resolution', *IJCP* 17(2010)1, 1–31.

law. Importantly, it draws extensively on a number of primary sources on current state practice gathered in the process of inquiries and interviews conducted with representatives of successor states that emerged after 1989, as well as eminent scholars from these jurisdictions. For these reasons, the actual writing of this book has been a challenge, foremost because of the significant degree of secrecy surrounding the interstate practice with reference to succession of tangible cultural heritage and related national policies in this matter. The fact-finding part of the research has at times been difficult, since the efforts to gain access to documents on the negotiations have not often been welcomed by the states' policy makers.

In order to afford the broadest perspective on how the international law on state succession has dealt with the issue of tangible cultural heritage, this book adopts a chronological method of analysis. It begins with the first attempts to regulate the principles of state succession to tangible cultural heritage in the nineteenth century and their elaboration in the mid-twentieth century (Part I). Then it discusses the evolution of the theory and practice of state succession in the context of decolonization, codifying works of the ILC (Part II) and recent post-Cold War cases (Part III). In the context of the latter, this book deals with the growing importance of international obligations towards cultural heritage and its impact on state succession. It explores the content and sources of such obligations and analyses their status at the time of state succession. In this regard, it provides critical research into the relationship between the protection of cultural heritage and general topics of international law, in particular human rights and humanitarian law. Special attention is paid to the link between the protection of cultural heritage and international obligations towards minorities in time of state succession. The book also investigates how the developments in different aspects of international cultural heritage law and practice affect the actual settlements of controversies with regard to tangible cultural heritage in cases of state succession. These particularly refer to the procedural principle of international cooperation and alternative means of dispute resolution. Thus, the book seeks to insert the addressed topic within the broader framework of the development of international law and to provide contextualization. The value of this approach primarily rests in the fact that in the research conducted to date, the issue of state succession to tangible cultural heritage has not been the object of any general comprehensive study which combines such a volume of different cases and critical references to other topics of international law.

While providing a broad historical and geographical perspective, this book seeks to advance the main argument that international cultural heritage law exercises a profound impact on the practice of state succession. It argues that the protection and enjoyment of cultural heritage do not constitute the exclusive concern of state sovereignty. On the contrary, such values are of general interest to the international community as a whole. Hence, a new doctrinal approach, based both on the principles of international cultural heritage law and human rights law, is needed. Such an approach shall imply the limitation of contractual freedom of states in the matter of cultural agreements in favour of the continuity of international cultural heritage obligations, irrespective of political circumstances and the title of state succession. Last but not least, this book provides a short policy document entitled 'Draft Proposal of Guiding Principles Relating to the Succession of States in respect of Tangible Cultural Heritage', which will hopefully serve as common ground for further bilateral negotiation.

PART I

EMERGENCE AND ELABORATION OF PRINCIPLES (1815–1939)

As we have seen, in certain cases, treaties have approved the idea of a general repatriation of works of art to the districts where they originated or the regions whose 'intellectual patrimony' they form. We have here much vaguer ideas which, for want of clarity, might sometimes favour unfounded claims. A work of art may be associated with a country by the most diverse bonds. From this point of view one may consider the subject treated, the nationality or birthplace of the artist, the bond between the work and the nation's history, the artistic tradition inspiring it, or even its allocation to a certain place or for a given use. Certainly, it is conceivable that such ideas can serve as the basis for negotiations entered into voluntarily and freely carried on. It is sincerely to be recommend that they be imposed or that their use by systematized.

Charles De Visscher, *International Protection of Works of Art and Historic Monuments* (The Department of State Publications, 1949), 836–7.

1

Territoriality, Nation-State, and the Integrity of National Patrimony in the Nineteenth Century

Raphael's *Madonna del Granduca*, one of the best-known treasures of the Florentine Galleria Palatina, was the subject of one of the first documented interstate settlements on state succession in cultural property.

The masterpiece dates back to Raphael's early Florentine period (*c.* 1505), when the painter became acquainted with the art and artistic milieu of the city at the beginning of Cinquecento, in particular with the *œuvre* of Leonardo da Vinci.[1] Indeed, it is acknowledged that the *Madonna del Granduca* combined the skills of the various Italian Renaissance schools and, for centuries, has served countless generations of artists as a standard of perfection and beauty. In 1799, the painting was purchased by Ferdinand III of Habsburg-Lorraine, Grand Duke of Tuscany, from whom it takes its name. The Grand Duke was so devoted to this picture that he always kept it in his private bedroom and carried it with him when he travelled. After Ferdinand's death, the painting remained in the Habsburg-Lorraine collections of the ruling house of Tuscany and the Austrian Empire.

As a result of the war between Sardinia and Austria, the territory of the Grand Duchy along with all state property passed first to Sardinia (1860) and subsequently to the newly proclaimed Kingdom of Italy (1861). However, the status of the private property belonging to the monarch of Tuscany or to the members of his house, deposited after the lost war, was the subject of controversy between Italy and Austria. In fact, the representatives of both states entered into lengthy negotiations on the settlement of financial disputes arising from the succession of Italy in territories previously ruled by the Habsburg dynasty. In their agendas, both states rendered special attention to the status of Raphael's masterpiece.[2] The last deposed Grand Duke of Tuscany, and Archduke of Austria, Ferdinand IV

[1] See Jürg Meyer zur Capellen, *Raphael, A Critical Catalogue of His Paintings,* vol. 1, *The Beginnings in Umbria and Florence, ca. 1500–1508* (Arcos, 2001), 208.

[2] Wojciech Kowalski, 'Repatriation of Cultural Property Following a Cession of Territory or Dissolution of Multinational States', *AAL* 6(2001)2, 139–66, at 141–42, and Wojciech Kowalski, 'Restitution of Works of Art Pursuant to Private and Public International Law', *RCADI* 288(2001), 9–244, at 77.

demanded its restitution, arguing that the painting, to which his family was particularly devoted, constituted his private property, hence he claimed that the artwork in question could not pass to Italy by virtue of the law of state succession. An opposite view was put forward by Italy, which claimed its successor rights and historic rights to the artistic property of the Grand Duchy of Tuscany, including art collections located in state buildings and residences. In 1871, both states reached an agreement (1871 Convention of Florence).[3] The representatives of Austria–Hungary announced that Ferdinand authorized them to declare that he was disposed to redraw his claim in order not to deprive Florence, his native city, from one of its most beautiful treasures (*'est disposée à ne pas priver Florence, sa ville natale, d'un de ses plus beaux ornements'*).[4] In reply to this declaration, Italy pledged that the painting would always remain in the Palatina Gallery under the name *Madonna del Granduca*, in the distinguished setting that it occupied.[5]

The case of Raphael's masterpiece is in a way emblematic of important developments in both the nineteenth-century practice of state succession and the general apprehension of the concept of cultural patrimony. Indeed, Italy and Austria–Hungary not only reaffirmed rudimentary customary rules on succession to state property in the case of territorial incorporation—succession to the property of the predecessor located in the succeeded territory and observance of private property rights—but also implicitly recognized the importance of historical and national ties between a work of art and its territorial context. Moreover, the case of the *Madonna del Granduca* demonstrated a significant change in the perception of art collections advanced during the centuries by monarchs and ruling dynasties. In fact, since the Age of the Enlightenment, the legal status of such collections in domestic laws gradually became detached from the property of ruling houses and became classified as part of the public domain, recognized as a 'common good' of a nation—national patrimony.

In terms of normative developments, the agreement between Italy and Austria–Hungary provides evidence for the emergence of two fundamental principles driving the allocation of cultural property in state succession: territoriality and the major importance attached to national patrimony of a successor state. This chapter endeavors to reconstruct the process of their evolution and application in the international practice of state succession during the nineteenth century.

1.1 Concept of territoriality

The origins of the principle of territoriality[6] determining the allocation of cultural treasures in post-war peace settlements and territorial reconfigurations in

[3] Convention pour régler les questions financières pendantes entre les deux pays à la suite de articles 6, 7, et 22 du traité paix du 3 octobre 1866, Autriche-Hongrie—Italie, Florence, 6 janvier 1871, 1 Martens NRGT (2e série) 328.

[4] Ibid. Protocole additionnel. [5] Ibid.

[6] Read more Ludwig Englstler, *Die territoriale Bindung von Kulturgütern im Rahmen des Völkerrechts* (C. Heymann, 1964).

Europe stem from two groups of problems. The first is the emergence of the legal principle of territoriality with regard to the situation of archives and public movable property at the time of the consolidation of nation-states after the Thirty Years' War (1618–48). The second concerns the process of humanization of the rules on war conduct in respect of art treasures, on the one hand, and the recognition of the link between cultural patrimony and its territorial and geographic contexts, on the other. These latter developments were closely bound to the appreciation and veneration of universal values of art in the modern era and in the Age of Enlightenment. All of these considerations reached their peak in the post-Napoleon settlements with regard to displaced cultural patrimony.

1.1.1 The Westphalian State, territorial transfers, and the allocation of archives and movable property

The Peace of Westphalia, concluding the Thirty Years' War, marked the start of the modern international community.[7] It is credited as a milestone in building the foundations of the international legal system in the form of 'a plurality of independent States, recognizing no superior authority over them'.[8] Indeed, the effectiveness of the Westphalian system depended on clearly defined, usually centrally governed, independent states which recognized each other's sovereignty and territorial competences.[9] In exercising their territorial sovereignty, states aimed at gaining all their resources and means of effective administration as well as protecting their economic interests. Accordingly, the peace treaty practice after the Thirty Years' War sanctioned the principle providing that transfer of territory between European states ought to respect its integrity in terms of the archival fonds belonging or relating to the ceded territories, and of public property located therein. In addition, the majority of peace treaties concluded in the seventeenth and eighteenth centuries also contained restitution clauses with reference to private property seized in the event of war operations, accompanying territorial transfers.

For the purposes of analysing the foundations of the principle of territoriality in respect of state succession in cultural property, the development of the regime on the allocation of archives and public movable property requires particular attention.

a) Archives

The legal principle of territoriality binding a property to a given territory emerged originally with regard to public archives. From the Middle Ages, international treaties on the transfer of territories contained special provisions on the allocation

[7] Antonio Cassese, *International Law* (2nd edn, OUP 2005), 22–25. [8] Ibid. 24.

[9] See Christine Bell, *On the Law of Peace: Peace Agreements and the Lex Pacificatoria* (OUP, 2008), 88.

of archives. Later on, in the process of acquiring the territories by centralized monarchies such as France and Poland, the transfer of archives of the ceded lands constituted a common practice.[10] This was continued in the modern era; from the beginning of the seventeenth century, the transfer of archives followed the vast majority of territorial cessions. The *Non-Exhaustive Table of Treaties Containing Provisions Relating to the Transfer of Archives in Cases of Succession of states*,[11] prepared in 1979 for the purposes of drafting the 1983 Vienna Convention by the ILC, enumerates several treaties and agreements on the exchange, division, and distribution of public archives, starting from the 1601 Treaty of Lyon between Savoy and France,[12] which provided for the cession of certain territories and the transfer of legal documents pertaining to those lands.

This and many other settlements on the transfer of archives primarily referred to the documents indispensable for the functioning of public administration and courts. There were, however, some exceptions. For instance, the 1648 Treaty of Münster between the Holy Roman Emperor and the King of France and their respective Allies (Articles XCV and CXIV)[13] and the 1648 Treaty of Osnabrück between the Holy Roman Emperor and Sweden (Article XVI)[14] provided for the transfer of all archives and documents belonging to the ceded territories or those returned after a temporary occupation. It appears that at the end of the eighteenth century, the principle of transfer of public archives together with territorial cession was well established. According to Mohammed Bedjaoui, Special Rapporteur to the ILC, 'the principle of the transfer of archives concerning the part of territory ceded is itself justified by the application of two basic principles: (a) the principle of territorial origin or of the territoriality of archives, according to which all papers and documents originating in the territory to which the succession of states relates must pass to the successor state, and (b) the principle of pertinence, according to which papers concerning the territory in question, irrespective of where they are kept, are likewise handed over'.[15] In addition, analysing the texts of treaties, it is possible to indicate some other principles which are regularly applied. These can be summarized as follows: 1) the integrity of collections (which usually led to reproducing records and providing the copies to a successor

[10] For an exhaustive analysis of state practice on this matter, see Luis Jacob, *La clause de livraison des archives publiques dans les traités d'annexion* (M. Giard et E. Briere, 1915).

[11] ILC, Documents of the Thirty-First Session, *YILC* 2/1(1979), 82–93.

[12] Traité entre Henri IV. Roi de France, et Charles-Emanuel, Duc de Savoye, pour l'échange du Marquisat de Saluces avec la Breffe, Bugey, Valromay et Gex. Fait à Lyon le 17 Janvier 1601, 5(2) Corps universel diplomatique 10.

[13] Traité de Paix entre Ferdinand III. Empereur, Louis XIV. Roi de France, les Electeurs, Princes et États du Saint Empire Romain. Fait à Munster le 24 Octobre 1648, 6 Corps universel diplomatique 450, English translation: Yale Law School, The Avalon Project, available at: <http://avalon.law.yale.edu/17th_century/westphal.asp>, accessed on 31 January 2015.

[14] Traité de Paix entre l'Empire et la Suede, conclu et signé à Osnabrug, le 24 Octobre l'an 1648. Le Roi de France a été compris dans ce Traité comme Allié de la Suede, 6 Corps universel diplomatique 469.

[15] Mohammed Bedjaoui, 'Eighth Report on Succession of States in Respect of Matters Other Than Treaties', UN Doc. A/CN.4/292, 74.

state); 2) immunity of personal property of sovereigns as well as of political and secret documentation—these archives were usually exempted from state succession mechanisms; 3) good faith and reciprocity—transfer of archives was based on good faith and reciprocity of state parties; 4) swift delivery of archives to the successor.

Apart from these statements, it is also important to mention that from the second half of the seventeenth century, the agreements on transfer of archives gradually recognized a distinction between historic archives and merely administrative documents. This extremely important differentiation was explicitly included in two 1679 Treaties of Nijmegen, signed between France and Holy Roman Empire on 5 February[16] and 17 July.[17] Both treaties (Articles XXII and VI, respectively), distinguished historical documents (called '*literary*'), which remained with the predecessor, and archives necessary for regular administration which passed to the successor states. Accordingly, it seems that post-Westphalian states tended to retain archives of historical or political interest (inherently of cultural content and value), whereas those of an administrative or judicial nature were usually rendered to successor states.

b) Public movable property

The Peace of Westphalia also had an important impact on state practice concerning the fate of public movable property situated in the territories subject to state succession. The treaty of Münster (Article CXIV) and the treaty of Osnabrück (Article XVI) contained identical provisions stating that ceded and restituted lands (in particular, cities and castles) ought to be transferred with all movables which had been found there, and which were still situated in these places at the date of the peace agreement: 'the Records, Writings and Documents, and other Moveables, be also restor'd; as likewise the Cannon found at the taking of the Places, and which are still in being'. However, the duty to restore did not refer to those movables which had been removed in the course of war. Accordingly, 'they shall be allow'd to carry off with them, and cause to be carry'd off, such as have been brought thither from other parts after the taking of the Places, or have been taken in Battels, with all the Carriages of War, and what belongs thereunto'. The execution of the treaties' provisions was based on the principles of 'reciprocity' and 'bona fide'. Thus, both treaties provided for the integrity of ceded territories,

[16] Pax Noviomagensis inter Leopoldum Romanorum Imperatorem, suo et Imperii nomine, et Ludovicum XIV. Regem Galliae pro se, et Confoederatis ejus; Quâ, Pace Westphalica pro firma Basi et norma utrinque positâ, omnes discordiae componuntur, Philippi-Burgum Caesari, Friburgum verò Regi ceduntur; Restitutio Ducis Lotharingiae certis sub Conditionibus stipulatur, Negotium Ducatûs Bullionensis amicabili Compositioni remittitur; Nec non omnia, que per Pacem Monasteriensem de Causa Montisferrati cauta sunt, confirmatur. Actum Noviomagi die 5. Februarii 1679, 7(1) Corps universel diplomatique 376.

[17] Traité pour l'Execuation de la Paix entre Serenissime et Très-Puissant Prince Leopold Empereur des Romains, et le Serenissime et Très-Puissant s-Puissant Prince Louis XIV. Très-Chrêtien Roi de France et de Navarre. Fait à Nimègue le 17 Juillet 1679, 7(1) Corps universel diplomatique 412.

including the furnishing of castles and churches, on the one hand, and recognized the right to war booty, on the other. In reference to the latter observation, it is however to recall two treaties from that period, which challenged, to certain extent, the right to war plunder: treaty of peace concluded in Oliva in 1660 between Poland and Sweden[18] and the treaty of Whitehall between England and the United Provinces of Netherlands.[19] The first obliged Sweden to restore to Poland not only state archives but also the royal library (Articles VIII–IX), the second explicitly referred to the issue of art objects, that is the collections of Stewart dynasty (Separate Article).[20]

In the modern era, European peace treaty practice applied the principles formulated at the time of the Peace of Westphalia extensively. Furthermore, the question of just settlements of property controversies arising from war conduct and territorial transfers gained more importance in further treaty regulations. In fact, such problems were often sent to special adjudicating bodies established by parties to a treaty. For instance, this was the case of the 1659 Treaty of Pyrenees,[21] which concluded a series of French–Spanish conflicts and provided for the cession of determined territories. This, under the Article CXII, introduced the formula of bilateral mixed commissions to settle property controversies.

Arguably, it seems that the post-Westphalian treaty peace practice with regard to the allocation of movable property significantly contributed to the formulation of principles of state succession to cultural property in both substantive (principle of territoriality) and procedural aspects (consensual form of dispute resolution).

1.1.2 Pre-1815 veneration of art and condemnation of war plunder

For centuries, war plunder and conquest were generally recognized as legitimate means of acquisition of artistic objects. Moreover, territorial transfers between states based both on the use of force and contractual agreements entitled a successor to appropriate the art treasures located therein as well as gave him a right to dispose and displace them. However, the war plunder of objects designed for religious worship or those of great artistic value was condemned by legal authorities since the ancient times. In her excellent monograph *Art as Plunder: The Ancient Origins of Debate about Cultural Property* (2008),[22] Margaret M. Miles discusses

[18] Tractatus Pacis inter Regem Poloniae Joannem Casimirum ejusque Foederatos Leopldum Romanarum Imperatorem, et Electorem Brandenburgicum Fredericum Wilhelmum ab una, et Carolum XI. Sueciae Regem à parte altera conclusae. Quô omnes omnino inimicitiae inter eosdem exortae abolentur, et à Rege Poloniae pro se et Successoribus suis, omnibus in Regnum Sueciae Praetensionibus renunciatur, Livoniaque Coronae Suedicae ceditur. Actum Olivae 23. April. 3. Maii 1660, 6(2) Corps universel diplomatique 303.

[19] Traité de Paix et d'Alliance entre Charles II. Roi d'Angleterre et les États Généraux des Provinces-Unies. Fait à Whitehall, le 14 Septembre 1662, 6(2) Corps universel diplomatique 422.

[20] See Stanisław, E. Nahlik, 'La protection internationale des biens culturels en cas de conflit armé', *RCADI* 120(1967)1, 64–163, at. 77–78.

[21] 6(2) Corps universel diplomatique 264.

[22] Margaret M. Miles, *Art as Plunder: Origins of Debate about Cultural Property* (CUP, 2008).

the arguments against art plunder raised by Greek and Roman authors in some detail. She focuses on Cicero's works, in particular on his theses of persecution of a Roman governor of Sicily, Gaius Verres, in which the ancient author condemned the pillage of Greek cities of the island, invoking ethical considerations, such as the observance of the social function of art, and temperance in war conduct. She also explains that this argumentation had a profound impact on future European debates about art collecting and reactions to the spoliations of art treasures.[23] Indeed, during the Renaissance, extant Christian theories on the immunity of *res sacrae* from war destruction and pillage[24] were extended by those claiming the exemption of objects of art and literature from the right to wartime booty.[25] These were caused by the widespread indignation felt in respect of damages and plunder of monuments of art committed by French and imperial forces in Italy. In their theses, humanists recalled the examples from antiquity in which victorious commanders respected famous statues and paintings and protected them from plunder.[26] What is even more important, the Renaissance condemnation of destruction and plunder was coupled with the exaltation of superior qualities and values of works of art, which should be respected by civilized monarchs.[27]

Notwithstanding these developments, the prevailing doctrine of law of nations (*ius gentium*), had until the eighteenth century considered pillage and the destruction of the adversary's property as legitimate,[28] although enemy acts against *res sacrae* or property of monarchs were widely criticized, on an ethical basis. As regards state practice, there were only a few cases of post-conflict settlements which addressed the question of plundered art treasures. For instance, in 1553, Anne de Montmorency, Constable of France, had to hand over to the Pope the series of Raphael's tapestries robbed from the Sistine Chapel during the Sack of Rome (*Sacco di Roma*) in 1527.[29] The need for the reconstitution of stolen or otherwise displaced cultural objects was also widely discussed during the negations of the Peace of Westphalia (1648),[30] since Europe, during the Thirty Years' War, experienced huge migrations of art collections caused by war pillage and territorial annexations.[31] The most striking example is the policy of Sweden, which in

[23] Ibid. 285 ff.

[24] These developed the earlier theories on the classification of non-private property destined for religious worship introduced by Roman law, see Henry John Roby, *Roman Private Law in the Times of Cicero and of the Antonines*, vol. 1, (CUP, 1902), 408–12.

[25] See Kowalski, 'Restitution of Works of Art' (n 2) 56–67.

[26] Ibid. 56.

[27] Ibid.

[28] See Hugo Grotius, *The Rights of War and Peace, Including the Law of Nature and of Nations. Translation of De Jure Belli Ac Pacis* (Amstelaedami 1680), trans. Archiblad Colin Campbell (Washington and London, 1901 (reprint edition 1979)), book III, chap. iv–vi, 323–44.

[29] Eugène Müntz, 'Les annexions de collections d'art ou de bibliothèque et leur rôle dans les relations internationales', *Revue d'Histoire Diplomatique* 8(1894), 481–97, at 492–93.

[30] See Susanne Tauss, '"Robbery Is the Most Noble Occupation": The Looting of Art During the Thirty Years' War', in Klaus Bussmann and Heinz Schilling (eds), *1648 War and Peace in Europe. Catalog of the Council of Europe Exposition; Münster, Osnabrück 1998/99*, vol. 2 (S.N. Publishing Company, 1998), 281–88.

[31] Hugh Trevor-Roper, *The Plunder of the Arts in the Seventeenth Century* (Thames and Hudson, 1970), 22–40.

a relatively short time managed to create an outstanding national collection of works of art by the means of legitimate war booties.[32] However, adequate treaty provisions were not formulated.

In the Age of Enlightenment, the doctrine of the law of nations gradually formulated more 'humanitarian' principles of war conduct, postulating the exemption of private property of individuals and property designed for public use from war operations. In particular, Emerich de Vattel, in his monumental treatise *The Law of Nations or Principles of the Law of Nature, Applied to the Conduct and Affairs of Nations and Sovereign* (1758),[33] postulated that: 'for whatever cause a country is ravaged, we ought to spare those edifices which do honour to human society, and do not contribute to increase the enemy's strength,—such as temples, tombs, public buildings, and all works of remarkable beauty. …) What advantage is obtained by destroying them? It is declaring one's self an enemy to mankind, thus wantonly to deprive them of these monuments of art and models of taste'.[34] Furthermore, 'the wanton destruction of public monuments, temples, tombs, statutes, paintings, &c. is absolutely condemned, even by voluntary law of nations, as never being conductive to the lawful object of war'.[35] Although these injunctions explicitly concern the destruction of art treasures, it seems that they may also cover the prohibition of their plunder. As the destruction of monuments does not contribute to war, then pillage does not either.[36] More importantly, Vattel linked the protection of art treasures to the interest of mankind. In this broad view, such objects shall not be considered as ordinary property since they embody special qualities recognized universally.[37]

The enlightened condemnation of art plunder needs to be seen in relation to the cosmopolitan culture of the eighteenth century, of which the veneration of art was one of the most important features. The representatives of European elites followed similar models of education, and shared similar tastes and values. These were extensively formed during educational travel, such as the Grand Tour. It was believed that the essential value of such journeys lay in the exposure both to the cultural legacy of classical antiquity and the Renaissance, and to the fashionable and polite aristocratic culture of the major European centres. With time, the artistic aspect of the Grand Tour gained a predominant position. During such travels, Europeans from the upper social and political classes became acquainted with ancient monuments, Old Masters, contemporary art, literature, and music. The Grand Tour itineraries essentially led to Italy, but they also covered the most

[32] See Wilhelm True, *Art Plunder: The Fate of Works of Art in War, Revolution, and Unrest*, trans. Basil Creighton (The John Day Company, 1961), 91.

[33] Emer (Emmerich) de Vattel, *The Law of Nations or Principles of the Law of Nature, Applied to the Conduct and Affairs of Nations and Sovereigns* (London, 1797), book III, ch. IX, §173, 370.

[34] Ibid. book III, ch. IX, §168, 368. [35] Ibid. book III, ch. IX, §173, 370.

[36] Wayne Sandholtz, *Prohibiting Plunder: How Norms Change* (OUP, 2007), 40.

[37] Ibid. 40; Tullio Scovazzi, 'La notion de patrimoine culturel de l'humanité dans les instruments internationaux—Rapport du directeur d'études de la section de langue française du Centre', in Tullio Scovazzi and James A. R. Nafziger (eds), *Le Patrimoine Culturel de l'Humanité/the Cultural Heritage of Mankind* (Nijhoff, 2008), 3–144, at 15–16.

important German or French cultural centres where famous art collections were located. Travellers from every country visited the same sites, palaces, galleries, and monuments. Thus, for such 'cultural pilgrims', the link between art treasures and their local and historical contexts was something natural—inherent. In fact, the shared cultural values of European elites constituted an important basis for the opposition to the Napoleonic art spoliations and displacements committed during the war campaigns of 1793–1815.

As regards the situation of art treasures during the eighteenth century wars and territorial reconfigurations, state practice usually provided such properties with a certain level of immunity. As William Hall observed several decades later: 'works of art and the content of collections were spared, as royal palaces were spared, on the ground of the personal courtesy supposed to be due from one prince to another'.[38] Indeed, even in cases of evident conquest, enlightened monarchs tended to find legal justifications for territorial annexations and appropriation of property. The most important example concerns the three partitions of the Polish–Lithuanian Commonwealth to Prussia, Austria, and Russia (1772–95), which led to a total dismemberment of this state. The annexing powers imposed on the Polish–Lithuanian parliament forced it to ratify each partition in order to provide a valid title to the territory. After the extinction of the Commonwealth, the three powers divided its state property, including art collections, archives, and libraries. Importantly, a special joint commission established by the annexing powers distinguished the properties of Crown from those belonging to the last deposed king of Poland, Stanislaw Augustus. In fact, he was entitled to retain a large part of his rich art collections.[39]

1.1.3 The Congress of Vienna (1815) and allocation of cultural treasures

The plunder of art treasures committed by Revolutionary and Imperial France (1794–1815) and the scale of their restitution decided at the 1815 Congress of Vienna laid the foundations for the development of international cultural heritage law. The main aspect of the post-Napoleonic regulations referred to the protection of art treasures in the event of armed conflict and occupation. Indeed, the 1815 Congress of Vienna applied, for the first time, the general rule of restitution of cultural treasures as a remedy to war plunder.[40] However, the negotiations and the final settlements with regard to objects looted by the French army did not only address the question of post-war restitutions but also advanced the principle of territoriality in respect of allocation of cultural property in state succession.

[38] William Hall, *A Treatise on International Law* (4th edn, Clarendon Press, 1895), 439.

[39] See Stanisław E. Nahlik, *Grabież Dzieł Sztuki: Rodowód Zbrodni Międzynarodowej/La pillage des œuvres d'art historique d'un crime international* (Ossolineum, 1958), 23–25.

[40] This aspect of post-Napoleonic art restitution has been extensively explored in legal literature; see, for instance, Sandholtz, *Prohibiting Plunder* (n 36) 71 ff.

a) Pillage of art and its justification

During the wars of the Revolution, the Consulate, and the First Empire, France acquired numerous artistic masterpieces, scientific specimens, libraries, and archives from all the annexed or controlled territories.[41] French armies were followed by special official commissioners, often eminent artists and scientists, who organized the gathered 'extraction'[42] of these objects from both public and private collections and their subsequent removal to France. These were annexed to different French institutions, but the finest masterpieces were destined for the Musée Français (Louvre) and the Bibliothèque Nationale, in Paris—a new cultural centre of Europe.[43]

France justified the pillage on ideological, scientific, and legal bases. The ideological fundaments of spoliation were grounded in a theory claiming that sovereignty in all arts should pass to France in order to honour the rule of freedom and liberty.[44] Moreover, the official propaganda claimed that France was the only true 'fatherland of the arts and genius',[45] and therefore the art treasures from different locations should 'return to the Domain of Freedom'.[46] As regards the scientific arguments, these maintained that France, due to its power and the superiority of its educational system, its science and art, was the only place in the world which was able and entitled to gather, protect, and study all the masterpieces of art.[47] Acts of pillage were also justified by legal argument, which invoked the right of war booty,[48] on the one hand, and legality of transfer of art treasures formally contracted under armistices and peace treaties, on the other. Accordingly, the objects were removed as war contributions or on the basis of a territorial cession. The latter practice was particularly developed during the Italian campaigns (1792–1802). In particular, under the 1797 Treaty of Tolentino,[49] Pope Pius VI agreed to hand over to France 100 treasures from the Vatican, including the most iconic ancient masterpieces such as the *Apollo Belvedere* and the *Laocoön*, as well as the finest works of the Old Masters such as Raphael's *Transfiguration*.

[41] See Paul Wescher, *Kunstraub unter Napoleon* (Mann, 1976).

[42] Eugène Müntz, 'Les annexions de collections d'art ou de bibliothèque et leur rôle dans les relations internationales', *Revue d'Histoire Diplomatique* 9(1895), 375–93, at 377.

[43] See Cecil Gould, *Trophy of Conquest: The Museé Napoleón and the Creation of the Louvre* (Faber & Faber, 1965); Francis Henry Taylor, *The Taste of Angels. A History of Art Collecting from Ramses to Napoleon* (Little, Brown & Co, 1948), 539–70.

[44] Taylor, *The Taste of Angels* (n 43) 539.

[45] Sandholtz, *Prohibiting Plunder* (n 36) 53–55.

[46] Ibid.

[47] Taylor, *The Taste of Angels* (n 43) 542; also see *Lettres au General Miranda sur le préjudice qu'occasionneraient aux arts at à la science le délacement des monuments de l'art de Italie* (Paris, 1796), quoted in Charles De Visscher, *International Protection of Works of Art and Historic Monuments* (Department of State Publications, 1949), 824, and in Ana F. Vrdoljak, *International Law, Museums and the Return of Cultural Objects* (CUP, 2006), 24.

[48] Sandholtz, *Prohibiting Plunder* (n 36) 53–55.

[49] Traité de paix entre la République Française et la Saint-Siège, Tollentino, le 19 février 1797, 2 Martens RMPT (2e série) 130.

b) Negotiations during the 1815 Congress of Vienna

Initially, the peace negotiations between France and the Sixth Coalition did not concern the question of cultural property. The 1814 Treaty of Paris,[50] under Article XXXI, provided for the transfer of 'all archives, maps, plans, and documents' to the ceded territories. This confirmed the well-established principle of the assignment of administrative archives to the territory which they concerned, but the issue of the restitution of looted art treasures was not raised since the Allied Powers did not want to weaken the position of the restored Bourbon government. They were afraid that the dismantling of the Louvre collections would be very unpopular since the French public opinion was justly proud of the new museums. Certain objects were, however, restored under the secret agreements with the monarchs of Prussia, Austria, Brunswick, Spain, and Bavaria.[51]

The situation completely changed with the defeat of Napoleon's Hundred Days. Although the Paris Convention of 3 July 1815 and the final Paris Peace Treaty of 20 November 1815 did not contain explicit provisions on the return of artworks, the Allies firmly rejected the proposals of French representatives to include in the text of the Treaty a principle of integrity of French museum and library collections. During the summer of 1815, states of the anti-Napoleonic coalition issued a number of claims, which were dismissed by France or ignored by the Louvre officials. During the negations France invoked arguments of a scientific nature, on the one hand, and the arguments on the merits of the 1814 Paris Peace Treaty, on the other.

The scientific arguments were based on an innovative concept of safeguarding the integrity of art, historic, and scientific collections. It was claimed that housing collections in single museums would permit the comparison and study of different aspects of art and science in a single convenient location.[52] Therefore, in the interests of the entire human community, such collections should not be divided. As regards the *de jure* arguments, these referred to the right of war booty and legitimate acquisition by respective peace treaties and agreements. Furthermore, French representatives recalled the text of the 1814 Treaty, which did not provide for any restitution of art collections; *a contrario* it sanctioned their location in Paris.[53] These arguments were generally rejected by the Allied Powers, whose attitudes in respect of return of art treasures evolved at the 1815 Vienna Congress

[50] Traité de paix signé à Paris, entre la France et chacune des puissances alliées, le 30 Mai 1814; suivi d'articles additionnels disctincts et spéciaux avec l'Austriche, la Russie, la Grande-Bretagne et la Prusse, et d'articles secrets, 3 Martens RMPT (2e série) 11.

[51] Xavier Perrot, *De la restitution internationale des biens culturels aux XIXe et XXe siècles: vers une autonomie juridique. These pour obternir le grade de docteur de l'Université de Limoges*, Vol. 1 (Université de Limoges, 2005), 30; available at <http://www.unilim.fr/theses/2005/droit/2005limo0505/html/index-frames.html>, accessed on 10 February 2015.

[52] Bénédicte Savoy, 'The Looting of Art: the Museum as a Place of Legitmization' and Andrew Maclellan, 'For and against the Universal Museum in and after the Age of Napoleon', in Ellinoor Bergvelt, Debora J. Meijers, Lieske Tibbe, et al. (eds), *Napoleon's Legacy: The Rise of National Museums in Europe 1794–1830* (GH Verlag, 2009), 29–40, 91–100.

[53] See Nahlik, *La pillage des œuvres d'art* (n 39) 154–55.

from a basic desire to restore pre-Revolutionary status quo in Europe to the formulation of new principles with regard to the situation of cultural property at the time of war and state succession.

The Allied Powers were determined to recover the art collections from France, yet they had to face a question of legal grounds for such restitution. It seems that from the very beginning the position of the British delegation to the Congress was crucial. Although Great Britain did not have any particular interest in the restitution settlement, its representatives actively participated in the entire process. Importantly, they aimed at inserting restitution provisions in some general framework of principles of law. Conversely, one may argue that for the delegations of other states, the paramount reason for action against was revenge. In this context, the position of the British representative, Robert Stewart, Viscount of Castlereagh, requires special attention. He deeply influenced the legal settlements with regard to cultural treasures. Castelreagh questioned a traditional principle of conquest which would allow the Allied Powers to confiscate and divide the property of defeated France, although in his own country even the British royal family hoped to acquire a part of the Vatican collections transferred to the Louvre. First of all, he argued that the confirmation of the principle of conquest would sanction the condemned practice of Revolutionary France and would not give the Allies a sound claim to the objects in question. Moreover, the problem of share in the French booty could be a potential source of conflict among the Allies.[54] The principle of restitution to place of origin seemed, in his view, more appropriate. He argued: 'it does not appear that any middle line can be adopted, which does not recognize a variety of spoliations under the cover the treaties, if possible more flagrant in their character than the acts of undisguised rapine. The principle of property regulated by the claims of the territories from whence these works were taken is the surest and only guide of justice'.[55]

Importantly, the position of the Allies during the negotiations with France was encouraged by a petition signed by 39 famous artists residing in Rome. The petitioners insisted 'on the necessity of leaving each school's works "under the sky that had witnessed their birth" and in the surrounding intended for their creators'.[56] The most perspicacious statements were, however, issued by the renowned archaeologist, Antoine-Chrysostome Quatremère de Quincy. He vigorously opposed the French spoliations, claiming that artistic integrity *in situ* should be predominant, since the value of treasures of art also stems from their place of creation.[57] He also criticized the protests against the return of the pillaged artworks back to Italy. He observed that the nonsense and wounded vanity increased to the point where the return of art treasures to Rome was seen as an act of spoliation of what, in fact,

[54] Vrdoljak, *International Law* (n 47) 26.

[55] Citation after John H. Merryman and Albert E. Elsen, *Law, Ethics and the Visual Arts* (5th edn, Kluwer Law International, 2007), 10.

[56] Visscher, *International Protection of Works of Art* (n 47) 826.

[57] Quatremère De Quincy, *Canova et ses ouvrages, ou mémoires historiques sur la vie et les travaux de ce célèbre artiste* (Le Clere, 1834), 279–81.

had been stolen from Rome.[58] He also argued that artistic patrimony belonged to all peoples and none has a right 'to appropriate it for itself or to dispose of it arbitrarily'.[59]

The opposite view was voiced by the French representatives. Throughout the nineteenth century it was also sustained by the French doctrine of international law. The spoliations were considered as legitimate under certain circumstances, especially if they were sanctioned by treaty provisions. Conversely, the 1815 settlements were recognized as 'robbery' and 'disgraceful'.[60] Some changes in the French theory of international law appeared only in the twentieth century.[61] The feeling of injustice of the restitution imposed on France by the Allies was also shared by French museum officials and public opinion.[62] The acquisitions of the Revolutionary era were perceived as part of French imperial identity. The removal of artworks in public galleries met strong resistance. In the end, only a part of the French spoliations was returned. For instance, more than half of the objects plundered in Italy remained in French collections.[63] It seems that from a normative perspective, the principle of non-dismemberment of public, scientifically catalogued collections was partially recognized by the Allies.

The question that the plunder of the art treasures during an enemy occupation should be distinguished from the cession of such objects under a treaty was also raised in Great Britain. It was argued that the acquisition of property formally conceded to France in accordance with the laws in force at the time of the transfer should not be treated in the same way as the fruits of an unjust war. In 1815, these considerations were challenged in favour of the view that the pillage of art treasures, also under the cover of a treaty, could not be considered as legitimate under international law.[64] Moreover, the condemnation of Napoleonic pillage practice, which had, as Ana Vrdoljak noticed, 'much in common with the colonising zeal of the European Powers in non-European territories, both in its systematic execution and in the use of treaties to cede property to the conquering State',[65] did not cover colonial acquisitions of art treasures. Accordingly, at the time of the 1815 settlement no state addressed the question of the return of Egyptian ancient treasures, removed by Napoleon in 1799–1801, to their place of origin.[66] Thus, at least

[58] Ibid. [59] Visscher, *International Protection of Works of Art* (n 47), 824.

[60] See Paul Pradier-Fodéré, *Traité de droit international public européen et americain suivant les progrés de la science et de la pratique contemporaines*, vol. 7 (Pedone, 1897), 986–96; Eugène Müntz, 'Les invasions de 1814–1815 et la spolation de nos musées. Episodes d'histoire diplomatique', *La Nouvelle Revue* (1897), 703–16.

[61] See further Nahlik, *La pillage des œuvres d'art* (n 39) 155, at footnote 16.

[62] Monica Preti-Harnard, '"The Destruction of the Museum Has Become an Historical Monument": The Restitution of Art Works as Seen by Louvre Officials (1814–1815)', in Ellinoor Bergvelt, Debora J. Meijers, Lieske Tibbe, et al. (eds), *Napoleon's Legacy: The Rise of National Museums in Europe 1794–1830* (GH Verlag, 2009), 137–56.

[63] Gould, *Trophy of Conquest* (n 43) 129.

[64] William Edward Hall, *A Treatise of International Law* (Clarendon Press, 1909), 417.

[65] Vrdoljak, *International Law* (n 47) 23–24.

[66] For more on Egyptian collections of France and the legal culture, see Antoinette Maget, *Collectionnisme public et conscience patrimoniale* (Harmattan, 2009).

from the 1815 Congress of Vienna settlements one can observe the creation of double-standards in respect of rights to cultural treasures of European (or broadly Western) sovereigns and nations, on the one hand, and colonized territories, on the other.

c) *Return of cultural objects and state succession*

Generally speaking, the 1815 settlements applied the paramount principle of territoriality in respect of return of cultural treasures. Accordingly, the art objects were returned to the countries and places from which they were removed. However, the political and territorial order after the 1815 Congress of Vienna differed enormously from the pre-Revolutionary one. Therefore, many treasures were returned to completely new political organisms and sovereigns. In this way, a new trend in international relations emerged: it was implicitly recognized that in cases of state succession, a successor state was entitled to claim the reintegration of the artistic and historic patrimony of its predecessor with respect to the succeeded territory. There are several cases of such settlements adopted in 1815, but the following four are particularly emblematic.

First, the set of paintings removed from the Austrian Netherlands were returned to the newly established United Kingdom of the Netherlands. Second, the famous St Mark's (Corinthian) horses confiscated from the Republic of Venice were returned to the city of Venice under the sovereignty of the Austrian Empire. The solutions applied in the third case—*Bibliotheca Palatina*—went much beyond mere territorial connections. The precious library collection had been created between the fifteenth and seventeenth centuries in Heidelberg at the residence of Electors of Palatinate. In 1622, it was removed from Heidelberg Castle during the Thirty Years' War as a war trophy by Maximilian I of Bavaria and subsequently donated to the Pope and incorporated into the *Biblioteca Apostolica Vaticana* in Rome. Under the 1797 Treaty of Tolentino, Pope Pius VI was forced to cede the collection to Revolutionary France. On the basis of the 1815 settlements, the *Bibliotheca Palatina* was not returned to the Vatican but instead to Heidelberg, at the time in the territory of the Grand Duchy of Baden. Moreover, in 1816 Pope Pius VII donated a further nearly 1000 manuscripts, mostly in German, to the University of Heidelberg. Thus, in this case not only the principle of place of origin was applied but so too was a new one: reintegration of dispersed cultural patrimony of a ceded territory. The fourth case referred to the famous triptych *The Last Judgment* (1467–71) by Hans Memling[67] in St Mary's Cathedral in Gdansk (Danzig), from where it was removed by French forces during the Napoleonic administration of the city (1807–14). The masterpiece was produced in Bruges commissioned by the Florentine Medici family for the Badia Fiesolana Church. In 1473, the Burgundian ship transporting the painting was captured by Gdansk's kapers (privateers) and subsequently donated to Sr Mary's Cathedral. At

[67] In the first part of nineteenth century the triptych was attributed to the Van Eyck brothers.

that time, the robbery caused a diplomatic scandal between Hansa and Gdansk, on the one side, and Burgundy, the Medici family, and the Pope, on the other. The latter condemned the city council of Gdansk and demanded the restitution of the artwork.[68] However, Gdansk's burghers became very attached to the painting and managed to keep it as one of the major treasures of the city for the subsequent three centuries. Moreover, the city successfully defended its rights to the triptych, notwithstanding the constant pressure from powerful monarchs to sell it.[69] After 1815, the painting was eventually returned to the city of Gdansk, where it was fervently welcomed by the citizens.

1.2 State and national patrimony

The previous section dealt with the emergence and consolidation of the principle of territoriality in respect of the allocation of art treasures in post-war settlements and the transfer of territory. In the nineteenth century, this rudimentary principle was supplemented by national considerations, emanating from the rise of national movements in Europe, following the Napoleonic wars and the consolidation of the theory of nation-state, deriving its political legitimacy from the geographical coincidence of territorial power and cultural and/or ethnic integrity. In these processes, the historic and artistic legacies of the past as well as current cultural manifestations played a crucial role.

On normative grounds, the formation of legal rules on the protection and enjoyment of national patrimony arises from the legislative efforts of pre-unitary Italian states from the sixteenth century.[70] These were particularly developed in the Papal State, where the removal of portable antiquities was prohibited, and in the Grand Duchy of Tuscany, whose regulations limited the export of works by the Old Masters. The aim of these regulatory measures was to protect the economic interests of the state against the increasing market demand for ancient and Italian art. However, the domestic legislation of Italian states also protected their artistic integrity, claiming it as part of a country's identity. In fact, by the end of the eighteenth century, all Italian states had introduced adequate regulations on the protection of artistic patrimony, recognizing the possession of art treasures as a vital aspect of Italian society and emerging national identity. Accordingly, the monuments of antiquity and collections of ancient objects constituted a

[68] See Jan Bialostocki, *Les Musées de Pologne (Gdansk, Krakow, Warszawa)* (Centre National de Recherches, 1966), 55–123.

[69] Ibid. These refer to an offer presented by the Emperor of the Holy Roman Empire, Rudolf II, and further demands of the Tsar of Russia, Peter the Great. Interestingly, the latter attempted to obtain the painting under the cover of due war reparations, but Gdansk firmly rejected this claim, invoking the importance of the triptych for the history of the city and cathedral.

[70] For a historical perspective, see Simonella Condemi, *Dal «decoro et utile» alle «antiche memorie». la tutela dei beni artistici e storici negli antichi stati italiani* (Nouva Alfa, 1987); for a giuridical analyis consult Mario Speroni, *La tutela dei beni culturali negli stati italiani preunitari* (Giuffré, 1988).

fundamental element of the identity of eighteenth-century Romans, who considered themselves successors to the glorious past.[71] Similarly, the 1746 sale of the finest pieces from the Estense Gallery by Francis III, Duke of Modena, to August III, Elector of Saxony and King of Poland (the so-called Dresden purchase, *vendita di Dresda*),[72] was widely criticized. In this context, the legacy of Anna Maria Luisa de' Medici, Electress Palatine and last member of the Medici ruling house of Tuscany, is of particular note. In 1732, she bequeathed her large family collections of art, including the content of the Uffizi, Palazzo Pitti, and the Medicean villas, to the Grand Duchy of Tuscany, on the condition that 'no part of it could be transported or removed from the capital (Florence) or from the grand ducal State'.[73] In this way, she sought to guarantee the protection of the artistic integrity of Tuscany for the benefit of the country and its citizens, endangered by the dynastic succession of power, and potential territorial reconfigurations.[74] The successors of the Grand Duchy of Tuscany respected the Electress's will, even during the period of frequent changes of sovereignty in 1799–1815, and Napoleon recognized the validity of transfer of art treasures to the people of Tuscany.[75]

In France, since the reign of Luis XIV, artistic and scientific achievements were extensively used to promote and foster the development of state economy and the political position of the kingdom. This example was followed by other European countries in the Age of Enlightenment. Accordingly, culture and science were seen as engines of progress, on the one hand, and symbols and sources of wealth and prestige, on the other, as Emer de Vattel noticed:

> In the present age the utility of literature and the polite arts is pretty generally acknowledged as is likewise the necessity of encouraging them. The immortal Peter I. thought that without their assistance he could not entirely civilise Russia and render it flourishing. In England, learning and abilities lead to honour and riches. Newton was honoured, protected, and rewarded while living, and after his death his tomb was placed among those of kings. France also, in this respect, deserves particular praise: to the munificence of her kings she is indebted for several establishments that are no less useful than glorious. The Royal Academy of Sciences diffuses on every side the light of knowledge, and the desire of instruction. Louis XV furnished the means of sending to search under the equator and the polar circle, for the proof of an important truth; and we at present know what was before only believed the strength of Newton's calculations. Happy will that kingdom be, if the too general taste of the age does not make the people neglect solid knowledge, to give themselves up to that which is merely amusing, and if those who fear the light do not succeed in extinguishing the blaze of science![76]

[71] Sabrina Norlander Eliasson, *Portraiture and Social Identity in Eighteenth-Century Rome* (Manchester University Press, 2009), 50.

[72] See Johannes Winkler (ed), *La vendita di Dresda* (Panini, 1989).

[73] Anita Valentini, *Il testamento di Anna Maria Luisa De' Medici: Una Principessa caparbia e determinata che ha segnato il destino delle collezioni d'arte medicee in Firenze* (Polistampa, 2006).

[74] Taylor, *The Taste of Angels* (n 43) 116.

[75] Nahlik, *La pillage des œuvres d'art* (n 39) 29.

[76] Vattel, *The Law of Nations* (n 33) book I, Chap. IX, §113, 49.

Apparently, the concept of protecting monuments of the past as a public duty only emerged during the French Revolution. Within a new concept of the state, minus the institutions of crown and church, France formed its idea of the 'nation.' This was initially seen as a conjecture of individuals forming the political community under a new centralized administration. However, the Revolutionary government acknowledged a need for certain common values and ideas which would replace former hierarchies and their symbols of power, and contribute to the formation of a unified, republican, French identity. The guidelines for this new 'cultural' policy were based extensively on the cycle of reports prepared by Henri Grégoire (often referred to as Abbé Grégoire), a Catholic priest and revolutionary leader. He advocated the unification of French identity by two major means: language and the protection of artistic patrimony. As regards language, in the report of 1794[77] Grégoire postulated a gradual ban on the use of local dialects and patois in public life and public schools in favour of standardized French, perceived as essential to the concept of 'France'.[78] This postulate was widely implemented and the use of French became a symbol of national unity of the French state. The question of artistic patrimony was related to criticism of the revolutionary destruction of many monuments associated with the *Ancien Régime*, on the one hand, and the enormous flow of works of art, monuments, libraries and archives into the public domain through the expropriation of feudal and ecclesiastical goods and war art plunder, on the other. Grégoire is credited to be the first to propose a rationale for the preservation of artistic patrimony as a public duty.[79] Joseph Sax, analysing Grégoire's views, explains that 'the body of artifacts that embodied the best of the people was the quintessence of France, its true heritage and patrimony,' and 'those who were willing to see these artifacts destroyed, or sold abroad as if the nation cared nothing for them ... were imperiling the most important symbols of the national identity, those things that spoke for what France should aspire to be.'[80] In fact, this link between nation, state, and cultural patrimony is one of the most important aspects of Grégoire's thought. He advanced the view that such objects were not only the property of the new republican nation in a legal sense, but that they constituted something that had always belonged to the French nation as a whole.[81] Moreover, he perceived their seizure from the former feudal settings as their liberation and return to the people.[82] In fact, as early as 1795, a new *Musée des monuments français* was opened in Paris. The museum, dreamed up and organized by Marie Alexandre Lenoir (1761–1839), a self-taught archaeologist, brought together a number of historic monuments, sculptures, and tombs from French Medieval and Renaissance art, removed from churches and private estates

[77] *Rapport sur la nécessité et les moyens d'anéantir les patois et d'universaliser l'usage de la langue française* (Report on the necessity and means to annihilate the patois and to universalize the use of the French language), after Joseph L. Sax, 'Heritage Preservation as a Public Duty: The Abbé Gregoire and Origins of an Idea', *Michigan Law Review* 88(1990)5, 1142–69, at 1162.

[78] Eric Hobsbawm, *Nations and Nationalism since 1780: Programme, Myth, Reality* (CUP, 1997), 80–81.

[79] Sax, 'Heritage Preservation as a Public Duty' (n 77) 1155.

[80] Ibid. 1156.

[81] Ibid. 1158.

[82] Ibid.

in course of the Revolution. Hence, from the Revolution onwards, public collections have constituted an important component of French national and imperial identity.[83]

By challenging former feudal systems and secularization of public life, the French Revolution and Napoleonic wars stimulated waves of nationalism. In addition, the plunder of artworks indirectly provoked a more profound reconsideration of the nature of patrimony, national identity, and its relationship to the material legacy of the past. Upon the collapse of the First French Empire, other nations' claims for the return of art treasures was widespread and their eventual return was often the cause of public celebration. For instance, at the Brandenburg Gate in Berlin crowds welcomed the returning treasures with flowers, and in Düsseldorf, the artworks were celebrated on the banks of the Rhine with street illumination, bell ringing, and cannon volleys.[84] In fact, the reintegration of cultural and artistic patrimony was not only acclaimed by states' representatives, but also by the general public as well as artists such as Antonio Canova, who himself negotiated the return of artworks to Italy.[85]

The rise of national patrimony is linked to the rise of new cultural trends in Europe which emerged from the criticism of the cosmopolitan ideas of the Enlightenment and opposition against the French invader. In particular, German Romanticism questioned the entire political conception of the nation and pointed out the value of tradition, history, and cultural differences between peoples. Moreover, it perceived the 'nation' as having a greater value than that of a mere conjecture by individuals. In this view, 'nation' was defined as a transcendental entity determined by common culture, historic identity, and a certain common spirit or destiny.[86] This Romantic nationalism contributed greatly to the development of the modern concept of nation-state, understood as a geopolitical and cultural entity whose identity was based on cultural patrimony and on the relationship with the past. Accordingly, the possession of certain cultural objects marked a given nation or nation-state as different and autonomous from other groups.[87] In this regard, the French example of building national museums was fundamental.[88] Nineteenth-century public museums of arts were perceived not

[83] See Alexandra Stara, *The Museum of French Monuments 1795–1816* (Ashgate, 2013).

[84] True, *Art Plunder* (n 32) 190. On the policy of spoliations of German lands by Revolutionary France, reactions of public opinion in respect of plunder, and collection of documents, see an excellent publication by Bénédicte Savoy, *Patrimoine annexé: les saisies de bien culturels pratiqués par la France en Allemagne autour de 1800*, vols 1–2 (Editions de la Maison des Sciences de l'Homme, 2003).

[85] Christopher M. S. Johns, *Antonio Canova and the Politics of Patronage in Revolutionary and Napoleonic Europe* (University of California Press, 1998), 171–94.

[86] See in particular Johann Gottlieb Fichte, *Addresses to the German Nation (1808)* (Hackett Publishing Company, 2013).

[87] Vrdoljak, *International Law* (n 47) 21–23, Halina Nieć, *Ojczyzna Dzieła Sztuki: Międzynarodowa Ochrona Integralności Narodowej Spuścizny Kulturalnej [Fatherland of the Work of Art: International Protection of the Integrity of National Cultural Heritage]* (Państwowe Wydawnictwo Naukowe, 1980), 105–6.

[88] Florence F. J. M. Pieters, 'The Dutch Method of Developing a National Art Museum: How Crucial Were the French Confiscations of 1795?,' in Ellinoor Bergvelt, Debora J. Meijers, Lieske Tibbe, et al. (eds), *Napoleon's Legacy: The Rise of National Museums in Europe 1794–1830* (GH Verlag, 2009), 41–54.

only as manifestations of wealth and power but also as reservoirs of historic patrimony of a given country or nation.[89] The construction or reconstruction of a new state, of a new political order, was followed by state activity in the field of artistic patrimony.

The concept of nation-state and the rise of national patrimony led, however, to practices of exclusion and assimilation in respect of groups and minorities, whose cultural identity was perceived as a potentially threat to state unity. In these circumstances, the creation of museums or private collections with objects venerated as the embodiments of national identity and memory[90] became a method of maintaining cultural autonomy for many nations and minority groups within multinational states and empires. In contrast to state-based institutions, these were created through private and civic initiatives, and in a similar way contributed to the consolidation of cultural identity of these nations and groups in the nineteenth century.

1.3 The principle of territoriality and the integrity of national patrimony in the practice of state succession

The French Revolution and the rise of romantic nationalism launched a chain of national and social movements which determined the history of Europe in the nineteenth century. The international recognition of the independence of Greece and Belgium in the 1930s confirmed the nation-based concept of the modern state, with its cultural and ethnic boundaries. After 1848, the Year of Revolution and the Crimean War (1853–56), the post-Vienna international political order collapsed. New states emerged on the map of Europe: in the south-east, the new national monarchies of Romania, Bulgaria, Serbia, and Montenegro appeared; in the west, big political and national movements in Italy and Germany, initiated in 1848, led to the unification and rise of these two modern nation-states.

These developments led to the consolidation of the theory of succession of states in nineteenth-century diplomacy. This provided for the theory of transfer of rights, property, and obligations from one sovereign state to the other. The succession of states also included certain historic and artistic items, symbolizing the tradition, religious devotion, and legitimacy of government or dynastic rights of sovereigns, in particular state regalia and historic documents. The rise of nationalism also addressed the question of reintegration of national patrimony dispersed in the past. This was reflected in peace treaty practice where the issue of allocation

[89] Italian states were the first to create a complex system of legislation aiming at the protection of national (state) cultural patrimony through limitation of the flow of the art treasures and antiquities abroad. Read further Andrea Emiliani, *Leggi, bandi e provvedimenti per la tutela dei beni artistici e culturali negli antichi stati italiani, 1571–1860* (Nuova Alfa Editoriale, 1996).

[90] Read, for instance, the history of the Czartoryski collection—one of the first museums to gather objects of national history and memory, see Adam Zamoyski, *The Czartoryski Museum* (Azimuth Editions, 2001).

of cultural property, based on territorial and national considerations, became one of the essential components.

1.3.1 Unification of Germany

The series of treaties concluded by the Kingdom of Prussia contained several provisions on the transfer of historical and artistic treasures in cases of state succession. Under Article XI of the 1864 Vienna Peace Treaty between Austria, Denmark, and Prussia,[91] ending the second war of Schleswig, Denmark was to render to the city of Flensburg, ceded to Prussia, a famous collection of antique artifacts. The Article stated that the collection relating to the history of Schleswig, largely dispersed in the previous events, would be reunified with the support of the Danish government. Accordingly, it provided for the restoration of the cultural and historical integrity of the ceded territory.

Similar provisions were included in the 1866 Peace Treaty between Hesse-Darmstadt and Prussia. The subject of these settlements was the collection of books, manuscripts, letters, and other objects housed until the 1794 wars in the Library of Cologne Cathedral. After 1815 the Rhineland with Cologne was annexed to Prussia, but the treasure was not returned. At the time of the 1864 Vienna Peace Treaty, it was preserved in the Grand-Ducal museum and library of Hesse-Darmstadt. The Treaty, under Article XVII, stated that the collection was to be returned, but the ownership of every piece was to be decided by a commission composed of the representatives of both monarchs. Any potential controversy was to be definitively settled by an impartial arbiter.[92]

The unification of the German Empire was concluded after the victorious war against France and the annexation of the Franco–German provinces of Lorraine and Alsace. Generally speaking, the 1871 Frankfurt Peace Treaty,[93] ending the war and regulating the cession of territories, did not contain any special provisions on the distribution of objects of cultural value. However, the peace negotiations addressed the question of the integrity of historical archives. This referred to the collection of historical documents the French Department of Meurthe kept in Nancy which was seized by Germans at the time of the military occupation of the city in 1870. During the further settlements,[94] the arguments raised by France relating to the protection of the integrity of the historic collections of documents were recognized by Germany even though the majority of the former Department of Meurthe passed to Germany.[95] Accordingly, under the 1871 Frankfurt Treaty,

[91] Traité de paix, Autriche—Prusse—Dannemark, Vienne, signé à Vienne le 3 octobre 1864, 1 Martens RMPT (2e série) 307.

[92] Traité de paix, Hesse-Darmstadt—Prusse, signé à Berlin le 3 Septembre 1866, 1 Martens RMPT (2e série) 377.

[93] Signed on 10 May 1871, 143 Parry's CTS 163.

[94] Traité de paix, Autriche—France—Sardaigne, signé à Zürich le 10 novembre 1859, 1 Martens RMPT (2e série) 121.

[95] See Gaston May, 'La saisie des archives du départment de la meurthe pendant la guerre de 1870-1871', *RGDIP* 18(1911)1, 22–36.

the archives of general administrative nature referring to the ceded territories had to be rendered to Germany (Article III of the 1871 Treaty of Frankfurt and Article VIII of the Supplementary Convention), thus implicitly, the integrity of historic collections was respected. To quote Charles de Visscher: 'This is a solution justified by both the scientifically reorganized necessity of preventing the breaking up of historic collections and the absence of any political interest, on the part of the state making the annexation, in the surrender of documents of this type'.[96]

The series of peace treaties concluded in the second half of the nineteenth century, first by the Kingdom of Prussia, and after 1871, by the German Empire, showed a strong trend towards historical and artistic restoration of ceded territories.[97] It is clear that the most important criterion of these settlements was the principle of territoriality. However, the Franco–German negotiations on the historic archives of Nancy also illustrated another tendency aimed at preserving the integrity of historic document collections on the basis of their cultural and scientific values, which should not be affected by the state succession process.

1.3.2 Italian *Risorgimento*

The question of rights to cultural patrimony of ceded territories was starkly raised at the time of the unification of Italy. Under the 1866 Treaty of Vienna between Italy and Austria,[98] the latter ceded the territories of the former Kingdom of Lombardy–Venetia. Italy's goals were to establish its position as an important state actor on the geopolitical international stage and to foster the creation of a unified Italian identity. With these objectives in mind, it acted to restore its full historical and cultural integrity after so much of its cultural heritage has been dispersed dramatically, in particular during the nineteenth century. The 1866 Treaty of Vienna, among other provisions on state succession to state movable property and public archives, referred explicitly to works of art and science, and to political and historical documents of the transferred territories. Accordingly, under Article XVIII, Austria was bound to render to Italy administrative and judicial records as well as historical archives of the former Republic of Venice. Similarly, Austria had to hand over the objects of art and science 'specially assigned' to the ceded territories. The Treaty also provided for a special bilateral commission created for this purpose:

> The archives of the ceded territories containing the titles to property, and documents regarding the administration of justice as well as the political and historical documents of the old Republic of Venice, will be handed over to the Commissioners who shall be

[96] Visscher, *International Protection of Works of Art* (n 47) 830.

[97] Reinhard Alings, *Monument und Nation: Das Bild Vom Nationalstaat im Medium Denkmal—zum Verhältnis von Nation und Staat im deutschen Kaiserreich, 1871-1918* (De Gruyter, 1996).

[98] Traité de paix, Autriche-Hongrie—Italie, signé à Vienne le 3 octobre 1866, 1 Martens RMPT (2e série) 383.

appointed thereto, to who care shall be delivered the objects of art and science assigned to the ceded territory.[99]

The Treaty applied the principle of reciprocity: Italy also had to render to Austria all administrative and legal documentation concerning the territories of Austria within the boundaries as of 1866. In this mutual 'exchange' of documents both states agreed to collaborate (Article XVIII, paragraph 2):

Reciprocally, the titles to property, and documents connected with the administration and civil justice applying to the Austrian territories, which may be in the archives of the ceded territory, will be handed over the Commissioners of His Imperial and Royal Apostolic Majesty.

The Governments of Italy and Austria engage to consult each other, at the request of the superior administrative authorities, respecting all the documents and information relative to the affairs which concern both the ceded territory and the adjoining country.[100]

However, Italy was not bound to render any artistic or scientific material which may have originated in the territory of Austria. Thus, particular emphasis was given to the restoration of the historical integrity of the ceded territory.[101] Accordingly, the general aim of the recovery of the cultural and scientific legacy of Venice was balanced by the reciprocally recognized scientific value of the integrity of collections (in this case of documents),[102] on the one hand, and the immunity of private property (both movable and immovable) of the members of the Austrian imperial family (sanctioned under Article XXII of the 1866 Treaty of Vienna), on the other.

As mentioned at the beginning of this chapter, the biggest obstacle for the integration of Italian national patrimony was caused by the principle of protection of Habsburg collections comprising works of art acquired in different historical circumstances and kept in Austrian residences, museums, libraries, and other institutions, or deposited in the territories ceded to Italy. This was not only due to the special status of the Imperial family but also to the very problematic distinction between state (domain public) and private property of monarchs. As a result of the difficult bilateral negotiations, several additional agreements were signed. Two of them dealt with the question of the artworks.

As early as 14 July 1868, Italy and Austria–Hungary signed an agreement on the restitution of documents and objects of art in the execution of Article

[99] The translation of the treaty of Vienna (1866) largely follows that of Coleman Phillipson, *Termination of War and Treaties of Peace*. Dutton, 1916. xix, Reprinted 2008, 2010, The Lawbook Exchange, Ltd.

[100] Ibid. [101] See Kowalski, 'Repatriation of Cultural Property' (n 2) 141.

[102] Art. XVIII, para. 4:

'They also engage to allow authentic copies to be taken of historical and political documents that may interest the territories remaining respectively in the possession of the other Contracting Power, and which, in the interest of science, cannot be taken from the archives to which they belong.'

XVIII of the 1866 Treaty of Vienna.[103] The first four articles of the agreement addressed the question of reciprocal restitution of archives and documents. In the subsequent group of articles (Articles V–VII), Austria undertook to return certain objects which had been removed from Venice just before the territorial cession.

One of the most important objects returned by Austria was the Iron Crown of Lombardy, originally housed in the Cathedral of Monza. The crown was part of ancient regalia used from the seventh century onwards for the coronation of the Kings of Italy and of the Emperors of the Sacred Roman Empire. Its possession had great symbolic value, conferring royal legitimacy to Lombardy. In fact, Napoleon had used it for his own coronation in 1805, sanctioning his conquests. After 1815 it was returned to the Habsburg rulers of Lombardy and in 1838 used for the coronation of Ferdinand I of Austria as King of Lombardy–Venetia.[104] Thus, its handing to Italy after the 1866 territorial cession was a symbolic and definitive transfer of political and dynastic rights to the ceded territory.

As regards other settlements, Austria retained the collections of paintings taken from Venice and moved to Vienna in 1838,[105] because for a long time they were housed in the Vienna Academy of Fine Arts and other galleries of the Empire (Article V). The other agreed objects of restitution were to be gathered in Vienna without delay and examined by the bilateral commission. At the same time, both states signed an additional protocol[106] which regulated the restoration of Venetian archives. It also addressed the issue of a series of tapestries (*arrazzi*) based on the cartoons of Rafael, which had been removed from the Ducal Palace of Mantua just before the cession of Lombardy in 1859.[107] As regards the tapestries, the commissioners did not reach any conclusion. The Austrian delegation claimed first, that this question did not enter into the provisions of the 1866 Treaty of Vienna, and second, the Palace of Mantua and its furnishing were of private property of the Emperor as heir to the Gonzaga dynasty, Mantua's ruling house.[108]

In 1871 Austria and Italy signed the Convention of Florence, which included several provisions on the restitution to Austria of different artworks and historic archives of the private property of Habsburg family members as well as on the compensation owed by Italy for keeping the majority of the disputed property.

[103] Convention passée entre l'Autriche-Hongrie et l'Italie pour la restitution des documents et objets d'art en vertu de l'article 18 du traité de paix du 3 Octobre 1866 (Florence, le 14 juliet 1868), for the text of this agreement, see Hans Tietze, *Die Entführung von wiener Kunstwerken nach Italien: eine Darlegung unseres Rechtsstandpunktes; mit einem offenen Brief an die italienischen Fachgenossen von Max Dvorák* (Schroll, 1919), 13–16.

[104] Graziella Buccellatin and Holly Snapp (eds), *The Iron Crown and the Imperial Europe* (Mondadori, 1995).

[105] Henri d'Arnoux de Fleury de l'Hermite, *Objets et monuments d'art devant le droit des gens* (L. Clercx, 1934), 56–57.

[106] Protocole Additionnel. Séance du 14 julliet 1868 à Florence, for the text of protocol, see Tietze, *Die Entführung von wiener Kunstwerken* (n 103) 16–17.

[107] On the history of the famous tapestries of the Ducal Palace of Mantua and their final restitution after the First World War, read Alessandro Luzio, *Gli Arazzi dei Gonzaga restituiti dall'Austria* (Arti Grafiche, 1919).

[108] Protocole Additionnel. Séance du 14 juillet 1868 à Florence (n 106).

In particular, these concerned private property of the Grand Dukes of Tuscany, including the Raphael's *Madonna del Granduca*.

The effects of the negotiations did not, however, satisfy all Italy's claims. In 1893 Austria was approached again with regard to the restitution of paintings removed in 1838. The Austrians delayed negotiations and the issue remained unresolved until the end of the First World War. Despite this, the very distinctive character of Italo–Austrian disputes as well as the innovative final settlements on the restoration of the historical and artistic integrity of the ceded territories makes them one of the key milestones of state succession with regard to cultural property.

1.4 Conclusion

The aim of this chapter was to explore the emergence of principles concerning the allocation of tangible cultural heritage in state succession. Accordingly, by the end of the nineteenth century certain guidelines and principles were formulated and applied in international practice. The first and predominant principle referred to territoriality, understood in terms of a special link between people, land, and cultural patrimony. The concept initially developed with reference to the restitution of movables on the occasion of peace settlements and was subsequently extrapolated to situations of territorial transfers. In this context, the state practice of rendering public archives related to the ceded territory played a paramount role. At the time of consolidation of the European nation-state, such a practice also incorporated cultural patrimony originated from a territory to which state succession related. The second consideration concerned the importance of cultural property for the national identity and heritage of a successor state. This particularly referred to the settlements between the newly unified Kingdom of Italy and Austria–Hungary, in which dynastic and legal considerations were partially challenged by those of an historic and national nature. The principles of territoriality and major importance attached to national patrimony of the successor state were, however, limited by considerations consisting in the protection of the integrity of collections of universal value, whose dismemberment would cause great losses for research and science.

Finally, international practice of state succession developed a procedural principle of dispute resolution. Accordingly, the controversies between states were settled through consensual bilateral commissions of experts (eg Italy and Austria–Hungary), or on the basis of decisions made by a special impartial arbiter (eg Hesse-Darmstadt and Prussia).

2

State Succession in Cultural Property

Peace Treaty Practice (1918–1939)

The case of Raphael's *Madonna del Granduca* is emblematic for the practice of state succession to cultural patrimony in the nineteenth-century. The vicissitudes of a bronze equestrian statue commemorating Józef Poniatowski, Polish Prince and Marshall of France, serves as an illustration of the complexity of post-First World War cultural heritage considerations.

The monument was constructed in 1817–32 by Bertel Thorvaldsen (1770–1844), one of the most illustrious Neoclassical artists. It represents Prince Józef Poniatowski, the nephew of the King of Poland, Stanislaw Augustus. Poniatowski was born and raised in the cosmopolitan milieu of Vienna, and in his youth served as aide-de-camp to the Emperor of the Holy Roman Empire and as general to his Polish uncle. Initially, he was firmly opposed to the ideas of the French Revolution and in 1801–02 even sheltered in his Warsaw residence the future King of France, Louis XVIII, the exiled brother of guillotined Louis XVI. However, in 1806, Poniatowski joined Napoleon Bonaparte and became one of his most loyal commanders in the wars of 1807–13. He also acted as a major leader of the newly created Duchy of Warsaw, a puppet Polish state under French rule. During the Napoleonic invasion of Russia, Poniatowski headed a Polish army of 32,000, and distinguished himself in a number of battles. He shared with Napoleon his hey days but also his defeat. During the retreat from the Russian campaign, the Prince lost the majority of his forces and eventually fell in the Battle of Nations of 1813 (the battle of Leipzig).[1]

The end of the First French Empire also quashed Polish expectations of recovering lost sovereignty. The 1815 Congress of Vienna created a semi-autonomous constitutional monarchy, the Kingdom of Poland, in personal union with Russia through the rule of the Russian Emperor. In these circumstances, the romantic myth of victorious Poniatowski symbolized Polish aspirations of freedom and self-governance. In 1816, a Polish civic committee obtained permission from the Tsar of Russia to erect a monument in Warsaw to commemorate the Prince.[2] It was destined for a square in front of the imperial-style residence of the Viceroy

[1] Richard Phillipson Dunn-Pattison, *Napoleon's Marshals* (Methuen & Co., 1909), 294 ff.
[2] Stanisław Lorentz and Andrzej Rottermund, *Neoclassicism in Poland* (Arkady, 1986), 47.

(Namestnik) of the Kingdom of Poland.[3] Thorvaldsen was commissioned to create the sculpture which was financed by resources obtained through civic fundraising. The figure of the Prince was modelled after the statue of Marcus Aurelius on the Roman Capitol, the heroic emperor leading his army to victory. This representation, rigidly Neoclassic in form, was perceived as romantic in its significance, embodying the brave spirit of the Poles, their love of freedom, but also the frustration of a nation without a state.[4]

The bronze cast of the statue was completed in 1832, but due to political circumstances—namely war between the Kingdom of Poland and the Russian Empire (the November Uprising) in 1830–31—Tsar Nicholas I withdrew the previous consent to erect the monument. The sculpture was moved to a fortress near Warsaw with the intention of destroying it as a symbol of Polish rebellion. Eventually, the Tsar changed his mind and gave the statue, as war booty, to his Field Marshal Ivan Paskevich, responsible for the pacification of Warsaw. In 1840, the monument was transported to the private residence of the Field Marshal in Gomel (today Belarus),[5] where it remained until 1922. In Warsaw, on the site destined for Poniatowski's monument, the Russian administration placed the statue of Paskevich, which was demolished by the Poles in 1917.

After the 1921 Treaty of Riga between newly independent Poland and Soviet Russia and Ukraine,[6] the statue of Poniatowski became the subject of bilateral negotiations. Poland claimed that its removal was unlawful under customary international law, and therefore it should be restored to the original site. The monument was finally shipped to Warsaw where it was welcomed as a symbol of regained independence and national dignity. In the interwar period, the statue did not return to its originally planned setting but was instead positioned in front of the headquarters of the Polish General Staff and the Tomb of the Unknown Soldier, on the site previously occupied by the immense Orthodox Cathedral of Alexander Nevsky. This church, designed as a symbol of Russian domination over the city, was completed by the imperial government in 1912, and subsequently demolished by the new Polish administration in 1924–26. Thus, after the First World War, the statue of Poniatowski was explicitly used to reclaim the Polish roots of Warsaw's cultural and political landscape. Alas, this did not last long. German soldiers blew the statue up during the Nazi occupation in 1944.[7]

[3] Now, the Presidential Palace, the official seat of the President of the Republic of Poland.

[4] Donald Pirie, *The Agony in the Garden: Polish Romanticism*, in Roy Porter and Mikuláš Teich (eds), *Romanticism in National Context* (CUP, 1988), 317–44, at 317–18.

[5] Urszula Szulakowska and Peter Martyn, *Power and Persuasion: Sculpture in Its Rhetorical Context* (Henry Moore Institute, 2004), 230.

[6] Peace Treaty between Poland, Russia, and the Ukraine, signed in Riga on 18 March 1921, in force upon signature, 6 LNTS 51 (hereinafter 1921 Treaty of Riga).

[7] The epilogue to the story of Poniatowski's monument was written after the Second World War. In 1946, the city of Copenhagen and the government of Denmark decided to present Warsaw with a new bronze statue of the Prince casted on the original Thorvaldsen's plaster model. In 1951, the monument financed by Denmark came to Warsaw, but it was accepted as an unwanted gift by the Polish pro-Soviet administration. In fact, the figure of a Polish aristocrat fighting against Russia was more than inconvenient in the Cold War political circumstances. Thus, the statue was located in the park of the former Poniatowski's residence, far away from any official buildings. The discussion on a

The changing fate of Poniatowski's monument embody all the crucial legal and ideological considerations of the post-First World War developments in respect of state succession to cultural property. The first regards the recognition of the link between the principle of self-determination of nations and enjoyment of national culture and patrimony. The second concerns the post-war reconstruction of Europe, particularly with regard to the rebuilding of its culture. The third consideration refers to the allocation of cultural patrimony in cases of dissolution of multinational states in the light of nationalistic rivalry between states over control of cultural objects, and over national memories.

This chapter explores how post-First World War peace treaty practice approached these overlapping and complex cultural heritage considerations. It aims to individuate the major principles that may be brought to bear on post-First World War peace treaty practice in terms of normative developments with regard to cultural property. It also gathers some examples of best practice and solutions achieved in the process of interstate negotiations in terms of consensual settlements of cultural heritage related disputes.

2.1 Self-determination and cultural patrimony

In the nineteenth-century, the international practice of state succession in cultural patrimony primarily concerned a few cases of cession of territory between European states. However, for more profound changes in international law to take place, more violent political movements and forces are usually required. The First World War marked an important shift in the global order. Following the war, the dismantling of great empires, and changes of territorial borders and political systems, the right to cultural patrimony was widely addressed. This was often linked to the emerging principle of self-determination of peoples in its 'external' meaning—referring to situations in which a people breaks free from an existing state and forms its own state by means of secession of part of the territory of a predecessor state, or its complete dissolution. It was mooted that on such occasions, a people may have a claim to recover its identity by repatriation of cultural objects lost and removed in the past. On the other hand, the nation-based conception of statehood often created tensions within its boundaries in regions of mixed ethnic populations, such as the Balkans. In order to provide international stability and peaceful coexistence of ethnic and religious minorities, successor states have usually been bound to grant certain rights to these communities, which also covered the right to enjoy their culture, heritage, and traditions. In this context, the principle of self-determination was perceived as an 'internal dimension'; as

proper setting for the monument could begin only after the end of Stalinism in the Soviet Union in the late 1950s. Finally, in 1965, the equestrian statue of the Napoleonic hero returned to its original location, in front of the Presidential Palace, as planned nearly 150 years previously.

such groups were entitled to develop their cultural identity within existing state boundaries.

2.1.1 External self-determination and reconstitution of national patrimony

The link between cultural heritage and the freedom of every people to determine their own political status was explicitly addressed in the post-First World War reconstruction of Europe. On political and ideological levels, the correlation between rights to cultural heritage and the right to self-determination can be found for the first time in the Marxist–Leninist theory of law and international relations. Vladimir I. Lenin advocated the adoption of self-determination of peoples as one of the paramount principles guiding international relations,[8] particularly designed as a tool for the liberation of all colonial countries.[9] The principle referred to all ethnic groups who should be free to determine their own fate, even by secession from another state.[10]

When the Bolsheviks came to power in November 1917 in Russia, they demanded an immediate, general, and democratic peace with Germany and its allies, and subsequently suspended war operations. During this period, they used the concept of self-determination on behalf of peace. In the six-point proposal for world peace published at the time, the Bolsheviks postulated the full implementation of the principle of self-determination of nations.[11] This principle was also included in a number of legal acts issued by the new Bolshevik government. Importantly, the 1918 Constitution of the Russian Socialist Federal Soviet Republic acknowledged the right of secession for its constituent republics.[12] Moreover, in the 1918 Treaty of Brest-Litovsk concluded with Germany and its Allies, Russia renounced its territorial claims to Finland, Estonia, Latvia, Lithuania, and Ukraine as well as implicitly supporting the right of the Armenians in the Ottoman Empire and Russia to determine their status.[13] In the same year, Russia also nullified the eighteenth-century treaties with Austria and Prussia on the partition of Poland as 'contrary to the principle of self-determination of nations'.[14] With reference to the Polish question, by a special decree of 1918 the Bolsheviks recognized the

[8] See Vladimir I. Lenin, *The Right of Nations to Self-determination. Selected Writings* (International Publishers, 1951).

[9] Antonio Cassese, *Self-Determination of Peoples. A Legal Reappraisal* (CUP, 1995), 14–19.

[10] Ibid.

[11] The Russian Conditions of Peace (Joffe's Statement of the 'Six Points', 22 December 1917), in *The Bolshevik Revolution, 1917–1918: Documents and Materials* (Stanford University Press, 1934), 477–78.

[12] Constitution (Fundamental Law) of the Russian Socialist Federative Soviet Republic of 10 July 1918, see Aryeh L. Unger, *Constitutional Development in the USSR: A Guide to the Soviet Constitutions* (Methuen & Co. Ltd, 1981), 25–41.

[13] Peace Treaty between Germany, Austria–Hungary, Bulgaria, Finland, Turkey, and Russia, Brest-Litovsk, signed on 3 March 1918, 223 Parry's CTS 80, also see Yale Law School, The Avalon Project, <http://avalon.law.yale.edu/20th_century/bl34.asp#treatytext>, accessed on on 29 January 2015.

[14] Jerzy Borzęcki, *The Soviet–Polish Peace of 1921 and the Creation of Interwar Europe* (Yale University Press, 2008), 7.

rights of the Poles to reconstruct their cultural patrimony dispersed under the rule of the Russian Empire.[15] Moreover, the decree provided for special commissions appointed to collect and catalogue the cultural property of Polish nationals in Russia as well as the property removed from the territory of the former Polish Crown.[16] Arguably, it appears that the Bolsheviks *de facto* recognized that the principle of self-determination also implied the right to restore dispersed artistic and historic objects as an important element of national identity. However, with the consolidation of power, Russia did not continue this policy, as can be observed in the further practice of its negotiations with newly independent states that emerged as a result of the dismemberment of the Empire.

During the Paris Peace Conference, decisive impetus for the introduction of the theory of external self-determination was provided by the US delegation.[17] Its argumentation was based on a traditional American commitment to self-determination processes and the doctrine of President Woodrow Wilson's Fourteen Points announced in January 1918.[18] These, among other issues, postulated: 'a free, open-minded, and absolutely impartial adjustment of all colonial claims, based upon a strict observance of the principle that in determining all such questions of sovereignty the interests of the populations concerned must have equal weight with the equitable claims of the government whose title is to be determined' (Point 5); 'the freest opportunity to autonomous development' of the nations of Austria–Hungary (Point 10) and the erection of an independent Polish state (Point 13). Moreover, the US administration opted for 'a general association of nations must be formed under specific covenants for the purpose of affording mutual guarantees of political independence and territorial integrity to great and small states alike' (Point 14). Developed by the Paris Peace Conference, this concept took the form of the League of Nations (LoN), established by the 1918 Treaty of Versailles.[19] According to the Covenant of the League of Nations of 1919 (the 1919 LoN Covenant),[20] its member states were expected to 'respect and

[15] See a series of decrees and documents: Wiesław Balcerek (ed), *Dokumenty i materiały* (Warszawa: Książka i Wiedza, 1977), at 3–4, 25, 30, 31. The principle of restoration of cultural treasures to the nations formerly dominated by the Russian Empire was subsequently challenged by both the principle of preservation of integrity of the former imperial collections and the process of nationalization of all artistic and historic objects situated in the territory of Soviet Russia as part of a new social order. See Borzęcki, *The Soviet–Polish Peace of 1921* (n 14) 258–66.

[16] Andrzej Jakubowski, 'Restytucja i repatriacja polskich zabytków i dzieł sztuki z Rosji Radzieckiej po 1921 roku. Artykuł XI Traktatu Ryskiego', in Ewa Manikowska and Piotr Jamski (eds), *Polskie dziedzictwo kulturowe u progu niepodległości* (Ministerstwo Kultury i Dziedzictwa Narodowego, Instytut Sztuki PAN, 2010), 92–126, at 104–8.

[17] The notion and perception of self-determination differed substantially in the Western and Bolshevik theories of international relations; see Thomas D. Musgrave, *Self-Determination and National Minorities* (OUP, 2000), 17 ff.

[18] President Woodrow Wilson's Fourteen Points, 8 January 1918, Yale Law School, The Avalon Project, <http://avalon.law.yale.edu/20th_century/wilson14.asp>, accessed on 31 January 2015.

[19] Treaty of Peace between the Allied and Associated Powers and Germany, signed in Versailles on 28 June 1919, entered into force 10 January 1920, 225 Parry's CTS 188.

[20] Adopted in Versailles on 28 June 1919, 225 Parry's CTS 195.

preserve as against external aggression' the territorial integrity of other members. They were also required to submit complaints for arbitration or judicial inquiry before going to war. Importantly, the LoN introduced the systems of mandates in respect of non-self-governing territories (former German colonies and Ottoman provinces) in order to assist them in gaining full independence.

Although the link between self-determination of peoples and allocation of cultural property following state succession was not explicitly mentioned at the Paris Peace Conference, it can arguably be deduced from the general principle of liberation and the restoration of patrimony of a number of European states under enemy occupation addressed by Wilson (Points 6, 7, 8, 11). In fact, in 1919, the principle of postwar restoration became paramount.[21] The US delegate to the Peace Conference, David Hunter Miller, argued that this term did not only relate to the physical dimension, but that it also implied the 'psychological restoration of the liberated territories, including the reconstitution of national cultural patrimonies'.[22] Thus, the allocation of art treasures was from the beginning a significant aspect of peace negations, reaffirming the importance between state, nation, and cultural patrimony.

2.1.2 Internal self-determination and the protection of cultural minority rights

The text of the 1919 LoN Covenant remained silent in respect of the principle of self-determination. In the subsequent jurisprudence of the League of Nations, its application in the external sphere was severely limited. Accordingly, the LoN International Commission of Jurists in the report on the right of the Swedish population of the Åland Islands to secede from Finland (1920) noted that the principle of self-determination was not 'a positive rule of the Law of Nations'.[23] It explained that international law did not recognize the right to secede as it could infringe the state's sovereignty and jeopardize the stability of international relations.[24] Moreover, the issue was usually a domestic (internal) concern. Nevertheless, the Commission noted that in some cases, such as the post-First World War transformation of the international order, this principle was not just an internal matter,[25] and the right to self-determination of new states that emerged after 1918 could not be questioned. Therefore, the exercise of self-determination always depended

[21] Susanna Mancini, 'Rethinking the Boundaries of Democratic Secession. Liberalism, Nationalism, and the Rights of Minorities to Self-Determination', *International Journal of Constitutional Law* 6(2008)3–4, 553–84, at 555.

[22] After Ana F. Vrdoljak, *International Law, Museums and the Return of Cultural Objects* (CUP, 2006), 78.

[23] Report of the International Commission of Jurists Entrusted by the Council of the League of Nations with the Task, of Giving an Advisory Opinion upon the Legal Aspects of the Åland Islands Question, LNOJ, Spec. Supp. No. 3, October 1920, 5. See Ana Filipa Vrdoljak, 'Self-Determination and Cultural Rights', in Francesco Francioni and Martin Scheinin (eds), *Cultural Human Rights* (Nijhoff, 2008), 41–78, at 44.

[24] Report of the International Commission of Jurists (n 23).

[25] Ibid.

on geopolitical circumstances. In this regard, the Commission proposed a compromise for the Åland Islands which would grant autonomous status and minority guarantees to the Swedish community under the sovereignty of Finland. This solution was eventually settled by the LoN Council (1921).[26]

The arrangements applied in respect of the Åland Islands are emblematic for the post-First World War system of the protection of minorities, and perceived as completing the principle of self-determination when it arose within states as opposed to between them. Denying the right to secede provided for certain rights and autonomy within the territorial integrity of a state. Although the issue of internal self-determination does not deal as such with the allocation of cultural property in state succession, it does refer to the rights of national, ethnic, religious and linguistic minorities to enjoy and develop their cultures. Accordingly, it does not concern the cultural patrimony as an exclusive matter of interstate relations but instead recognizes the existence and need for protection of certain rights such as education, language, etc, which are to be ensured, irrespective of the question of state succession.

The origins of international regimes for the protection of minority rights are closely linked to the nineteenth-century national movements within the Ottoman Empire. The 1878 Treaty of Berlin[27] provided for guarantees in respect of equal treatment of all citizens and religious minorities. In order to maintain security in the Balkans, the great European powers and the Ottoman Empire as the predecessor state imposed certain minority clauses on the newly independent national states of Serbia, Romania, and Montenegro. These were conditions of their international recognition and transferal of territory.[28] In the meantime, the European powers applied discriminatory assimilation policies in these territories.[29] Thus, the minority clauses were seen only as obligations imposed on newly independent states, to provide 'standards of civilization,' under the tutelage of the old 'civilized' powers who were entitled to intervene.

The breach of integrity of the European empires in 1918 raised a question as regards the principles of the post-war redrafting of borders. It was acknowledged that the development of national movements conflicting with the assimilation polices of multinational empires was one of the main reasons for the First World War. During the 1919 Paris Peace Conference, Wilson's principle of self-determination of peoples within states was partially recognized, although minority guarantees were not incorporated into the 1919 LoN Covenant. In

[26] *Åland Islands*, Decision of 24 June 1921 (including Sweden's Protest), LNOJ September 1921, 697.

[27] Traité de Berlin (Allemagne, Austriche-Hongrie, France, Grande-Bretagne, Italie, Russie, Turquie) du 13 juillet 1878, 1 Martens NRGT (2e série) 449.

[28] Carole Fink, *Defending the Rights of Others. The Great Powers, the Jews, and International Minority Protection 1878–1938* (CUP, 2004), 37.

[29] For instance, assimilation polices and legislation of Germany adopted towards the Danes in Schleswig, the Poles in the Grand Duchy of Poznań and the French in Alsace-Lorraine, or the official Russification of Baltic and other Western provinces by the Russian Empire; see Musgrave, *Self-Determination and National Minorities* (n 17) 9 ff.

practice, the European powers, the United States, Japan, and their colonies were not covered by such guarantees, whereas a minority system was applied in the LoN mandate territories. Moreover, minority provisions were imposed on all the new successor states in Central and Eastern Europe as a precondition of diplomatic recognition of statehood, and special bilateral treaties had to be signed with the LoN. Accordingly, such treaties were concluded with some of the newly independent states: Poland, Kingdom of Serbs, Croats, and Slovenes (from 1929 the Kingdom of Yugoslavia), and Czechoslovakia. Other treaties were imposed on the defeated powers, Hungary, Austria, Bulgaria, Turkey, and those states that were granted with new territorial acquisitions, Greece and Romania. Other newly independent states such as Albania, Iraq, Estonia, Latvia, and Lithuania had to accept minority obligations as a requirement of their admission to the League.[30] Thus, the protection of minority rights, which could not be altered by domestic legislation, became a crucial condition for the international recognition of territorial sovereignty and evidence of the level of civilization.[31]

The LoN minority treaties were modelled on that concluded with Poland on 28 June 1919.[32] This provided for two major obligations: 1) equal political, civil, and religious rights to individual members of a minority group with other citizens of the state, 2) protection of the rights to education, language, and development of national identity also by ensuring state aid in this matter. In the case of a breach of these obligations, minorities could direct their complaints to the League of Nations Council. A perspicacious interpretation of these minority guarantees was developed by the Permanent Court of International Justice in *Minority Schools in Albania* (1935):[33]

> The idea underlying the treaties for the protection of minorities is to secure for certain elements incorporated in a state, the population of which differs from them in race, language or religion, the possibility of living peaceably alongside that population and coopering amicably with it, while at the same time preserving the characteristics which distinguish them from the majority, and satisfying the ensuing special needs.
>
> In order to attain this object, two things were regarded as particularly necessary, and have formed the subject of provisions in these treaties.
>
> The first is to ensure the nationals belonging to racial, religious or linguistic minorities shall be placed in every respect on a footing of perfect equality with the other nationals of the state.
>
> The second is to ensure for the minority elements suitable means for the preservation of their racial peculiarities, their traditions and their national characteristics.

[30] Jennifer Jackson Preece, 'Minority Rights in Europe: From Westphalia to Helsinki', *Review of International Studies* 23(1997)1, 1–18.

[31] Compare Nathaniel Berman, 'Beyond Colonialism and Nationalism? Ethiopia. Czechoslavakia and Peaceful Change', *Nordic Journal of International Law* 65 (1996)3/4, 421–79, at 432–37.

[32] Treaty between the Principal Allied and Associated Powers and Poland, signed in Versailles on 28 June 1919, 225 Parry's CTS 412 ('Polish Minority Treaty' or 'Little Versailles'), also available at: <http://www.forost.ungarisches-institut.de/pdf/19190628-3.pdf>, accessed on 27 January 2015.

[33] *Minority Schools in Albania*, Advisory Opinion of 6 April 1935, PCIJ ser.A/B, No. 64.

These two requirements are indeed closely interlocked, for there would be no true equality between a majority and a minority if the latter were deprived of its own institutions, and were consequently compelled to renounce that which constitutes the very essence of its being as a minority.

Thus, apart from political rights, it appears that the recognition of minority rights was also manifested in the sphere of cultural matters. The court interpreted the minority obligations as a duty to ensure 'suitable means for the preservation of their rational peculiarities, their traditions and their national characteristics.' These groups' rights may be arguably perceived as cultural rights.[34] In other words, the minority guarantees provided for the 'recognition of the right to internal self-determination with regard to certain cultural matters, for such groups'.[35]

With respect to the dissolution of the Russian Empire, the protection of certain minority rights was provided by the treaties between Russia and some new states that emerged after 1917, independently from the LoN regime. In particular, the relevant provisions were drafted on the occasion of the conclusion of the 1920 Treaty of Tartu, between Finland and Russia (the 1920 Treaty of Tartu II),[36] and the 1921 Treaty of Riga between Poland, Russia, and Ukraine. Accordingly, in two special declarations of 14 October 1920 inserted in the *procès-verbal* by the Finnish and Russian delegations at the peace negotiations in Tartu (Dorpat), both states reciprocally recognized a broad catalogue of minority rights of Finish and Russian national minorities in Eastern Karelia, and Ingria, respectively. Whereas, in the 1921 Treaty of Riga, under Article 7 § 1, Poland, Russia, and Ukraine undertook reciprocal obligations concerning the freedom of intellectual development, use of language, and practice of religion. The nature of these obligations can also be perceived in terms of the reciprocal protection of cultural rights of national minorities.

In practice, the post-First World War minority system was not widely used. In fact, from the beginning of the 1930s, with the recurrent rise of nationalism, internal assimilationist policies were widely applied. Moreover, there was an opposite tendency to the LoN principles in the exchange of ethnic and religious minorities—seen as a source of destabilization of the territorial and political order. An ethnically homogeneous society was considered optimal. In particular, extensive displacements of populations were applied with regard to the dissolution of the Ottoman Empire in the case of Greece, Turkey, and Bulgaria. Thus, the link between people, cultural heritage and territory was broken. Exchange or displacement of populations, though not supported by legal doctrine, was often applied in international practice until the times of the post-Second World War settlements.

Notwithstanding these facts, the inclusion of certain obligations towards the protection of cultural rights in the context of minority treaties marked an important shift in the practice of state succession. It became acknowledged that the

[34] Vrdoljak, *International Law* (n 22) 77. [35] Ibid.

[36] Treaty of Peace between Finland and Soviet Government of Russia, signed in Dorpat (Tartu) on 14 October 1920, 3 LNTS 5.

replacement of one state by another should not affect the right to protect and enjoy the culture and identity of peoples inhabiting the territory to which state succession related.

2.2 Allocation of cultural property—the complexity of the post-First World War regulations

The great destruction of European cultural heritage during the Second World War often diminishes the losses in national patrimony suffered by many states during the First. Casualties of important works of art were committed by all sides on all First World War fronts. The scale of damages was particularly shocking for West European societies, who from the mid-nineteenth century widely acknowledged the value of preserving monuments of the past as a vital part of national identity and national pride. Moreover, the destruction and pillage of property and buildings dedicated to religion, education, art, and science were prohibited under binding international instruments on war conduct since the Peace Conferences of 1899[37] and 1907.[38] The popular reaction to the bombarding of national cultural icons such as the Cathedral in Reims (France) or to the burning of the Cloth Hall in Ypres and the University Library of Louvain (Belgium) was extremely violent. This sentiment was effectively exploited by official war propaganda. In particular, France and Germany accused each other of 'barbarian' practices and 'vandalism'.[39] The Paris Peace Conference was heavily affected with a tense atmosphere dominating meetings of the Reparation Committee, in which all the claims were addressed.[40]

The post-First World War peace treaties formed a very complex system of regulations referring to cultural property. Generally speaking, they may be summarized into four major groups:[41] 1) restitution of cultural treasures and reparation for cultural loss in response to war damages in Europe; 2) repatriation based on the general principle of territoriality in cases of state succession; 3) repatriation of cultural treasures aimed at reconstruction of national heritage, primarily in Central and Eastern Europe; 4) protection and access to cultural treasures and

[37] Regulations annexed to the II Hague Convention (1899) on war on land, Art. 56 of the Convention (II) with Respect to the Laws and Customs of War on Land, with Annex, adopted in The Hague on 29 July 1899, entered into force 4 September 1900, 187 Parry's CTS 429.

[38] Regulations annexed to the IV Hague Convention (1907) on war on land, Arts 27 and 56 of the Convention (IV) Respecting the Laws and Customs of War on Land, and Annex, signed in The Hague on 18 October 1907, entered into force 26 January 1910, 208 Parry's CTS 77.

[39] Nicola Lambourne, 'Production Versus Destruction: Art, World War I and Art History', *Art History* 22(1999)3, 347–63.

[40] See Philip Burnett, *Reparations at the Paris Peace Conference from Standpoint of the American Delegation*, vol. I (Octagon Books, 1940), 876.

[41] Compare Wojciech Kowalski, 'Repatriation of Cultural Property Following a Cession of Territory or Dissolution of Multinational States', *AAL* 6(2001)2, 139–66, Vrdoljak, *International Law* (n 22) 79.

archaeological sites in the colonial and Middle East territories ceded by Germany and Turkey. These different groups of regulations overlap and it sometimes seems almost impossible to systematize them methodologically. In fact, in the entire set of post-First World War peace treaties, only the 1919 Treaty of Neuilly concluded between the Allied Powers and Bulgaria[42] dealt exclusively with the restitution of art treasures removed during the war. Other peace treaties included general restitution provisions, which in part related to war plunder, in part to state succession.

2.3 Restoration of national patrimonies displaced or lost in relation to the First World War

All the peace treaties concluding the First World War provided for the restitution of movable cultural property removed during the war from occupied and ceded territories. Apparently, these were drafted not only in order to restore the former integrity of invaded territories, but also to deal with some older claims which existed prior to the First World War. In addition, several regulations introduced to some extent restitution-in-kind as a form of reparation for irretrievable losses of cultural patrimony.[43]

As regards the settlements with Germany, a more extensive list of claims was issued by Belgium and France. Accordingly, under Article 245 of the 1919 Treaty of Versailles, Germany had to hand over to France not only the 'trophies, archives, historical souvenirs or works of art' removed during the First World War, but also those taken in the war of 1870–71. However, the French proposals to broaden these provisions via the inclusion of the principle of restitution-in-kind for cultural property damaged by German forces were rejected.[44]

With reference to Belgium's claims, Germany, under Article 247, had to replace the manuscripts, incunabula, printed books, maps, and objects of collection 'corresponding in number and value' to those destroyed in the Library of Louvain in 1914.[45] Moreover, Belgium was compensated for its losses in artistic patrimony with famous Flemish paintings, legally acquired by German public collections in the nineteenth century. Accordingly, Germany had to restore to Belgium not only the panels of the famous triptych *Adoration of the Mystic Lamb*, also known as *Ghent Altarpiece* (1432), by the Van Eyck brothers from the Cathedral of St Bavon in Ghent, which German forces seized during the First World War, but also other

[42] Treaty of Peace between the Allied and Associated Powers and Bulgaria, signed at Neuilly-Sur-Seine on 27 November 1919, 226 Parry's CTS 332.

[43] Ana Filipa Vrdoljak, 'Enforcement of Restitution of Cultural Heritage through Peace Agreements', in Francesco Francioni and James Gordley (eds), *Enforcing International Cultural Heritage Law* (OUP, 2013), 22–39, at 25–26.

[44] Douglas Rigby, 'Cultural Reparations and a New Western Tradition', *American Scholar* 273(Summer 1944), 278–84.

[45] The reconstructed Library of Louvain was, however, burnt down by Germans in 1940; 900,000 books and manuscripts were destroyed.

panels of these triptychs purchased by the King of Prussia 100 years earlier and held in the Gemäldegalerie in Berlin.[46] Analogously, Germany was bound to hand over four panels of the triptych *Last Supper* (1464–67) by Dierick (Dirk) Bouts, two from the collections of the Berlin Gemäldegalerie, two from the Old Pinakothek in Munich, with the objective of completing the central panel of the altarpiece preserved in its original location in the Church of St Peter at Louvain (itself heavily damaged by German artillery fire in 1914).[47] The surrender of the painting to Belgium was perceived both as a form of reparation for the infringement of rules of law by Germany and reconstruction of dismemberment of works of art of immense universal value.[48]

Similarly founded claims were also raised by Italian representatives, who demanded cultural reparation for the destruction of a number of valuable frescoes and churches caused by German and Austrian air raids and bombardments in the regions of Veneto and Emilia-Romagna: the colossal fresco *Transportation of the Holy House of Loretto* (1743) by Giambattista Tiepolo, in the Church of the Scalzi in Venice, bombed in 1915.[49] In press interviews, it was suggested that Italy should be compensated by being given the finest Renaissance paintings from the Dresden Gallery, including the renowned *Sistine Madonna* by Raphael, and *Holy Night* by Correggio. These had been acquired in the mid-eighteenth century by the Elector of Saxony, and Italy sought to have them restored. It appears, however, that these claims against Germany were never considered seriously at the Paris Peace Conference.

As regards the peace with Austria and Hungary, the regulations on the restitution of works of art were included in two peace treaties: the 1919 Treaty of Saint-Germain,[50] with Austria, and the 1920 Treaty of Trianon, with Hungary.[51] These provided under Article 191 and Article 175, respectively, for the return of 'all records, documents, objects of antiquity and of art, and all scientific and bibliographical material taken away from the invaded territories, whether they belong to the state or to provincial, communal, charitable or ecclesiastical

[46] Michael J. Kurtz, *America and the Return of Nazi Contraband: The Recovery of Europe's Cultural Treasures* (CUP, 2006) 24.

[47] Ibid. 30. The nature of restitution to Belgium became very problematic and Art. 247 was added very late to the text of the 1919 Treaty of Versailles. The problem of restitution in kind and reparations paid in cultural property was intensely discussed during the Paris Conference and was not accepted as a general rule of the post-war settlements. On the different views on this problem and the Paris negotiations, see Wojciech Kowalski, 'Restitution of Works of Art Pursuant to Private and Public International Law', *RCADI* 288(2001), 9–244, at 70–74, and the bibliography provided therein.

[48] Thomas Bodkin, *Dismembered Masterpieces: A Plea for their Reconstruction by International Action* (Collins, 1945), 13–15; see also Vrdoljak, 'Enforcement of Restitution' (n 43) 26–27.

[49] 'Art Seizures by Italy. Armistice Commission Begins Taking Masterpieces from Vienna and May Demand Others, Including Sistine Madonna', *The New York Times*, 13 April 1919, 6–7.

[50] Treaty of Peace between the Allied and Associated Powers and Austria together with Protocol and Declarations, signed at St Germain-en-Laye on 10 September 1919, entered into force on 8 November 1921, 226 Parry's CTS 8.

[51] Treaty of Peace between the Allied and Associated Powers and Hungary together with Protocol and Declarations, signed at Trianon on 4 June 1920, entered into force on 26 July 1921, 6 LNTS 187.

administrations or other public or private institutions'. Moreover, under Article 192 of the 1919 Treaty of Saint-Germain and Article 176 of the Treaty of Trianon, Austria and Hungary had to 'restore objects of the same nature as those referred to in the preceding Article which may have been taken away since 1 June 1914 from the ceded territories, with the exception of objects bought from private owners'. Thus, both treaties not only provided for the repatriation of objects removed during the war from the ceded territories, but also for a certain 'cultural compensation'—restitution-in-kind for the lost or destroyed cultural property.

Other peace treaties concluded after the First World War also contained restitution provisions: the 1919 Treaty of Neuilly, with Bulgaria, under Article 126; the 1920 Treaty of Sèvres, with Turkey, under Article 420.[52] These reaffirmed the paramount criterion of territoriality, which was to govern the postwar settlements with regard to the allocation of cultural property.

2.4 Territorial cession and the allocation of cultural property

The subsequent group of treaty regulations consists in the allocation of cultural property displaced from the ceded territories, on the basis of the rudimentary principle of territoriality. This provided that territorial cession not only entailed the transfer of cultural property located in the territory in question, but also the repatriation of property removed from that territory prior to the date of cession. As regards the 1919 Treaty of Versailles, such provisions were drafted under the already mentioned Article 245, which regulated the cession of the territory of Alsace-Lorraine to France. The peace treaties with Austria and Hungary demanded that both states would hand over to the Allies 'all the records, documents and historical material possessed by public institutions which may have a direct bearing on the history of the ceded territories' (Article 193 paragraph 1 of the 1919 Treaty of Saint-Germain, and Article 177 paragraph 1 of the 1920 Treaty of Trianon). Accordingly, these provisions referred to the materials removed from the ceded territories during the previous ten years in the case of Austria, and in the period from 1 January 1868 with regard to Hungary.[53] In both treaties the period was extended in respect of Italy to the date of the proclamation of the Kingdom in 1861. In addition, it is important to highlight that the repatriation of these materials was also based on reciprocity (Article 193 paragraph 2 of the 1919 Treaty of Saint-Germain and Article 178 of the 1920 Treaty of Trianon):

> The new states arising out of the former Austro-Hungarian Monarchy and the states which receive part of the territory of that Monarchy undertake on their part to hand over to Austria the records, documents and material dating from a period not exceeding twenty

[52] Treaty of Peace with Turkey, signed on 10 August 1920, not ratified; replaced by the Treaty of Peace, signed at Lausanne on 24 July 1923, entered into force on 6 August 1924, 28 LNTS 11.

[53] The date when the constitutional reform introducing the dual Austro-Hungarian Monarchy came into force.

years which have a direct bearing on the history or administration of the territory of Austria and which may be found in the territories transferred.

Similarly, Turkey was obliged to restore administrative records as well as cultural treasures and historic archives related to the ceded territories. This, however, referred only to the disposals made during the First World War. Under Article 422 of the 1920 Treaty of Sèvres, 'all objects of religious, archaeological, historical or artistic interest which have been removed since August 1, 1914, from any of the territories detached from Turkey' had to be restored by Turkey to the state which succeeded in the territory from which the objects in question had been removed. Moreover, Turkey was obliged to hand over such items even if they had passed into private ownership.

With reference to the administrative records referring to the ceded territories, under the 1920 Treaty of Sèvres these had to be handed over to the Allies. In the case where such documents would concern 'equally the administrations in Turkey', and because of that they could not be returned 'without inconvenience to such administrations', Turkey accepted that the states concerned would have access to such documents, on the basis of reciprocity.[54]

Similar provisions on the repatriation of cultural property and archives removed during the war from the ceded territories were inserted into the group of treaties concluded between Russia and four successor states: Latvia,[55] Lithuania,[56] Estonia, and Poland. Accordingly, Russia had to restore to these states all cultural objects, scientific collections, and archives as well as property of cultural and scientific institutions illegally removed or officially evacuated during the war operations (in the case of Latvia and Lithuania between 1914–17,[57] and Poland between 1914–15).[58] With regard to Estonia, the 1920 Treaty of Tartu (1920 Treaty of Tartu I)[59] attached special importance to the repatriation of the precious collections of antiquities and paintings from the University of Tartu (Dorpat University), evacuated by Russia to Voronezh in 1918 (Article 12 paragraph 4). In the cases of Latvia, Lithuania, and Estonia, the obligation of Russia to return the demanded cultural objects was, however, limited. Accordingly, return was due insofar as these items were in actual possession or would be reported to be possessed by the Russian state or its institutions.[60]

[54] Under Arts 423 and 425, it also provided for access to certain particular groups of historic archives and records: Library of the Russian Archaeological Institute at Constantinople, and documents related to the administration of Wakfs, localized religious communities in territories ceded from Turkey. In the last case, it reciprocally applied also to the states, which took control over former Ottoman territories.

[55] Peace Treaty between Latvia and Soviet Government of Russia, negotiated at Moscow and completed and signed at Riga on 11 August 1920, 2 LNTS 195 (hereinafter the 1920 Treaty of Riga).

[56] Peace Treaty and Protocol between Lithuania and Soviet Government of Russia, signed at Moscow on 12 July 1920, 3 LNTS 105 (hereinafter the 1920 Treaty of Moscow).

[57] Art. 11 § 1 and Art. 12 § 2 of the 1920 Treaty of Riga, Art. 9 § 1, Art. 10 § 1 of the 1920 Treaty of Moscow.

[58] Art. 11 § 9 of the 1921 Treaty of Riga.

[59] Treaty of Peace between Russia and Estonia, signed at Tartu on 2 February 1920, 11 LNTS 29 Art. 12 para. 4.

[60] Art. 11 § 1 and Art. 14 § 1 of the 1920 Treaty of Riga, Art. 9 § 1 and Art. 10 § 1 of the 1920 Moscow Treaty, Art. 12 § 4 of the 1920 Treaty of Tartu I.

Conversely, there was no similar limitation in the 1921 Treaty of Riga with Poland. Furthermore, Russia had to hand over to Poland a 'suitable equivalent' for any object of particular cultural or historic value, lost or destroyed as a result of the forceful evacuation of cultural property in 1914–15.[61]

It seems clear that these regulations referred both to the restitution of objects plundered in time of war and to the repatriation of those displaced and/or evacuated relatively shortly before the date of state succession in different factual circumstances. Thus, the allocation was governed by a very clear criterion: what belongs to the territory and was removed shall be handed over.

2.5 Dissolution of a multinational state and reintegration of national patrimonies

The post-First World War settlements consistently addressed the concept of reintegration of national historic and artistic patrimony in cases concerning the dismantling of multinational empires. Certain similar practices had obviously appeared before—for instance, the return of the *Bibliotheca Palatina* to Heidelberg in 1815—but never on such a scale. In fact, the solutions adopted after 1918 were founded on the idea of correction/repair of historic wrongs experienced under the rule of the defeated empires.

2.5.1 Dissolution of the German Empire

Under the 1919 Treaty of Versailles, the biggest territorial cession made by Germany concerned the transfer of the Eastern provinces of the former Kingdom of Prussia to Poland. At the 1919 Paris Conference, the Polish delegation presented a proposal to include the issue of restoration of Polish cultural property removed by the Prussian army and administration from the end of the eighteenth century. In the presented memorandum, Poland demanded the repatriation of 'all libraries, museum collections, and all objects of art, science and religion, as well as historical relicts, which for any reason whatsoever have been sequestrated, confiscated, taken away... from any territory of Poland.'[62] These claims were not, however, considered at the Conference on a formal basis, since at the time when the requested properties were displaced, Poland 'did not fulfil the requirement of being an independent, allied or associated state or of country in a state of war in Germany'.[63] Therefore, these issues were delegated to bilateral Polish–German negotiations. In 1920, both states signed financial agreements which under Article VI provided that Germany would restore 'all acts, documents, monuments, works

[61] Art. 11 §9 of the 1921 Treaty of Riga.
[62] Burnett, *Reparations at the Paris Peace Conference* (n 40) 886, document no. 257, Art. 1.
[63] Kowalski, 'Repatriation of Cultural Property' (n 41) 156.

of art and other scientific or library materials which had been removed from the lands conveyed to Poland.'[64]

In practice, Poland encountered a number of problems in delivering the relevant documentation. As Wojciech Kowalski relates, the only attempt in this matter was made in respect of Sandro Botticelli's *Madonna with Singing Angels*, also known as *Tondo Raczynski* (*c.*1478). The masterpiece, owned by the Polish aristocratic family Raczyński, was deposited in the Kaiser-Friedrich-Museum in Berlin, prior to 1918. Poland did not succeed in the negotiations and the painting remained in Germany as a loan, until Poland was granted its formal supervision, under §19 of the 1925 agreement on family estates:[65]

> (1) The picture by Sandro Botticelli entitled 'Madonna and Child, surrounded by a choir of singing angels', belonging to the family trust estate 'Graf Athanasius von Raczynski' which is in the picture gallery of the Kaiser Friedrich Museum in Berlin, shall be transferred to Polish control.
> (2) Inasmuch as the Prussian revenue authorities assert contractual rights to the possession of the picture in question while the Polish Government contest these rights, the parties reserve the right to conclude a special agreement with regard to the legal questions involved and with regard to the question whether, and under what circumstances, the transfer of the picture is to be effected.

This special act regulated the situation of private estates affected by the change of state borders. The principle of territoriality was paramount, and accordingly, each state assumed control over the property in question situated on its territory at the time of the coming into force of the 1925 Agreement. Although it provided for future negotiations on the status of the Botticelli painting, no subsequent agreement was signed. After the Second World War, the painting was eventually sold by the Raczyński family to the Government of the Federal Republic of Germany and it now sits to the collection of the Gemäldegalerie in Berlin.[66]

[64] Polish–German Financial Agreements dated 9 January 1920 in *Rokowania polsko-niemieckie z 9 stycznia 1920* (Warszawa, 1925); English translation after Kowalski, 'Repatriation of Cultural Property' (n 41) 156, footnote 34.

[65] Agreement between Germany and Poland Concerning Family Estates, signed in Berlin on 16 December 1925, 46 LNTS 139. As regards *Tondo Botticelli*, the special provisions were to be found under §19:

> '(1) The picture by Sandro Botticelli entitled "Madonna and Child, surround by a choir of singing angels", belonging to the family trust estate "Graf Anthanasius von Raczynski' which is in the picture gallery of the Kaiser Friedrich Museum in Berlin, shall be transferred to Polish control.
> (2) Inasmuch as the Prussian revenue authorities assert contractual rights to the possession of the picture in question while the Polish Government contest these rights, the parties reserve the right to conclude a special agreement with regard to the legal questions involved and with regard to the question whether, and under what circumstances, the transfer of the picture is to be effected'.

[66] Nicolas Powell, 'Notes on German Art Collections since 1945', *The Burlington Magazine* 96(1954)620, 338–44, at 339.

2.5.2 Dissolution of Austria–Hungary

The question of the reintegration of national cultural patrimony and the distribution of imperial collections became crucial with regard to the dismemberment of Austria–Hungary and the Russian Empire. In both cases, the successor states claimed for the return of cultural treasures which had been removed by the predecessor state from their respective territories with no time limits with regard to the date of removal. However, the final solutions and settlements of claims substantially differed.

a) Treaty provisions

The 1919 Treaty of Saint-Germain and the 1920 Treaty of Trianon embodied the general tenet of repatriation of archives and cultural property belonging to the Austro–Hungarian government or the Crown to their places of origin, if they were illegally removed from the ceded territories.[67] Under Article 195 of the Treaty of Saint-Germain, the claims of Italy, Belgium, Poland, and Czechoslovakia (the reciprocal demands by Hungary were moved to the 1920 Treaty of Trianon) on the return of 'objects or manuscripts in possession of Austria' and listed in the attached annexes, were to be examined and settled 'within a period of twelve months from the coming into force of the present Treaty' by a special Committee of Three Jurists appointed by the Reparation Commission. The decision of the Committee was binding.

The longest list of documented claims was submitted by Italy in Annex I to Article 195, which settled former claims, pending from the 1866 Treaty of Vienna. The said Annex included three major groups of items: 1) number of objects removed between the eighteenth and nineteenth centuries from the Grand Duchy of Tuscany[68] and the Duchy of Modena,[69] governed until 1859 by the members of the Habsburg dynasty; 2) 'objects made in Palermo in the twelfth century for the

[67] For an extensive analysis of the topic, see Yves Huguenin-Bergenat, Kulturgüter bei Staatensukzession: *Die internationalen Verträge Österreichs nach dem Zerfall der österreichisch-ungarischen Monarchie im Spiegel des aktuellen Völkerrechts* (De Gruyter, 2010).

[68] ANNEX I [to Part VIII, Section II]

TUSCANY

The Crown jewels (such part as remains after their dispersion); the private jewels of the Princess Electress of Medici; the medals which form part of the Medici heirlooms and other precious objects—all being domanial property according to contractual agreements and testamentary dispositions—removed to Vienna during the eighteenth century.

Furniture and silver plate belonging to the House of Medici and the 'jewel of Aspasios' in payment of debts owed by the House of Austria to the Crown of Tuscany.

The ancient instruments of astronomy and physics belonging to the Academy of Cimento removed by the House of Lorraine and sent as a present to the cousins of the Imperial House of Vienna.

[69] ANNEX I [to Part VIII, Section II]

MODENA

A 'Virgin' by Andrea del Sarto and four drawings by Correggio belonging to the Pinacothek of Modena and removed in 1859 by Duke Francis V.

Norman kings and employed in the coronation of the Emperors, which were carried off from Palermo' in 1718, and at the time of the treaty preserved in Vienna; 3) objects and manuscripts removed from Naples during Austrian rule in the first part of the eighteenth century; 4) 'various documents carried off at different times from the state Archives of Milan, Mantua, Venice, Modena and Florence'.

The Annex II to Article 195 enumerated the assertions of Belgium, which not being a successor state of Austria claimed a share in the imperial collections. Accordingly, it demanded several objects removed from the southern Netherlands by the Austrian administration in the eighteenth century.[70] Thus, Belgium aimed to reconstruct its cultural patrimony, affected by the centralized politics of the Habsburgs, and to settle claims which could be raised at the time of its independence in the nineteenth century.

The Annexes III and IV contained a list of objects claimed by the new successor states of Austria–Hungary, Poland, and Czechoslovakia. Poland managed to list only one well-documented item: the gold cup of King Ladislaus IV, removed from the territory forming part of Poland subsequent to the first partition of the Polish–Lithuanian Commonwealth in 1772. Instead, Czechoslovakia claimed a number of objects and documents taken from its territory by Habsburg emperors between the seventeenth and twentieth centuries.[71]

The three following MSS. belonging to the Library of Modena: Biblia Vulgata (Cod. Lat. 422/23), Breviarium Romanum (Cod. Lat. 424), and Officium Beatae Virginis (Cod. Lat. 262), carried off by Duke Francis V in 1859.

The bronzes carried off under the same circumstances in 1859.

Certain objects (among others two pictures by Salvator Rosa and a portrait by Dosso Dossi) claimed by the Duke of Modena in 1868 as a condition of the execution of the Convention of 20 June 1868, and other objects given up in 1872 in the same circumstances.

[70] ANNEX II [to Part VIII, Section II]

I. The Triptych of S. Ildephonse, by Rubens, from the Abbey of Saint Jacques sur Cowdenberg at Brussels, bought in 1777 and removed to Vienna.
II. Objects and documents removed for safety from Belgium to Austria in 1794:
  (a) Arms, armour and other objects from the old Arsenal of Brussels.
  (b) The Treasure of the 'Toison d'or' preserved in previous times in the 'Chapelle de la Cour' at Brussels.
  (c) Coinage, stamps, medals and counters by Theodore van Berckel which were an essential feature in the archives of the 'Chambre des Comptes' at Brussels.
  (d) The original manuscript copies of the 'carte chorographique' of the Austrian Low Countries drawn up by Lieut.-General Comte Jas de Ferraris between 1770 and 1777, and the documents relating thereto.

[71] ANNEX IV [to Part VIII, Section II]

1. Documents, historical memoirs, manuscripts, maps, etc, claimed by the present State of Czecho-Slovakia, which Thaulow von Rosenthal removed by order of Maria Theresa.
2. The documents originally belonging to the Royal Aulic Chancellery of Bohemia and the Aulic Chamber of Accounts of Bohemia, and the works of art which formed part of the installation of the Royal Château of Prague and other royal castles in Bohemia, which were removed by the Emperors Mathias, Ferdinand II, Charles VI (about 1718, 1723 and 1737) and Francis Joseph I, all of which are now in the archives, Imperial castles, museums and other central public institutions at Vienna.

Apart from the above-mentioned provisions, the successor states of the Habsburg Monarchy were entitled to receive a portion of the predecessor state collections, based on the principle of the historical and 'intellectual' links with ceded territories. Such returns had to be reciprocal. This was clearly stated by Article 196:

With regard to all objects of artistic, archaeological, scientific or historic character forming part of collections which formerly belonged to the Government or the Crown of the Austro–Hungarian Monarchy and are not otherwise provided for in the present Treaty, Austria undertakes:

(a) to negotiate, when required, with the states concerned for an amicable arrangement whereby any portion thereof or any objects belonging thereto which ought to form part of the intellectual patrimony of the ceded districts may be returned to their districts of origin on terms of reciprocity, and

(b) for twenty years, unless a special arrangement is previously arrived at, not to alienate or disperse any of the said collections or to dispose of any of the above objects, but at all times to ensure their safety and good condition and to make them available, together with inventories, catalogues and administrative documents relating to the said collections, at all reasonable times to students who are nationals of any of the Allied and Associated Powers.

Similar general provisions as to the repatriation of material forming 'part of the intellectual patrimony of the ceded districts' to 'their districts of origin on terms of reciprocity' were inserted into the text of the 1920 Treaty of Trianon under Article 177 paragraphs 2, 2(a), and 2(b). Moreover, under paragraph 3, Hungary was, on the basis of reciprocity, entitled to 'to apply to the said states, particularly to Austria, in order to negotiate, in the conditions mentioned above, the necessary arrangements for the return to Hungary of the collections, documents'. Thus, this treaty acted as a basis for the future distribution of the common treasures of the dual Habsburg Empire.

Both treaties (Article 194 of the Treaty of Saint-Germain, Article 179 of the Treaty of Trianon) also confirmed that Austria and Hungary were bound by the former treaty obligations on the return of cultural material to Italy, namely, under Article 15 of the 1859 Treaty of Zurich, Article 18 of the 1866 Treaty of Vienna, and the 1868 Convention of Florence, concluded between Italy and Austria–Hungary, since 'in so far as the Articles referred to have not in fact been executed in their entirety', and these items were still situated in the territory of Austria and Hungary.

Thus, the claims by the successor states practically referred to the entire period of Habsburg rule without time limitations on the date of removal. Their objectives to reconstruct the dispersed national cultural patrimonies and to take a share of former imperial collections appear very obvious.

b) Decisions of the International Arbitrage Committee (1921–22)

On the basis of Article 195 of the 1919 Treaty of Saint-Germain, the settlement of claims was executed by the Committee of Three Jurists (the Committee), nominated by the Reparation Commission. The Committee was formed by representatives of the Allied Powers, not being directly involved in the dissolution of Austria–Hungary. This was to guarantee their competence and impartial judgment. Accordingly, it comprised three eminent jurists from the United States, Great Britain, and France, all with experience in international treaty law.[72] However, the claimant states preferred to start bilateral negotiations directly with Austria. For instance, Polish and Belgian demands, in part related to coins, armour, stamps, and maps, were separately settled by friendly bilateral agreements, immediately after the first hearings by the Committee.[73]

Hence, only the claims by Czechoslovakia and the remaining demands of Belgium—Rubens's *Triptych of St. Ildefonso*, also known as the *Ildefonso Altar* (1630–32)—and the Order of the Golden Fleece were actually submitted to the arbitration of the Committee.[74] The Committee did not find grounds for restitution, and entirely shared Austria's view, which basically maintained that those treasures formed part of the property of the Habsburg dynasty and their removal was lawful according to the law in force at the time of their transportation to Vienna. The reasoning of the Committee is of great interest, since the arbiters had to deal with two fundamental questions constantly repeated in the legal disputes on the allocation of cultural treasures at the time of state succession: the right and validity of disposal of cultural items made by the predecessor state; and identification of law applicable for the assessment of such disposal and/or displacement of cultural property.

The first considerations concerned the *Ildefonso Altar*. The painting was made on the commission of the Habsburg family for the church of St Jacob in Caudenberg, Brussels. Eventually, it was purchased by the Empress Maria Theresa in Brussels in the territory of Austrian (Catholic) Netherlands and transported to Vienna. Belgium argued that the artwork had been purchased by the Empress from the funds derived from the Catholic Low Countries, the predecessor of Belgium. Therefore, it constituted Belgian 'public domain', and could not be classified as the property of the Habsburg dynasty.[75] Moreover, it was argued that 'the purchase was intended or, in view of the early history of the pictures, must be presumed to have been intended, by Maria Theresa, as a purchase on behalf of the Belgian state or "Public Domain".'[76]

The Committee found that Belgium was not able to prove that the artwork had been taken from Brussels to Vienna in violation of the rights of the Low

[72] The arbiters were: Hugh A. Bayne of the New York Bar, J. Fischer Williams from London and Jacques Lyon, Advocate at the Court of Appeal of Paris; see *Report of the Committee of Three Jurists. Belgian Claims to the Triptych of Saint Ildephonse and Treasure of the Order of the Golden Fleece* (Paris, 1921), 2; also 'O', 'International Arbitration under the Treaty of St. Germain', *BYIL* 4(1923/24), 124–30, at 125.

[73] 'O', 'International Arbitration' (n 72) 125.

[74] See Huguenin-Bergenat, *Kulturgüter bei Staatensukzession* (n 67) 159 ff.

[75] *Report of the Committee of Three Jurists* (n 72) 8–14.

[76] Ibid. 14.

Countries, and Belgium as their legal successor.[77] It argued that under the laws in force in the Habsburg Empire and the Low Countries, the Empress Maria Theresa:

was free to dispose at her pleasure of the fiscal resources of the Low Countries. Thus she could employ the resources either for the Low Countries or for objects of public interest in, and for the benefit of, any other of her Possessions or states (eg Bohemia or Hungary) or in the purchase of real estate or chattels intended as additions to the property, settled or unsettled, of Habsburgs, or as presents to a member of the imperial family or a servant of the dynasty.[78]

As regards the argument that the purchase of the artwork in question had been intended to be made on behalf of the 'public domain' of the Low Countries, the Committee held that the Empress never showed:

any intention of reviving the past and indirectly placing beyond dispute the rights of the Fisc of the Low Countries over the Triptych … The correspondence which passed at the time clearly shows that the Triptych was bought for 'the Court', for 'Her Majesty', for the 'Imperial and Royal Gallery of Vienna' (which at this date beyond all dispute was an integral part of the private settled property of the Habsburg family); the repeated use of the these expressions cannot be reconciled with an intention to transfer the Triptych to, or leave it in the possession of, the 'Public Domain'—if any such existed—of the Low Countries.[79]

Similar reasoning was applied in the case of Czechoslovak claims over the return of a number of artworks from the Vienna collections, which had been removed on various occasions from royal residences in the territories of Bohemia and Slovakia by Habsburg sovereigns. After the examination of the facts and legal background, the Committee did not find any basis for the repatriation of the art treasures. The arbiters concluded that the question they had to decide was:

one of the public law in force in Bohemia at the date of the removal of the works of art in question … It has not been established that works of art purchased by sovereigns out of their Bohemian revenues became the property of the 'Public Domain', 'Crown' or 'state' of Bohemia or that there existed at any material time a rule of Bohemian constitutional law prohibiting the sovereign of Bohemia from removing permanently from the country all or any part of the works of art or other movable property so purchased … The Treaty does not create, and international law does not recognize, any right of states whose union, whether federal or otherwise, is dissolved, to share in property acquired for the former common sovereign out of revenues contributed by those states, whether in proportion to their several contributions.[80]

A different case constituted the second Belgian claim on the return of the treasure of the Order of the Golden Fleece. The Order was founded by Philip the

[77] Ibid. 21. [78] Ibid. 20. [79] Ibid. 20–21.
[80] Ibid. 126–27; in part related to Czechoslovak claims, see 'O', 'International Arbitration' (n 72) 126–27.

Good, Duke of Burgundy, in the fifteenth century. It was evacuated to Vienna in 1794 just before French invasion, and it never returned. Belgium considered it a national institution of the Low Countries and, consequently a national Belgian treasure. It therefore argued that the preservation of the Order in Vienna would violate legitimate Belgian rights. Conversely, Austria maintained that the treasure was an institution of the House of Burgundy, to which Habsburgs were successors. Accordingly, it should follow the destiny of the dynasty.

On deciding this case, the Committee did not pronounce on the title to the Treasure but instead on its territorial allocation. After a long examination of the historic fortunes of the Order, it held:

> The Order of the Golden Fleece was in its origin a dynastic Order of Chivalry or Knighthood, and even after account is taken of the profound modifications which time has imposed, it remains an Order of Chivalry, i.e. a courtly Order of 'Knights', not necessarily of one nationality, conceived as grouped round a Sovereign. It was not a 'national Order' in its origin, and it never evolved into a 'national' or political institution of the Low Countries or of any other country. It never had any exclusive connection with the soil or population of the Low Countries; it never was irremovably established there … Even if the word 'national' be used in the secondary sense in which it may be applied to an aristocratic Order attached to what has become in modern times, and with the growth of the idea of nationality, a national dynasty, the Golden Fleece cannot in the eighteenth century justly lay claim to this epithet of 'national' in relation to the Low Countries. The Committee does not seek to deny that on many pages of the history of the Low Countries the destinies of the Order were intimately connected with destinies of those countries … but this brilliant past dates from the second half on the fifteenth century. It did not, and could not, give, to Low Countries at the end of the eighteenth century rights which have descended to contemporary Belgium.[81]

As evident in the decisions of the Committee of Three Jurists, the reasoning applied did not take into consideration the national cultural interests of Austria–Hungary's successor states. It aimed at identifying the 'actual legal position at the date of the events themselves.'[82] In other words, the arbiters sought to find out whether the removal of the artworks in question was legal or not in accordance with the laws in force at the time of transfer. Other considerations, such as the right to recover the dispersed national patrimony, were not applied. With reference to this, as one of the members of the Committee noticed:

> It may indeed be marked that though the contest was international inasmuch as the disputants were sovereign states, the problems to be solved did not arise out of the relations of the two state parties to the disputes or their respective nationals, but were rather a resuscitation or reincarnation of internal constitutional disputes between subjects and sovereigns in which modern state was standing in the shoes of the subjects and another in the shoes of the sovereign.[83]

[81] *Report of the Committee of Three Jurists* (n 72) 51–52; quoted also in 'O', 'International Arbitration' (n 72), 128–29.

[82] 'O', 'International Arbitration' (n 72) 126.

[83] Ibid. 129.

c) *The 1920 Austro–Italian Artistic Convention*

In order to secure its pending claims against Austria, Italy through the Royal Italian Armistice Commission in Vienna, seized a number of masterpieces of Italian origin preserved in the imperial collections of the city (in particular in the Kunsthistorisches Museum), even before the 1919 Treaty of Saint-Germain was ratified.[84] The removal was executed by Italian *carabinieri*, headed by some distinguished scholars, and objects were partially deposited in the Italian Embassy, partially sent immediately by train to Italy.[85] The seized property included 66 paintings by artists such as Bellini, Tintoretto, Carpaccio, and Veronese (in large part transported by Austria from Venice in the early nineteenth century). In addition, Italy captured several manuscripts and document records from Austrian state libraries and archives as well as the famous Gonzaga Tapestries from Mantua, deposited in the Castle of Schönbrunn.[86] The advances of Italy were, however, perceived as very controversial by other great powers. In order to formalize the situation, Italy and Austria signed a special bilateral convention on 4 May 1920 in Vienna (*Convenzione Artistica*).[87] This was based on four general principles: 1) full execution of the provisions of the former bilateral agreements; 2) repatriation based on territorial and historical links; 3) reciprocity, and 4) general interest of civilization to maintain the integrity of historically formed famous art collections.

Accordingly, Italy managed to keep all the objects seized by its armistice mission in Vienna in 1919 as well as the remaining part of the treasure of the Iron Crown of Lombardy, historic movables of Venice (Article 3 paragraph 1 of the *Convenzione Artistica*), and some other objects. Thus, Italy succeeded in recovering a great majority of the objects demanded from the mid-nineteenth century. Austria also had to hand over all the historic and archival materials originating from the transferred territories, if they were included in the collections in public Austrian institutions (Article 5 of the *Convenzione Artistica*). Excluded from the repatriation were the following: objects moved to Austria in 1790; objects bought or donated by private owners; objects originating from the territories transferred

[84] Johann Rainer, 'Die Italienische Militärmission in Wien 1918–1920', in Alexander Novotny and Othmar Pickl (eds), *Festschrift Hermann Wiesflecker Zum 60. Geburtstag* (Selbstverlag des Historischen Instituts der Universität Graz, 1973), 267–80.

[85] Huguenin-Bergenat, *Kulturgüter bei Staatensukzession* (n 67) 79 ff; Jonathan Blower, 'Max Dvořák and Austrian Denkmalpflege at War', *Journal of Art Historiography* 1(2009), 1–19, at 8 ff.

[86] For the full list of confiscated objects and Austrian position in the case, see Hans Tietze, *Die Entführung von wiener Kunstwerken nach Italien: eine Darlegung unseres Rechtsstandpunktes, mit einem offenen Brief an die italienischen Fachgenossen von Max Dvorák* (Schroll, 1919); on the return of Gonzaga Tapestries, see Alessandro Luzio, *Gli arazzi dei Gonzaga restituiti dall'Austria* (Arti Grafiche, 1919); for the description of the Italian contingent activity, see, for instance, 'Seize More Art Treasures. Italian Military Mission in Vienna Continues Confiscation', *The New York Times*, 17 February 1919, 2; 'Art Seizures by Italy. Armistice Commission Begins Taking Masterpieces from Vienna, and May Demand Others, Including Sistine Madonna', *The New York Times*, 13 April 1919, 77.

[87] Convention speciale afin de résoudre les controverses relatives au patrimoine historique et artistique de l'ancienne monarchie austro-hongroise, signée à Vienne, le 4 mai 1920, 19 Martens NRGT (3e série) 682; see further Huguenin-Bergenat, *Kulturgüter bei Staatensukzession* (n 67) 123 ff.

to Italy, but not comprising the intellectual patrimony of Italy (Article 5, points 1–3). The special bilateral committee had to be established in order to prepare a list of objects.

Under Article 3 paragraphs 2 and 3, and Article 4 paragraph 2, Italy agreed, on the basis of reciprocity, to return to Austria a few objects, among them Canova's bust of Emperor Francis I which was held in Venice. Italy also abandoned other claims, especially those related to the regalia of the Norman Kings of Sicily in order not to disperse Vienna's collection of imperial regalia. Moreover, in a special Article 1 of the *Convenzione Artistica* both states reaffirmed the importance of the integrity of historical, artistic, and archaeological collections. Importantly, Italy agreed to support Austria against the claims issued by other states, which would endanger the integrity of Austrian collections, whose conservation lay 'in the interest of science'. Such compromise obviously strengthened the Austrian position in negotiations with other countries.[88]

The *Convenzione Artistica* addressed practically all Italian claims, and within a few years following its conclusion it was fully implemented.[89] The regulations negotiated by Austria and Italy confirmed the paramount nature of the principles of territoriality and the major significance for national cultural heritage of the successor state, which were however limited by universal interests of science in the preservation of the integrity of public collections.

d) The 1932 Austro–Hungarian Agreement

On the basis of the 1920 Treaty of Trianon provisions (Article 177 paragraph 3); Austria and Hungary negotiated and finally in 1932 signed a bilateral agreement on the distribution of museum and library collections of the former Habsburg Monarchy (the 1932 Austro–Hungarian Agreement).[90] This was the first international act which dealt entirely with state succession to cultural patrimony. Not only did it provide for the repatriation of cultural items to their places of origin but it also settled the question of common heritage of both nations and states. Moreover, it constituted a very rare example of an international settlement related to the rights to cultural treasures which, in general, satisfied both parties,[91] and thus it can be perceived as a model solution.

[88] Kowalski, 'Repatriation of Cultural Property' (n 41) 144, footnote 15.

[89] Certain difficulties however concerned the allocation of the remaining objects from the treasury of the Grand Duchy of Tuscany. See commented review of documental diplomatic records in: 'Il Diamante Fiorentino', *Prassi italiana di diritto internazionale by Istituto di Studi Giuridici Internazionali*, online resource: <http://www.prassi.cnr.it>, accessed on 27 January 2015.

[90] Agreement between Austria and Hungary Concerning Certain Objects from Museum and Library Collections, with Three Protocols and Three Annexes, signed in Venice on 27 November 1932, 162 LNTS 395, see Huguenin-Bergenat, *Kulturgüter bei Staatensukzession* (n 67) 180 ff.

[91] Hans Tietze, 'L'accord austro-hongrois sur la répartition des collections de la Maison des Habsbourg', *Mouseion* (1933)23–24, 92–97; Kowalski, 'Repatriation of Cultural Property' (n 41) 146, fn 23. Kowalski also quotes the opinions of Austrian and Hungarian officials confirming the satisfactory conclusion of negotiations.

It is possible to distinguish four major principles which governed the 1932 Austro–Hungarian Agreement: 1) repatriation based on territoriality and historic links; 2) reciprocity; 3) protection of the integrity of common heritage; and 4) equal access to the collections forming the common heritage of both nations and interstate cultural collaboration.

During the negotiations Hungary claimed that it was entitled both to the recovery of patrimony removed by the Habsburgs to Vienna, and to a proportional share in the former imperial collections. The view of Austria was the opposite. Its representatives argued that under Article 177 of the 1920 Treaty of Trianon, it was only bound to restitution of objects which had been removed from the territory of Hungary according to the post-First World War territorial boundaries. The Treaty did not provide a share for Hungary in the well-established Vienna collections, whose integrity needed to be preserved.[92] The parties finally hammered out a compromise. Accordingly, both states agreed to reciprocal repatriation of objects originated from their respective territories as of 1920. The list of objects was included in the three annexes to the 1932 Austro–Hungarian Agreement. Hungry received 36 manuscripts and more than 150 works of art, closely bound to its history and territory. As regards the objects from imperial collections, forming part of Hungarian patrimony but not handed over to Hungary, it was stated that Austria would keep them as a joint inalienable 'common heritage' of both states (Article III paragraphs 1 and 2). In case of disagreement over particular items, the dispute had to be submitted under an impartial arbitrage (Articles III paragraph 3 and VI).

As a form of compensation for such a solution, and to avoid potential claims in the future, Austria handed over to Hungary certain historical objects of universal value. For instance: two wings of the triptych of *Crucifixion* (1491), also known as the *Calvary Triptych*, by Hans Memling, whose central scene was preserved in Budapest; Tintoretto's *Hercules Thrusting The Faun off the Bed of Omphale* (*c.*1585), which supplemented an aspect of the famous artist's *oeuvre* thus far missing in the collection of the Budapest Museum of Fine Arts; and a set of armour pieces completing the Hungarian royal armoury.[93] Thus, both negotiating states applied very sophisticated collection-oriented considerations, going beyond mere division based on the principle of territoriality or nationality of an artist. Apparently, the solutions applying archival criteria are unique to the whole evolution of the international practice of state succession to cultural property.

The 1932 Austro–Hungarian Agreement also secured the citizens of both states equal access to the patrimony preserved in Vienna as well as giving Hungary the right to control the general utilization of the collections (Article IV). In addition, it provided for the facilitation of interstate cultural collaboration in the form of temporary art exhibitions (Article V).[94] In a few other cases in which Hungarian claims clashed with those issued by other successor states of Austria–Hungary,

[92] Tietze, 'L'accord austro-hongrois' (n 91) 92–94.

[93] Ibid. 95; Kowalski, 'Repatriation of Cultural Property' (n 41) 147.

[94] 'The Austrian Federal Government is prepared to give favourable consideration to any requests from the Royal Hungarian Government for the loan for a specified period of objects forming part

these were to be settled in the direct negotiations between interested claimants (Protocol I and II to the 1932 Austro–Hungarian Agreement).

e) *Historic archives of Austria–Hungary*

In the years following the 1919 Treaty of Saint-Germain, Austria concluded several agreements with other successor states of the Habsburg Empire, primarily with reference to the archival records. For instance: with Czechoslovakia in 1920,[95] with Romania in 1921, a general convention with Hungary, Italy, Poland, Romania, the Kingdom of Serbs, Croats, and Slovenes, and Czechoslovakia in 1922, and an agreement with Poland in 1932.[96] In all these negotiations, the difference between historic archives constituting a cultural national patrimony and administrative and judicial records confirming state sovereignty over a territory was widely accepted.

In this context, it is worth recalling the proceedings of the 5th International Congress of Historical Sciences, held in 1923 in Brussels, where the representatives of new European states were very active. The delegate of Czechoslovakia, Jan Opocensky, describing the 1920 Austro–Czechoslovak agreement, clearly distinguished these two kinds of records.[97] Other delegates confirmed the legitimate rights of new states to recover their historic and administrative records, following state succession processes.[98] They argued that the cessions of archives arising from the changes of borders between states should be determined not only according to administrative purposes, but also 'intellectual, religious and artistic needs of the states concerned' ought to be taken into account.[99]

However, the most coherent, visionary principles, which would govern the distribution of archives in the case of state succession, were presented by the Polish delegate, Józef Paczkowski.[100] His proposals may be summarized into four general points: 1) succession to archives should consider the needs of both administration and science; 2) negotiations on the distribution of archives must be expert based;

of Hungary's intellectual patrimony with a view to temporary exhibitions organized by the administrations of Hungarian public collections.'

[95] Convention entre Austriche et Tchécoslovaquie concernant l'exécution de certaines dispositions du Traité de Saint-Germain, signée à Prague, le 18 mai 1920, 19 Martens NRGT (3e série) 694. This agreement under Art. A provided also for a repatriation of certain objects of the artistic, archaeological, scientific, and historic character, preserved in the former collection of Austria–Hungary, see Huguenin-Bergenat, *Kulturgüter bei Staatensukzession* (n 67) 130 ff.

[96] Agreement between Austria and Poland Regarding Questions of Archives, signed in Vienna on 26 October 1932, 138 LNTS 193. At the same time, Poland also recovered some other historical objects, see Kowalski, 'Repatriation of Cultural Property' (n 41) 145, footnote 17.

[97] Jan Opocensky, 'La remise des archives à la Tchécoslovaquie par l'Autriche', in François Louis Ganshof and Guillaume Des Marez (eds), *Compte rendu du Ve Congrès international des sciences historique* (Weissenbruch, 1923), 450–52.

[98] Joseph Paczkowski, 'Les principes de la remise des actes en connexion avec les changements de frontière entre les états', in François Louis Ganshof and Guillaume Des Marez (eds), *Compte rendu du Ve Congrès international des sciences historique* (Weissenbruch, 1923), 457–60.

[99] Ibid. [100] Ibid.

3) archives can never be treated as war trophies; and 4) distribution of historic collections of archives must respect their integrity.[101] Thus, Paczkowski argued that in state succession not only national, historic, and administrative considerations in respect of allocation of archives must be satisfied, but also their scientific integrity and use must be equally protected. He also postulated a publication of an updated *compte-rendu* of the ongoing state practice in this matter.[102]

2.5.3 Dissolution of the Russian Empire

At the end of the First World War many nations of the former Russian Empire claimed the right to self-determination. In 1917–19, the following states proclaimed independence from Russia: Armenia, Azerbaijan, Belarus, Georgia, Estonia, Finland, Latvia, Lithuania, Moldavia, Poland, and Ukraine. However, only a few of them effectively managed to maintain this status in the interwar period. Accordingly, in the period 1920–21, Russia concluded a set of peace treaties with the Baltic States, Finland, and Poland, recognizing the separation of its former western provinces. All these treaties provided for the reconstruction of national patrimonies impoverished under imperial rule, during ongoing war operations and revolutionary turmoil.

a) Treaties with the Baltic States and Finland

Less restrictive regulations were provided by the 1920 Treaty of Tartu II with Finland. Under Article 29 §1 of this treaty, Russia and Finland agreed only 'at the first opportunity to restore the archives and documents which belong to public authorities and institutions which may be within their respective territories, and which refer entirely or mainly to the other Contracting Power or its history'. These documents, 'entirely or mainly concerned with Russia or its history', had to be preserved in Russia, and Finland was 'entitled to provide herself with copies of the documents thus handed over to Russia'. Such a limited set of regulations in respect of the allocation of cultural property between these two states may be arguably explained by the particular position of Finland within the Russian Empire. In fact, the Grand Duchy of Finland enjoyed a high degree of autonomy throughout the nineteenth century.[103] The policy of political and cultural assimilation was applied by the imperial administration as late as 1898.[104] Moreover, there were no extensive displacements of cultural objects between these countries.

In the case of Baltic States, their national patrimony was widely scattered, due to the long-lasting Russian policy of cultural and national assimilation and the effects of the First World War and revolution. Thus, these new states demanded a more extensive restoration of their lost cultural property. As explained, Russia,

[101] Ibid. 459. [102] Ibid. [103] Grand Duchy of Finland.

[104] Tuomo Polvinen, *Imperial Borderland: Bobrikov and the Attempted Russification of Finland 1898-1904* (C. Hurst & Co. Ltd, 1995).

under special treaty provisions, was obliged to hand over to Latvia and Lithuania property removed during the First World War. Furthermore, it also had to repatriate to these states cultural material displaced prior to 1914. Accordingly, under similarly drafted provisions of peace treaties, Russia agreed to hand over 'libraries, archives, museums, creations of art and documents which are of important scientific, artistic or historical value' to Latvia and Lithuania providing that their return did not 'cause serious loss to Russian archives, libraries, museums or art galleries where they are presently kept'. All matters concerning the return of these items had to be determined by 'a special joint commission having an equal number of members from both Parties to this Treaty' (Article 11 §1 paragraphs 2 and 3 of the 1920 Riga Treaty, Article 9 §1 paragraphs 2 and 3 of the 1920 Treaty of Moscow). No restitution-in kind was provided for. As regards the 1920 Treaty of Tartu I with Estonia, Russia was obliged under Article 12 §4 to hand over, apart from the already mentioned property of the University of Tartu, 'other educational establishments which are or were situated in Estonian territory, and which have been removed to Russia'. This property included 'libraries, archives, documents and, in general, all other objects which are of scientific or historical interest to Estonia'. This obligation was, however, very limited. Accordingly, such cultural property was to be restored only insofar as its situation was known or could be revealed to the Russian Government or public institutions.

To summarize, all the peace treaties concluded by Russia with the Baltic States imposed on the Russian state a general obligation to restore the cultural patrimony of ceded territories. There were no time limitations as regards the date of removal of the objects. However, the obligation of handing over was seriously limited by the principle of the integrity of collections and the evidence of physical possession of the claimed objects by Russian institutions. In practice, only a portion of the items in question returned to their place of origin.[105] The collections of the University of Tartu, kept in Voronez until the present day, constitute one such case.

b) *The settlements with Poland—the 1921 Treaty of Riga and its aftermath*

The most complex and far-reaching provisions on the restoration of national cultural patrimony in state succession were introduced by the 1921 Treaty of Riga between Poland, Russia, and Ukraine. This was signed after the Polish–Bolshevik war (1919–21). Initially, it was intended that a peace treaty would be concluded by four successor states of the former Russian Empire: Poland, Belarus, Russia, and Ukraine. As a result of the consolidation of power by the Bolsheviks, on the one hand, and Polish military advancements, on the other, the interests of Belarusians

[105] For instance, Russia returned, in accordance with the 1920 Treaty of Tartu I with Estonia, part of the cultural material that had been evacuated from the territory of Estonia during the First World War, including the historical archives from sixteenth century and the Tallinn City Archives, in the early 1920s, after: <http://estonia.eu/about-estonia/culture-a-science/estonian-cultural-treasures-outside-estonia.html>, accessed on 27 January 2015.

and Ukrainians were not taken into account. Thus, the entire series of negotiations were performed between Polish delegates and Russian Bolsheviks, who formally represented the Soviet republics of Ukraine and Belorussia.[106]

The regulations on the allocation of cultural property were highly advantageous for Poland due to the political and military situation of the Bolsheviks in 1921. The core objective of Polish negotiators was to restore the highest possible number of Polish national treasures dispersed during more than 100 years of Russian domination, as well as to recover the objects displaced or plundered in relation to the First World War and the war of 1919–21. Poland also sought to preserve the cultural property of Polish nationals in the territories controlled by the Bolsheviks in light of the damages caused by the revolution and forced nationalization and collectivization of private property. Accordingly, the treaty provided for the transfer of cultural property gathered by Polish nationals in the territory of Russia (in particular Moscow and St Petersburg) and bequeathed to the Polish nation prior to the 1917 revolutionary decrees on collectivization. Thus, the 1921 Treaty of Riga, apart from the already mentioned provisions on the repatriation of objects removed during the two recent wars, provided for the unconditional return of cultural objects which were removed by the Russian administration from the territory of the Polish–Lithuanian Commonwealth in the boundaries of 1772, and the handing over to Poland private and public art and scientific collections gathered in Russia by Polish nationals and societies.

Consequently, there were four general principles on which the restoration of Polish cultural heritage was based: 1) repatriation of cultural treasures and archives based on the principles of territoriality and nationality; 2) reciprocity of repatriation; 3) no distinction between private and public property; and 4) protection of the integrity 'systematic, scientifically prepared and complete collections' of universal importance.

With reference to these, Russia and Ukraine had to restore to Poland, on the basis of reciprocity, all war trophies, libraries, art, and archaeological collections as well as 'collections of any nature and objects of historical, national, artistic, archaeological, scientific and general educational value' (Article 11 §1). The objects belonging to these categories had to be restored 'irrespective of the conditions under which, and the pretexts upon which they were carried off and irrespective of the authorities responsible for such removal and without regard to the person whether physical or legal to whom they belonged prior to, or subsequent to their removal.'

The repatriation was excluded only for two categories of objects (Article 11 §2). The first regarded the items of Belarusian and Ukrainian cultures originating from the territories of the former Polish–Lithuanian Commonwealth to the east of the borders of Poland, established in the 1921 Treaty of Riga, providing that that they had not been removed unlawfully (not by regular way of transaction

[106] On the circumstances, negotiations and final execution of the 1921 Treaty of Riga, see Borzęcki, *The Soviet–Polish Peace of 1921* (n 14) 185 ff.

or succession). The second category referred to the objects transferred to the territory of Russia and Ukraine as of 1921 by voluntary transaction, succession, or those taken by their legal owner. However, the parties to the treaty declared an option to conclude 'special conventions concerning the restitution, purchase, or exchange' of certain objects belonging to the cultural patrimony of one of the parties, which had been transferred to the territory of the other as a result of transaction or of succession (Article 11 §8). The restoration of historical, administrative, and judicial archives, plans, seals, etc, of both private and public provenance had to be performed in a similar way (Article 11 §5).

Article 11 of the 1921 Treaty of Riga applied in two paragraphs the principle of the protection of the integrity of collections. First, the treaty regulated the restoration of maps, plans, seals, collections of documents, etc (Article 11 §4). It provided that those items which could not be divided had to be restored to Poland in their entirety, even though they were not exclusively linked to the territory of Poland. Second, Article 11 §7 reciprocally recognized 'the value of systematic, scientifically prepared and complete collections, such as form a fundamental part of collections of world-wide scientific importance, ought in no way to be impaired'. The parties agreed that Poland would be compensated with an item of 'the same artistic or scientific value' if an object in question could not be removed without damage to the integrity of the collection. There were, however, exemptions from this principle when an object was 'closely bound up with the history and culture of Poland.' Again, the restoration of Polish national cultural patrimony was a predominant principle of these repatriation provisions.

On the basis of Article 11 §15 of the 1921 Treaty of Riga, a joint Mixed Commission in Moscow was appointed to settle all the claims arising from the treaty. The Commission then chose special expert-based sub-commissions to solve the controversies surrounding the restoration of cultural patrimony and archives. However, as the restoration provisions of the 1921 Treaty of Riga were very far-reaching, its execution was extremely difficult, time-consuming, and incomplete. The Commission worked for 13 years (1921–34) and only partially managed to settle the submitted claims. Poland presented a list of 170 different claims, issued by state, private, and ecclesiastic institutions as well as individual private owners.[107] However, the Bolsheviks controlled all the archives and information needed for the successful allocation of property. Moreover, many objects had been hidden in different former imperial residencies and warehouses, and many among inventories and archival records were being constantly 'cleansed' to impede Polish representatives from locating the claiming property.[108]

[107] All lists and proceedings of the Commission were immediately published, see *Dokumenty dotyczące akcji delegacyj polskich w Komisjach Mieszanych Reewakuacyjneh i Specjalnej w Moskwie. Les trovaux des Délégations Polonaises aux Commissions Mixtes de Reevacuation et Speciale à Moscou*, vols I–VII (Warszawa, 1922–23).

[108] The procedure of 'sterilization' or cleansing of archives was ordered by the Chief of the Russian Delegation, Piotr Wojkov, who explicitly stated that 'all the information that would make it possible for Poland to submit any pecuniary or material claims' against Russia had to be removed from the records. Wojkov's confidential report on the Bolshevik strategy of setting claims with Poland

Finally, in 1921–29 Poland recovered several hundred important cultural objects, among them part of the great royal collection of Flemish tapestries removed from the Wawel Castle in Cracow, some historic regalia, paintings, books, militaria, etc, about half of what was actually claimed. Many of the objects were of important symbolic value, since they had been confiscated by Russia as a form of punishment for Polish uprisings against imperial rule, similar to Poniatowski's monument. In addition, Polish negotiators had to make difficult choices. When the restoration of claimed objects clashed with the protection of the integrity of Russian collections, Poland could be compensated with an equivalent. On this basis, Polish delegates resigned from the claims to a set of Old Masters removed from royal residences in Warsaw in favour of an ancient sword, constituting a part of Poland's regalia, which was, however, legally purchased by the Russian government in the nineteenth century. As regards Russia's claims, Poland, following the principle of reciprocity, had to hand over to Russia several historic documents, including the collections of letters by Lenin.[109]

The bilateral negotiations were widely reported by the Russian and Polish press. Special attention was paid to the restoration of artistic and library collections from the state institutions of Petrograd (St Petersburg), namely the Public Library and Academy of Fine Arts. The Council of the Petrograd University stood up in defense of the integrity of the collections, arguing that dissolution of it would constitute one of the barbarities of the twentieth century. In response to this proclamation, Polish scientific societies from Warsaw and Cracow issued counter-statements, claiming that the principle of the integrity of collections had to be challenged whenever their mode of acquisition consisted in crime: war plunder, robbery, and violent reprisal against national cultural institutions.[110] Arguably, this exchange of views and arguments constituted the essence of conflicts regarding the allocation of cultural property between all imperial powers and conquered peoples.

2.6 Succession to colonial territories and the status of cultural patrimony

The post-First World War state succession arrangements were only applied with regard to the European context. The dismemberment of the German colonial empire in Africa and the Pacific and the Ottoman Empire in the Middle East and

was published for the first time in 1991; see Piotr Wojkov, '1921–1923: Dwa lata prac Delegacji Rosyjsko-Ukraińskiej [do] Rosyjsko-Uraińsko-Polskich Komisji Mieszanych Reewakuacyjnej i Specjalnej nad Wykonaniem Ryskiego Tratatu Pokojowego: Sprawozdanie', in Jan Kumaniecki, *Tajny Raport Wojkowa, czyli radziecka taktyka zwrotu polskiego mienia gospodarczego i kulturalnego po Pokoju Ryskim* (Gryf, 1991), 171; see also Borzęcki, *The Soviet–Polish Peace of 1921* (n 14) 261; Kowalski, 'Repatriation of Cultural Property' (n 41) 153, footnote 40.

[109] Borzęcki, *The Soviet–Polish Peace of 1921* (n 14) 263.

[110] Texts of all the three proclamations published in Wiesław Balcerek (ed), *Polsko–Radzieckie Stosunki Kulturalne 1918–1939* (n 15) 90–93, 117–26.

North Africa did not lead to the independence of these territories. Accordingly, the Allied Powers dominated the new political and territorial order and considered the formerly colonized peoples as backward, unable of withstanding the challenges of the modern world. Consequently, they were not granted the right of self-determination. Accordingly, under Article 22 of the 1919 Covenant of the League of Nations, a system of mandates was established. This covered the former German and Ottoman non-European territories, and the 'trust' and 'tutelage' over these mandates were given to the group of mandating powers (France, Great Britain, Belgium, Japan, New Zealand, Australia, South Africa), responsible for their full administration. Besides the mandate system, the Allied Powers also formalized their earlier territorial acquisitions made at the expense of the Ottoman Empire. Under the 1923 Treaty of Lausanne, the newly founded Republic of Turkey had to relinquish its claims to a number of vast territories, including Egypt, Sudan, and Cyprus, which passed to the British Empire, and Libya which formally became an Italian colony.[111]

In the same way as the Paris Peace Conference did not recognize the political rights of colonized peoples, their cultural rights to reconstitution of national patrimony were not taken into account. Consequently, the control over their cultural patrimony was assigned to the mandating powers. Once again, international law employed legal double standards, which applied different rules to 'civilized' nations and underdeveloped peoples.

As a matter of fact, the 1919 Treaty of Versailles under Article 246 provided for the return by Germany of two objects of colonial origin: 1) the original Koran of the Caliph Othman, removed by Turks from Medina and subsequently presented to the German Emperor William II, had to be returned to the King of Hedjaz (Hejaz);[112] 2) the skull of the Sultan Mkwawa, a tribal chief, who had committed suicide fighting against German colonization in East Africa, had to be handed over to the British government, a successor colonial power.[113] The return of the Koran can arguably be seen in terms of reconstitution of cultural heritage of the newly formed Arab kingdom; the provisions on the skull of Sultan Mkwawa confirmed only British territorial sovereignty over the former German colony of Tanganyika.

An extensive system with reference to cultural patrimony and archives was contained in the 1920 Treaty of Sèvres. Apart from the already mentioned provisions on the restitution of objects plundered during the war and repatriation based

[111] More on the post-colonial state succession with regard to the Libyan cultural property, see Chapter 6, section 6.4.2.

[112] The Kingdom was created in 1916 as a result of the Arab rebellion against Ottomans on the Eastern coast of the Red Sea; in 1932, it became part of the unified Kingdom Saudi Arabia.

[113] The skull was never located and not handed over to Britain, see Vrdoljak, *International Law* (n 22) 85; Wojciech, *Art Treasures & War. A Study on the Restitution of Looted Cultural Property, Pursuant to Public International Law* (Institute of Art & Law, 1998), 31; Kowalski, 'Repatriation of Cultural Property' (n 41) 150; Barnett Hollander, *The International Law of Art for Lawyers, Collectors and Artists* (Bowes & Bowes, 1959), 32; see also 'Letters to Editor', *The Times (London)*, 13, 18, and 21 June 1988.

on territoriality, this also dealt with archaeological patrimony. Under Article 421, it imposed on Turkey the obligation to 'abrogate the existing law of antiquities' and enact new legislation based on a set of principles attached as an annex to this Article. Turkey also had to guarantee the execution of this new law 'on a basis of perfect equality between all nations'.

The Annex contained eight principles, which generally set out the objectives of legal excavations such as permissions for archaeological research, acquisition and exportation of antiquities, as well as a penal regime for unauthorized digging or damage to archaeological sites. These regulations provided scholars of all nations free access to archaeological sites. Furthermore, they also secured the option of '*partage*' of the proceeds of excavations between Turkish authorities and the excavators. Where the division of such findings would result 'impossible for scientific reasons', the excavator had to receive 'a fair indemnity in lieu of a part of the find'. In this way, the Allied powers ensured the protection of archaeological sites, on the one hand, and their own scientific interests, on the other. These arrangements cannot arguably be treated in any aspect as state succession to cultural patrimony, but rather 'colonial' succession[114] to rich archeological sites (guaranty of the legality of excavations and subsequent exportation of antiquities by foreign missions).

The 1920 Treaty of Sèvres, due to new political circumstances in Turkey, was never ratified. However, Article 421 and the Annex were widely used as a model for new archaeological legislation in the Middle East mandate of the League of Nations (for instance, in Iraq and Palestine).[115] Consequently, in the territories ceded by Turkey, the archaeological heritage had to be shared with other countries on the basis of the principle of scientific professional research. In practice, the mandating powers could freely conduct the excavations to enrich their national imperial collections. The cultural integrity of the mandate territories and peoples was not considered as an important objective.

2.7 Conclusion—a legal appraisal

The interwar peace practice is perceived as a 'decisive turning point'[116] in the development of international legal system. Christine Bell, following earlier scholarship, stresses the novelty of the post-First World War peace practice in relation

[114] Vrdoljak, *International Law* (n 22) 85–86.

[115] Ibid. 86–87, Lyndell V. Prott and Patrick J. O'Keefe, *Law and the Cultural Heritage* (Vol. I; *Discovery and Excavations*; OUP, 1984), 45–50; Charles De Visscher, 'La protection des patrimoines artistiques et historiques nationaux: nécessité d'une réglamentation internationale', *Mouseion* (1938) 43–44, 7–34, at 15–16.

[116] Christian Tomuschat, 'The 1871 Peace Treaty between France and Germany and the 1919 Peace Treaty of Versailles', in Randall Lesaffer (ed), *Peace treaties and international law in European history: from the late Middle Ages to World War One* (CUP, 2004), 382–98, at 384.

to the treaty of 'classical period', that is, treaties constructed on the Westphalia model.[117] She notes that these treaties 'marked a turning point from a concept of "balance of powers" as sufficient restraint on war, in a step towards bringing the law on war into line with increasing political concerns about war as a permissible course of action'.[118] Moreover, the concept of the 'balance of power' became weakened by the creation of the League of Nations, marking further formalization of organizations of the international community.[119] This post-First World War conceptualization of peace was also founded on the presumption that a new international order and stability could not be achieved without a restoration of 'communities, territories, and cultural objects and archives'.[120] Thus, a new universal language of political and cultural self-determination was established. In other words, the solutions applied at that time limited their scope as peace settlements, but they also aimed to secure international stability through the enforcement of rights of human communities, including the restoration and enjoyment of their cultural heritage.

The post-First World War peace treaty practice constituted indeed the most important part of extensive legislation with regard to state succession to tangible cultural heritage in cases of cession and dissolution of the multinational state. However, this essentially concerned the European context, and had little effect on the colonial territories. On the basis of the above quoted practice, a few general conclusions in terms of normative developments can be advanced.

First, it appears that at the time of the conclusion of the First World War, the distinction between the legal regime of restitution applicable to cultural property seized in the event of war and that of state succession became fully recognized. Nevertheless, the fact that both regimes were founded on the paramount principle of territoriality binding cultural property with a given territory, their objectives were different. Accordingly, the norms of international law on the restitution of cultural property to the territory from which it had been removed in the event of war constituted the corollary of the universally binding rules prohibiting destruction and looting of property and buildings dedicated to religion, education, art and science. Inversely, the principle of territoriality in cases of state succession provided that territorial transfers not only entailed the transfer of cultural property located in the lands in question, but also the repatriation of property removed prior to the date of succession. Thus, this principle safeguarded the economic and cultural integrity of territory. The differences between these two regimes did not, however, mean that in settling determined cases they could not be jointly taken into consideration, especially when state succession escalated in armed conflict, as usually happened.

Second, post-First World War peace treaty practice in the matter of allocation of cultural property applied the principle of major significance to the

[117] Christine Bell, *On the Law of Peace: Peace Agreements and the Lex Pacificatoria* (OUP, 2008), 90–91.

[118] Ibid. 91.

[119] Ibid.

[120] Vrdoljak, 'Enforcement of Restitution' (n 43) 25.

cultural heritage of a successor state, supplementing the paramount principle of territorial links. In the interwar period, it was essentially understood in terms of nationality of cultural treasures. In fact, this principle constituted the main reason behind the majority of claims, though it was not always explicitly formulated in texts of peace treaties. Importantly, the adoption of the principle of nationality, decisive in interstate settlements, recognized for the first time in international practice the existence of collective rights to enjoy and physically control material manifestations of culture and group (national) identity. Arguably, such an affirmation of national collective rights was profoundly linked to the emerging principle of self-determination of nations in its external as well as internal dimensions. With reference to the latter, the system of minority guarantees provided for a limited protection of cultural rights of such groups to enjoy their religious, ethnic, and national particularities within the dominant culture of a successor state.

Third, the interwar state practice led to the reconceptualization of sovereign rights to dispose and displace of cultural property. In fact, all the settlements in this matter addressed the question of the legality of sovereign acts of predecessor states with reference to such property. It appears that the removals made by the use of force or under administrative discriminatory duress were widely considered as illegitimate and constituted a prerequisite for repatriation of a given object to its place of origin. Inversely, the property, displaced in a regular way through a commercial transaction in conformity with the applicable law in a given territory at the time of transfer, was exempted from the regime on state succession; for example, the *St Ildefonso Altar* which was legally purchased and transported by the Empress Maria-Theresa from Brussels to Vienna. However, in some cases these considerations could be challenged by the particular value of a given object for the national culture of a successor state, for example, Article 11 §8 of the 1921 Treaty of Riga. The methods of proving such an important link with national culture were, however, very difficult to establish, especially in respect of the objects of recognized universal artistic value, such as works of great masters, and were usually settled on a case-by-case basis.

Fourth, state succession arrangements usually affirmed the principle of integrity of internationally ranked collections. Arguably, this can be understood as the principle of protection of the interest of human society as a whole in universal reservoirs of art and science. This principle could only be challenged by the fact that certain objects were plundered in the event of war, or when a great national interest of a successor state was at stake. However, it seems that preservation of the interest of the international community was often respected at the expense of newly independent states and their national interests.

Fifth, the post-First World War practice of state succession widely applied the procedural principle of resolution of cultural property related disputes. This consisted in special bilateral commissions of experts (eg Austria–Italy, Austria–Hungary, Poland–Russia and Ukraine), or arbitral adjudication under the supervision of the League of Nations (Committee of Three Jurists).

Finally, it is worth mentioning one of the best practices applied by Austria and Hungary, the successors of the former Habsburg Monarchy. These concern the institution of privileged access to former imperial collections in Vienna secured to citizens of both states. Moreover, the 1932 Austro-Hungarian Agreement gave Hungary a right to control the general utilization of the collections. In addition, it provided for the facilitation of interstate cultural collaboration in the sphere of temporary art exhibitions.

PART TWO

CONSOLIDATION AND CODIFICATION OF THE LAW (1940–1989)

We might say that ... newly independent states have a claim, based on public international law, to receive back specified objects created on their territory and expressive of indigenous culture, as well as those bought with local funds and constituted public property. If today the states concerned advance such demands uninsistently, this is the result of their difficult situation, in which questions of economy take priority in discussion with the ex-colonial states. There need be no surprise when we find that no mention is made of cultural objects in agreements and other acts connected with succession. Such instruments are the outcome as a rule, of great concessions, and by no means express all the well-substantiated claims of the liberated states.

Halina Nieć, 'Sovereign Rights to Cultural Property', *PYIL* 3(1971), 245.

The peoples who were victims of this plunder, sometimes for hundreds of years, have not only been despoiled of irreplaceable masterpieces but also robbed of a memory which would doubtless have helped them to greater self-knowledge and would certainly have enabled others to understand them better.

The return of a work of art or record to the country which created it enables a people to recover part of its memory and identity, and proves that the long dialogue between civilizations which shapes the history of the world is still continuing in an atmosphere of mutual respect between nations.

Amadou-Mahtar M'Bow, 'A Plea for the Return of an Irreplaceable Cultural Heritage to those who Created It: An Appeal by the Director-General of UNESCO of 7 June 1978', *Museum* 31(1979)1, 58.

3

The Second World War, Decolonization, and State Succession in Cultural Property

The Koh-i-Noor, one of the largest diamonds in the world, is an icon of modern popular culture[1]. Since its first public display in 1851 at the Great Exhibition in London, it has attracted the attention of the media, writers, film-makers and even creators of computer games. Its complex history and the controversies with regard to its territorial pertinence and ownership make it one of the most significant protagonists of post-Second World War disputes in the matter of state succession in tangible cultural heritage.

The origins of the Koh-i-Noor ('Mountain of Light') are not well-documented but it is believed that the diamond was mined in central or south-eastern India long before the arrival of Alexander the Great. For centuries it was the most venerated gem in the royal regalia of different Indian, Mogul, Persian, and Afghan monarchies.[2] During the rule of the Maharaja Ranjit Singh (1780–1839), the Lion of Punjab, the diamond eventually became part of the treasury of the Sikh Empire which covered Punjab and other northern territories of present-day India and Pakistan.[3] As a consequence of the wars with the British East India Company, the Sikh lands were annexed to British India. In 1849, the last Maharaja, the eleven-year old Dalip Singh Bahadur, while ceding Sikh territories also had to surrender the Koh-i-Noor to the Queen of the United Kingdom of Great Britain and Ireland. It seems clear that at the time, the British administration perceived this acquisition as a mere spoil of war. Accordingly, the Maharaja was sent to London in order to present the diamond to Queen Victoria in person, as it was perceived 'more for the honour of the Queen that the Koh-i-noor should be surrendered directly from the hand of the conquered prince into the hands of the sovereign who was his conqueror, than it should be presented to her as a gift—which is always a favour—by any joint-stock company among her subjects.'[4] Since 1851,

[1] See Iradj Amini, *The Koh-i-noor Diamond* (Roli Books, 2013).

[2] Saby Ghoshray, 'Repatriation of the Kohinoor Diamond: Expanding the Legal Paradigm for Cultural Heritage', *Fordham International Law Journal* 31(2007–2008)3, 741–80, at 746–47.

[3] Jeanette Greenfield, *The Return of Cultural Treasures* (3rd edn, CUP, 2007), 129.

[4] Letter of James Broun-Ramsay, Lord Dalhousie, Governor-General of India to Sir George Cooper, 16 August 1849, in John G. A. Baird (ed), *Private Letters of the Marquess of Dalhousie* (Blackwood, 1910), 85–90, at 88.

the Koh-i-Noor has been worn only by female members of the British royal family. After Queen Victoria's death in 1901, this right fell to every Queen Consort. Currently, the diamond is fitted in the crown of 1937, kept in the Tower of London.

In 1947, India and Pakistan gained independence.[5] According to the provisions of the 1947 Indian Independence Act,[6] the majority of historic Punjab and cultural centre, Lahore, passed to Pakistan. Following this territorial partition, which was essentially based on religious divisions, the Sikh community from Pakistan was resettled in India, and Muslims from India moved to Pakistani Punjab. Thus, under the new political circumstances, the links between territory, people, and material cultural heritage was ruptured. Moreover, the transfer of powers from Great Britain to these newly independent states did not address the issue of allocation of cultural property in state succession. In fact, India and Pakistan managed to recover only a small number of cultural items displaced during colonialism.

The case of the Koh-i-Noor is, however, peculiar as it concerns the succession rights to cultural patrimony of the Sikh Empire raised by both India and Pakistan, on the one hand, and the United Kingdom, on the other. In 1976, Zulfiqar Ali Bhutto, the Prime Minister of Pakistan, formally requested that the gem be returned to Pakistan since it was in the geographical territory of present-day Pakistan that it had been surrendered to the British. Although Bhutto did not explicitly recall the rights of Pakistan to Punjab's royal regalia, arising from state succession, it undoubtedly appears that his demand was driven by this reasoning. He argued that the diamond had 'immense sentimental value for Pakistan',[7] and its retention by the UK caused a 'sense of cultural deprivation or historical disinheritance'.[8] Furthermore, he stressed the historical and cultural significance of the Koh-i-Noor for the city of Lahore (Punjab), 'Pakistan's cultural capital'.[9]

The British government rejected this claim on two general grounds.[10] First, that the history of the gem was very confused, since Pakistan was not the only state which could demand its return. Second, the diamond was not seized as a war trophy but was formally presented to the British Queen. Hence, its ownership was legitimately transferred, under international law applicable at the time of the annexation of Punjab, and as such it constituted an inalienable part of the Crown Jewels of the United Kingdom.[11]

From 1997–2002, several other claimants demanded the repatriation of the diamond. These included the representatives of India, Pakistan, and Afghanistan

[5] For an extensive analysis, see Hari Om Agarwal, *State Succession. A Study of Indian Cases* (Allahabad Law Agency, 1980).

[6] Indian Independence Act of 18 July 1947, 10 & 11 Geo. 6. Ch. 30; available at: <http://www.legislation.gov.uk/ukpga/1947/30/pdfs/ukpga_19470030_en.pdf>, accessed on 31 January 2015.

[7] Dominic Casciani, 'PM Debated Diamond's Ownership', BBC News, 12 December 2006, <http://news.bbc.co.uk/2/hi/uk_news/politics/6213055.stm>, accessed on 31 January 2015.

[8] Ibid. [9] Ibid.

[10] See Charles Rousseau, 'Refus de la Grande-Bretagne de restituer le Koh-I-Noor au Pakistan', *RGDIP* 81(1977)2, 545–47.

[11] Vivek K. Hatti, 'India's Right to Reclaim Cultural and Art Treasures from Britain under International Law', *The George Washington Journal of International Law and Economics* 32(2000)3, 465–95, 484 ff.

(including the Taliban),[12] an individual, Mr Beant Singh Sandhanwalia, the last recognized heir of the late Maharaja Duleep Singh, and officials of the Jagannath temple in Puri, India, to which the gem had allegedly been bequeathed prior to its surrender to the British.[13] The debate concerned the legality of transfer of the diamond, and the moral obligations of the UK towards its former colonies. The position of the British government towards those claims was somewhat pragmatic. It sustained that the multiplicity of competing claims would render it impossible to establish the gem's former ownership. Moreover, it has been stressed that the Crown Jewels, including the Koh-i-Noor, are part of British national heritage and held by the Queen as sovereign.[14] This position has been upheld most recently by David Cameron, the current British Prime Minister. He told Indian TV channel NDTV that if the UK agreed to meet such a claim, it would be a precedent for analogous demands, and that in that event, 'the British Museum would be empty'.[15]

In the light of these controversies, the case of the Koh-i-Noor arguably embodies most of difficulties relating to the allocation of cultural property in the post-Second World War practice of state succession. First of all, this refers to the profound territorial reconfigurations which often disregarded historic and ethnic divisions. In particular, the newly post-colonial states assumed administrative boundaries drafted by colonial powers, barely related to the pre-colonial state organisms. Consequently, ethnic or religious groups were often scattered between the territories of different newly independent states or, as in the case of India and Pakistan, the transfers of populations took place in order to provide a degree of cultural homogeneity within new state boundaries. Such situations caused great difficulties in establishing successor rights to determined cultural property. As regards the Koh-i-Noor, none of the states concerned can fully claim to be the direct legal, territorial, and cultural successor of the state in which the gem originated. Accordingly, Pakistan may invoke the principle of territoriality, whereas India may claim the restoration of the lost national heritage on behalf of its Sikh citizens. Ironically, similar national and historical argumentation can be also applied by the UK since the Koh-i-Noor, constituting part of the British royal regalia for more than 100 years, has become a significant element of British cultural heritage and British state identity. Arguably, such competition between the principle of territoriality and its major significance for the national cultural heritage constituted the crux of the majority of post-Second World War disputes on the allocation of cultural property.

This chapter deals with the deconstruction of the well-established inter-war law on state succession in tangible cultural heritage, caused by the effects of the Second World War and decolonization. It quotes the early post-war practice of state succession to cultural property, in light of the Allied restitution programme and Cold

[12] Ghoshray, 'Repatriation of the Kohinoor Diamond' (n 2) 752. [13] Ibid.

[14] Greenfield, *The Return of Cultural Treasures* (n 3) 131.

[15] <http://www.bbc.co.uk/news/uk-politics-10802469>, accessed on 31 January 2015.

War political considerations. It explores the major difficulties in the allocation of cultural property within the framework of state succession both in European and post-colonial contexts. It also identifies some new tendencies, generally defined *ex gratia* and *de facto* solutions, driven by economic and political calculations rather than any legal reasoning. This chapter observes that, ironically, by avoiding any comprehensive legal approach, such arrangements implicitly postulated the priority of national collective rights to cultural heritage over those arising from state succession. In fact, the *ex gratia* and *de facto* solutions usually accommodated only the most ardent and emotionally marked claims of the successor states. Finally, it recalls the case of the Old City of Jerusalem and Holy Places in Palestine as evidence of the emerging international concern for the safeguarding of universal cultural values in the post-colonial landscape.

3.1 Cultural property in the post-Second World War legal landscape

The major concern of post-Second World War settlements in the field of tangible cultural heritage consisted in the mitigation of the effects of unprecedented destruction and plunder of cultural property, especially on the European continent. The international efforts at that time reaffirmed the significance of restoring cultural material to the territories and peoples who were deprived of their treasures during military occupation. Certain attempts were also made at settling cultural property-related disputes resulting from state succession within the post-Second World War restitution programme, as Europe experienced profound changes of state boundaries followed by displacements of ethnic groups both between states and within their boundaries. However, the implementation of the principles on state succession to cultural property established prior to the Second World War met with great difficulties due to the outbreak of the Cold War, which hindered the resolution of the most pressing controversies. Moreover, the Eurocentric view of international law changed as a result of the Second World War; in fact, an upheaval in the international order and the emergence of new powerful actors on the international stage constituted one of the major effects of this conflagration. Europe lost the central position it occupied in global politics, which became dominated by two new superpowers, the United States and the Soviet Union. In addition, the newly independent states liberated in the process of decolonization looked to establish their own interests and claims in terms of proportional share in international politics, economy, and cultural resources.

3.1.1 Post-Second World War restitution programme

One of the major developments after the Second World War with regard to tangible cultural heritage was the criminalization of the plunder of cultural property, and the reaffirmation of the corresponding obligation of restitution. It was commonly understood that acts committed against cultural heritage profoundly affected human communities and that they were often used as a part of genocidal practices.[16] This was particularly relevant in view of Nazi ideology, according to which certain ethnic groups or nations were denied the right to possess and enjoy their cultural heritage and cultural identity. On legal grounds, a crucial development was made by the Nuremberg International Military Tribunal.[17] In particular, the trial against Alfred Rosenberg, head of the Nazi official organ *Einsatzstab Rosenberg*, responsible for the organized pillage of art treasures, explicitly marked the first time that the plundering of such properties was held to be a war crime and a crime against humanity.[18] In light of this, the duty of restitution was perceived not only as an important element of the post-war reconstruction process and a crucial factor in safeguarding the peace, but also as a binding international obligation towards the maintenance of human dignity.

The fundamental document for the post-Second World War restitution of cultural property was adopted as early as 5 January 1943, when the conflict was still in train. The Inter-Allied Declaration against Acts of Dispossession Committed in Territories under Enemy Occupation or Control (the 1943 Declaration of London), notwithstanding its merely declaratory nature, expressed the Allies' intention of doing everything in their power to reverse all acts of acquisition of property, including cultural objects, committed under duress or by use of force in the territories occupied by Germany and their allies, even though such acts appeared to be legitimate.[19] Moreover, it extended its scope to neutral countries warning that profiting from such unlawful acts of plunder and confiscation would be perceived as acting 'as fences or cloaks on behalf of the thieves'. In 1944, this duty of neutral states relating to the restitution of cultural property to its rightful owners was also recommend by the international conference in Bretton Woods.[20] Importantly, the 1943 London Declaration and the Final Act of the Conference in Bretton Woods put forward the principle that the duty of unconditional restitution was applicable to all property deriving from the occupied countries, acquired under force or duress. Accordingly, the Allies recognized the inequality of power between the parties to the transactions and excluded the legality of *bona fide* acquisition of objects originating from the occupied territories.[21]

[16] Raphael Lemkin, *Axis Rule in Occupied Europe: Laws of Occupation—Analysis of Government—Proposals for Redress* (Carnegie Endowment for International Peace, 1944), 84.

[17] For an examination of the case law of the Nuremberg Tribunal regarding crimes against cultural heritage, see Jacqueline Nowlan, 'Cultural Property and the Nuremberg War Crimes Trial', *Humanitares Volkerrecht* 4(1993), 221–23.

[18] *Trial of the Major War Criminals before the International Military Tribunal, Nuremberg 14 November 1945–1 October 1946*, vol. 22 (International Military Tribunal, 1948), 539–41.

[19] The text of the London Declaration is available at: <http://www.lootedartcommission.com/inter-allied-declaration>, accessed on 31 January 2015.

[20] Monetary and Financial Conference. Bretton Woods, July 1944, Final Act, Part VI, available at: <http://www.lootedartcommission.com/bretton-woods>, accessed on 31 January 2015.

[21] Wilfried Fiedler, 'Die Allierte (Londoner) Erklärung Vom 5.I.1943', in Jürgen Basedow (ed), *Privatrecht in Der Internationalen Arena, Liber Amicorum Kurt Siehr* (T.M.C. Asser Institut 2000), 197–218.

At the end of 1945, the Paris Conference on Reparation reaffirmed the principle of restitution of all property, which: 1) 'existed at the time of occupation of the country concerned, and were removed with or without payment;' 2) 'were produced during the occupation and obtained by an act of force'. In addition, it provided for the principle of restitution-in-kind, applicable to cultural property. Accordingly, it stated that the 'objects (including books, manuscripts and documents) of an artistic, historical, scientific (excluding equipment of an industrial character), educational or religious character which have been looted by the enemy occupying Power shall so far as possible be replaced by equivalent objects if they are not restored.'[22] In 1946, the Allied Control Council for Germany (Control Council) adopted a final definition of 'restitution' applicable to the entire German territory. According to this definition, which was complemented by other Allied legislation, the restitution would be based on six major principles. First, 'the public-international-law principle'[23] provided that the Control Council would deal only with the claims presented by the states from whose territories the objects had been looted. Moreover, the application of this principle ensured a much easier mechanism of restitution. In fact, the process of restoration of looted cultural property would be much more complicated and time-consuming if the Council's decisions were founded on the principles of private law aimed at protecting the security of commercial transactions: the protection of the bona fide purchaser, and time limitations. Second, the principle of 'identification' meant that objects found in Germany had to be identified with those actually removed; during the process of identification, the possessors of the objects were required to provide their protection and supervision.[24] Third, the Allied legislation confirmed the criterion of the use of force—the restitution concerned only the acquisitions of cultural objects that had been taken by force or under duress. Fourth, the restitution was based on the rudimentary principle of territoriality—cultural objects, irrespective of whether or not they were of public or private property, ought to be restored to the territory from which they were taken. Fifth, Germany was bound to participate in the costs of restitution. Finally, the restitution-in-kind could be ordered with regard to the goods of a unique character whose restoration was not possible.

Clearly, the 1946 definition of restitution fully reaffirmed the rudimentary principle of territoriality in respect of the restitution of looted property and provided for the reparation for cultural loss in cases of irreparable objects. This very far-reaching principle, applied only to a very limited number of cases prior to the Second World War, was questioned by the US administration as early as 1947 who argued that extensive application of cultural replacement would not be consistent

[22] Final Act and Annex of the Paris Peace Conference on Reparation of 21 December 1945, Annex 1: Resolution on the Subject of Restitution in John B. Howard, *The Paris Agreement on Reparations from Germany* (United States Government Printing Office, 1946), 19.

[23] István Vásárhelyi, *Restitution in International Law* (Akad. Kiadó, 1964), 87.

[24] Ibid.

with the principle of the protection of cultural property of all nations, including the German people.[25]

Importantly, the prohibition of the acquisition of cultural property under duress, the duty of restitution, and of equal protection of the cultural heritage of every people in the world, laid the foundations for subsequent restitution practices, including the Allied (US) programme on the recovery of cultural property plundered in Asia by Japanese armed forces and its occupying administration.[26] Moreover, those post-Second World War experiences were crucial for further international legislative efforts in terms of the restitution of cultural property displaced in the event of war. They also greatly affected the arrangements applied to the cases of state succession, as the elaboration of the criterion of the use of force—a prerequisite for restitution of cultural material—has been extensively invoked by newly independent post-colonial states.

3.1.2 The division of Europe and the Cold War

The arrangements made at the Yalta Conference in February 1945[27] influenced international relations for a long time. The foundation of the United Nations expressed the desire to prevent interstate violence and to provide for the equality of nations and safeguard fundamental human rights and human dignity. Moreover, the charters of both International Military Tribunals—Nuremberg and Tokyo—convened to prosecute the leaders of Nazi Germany and the Empire of Japan—introduced the concept of international criminal responsibility for war crimes, and crimes against peace and humanity. These efforts, based on universally recognized values, were however restrained by post-war political reality and interests. Hence, the implementation of the post-Second World War restitution programme remained incomplete.

In fact, the post-Yalta political order is often described as *cuius regio eius ordo (socialis)*—'whose realm, his social order.'[28] Under the rule of communism there was no space left for an attempt at reclaiming the stolen property, including art objects. In Central and Eastern Europe, new regimes took full control over the cultural treasures, which in 1944–49 were practically nationalized *in toto*. Similarly, all the arrangements in respect of the restitution of art treasures plundered during

[25] Wojciech Kowalski, 'Restitution of Works of Art Pursuant to Private and Public International Law', *RCADI* 288(2001), 9–244, at 154.

[26] See Victoria Reed, 'Ardelia Hall: From Museum of Fine Arts to Monuments Woman', *International Journal of Cultural Property* 21(2014)1, 79–93, at 87.

[27] The meeting was held from 4–11 February 1945. See Protocol of the Proceedings of the Crimea Conference at Yalta of 11 February 1945, British Parliamentary Paper Miscellaneous, No. 7 (1947) Cmd. 7088.

[28] This has sometimes been associated with the official sixteenth-century principle *cuius regio, eius religio*—'whose realm, his religion', agreed in the 1555 Peace of Augsburg, which ended armed conflict between the Catholic and Protestant forces in the Holy Roman Empire. See Hans Rothfels, 'Nationalität und Grenze im Späten 19. und frühen 20. Jahrhundert', *Vierteljahrshefte für Zeitgeschichte* 9(1961)3, 225–33; John Lukacs, *Decline and Rise of Europe. A Study in Recent History, with Particular Emphasis on the Development of a European Consciousness* (2nd edn, Greenwood Press, 1975).

the war, or their allocation in cases of state succession, followed 'fraternal' *ex gratia* dialogue between socialist peoples rather than legal considerations.

In this Cold War political landscape, the crucial question concerned the post-war status of Germany. On the basis of the Potsdam Agreement,[29] Germany and Austria were divided into four occupation zones, administered by the United States, Great Britain, France, and the Soviet Union. A similar division was applied to both capitals, Berlin and Vienna. The territories of pre-war Germany in the east from the Oder-Neisse line passed to Polish administration as compensation for the territories taken by the USSR, while East Prussia with Königsberg was annexed to the USSR. In addition, France was granted administrative powers in Saarland, temporarily detached from Germany. The decisions taken at Potsdam also sanctioned an immense displacement of German nationals. Accordingly, nearly 15 million people had to flee, primarily from Czechoslovakia, the USSR, and the territories ceded to Poland, to the four Allied Occupation Zones.[30] The tensions between the Western Allies and the USSR began immediately after the defeat of Germany and Japan. By 1948 it was clear that there would be no agreement on the future of Germany. Notwithstanding the previous arrangements on common control over that country, the Allies decided to keep their political interests and military presence in the administered territories. The Soviet blockade of Berlin, initiated in 1948, constituted the climax of the tensions.[31] In 1946–49, the USSR managed to introduce pro-Soviet leadership in its occupation zone. Thus, the division of Germany between two different political blocs was sealed. In autumn 1949, Western Allies formed the Federal Republic of Germany (FRG)—West Germany,[32] and the lands under Soviet control proclaimed the German Democratic Republic (GDR)—East Germany.[33] Berlin remained a divided city, whose split status was dramatically enhanced in 1961 by the construction of the Berlin Wall. Hence, no peace treaty was signed with Germany which would deal with territorial changes, transfer of population, or state succession, including the allocation of cultural property. Until 1972, the conflicting blocs of states did not recognize the sovereignty of either East or West Germany.

Europe experienced other profound changes of state boundaries followed by displacements of ethnic groups between and within states. These were only partially based on international agreements and in many cases mere *de facto* solutions were applied.[34] Moreover, thousands of individuals from Central Eastern

[29] The conference was held from 17 July–2 August 1945. See Protocol of Proceedings of the Berlin Conference, August 1, 1945, British Parliamentary Paper Miscellaneous No. 6 (1947) Cmd. 7087.

[30] See two works by Alfred M. De Zayas: *A Terrible Revenge. The Ethnic Cleansing of the East European Germans, 1944–1950* (St. Martin's Press, 1994), and *Nemesis at Potsdam: the Anglo-Americans and the Expulsion of the Germans; Background, Execution, Consequences* (Routledge & Kegan Paul, 1979).

[31] John Lewis Gaddis, *The Cold War: A New History* (Penguin Press, 2005), 33.

[32] Proclaimed on 7 September 1949.

[33] Proclaimed on 7 October 1949.

[34] These primarily regarded Central and Eastern Europe, ie Fins from the USSR, Italians from Istria and Dalmatia, Hungarians from Czechoslovakia, Poles from the USSR, Ukrainians from Poland, etc.

Europe were forced into political emigration. Thus, apart from being the deadliest conflict in history, the Second World War also caused the eradication of secular cultural ties and the post-war destruction of material cultural heritage. It must also be stressed that due to the Holocaust and post-war policies of states, almost the entire European population of Jews was erased from the cultural and ethnic landscape of that continent. Jewish cultural heritage was destroyed and dispersed. In many cases, the question of the allocation of cultural property remained tacit until the end of the Cold War.

3.1.3 Decolonization and the Cold War

The development of the doctrine and practice of state succession in tangible cultural heritage is strictly linked to European, or more broadly Western, diplomacy, in the nineteenth and the first half of the twentieth century. The end of the Second World War also brought about the independence of formerly colonized and occupied peoples outside Europe. In particular, the Japanese occupation of the Far East led to the removal of European administration and influences. Hence, with the defeat of Japan, the colonized nations of Indochina and Indonesia immediately proclaimed their independence. At the same time, national movements within British India resulted in the independence of Pakistan, India, and Burma. In Eastern Asia, the hegemony of Japan was replaced by new communist China.

From the very beginning, the emergence of new states was, however, profoundly influenced by Cold War political and ideological considerations. Traditionally, both super powers—the US and USSR, as well as Maoist China—opted for decolonization, but at the same time they also perceived it as a way of enlarging their spheres of interest. This rivalry was primary seen in the context of the political and social order which would follow the dissolution of the colonial system. Many post-colonial wars of independence expanded into general Cold War conflicts in which two blocs actively participated, supporting colonial rulers or Marxist guerrilla movements, respectively. These interventions often caused great damage to cultural patrimony, such as the 1968 US bombing of the historical Imperial City in Hue, Vietnam.

From the time of the Afro–Asian Conference (Bandung Conference) in 1950,[35] the majority of post-colonial states began to cooperate in order to oppose both blocs of states, aiming to find a new position in the world. By the mid-1960s, this growing movement also addressed the question of the recovery of and reparation for their lost patrimonies. However, the post-Second World War restitution programme remained silent on the legal principles governing the situation of cultural property originating from these formerly colonized and occupied territories.

Apart from the question of the retrieval of cultural material removed in the colonial period, the outbreak of the Cold War also had a profound impact on

[35] Kahin George Mcturnan, *The Asian–African Conference: Bandung, Indonesia, April 1955* (Cornell University Press, 1956).

the allocation of cultural property within formerly colonized or occupied territories beyond Europe. This primarily concerned the fate of historical treasures of China and Korea. Due to the 1953 division of the latter into the Republic of Korea (South Korea) and the Democratic People's Republic of Korea (North Korea), practically all venerated cultural objects of the Korean people remained in cultural institutions in the south of the country.[36] Similarly, the civil war in China led to the division of cultural treasures between the government of the Republic of China exiled in Taiwan and the government of the People's Republic of China, proclaimed in 1949. In 1948, museum officials from Beijing ordered the evacuation of the most important imperial treasures (over 600,000 artefacts) from the Palace Museum of the Forbidden City to Taipei, in Taiwan. Following the end of hostilities, the Chinese government in Taiwan decided to house them in the newly built National Palace Museum of Taipei,[37] which is currently one of the most visited art museum in the world.[38] Thus, in both cases the *de facto* division of state territory based on political and ideological considerations deprived for long part of the Korean and Chinese nations of their most significant cultural treasures.

3.2 Post-Second World War Europe and state succession in cultural property

With regard to the post-Second World War restitution programme, some of the international controversies on the matter of cultural property were regulated by a series of Paris peace treaties signed in 1947 with the former allies of Germany: Bulgaria, Finland, Hungary, Italy, and Romania. Similar regulations were also adopted in the 1955 Austrian State Treaty,[39] which concluded the Allied occupation and division of that country. All of these treaties were largely based on the principles adopted in the 1943 Declaration of London. Although they primarily dealt with the restitution of cultural property relating to violations of international humanitarian law, they also referred to cases of state succession. In addition to peace treaty practice, an important set of regulations was introduced via different arrangements between the states of the Eastern bloc. These were mostly driven by Cold War considerations, which favoured the unity of socialist democratic peoples, overriding any post-war national and cultural rancour.

[36] See Kungnip Chungang Pangmulgwan, *100 Highlights of the National Museum of Korea* (National Museum of Korea, 2006).

[37] <http://www.npm.gov.tw>, accessed on 31 January 2015.

[38] As of 2009; 'Exhibition and museum attendance figures 2009', *The Art Newspaper* 23 no. 212, April 2010.

[39] State Treaty (with Annexes and Maps) for the Re-Establishment of an Independent and Democratic Austria, signed in Vienna on 15 May 1955, entered into force 27 July 1955, 217 UNTS 223.

3.2.1 Peace treaty practice

All of the peace treaties signed in 1947 with the European Allies of Germany included provisions reflecting the principles of the post-war Allied restitution programme. Except for the 1947 Peace Treaty with Finland, which basically repeated the text of the earlier armistice, the remaining treaties followed the same model with regard to restitution provisions. Accordingly, the Paris peace treaties confirmed a peremptory obligation of restitution of property, including cultural objects, removed by force or duress from the occupied territories, and the paramount nature of the principle of territoriality. The procedure of restitution would be based on public international law. In addition, the 1947 Peace Treaties with Bulgaria, Italy,[40] and Hungary[41] contained identical provisions on the restitution-in-kind for cultural material of a unique character, of which restoration would not be possible. For instance, the 1947 Peace Treaty with Italy contained the following provisions: 'if, in particular cases, it is impossible for Italy to make restitution of objects of artistic, historical or archaeological value, belonging to the cultural heritage of the United Nation from whose territory such objects were removed by force or duress by Italian forces, authorities or nationals, Italy shall transfer to the United Nation concerned objects of the same kind as, and of approximately equivalent value to, the objects removed, in so far as such objects are obtainable in Italy' (Article 75.9).

In this group of regulations, only the treaties with Italy and Hungary explicitly dealt with the allocation of cultural property following state succession. It appears that in both cases, these regulations were greatly affected by the principles of the post-war restitution programme.

a) Italy

The 1947 Peace Treaty with Italy included the most detailed and far-reaching provisions concerning state succession to cultural property. Accordingly, Italy transferred certain territories to France, Yugoslavia, and Greece, and had to resign from any colonial claims to Libya, Eritrea, and Italian Somaliland. The treaty also formally concluded the Italian occupation of Albania and Ethiopia. Under Article 1 of Annex XIV to the treaty, the successor states 'shall receive, without payment, Italian state and para-statal property within territory ceded' to them, together with 'all relevant archives and documents of an administrative character or historical value concerning the territory in question'. The same Annex, under Article 4, provided for transfer to the successor states of 'all objects of artistic, historical or archaeological value belonging to the cultural heritage of the ceded territory, which, while that territory was under Italian control were removed from

40 Treaty of Peace with Italy, signed on 10 February 1947, entered in force on 15 September 1947, 49 UNTS 3.

41 Treaty of Peace with Hungary, signed on 10 February 1947, entered in force on 15 September 1947, 41 UNTS 135.

there, without payment and are held by the Italian Government or by Italian public institutions'. With reference to these provisions, it seems clear that the treaty rigorously applied the general principle of territoriality, at least in cases of war plunder. Moreover, the criterion for the return of a specific cultural object to the successor state was its removal without payment, which can arguably be perceived as analogous to the prerequisite of acquisition by force or under duress applicable to the transfers committed in the event of war.

As regards the settlements with France, apart from the general restoration of archives pertinent to borderline municipalities ceded by Italy, the 1947 Peace Treaty with Italy, under Article 7, provided for the reintegration of historic and administrative records related to the territories of the Duchy of Savoy and the County of Nice ceded to France in 1860.[42] Accordingly, Italy was bound to hand over to France 'all archives, historical and administrative, prior to 1860, which concern the territory ceded to France under the Treaty of 24 March 1860 and the Convention of 23 August 1860.' Hence, it appears that on the occasion of the Italian defeat and the new delimitation of state borders, France sought to resolve some cultural questions which were not linked to the actual territorial arrangements, but inversely referred to past territorial transfers. In fact, the allocation of certain archives pertinent to different territories on the Franco–Italian border and displaced since the time of the Napoleonic wars, was the subject of some pre-Second World War bilateral negotiations.[43] Eventually, in 1949, the settlements on this matter were subject to the efforts of a mixed bilateral Franco–Italian commission. Subsequently, Italy handed over to France certain documents of an administrative nature and those of historic value pertinent to the territory of Savoy and Nice, as well as those related to the municipalities ceded in 1947 (Tenda-Briga district).[44] In cases where the records were of both Italian and French interest, France was provided with microfilmed copies of original archival fonds.[45]

The settlements between these two states were driven by the paramount principle of territoriality, which was also applied to the documents of historical value. In other words, the cession of territory was followed by the transfer of the materials constituting its cultural and historic legacy.

The most restrictive provisions on state succession to cultural property were, however, applied by the 1947 Peace Treaty with Italy in respect of the territories ceded to Yugoslavia. As in the case of the French–Italian settlements, the treaty dealt not only with the current territorial transfer, but it also aimed at resolving some past claims. Bilateral relations between Italy and Yugoslavia were very sensitive at that time, due to ethnic tensions and very recent memories of war crimes

[42] Traité pour la cession de la Savoie et de Nice à la France, signé à Turin le 24 Mars 1860, 1 Martens RMPT 145; available at: <http://mjp.univ-perp.fr/traites/1860turin.htm>, accessed on 31 January 2015.

[43] Ministero dell'Interno, 'I danni materiali e le conseguenze della guerra', in *Gli Archivi di Stati al 1952* (2nd edn, Istituto Poligrafico dello Stato,1954), 4–26, available at: < http://www.icar.beniculturali.it/biblio/pdf/AdS_1952/02_danniMateriali.pdf>, accessed on 31 January 2015.

[44] Ibid. [45] Ibid.

committed by both parties to the conflict. Under the 1947 Peace Treaty, Italy had to cede the territories on the north-eastern coast of the Adriatic to Yugoslavia. In addition to this, the area of the city of Trieste formed a separate Free Territory of Trieste which, however, was not considered as ceded territory in the meaning defined in the treaty (Article 21.4).

Importantly, the treaty revised a number of *de facto* solutions applied by the Kingdom of Italy at the time of the dismemberment of Austria–Hungary. Hence, it provided for the repatriation to Yugoslavia of 'all objects of artistic, historical, scientific, educational or religious character (including all deeds, manuscripts, documents and bibliographical material) as well as administrative archives (files, registers, plans and documents of any kind)' on the basis of the rudimentary principle of territoriality. Accordingly, Italy was bound to hand over to Yugoslavia three groups of objects (Article 12): 1) items, 'which, as the result of the Italian occupation, were removed between 4 November 1918 and 2 March 1924 from the territories ceded to Yugoslavia under the treaties signed in Rapallo on 12 November 1920 and in Rome on 27 January 1924'; 2) 'all objects belonging to those territories and falling into the above categories, removed by the Italian Armistice Mission which operated in Vienna after the first World War'; 3) all objects of public property removed on 4 November 1918 from the territory which under the 1947 Treaty with Italy was ceded to Yugoslavia, and 'those connected with the said territory which Italy received from Austria or Hungary under the Peace Treaties signed in St. Germain on 10 September 1919 and in the Trianon on 4 June 1920 and under the convention between Austria and Italy, signed in Vienna on 4 May 1920.' With reference to the last group of objects, one may observe a certain 're-repatriation'.[46] The items, which had been handed over to Italy at the time of the collapse of Austria–Hungary, would be repatriated once again on the basis of the territorial connection following the subsequent state succession process. Moreover, the treaty, under Article 12.3, also provided for the repatriation-in-kind or substitute repatriation in favour of Yugoslavia. Accordingly, in cases where Italy was 'unable to restore or hand over to Yugoslavia' the objects determined by the treaty, it was obliged to hand over to Yugoslavia 'objects of the same kind as, and of approximately equivalent value to, the objects removed, in so far as such objects are obtainable in Italy'.

In the execution of this treaty, Italy and Yugoslavia signed an agreement in 1961 on the regulation of the restitution of cultural property.[47] This concerned the final settlement of the controversies to certain objects of art, archaeological items, and archival fonds. In some cases, Italy was bound to pay compensation for the objects which could not be restored. However, the crux of cultural heritage controversies between Italy and Yugoslavia consisted in the status of around 100 Venetian

[46] Wojciech Kowalski, 'Repatriation of Cultural Property Following a Cession of Territory or Dissolution of Multinational States', *AAL* 6(2001)2, 139–66, at 154.

[47] Accordo tra la Repubblica Italiana e la Repubblica Popolare Federale di Jugoslavia per il regolamento della restituzione alla Jugoslavia dei beni culturali, con scambio di note, Roma, il 15 Settembre 1961, GU No. 080 of 27 March 1962.

works of art from the fourteenth to eighteenth centuries, evacuated in 1940 by the Italian administration from several municipalities of Istria, which under the 1947 Peace Treaty formed part of the Free Territory of Trieste (FTT), and in 1975 were eventually incorporated to Yugoslavia under the Treaty of Osimo.[48] The question of the allocation of the so-called 'Istria's jewels' remained unsettled during the Cold War. It re-emerged on the occasion of the subsequent state succession process, which led to the dissolution of Yugoslavia, in 1991.[49]

The last set of provisions on the allocation of cultural property, under the 1947 Peace Treaty with Italy, regulated the situation of the Italian colonies in Africa. As mentioned, Italy had to withdraw its claims to Libya, Eritrea, and Italian Somaliland. However, the withdrawal of Italy from these territories was not followed by any regulations on the fate of cultural property. In fact, the final arrangements on this matter, as in the case of Libya, were undertaken 60 years later, under completely different political circumstances.[50]

The 1947 Peace Treaty with Italy only concerned the case of Ethiopia, annexed to Italian East Africa as a result of the Second Italo–Abyssinian War (1935–36). However, the conquest was made at the expense of the sovereign state, and the League of Nations member was condemned by many states, including the US government, who did not recognize the validity of this territorial acquisition. During the period of Italian control over Ethiopian territory, several cultural items were removed. These included a statute of the Lion of Judah (a national emblem), some royal and ecclesiastical crowns, the throne from the Imperial Palace in Addis Ababa, paintings from the building of the Ethiopian Parliament, state archives, and one of the famous Axum obelisks (dated the fourth century AD).[51] After the Second World War, Ethiopia argued that the Italian confiscations were made in violation of international law.[52] In response to these claims, under Article 37 of the treaty Italy was bound, within a period of 18 months from the coming into force of the treaty, to 'restore all works of art, religious objects, archives and objects of historical value belonging to Ethiopia or its nationals and removed from Ethiopia to Italy since 3 October 1935' (from the beginning of the Second Italo–Abyssinian War). It remains ambiguous, however, whether Ethiopia was treated as a successor state.

Following the conclusion of the 1947 Peace Treaty, Italy returned to Ethiopia some of the claimed cultural property. In 1956 both states signed an additional agreement.[53] Article VI of this agreement replaced the general obligations to

[48] Treaty between Italy and Yugoslavia on the delimitation of the frontier for the part not indicated as such in the peace treaty of 10 February 1947, with Annexes, Exchange of Letters and Final Act, signed on 10 November 1975, entered in force on 11 October 1977, 1466 UNTS 25.

[49] See Chapter 6, section 6.3.3. [50] See Chapter 6, section 6.4.2.

[51] Richard Pankhurst, 'Ethiopia, the Aksum Obelisk, and the Return of Africa's Cultural Heritage', *African Affairs* 98(1999)391, 229–39.

[52] Ibid.

[53] Agreement between Italy and Ethiopia Concerning the Settlement of Economic and Financial Matters Issuing from the Treaty of Peace and Economic Collaboration, signed on 5 March 1956, entered into force on 4 July 1956, 267 UNTS 190.

return the cultural property of the 1947 Peace Treaty into a detailed list of objects that were to be handed over to Ethiopia. According to Annex A to the 1956 Agreement, Italy returned 191 minor objects. Under Annex B Italy was obliged to return a number of valuable objects, such as imperial archives, the Lion of Judah Statue, imperial thrones, coaches, etc. The 1956 Agreement also referred to the famous Axum obelisk. In Annex C, within six months following the entry into force of the 1956 Agreement, Italy was obliged to remove it from Rome to Naples for its further transportation to Ethiopia. The costs of the delivery to the port were to be borne by Italy. Who was to pay for its subsequent shipment to Ethiopia, however, remained rather ambiguous. In the following years, the obelisk and many other objects were still not returned to Ethiopia. Thus, early in 1970, the Ethiopian parliament passed a resolution stating that the monument had to be recovered and the Emperor would cancel his planned visit to Italy unless Italy agreed on immediate restitution. Moreover, the parliament recommended severing diplomatic relations unless the monument was handed over. In 1997, both states signed an additional agreement. Finally, in 2005, the Axum obelisk was dismantled and transported by plane to Ethiopia, where it was re-erected.[54]

The 1947 Peace Treaty with Italy and its implementation was crucial for the post-Second World War approach to the allocation of cultural property in state succession. First, it widely followed the principles of the Allied restitution programme in terms of adopting the peremptory principle of territoriality in all cases of cession. However, such a rigorous regime disregarded another important consideration frequently applied in the pre-Second World War state succession settlements: the protection of cultural heritage of the predecessor state and the major significance of such property for national and ethnic groups. Under the 1947 Peace Treaty with Italy, this referred to Italian nationals expelled from the territories ceded to Yugoslavia. Second, the treaty also applied the principle of restitution-in-kind to the cases of state succession. Third, it provided for the first time for the duty to restore cultural property to a non-European state, following the withdrawal from colonized territories.

b) Hungary

As regards the allocation of cultural property in state succession, the 1947 Peace Treaty with Hungary contained special regulations in respect of Yugoslavia and Czechoslovakia. These were driven by the attempts to finally conclude the process of the dissolution of Austria-Hungary. Thus, on the occasion of the post-Second World War settlements, Czechoslovakia and Yugoslavia, which in 1920 succeeded to the territories of the former Kingdom of Hungary, aimed at settling several older claims. Accordingly, under Article 11 of the 1947 Peace Treaty, Hungary had to hand over the objects 'constituting the cultural heritage of Yugoslavia and Czechoslovakia which originated in those territories and which, after 1848, came

[54] For more detail, see Chapter 6, section 6.5.

into the possession of the Hungarian state or of Hungarian public institutions as a consequence of Hungarian domination over those territories prior to 1919'. These referred to four major groups of objects: 1) 'historical archives which came into being as integral wholes in Yugoslav or Czechoslovak territories'; 2) 'libraries, historical documents, antiquities and other cultural objects which belonged to institutions on Yugoslav or Czechoslovak territories or to historical personalities of the Yugoslav and Czechoslovak peoples'; 3) 'original artistic, literary and scientific objects which are the work of Yugoslav or Czechoslovak artists, writers and scientists;' 4) 'the archives of the Illyrian Deputation, the Illyrian Commission and Illyrian Chancellery, which relate to the eighteenth century'—records of the Habsburg offices detailing the issues of the Slavic, mostly Serbian community, under the Hungarian Crown (1745–91). The 'objects acquired by purchase, gift or legacy and original works of Hungarians' (Article 11.2) were exempted from the obligation of restitution.

Hungary was also bound to provide assistance to the representatives of Czechoslovakia and Yugoslavia in finding the property demanded. The lists of requested objects had to be presented to the Hungarian Government, which could raise objections (Article 11.4). The disputes between parties would be settled by a special commission. According to Article 40, this would be composed of 'one representative of each party and a third member selected by mutual agreement of the two parties from nationals of a third country'. A third member had to be chosen within one month; if parties failed to agree on that person, 'the Secretary-General of the United Nations may be requested by either party to make the appointment'. The decisions taken by this commission would be definitive and binding.

The actual implementation of these provisions is, however, very difficult to trace. It appears that no protocols of negotiations have ever been published. One may suppose that due to the ardent post-war tensions as to the status of the Hungarian national minority and its property in Slovakia, Hungary, and Czechoslovakia, no agreement regarding cultural heritage matters was reached. However, it has been reported that in 1956–60 Yugoslavia obtained several important archives, in particular those relating to the eighteenth century Illyrian institutions, which are of great significance for the history of Serbs.[55]

The regulations of the 1947 Peace Treaty with Hungary may be considered as instructive for the allocation of cultural property in state succession for two major reasons: 1) the concept of national ties was made concrete by adopting the criterion of the nationality of artists, writers, and scientists; 2) the development of the procedural principle of consensual dispute resolution by the means of a mixed commission headed by an impartial arbiter. Importantly, such an arbiter would be appointed by an external authority—the Secretary-General of the United Nations, if parties failed to choose such a person. This external international participation

[55] After Philip J. Adler, 'Serbs, Magyars, and Staatsinteresse in Eighteenth Century Austria: A Study in the History of Habsburg Administration', *Austrian History Yearbook* 12(1976), 116–47.

in the decision-making process marked the emergence of a more general tendency towards the internationalization of interstate cultural property related disputes, especially in the post-colonial context.

3.2.2 Beyond succession—*de facto* and *ex gratia* solutions

The outbreak of the Cold War in effect put an end to the Allied restitution programme. This affected the fate of cultural property in state succession. The crux of the controversies consisted in the post-Second World War status of Germany on the one hand, and the advancement of the military presence of the Soviet Union in eastern and central Europe on the other. Hence many interstate arrangements on the matter of the allocation of cultural property followed *de facto* solutions.

a) The theory of debellatio *and the Soviet rights to German cultural property*

Following the unconditional military surrender of the Third Reich in 1945,[56] full control of the territory of Germany passed to the Allies. In these circumstances, the question over the status of state and private cultural property under the Allied administration was raised. The post-war restitution programme did not initially deal with the restoration of property to Germany and its allies. It also remained silent on the responsibility for the destruction and plunder of cultural heritage committed by the Allies. Moreover, the application of the principle of restitution-in-kind for irreparable losses in material cultural heritage turned out to be abused in the territories under the Red Army's control. During the last months of the war and the short period following its conclusion, the Soviet forces launched an organized policy of confiscation and plunder of cultural property from the invaded territories.[57] In fact, hundreds of thousands of cultural objects were sent in special 'booty' trains back to the USSR.[58] The most emblematic cases referred to the 1945 capture and removal of two famous German art collections to Moscow: paintings from the National Gallery in Dresden, and the so-called Priam's treasure from the Pergamon Museum of Berlin.[59] These forced acquisitions in the occupied territories were treated as reparations for the intentional destruction and plunder committed by Nazi Germany in the USSR on the one hand, and as a legitimate disposal of property under Soviet sovereignty on the other. While the first consideration touches on the broader question of post-war

[56] See German surrender documents of 7 May 1945 (Reims), and of 8 May 1945 (Berlin), Yale Law School, The Avalon Project, <http://avalon.law.yale.edu/subject_menus/gsmenu.asp>, accessed on 31 January 2015.

[57] Konstantin Akinsha, Grigoriĭ Kozlov, and Sylvia Hochfield, *Beautiful Loot: The Soviet Plunder of Europe's Art Treasures* (Random House, 1995).

[58] Wayne Sandholtz, *Prohibiting. Plunder: How Norms Change* (OUP, 2007), 160.

[59] Klaus Goldmann, 'The Trojan Treasures in Berlin: The Disappearance and Search for the Objects after World War II', in Elisabeth Simpson (ed), *The Spoils of War. World War II and Its Aftermath: The Loss, Reappearance and Recovery of Cultural Property* (Harry N. Abrams, Inc., Publishers, 1997), 200–3.

restitution, the second concerns the issue of state succession, and is strictly linked to the international status of defeated Germany. In fact, there has been continuing controversy in legal scholarship and jurisprudence as to whether the unconditional surrender of the Third Reich constituted a case of *debellatio*—the complete destruction and extinction of a defeated state.[60]

According to the supporters of the theory of *debellatio*, sovereignty over the territory of Germany after the Second World War passed to the Allies because the German state ceased to exist. Consequently, the Allied Powers, in the absence of a peace treaty, could sovereignly decide on territorial reconfigurations and the disposal of German state property. Such acts taken within Germany were therefore internal issues not governed by the international law of military occupation. The Soviet Union claimed that the Allies also had the sovereign capacity to regulate the acquisition and displacement of German state cultural property.[61] In light of this, one also must note some restoration of items from the USSR to East Germany in the 1950s. This primarily referred to the collection of the Dresden National Gallery. Its restitution was presented as a gift *ex gratia* made by the USSR, which had lawfully acquired the paintings. In practice, it was pursued by the Soviet government to calm social tensions caused by the post-war economic exploitation of East Germany. No legal considerations were applied.[62]

Although it is not the aim of this analysis to discuss whether the defeat of the Third Reich was or was not a case of *debellatio*, it seems clear that the capitulation of this state did not exclude it from the general benefits of international humanitarian law in favour of its nationals,[63] including the rights to protect national cultural heritage. In addition, there are no doubts that both German states were entitled to demand the restoration of cultural property removed from their respective territories by acts of war or decisions of the Allied Powers acting as sovereigns.

b) One nation, one heritage, different states: the distribution of cultural property between German states

The complex political situation between the two German states was reflected in the sphere of cultural heritage. Due to the lack of any final peace treaty with Germany, and the 1949 proclamation of two separate states not recognized respectively by Western and Eastern blocs, the achievement of consensus on the allocation of state cultural property was virtually impossible. Thus, the post-war

[60] Eyāl Benveniśtî, *The International Law of Occupation* (2nd edn, Princeton University Press, 2004), at 91–96.

[61] Shawn S. Stephens, 'The Hermitage and Pushkin Exhibits: An Analysis of the Ownership Rights to Cultural Properties Removed from Occupied Germany', *Houston Journal of International Law* 18(1995–1996)1, 59–112; Margaret M. Mastroberardino, 'The Last Prisoners of World War II', *Pace International Law Review* 9(1997), 315–56.

[62] Konstantin Akinsha, 'Stalin's Decrees and Soviet Trophy Brigades: Compensation, Restitution in Kind, or "Trophies" of War?', *IJCP* 17(2010)2, 195–216.

[63] See Yutaka Arai-Takahashi, *The Law of Occupation. Continuity and Change of International Law, and its Interaction with International Human Rights Law* (Brill, 2009), 39.

solutions between East and West Germany were primarily conditioned by the fortuitous location of cultural materials in the respective territories.

The major problems were with regard to the Berlin collections, which at the end of the Second World War were removed from the eastern part of the city to the west. The best-known examples concerned priceless antiquities, including the famous bust of Nefertiti (*c.*1370 BC–*c.*1330 BC). As well as the entire collection of Egyptian art, the removed artefacts also included Greek vases and a few thousand paintings, among them works by Rembrandt, Dürer, and Friedrich.[64] The issue of ownership was never resolved between the two German republics. During the entire period of the Cold War, the displaced works of art remained in the possession of the FRG, to which the GDR continually claimed its sovereign rights.[65] Similar problems also referred to the collections of the Berlin (Prussian) State Library. During the final phase of the Second World War, these were distributed in different storage locations in the territory of the Third Reich. After the war, the question arose as to which German state was entitled to these collections. A small number remained in the original location, in East Berlin, and a larger portion was in the possession of Poland and West Germany. The latter, in 1957, passed a law providing that a special body, the 'Foundation for the Ownership of Prussian Cultural Property' would be a valid successor to the patrimony of the extinguished state of Prussia. This act was firmly contested by the GDR government.[66]

The controversies on state succession to cultural heritage also concerned Germany's state cultural property located abroad.[67] This included the libraries and artistic collections of scientific institutions in Italy: three libraries situated in Rome—the Bibliotheka Hertziana, the Library of the German Archaeological Institute, the Library of the German Historical Institute; the Library of the German Institute Art History in Florence; and the historic buildings in Rome—the Villino Amelung and Palazzo Zuccari. In 1953, the governments of the UK, the US, France, and Italy concluded an agreement with the Federal Republic of Germany,[68] which provided for the return of the libraries and estates as property of the FRG. This stipulated that they were to be kept in Italy, and maintained as 'international centres of scholarship and research open to all nationals…, in such a manner as to serve impartially and without discrimination the interests of scholars of all nations' (Article I (a)(b)). Italy was bound to 'assist in finding suitable premises for housing the Libraries… and to grant to the Libraries, within the limits of the law, the same facilities which they enjoyed in the past' (Article II). The rights of East Germany were not taken into account.

[64] See Reinhard Mussgnug, *Wem Gehört Nofretete?* (De Gruyter, 1977).

[65] Ibid. at 10 et seq.

[66] Mohammed Bedjaoui, *Third report on succession of States in respect of matters other than treaties*, UN. Doc. A/CN.4/226, para. 49.

[67] Wojciech Kowalski, *Art Treasures & War. A Study on the Restitution of Looted Cultural Property, Pursuant to Public International Law* (Institute of Art & Law, 1998), 77–78.

[68] Agreement between United Kingdom of Great Britain and Northern Ireland, France, United States of America, Italy and Federal Republic of Germany Relating to Certain Libraries and Properties in Italy, signed on 30 April 1953, 175 UNTS 89.

It is also important to mention that occasionally both German states acted in harmony.[69] *Kunstsammlungen zu Weimar v. Elicofon*[70] concerned the title to two portraits by Albrecht Dürer, stolen in 1945 from Schwarzburg Castle, located close to the city of Weimar in East Germany. The paintings were smuggled to the US and appeared in New York in 1966 in the possession of an American citizen, Mr. E. I. Elicofon, who purchased them, being unaware of their originality and provenance.

Without going into the very complex details of the case, it is important to note that a small number of claims on the return of the items were issued in the US courts as soon as information about the discovery was made public. One of them came from the government of East Germany, which asked for the restitution of the paintings, part of the Weimar public art collection—the Kunstsammlungen zu Weimar (KZW)—until 1943, when they were stored in the nearby Schwarzburg Castle for preservation. The suit of the GDR was however barred, since the government of East Germany was not recognized at the time by the US. Therefore, in 1969 the Federal Republic of Germany commenced litigation seeking custody of the paintings. It also acted on behalf of East Germany, as it was entitled to represent the KZW as a trustee of its interests.[71] In 1974, when the US formally recognized the GDR government, the KZW validly joined the procedure as plaintiff. After that, the FRG was granted leave to discontinue the claim.[72] Finally, in 1982, the US Court of Appeals decided that the Kunstsammlungen zu Weimar in East Germany was entitled to the paintings as 'their lawful owner by succession'.[73]

This case is of particular importance as it demonstrated the importance of the collective rights of a nation to its dispersed cultural heritage. When the territorial and institutional linking of the objects could not effectively be raised, both German states decided to act on the basis of the principle of the major importance for the national heritage.

c) De facto *succession: Poland*

Post-Second World War Poland constituted one of the most complex cases concerning the allocation of cultural material.[74] As a result of the 1945 Potsdam Agreement, Poland had its state boundaries and ethnic make up dramatically altered. It lost nearly half its territory to the USSR, and it obtained vast territories at the expense of Germany. This was decided on the basis of Chapter X.B. paragraph 2 of the Potsdam Agreement, which held that, 'pending the final

[69] After Kurt Siehr, 'International Art Trade and Law', *RCADI* 243(1993)6, 9-292, at 128.

[70] *Kunstsammlungen zu Weimar v. Elicofon*, 478 F.2d 231 (1973); 536 F.Supp. 829 (E.D.N.Y.1981), *aff'd*, 678 F.2d 1150 (2d Cir.1982), see analysis of the case in John H. Merryman and Albert E. Elsen, *Law, Ethics and the Visual Arts* (5th edn, Kluwer Law International, 2007), 143–52.

[71] *Federal Republic of Germany v. Elicofon*, 358 F.Supp. 747 (E.D.N.Y. 1972).

[72] *Federal Republic of Germany v. Elicofon*, 536 F. Supp. 813 (E.D.N.Y. 1978).

[73] *Kunstsammlungen Zu Weimar v. Elicofon* (n 70) at para. 27.

[74] See Andrzej Jakubowski, 'Territoriality and State Succession in Cultural Heritage', *ICJP* 21(2014)4, 375–96, at 384–86.

determination of Poland's western frontier', the former German territories situated east of the Oder-Neisse line, including that portion of East Prussia not placed under the administration of the USSR, comprising the area of the former Free City of Gdansk (Danzig) would pass to the administration of the Polish state. At the same time, pursuant to Chapter XIII of the 1945 Potsdam Agreement, the transfer of the German population was ordered. Consequently, Poland lost its historical territories and simultaneously obtained those of a predominantly German cultural character. The case of Poland is here discussed first with reference to the German states, and subsequently with reference to the USSR.

No peace treaty was signed with Germany after the Second World War thus the territorial changes were not sanctioned by either of the states concerned. The borders were therefore not confirmed until the 1950 agreement with the German Democratic Republic[75] and the 1970 treaty with the Federal Republic of Germany.[76] The final border treaty was concluded in 1990,[77] 45 years after the end of the Second World War. It was in these circumstances that Poland and both German states did not make any arrangements as to the status of German property, including cultural material, situated in the territories granted to Poland. In fact, the question was unilaterally decided by the new communist Polish government. Pursuant to two decrees of 1945[78] and 1946[79] on deserted and abandoned property, all assets situated in the former German territories, irrespective of its pre-war status, was nationalized and became Polish. This referred to state, municipal, ecclesiastical, and private property.[80] The first consideration under which such a solution was proposed was to cease the ambiguity of the status of property in the newly acquired territories. Second, German property was treated as partial compensation for both the property destroyed during the war and occupation, and the property left in the Polish provinces that had been transferred to the USSR.

Both the Polish government and Polish legal theory at the time argued that all the cultural material situated in the German territories annexed in 1945 validly passed to the Polish state,[81] as the decisions of the Allied Powers were decisive.

[75] The Agreement between Poland and the German Democratic Republic Concerning the Demarcation of the Established and the Existing Polish-German State Frontier, signed on 6 July 1950, 319 UNTS 93 (hereinafter the 1950 Treaty of Zgorzelec/Goerlitz).

[76] Treaty between Poland and the Federal Republic of Germany Concerning the Basis for Normalization of Their Mutual Relations, signed on 7 December 1970, 830 UNTS 327 (hereinafter the 1970 Treaty of Warsaw).

[77] Treaty between the Federal Republic of Germany and Poland Concerning the Demarcation of the Established and Existing Polish–German State Frontier, signed on 14 November 1990, 1708 UNTS 382.

[78] Dekret z dnia 2 marca 1945 r. o majątkach opuszczonych i porzuconych, *Journal of Laws of the Republic of Poland* (1945)9, item 45.

[79] Dekret z dnia 8 marca 1946 r. o majątkach opuszczonych i poniemieckich, *Journal of Laws of the Republic of Poland* (1946)13, item 87.

[80] The 1946 Decree nationalized 'all property of the former German Reich and Free City of Danzig, German and Danzig's natural and legal persons, as well as persons who fled to the enemy'; English translation after Kowalski, *Art Treasures & War* (n 67) 67–68.

[81] See Jan Pruszyński, 'Das Recht auf Kulturgüter in den westlichen und nördlichen Gebieten Polens', *PYIL* 22(1995/1996), 187–200.

This also referred to art objects evacuated by the German administration from other territories at the end of the war for their safeguarding as in the case of the part of the Berlin (Prussian) state Library. With reference to art objects originally located in the annexed territories, removed during the war by Germans or those looted by the Red Army—Poland did not take a clear position. Initially, it claimed only the return of archival records referring to the annexed territories, but in time it also asked for some art objects from former German public collections. In addition, one also has to remember that those lands, named by the Polish official propaganda as 'Regained Territories,' were, however, subjected to art plunder executed by the Red Army in the same way as in the other German territories under direct Soviet occupation. Thus, a number of objects originating from Lower Silesia or Pomerania were transported to the USSR.

Importantly, in bilateral relations between Poland and East Germany the question of state succession to cultural property was inserted into the broader problem of post-war restitution of displaced cultural property. During the Cold War there were exchanges of cultural objects between the governments of Poland and the GDR, but they had never taken the form of systematic settlement of war plunder and post-war territorial reconfigurations. Moreover, the exchanges resembled more of a political 'gift' *ex gratia* than of any legally based solution. Thus, many objects and collections originating in the territory of Poland as of 1945, evacuated or looted in the last days of war west of the Oder-Neisse line, did not return to their original locations. Similarly, some German collections stored in the territories taken over by Poland, in particular the priceless collection of the Prussian State Library, were not handed back to the GDR and remained in the possession of Polish institutions.

With reference to Polish–West German relations, the question of cultural property was not broached until the end of the Cold War. However, the legality (or otherwise) of Polish unilateral compensation and property transfer was perceived differently by Polish and West German lawyers. The core issue in these controversies constituted the interpretation of the 1945 Potsdam Agreement and its international consequences. Accordingly, the Polish doctrine argued that the Agreement, being a valid international instrument, had constitutive effects in respect of all the states concerned. Conversely, the FRG's state doctrine and West German legal scholarship claimed that the issue of border and property transfer could be settled only in a peace treaty signed with a unified Germany. In the meantime, Poland was only an administrator of the former German territories.[82] Consequently, all the arrangements in respect of property taken by Poland were deemed unlawful. This also refers to the nationalization of cultural property.[83] However, the question was never broached in official bilateral relations until 1990.[84]

[82] Dieter Blumenwitz, *What Is Germany? Exploring Germany's Status after World War II* (Kulturstiftung der Deutschen Vertriebenen, 1989), 40.

[83] Stefan Turner, 'Das Internationale Kulturgüterrecht und die Zerstreuung des deutschen Kulturbesitzes nach dem Zweiten Weltrieg', in Wilfried Fiedler (ed), *Internationaler Kulturgüterschutz Und Deutsche Frage* (Gebr. Mann, 1991), 154–82, at 180–82.

[84] See Chapter 6, section 6.3.1.

In post-Second World War relations between Poland and the USSR, the question of the allocation and distribution of cultural property resulting from territorial and population transfers was entirely settled on an *ex gratia* basis. By the end of 1939, the Soviet Union annexed nearly half of Polish territory with a mixed ethnic and cultural composition, and immediately took control over public art and library collections as well as nationalizing the private ones.[85] In 1940, the annexed territories were incorporated into three Soviet republics: Byelorussian SSR, Lithuanian SSR, and Ukrainian SSR. These decisions were sanctioned by the decisions of the Allied Powers at the 1945 Yalta Conference, followed by massive population transfers .Poland insisted on the mutual exchange of cultural property in order to secure the integrity of national cultural heritage, primarily with regard to art and library collections located in the cities of Lviv (Lwów) and Vilnius (Wilno).[86] In 1945, the Bureau of Revindication and Reparations of the Polish Ministry of Culture and Arts formulated its official position on the repatriation of certain cultural property from the territories ceded to the USSR. This referred to the objects and collections of public and private property public domain. The Bureau's reasoning was based on the fact that these collections were not of a local nature but constituted an important element of an all-Polish national identity.

The idea of reciprocal exchange repatriation of cultural treasures, which should follow population transfers, was expressed in a series of draft agreements prepared by the Bureau. A good example of the application of this 'national linking' principle, challenging the traditional territorial one, can be found under Article 1 of the 1945 Draft Agreement between Poland and the Ukrainian SSR on the mutual repatriation of cultural property:

> Ensuring the definitive regulation of the state border and mutual exchange of population between the two states, and understanding that creations of national spirit, that is, cultural values, belonging to a given nation notwithstanding their place of origin, and taking into account the large losses in the cultural heritage of Poland and the Ukrainian SSR inflicted by the German aggressor, and also willing to stress the fraternal relationship between the two nations, both parties to this agreement allow for the repatriation from their territories of those cultural goods that, owing to their national character, are part of the cultural property of the other party.[87]

It seems that such a solution was initially considered also by the USSR. However, it has never taken the form of an international treaty. Only in the series of analogously drafted 'repatriation agreements', concluded in 1944 by Poland, USSR and

[85] Tadeusz Piotrowski, *Poland's Holocaust: Ethnic Strife, Collaboration with Occupying Forces and Genocide in the Second Republic (1918–1947)* (Jefferson McFarland & Company Inc., Publishers, 1998), 11 ff.

[86] Kowalski, *Art Treasures & War* (n 67) 68–69.

[87] A Draft Agreement between the Provisional Government of the National Unity of the Polish Republic and the Government of the Ukrainian Soviet Socialist Republic on the repatriation of Polish cultural goods from the territory of the Ukrainian SSR and of the Ukrainian goods from the territory of Poland (1945). Citation and translation from Polish after Kowalski, *Art Treasures & War* (n 67) 70.

the three Soviet republics concerned, were evacuated people allowed to take to their country of destination works of art and antiquities providing that they were private property, and if their weight, together with their luggage, did not exceed the allowable limit of two tons per family. Similarly, priests were allowed to evacuate items from their parishes, including church furnishings as well as objects of religious worship.[88] Thus, state property, the important private collections, and property of different civic organizations, remained in the ceded territories.

After the war, Poland and the USSR concluded other 'repatriation agreements' in 1945–56,[89] but these did not address the allocation of cultural property and referred only to the transfer of personal belongings. Planned agreements with the three neighbouring Soviet republics were not concluded. In 1946, the Ukrainian SSR handed over to Poland some of the disputed collections, such as part of the great library and artistic collections of the National Institution 'Ossolineum' from Lviv, as a gift *ex gratia* of the Ukrainian nation to Poland. Ironically, the collections obtained in 1946 from Lviv were placed in Wrocław, a former German city—Breslau.

In the context of the allocation of cultural property between Poland and the USSR, it is necessary to mention the solutions applied under the 1946 Agreement regarding the Mutual Return of Property between Poland and Czechoslovakia.[90] The core aim of this document was to establish bilateral cooperation for the restitution of property removed from the territories of both states during the war. However, the territorial boundaries were defined as those that existed before the outbreak of the Second World War. Accordingly, it referred to the territories which in 1946 had already been formally annexed to the USSR.[91] Under Article 1, the Agreement provided for the restitution of all property removed 'without payment or compensation', including cultural and scientific objects, archives, and registers, irrespective of whether they were state or private property. According to Article 2, such objects—removed from the territory of one party prior to the beginning of the war—had to be unconditionally handed over to the other party, regardless of the actual situation of their owner. Arguably, this agreement, which applied as paramount the criterion of territoriality in respect of the restitution of objects plundered during the war, implicitly introduced the possibility of returning the objects on the basis of the principle of nationality in cases of territorial cession.

[88] Discussed in the example of the Agreement between the Polish Committee of National Liberation and the Government of the Byelorussian SRR regarding the evacuation of the Polish population from the territory of the BSSR and of the Byelorussian population from the territory of Poland, done at Lublin, on 9 September 1944: Układ pomiędzy Polskim Komitetem Wyzwolenia Narodowego a Rządem Ukraińskiej Socjalistycznej Republiki Rad dotyczący ewakuacji obywateli polskich z terytorium B.S.R.R. i ludności ukraińskiej z terytorium Polski; Polish texts of the agreements and annexes are published in *Biuletyn Biura Informacji Rady Europy* (2000)4.

[89] Kowalski, 'Repatriation of Cultural Property' (n 46) 155–58.

[90] Agreement regarding the mutual return of property between Poland and Czechoslovakia, done at Warsaw, on 12 February 1946, *Journal of Laws of the Republic of Poland* (1948)4, item 25.

[91] At this point, I would like to thank Nawojka Cieślińska-Lobkowicz for several very useful comments concerning this agreement.

d) Status quo *settlement: Finland–USSR*

The case of the allocation of cultural property between Finland and the Soviet Union demonstrates important affinities with those of Poland. Since the Napoleonic wars, the history of Finland was tightly bound to that of Russia. As discussed in Chapter 2, the Bolshevik revolution facilitated the independence of Finland, confirmed by the 1920 Treaty of Tartu (II). In general, the territory of the Finish state respected its ethnic composition, and no population transfers were applied. This changed after the Soviet invasion in 1940 which forced Finland to cede its historic territories of Karelia and Salla. The loss of Karelia was particularly painful since it is considered the heart and origin of Finnish culture. Moreover, the capital of Karelia, Vyborg (Viipuri), preserved important art and library collections. As a result of the Soviet invasion, around 400,000 people had to flee the region, taking with them the great majority of cultural movables, including historic archives and art collections from Vyborg. These are currently kept in different museums in Finland.[92] Collections of the public libraries were however left *in situ*.

As the Finish government supported the Third Reich against the USSR in 1941, it had to cede Karelia under the 1947 Paris Peace Treaty.[93] After the transfer of the territory, neither state officially discussed the status of evacuated or lost cultural items. Thus, each accepted the *status quo*—tacitly confirming the principle of national linking, which enabled Finland to keep the evacuated cultural property.

3.2.3 National cultural treasures entrusted abroad: Poland–Canada and Hungary–USA

Not only did Cold War political considerations influence the allocation of cultural property in the case of territorial changes, but they also influenced the rights of states behind the Iron Curtain to recover state cultural property entrusted abroad during the Second World War. This was the case of Poland and Hungary, who gave their national treasures to Western Allies as custodians. Arguably, both showed how the rights to state cultural property entrusted to care abroad was conditioned by the political and ideological controversies during the Cold War.

The first case, known as *Polish Art Treasures in Canada 1940–1960*, refers to a large collection of sixteenth-century tapestries (*arazzi*) from the Royal Wawel Castle in Cracow.[94] The collection enjoyed a quasi royal regalia status, as it had

[92] I would like to thank Professor Esko Häkli for this information.

[93] Treaty of Peace with Finland, signed on 10 February 1947, entered into force on 15 September 1947, 48 UNTS 203.

[94] The case was extensively discussed in legal literature by Sharon A. Williams and Stanisław E. Nahlik. See Sharon A. Williams, 'The Polish Art Treasures in Canada, 1940–1960', *CanYIL* 15 (1977), 146–72, 146 ff; Sharon A. Williams, *The International and National Protection of Movable Cultural Property: A Comparative Study* (Oceana Publications, 1978), 66 ff; Stanisław E. Nahlik, 'Le cas des collections polonaises au Canada', *Annuaire polonais des affaires internationales* (1959–60), 172–90; Stanisław E. Nahlik, 'The Case of the Displaced Art Treasures. History and Appreciation of a Polish-Canadian Strife', *GYIL* 23(1980), 255–95.

officially formed part of the Polish public domain since 1572. In September 1939, these tapestries were evacuated from Cracow before the German troops could seize them. In 1940, they eventually reached Canada where they were stored in governmental buildings. The problem arose in 1945, when Canada recognized the new pro-Soviet government of Poland. In the meantime, part of the collection was removed by the Polish non-communist government-in-exile and entrusted to private and ecclesiastic institutions in Canada. On the occasion of the claim issued by the new government of Poland, Canada had to decide to whom the treasure should be returned. Who was the successor of the pre-war Polish state in terms of the 1940 custody agreement? After long diplomatic negotiations, the disputed tapestries were finally returned to the Royal Wawel Castle in 1961, confirming the continuity of the Polish state regardless of the Cold War considerations between the West and the Soviet bloc on the nature and legitimacy of the succession of governments.

A similar case refers to the Holy Crown of St Stephen (Holy Crown of Hungary dating *c.* AD 1000). The crown is a symbol of Hungarian national identity and according to the centenary tradition (doctrine of the Holy Crown), constitutes the incarnation of the state of Hungary and its sovereignty. In 1945, after the surrender of the German forces, the Hungarian administration, which was afraid of the Soviet invasion, entrusted the crown and other coronation regalia to the United States for safekeeping.[95] After the war, the question arose as to whom and when the crown had to be returned. The issue did not however appear in the text of the 1947 Paris Peace Treaty with Hungary. This was done to prevent the USSR from asserting any claim to the crown. Moreover, it was suggested that there was a 'tacit agreement' in the 1947 Paris Peace Treaty that the US would retain custody of the coronation regalia until such time when Soviet troops withdrew from Hungary. During the Cold War, in particular the violent suppression of the 1956 Hungarian uprising by the USSR, the crown, kept in the US Gold Depository at Fort Knox, was not returned. In 1977, following a more open policy in respect of the Eastern bloc countries, US President Jimmy Carter decided that the regalia ought to be restored to Hungary. This decision caused enormous protests of Hungarian–Americans suspecting that the communist government of Hungary could simply melt down the royal jewels. Moreover, the US administration also met strong resistance in its Senate. Accordingly, Senator Robert Dole issued a lawsuit against the US President in order to prevent him from returning the Hungarian coronation regalia to the People's Republic of Hungary, on the ground that such a step had to be approved by the Senate.[96] However, the courts dismissed the case in both instances.[97] In 1978, the crown was handed over to the Hungarian people during a special ceremony in Budapest.[98] The US

[95] The circumstances of the case after Siehr, 'International Art Trade and Law' (n 69) 121–22; Charles Rousseau, 'États-Unis et Hongrie: remise de la couronne de Saint Etienne à la Hongrie par les Etats-Unis', *RGDIP* 82(1978)3, 883–85.

[96] *Dole v. Carter*, 444 F. Supp 1065 (D.C.Kan.1977).

[97] *Dole v. Carter*, 569 F.2d 1109 (10th Cir. 1977).

[98] Rousseau, 'États-Unis et Hongrie' (n 95) 885.

administration stressed that the treasure was returned to the people,[99] not to the communist government. Moreover, the latter had also to assert that the regalia would be put on permanent public display in the National Museum in Budapest.

In both cases, the national collective rights to cultural property played a fundamental role. It appears that the principle of the major role that the objects in question played in the national cultural heritage of Poland and Hungary overrode political controversies arising from Cold War confrontation. Yet, these two cases need to be considered as substantially distinct from those making a clear reference to the rules of state succession. In fact, their core importance lies in the recognition of the newly established governments of Poland and Hungary as bona fide representatives of both states in the international legal scene. Thus, they referred more to the issue of succession of governments, rather than succession of states.

3.3 Decolonization in matters of cultural property

The post-Second World War erosion of the colonial system broadly addressed the restoration of lost cultural patrimonies. As in the case of the dismemberment of European empires, the right to cultural resources was closely linked to peoples' rights of self-determination. The control of cultural material was perceived as a decisive factor for national and state identity. The retention of collections acquired during imperial domination was firmly defended by the colonial powers. However, international cultural order profoundly changed at the end of the Second World War. The Allied restitution programme reaffirmed the prohibition of the removal of cultural property by force and under duress and provided for its restoration following the end of occupation. This was crucial for colonized peoples, whose cultural treasures were often subject to war plunder and discriminatory colonial policies. As shown in the example of the measures adopted in respect of Ethiopia in the 1947 Peace Treaty with Italy, the return of cultural material to colonized territories could be perceived both in terms of due post-war restitution and the general allocation of property in state succession. The dilemma with regard to an adequate legal regime governing such arrangements constituted the crux of post-colonial controversies in respect of dispersed cultural heritage.

In the first stage of post-Second World War decolonization, the rights of newly independent states to cultural resources were not widely discussed. Following general mechanisms of state succession, the post-colonial states automatically acquired state cultural property situated on their territories; these *inter alia* included the collections of local museums and other cultural institutions established by the former colonial administration. However, the nationalization of the assets of non-state entities was strongly opposed by former powers, on the basis of the theory of acquired rights. This also referred to cultural properties owned

[99] See Michael Anton, *Internationales Kulturgüterprivat- und Zivilverfahrensrecht* (De Gruyter, 2010), 891.

by private persons or societies as well as properties of religious organizations. As regards the objects removed from the colonized territories before their independence, the question of ownership was initially omitted.

Importantly, post-colonial succession to cultural property differed in cases where societies were fully aware of their historic past and were prepared to demand their rights be respected. Primarily, this was the case of some of the former European colonies in Asia. A much more complicated situation characterized many newly independent states in Africa, which inherited colonial territories of mixed ethnic composition, lacking a uniform cultural identity. As the new states did not directly succeed the pre-colonial states but instead emerged from colonial administration units, their succession to the objects removed before independence was controversial. One situation concerned the cultural material which had entered major state collections as war booty or forced war reparations paid in the event of a colonial conflict. Another referred to the determination of a valid legal successor of the items coming into state property of colonial powers 'regularly'; that it, acquired by the virtue of private law. Yet another concerned the existence of cultural inheritance (links) between the objects created in the pre-colonial past and the newly independent state.

For these reasons, and because of obvious economic inequality between the former colonial powers and their subjects, post-colonial treaties rarely dealt with the question of cultural patrimony. In the mid-1960s, the question of the decolonization of cultural resources started finally and definitively to become detached from the law of state succession.

3.3.1 Self-determination of peoples and *uti possidetis juris*

The First World War saw the beginning of the colonial system's demise. The rights of colonized peoples were explicitly addressed by US President Woodrow Wilson, who in his Fourteen Points postulated 'a free, open-minded, and absolutely impartial adjustment of all colonial claims'.[100] In the East, imperialism and colonialism were condemned by Marxist–Leninist ideology, which perceived imperialism as the pinnacle of capitalism, a cause for a class-stratified society, in competition for capital accumulation.[101] The post-First World War arrangements did not, however, settle the question of colonies, nor did they address the allocation of cultural property outside the European context. Nonetheless, the gradual erosion of the colonial system enabled the movement by several territories towards a more autonomous system of governance, particularly in respect of the British white dominions and India. The dissolution of the German colonial empire and

[100] President Woodrow Wilson's Fourteen Points, 8 January 1918, Yale Law School, The Avalon Project, <http://avalon.law.yale.edu/20th_century/wilson14.asp>, accessed on 31 January 2015.

[101] Ronald D. Grigor Suny, '"Don't Paint Nationalism Red!": National Revolution and Socialist Anti-Imperialism', in Prasenjut Duara (ed), *Decolonization: Perspectives from Now and Then Rewriting Histories* (Routledge, 2004), 176–98, 191 ff.

Ottoman Turkey also led to a new framework of post-colonial rule under the League of Nations mandate system.

In 1945, the principle of self-determination of peoples at the national level became one of the most important concepts of modern international law. Accordingly, Article 1(2) of the UN Charter stated that the purpose of the Charter was 'to develop friendly relations among nations based on respect for the principle of equal rights and self-determination of peoples'. Furthermore, the principle was also recalled by Article 55 on economic and social cooperation. The Charter, however, did not explicitly link the right of self-determination with full independence. This changed at the peak of the decolonization process in 1960. With the acceleration of the liberation movements, the United Nations proclaimed that colonialism should be brought to a speedy and unconditional end; the supervision of the entire process was given to the Special Committee on Decolonization. The 1960 UN Declaration on the Granting of Independence to Colonial Countries and Peoples (UNGA Resolution 1514(XV))[102] and other later instruments recognized the right to self-determination as a key principle governing the dismemberment of the colonial system. The principle was understood as the freedom of all peoples to 'determine their political status and . . . pursue their economic, social and cultural development'.[103] The inter-war concept, which posited that the lack of adequate political, economic, or social preparedness could justify the delaying of independence, was challenged.[104] In fact, self-determination became a legal principle, which obliged former colonial powers to accept the will of colonized peoples. In addition, the territories in question received a special status, and as a consequence, international legitimacy.[105]

It is clear that the exaltation of the principle of self-determination broke the principle of state territorial integrity with regard to former colonial powers and their overseas territories. At the same time, it was also accepted that decolonization would follow the principle of *uti possidetis juris*, already tested with regard to the dissolution of the Spanish empire in Latin America. The principle ensured that the frontiers of newly independent states would respect the original boundaries of the former colonial territories from which they had emerged. In other words, territorial units created by the colonial empires were treated as permanent features of the international state system.[106] Such a solution was driven by the need to preserve as long as possible the stability of territorial relationships, even at the expense of the right to self-determination of peoples inside post-colonial borders. As in the *Burkina Faso v. Mali* case,[107] the International Court of Justice (ICJ) held that the obvious purpose of this principle was 'to prevent the independence

[102] Declaration on the Granting of Independence to Colonial Countries and Peoples, 14 December 1960, UNGA Res. 1514 (XV).

[103] Ibid. [104] Ibid.

[105] Malcolm N. Shaw, 'Peoples, Territorialism and Boundaries', *EJIL* 8(1997)3, 478–507, at 480.

[106] Susanna Mancini, 'Rethinking the Boundaries of Democratic Secession. Liberalism, Nationalism, and the Rights of Minorities to Self-Determination', *International Journal of Constitutional Law* 6(2008)3–4, 553–84, at 566.

[107] Judgment of 22 Decemer 1986, ICJ Reports 1986, 554.

and stability of new states being endangered by fratricidal struggles provoked by the changing of frontiers following the withdrawal of the administering power'.[108] In addition, the respect of colonial borders needed to be taken into account 'in the interpretation of the principle of self-determination of peoples.'[109]

The relevance of the principle of *uti possidetis juris* for the allocation of cultural property following the withdrawal of colonial powers was confirmed by the ICJ as early as 1962. This regarded the case of the delimitation of frontiers between post-colonial Cambodia and Thailand in the area of the Buddhist temple of Preah Vihear.[110] The large temple complex was created between the tenth and twelfth century by the rulers of the Khmer Empire, one of the most powerful political and cultural organisms in South-east Asia. Both Cambodia and Thailand considered themselves the heirs of this glorious past. The temple was rediscovered at the turn of the nineteenth century, but its cultural and historical value was not taken into account by Siam (official name of Thailand until 1939) when it demarcated its state borders with French Indochina some years later.[111] The conflict broke out after the decolonization of Cambodia. With the withdrawal of the French forces in 1954, Thailand took advantage of the chaos and 'recovered' the cultural site. Cambodia protested and brought the case to the ICJ, asking for the resolution of this territorial dispute. In taking its decision, the court did not explicitly deal with the question of the assignment of the temple to one of the states or the succession to the former Khmer empire, but instead it examined the technicalities of the frontier demarcation between French Indochina (the predecessor of Cambodia) and Thailand. In its decision of 1962, the court found that Preah Vihear was situated in the territory under the sovereignty of Cambodia.[112] Consequently, Thailand was obliged to withdraw its forces from the area of the temple. What is even more important was that Thailand was obliged to restore to Cambodia the objects (antiquities) removed from the temple and from its area.[113]

Apparently, the principles of self-determination and *uti possidetis juris* in respect of the former colonized territories had an important impact on the allocation of cultural property, following state succession. First, the recognition of the right to self-determination of colonized peoples and the integrity of territory gave newly independent states control over the natural and cultural resources situated in their respective territories. In addition, it implicitly paved the way for the restoration of their dispersed cultural patrimonies. Second, post-colonial state borders reflecting previous imperial interests did not usually correspond to cultural, ethnic, and religious divisions. Therefore, newly independent states faced enormous difficulties in establishing their uniform national and state identities, and often

[108] Ibid. 566–67. [109] Ibid.

[110] *Temple of Preah Vihear (Cambodia v. Thailand)*, Judgment of 15 June 1962, ICJ Reports 1962, 6; Surya P. Sharma, *Territorial Acquisition, Disputes, and International Law* (Kluwer Law International, 1997), 127–28, 204, 210.

[111] After Peter Cuasay, 'Borders on the Fantastic: Mimesis, Violence, and Landscape at the Temple of Preah Vihear', *Modern Asian Studies* 32(1998)4, 849–90.

[112] *Cambodia v. Thailand* (n 110) 34–35. [113] Ibid. 35.

suffered long-lasting ethnic and religious conflicts. Third, the political instability caused by the removal of the colonial administration from multi-ethnic and multi-religious territories was used by former powers as a justification of the retention of cultural treasures while also weakening the negotiating position of newly independent states.

3.3.2 The practice of decolonization

There is very limited international practice regarding the allocation of cultural property in terms of state succession. In fact, Lyndell Prott and Patrick O'Keefe, in their monograph *Law and Cultural Heritage*, classify as such only the agreements concluded between Laos and France in 1950.[114] It appears that another two cases may be added to this list, cases arguably affected by the post-Second World War peace treaty practice. However, the majority of post-colonial controversies surrounding the fate of cultural property have never been settled in formal succession agreements. Inversely, they were solved under non-succession *ex gratia* arrangements, included within a broader context of economic and cultural cooperation.

The following cases explore the first attempts at settling the post-colonial cases in the framework of law on state succession, and the further abandonment of this practice in favour of less dogmatic solutions driven by post-colonial reconciliation.

a) Joint ownership: France–Cambodia–Laos–Vietnam

As a result of the First Indochina War (1946–54), France was forced to grant limited independence to its protectorates—the monarchies of Cambodia, Laos, and Vietnam, in the form of the Associated States of Indochina (États Associés d'Indochina)—members of the post-colonial French Union. One of the crucial issues concerned the management and protection of archaeological sites.

As early as 1900, the French authorities adopted a regulation on the conservation of monuments and objects of historic and artistic interest situated on the territory of Indochina.[115] According to its provisions, such properties were classified, treated as *res extra commercium*, and subjected to the supervision of the French School of the Far East—École française d'Extrême-Orient (EFEO)—an important governmental institution established in 1900, with its principal seat in Hanoi.[116] The School conducted research in art, archaeology, ethnology, literature,

[114] Lyndell V. Prott and Patrick O'Keefe, *Law and the Cultural Heritage*, vol. 3 *Movement* (Butterworths, 1989), 805.

[115] Arrêté du Gouverneur Général de l'Indochine sur la conservation des monuments et objets ayant un intérêt historique ou artistique, le 9 mars 1900, available at: <http://www.unesco.org/culture/natlaws/media/pdf/cambodia/cambodia_arreteconservation_1900_frorof>, accessed on 27 January 2015.

[116] The French School of the Far East, available at: <http://www.efeo.fr/en/presentation/historique.shtml>, accessed on 27 January 2015.

and Buddhist studies. It had gathered important collections of artefacts and documentation since it was in charge of conservation work at Angkor and other archaeological sites in the territory of French Indochina. After the First World War, more specific regulations in matters of cultural property were adopted with regard to each French protectorates therein: Cambodia, Laos, and Vietnam.[117]

The situation changed in late 1940s when France initiated the process of handling the power to the governments of newly independent states in Indochina. For instance, on 19 July 1949, France and Laos signed the general convention regulating the passing of sovereignty,[118] and on 6 February 1950 both states concluded a series of detailed annexed conventions, which included cultural questions,[119] followed by the *procès-verbal* on the transfer of powers dated 20 July 1950.[120]

The major issue related to cultural heritage referred to the EFEO. On the basis of the EFEO status annexed to the 1950 Convention Relating to the French School of the Far East signed between France, Cambodia, Laos and Vietnam,[121] the competences in respect of conservation of monuments passed from the EFEO to the successor states (Title V, Annex II, Article 1 paragraph 1). The 1950 Convention regulated the questions of budget and joint supervision of the School by the four states concerned as well as the conducting of scientific research and archaeological excavations.

As regards the most important museums and collections of the EFEO (in Hanoi and Phnom Penh), these came under joint ownership of the four states concerned, administered by the School (Article 2a paragraph 1). The joint ownership could not, however, affect the rights of third parties to the objects preserved

[117] Documents administratifs, in *Bulletin de l'École française d'Extrême-Orient*, 26(1926), 525–688, available at: <http://www/persee.fr/web/revues/home/prescript/article/befeo_0336-1519_1926_num_26_1_3110>, accessed on 27 January 2015.

[118] Convention générale entre la République Française et le Royaume du Laos du 19 juillet 1949, in France (Éditeur Scientifique) and Laos (Éditeur Scientifique) (eds), *Accords Franco-Laotiens: Convention Générale Franco-Laotienne du 19 Juillet 1949 et Conventions Annexes du 6 février 1950* (École d'Extrême-Orient, 1950), 7 ff.

[119] Accords Franco-Laotiens: Convention Générale Franco-Laotienne du 19 juillet 1949 et Conventions Annexes du 6 février 1950, 75 ff; see also a series of agreements concluded separately with Cambodia:

Accord culturel entre le Cambodge et la France, le 15 juin 1950, available at: <http://www.unesco.org/culture/natlaws/media/pdf/cambodia/cambodia_accordfrance_1950_frorof>, accessed on 31 January 2015; accord bilatéral du 23 octobre 1956 entre le Gouvernement Royal du Cambodge et l'École Française d'Extrême Orient concernant le régime des fouilles archéologiques sur le territoire de cet État, available at: <http://www.unesco.org/culture/natlaws/media/pdf/cambodia/cambodge_accord1956_freorof.pdf>, accessed on 31 January 2015; accord du 16 mars 1967 entre le Gouvernement Royal du Cambodge et l'École Française d'Extrême-Orient relatif à la reconduction des accords bilatéraux de 1956 sur la conservation d'Angkor et sur le régime des fouilles archéologiques, available at: <http://www.unesco.org/culture/natlaws/media/pdf/cambodia/cambodge_accord1967_freorof.pdf>, accessed on 31 January 2015.

[120] Quoted after: UNGA, Doc. A/10224, 5 November 1975, at 4, see also UNESCO Committee of Experts to Study the Question of the Restitution of Works of Art (23 March 1976), UNESCO Doc. SHC-76/CONF.613/3, at 4, Annex I.

[121] Convention annexée du 6 février 1950 Convention relative a l'Ecole Française d'Extrême-Orient entre le Gouvernement du Cambodge, le Gouvernement de la France, le Gouvernement du Laos et le Gouvernement du Viêt-nam, in *Accords Franco-Laotiens* (n 118) 79 ff.

in these museums on loan or in the form of a deposit (Article 2a paragraph 2). Other museums and collections situated on the territory of the states concerned passed to these states, with the exception that the rights of third persons would be respected (Article 2b paragraph 1). Other detailed dispositions were regulated in the *procès-verbal* on the Transfer of Powers of 20 July 1950.[122]

As a result of the subsequent military conflicts in the region, the French succession solutions have never really been implemented. In 1975, the EFEO had to leave Indochina forever. Finally, the collections were nationalized by the local governments after the dissolution of the post-colonial Associated States of Indochina. It seems that there were no further claims put forward by Laos, which treated the question as properly settled.[123]

This solution confirmed the paramount criterion of territoriality. In addition, it explicitly introduced the vanguard concept of joint ownership of collections and the joint administration of public cultural institutions and scientific research conducted therein. However, it did not address the issue of the allocation of the artworks removed by France prior to 1950 from the territory of the newly independent states. Therefore, it clearly seems that the core aim of these solutions was to preserve French cultural and scientific interests.

b) The integrity of state cultural property: France–Algeria

The dissolution of the French colonial empire in Africa also resulted in at least one international instrument by which the allocation of cultural treasures could arguably be treated in terms of state succession. This is the 1968 Franco–Algerian agreement with respect to the restitution of 300 artworks, paintings, and drawings, gathered by the Algiers Museum of Fine Art between 1930 and 1962.[124] The objects concerned had been preserved in Algiers until April 1962, when the French administration evacuated them to the Museum of the Louvre in Paris for safekeeping at the final stage of the Algerian War of Independence (1954–62).[125] Yet the Évian Accords, signed between France and the Provisional Government of the Algerian Republic in March 1962,[126] had already transferred the property of state institutions in Algeria to the new Algerian state-to-be.

[122] See UN, Doc. A/10224, 5 November 1975.

[123] Ibid. In 1975, Laos informed the Secretary General of the United Nations that 'the matter of the restitution of works of art by France, the former protecting power, was settled in Laos over twenty years ago by the Franco-Laotian Convention of 6 February 1950 and the documents attached thereto, in particular the *procès-verbal* of the transfers of powers dated 20 July 1950'; see also UNESCO Doc. SHC-76/CONF6153, at 4.

[124] Accord franco-algérien du 11 juillet 1968, cédant à l'Algérie 300 œuvres d'art ayant appartenu au Musée d'Alger de 1930 à 1962, *Recueil général des traités de la France* (Accords unilatéraux non publiés, 1958-1974), vol. 2 (La Documentation Française, 1977), at 330, no. 680.

[125] On the history of French museology in Algeria, see an excellent monograph by Nabila Oulebsir: *Les usages du patrimoine: monuments, musées et politique coloniale en Algérie (1830-1930)* (Fondation de la Maison des sciences de l'homme, 2004).

[126] Déclaration générale des deux délégations du 18 mars 1962, Journal officiel de la République française, 20 March 1962, 3019; available at: <http://www.legifrance.gouv.fr/jopdf/common/jo_pdf.jsp?numJO=0&dateJO=19620320&pageDebut=03019&pageFin=&pageCourante=03019>, accessed on 5 February 2015.

In July 1962 Algeria gained independence and by the end of this year it asked for the restitution of the artworks, deposited in the Louvre, arguing that they were part of the artistic patrimony of Algeria.[127] Interestingly, the items in question were of French and European origin (fourteenth to twentieth centuries).[128] This claim was issued simultaneously with the exodus of non-Muslims from Algeria and was widely criticized in the French public opinion. Voices claiming the risks to which Christian art could be exposed if left in a newly Muslim country gained some traction and the nationalization of the Algerian collections was initially seriously considered. Yet, after years of negotiations, in 1968 France agreed to hand over the requested objects, which were subsequently placed in the reopened Algiers National Museum of Fine Arts, at that time, the largest collection of Western art in Africa.

In the French literature, this restitution has mainly been perceived as one based on 'the application the rules commonly recognized in the matter of state succession'.[129] Accordingly, the artworks in question, being state property, automatically passed to Algeria at the date of its independence. Moreover, it has been admitted that the evacuation of the artworks to France was carried out with the objective of safeguarding them from military operations. It was claimed that the colonial administration had no intention of appropriating them on behalf of the French state. Consequently, the claim of Algerian title to objects concerned could not be questioned.[130] At the same time, however, there were those arguing that all returns of cultural objects in peace time are purely of an *ex gratia* nature, including the 1968 Franco–Algerian agreement. Accordingly, it was suggested that when the removal was made by extortion, the beneficiary state could be entitled to adequate reparation, but the returning state always acted *ex gratia*.[131]

c) Cultural cooperation: The Netherlands–Indonesia (1949)

At the first stage of the dissolution of the Dutch East Indies, certain arrangements concerning state succession to cultural material were planned. As a result

[127] See Xavier Perrot, *De la restitution internationale des biens culturels aux XIXe et XXe siècles: vers une autnomie juridique. These pour obternir le grade de docteur de l'Université de Limoges*, Vol. 1 (Université de Limoges, 2005), at 232–33, note 68, available at: <http://www.unilim.fr/theses/2005/droit/2005limo0505/html/index-frames.html>, accessed on 5 February 2015.

[128] The collection comprised: number of paintings of Dutch, Flemish, German and Italian schools (fourteenth–seventeenth centuries), including works of Jacopo Pontormo, Sebastiano Ricci, Jan van Goyen, and others; many paintings and drawings of French school (fifteenth–twentieth centuries), including the fifteenth century triptych *Christ by Mary Magdalene* of the famous School of Amiens, works by Eugène Delacroix, Edgar Degas, Claude Monet, Paul Gauguin, and Auguste Renoir.

[129] Geneviève Burdeau, 'Droit International Public: Rapport Français, in *La protection des biens culturels. Journées Polonaises de 1989, Travaux de l'Association Henri Capitant des Amis de la culture juridique française* 40(1989), 69–70, at 68–69.

[130] Ibid.

[131] Raymond Goy, 'Le régime international de l'importation, de l'exportation et du transfert de propriété des biens culturels', *AFDI* 16(1970), 605–24, at 613.

of the Dutch–Indonesian Round Table Conference, held in the Hague in autumn 1949,[132] the Netherlands formally transferred sovereignty to the newly independent United States of Indonesia. Furthermore, both states accepted a series of draft agreements, including a cultural one.[133]

The Draft Cultural Agreement provided for a vast array of cultural cooperation and reciprocal cultural promotion measures, coordinated by a special joint committee. This, regulated under Article 5, was also responsible for the 'transfer of objects of cultural value.' Accordingly, Article 19 stated:

> Objects of cultural value originating from Indonesia and which have come into the possession of the Netherlands Government or of the former Netherlands–Indies Government otherwise than by reason of private law shall be transferred to the Government of the Republic of the United States of Indonesia in consequence of the transfer of sovereignty from the Kingdom of the Netherlands to the Republic of the United states of Indonesia.
>
> For the implementation of the provision of the preceding paragraph the joint committee shall propose a separate regulation on the basis of article 5. In this regulation provisions shall be included concerning a possible exchange of objects of cultural or historical value being the property or in the possession of the one country and originating from or of importance to the other country.

It is clear that the 1949 Draft Cultural Agreement applied the traditional European criterion of territoriality in respect of the allocation of state cultural property. Thus, all items removed by the colonial administration had to be handed over to Indonesia. In practice, the full text of this draft agreement has never taken the form of a binding international instrument. In fact, the increasing political tensions between two states led the Indonesian government to reject the 1949 Draft Cultural Agreement, since it was perceived to still represent a measure of cultural imperialism.[134] However, the obligations under Article 19 were retained by both states and embodied in a special protocol of 1954.[135] In the 1960s the climate of bilateral relations changed and the Netherlands and Indonesia signed a new cultural agreement (1968).[136] This repeated the procedural principle of cooperation, but it did not explicitly address the issue of the allocation of cultural property in relation to the process of decolonization. Arguably, it seems that the

[132] Netherlands and Indonesia. Round Table Conference Agreement: Covering Resolution, with the Attached Agreements and Exchanges of Notes Accepted at the Second Plenary Meeting of the Round Table Conference, signed at the Hague, on 2 November 1949, Protocol, Amsterdam, 27 December 1949, and Act of Transfer of Sovereignty and Recognition, signed at Amsterdam, on 27 December 1949, 69 UNTS 3.

[133] Draft Cultural Agreement between the Republic of the United States of Indonesia and the Kingdom of the Netherlands (1949), 69 UNTS 258.

[134] Cynthia Scott, 'Sharing the Divisions of the Colonial Past: an Assessment of the Netherlands–Indonesia Shared Cultural Project, 2003–2006', *International Journal of Heritage Studies* 18(2012)1, 1–15, at 4.

[135] See further Susan Legene and Els Postel-Coster, 'Isn't it all Culture? Culture and Dutch Development Policy in the Post-Colonial Period', in Jan Nekkers and Peter Malcontent (eds), *Fifty Years of Dutch Development Cooperation, 1949–1999* (SDU, 2000), 271–88, at 275.

[136] Agreement between Netherlands and Indonesia on cultural co-operation, signed on 7 July 1968, 739 UNTS 3.

protocol of 1954 remained in force, notwithstanding the signing of a new agreement. In fact, in 1974, Indonesia formally asked for the return of cultural treasures removed from Indonesia prior to independence.[137] Bilateral consultations began in 1975, which apparently led to the formulation of a recommendation on subsequent settlements.[138] Accordingly, it was agreed that objects of the most important historical and cultural value should be returned to their country of origin if they were state property. With reference to the cultural treasures in private hands or those items plundered during the Indonesian war of independence (1945–49), the Netherlands would render assistance in establishing necessary contacts and facilitating their return. Moreover, both states would closely cooperate in a programme of visual documentation of cultural heritage.[139]

In the late 1970s both states began an intensive exchange of archival materials, including some returns from Indonesia to the Netherlands. In 1978, a few important cultural objects were eventually returned to Indonesia. Primarily, these concerned the so-called Lombok Treasures, removed from the Indonesian island during a military expedition at the end of the nineteenth century.[140] The collection was sent to Amsterdam and displayed in the Rijksmuseum and then it was kept in Leiden. Aside from this, the Netherlands handed over the objects related to Prince Dipo Negoro, a national hero in the fight against colonial rule.[141] The return of these items had symbolic value since their removal was directly bound to the loss of independence. In addition, the Netherlands transferred one of the finest and most famous examples of Indonesian Buddhist art, the thirteenth-century Prajñāpāramitā statue from Java, currently displayed in the National Museum of Indonesia (previously, the Pusat Museum), Jakarta.[142] This statue represents the Buddhist transcendental 'Perfection of Wisdom'. It is believed that the returned statue is also a portrait of the Queen Ken Dedes of Singhasari, a legendary beauty and seminal figure in Javanese history, considered a matriarchal ancestor of the rulers governing in Indonesia and Malaya between the thirteenth and fifteenth centuries, the period described as the Indonesian 'Golden Age'. Therefore, the return of the statue was of great significance for the reconstruction of national heritage, memory, and identity.

Arguably, it appears that the outcome of the bilateral negotiations between the Netherlands and Indonesia followed the principles of succession to state cultural property. Yet the obligation to hand over the demanded objects, embodied in the initial agreements, was enforced primarily on the basis of a broader framework of bilateral cultural cooperation, as provided by the agreement of 1968. Importantly, the scale of actual returns and exchanges in 1970s was limited and

[137] Peter H. Pott and M. Amir Sutaarga, 'Arrangements Concluded or in Progress for the Return of Objects: The Netherlands–Indonesia', *Museum* 31(1979)1, 38–42, at 40.

[138] Ibid. [139] Ibid. 41–42. [140] Ibid. 38–39, 41–42.

[141] Ibid. 41–42, Greenfield, *The Return of Cultural Treasures* (n 3) 372–74.

[142] See Natasha Reichle, 'Ideas of Portraiture: Prajñāpāramitā in Java and Sumatra', in Natasha Reichle (ed), *Violence and Serenity: Late Buddhist Sculpture from Indonesia* (University of Hawai'i Press, 2007), 51–84, at 69–70.

bilateral cooperation between the Netherlands and Indonesia and their respective cultural institutions proceeded very slowly.[143] In fact, a new era began at the end of twentieth century within new shared-heritage cooperation efforts.[144]

d) Cultural cooperation and scientific assistance: Belgium–Zaire

The post-colonial situation of 'Black Africa' was very different from that in the European colonies in Asia and the South Mediterranean. The Belgian Congo encompassed a very large territory which did not reflect pre-colonial state and ethnic divisions. There were more than 250 ethnic groups and many religions and languages which were not limited to colonial boundaries. In 1960, Congo gained independence, and immediately different ethnic and secessionist conflicts started. In these circumstances, as in many other post-colonial cases, the reintegration of lost cultural patrimony was perceived as a way to construct and consolidate a new national state identity.

Initially, the process of decolonization of the Belgian Congo did not provide for any cultural arrangements. The claims of the independent Republic of Congo referred to the collections of the Royal Museum of Central Africa (RMCA) in Turvuren, Belgium,[145] as well as some other collections situated in the territory of Congo, prior to its independence.[146] In 1970, after some years of negotiations, both states finally reached an agreement. This provided for the organization of a museum network in the territory of Congo (in 1971 renamed Zaire), and for the transfer of ethnographical and art collections.[147] Subsequently, the National Museum Institute of Zaire (NMIZ) was founded in Kinshasa, to which Belgium transferred a few hundred objects, primarily of ethnographical interest.[148] Importantly, many of the items transferred to Zaire had not come into the possession of the RMCA during colonization but did so much later in the event of violent conflicts experienced in this former Belgian colony after its independence. The implementation of the agreement was faced with enormous problems of illicit trafficking. It has been reported that even some objects returned by Belgium have subsequently appeared on the international art market.[149]

It appears that the agreement concluded between Belgium and Zaire may be, to a certain extent, interpreted in terms of state succession (only in respect of

143 Scott, 'Sharing the Divisions of the Colonial Past' (n 134) 4.

144 See Chapter 6, section 6.4.3.

145 'Royal Museum for Central Africa (RMCA), originally known as museum of the Congo (until 1908), and Museum of the Belgian Congo (until 1960), see <http://www.africamuseum.be>, accessed on 31 January 2015.

146 Huguette Van Geluwe, 'Belgium's Contribution to the Zairian Cultural Heritage', *Museum* 31(1979)1, 32–37, Shaje Tshiluila, 'Inventorying Movable Cultural Property: National Museum of Zaire', *Museum* 39(1987)1, 50–51, at 50.

147 After Van Geluwe, 'Belgium's Contribution to the Zairian' (n 146) 35.

148 Ibid. 37.

149 See, for instance, Greenfield, *The Return of Cultural Treasures* (n 3) 371, 410.

property transferred to Belgium before 1960).[150] However, its provisions regarding the participation of the predecessor state in establishing the structures of a museum system and of the education of scientific units of the successor went far beyond general principles on the allocation of cultural property. Arguably, the contribution of Belgium ought to be seen rather within the framework of political and economic cooperation ('fruitful relations'),[151] as well as through means of mitigating the effects of discriminatory colonial policies. In fact, such gestures also appeared politically necessary to enable continuity of research of Belgian scientists in the former colony subsequent to its independence.

3.3.3 Decolonization and the safeguarding of universal cultural values: the Old City of Jerusalem and the Holy Places

After the Second World War, the scale of the destruction of cultural property during military operations mobilized the international community to take more decisive joint measures towards the protection of material cultural heritage of great importance to all mankind. Initially, the concept of protection was strictly related to humanitarian law, providing immunity for cultural sites and cultural institutions from military operations in the event of armed conflict. For instance, this was the case regarding Allied bombardments of Rome and the City of the Vatican. On 18 May 1943, Pope Pius XII, deeply concerned about the threat the war posed to Rome, asked the US President Franklin D. Roosevelt for the Italian people to be 'spared as far as possible further pain and devastation, and their many treasured shrines of Religion and Art—precious heritage not of one people but all human and Christian civilization' would be 'saved from irreparable ruin.'[152] Roosevelt responded that the Allied pilots were 'thoroughly informed as to the location of the Vatican', and 'specially instructed to prevent bombs from following within the Vatican City.'[153] Before the bombing, Allied planes dropped leaflets explaining that no attempt was being made to bomb 'those cultural monuments which are the glory not only of Rome but of the civilized world.'[154]

This recognition of the duty of the international community to provide adequate measures for the protection of cultural property from the effects of military operations resulted in the adoption of the 1954 Hague Convention.[155] However, it also appears that the need for a special international regime to safeguard certain

[150] Philippe Gautier, 'Droit international public: rapport belge', in *La protection des biens culturels. Journées Polonaises de 1989, Travaux de l'Association Henri Capitant des Amis de la culture juridique française* 40(1989), 35–48, at 47–48.

[151] Van Geluwe, 'Belgium's Contribution to the Zairian' (n 146) 37.

[152] Myron C. Taylor (ed), *Wartime Correspondence between President Roosevelt and Pope Pius XII* (Macmillan Company 1947), 90.

[153] Ibid. 92.

[154] 'On Our Pages: 100, 75 and 50 Years Ago; 1943: Allies Bomb Rome', *International Herald Tribune*, 20 July 1993.

[155] UNESCO Convention for the Protection of Cultural Property in the Event of Armed Conflict, signed on 14 May 1955, entered in force on 7 August, 1956, 249 UNTS 240.

cultural heritage sites of great importance to all humanity also developed in relation to the self-determination of formerly dependent territories. In fact, the recognition of self-determination as a governing principle of decolonization resulted in the increasing interest of the international community in the fate of universally significant cultural heritage sites, following the emancipation of the former colonial territories. Prior to 1945, Western 'civilized' powers and their scientific institutions claimed free access to cultural resources of colonized territories. This had a profound impact on the modern perception of culture and its manifestations in the history of art, archaeology, ethnography, and anthropology. Importantly, many collections were founded to protect dispersed cultural material and as manifestations of a growing interest in non-European cultures and artworks beyond the Western canon. Imperial and colonial museums were perceived as universal reservoirs of knowledge and beauty, where everyone could study and compare items from different parts of the globe. In fact, as Ana Vrdoljak has noted, imperial states 'artfully reinvented the importance of these collections: from national imperial collections to those forming part of the "common heritage of all mankind"'.[156]

This approach also resulted in the first attempts to protect certain cultural sites considered of great importance for the international community due to their scientific and artistic values. In particular, efforts were undertaken with regard to archaeological sites in the Middle East following the dissolution of the Ottoman Empire. After the Second World War, it was decided that the international control and protection of these sites could no longer be provided in light of the ongoing process of decolonization. Some former colonial powers attempted to settle these issues within the framework of succession agreements with newly independent states; for example, France in respect of cultural heritage sites in the former French Indochina. In some others, the international community sought alternative legal and technical formulas aimed at preserving such cultural heritage sites within new political and territorial circumstances.

In 1972, the protection of such monuments and sites of exceptional importance and value for humanity as a whole became an important component of international law under the World Heritage Convention (WHC).[157] This provided for the joint interest and obligation of the international community in safeguarding such cultural manifestations. Notwithstanding the fact that the WHC regime fully respects state sovereignty over world heritage sites, it introduces a certain internationalization of the protection justified by the interest of the world community. This remains a challenge for the Convention.[158] In fact, the dialectic

[156] Ana Filipa Vrdoljak, *International Law, Museums and the Return of Cultural Objects* (CUP, 2006), 99.

[157] UNESCO Convention Concerning the Protection of World Natural and Cultural Heritage, adopted on 16 November 1972, entered into force on 17 December 1975, 1037 UNTS 151.

[158] Francesco Francioni, 'The 1972 World Heritage Convention: An Introduction', in Francesco Francioni and Federico Lenzerini (eds), *The 1972 World Heritage Convention: A Commentary* (OUP, 2008), 3–8, at 5–6.

between territorial sovereignty, on the one hand, and the interest of international community, on the other, may also be relevant when certain cultural properties, located in the territory subject to state succession, form part of world heritage.

While it is true that the initial international efforts to protect such sites referred to campaigns of safeguarding outstanding ancient and early Christian monuments of Egypt and Sudan undertaken in the early 1960s[159] and to the subsequent adoption of the 1972 World Heritage Convention, the first attempts in this regard concerned the post-colonial status of Jerusalem and its Holy Places. In fact, the tensions between Jewish and Arab peoples inhabiting Palestine were perceived as a potential threat for the peaceful dissolution of the League of Nations mandate system and, as a consequence, a danger to the Holy Places of Jerusalem. For these reasons, the United Nations aimed at finding a Solomonic (*nomen omen*) solution which would ensure the peaceful transition to full independence of Palestine and the preservation of its sacred heritage. In this way, the universal interest in safeguarding the religious and cultural sites led to an active participation of the international community in the process of state succession.

a) Historical background

The territory of Palestine under Ottoman rule had been of a predominantly Arab (Muslim) character. The second half of the nineteenth century[160] saw increased immigration of Jews to Palestine, driven by the Zionist movement and aimed at re-establishing the homeland of the Jewish people in the Biblical and historical Land of Israel. After the First World War, on the basis of the 1923 Treaty of Lausanne,[161] the Turkish Middle East territories passed under the control of the League of Nations, administrated by Great Britain and France. Palestine and Transjordan constituted the British Mandate of Palestine, where Jews were allowed to settle but only in the boundaries delimited from the east by the River Jordan. It is notable that the League of Nations Permanent Mandates Commission recognized the right to self-determination of Jewish and Arab communities of Palestine, entitling them to establish their respective sovereign states. The mandate system was treated as 'a transitory period', leading to full independence.[162]

Under the British administration, the growing presence of Jewish immigrants and their political and cultural activities caused several violent conflicts with the Arab population of Palestine. Tensions increased during the Second World War. In 1946, the League of Nations was dissolved but France and the United

[159] UNESCO, *Protection of Mankind's Cultural Heritage: Sites and Monuments* (UNESCO, 1970), 39 ff.

[160] For the general facts, see David E. Guinn, *Protecting Jerusalem's Holy Sites. A Strategy for Negotiating a Sacred Peace* (CUP, 2006), 21 ff.

[161] Treaty of Peace with Turkey, signed at Lausanne, on 24 July 1923, 28 LNTS 11.

[162] LoN Permanent Mandates Commission, *Minutes of the Thirty-Second (Extraordinary) Session Devoted to Palestine. Held at Geneva from July 30th to August 18th, 1937, Including the Report of the Commission to the Council, First Meeting of July 30th, 1937* (LoN, 1937).

Kingdom agreed to administer the Mandate Territories of the Middle East until other arrangements would be made by the newly formed United Nations.[163] In the same year, French and British troops began a withdrawal of military forces from the administered territories in question, and the part of the British Mandate of Palestine—Transjordan—gained independence as the Hashemite Kingdom of Jordan. The future of Palestine was pending. In 1947, the United Kingdom asked the UN to put the question of the future government on the agenda of the next session of the General Assembly.[164] In the following year, on 29 November 1947, the UN General Assembly adopted the so-called Partition Resolution,[165] which provided for the division of Palestine into two states—Jewish and Arab. The City of Jerusalem—the Holy Place of the three great religions—Judaism, Christianity, and Islam—would be internationalized.

b) International regime of the City of Jerusalem

Accordingly, the Partition Resolution introduced a special regime for Jerusalem, including the city of Bethlehem, 'as a *corpus separatum* under a special international regime and shall be administered by the United Nations' (Part III.A). The head of that administration would be the Governor of the City of Jerusalem, and would not be a citizen of either of the states in Palestine (Part III.C §2). The special regime would be adopted for ten years, after which certain modifications could be introduced on the basis of a referendum among the residents of the City (Part III.D). An international administration was primarily responsible for the protection and preservation of 'the unique spiritual and religious interests located in the city of the three great monotheistic faiths throughout the world, Christian, Jewish and Moslem; to this end to ensure that order and peace, and especially religious peace, reign in Jerusalem' (Part III.C §1(a)). As regards the Holy Places, the Partition Resolution provided, under Part III.C §13 that:

(a) Existing rights in respect of Holy Places and religious buildings or sites shall not be denied or impaired.
(b) Free access to the Holy Places and religious buildings or sites and the free exercise of worship shall be secured in conformity with existing rights and subject to the requirements of public order and decorum.
(c) Holy Places and religious buildings or sites shall be preserved. No act shall be permitted which may in any way impair their sacred character. If at any time it appears to the Governor that any particular Holy Place, religious building or site is in need of urgent repair, the Governor may call upon the community or communities concerned

[163] 'The League of Nations and the Mandates', *YBUN* (1946–1947), 575.

[164] See Elihu Lauterpacht, *Jerusalem and the Holy Places* (Anglo–Israel Association, 1968), 14.

[165] 'Future Government of Palestine', UNGA Res. 181 (II), 29 November 1947, UN Doc. A/RES/181(II). See further Shabtai Rosenne, 'Israel: Some Legal Aspects of the Transition from Mandate to Independence: December 1947–15 May 1948', in Alfred E. Kellermann, Kurt Siehr, Talia Einhorn (eds), *Israel among the Nations—International and Comparative Law Perspectives on Israel's 50th Anniversary* (Kluwer Law International, 1998), 311–42.

to carry out such repair. The Governor may carry it out himself at the expense of the community or communities concerned if no action is taken within a reasonable time.

(d) No taxation shall be levied in respect of any Holy Place, religious building or site which was exempt from taxation on the date of the creation of the City. No change in the incidence of such taxation shall be made which would either discriminate between the owners or occupiers of Holy Places, religious buildings or sites, or would place such owners or occupiers in a position less favourable in relation to the general incidence of taxation than existed at the time of the adoption of the Assembly's recommendations.

Moreover, the Resolution gave special powers to the Governor of the City of Jerusalem in respect of Holy Places, religious buildings and sites in the City and in any part of Palestine (Part III.C §14). These were defined as follows:

(a) The protection of the Holy Places, religious buildings and sites located in the City of Jerusalem shall be a special concern of the Governor.

(b) With relation to such places, buildings and sites in Palestine outside the city, the Governor shall determine, on the ground of powers granted to him by the Constitutions of both states, whether the provisions of the Constitutions of the Arab and Jewish states in Palestine dealing therewith and the religious rights appertaining thereto are being properly applied and respected.

(c) The Governor shall also be empowered to make decisions on the basis of existing rights in cases of disputes which may arise between the different religious communities or the rites of a religious community in respect of the Holy Places, religious buildings and sites in any part of Palestine.

In this task he may be assisted by a consultative council of representatives of different denominations acting in an advisory capacity.

Thus, the initiative of the United Nations proposed an important and complex solution aimed at providing equal access to the Holy Places of Jerusalem, and the protection of the unique multicultural patrimony of this territory in the post-dependent, transitional period, in which external participation was crucial.

The partition of Palestine and the concept of the international control over the Holy Places did not meet the expectations of either the Jews and or the Arabs. The Jewish leaders, however, accepted the conditions of partition, driven by the consideration that it was better to have a Jewish state, even if in a limited territory.[166] Conversely, the Partition Resolution was unacceptable for the Arabs, who argued that their right to self-determination had been violated by the UN.[167] Moreover, Arab politicians perceived the foreign intervention and the presence of international administration in Jerusalem as a continuation of the quasi-colonial mandate system. Consequently, Palestinian Arabs, supported by other countries of the region, entirely rejected the division of Palestine, claiming that there could only be one state with Jerusalem as its capital. Thus, the UN plan was not implemented. In 1948, the UK completely withdrew from Palestine and Jews proclaimed the independence of the new state of Israel, while the Arab–Israeli war

[166] Lauterpacht, *Jerusalem and the Holy Places* (n 164) 15–16.

[167] Ibid. 16 ff.

erupted. In 1949, Jerusalem became divided between Israel and Jordan. The latter took control over the eastern part the city (East Jerusalem) containing the sacred Old City, and the majority of Holy Places.

c) The de facto *division of the City and hostilities against the Holy Places*

In 1949, the UN General Assembly pronounced once again on the future of the city of Jerusalem and the protection of the Holy Places, calling for the execution of the 1947 Partition Resolution.[168] In the same year, an agreement between Israel and the United Nations was also drafted,[169] providing for the preservation and protection of the Holy Places. The UN continued these efforts in 1950. However, in this year the partition of the city was sealed. Jordan formally annexed East Jerusalem, taking control over the majority of the Holy Places. Notwithstanding these facts, the Jewish parliament (Knesset) officially proclaimed Jerusalem as the capital of Israel in 1950.

Formally, free access to the Holy Places and cultural institutions was granted. Accordingly, the 1949 Armistice Agreement, under Article VIII.2, provided for the 'resumption of the normal functioning of the cultural and humanitarian institutions on Mount Scopus and free access thereto; free access to the Holy Places and cultural institutions and use of the cemetery on the Mount of Olives.'[170] In practice, the border between the two parts of the city was protected with wire and concrete barriers. The cultural and religious sites on both parts of the city were subjected to devastation and negligence; the Jewish community was barred from its sacred places. Arguably, after 1949, one could observe a certain 'exhaustion of the UN interest in internationalization' of Jerusalem and the Holy Places.[171] In the following years, this question was not discussed by the General Assembly nor by the Security Council. It seems that the *de facto* division of Jerusalem between Israel and Jordan and the abandonment of its internationalization were commonly acknowledged.

As a result of the Six-Day War, in 1967, Israel incorporated East Jerusalem. In 1980, the Knesset passed the so-called 'Jerusalem Law',[172] proclaiming the unification of the city as the capital of Israel. Under Article 3, the Jerusalem Law provided for the protection of the Holy Places 'from desecration and any other violation and from anything likely to violate the freedom of access of the members

[168] 'Palestine: Question of an International Regime for the Jerusalem Area and the Protection of the Holy Places', UNGA Res. 303(IV), 9 December 1949, UN Doc. A/RES/303 (IV).

[169] Annex Text of Draft Agreement between the United Nations and Israel. Israel Draft Resolution, UN Doc. A/Ac.31/L.42.

[170] Israel and Jordan. General Armistice Agreement (with Annexes), signed on 3 April 1949, 42 UNTS 303.

[171] Lauterpacht, *Jerusalem and the Holy Places* (n 164) 23 ff.

[172] Basic Law—Jerusalem—Capital of Israel, 5 August 1980, available online on the website of the Israel Ministry of Foreign Affairs, available at: <http://www.mfa.gov.il/MFA/MFAArchive/1980_1989/Basic+Law-+Jerusalem-+Capital+of+Israel.htm>, accessed on 4 February 2015.

of the different religions to the places sacred to them or their feelings towards those places.' Israel did not, however, ensure proper protection of the Muslim Holy Places. In fact, the Israeli government ordered the expropriation and demolition of the 800-year-old part of Jerusalem (Moroccan Quarter), entirely inhabited by the Arab population. This was to make place for an open-air synagogue leading to the Jewish holy site of the Western Wall.

The Israeli annexation was condemned by the United Nations in several documents adopted by the Security Council from 1968–80. Of special importance were two resolutions adopted in 1980. Accordingly, Resolution 476 of 30 June 1980[173] stated that 'all legislative and administrative measures and actions taken by Israel, the occupying Power, which purport to alter the character and status of the Holy City of Jerusalem have no legal validity'. This view was stressed by Resolution 478 of 20 August 1980,[174] which pronounced that 'all such measures which have altered the geographic, demographic and historical character and status of the Holy City of Jerusalem are null and void and must be rescinded in compliance with the relevant resolutions of the Security Council.' In 1988, the situation of Jerusalem became even more complicated as the Palestinians proclaimed the independence of a Palestinian state with East Jerusalem as the capital.

Thus, UN efforts to provide a special status to the City of Jerusalem, driven by the common interest of the international community in the protection of its Holy Places, ended in the fiasco of the continuing peace process in the Middle East. Nonetheless, these initiatives showed a new trend in international practice, promoting the view that the protection of certain cultural sites of great importance for humanity as a whole shall not constitute an exclusive concern of state sovereignty. Moreover, the preservation of such heritage shall be provided irrespective of ongoing conflicts and transfers of sovereignty.

3.4 Conclusion

It is a truism to say that the Second World War had far-reaching implications for most of the world, and that it profoundly changed the international legal order. These developments were also reflected in the post-war practice of state succession to cultural property, both in the European as well as colonial contexts. Accordingly, two major normative conclusions can be drawn.

First, the Allied restitution programme proclaimed by the 1943 London Declaration fully reaffirmed the paramount nature of the principle of territoriality, which governed both the restoration of cultural property removed by the use of force or under duress in the event of war, and the allocation of such materials in state succession. In particular, some of the post-Second World War peace treaties provided for the unconditional restoration of such properties originating

[173] UN Security Council Resolution 476 (1980), UN Doc. S/RES/476 (1980).
[174] UN Security Council Resolution 478 (1980), UN Doc. S/RES/478 (1980).

from the ceded territories. On the other hand, the profound changes of territorial boundaries in Europe, followed by the displacements of entire national and/or ethnic groups, also led to certain *de facto* solutions. These were greatly influenced by Cold War political considerations and they tacitly recognized the priority of collective cultural rights of a group over the general principle of territoriality. Indeed, cultural property often followed the destiny of displaced communities, although such a principle for allocation was not explicitly formulated by the inter-state arrangements.

Second, the process of decolonization showed the often and firm disagreement of predecessor states (former colonial powers) to share the cultural resources acquired during colonialism with newly independent postcolonial states. There were only a few cases which regulated the allocation of cultural property within the legal framework of state succession. While it is true that some of these arrangements introduced innovative solutions in respect of joint custodianship and management of cultural heritage, the majority of claims issued by newly independent states relating to the restoration of cultural property removed by the predecessor state during colonialism were not satisfied. The former colonial powers preferred to solve such disputes on a case-by-case basis or within a broader framework of economic and cultural cooperation. The rare returns of cultural property were usually perceived in terms of *ex gratia* gestures towards previously colonized countries rather than as legal obligations arising from state succession. For these reasons, the newly independent states in the subsequent decades attempted to establish alternative grounds for a just and adequate distribution of cultural objects. A need for a 'third way' to enforce post-colonial cultural heritage claims became evident.

Finally, the independence of the territories formerly controlled by European powers led to the reconsideration of legal measures for the safeguarding of monuments and sites of universal cultural value, for the benefit of international community as a whole. The first efforts in this regard concerned the UN internationalized regime for Old City of Jerusalem and the Holy Places in Palestine. The failure of this initiative laid the foundations for the world heritage system and the formalization of legal duties of territorial states as well as a common commitment of all states to protect determinate monuments and sites for the benefit of future generations, beyond from any territorial and political reconfigurations.

4

In Search of a New Global Order

The Codification of State Succession and the Development of International Cultural Heritage Law

In 1977 the Republic of Nigeria hosted the Second World Bank African Festival of Arts and Culture (FESTAC). On this occasion, it asked the British Museum for the loan of a fifteenth-century ivory mask for an exhibition organized in Lagos. The mask was one of the best known artefacts produced in the territory of present-day Nigeria, and its display was particularly anticipated. However, the British Museum rejected the loan request for security and conservation reasons.[1] This refusal cooled the relationship between the newly independent state of Nigeria and its colonial predecessor—the United Kingdom, responsible for the extensive spoliation of African cultural property in the colonial era. In fact, Nigeria's historical pretensions not only referred to singular objects, like the ivory mask, but they generally contested the overall removal of cultural property committed during the European scramble for Africa (1881–1914). In this context, the central issue of Nigeria's claims for access to the dispersed cultural patrimony concerned the fate of the so-called Benin Bronzes, a collection of bronze plaques from the royal palace of the City of Benin. The artistic value as well as the renowned, dramatic vicissitudes of these artefacts made this case the most emblematic example of the post-colonial restitution debate.[2]

The bronze plaques originated from the pre-colonial Kingdom of Benin, founded in the fifteenth century, which covered most of the territory of modern Nigeria. The artworks, which depicted a variety of scenes, including animals, humans, and scenes of court life, decorated the royal palace of the sacred City of Benin until 1897. More than 2,500 objects, together with other treasures, were seized by the British forces in a punitive action against the king of Benin (the

[1] Jeanette Greenfield, *The Return of Cultural Treasures* (3rd edn, CUP 2007), 122.

[2] Recently, the question of Nigeria's dispersed cultural heritage has gained much public attention due to the travelling exhibition and artistic project organized in different Nigerian cities, entitled: Benin1897.com: Art and the Restitution Question, 8 March–10 October 2010, Peju Layiwola. Peju Layiwola, ʃSola Olorunyomi, *Benin1897.com: Art and the Restitution Question* (Wy Art Editions, 2010), also see the movie 'Invasion 1897' by Lancelot Oduwa Imaseun, premiered on 17 September 2014 at the Freer and Sackler Galleries, Smithsonian Institution, Washington DC, available at: <http://invasion1897movie.com/about.html>, accessed on 5 February 2015.

Oba), and subsequently taken to London. The royal palace and the city were largely destroyed and later, the Kingdom of Benin turned into a British colony. The majority of the captured objects were auctioned to cover the cost of this military expedition,[3] and the Benin Bronzes were subsumed into different European and American collections, including the British Museum. Their presence in the West resulted in a greater appreciation of African culture, which influenced many modernist artists. Today, the Benin Bronzes are considered the finest manifestations of pre-colonial African art.

At the time of the decolonization of Nigeria, the question of the restitution of artworks removed prior to independence was not explicitly raised in terms of legal claim. Nonetheless, Nigeria started a campaign to recover the dispersed cultural heritage of the Kingdom of Benin, considered a fundamental element of its national identity. With this objective, it purchased some of the bronzes directly from the British Museum; other pieces were bought at public auctions.[4] In addition, the government of Nigeria issued an appeal through the International Council of Museums (ICOM) for the restitution of its cultural patrimony via long-term loans or donations of some examples of Benin art. By the mid-1970s, the issue had been raised on various occasions, though it never took the form of an official request to a foreign government or museum in terms of due restitution of looted cultural property or in terms of the allocation of cultural property in state succession. In practice, the claims founded on the law of state succession could be presented only to public institutions of Nigeria's predecessor, the UK. These institutions preserved only a part of the treasures plundered in 1897. In fact, the vast majority of the Benin Bronzes were in the possession of different museums in third countries, such as Germany and the United States, who were not involved in the colonization of the Kingdom of Benin or in the plunder committed at the end of the nineteenth century. For these reasons, while claiming the return of its cultural objects, Nigeria recalled the moral duty of current holders of such items to reverse colonial discriminatory policies towards the cultural heritage of African peoples. For instance, it has recently been reported that in 2008, at the opening of the exhibition *Benin Kings and Rituals* in Berlin, the Minister of Culture and Tourism of Nigeria, Prince Adetokumbo Kayode, made the following demand for the restitution of the Benin objects:

> I wish to appeal to the conscience of all as the Berlin plea of return of Nigeria's cultural objects that while Nigeria prepares itself and perhaps, Africa prepares an official request for the return of its stolen artefacts, those hearts that are touched by that reckless act of colonization should on their own return all or part of the objects in their collection to Nigeria and Africa. It should not be seen as another declaration of war but a passionate plea.[5]

[3] Greenfield, *The Return of Cultural Treasures* (n 1) 124–25. [4] Ibid. 124 ff.

[5] See <http://www.modernghana.com/news/189971/1/does-collaboration-between-nigerian-and-european-a.html>, accessed on 5 February 2015.

In June 2014, this appeal produced some important symbolic results: two bronze works plundered from Benin, were voluntarily returned by Adrian Mark Walker, great grandson of one the soldiers who participated in the 1897 expedition.[6] During a special ceremony, the artefacts were handed over to the Oba Erediauwa, whose great grandfather, Oba Ovenramwen, was the Oba of Benin during the British invasion. Alas, the requests addressed to cultural institutions in the UK, Nigeria's predecessor state, and other collections in Europe and USA all still remain in a legal limbo.

The case of the Benin bronzes exemplifies the complexity of disputes relating to cultural property removed from different territories before their independence. These controversies emerged particularly as a result of decolonization although similar problems have also been addressed in the European context in relation to removals made during dependence on foreign sovereigns.[7] In the majority of cases, the demands arising from such situations could rarely be accommodated within the legal framework of state succession. In fact, as with the Benin bronzes shows, the vast majority of removed objects were acquired by different entities in third states. In other cases, the property was legally purchased at the time of dependence on a foreign power. Thus, the question of the restitution of such property could not be resolved by means of a 'regular' succession agreement with a predecessor state. Accordingly, the claims of newly independent states met different legal obstacles as they had to be addressed to each holder of the requested objects. For these reasons, the post-colonial states in Asia and Africa tied their demands relating to their dispersed cultural heritage to the right of self-determination and the recognition of their cultural identities which had been suppressed by colonialism.

The increasing role a group's collective rights to dispersed cultural property played in the development of the human rights regime and the codification of cultural heritage law can be observed since 1945. The codification of efforts in both matters was driven by the devastating experiences of the Second World War. There was a common conviction that global peace and security could also be achieved by promoting international collaboration in the cultural arena. Hence, the protection of the cultural heritage of every nation came to be perceived as being in the general interest of humanity, 'since each people makes its contribution to the culture of the world'.[8] The international community also recognized the view that certain cultural sites of outstanding universal value required global attention and safeguarding for future generations. Thus, the end of the Second World War marked the beginning of the process of internationalization of the

[6] 'Britain returns two pieces of bronze looted from Benin in 1897 to Oba Erediauwa', 21 June 2014, available at: <http://www.nigerianwatch.com/news/4640-britain-returns-two-pieces-of-bronze-looted-from-benin-in-1897-to-oba-erediauwa>, accessed on 5 February 2015.

[7] See Kurt Siehr, 'International Art Trade and Law', *RCADI* 243(1993)6, 9–292, 147 ff.

[8] 2nd and 3rd Recitals, Preamble, Convention for the Protection of Cultural Property in the Event of Armed Conflict, Hague (the 1954 Hague Convention), signed on 14 May 1955, entered into force on 7 August, 1956, 249 UNTS 240.

protection of cultural heritage in national as well as universal dimensions, for the benefit of all humanity.

The controversies that arose at the time of post-war territorial transfers in Europe, as well as the ongoing process of decolonization, demonstrated the need for a more profound reconsideration of the existing legal regime for state succession, including the issue of tangible cultural heritage. Hence, the United Nations launched the process of codification of the international law on state succession. In 1961, the UN General Assembly recommended the International Law Commission (ILC) 'to include on its priority list the topic of succession of states and Governments.'[9] In 1962, the ILC decided to include the topic in its programme work.[10] The work resulted in the adoption of two Vienna Conventions on Succession of States in respect of Treaties (1978) and in respect of state property, archives, and debts (1983). The preparatory work on the text of the latter dealt with the question of state succession to cultural property and historic archives.

This chapter explores the interplay between the development of international cultural heritage law in relation to the parallel codification of the law on state succession in the matter of state property and archives. Its objective is to investigate the major legal rules and principles applicable to the controversies on the allocation of cultural property, following state succession, elaborated from 1945 to 1989. To this end, it first analyses the impact of the growing complexity of international law for the protection of cultural heritage on state succession to state property. This refers to three aspects: the elaboration of legal and human rights ties connecting a cultural property to a given state territory or human community; the development of the procedural principle of cooperation in settling cultural heritage-related disputes; and the notion of world heritage in relation to territorial sovereignty. Second, this chapter explains the relevance of the right of self-determination in asserting the claims for the return of cultural property by newly independent states and the role of the international restitution debate during the works of the ILC on the codification of rules on state succession. Finally, it concludes with a discussion of the regime of state succession to property and archives under the 1983 Vienna Convention.

4.1 Cultural genocide, war plunder, and restitution

In European practice of state succession, the core principle regarding the allocation of cultural property was the territorial provenance of such material. In other words, cultural property should be assigned to the territory from which it had been displaced during the rule of the predecessor state. The allocation of cultural material based on the principle of territoriality was, however, limited to state or other public (so-called *para-state*) cultural property. Furthermore, the actual distribution had to be weighed up against other principles, in particular the

[9] UN Doc. A/RES/1686(XVI), para. 3(a).

[10] UN Doc. A/5209, para 60.

protection of internationally regarded art and scientific collections. As explained in the previous chapters, the scope of the principle of territoriality in respect of the allocation of cultural property in state succession may be perceived as analogous to that governing the restitution of material removed during war and enemy occupation. The post-Second World War Allied restitution programme recognized that the destruction and plunder of cultural property committed in armed conflict constituted discriminatory measures towards determined ethnic and national groups. In this view, by introducing the obligation to restore all cultural property acquired by use of force or under duress in international armed conflict, the post-war legislation aimed at reversing the effects of such measures. It raised, however, a question as to whether similar considerations could also be applied to the discriminatory measures undertaken towards the territories and peoples subjected to foreign rule.

A positive answer to this question would provide a legal ground for the claims of new states to recover their cultural patrimonies dispersed on the occasion of internal conflicts and during dependence on a foreign power. Accordingly, if such discriminatory measures were equated with the removal of cultural property by the use of force or under duress at the time of enemy occupation, the formerly dependent and colonized countries would have a better title for their demands against predecessor states.

4.1.1 The crime of genocide and its cultural dimension

At the end of the Second World War, the discriminatory nature of the destruction and plunder of cultural property was interpreted in terms of genocidal practices. From this perspective, the systematic destruction and plunder of property of major importance for the cultural heritage of a specific group was equated with biological extermination and was denominated 'cultural genocide'. According to Raphael Lemkin, the first lawyer to propose the adoption of a multilateral convention criminalizing the extermination of human groups, acts against cultural heritage needed to be classified as crimes of significance to more than one nation. Lemkin argued that such crimes needed to be considered as severe violations of international law, threatening the interest of the international community as a whole.[11]

The issue raised its head at the time of the drafting of the UN Convention on the Prevention and Punishment of the Crime of Genocide (1948 Genocide Convention).[12] This international instrument reaffirmed the view that the history of genocide inflicted enormous losses on humanity, and whether it was committed

[11] Raphael Lemkin, *Axis Rule in Occupied Europe: Laws of Occupation—Analysis of Government—Proposals for Redress* (Carnegie Endowment for International Peace, 1944); see further an extensive collection of studies edited by Agnieszka Bieńczyk-Missala and Sławomir Dębski, *Rafał Lemkin: A Hero of Humankind* (Warszawa: Polski Instytut Spraw Międzynarodowych, 2010).

[12] Convention on the Prevention and Punishment of the Crime of Genocide, UNGA Resolution 260 A (III) of 9 December 1948, entered into force on 12 January 1951, 78 UNTS 277.

in times of peace or in times of war, constituted a crime under international law (Article 1). It seems that initially the inclusion of the cultural element in the definition of genocide was seriously considered.[13] However, it was deliberately omitted from the final text.[14] As the Convention was being finalized, a debate emerged over its proper scope. Some states opposed the idea of including cultural genocide in the text of the convention, arguing that acts against culture were analytically distinct from those committed against human lives.[15] Moreover, some claimed that the notion of cultural genocide was too broad and too vague a concept to be criminalized. Apart from legal controversies, the exclusion of cultural genocide from the Convention was driven by Cold War tensions between the Western and Soviet bloc states. Colonial powers as well as other states with large minorities or indigenous groups were afraid of the international condemnation of cultural genocide since it could affect their internal assimilationist policies or treatment of colonized peoples.[16] In addition, it was argued that the explicit criminalization of cultural genocide could potentially be used by Soviets as a tool to interfere with relations with their internal states.[17]

The achieved compromise led to the adoption of the 1948 Genocide Convention, which referred only to acts 'committed with intent to destroy, in whole or in part, a national, ethnical, racial or religious group as such: killing members of the group; causing serious bodily or mental harm to members of the group; deliberately inflicting on the group conditions of life, calculated to bring about its physical destruction in whole or in part; imposing measures intended to prevent births within the group; [and] forcibly transferring children of the group to another group' (Article 2). Thus, acts against cultural heritage of human communities were not included in the list of genocidal practices, though condemned by international law.[18]

Moreover, Article 12 of the 1948 Genocide Convention limited its binding force in respect of colonial territories, as it was up to the contracting parties as to whether or not they would extend the application of the Convention to the dependent territories of those foreign relations for which they were responsible.

[13] UNGA Resolution 96(I), of 11 December 1946, UN Doc. A/BUR/50.

[14] Ana Filipa Vrdoljak, *International Law, Museums and the Return of Cultural Objects* (CUP, 2006), 168 ff.

[15] Caroline Ehlert, *Prosecuting the Destruction of Cultural Property in International Criminal Law: with a Case Study on the Khmer Rouge's Destruction of Cambodia's Heritage* (Nijhoff, 2013), 33 ff., David Nersessian, 'Rethinking Cultural Genocide under International Law Human Rights Dialogue', *Cultural Rights Series* 2(Spring 2005)12, 7–9, available at: <http://www.carnegiecouncil.org/resources/publications/dialogue/2_12/section_1/5139.html>, accessed on 5 February 2015.

[16] Nersessian, 'Rethinking Cultural Genocide under International Law Human Rights Dialogue' (n 15).

[17] Ibid.

[18] Such an approach to the catalogue of acts falling within the categories of acts of genocide was subsequently upheld by the ILC. Accordingly, it explained that 'as clearly shown by the preparatory work for the Convention… the destruction in question is the material destruction of a group either by physical or by biological means, not the destruction of the national, linguistic, religious, cultural or other identity of a particular group.' 'Report of the International Law Commission on the work of its Forty-eighth Session', *YILC* 2(1996)2, 45–46, para. 12.

The exclusion of cultural genocide from the text of the 1948 Genocide Convention was particularly meaningful for new states emerging in the process of decolonization. Indeed, it meant that the discriminatory policies towards their cultural heritage undertaken during colonialism could hardly be viewed as genocidal practices, unlike Second World War art plunder, condemned as a crime against humanity. Consequently, those new states whose inhabitants and cultural heritage were affected by such colonial policies were not provided with measures to redress their claims, including the restoration of dispersed cultural patrimonies, on the ground of an international regime of prevention and punishment of genocide.

4.1.2 The 1954 Hague codification

a) Prohibition of war plunder

The post-Second World War restitution programme, with the exception of the Ethiopian case, remained silent about the allocation of cultural property within the colonial context. The question was also omitted at the time of the Hague codification of the rules of international humanitarian law with regard to the protection of cultural property during war.

In its preamble, the 1954 Hague Convention reaffirmed a pluralistic conception of culture, stating that 'damage to cultural property belonging to any people whatsoever means damage to the cultural heritage of all mankind, since each people makes its contribution to the culture of the world'. Moreover, cultural heritage 'should receive international protection' because its preservation 'is of great importance for all peoples of the world'. The Convention then provided for the regime of protection and immunity of such property from military operations. The Convention encouraged parties to prevent theft and vandalism of cultural property and proposed a distinctive blue and white shield-shaped emblem to identify protected cultural property. Such property and cultural institutions are to be protected in armed conflicts between states, as long as they are not put to military purposes. Special protection is to be given to those cultural properties that are listed on the 'International Register of Cultural Property under Special Protection'. Importantly, under Article 4.3, the High Contracting Party to the 1954 Hague Convention is bound to 'prohibit, prevent and, if necessary, put a stop to any form of theft, pillage or misappropriation of, and any acts of vandalism directed against, cultural property'. It shall also abstain 'from requisitioning movable cultural property situated in the territory' of another High Contracting Party. According to Article 14, the immunity from seizure, placing in prize, or capture shall be granted to the cultural property transported under special protection or in urgent cases. Yet, the non-retroactive regime of this treaty did not apply to past pillages of cultural material, including the events occurred at the time of earlier colonial wars and conflicts.

b) Restitution of cultural property

The Convention was supplemented by the Protocol for the Protection of Cultural Property in the Event of Armed Conflict (1954 Hague Protocol),[19] which dealt with an international duty to return cultural material exported from an occupied territory. Each document had to be signed by each state independently, and this enabled many to postpone accession to the more restricted Protocol.

According to the provisions of the 1954 Hague Protocol, each High Contracting Party undertook 'to prevent the exportation, from a territory occupied by it during an armed conflict, of cultural property' (Article 1). It was also bound to take into custody the cultural property imported into its territory 'either directly or indirectly from any occupied territory' (Article 2). Following the end of hostilities, each High Contracting Party would return to 'the competent authorities of the territory previously occupied', the cultural property located in its territory, if this property was unlawfully removed. This also referred to cultural property temporarily entrusted to one High Contracting Party to the 1954 Hague Protocol in the territory of another Party, 'for the purpose of protecting such property against the dangers of an armed conflict' (Article 5). Importantly, the protocol limited the application of the principle of restitution-in-kind because it provided that property unlawfully removed from an occupied territory 'shall never be retained as war reparations' (Article 3). As regards the obligations of an occupying state, the 1954 Hague Protocol obliged it to prevent the export of cultural property from the territory occupied by it. In cases where certain objects were to be returned, the occupying state was bound to pay an indemnity to their purchasers in bona fide (Article 4).

The 1954 Hague Protocol limited its application only to states parties and did not provide any obligations towards third states. It was not explicitly retroactive and its operational nature in respect of displacements of cultural property and war plunder committed prior to its adoption has been hotly debated. Moreover, the 1954 Hague Protocol did not deal with internal conflicts, and its application in respect of conflicts in colonial territories depended on the colonial powers responsible for their international relations (Articles 12–13).

At the time of the adoption of the 1954 Hague Protocol, it became clear that its regime would have little impact on settlements arising from the emancipation of former colonies. This was due not only to the limited character of obligations and the disputable retroactivity of the Protocol, but also to the fact that the two major state actors in the restitution debate—the UK and the US—did not ratify any of the Hague regulations. In the case of the US, the ratification of the 1954 Hague Convention, without the Protocol, took place in 2009. The UK only signed the Convention, which still remains to be ratified even now.

[19] Adopted on 14 May 1954, entered into force 7 August 1956, 249 UNTS 358.

The Hague codification of the rules governing the international protection of cultural property in the event of armed conflict confirmed already existing obligations under customary international law: prohibition of war plunder and duty to return. This reaffirmation is crucial for situations where state succession escalates into armed conflict and leads to the displacement or pillage of cultural material. It appears that in such cases, state succession considerations regarding the allocation of cultural assets could be challenged by those regulating the protection of cultural property in the event of armed conflict. In particular, preference must be given to the rule of international law ordering the restitution of cultural property removed from an occupied territory. Paradoxically, as the principles on state succession might appear disputable, the result of legal actions pursued by a successor state aimed at recovering cultural properties would often prove to be more predictable when the removal took place in the violent circumstances of a military conflict.[20]

4.2 Normative framework for the protection of the cultural heritage of mankind—the World Heritage Convention

The terrible consequences of the Second World War as well as the effects of decolonization nourished international efforts to provide a legal framework for the protection of cultural heritage of outstanding universal value. Apart from the UN internationalized regime for the Old City of Jerusalem and the Holy Places, the first international instruments which dealt with the duty to protect cultural property of global importance in time of peace concerned archaeological heritage. As early as 1956, UNESCO adopted the Recommendation on International Principles Applicable to Archaeological Excavations (1956 New Delhi Recommendation).[21] This associated the general interest of the international community with scientific research and knowledge. It appears that the cognitive significance of archaeological heritage was perceived to be of much greater value than its aesthetic and economic aspects. The 1956 New Delhi Recommendation, fully recognizing state sovereignty over archaeological resources, emphasizes the universal values of scientific research. In the preamble, it states that 'the history of man implies the knowledge of all different civilizations; and that it is therefore necessary, in the general interest, that all archaeological remains be studied and, where possible, preserved and taken into safe keeping'. A similar concept was also applied by the Council of Europe in the first version of the European Convention on the Protection of Archaeological Heritage (1969 London Convention).[22] This recognized that 'while the moral responsibility for protecting the European

[20] See Chapter 5, section 5.3.3(d).

[21] Recommendation on International Principles Applicable to Archaeological Excavations, New Delhi, 5 December 1956, UNESCO Doc. 9C/Resolution.

[22] European Convention on the Protection of Archaeological Heritage, signed on 6 May 1969, entered into force on 20 November 1970, 788 UNTS 227.

archaeological heritage, the earliest source of European history, which is seriously threatened with destruction, rests in the first instance with the State directly concerned, it is also the concern of European States jointly'.

As already mentioned, this perception of the general interest of the international community in relation to safeguarding cultural heritage sites of great importance to humanity as a whole, stimulated a series of worldwide campaigns (1958–62) for saving archaeological sites in Egypt and Sudan. In 1954, the government of Egypt decided to build the Aswan Dam (Aswan High Dam), which would cause the flooding of the Nile valley which contained treasures of ancient Egypt such as the Abu Simbel temples as well as the Nubian sites of the Upper Nile. The most famous part of these campaigns consisted in the relocation of the Abu Simbel and Philae temples, which were taken apart and re-assembled piece by piece in a safe location.[23] The enormous costs of the project were financed with the funds contributed by 50 countries. The project provided the impulse for the subsequent campaigns of safeguarding Venice and Florence, both critically affected by the floods of 1966.[24]

In 1970, UNESCO initiated the elaboration of a draft treaty on the international protection of monuments and sites of universal value, constituting the heritage of mankind.[25] Finally, the 1972 Stockholm conference on the human environment established a connection between the protection of cultural property and aspects of the natural environment of extraordinary importance, advocating an international system of cooperation for the safeguarding and conservation of these properties and sites. In the same year, the General Conference of UNESCO adopted the Convention Concerning the Protection of the World Cultural and Natural Heritage.[26] This introduced the principle that the international community as a whole has an interest and duty to cooperate in order to safeguard and guarantee the conservation of certain elements of cultural and natural heritage of universal and outstanding value.

The core of this regime consists in the World Heritage List (WHL). Under Article 11, the decision relating to inscription rests with the World Heritage Committee, an organ elected by the states parties to the Convention. The Committee also disposes a special budget ('the World Heritage Fund'), destined for the purposes of the Convention (Article 15). The process of nominating properties for inclusion on the WHL begins with the states parties, which sovereignly identify and delineate the properties in their own territories which would form part of world heritage (Article 3). The process of selection of monuments and sites is made on the basis of selection criteria confirming outstanding universal value (Article 11(2) (5)). The inclusion of a property on the WHL requires the consent of the territorial state (Article 11(3)).

[23] *Protection of Mankind's Cultural Heritage: Sites and Monuments* (UNESCO, 1970), 46–50.

[24] Ibid. 52 ff.

[25] Preliminary Draft Convention Concerning the Protection of Monuments and Sites of Universal Value, UNESCO Doc. SHC/MD/17 (1971), Annex II.

[26] Signed on 16 November 1972, entered into force on 17 December 1975, 1037 UNTS 151.

It is clear that the 1972 Convention fully respects the sovereignty of the territorial state over properties inscribed in the WHL, and the state's sovereign rights in the process of nomination and inscription. However, the recognition that inscribed properties constitute 'heritage of mankind' and their protection lies in the general interest of the international community, entails certain limitations on state sovereignty. Accordingly, territorial states cannot invoke their sovereign rights to justify measures taken towards a given cultural property on the WHL that could threaten the property's outstanding universal value. When such a property forming part of the cultural and natural heritage 'is threatened by serious and specific dangers', the World Heritage Committee may at any time, in case of 'urgent need', inscribe this property on the List of World Heritage in Danger (Article 11(4)), without the consent of the state concerned.[27] The interpretation also stands that in particular cases, when if an inscribed property loses its outstanding universal value, the World Heritage Committee may also decide to remove the property from the WHL.[28] Here too, the consent of the territorial state is not required.[29]

It seems that the special regime for world heritage may affect the arrangements taken in cases of state succession. Accordingly, inscription of a cultural property on the WHL by a motion of the predecessor state entails a certain internationally protected status of this property, which shall not be threatened by the replacement of one territorial state by another. Consequently, one may argue that inscription on the WHL shall continue, irrespective of the fact of state succession, as long as the requirements for its selection are fulfilled. Obviously, the successor territorial state can request deletion of the property from the WHL, but such an act would infringe the general interest of the international community and may have profound political repercussions for such a state.

For these reasons, one may also deduce that the international regime under the World Heritage Committee would play an important role in scenarios of state succession which include the use of force, since the acts against a cultural property inscribed on the WHL would concern not only the states involved in the succession processes but also the international community as a whole. Therefore, inscription of a cultural property on the WHL shall entail its protection at the time of state succession.

4.3 Self-determination and tangible cultural heritage

As with the post-First World War arrangements regarding the allocation of cultural property, it is also necessary to investigate the relationship between state

[27] Gionata P. Buzzini and Luigi Condorelli, 'Article 11: List of World Heritage in Danger and Deletion of a Property from the World Heritage List', in Francesco Francioni and Federico Lenzerini (eds), *The 1972 World Heritage Convention: A Commentary* (OUP, 2007), 175–200, 177.

[28] Ibid. 196–99.

[29] Ibid. 199.

succession and the principle of self-determination in its cultural dimension. After the First World War, the link between the principle of self-determination and cultural heritage was generally understood in terms of the post-war reconstruction of Europe and the peaceful coexistence of its nations. This referred both to the internal and the external dimensions of self-determination. In the first context, the principle of self-determination concerned the League of Nations' (LoN) system of minority guarantees, aimed at protecting the rights of such groups, including their cultural rights, within larger state organisms. In its external dimension, it was argued that the exercise of self-determination also entailed the right of a new state to the restoration of cultural and historic objects of great importance to national identity, removed by a predecessor state. While such an external interpretation of the principle of self-determination was rarely invoked in the practice of state succession prior to 1945, it gained special importance during decolonization.

As mentioned in the previous chapter, the UN Charter incorporated the concept of self-determination as a binding principle of international law applicable to all peoples, and this included their cultural development. Accordingly, it has been recognized that peoples have the right to decide freely on their international political status and on their sovereignty, without external compulsion or outside interference.[30] This affirmation has been critical for the process of decolonization. Pursuant to the 1960 UNGA Declaration on the Granting of Independence to Colonial Countries and Peoples,[31] self-determination became a legal principle which obliged former colonial powers to accept the will of colonized peoples, and facilitated international recognition of newly independent states. Importantly, the 1960 Declaration linked the principle of self-determination to the economic, social, and cultural rights of all peoples. With reference to this, the newly independent post-colonial states directly linked the right of self-determination to the right to develop and reconstruct their cultural identity and cultural heritage. The recognition of the collective identity of a people and its sovereignty over its territory was implied in the recognition of cultural autonomy and sovereignty over cultural resources. In this context, a question was raised as to whether the principle of self-determination also entitled the right of every people to regain its cultural property dispersed during the time of dependence on a foreign power, and whether such a right could provide a basis for legal claims for the restoration of cultural property following state succession.

[30] For the post-Second Word War international debate on the extent of the principle of self-determination and identification of groups entitled to exercise this right, see Antonio Cassese, *Self-Determination of Peoples. A Legal Reappraisal* (CUP, 1995), 37 ff.

[31] UN Doc. A/RES/1514(XV).

4.3.1 Self-determination, cultural development, and dispersed cultural property

With the adoption of both International Covenants on Human Rights (1966),[32] the principle of self-determination was sanctioned as a right of all peoples—an integral part of human rights law of universal application. Both instruments, under an identically formulated Article 1, provided that by virtue of the right of self-determination, all peoples 'freely determine their political status and freely pursue their economic, social and cultural development'. The Covenants also linked this right with the freedom of disposal vested to all peoples of 'their natural wealth and resources without prejudice to any obligations arising out of international economic co-operation, based upon the principle of mutual benefit, and international law'. Moreover, it was provided that 'in no case may a people be deprived of its own means of subsistence'.

From the mid-1960s on, the post-colonial states, organized into the Non-Aligned Movement, started an international campaign aimed at recognizing their rights and position in international law and international Cold War relations. A significant part of this campaign referred to their claim over the control of cultural resources removed from their territories before independence.[33] Although the Covenants did not provide for the right to cultural resources, such a concept was subsequently developed by the representatives of newly independent states. Analogous to the Allied restitution programme, which aimed at reversing the effects of artwork plunder committed during the Second World War, the representatives of former colonies claimed the need for vast compensation for the consequences of cultural exploitation in the colonial era, through social and cultural development.[34] They developed the cultural dimension of 'external' self-determination, defined as the right of every independent people to 'regain, enjoy and enrich their cultural heritage'.[35] The right to 'cultural resources' ran parallel to the right to natural resources; both were perceived as essential for the development of the post-colonial countries.[36]

The United Nations and UNESCO were the two major forums in which the newly independent states presented their demands.[37] In 1973, the United Nations

[32] International Covenant on Civil and Political Rights (ICCPR), adopted on 16 December 1966, entered into force on 23 March 1976, 999 UNTS 171, International Covenant on Economic, Social and Cultural Rights (ICESCR), adopted on 16 December 1966, entered into force on 3 January 1976, 993 UNTS 3.

[33] In particular, see the resolutions adopted by two Conferences of Heads of State or Government of Non-Aligned Countries: Resolution of the Fourth Conference (Algiers Conference, 5–7 September 1973), reproduced in part in UNGA Doc. A/9199, 2, and Fifth Conference (Colombo, 16–19 August 1976), UNGA Doc. A/31/1976, Annex IV.

[34] Ana Filipa Vrdoljak, 'Self-Determination and Cultural Rights', in Francesco Francioni and Martin Scheinin (eds), *Cultural Human Rights* (Nijhoff, 2008), 41–78, at 53 ff.

[35] Aureliu Critescu, *The Right to Self-Determination Historical and Current Development on the Basis of United Nations Instruments*, (UN Doc. E/CN.4/Sub.2/404/Rev. 1, 1981) at 111, paras. 641–77.

[36] Vrdoljak, *International Law* (n 14) 201.

[37] Nabil Bouaïta, 'La restitution des archives nationales et biens culturels à leurs pays d'origine dans le cadre du nouvel ordre culturel', *Revue de droit international, de sciences diplomatiques et politiques* 61(1983)1, 27–48.

General Assembly, primarily driven by the motions of African states,[38] adopted the first of a series of resolutions on this matter. Recalling the 1960 Declaration on the Granting of Independence to Colonial Countries and Peoples, the 1973 Resolution on the Restitution of Works of Art to Countries Victims of Expropriation' (UNGA Res. 3187 (XXVIII)),[39] deplored 'the wholesale removal, virtually without payment, of *objects d'art* from one country to another, frequently as a result of colonial or foreign occupation'. It recognized 'special obligations in this connection of those countries which had access to such valuable objects only as a result of colonial or foreign domination'. Furthermore, it asked 'all the states concerned to prohibit the exportation of works of art from territories still under colonial or foreign occupation'.

It may seem that UNGA Resolution 3187 (XXVIII) handled colonial rule and war occupation in the same way.[40] Thus, colonial expropriation were deemed to be similar to war plunder and consequently illegal. However, the resolution did not explicitly formulate an obligation of restitution arising from the wrongful act; rather it focused on two objectives: 1) international cooperation, and 2) cultural reparation. Accordingly, it affirmed that 'the prompt restitution to a country of its *objects d'art*, monuments, museum pieces and manuscripts by another country, without charge' would strengthen international cooperation and would constitute 'just reparation for damage done'. This view continued to be upheld in a few other UNGA Resolutions adopted in the 1970s,[41] and led to an important change of discourse on the right of newly independent states to reconstruct their cultural patrimonies, dispersed during colonial domination. This was also linked to the concept of the New International Economic Order (NIEO),[42] put forward by some developing states, arguing that their social and economic interests and rights should no longer be suppressed by the interests of developed countries, in particular former colonial powers. Although the proposals of the NIEO generally focused on the aspect of international trade, it was argued that the changes in economic relations should also lead to the reconsideration of a new international cultural order, in which the rights of developing states would be respected.[43]

Consequently, the debate on the exercise of the right to self-determination and on social, economic, and cultural development went far beyond the body of the international law of state succession, and beyond considerations of the legality of colonial acquisitions. The issue of international cooperation and moral duty to

[38] Lyndell V. Prott and Patrick O'Keefe, *Law and the Cultural Heritage*, Vol. 3 *Movement* (Butterworths, 1989), 814.

[39] UNGA Res. 3187 (XXVIII) of 18 December 1973, UN Doc. A/Res/3187(XXVIII).

[40] Wojciech Kowalski (ed), 'Claims for Works of Art and Their Legal Nature', in The International Bureau of the Permanent Court of Arbitration, *Resolution of Cultural Property Disputes. Papers Emanating from the Seventh PCA International Law Seminar May 23, 2003* (Kluwer Law International, 2004), 31–51, at 47–48.

[41] Primarily, see UNGA Res. 3391 (XXX) of 19 November 1975, UN Doc. A/Res/3391(XXX).

[42] Declaration for the Establishment of a New International Economic Order, UN Doc. A/RES/S-6/3201

[43] Mohammed Bedjaoui, *Towards a New International Economic Order Paris* (UNESCO, 1979), 75, 245 ff.

compensate historic injustices, which not only referred to former colonizers but also to those who took advantage from the expropriation (such as other states, museums. or individuals possessing cultural objects), began to play a key role in post-colonial cultural discourse.

4.3.2 Self-determination and cultural rights

During the emancipation of former colonized territories, self-determination and cultural development were rights generally limited to states and their national cultures. The exercise of the right of self-determination was associated with its external dimension and did not concern the rights of national, ethnic or religious minorities within a state territory, following territorial transfers. In fact, after 1945, in part as a response to the Holocaust, minority protection was replaced by a system of human rights of universal application. It was believed that such a global regime would provide more effective protection and the realization of human rights within existing and newly independent states, rather than the pre-Second World War system of minority treaties. Moreover, in the circumstances of the Cold War and ongoing liberation movements, states were afraid of universalizing minority protection, which was perceived as a threat to their internal stability and development.[44] Thus, under post-1945 international legislation, cultural rights became human rights, inherent in every individual human being. The question raised, however, was whether these new cultural rights would also include the right to tangible cultural heritage, in particular heritage that had been dispersed in the past.

Under the 1948 Universal Declaration of Human Rights (UDHR),[45] cultural rights were defined as the individual right to participate in cultural life, to enjoy the arts and to share in scientific advancement and its benefits (Article 27). A similar notion of cultural rights was also adopted under Article 15 of the ICESCR. In contrast to the provisions of Article 27 of the UDHR, it implied certain proactive duties on states parties. Accordingly, they were required to take necessary steps 'for the conservation, the development and the diffusion of science and culture' (Article 15.2), as well as for 'the encouragement and development of international contacts and co-operation in the scientific and cultural fields' (Article 15.4).

However, this perception of cultural rights as individual rights was gradually interpreted in a collective sense, which recognized certain rights of minorities and indigenous peoples. At the early stage of development of the international system of human rights, the crucial regulation on this matter was adopted under Article 27 of the ICCPR. States parties were obliged to comply with a limited number of obligations in respect of 'ethnic, religious or linguistic minorities'. Accordingly, members of

[44] See Anthony Evelyn Alcock, *A History of the Protection of Regional Cultural Minorities in Europe: From the Edict of Nantes to the Present Day* (MacMillan, 2000), 100 ff.

[45] Adopted in Paris on 10 December 1948, UNGA Res. 217A(III), UN Doc.A/810, 71.

such groups 'shall not be denied the right, in community with the other members of their group, to enjoy their own culture, to profess and practice their own religion, or to use their own language.' It would appear that the notion of cultural rights in the collective sense, comprising the right to enjoy the group's culture, also entailed the right to the cultural heritage of such a group.

In this view, it is possible to identify three major spheres in which cultural rights in the collective sense may interplay with state succession on the matter of tangible cultural heritage. The first is strictly linked to the post-Second World War redrafting of state boundaries in Central Eastern Europe, followed by the displacements of entire national and/or ethnic groups. As explained in the previous chapter, these arrangements resulted in certain *de facto* solutions in respect of the allocation of cultural property. In several cases, such interstate settlements accepted situations in which tangible cultural property was displaced, or more precisely taken, by the transferred populations. It appears that in this way states participating in such transfers tacitly recognized the priority of collective cultural rights of a displaced group over the general principle of territoriality. The relevance of this trend for the more profound changes in the law of state succession was, however, undermined by the subsequent prohibition of involuntary population transfers under Article 49 of the Fourth Geneva Convention (1949).[46] Accordingly, forced population transfers, accepted as legitimate means of settling ethnic and national conflict after the First and Second World Wars, became criminalized as a violation of international law.

The second sphere refers to the broader discourse on the exercise of the right of self-determination by the newly independent post-colonial states, and their right to develop and reconstruct cultural heritage suppressed during dependence on a foreign power. Accordingly, such states could not only demand the items constituting state and/or other public property, but also the objects created on their territory and expressive of local and indigenous cultures.[47] For instance, UNESCO in the document entitled *Cultural rights as human rights* (1970) noted that self-determination 'also involved a new sense of dignity, a new searching for ideas handed down from the past, pride in art forms perfected both before and during colonial rule, and the determination to rebuild the traditional cultures so often disparaged in recent centuries, or to protect new indigenous cultures from the onslaught of urbanization and industrialization'.[48]

This last dimension concerns the re-emerging regime for the protection of minorities in international law. Although the UN Charter and both the 1966 Covenants remained silent in respect of the right to self-determination of minorities within states, the need for a special system for minority protection within the international human rights framework was gradually acknowledged. The clash

[46] Geneva (IV) Convention Relative to the Protection of Civilian Persons in Time of War, signed on 12 August 1949, entered into force 21 October 1950, 75 UNTS 287.

[47] Halina Nieć, 'Sovereign Rights to Cultural Property', *PYIL* 4(1971), 239–50, 245.

[48] UNESCO, *Cultural Rights as Human Rights* (UNESCO, 1970), UNESCO Doc. SHC/XIX/3A, at 8–9.

between official cultural policies and minority and indigenous cultures became especially evident in the newly independent post-colonial states. The emancipation of former colonies (re)activated deep tensions between different groups within new states, which often led to the suppression of minority cultures by those of the dominant majorities or by newly created uniform cultural policies. Therefore, UNESCO promoted the principle of equality of cultures in its documents. In particular, the 1976 Recommendation on Participation by the People at Large in Cultural Life and their Contribution to It[49] asked states parties to provide legislative measures in order to 'guarantee the recognition of the equality of cultures, including the cultures of national minorities and of foreign minorities if they exist, as forming part of the common heritage of all mankind, and ensure that they are promoted at all levels without discrimination; ensure that national minorities and foreign minorities have full opportunities for gaining access, to and participating in the cultural life of the countries in which they find themselves in order to enrich it with their specific contributions, while safeguarding their right to preserve their cultural identity.' Consequently, it was argued that states, including those that had recently emerged, had a responsibility towards minorities to assist their cultural development.[50] Moreover, they were actively to participate in such development in the same way as they would act for the development of national cultures.[51]

4.4 The protection of movable cultural property and the restitution debate: action by UNESCO

The principle of self-determination and cultural development also laid the foundations for the activity of non-European states in the matter of cooperation in times of peace for the prevention and remediation of the illicit traffic of movable cultural property. The campaigns of post-colonial countries and others affected by the illicit trade and impoverishment of national cultural heritage were extensively pursued within the forum of UNESCO. As early as 1964, the General Conference of UNESCO in its 13th session adopted the Recommendation on the Means of Prohibiting and Preventing the Illicit Export, Import and Transfer of Ownership of Cultural Property.[52] This document recognized the importance of the link between state territory and cultural property as it is 'incumbent upon every State to protect the cultural property existing within its territory and which constitutes its national heritage against the dangers resulting from illicit export,

[49] Recommendation on Participation by the People at Large in Cultural Life and Their Contribution to It, Nairobi, 26 November 1976, UNESCO Doc 19C/Resolutions, Annex I.

[50] Ryszard Cholewinski, 'State Duty Towards Ethnic Minorities: Positive or Negative?', *Human Rights Quarterly* 10(1988)3, 346–59.

[51] Compare Vrdoljak, 'Self-Determination and Cultural Rights' (n 34) 64.

[52] Recommendation on the Means of Prohibiting and Preventing the Illicit Export, Import and Transfer of Ownership of Cultural Property, UNESCO Doc.13C/Resolutions, 206, 207.

import and transfer of ownership.'[53] To provide efficient measures for preventing the impoverishment of national heritage, UNESCO recommended close multilateral collaboration and cooperation at domestic and international levels.[54]

Hence, the procedural principle of cooperation, already promoted by various post-Second World War international instruments including the 1945 UNESCO Constitution,[55] gained particular relevance with regard to cultural matters. This was reinforced by the subsequent 1966 UNESCO Declaration of Principles of International Cultural Co-operation (1966 UNESCO Declaration on Cultural Co-operation),[56] which integrally related the exercise of the right to self-determination with cultural development of all mankind. Importantly, the Declaration reaffirmed that 'every people has the right and the duty to develop its culture' (Article 1(2)), thus the aim of international cultural cooperation is 'to spread knowledge, to stimulate talent and to enrich cultures', and 'to enable, everyone to have access to knowledge, to enjoy the arts and literature of all peoples, to share in advances made in science in all parts of the world and in the resulting benefits, and to contribute to the enrichment of cultural life' (Article 4 (1) (4)).

The importance of international cultural cooperation was subsequently recognized as a fundamental duty in further UNESCO instruments designed to prevent the impoverishment of national cultures endangered by illicit traffic in movable cultural property, as well as in settling international controversies in respect of the restoration of cultural material of peoples subjected to foreign domination.

4.4.1 The 1970 UNESCO Convention

As regards the issue of illicit transfer of cultural property, the efforts of developing countries led to the adoption of a multilateral international treaty which bound states parties to cooperate on the grounds of public law in order to prevent the traffic of cultural objects stolen or illicitly exported from other countries: the 1970 UNESCO Convention on the Means of Prohibiting and Preventing the Illicit Import, Export and Transfer of Ownership of Cultural Property. Under Article 2, this Convention recognized that international cooperation constituted 'one of the most efficient means of protecting each country's cultural property against all the dangers' which may result from the illicit trafficking of cultural property.

The text of this instrument nevertheless constituted a compromise between the former colonial powers—generally speaking, the developed countries which constituted the market for cultural goods—and in a greater capacity newly independent states—developing countries which constituted the source of these goods. For this reason, the 1970 Convention limits its application to illicit trafficking in cultural objects illicitly imported after the Convention's entry into force. In fact,

[53] Ibid. preamble. [54] Ibid. Art. 11(b)(ii) and Art. 19.

[55] Constitution of the United Nations Educational, Scientific and Cultural Organization, signed on 16 November 1945, entered into force on 4 November 1946, 4 UNTS 275.

[56] Declaration of Principles of International Cultural Co-operation, Paris, 4 November 1966, UNESCO Doc. 14C/Resolution 8.

while drafting the Convention, the post-colonial states advocated the extension of the Convention's application to the illicit transfers committed prior to their independence as well as general retroactive effects of this instrument. Conversely, the former dominant powers insisted on the inclusion of a non-retroactivity clause.[57] Eventually, none of these clauses was introduced. The non-retroactive application of the 1970 Convention was, however, assumed on the basis of customary international law and on the provisions of Article 28 of the 1969 Vienna Convention on the Law of Treaties.[58] Alternatively, the 1970 UNESCO Convention, under Article 15, refers its states parties to bilateral agreements on particular questions referring to the situation prior to its operation:

> Nothing in this Convention shall prevent states Parties thereto from concluding special agreements among themselves or from continuing to implement agreements already concluded regarding the restitution of cultural property removed, whatever the reason, from its territory of origin, before the entry into force of this Convention for the states concerned.

The 1970 Convention did not solve the problems that emerged from post-Second World War state succession and decolonization; the limitations of such bilateral relations were clear for all the parties concerned. The regime of the 1970 Convention nevertheless introduced an important legal basis for establishing the principles governing the allocation of cultural property that may be applicable for future cases of state succession. Arguably, a successor state may have a claim to recover those objects that were illicitly exported or acquired in the territory subject to state succession, provided that such a transfer took place after the ratification of the 1970 Convention by the predecessor state. Yet, in such cases the successor state would have to compensate the purchaser where the purchase had been made in good faith, as held under Article 7(a)(ii) of the Convention. The procedural principle of cooperation reinforced by Article 2 may provide an indispensable tool for dealing with such controversies.

4.4.2 Further developments

In the 1970s, the disappointment of many states over the scope of the 1970 UNESCO Convention continued. In 1976, the conference of the Committee of Experts to Study the Question of the Restitution of Works of Art (Committee)[59] addressed the need for a concrete form, 'in a spirit of international solidarity and good faith', to accommodate the claims on the recovery of irreplaceable cultural objects.[60] UNESCO approached the question in two ways. First, it advocated the

[57] Patrick J. O'Keefe, *Commentary to the UNESCO 1970 Convention on Illicit Traffic* (Institute of Art and Law, 2000), 14, Vrdoljak, *International Law* (n 14) 206–207.

[58] Vienna Convention of Law Treaties, signed on 23 May 1969, entered into force on 27 January 1980, 1155 UNTS 331.

[59] Venice, 29 March–2 April 1976, UNESCO Doc.SHC-76/CONF.615/5.

[60] Ibid. General Principles, paras. 18-24.

international exchange of cultural property also by means of inter-institutional loans. Second, it established a new international forum to facilitate questions not resolved by the adoption of the 1970 Convention.

a) The international exchange of cultural property

In 1976, the General Conference of UNESCO adopted the Recommendation Concerning the International Exchange of Cultural Property.[61] It was recognized that closer relations between states in the sphere of official exchange of cultural property would contribute to the enrichment of the cultures involved and provide access to cultural property for poorer countries and institutions.[62] Cooperation on this matter would also enable more efficient action against illicit trafficking in cultural property.[63] To this end, UNESCO recommended an array of different forms of exchange at unilateral, bi/multilateral levels, comprising short- and long-term loans, deposit, sale, and donation. Moreover, Article 12(4) of the 1976 Recommendation provided that 'the attention of cultural institutions in all countries should be drawn especially to the opportunities for reassembling a presently dismembered work which would be afforded by a system of successive loans, without transfer of ownership, enabling each of the holding institutions to take its turn to display the work in its entirety.'

Although it was not mentioned in the text of the 1976 Recommendation, international exchange was also aimed at providing countries which had been deprived of their cultural treasures during foreign domination access to such property.[64] As seen in the case of the Benin Bronzes, such loans were eagerly awaited by the newly independent post-colonial states, as temporary exhibitions and long-term deposits constituted the only form in which these states could gain access to the cultural treasures of their past. Therefore, such quasi restitution of cultural property, without the transfer of title, came to be perceived as an alternative solution in cases of historical removal and appropriation.

b) The UNESCO Intergovernmental Committee and cooperation

In the mid-1970s, UNESCO began the search for a new system to accommodate the claims of newly independent states for the restitution of cultural property removed prior to their independence. At its meeting in Venice in 1976, the UNESCO committee of experts set up to study the question of the restitution of works of art recognized that 'as the testimony of the creative genius and the history of peoples, cultural property is a basic element of their identity and full enjoyment of this heritage is for each people an indispensable condition for its

[61] Recommendation Concerning the International Exchange of Cultural Property, Nairobi, 26 November 1976, UNESCO Doc. 19C/Resolutions, Annex I.

[62] Ibid. preamble. [63] Ibid. Art. 15. [64] See UN Doc. A/CN.4/322, para 53.

self-realisation.'[65] Therefore, the facilitation of restitution of cultural property should be the aim of UNESCO. The Committee asked the Director General of UNESCO to consider setting up a special body for this purpose.[66]

Two years later, in Dakar, this concept was endorsed by the UNESCO committee of experts on the establishment of an intergovernmental committee concerning the restitution or return of cultural property.[67] The terms of approaching the problems not covered by the 1970 Convention were expressed in the document prepared by the International Council of Museums (ICOM), entitled 'Study on the Principles, Conditions and Means for the Restitution or Return of Cultural Property in View of Reconstructing Dispersed Heritage' (1978 Study).[68] This was based on two paramount considerations: 1) the coherence of reconstituted heritage, and 2) the primacy of the objects. The first was understood as 'the return to their countries of origin of those objects and documents' which were 'indispensable to people in understanding their origin and culture.'[69] The second was defined as 'protection, accessibility to the public and transmission of the object.'[70] Importantly, the 1978 Study affirmed that 'the reassembly of dispersed heritage through restitution or return of objects which are of major importance for the cultural identity and history of countries having been deprived thereof' was commonly recognized as an ethical principle. It continued that this principle would 'soon become an element of *jus cogens* of international relations.'[71]

This view was highly criticized by some legal scholars. For instance, James Nafziger noticed that although there was much dispute about the identity of the peremptory norms of general international law as provided by Article 53 of the Vienna Convention on the Law of Treaties, 'they would include, for example, restraints on the illegal threat or use of force under article 2(4) of the United Nations Charter, the principle of *pacta sunt servanda*, prohibitions on such egregious violations of human rights as apartheid, slavery and use by states of torture and the principles of self determination and minimum human welfare.' However, he argued that it seemed 'very doubtful that the notion of a right to return and restitution of cultural property constitutes a peremptory norm of general international law, from which no derogation is permitted.'[72]

The Dakar Conference did not, however, lay claim for the wholesale transfer of cultural material from museums to the countries of origin. In this regard, the Conference can arguably be viewed as the site of a battle between the interests of the market countries and former colonial powers seeking to protect their collections from dispersal, on the one hand, and the rights of states deprived of their material patrimony, on the other. The former emphasized the universal significance

[65] UNESCO Doc. SHC-76/CONF.615/5, para. 19.
[66] UNESCO Doc. SHC-76/CONF.615/5, para. 25.
[67] UNESCO Doc. CC-78/CONF.609/3.
[68] UNESCO Doc.CC-78/CONF.609/3, Annex I.
[69] Ibid. para. 10.
[70] Ibid. paras. 19–20.
[71] Ibid. para. 38.
[72] James A. R. Nafziger, 'The New International Framework for the Return, Restitution, or Forfeiture of Cultural Property', *N.Y.U. Journal of International Law and Politics* 15(1982/83)4, 789–812, at 805–6.

and value of collections of art and knowledge; the latter highlighted the historical injustices and their right to control an adequate share in their own national heritage.[73] The Dakar Conference expressed a compromise solution and stressed the importance of the moral obligations of those states and museums which had acquired cultural treasures to render the most important items to nations deprived of their patrimony. This was particularly valid for the territories in Africa and the Pacific islands, whose material patrimony had been removed and was preserved practically *in toto* in Western museums.

In a similar vein, one must also note the 1978 appeal by the Director General of UNESCO, Amadou-Mahtar M'Bow. In this document entitled 'A Plea for the Return of an Irreplaceable Cultural Heritage to Those Who Created It',[74] he emphasized the moral rights of peoples to enjoy their cultural heritage. For this purpose, he stressed the need for international cooperation. Yet, M'Bow did not limit his appeal to the rights of states (nations) to reconstruct their cultural patrimony. He approached the question from a much broader context, recalling non-state actors 'the men and women of these countries', whose right to recover cultural assets should be taken into account.

Finally, the General Conference of UNESCO set up the Intergovernmental Committee for Promoting the Return of Cultural Property to its Countries of Origin or its Restitution in case of Illicit Appropriation (UNESCO Intergovernmental Committee).[75] According to the statues of the Committee,[76] the main sphere of its activities concerned the facilitation of 'bilateral negotiations for the restitution or return of cultural property to its countries of origin', and the promotion of 'multilateral and bilateral co-operation with a view to the restitution and return of cultural property to its countries of origin' and in the area of international 'exchanges of cultural property in accordance with the Recommendation on the International Exchange of Cultural Property'. In fact, in the subsequent practice of the Committee, its basic role consisted of promoting bilateral agreements between states in respect of objects removed prior to the 1970 Convention. The work was carried out on a case-by-case basis.

As regards state practice in such bilateral agreements, the most well-known cases concerned the already cited arrangements between Belgium and Zaire, and between the Netherlands and Indonesia. Similarly, in the process of the peaceful separation of Papua New Guinea from Australia, the latter committed itself to protecting the cultural heritage of its former colony. Within two years of the independence of Papua New Guinea in 1975, the National Museum and Art Gallery was opened in Port Moresby thanks to the assistance of its former colonizer, and

[73] See UNESCO Doc. CC-78/CONF/609/6, para 14-19.

[74] Amadou-Mahtar M'bow, 'A Plea for the Return of an Irreplaceable Cultural Heritage to Those Who Created It, 7 June 1978', *Museum* 31(1979), 58.

[75] UNESCO Doc. 20C/Resolution 4/7.6/5.

[76] Ibid. Annex, Statutes of the Intergovernmental Committee for Promoting the Return of Cultural Property to its Countries of Origin or its Restitution in Case of Illicit Appropriation, Art. 4.

a large number of cultural objects were handed over by Australian institutions.[77] In the Europe, the most important case and virtually the only one settled in the form of a treaty concerned the settlement between the new state of Iceland and Denmark. At the centre of the controversy were the Arnamagnæan Manuscripts, a collection of mediaeval literary sagas, one of the most important manifestations of Icelandic culture. In the eighteenth century, when Iceland formed part of the Danish–Norwegian kingdom, many of the manuscripts were gathered by Arne Magnussen, an Icelandic scholar, who bequeathed them to the University of Copenhagen. Years later a special foundation was created to ensure their preservation and research. In 1814, when Norway became a separate state, Iceland remained under Danish sovereignty until 1945, when it gained independence. Even before its separation from Denmark in 1944, Iceland had begun to petition for the return of these manuscripts. Its claim was strictly bound to the right of self-determination and reconstruction of its cultural identity. The issue was complicated however, as the collection constituted the property of a private entity. Therefore, it was claimed that Iceland had no legal rights to the manuscripts and the question could only be considered in terms of a Danish gift.[78] After many legal obstacles, in 1971 Iceland and Denmark finally ratified a treaty which provided for the return of the manuscripts within a period of 25 years from its ratification. From 1971 to 1997 these provisions were gradually implemented. It was argued that after 'issues of fishing boundaries around and the defence of Iceland itself the issue of the return of the manuscripts' constituted 'the biggest and most serious problem in the foreign relations of independent Iceland'. By returning these treasures, 'the Icelandic people realize that the Danish people have shown them such consideration as is rarely found in international circles.'[79]

By the end of the 1970s an international debate on the restoration of lost cultural materials became more fragmented. At UNESCO's General Conference in 1978, an important distinction between the two institutions of 'restitution' and 'return' was made.[80] These were subsequently defined by the 1986 Guidelines for the Use of the 'Standard Form Concerning Requests for Return or Restitution' (1986 Guidelines).[81] Accordingly, 'restitution' was to be used 'in case of illicit appropriation' during war as provided by the 1954 Hague Convention or during times of peace, with particular reference to the 1970 UNESCO Convention, 'i.e. when objects have left their countries of origin illegally, according to the relevant national legislations.' Conversely, the term 'return' applied to 'cases where objects left their countries of origin prior to the crystallization of national and international law on the protection of cultural property'. It explicitly referred to 'transfers

[77] Vrdoljak, *International Law* (n 14) 219–20.

[78] Greenfield, *The Return of Cultural Treasures* (n 1) 28.

[79] Erland Kolding Nielsen, 'Denmark to Iceland. A Case without Precedence: Delivering Back the Islandic Manuscripts 1971–1997', in *68th International Federation of Library Associations and Institutions Council and General Conference, Glasgow,* 18–24 August, 2002, at 5, available at: <http://archive.ifla.org/IV/ifla68/papers/Kolding_Nielsen02.pdf>, accessed on 4 February 2015.

[80] UNESCO Doc. 20C/Resolution 4/7.6/5.

[81] UNESCO Doc. CC-86/WS/3, A.9.

of ownership' made from the colonial territories to the colonial powers, or the territories under foreign occupation. The Guidelines explained that:

> in many cases, they were the result of an exchange, gift or sale and did not therefore infringe any laws existing at the time. In some cases, however, the legitimacy of the transfer can be questioned. Among the many variants of such a process is the removal of objects from a colonial territory by people who were not nationals of the colonial power. There may have also been cases of political or economic dependence which made it possible to effect transfers of ownership from one territory to another which would not be envisaged today.

It is clear that UNESCO adopted a position according to which the rights of former colonizing peoples had to be treated in a separate way, beyond the regimes of illicit appropriation, and beyond the law of war. It also seems that such rights, arising from the common awareness of the importance of cultural heritage for those who had created it, should be treated differently from state succession considerations.

The special regime proposed by UNESCO for post-colonial claims did not, however, address all the issues relating to the distribution of cultural treasures arising from colonial domination. The UNESCO framework dealt with the interests of states, which were also entitled to represent non-state actors under their sovereignty. Since M'Bow's appeal in 1978, the rights of other stakeholders—primarily the rights of indigenous peoples—have been more often recalled.[82] This led to important developments at the domestic level in some of the settler states such as Australia, New Zealand, the US, and Canada, which began to recognize the cultural heritage rights of their indigenous communities.[83] In relation to the terminology of international cultural law, the mechanisms for the recovery of cultural property by indigenous peoples or ethnic groups within states have been embraced under the term 'repatriation.' Interestingly, the same term was often used with reference to the allocation of cultural material, following state succession, in the European context.[84]

4.5 The International Law Commission and state succession to cultural property

The process of codification of international law on state succession, akin to the parallel development of cultural heritage law, was profoundly affected by decolonization. The controversies between developed and developing countries led to

[82] Vrdoljak, *International Law* (n 14) 217 ff.

[83] See materials of the conference 'Material Culture in Flux-Repatriation of Cultural Property held on 20–21 May 1994 at the University of British Columbia' *University of British Columbia Law Review* (1995) special issue.

[84] See Wojciech Kowalski, 'Repatriation of Cultural Property Following a Cession of Territory or Dissolution of Multinational States', *Art, Antiquity and Law* 6(2001)2, 139–66, 143 ff.

great difficulties in the drafting of texts of international instruments and later complicated their ratification and actual implementation. Hence, in the processes of codification of law on state succession as well as that of cultural heritage, it became clear that the major former colonial states remained outside the codified legal framework. In fact, none of the conventions on state succession prepared by the International Law Commission enter into force prior to 1989.

4.5.1 The impact of decolonization on the theory of state succession

The relevance of the post-colonial issue was particularly addressed in the legal and academic discourse on the phenomenon of decolonization and state succession.[85] The ILC, in its report to the United Nations General Assembly, noted the need to 'avoid confusing state succession with decolonization,' as the latter demonstrated the 'elements of continuity and rupture.'[86] On a theoretical level, a debate on the post-colonial notion of state succession was held between Mohammed Bedjaoui, an Algerian legal expert and representative of postcolonial states, and David P. O'Connell, a prominent British scholar and author of a monumental monograph on state succession.[87]

In 1970, both experts were asked by the Hague Academy of International Law[88] to present lectures on precisely the same subject.[89] The positions of both authors were very different. O'Connell did not perceive decolonization as a rupture in the theory of state succession, but only as an historical 'experience', which should not be treated as a conditioning factor.[90] He argued that the law of state succession could not only accommodate ephemeral interests of post-colonial states, but rather it needed to 'centre upon one basic concept, namely the reconciliation of the independence of successor states with the expectations of other states and peoples.'[91] He claimed that the law of state succession needed to provide a 'minimal disturbance of existing legal situations.'[92] Consequently, the codification of international law on state succession should find some universal solutions and rules.

As regards state succession to public property, his views were very much based on the theory of 'acquired rights,'[93] which shall be respected by newly independent states. Accordingly, he argued that the continuity of legal relations, including property rights, could not lapse by the mere fact of state succession.[94] On the basis of international practice prior to the Second World War, as well as post-colonial

[85] See an extensive analysis by Matthew Craven: *The Decolonization of International Law: State Succession and the Law of Treaties* (OUP, 2007) 93–206.

[86] UN Doc. A/7209/Rev.1, ICL Report, 20th Session, 27 May–2 August 1968, para. 64.

[87] Daniel Patrick O'Connell, *State Succession in Municipal Law and International Law*, Vols 1, 2 (CUP, 1967).

[88] Craven, *The Decolonization* (n 85) 82.

[89] Daniel Patrick O'Connell, 'Recent Problems of State Succession in Relation to New States', *RCADI* 130(1970)2, 95–206.

[90] Ibid. 103. [91] Ibid. 120. [92] Ibid. 120. [93] Ibid. 134–46.

[94] Ibid. 166–69.

arrangements between France and its former African territories,[95] O'Connell explained the difference between public and private domains of a state. The first referred to state property strictly bound to the functions of governments, while the latter was owned by a state in the same manner as private property was owned by an individual. In the case of state succession, the first category passed from the predecessor state to the successor one. The private property rights of the predecessor state continued after the change of sovereignty. It is clear that such an approach could have a tremendous impact on the rights of newly independent states to cultural resources.

Conversely, Bedjaoui perceived the process of decolonization as an extremely important legal and social phenomenon, different from classically (traditionally) perceived state succession.[96] He claimed that the process of decolonization had to alter the rules of international law, which primarily accommodated the interest of the former colonial powers. He linked the right of self-determination of peoples with the concept of the control over natural resources,[97] and the right to maintain or reject economic obligations and property relations established prior to decolonization. Therefore, he attacked the theory of acquired rights as an emanation of post-colonial interests rather than an attempt to safeguard legal stability and justice.[98]

In this context, one of the fundamental questions concerned the catalogue of categories (types) of state succession. While the number of doctrinal voices were of the opinion that a clear distinction between different types of state succession was largely formalistic and did not entail distinct legal consequences,[99] the experience of the ongoing process of decolonization inclined the ILC to reconsider introducing such a new category in relation to formerly dependent colonial territories. The ILC followed the view expressed *inter alia* by the 1970 UNGA Declaration on Principles of International Law concerning Friendly Relations and Co-operation among States in accordance with the Charter of the United Nations,[100] that the territory of a colony had a status separate and distinct from the territory of the state administering it. Thus, the independence of such a territory did not constitute a case of secession/separation from the territory of the predecessor. Inversely, this led to the creation of a completely new political and legal situation. Accordingly, a new legal regime was advocated to enable former colonial nations to exercise their right to self-determination freely and break the ties of colonial economic dependency and domination.[101] The ILC shared this view and

[95] See *inter alia* Gérard Fouilloux, 'La succession aux biens publics français dans les états nouveaux d'Afrique', *AFDI* 11(1965), 885–915, Jean-Claude Gautron, 'Sur quelques aspects de la succession d'états au Sénégal', *AFDI* 8(1962), 836–64.

[96] Mohammed Bedjaoui, 'Problèmes récentes de succession d'états dans les états nouveaux', *RCADI* 130–2(1970), 455–586, at 489–92.

[97] Ibid. 493–96. [98] Ibid. 544–61.

[99] See Patrick Dumberry, *State Succession to International Responsibility* (Nijhoff, 2007), 15–22.

[100] UNGA Res. 2625 (XXV), 24 October 1970, UN Doc. A/RES/25/2625.

[101] Yilma Makonnen, 'State Succession in Africa: Selected Problems', *RCADI* 200-V(1986), 93–243, at 130–31.

eventually identified such a specific category of state succession.[102] Accordingly, both Vienna Conventions[103] define a 'newly independent state' as 'a successor State the territory of which immediately before the date of the succession of States was a dependent territory for the international relations of which the predecessor State was responsible'.[104]

The establishment of the separate category of newly independent states and its separate legal regime has been much discussed and never fully accepted in state practice and legal scholarship.[105] In fact, the more recent ILC Draft Articles on Nationality of Natural Persons in relation to the Succession of States[106] do not adopt specific rules applicable to newly independent states. Arguably, the differences between the two theories of international law on state succession—the classical Western-based international law and new concepts arising from the aspirations and interests of post-colonial states, dominating the work of the ILC—have eventually led to a failure of the entire codification efforts at the end of the era of decolonization.

4.5.2 Topics covered by the codification works

The fundamental issue at the heart of the ILC work concerned state succession to international treaties. While the Commission, from the beginning, confirmed the succession rule with regard to treaties setting territorial boundaries,[107] the topic of political and other treaties remained extremely controversial. Again, the main controversy concerned newly independent states and their position with regard to the treaties concluded by former colonial powers. The ILC noted that 'majority of writers take the view, supported by State practice, that a newly independent State begins its life with a clean slate, except in regard to "local" or "real" obligations'.[108] In fact, as early as 1947 the UN Secretariat, while discussing Pakistan's position in relation to the organization, noted that 'the territory which breaks off, Pakistan, will be a new state; it will not have the treaty rights and obligations of the old state'.[109] The ILC shared this opinion and the eventually adopted a general regime

[102] See further, Zidane Meriboute, *La codification de la succession d'États aux traités: décolonisation, sécession, unification* (Presses Universitaires de France, 1984), 29–30, 49, 56, 63.

[103] Vienna Convention on Succession of States in Respect of Treaties, signed on 23 August 1978, entered into force on 6 November 1996, 1946 UNTS 3; Vienna Convention on Succession of States in Respect of State Property, Archives and Debts, adopted on 8 April 1983, not in force, UN Doc. A/CONF.117/14 (1983).

[104] See Art. 2(1)(f) of the 1978 Vienna Convention and Art. 2(1)(e) of the 1983 Vienna Convention.

[105] See further, Vladimir, D. Degan, 'Création et disparition de l'Etat (à la lumière du démembrement de trois fédérations multiethniques en Europe)', *RCADI* 279(1999), 195–375, at 298–99.

[106] UN Doc. A/54/10, ILC Report, 51st session, 3 May–23 July 1999, *YILC* (1997)2, 41.

[107] Sir Humphrey Waldock, Special Rapporteur, 'First Report on Succession of States and Governments in respect of Treaties', UN Doc. A/CN.4/202, *YILC* (1968)2, at 92–93.

[108] UN Doc. A/9610/Rev.1, ILC Report, 26th Session, 6 May–26 July 1974, *YILC* (1974)2/1, at 211, para. 3.

[109] Ibid. para. 4.

for such states under Article 16 of the 1978 Vienna Convention. This provided that a newly independent state was not bound to maintain in force, or to become a party to, any treaty by reason only of the fact that the treaty had been in force in respect of the territory in question at the date of the succession. The following provisions of the Convention regulated the rights of newly independent states in respect of defining their participation in multilateral and bilateral relations, according to the clean slate (*tabula rasa*) principle. Yet the experience of the decolonization has shown that new states might apply various strategies, mitigating the effects of this principle, depending on the circumstances in which they achieved independence; eg devolution agreements concluded within the British Commonwealth, which generally provided for the continuity of international treaty obligations.[110]

In 1967, the ILC appointed Bedjaoui as Special Rapporteur and assigned him the task of preparing an introductory report in respect of other rights and duties resulting from sources other than treaties, with special reference to decolonization.[111] Bedjaoui presented his introductory report to the ILC in 1968.[112] He proposed that the codification should address six different topics: public property, public debts, natural resources, territorial problems related to state succession, specific issues referring to decolonization, and nationality and the legal regime of the predecessor state.[113] As a result of the discussion within the ILC, it was decided that the codification would focus only on the economic aspect of state succession: public property and debts.[114] From the category of public property, the question of archives was subsequently addressed. In 1973, the ILC decided to limit the scope of the convention only to one category of public property, state property,[115] 'which could be properly regarded as a concept of international law'.[116]

4.5.3 Property of cultural significance—a separate category of property?

The question of state succession to cultural property became the subject of intense research carried out at the time of drafting the articles of the 1983 Vienna Convention. In this regard, the Special Rapporteur referred extensively to the parallel debate on the rights of formerly colonized peoples to the cultural material dispersed prior to decolonization. The ILC considered the issue at its several sessions in the years 1968–81. These discussions covered both the topic of

[110] See Malcolm, N. Shaw, *International* Law (6th edn, CUP, 2008), at 979, O'Connell, *State Succession* (n 87) vol. 1, 36–57.

[111] UN Doc. A/CN.4/199, ILC Report, 19th Session, 8 May–14 July 1967, *YILC* (1967)2, at 368.

[112] Mohammed Bedjaoui, Special Rapporteur, 'First Report on Succession of States in respect of Rights and Duties Resulting from Sources other than Treaties', UN Doc. A/CN.4/204, *YILC* (1967)2, at 94.

[113] UN Doc. A/CN.4/204.

[114] UN Doc. A/7209/REV.1, para. 79.

[115] UN DOC.A/CN.4/L.196, YILC (1973)1.

[116] Ibid. 149.

cultural property and that of state archives, and their role for cultural heritage of successor states.

a) *Cultural property*

It appears that from the beginning of the work of the ILC, no separate provisions in respect of cultural property were seriously considered. Arguably, this can be explained by the choice made by the ILC to restrict the scope of the convention to state property only. As mentioned, the ongoing debate on the right of post-colonial states to their dispersed cultural heritage could hardly be embodied in the legal framework of succession to state property. Nonetheless, Bedjaoui in his reports explicitly argued that the transfer of movable property from the dependent territories was to be 'carried out fully in accordance with the canons of justice, morality and law.'[117] He also stressed that dependent (colonial) territories had a separate legal status independent from that of an administrating power. Consequently, the latter was entitled to exercise the 'acts for the disposal of the territory, its property or the rights of its population'.[118] Furthermore, he referred to the ongoing activity of the United Nations General Assembly and UNESCO in respect of the return and restitution of cultural property removed prior to decolonization. He explained that though many former colonial powers refused to pursue restitution *de jure*, the question of such a reversal of colonial domination was associated with 'psychological aspects' and 'the feelings of guilt,'[119] which implied that 'the possession of the cultural property, historical archives, works of art etc. by the predecessor State was unlawful.'[120] Hence, the maintenance of the *status quo* would not improve the situation. Thus, such disputes ought to be settled by new measures of regulation in the spirit of cooperation, within the framework of a new international order in which 'the right to collective memory' would be respected.[121] It appears that action by UNESCO was perceived as the best framework within which to deal with the complex cases of the allocation of cultural property removed from the dependent territories.

Bedjaoui argued that for the purposes of drafting international legal instruments the definition of cultural property as such presented 'almost insurmountable problems' because some objects 'have a universal value, either because of the message they transmit or the personality of their authors'. On the other hand, 'national cultural assets ... are objects constituting the essential wealth of a country's cultural memory and identity'.[122] Nevertheless, he explained that in relation to the provisions on the transfer of state property in the event of succession, the regime of state succession would also relate to 'problems connected with the cultural heritage—pictures, sculptures, statues, works of art, zoological, botanical,

[117] UN Doc. A/CN.4/292, para. 136.
[118] Ibid. paras 125–126.
[119] UN Doc. A/CN.4/322, para. 52.
[120] Ibid. para. 52.
[121] Ibid. para. 46.
[122] Ibid. para. 49.

archaeological or mineralogical specimens, etc.... provided that, and in so far as, these works of art constitute State property'.[123] According to the definition of 'state property', under Article 8 of the 1983 Vienna Convention, such objects would be regulated by the regime of state succession if 'at the date of the succession of States, [they] were, according to the internal law of the predecessor State, owned by that State'. Such an approach was also confirmed by the ILC, which commented that the passing of the works of art be 'covered either by the provisions relating to State property or is dealt with as the question of their return or restitution, rather than as a problem of State succession'.[124] In this view, it also alluded to the activity of UNESCO in the field of return and restitution of cultural property.

b) Historic archives

The question of state succession to archives constitutes one of the three major topics covered by the 1983 Vienna Convention. Bedjaoui carried out in-depth research on the subject, though the actual preparatory works on draft articles on this matter were facilitated by the well-established state practice of distribution of archives, based on the principles of territorial provenance and functional pertinence. Moreover, the issue was subject to the parallel regulatory activity of UNESCO and the International Council of Archives,[125] and the final text of the 1983 Vienna Convention was revised by a special international working group.[126]

Importantly, UNESCO stressed the great importance of archives 'for the general, cultural, political and economic history of the countries which were under foreign occupation, administration and domination', and called for restoration of such fonds.[127] In 1978, in his report to the 20th UNESCO General Conference, M'Bow noted that archives were 'universally recognized as an essential part of the heritage of every national community.' In addition, they were 'indispensable in the development of national awareness and identity, they constitute a basic part of the cultural property of States.'[128] He recalled that the inclusion of archives within the broad definition of cultural property was fully recognized.[129] In fact, the 1954

[123] Ibid. para. 40.

[124] Report of the International Law Commission on the Work of Its Thirty-Third Session, 4 May–24 July 1981, UN Doc. A/36/10, at Art. 9 Commentary, para. 6, *YILC* (1981–2), at 51, UN Doc. A/CONF.117/4, at 51.

[125] For the list of major documents, see Council of Europe (ed), *Reference Dossier on Archival Claims* (Council of Europe Publ, 1997), reprinted in *Proceedings, Thirty-First International Conference of the Round Table on Archives*, 208–68.

[126] 'Professional advice formulated in 1983 on the Vienna Convention on succession of States in respect of State property, archives and debts', Part III, State archives (Art. 19 to 31)', in *Proceedings* (n 1254) 248–49.

[127] UNESCO Doc.18C/Resolutions, 4.212.

[128] Report of the Director-General on the Study Regarding Problems Involved in the Transfer of Documents from Archives in the Territory of Certain Countries to the Country of Their Origin, UNESCO Doc. 20 C/102 (1978), para. 7.

[129] Ibid. para. 8.

Hague Convention and the 1970 UNESCO Convention included archives in their definitions of cultural property.[130]

In this view, Bedjaoui differentiated so-called administrative and judicial records from historical archives, comprising public libraries and museums, which form part of national identity and national cultural heritage.[131] Special emphasis was placed on the archives relating to the former colonies, removed by colonial powers before the termination of their territorial sovereignty. Accordingly, Bedjaoui made a clear distinction between: 1) 'historical archives proper, which antedate the beginning of colonization of the territory;' 2) archives of the colonial period, relating to the *imperium* and *dominium* of the metropolitan country and to its colonial policy in the territory more generally; and 3) 'purely administrative and technical archives relating to the current administration of the territory.'[132] With reference to the first group, 'which may have been removed by the former metropolitan country', he held that: 'the principle of transfer should be firmly and immediately applied. These archives antedate colonization, they are the product of the land and spring from its soil; they are bound up with the land where they came into existence and they contain its history and its cultural heritage.'[133] This approach was subsequently included in the provisions of the Convention, specially drafted for the newly independent states recognizing the priority of the right of peoples to 'development, to information about their history and to their cultural heritage' over contractual agreements between the predecessor state and the successor state with regard to the distribution of state archives (Article 28).

In 1979,[134] Bedjaoui presented a very detailed reconstruction of international practice with regard to the transfer of state archives and libraries.[135] Moreover, he alluded to the UNESCO and UN actions explicitly linking the question of allocation of archives with the problem of the protection and restitution of cultural heritage.[136] Accordingly, the distribution of historical archives which are of great cultural value should be determined in the same way as other cultural objects.

The final solution proposed by Bedajaoui was to provide a very broad definition which would cover all 'documents' presenting a feature of 'writing'. This definition was intended to comprise all materials from all time-periods, but it excluded works of art 'as such and not as archival pieces'.[137] Nonetheless, Bedjaoui noticed that in some civilizations 'documents had been also expressed through the medium of objects of art'.[138] Therefore, he argued that the Convention should

[130] Art. 1(a) of the 1954 Hague Convention, and Art. 1(j) of the 1970 UNESCO Convention.

[131] Mohammed Bedjaoui, 'Third Report on the Succession of States in Respect of Matters Other Than Treaties', UN Doc. A/CN.4/226, *YILC* (1970)2, 151 ff.

[132] Ibid. at 158. [133] Ibid. at 158.

[134] Mohammed Bedjaoui, 'Eleventh Report on the Succession of States in Respect of Matters Other Than Treaties', UN Doc. A/CN.4/322 and Corr. 1 and Add. 1 and 2.

[135] UN Doc. A/CN.4/322.

[136] Mohammed Bedjaoui, 'Eleventh Report on the Succession of States' (n 134).

[137] UN Doc. A/36/10, at 51, para 6.

[138] Mohammed Bedjaoui, 'Thirteenth Report on the Succession of States in Respect of Matters Other Than Treaties', UN Doc. A/CN.4/345 and Add. 1-3, para. 227.

leave the determination of this concept to the internal law of each state.[139] It was further explained that:

> [d]epending on the country, the 'state archives' may or may not include works of art, such as curios, valuable ancient manuscripts, illuminations, medal collections, etc.... Such works of art are to be treated in the same way as actual documents when they have been defined by the internal law of the predecessor state as state 'archives.'
>
> Naturally, the absence of such a definition in no way implies that works of art such as paintings, statuettes, sculptures, icons, the contents of collections, etc., are excluded from succession. As 'state property,' works of art of these kinds will be affected by a succession of states as specified in the articles governing state property. It is in any case clear that, all questions of the internal law of state aside, paintings by the great masters have nothing in common with the papers or documents that make up 'state archives'. They can be only governed by that part of draft that deals with succession in respect of state property.[140]

The final definition of archives under the 1983 Convention contained important restrictions however. Accordingly, it referred only to 'documents of whatever date and kind, produced or received by the predecessor State in the exercise of its functions which, at the date of the succession of States, belonged to the predecessor State according to its internal law and were preserved by it directly or under its control as archives for whatever purpose' (Article 20). Thus, the regime under the 1983 Convention did not cover the allocation and distribution of cultural property other than state-owned property and did not provide an explicit distinction between historical archives and 'ordinary' ones. Moreover, the fact that the definition of state archives depended on the internal law of the predecessor state virtually excluded libraries and museums from the operation of the convention. However, it was acknowledged that there were certain areas in which these concepts overlapped.[141]

4.6 The 1983 Vienna Convention

At the start of the 1980s, work accelerated on the final articles on succession of states in respect of state property, archives, and debts. From 1980 to 1982, the UN General Assembly accepted the work already undertaken by the ILC and decided to convene a United Nations Conference on the Succession of States in respect of State Property, Archives and Debt.[142] The conference was held in Vienna from 1 March to 8 April 1983 and resulted in the adoption, on 7 April 1983, of the Vienna Convention on Succession of States in respect of State Property, Archives and Debts. The core aim of this instrument was to regulate the most critical economic aspects of the ongoing process of decolonization. Indeed, the Final Act of

[139] Ibid. at 248. [140] Ibid.

[141] UN Doc. A/CN.4/226, Bedjaoui, 'Third Report on Succession of States' (n 131) 161, UN Doc. A/CN.4/322, paras 6–17, 132, UN Doc. A/CONF.117/C.1/SR.18, paras 17–19.

[142] UN Doc. A/RES/36/163, UN Doc. A/RES/36/113 and UN Doc. A/RES/37/11.

the 1983 Conference included a special resolution concerning peoples struggling against colonialism, alien domination, alien occupation, racial discrimination, and apartheid.[143] In particular, it recognized that such peoples 'possess permanent sovereignty over their resources and natural wealth and their rights to development, information concerning their history and to the conservation of their cultural heritage.' Therefore, the implementation of the 1983 Vienna Convention needed to be followed by the observance of these rights by former metropolitan states.

This post-colonial aspect of state succession was also explicit in the preamble to the Convention, which emphasized the importance of the principle of self-determination and the universal respect and observance of human rights and fundamental freedoms. As regards the definitions applied, the 1983 Vienna Convention provided the already accepted notion of 'succession of States', which consisted in 'the replacement of one State by another in the responsibility for the international relations of territory' (Article 2(1)(a)). In this regard, special consideration was attached to the process of decolonization by introducing the concept of 'newly independent State', defined as 'a successor State the territory of which, immediately before the date of the succession of States, was a dependent territory for the international relations of which the predecessor State was responsible' (Article 2(1)(e)). The regime of the 1983 Vienna Convention applies only to relations between states[144] and it is not retroactive (Article 4), which means that in all cases of state succession preceding the entry into force of the Convention, the customary rules of international law operative up until that date would be applicable. However, it was provided that every successor state may make a declaration that its own succession would be regulated by the 1983 Vienna Convention, even prior to it entering into force, 'in relation to any other contracting State or State Party to the Convention which makes a declaration accepting the declaration of the successor State' (Article 4(2)). Yet, these exemptions from the rule of non-retroactivity were of scant relevance for the process of decolonization, which in practice was concluded beyond the codified regime.

Although the Final Act of the 1983 Vienna Conference explicitly made reference to the right of peoples to their cultural heritage, the Convention itself did not provide special regulations in terms of the passing of cultural property. Nonetheless, it was recognized that some of its sections could also be extrapolated to regulate state succession to certain aspects of cultural property.[145]

[143] UN Doc. A/CONF.117/15.

[144] Compare Rudolf Streinz, 'Succession of States in Assets *and* Liabilities—A New Régime? The 1983 Vienna Convention on State Succession in respect of State Property, Archives and Debts', *GYIL* 26(1986), 198–237, at 208.

[145] UN Doc. A/CN.4/226, at 68–71; UN Doc. A/CN.4/259, para. 12; UN Doc. A/CN.4/322, para. 6.

4.6.1 State succession to state property

As already mentioned, the 1983 Vienna Convention provides for rules on the transfer of only one category of public property; property owned by the predecessor state according to its internal law at the date of state succession (Article 7). Other introductory articles on state succession to state property confirm general principles of customary international law, including the principle of the passing of state property without compensation (Article 11), and the protection of the rights of third states (Article 12). Moreover, under Article 13, the 1983 Vienna Convention introduced the principle of preservation and safety of state property, defined as a duty of the predecessor state to 'take all measures to prevent damage or destruction to State property' subject to state succession.

The 1983 Vienna Convention regulates the passing of state property with reference to five specific categories of state succession: 1) transfer of a part of the territory of a state (Article 14); 2) a newly independent state (Article 15); 3) the uniting of states (Article 16); 4) separation of a part or parts of the territory of a state (Article 17); 5) dissolution of a state (Article 18).[146] Within the framework of such a division, it then introduces different regimes for succession to state property. As a general rule, the passing of immovable property is determined by its location and passes to the successor state. The more complex regulations refer to movable property. In respect of cession, the 1983 Vienna Convention adopts the principle of primacy of a succession (devolution) agreement concluded between the predecessor state and the successor state. Accordingly, 'the passing of state property of the predecessor state to the successor state is to be settled by agreement between them' (Article 14(1)). In the absence of such an agreement, the successor state receives the movable state property of the predecessor connected with its activity in respect of the territory subject to state succession (Article 14(2)(a)). In the case of unification, all state property of the predecessor passes to the successor state.

The regime on the passing of state property in cases of secession and dissolution (Articles 17 and 18) also provides for the primacy of the contractual agreement between the predecessor and successor states. If, however, there has been no agreement, state property of the predecessor is distributed according to its location. Hence, the movable state property of the predecessor state, connected with its activity in the territory subject to state succession and located therein passes to the successor state (Article 17(1)(b), Article 18(1)(c)). Moreover, the successor state is entitled to other state property of the predecessor situated outside its territory in equitable proportions (Article 17(1)(c), Article 18(1)(d)).[147]

Finally, a special regime on state succession of state property was introduced with regard to states that emerged in the process of decolonization. In such cases, the 1983 Vienna Convention does recognize the primacy of succession agreements.

[146] As explained in the Introduction to this book, such a classification of different types of state succession is not perceived as exhaustive; ie it does not include incorporation of a territory.

[147] Władysław Czapliński, 'Equity and Equitable Principles in the Law of State Succession', in Mojmir Mrak (ed), *Succession of States* (Nijhoff, 1999), 61–73.

Furthermore, it provides that even if such an agreement is concluded between the predecessor state and the newly independent state, it 'shall not infringe the principle of the permanent sovereignty of every people over its wealth and natural resources' (Article 15(4)). The representatives of newly independent states perceived such a right as constituting *jus cogens*, and therefore it was claimed that an agreement violating such a peremptory norm of international law should be void *ab initio*.[148] Other provisions were also very favourable for newly independent states (Article 15(1)). Accordingly, state property of a predecessor located in the territory of a newly independent state passes to that state. A former colony is also entitled to property that belonged to its territory and which, during the period of dependence, became the property of the predecessor state. In addition, it also succeeds to any state property of the predecessor state situated outside its territory if it has contributed to its creation during colonial dependence. The passing of such property is determined in proportion to the contribution of the dependent territory.

According to the definition of state property under the 1983 Vienna Convention, it seems that its regime may also cover cultural property owned by the predecessor state, such as state museums, monuments, collections, etc. Moreover, the general principle of preservation and safety of state property formulated as a duty of the predecessor state, already recognized in international practice, may potentially play a crucial role for the protection of vulnerable cultural items in interstate negotiations following state succession. However, the two main criteria for the passing of state property under the 1983 Vienna Convention—the territorial location of the property at the date of succession, and the connection with the activity of the predecessor state in the territory subject to state succession—hardly reflect the nature of cultural heritage disputes in cases of state succession. In fact, such controversies between successor and predecessor states in the matter of the allocation of cultural material usually focus on the issue of territorial provenance and significance for national cultural heritage. Yet the principle of equity applicable to the distribution of property in cases of secession and dissolution may be very useful, and it has already been tested in international practice, particularly in the case of the division of artistic collections between Hungary and Austria in the 1930s.

It appears that the provisions on the passing of state property in cases of decolonization potentially have the most far-reaching consequences for the problems of the allocation and distribution of cultural property. Indeed, a newly independent state is entitled to property that 'belonged' to its territory before and during dependence on a foreign power and to which it 'contributed'. These two principles may arguably constitute a convenient basis for claims for the recovery of cultural material. Such a demand would not, however, be founded on the principle of cultural links; rather, it would be driven by the concept of reversing colonial exploitation. In other words, an ex-colony shall succeed to state property of the

[148] See Gennadii Mikhailovich Danilenko, *Law-Making in the International Community* (Nijhoff, 1993), at 243.

predecessor that came from its territory during the period of dependence, and/or property created with the contribution of its resources.[149]

4.6.2 State archives

The section of the 1983 Vienna Convention on succession of states to state archives referred more explicitly to the question of cultural heritage. However, it did not make any distinction between administrative and judicial records, and historic archives. As already noted, the Convention provided a very broad definition of state archives (Article 20). A certain vagueness in the definition was deliberate. According to Bedjaoui, a clear distinction between these two groups of state archives would not be feasible in terms of the general scope of the Convention.[150] Moreover, he also rejected the possibility of an enumerative definition since 'this would be unwise, for lists are never exhaustive and anything that might be overlooked or omitted could well be considered as unaffected by state succession.'[151]

Generally speaking, the 1983 Vienna Convention confirmed the customary principle of succession of state archives based on territorial pertinence. With regard to all categories of state succession, the part of state archives of the predecessor state indispensable for the normal administration of the territory passed to the successor state (Article 27 (2) (a)), Article 28 (1) (b), Article 30 (1) (a), Article 31 (1) (a)). Moreover, other archives of the predecessor state, which relate 'exclusively or principally' (Article 27 (2) (b), Article 28 (1) (c)) or 'directly' (Article 30 (1) (b), Article 31 (10 (b)) to the territory concerned also pass to the successor state. The successor states are also entitled to obtain, on a reciprocal basis, appropriate reproductions of state archives of the predecessor states, connected with the interests of the territory subject to state succession.

The cultural heritage aspect of state succession to state archives is to be found under the articles of the 1983 Vienna Convention on a newly independent state (Article 28(7)), separation of part or parts of the territory of a state (Article 30(3)), and dissolution of a state (Article 31(4)). Accordingly, they provide that agreements concluded between the predecessor state and successor state 'in regard to state archives of the predecessor state shall not infringe the right of the peoples of those states to development, to information about their history, and to their cultural heritage.' At the 1983 Vienna Conference, almost all the developing states treated the right to cultural heritage as a part of *jus cogens*, analogous to the already discussed right to natural resources.[152] The rights of newly independent states to dispersed historical archival material are also stressed under Articles 28 (1) (a), and Article 28 (4). The first provides that the archives, belonging to the territory to which the succession of states relates and which subsequently passed

[149] Nieć, 'Sovereign Rights to Cultural Property' (n 47) 245.
[150] Bedjaoui, 'Thirteenth Report on the Succession of States' (n 138) para. 247.
[151] Ibid. para. 245.
[152] See Danilenko, *Law-Making in the International Community* (n 148) 243.

to the predecessor state during the period of dependence, shall pass to the successor state. The second imposes on the predecessor state an obligation to 'cooperate with the successor state in efforts to recover any archives which, having belonged to the territory to which the succession of states relates, were dispersed during the period of dependence.' For this reason, the ILC noted that 'special rules for cases in which third states had profited from colonial occupation' should be constructed.[153] It seems, however, that the rights of former colonial territories to obtain important archival records have been significantly restricted by the general principle of the preservation of the integral character of groups of state archives, under Article 25 of the 1983 Vienna Convention.

4.6.3 The failure of the 1983 Vienna Convention

The actual proceedings of the 1983 Vienna Conference were determined in large part by the controversies between developing countries supported by the Soviet bloc, on the one hand, and the developed Western countries, on the other. The crux of this debate centred on the provisions on newly independent states. The former colonial countries argued that such a special regime was essential to their development. Moreover, they claimed that the controversial provisions of the 1983 Vienna Convention were in full harmony with the progressive tendencies in international law, aimed at reversing the legacy of colonialism.[154] Western states perceived the solutions applied by the 1983 Vienna Convention in respect of post-colonial territories as tools merely destined to achieve certain political goals and openly directed against their interests.[155] Thus, they did not support the final text of the Convention. Accordingly, the Convention was adopted with 54 votes in favour (mainly developing and socialist states), with 11 votes against (Western states). This lack of agreement resulted in the fact that until the end of the Cold War, the Convention did not obtain any accession and it has never entered into force.

4.7 Conclusion

The period 1945–89 saw an extensive drive towards codification and development of international law in the spheres of cultural heritage and state succession. It raises the question, however, as to whether and how the principles governing state succession in matters of tangible cultural heritage really altered in relation to those already evolved prior to the Second World War.

Undoubtedly, international legislation on the protection of cultural heritage reaffirmed the importance of the links between cultural material and national territory. It has been widely recognized that each culture deserves equal treatment

[153] UN Doc. A/7209/Rev.1, para. 67, Vrdoljak, *International Law* (n 14) 203.
[154] UN Doc. A/CONF.117/C.1/SR.13. [155] Ibid.

and protection. Moreover, the impoverishment of cultural heritage of one country is not only an internal issue but is the concern of humanity as a whole, as 'damage to cultural property belonging to any people whatsoever means damage to the cultural heritage of all mankind, since each people makes its contribution to the culture of the world'. These considerations resulted in the international obligations towards cultural property under the 1954 Hague Convention, the 1954 Hague Protocol and the 1970 UNESCO Convention: 1) the obligation to protect cultural property in the event of armed conflict and to restore such items removed from militarily occupied territories; 2) the obligation to protect cultural property in times of peace against illicit traffic of movable cultural property through the means of the procedural principle of co-operation. Apparently, these two regimes reinforced the principle of territoriality governing the allocation of cultural property in state succession, particularly in situations when the object in question was removed from the territory subject to succession in the event of armed conflict or in violation of national law on the protection of cultural heritage.

In addition, the recognition and exaltation of the general interest of humanity as a whole in the safeguarding and conservation of certain cultural manifestations of outstanding universal value arguably modified the principles of state succession. While it is true that the interwar international practice of state succession to cultural property often applied the non-binding principle of non-dispersal of universally ranked collections, the World Heritage regime provided a legal duty on the territorial state as well as a common commitment of all states to protect specific monuments and sites for the benefit of future generations. It appears that inscription of a cultural property on the WHL entails its protection at the time of state succession.

The following observations relate to the principle of self-determination and collective cultural rights. This issue needs to be discussed with regard to both its external and internal dimensions. The first recognizes the existence of the right of every people to its culture, and cultural heritage. From such a standpoint, the newly independent states developed the concept of moral rights vested in them against the former colonial powers in terms of restitution of cultural property removed during the era of colonial exploitation and oppression. Accordingly, it has been argued that at the time of independence they are entitled to regain their cultural identity and dispersed cultural property. The second dimension refers to collective cultural rights of human groups and communities. As explained, the post-Second World War practice in Central and Eastern Europe tacitly recognized the right of displaced populations to migrate in possession of their most venerated cultural properties. To the same end, a new post-1945 human rights regime recognized the rights of minorities to develop and enjoy their culture on an equal footing with the rights of states to develop their national cultures. Thus, successor states acceding to international human rights instruments undertake the obligations towards minority cultures and their tangible heritage. In the period from 1945 to 1989, the nature and extent of these obligations were, however, disputable.

Finally, it became clear that the codification of international law on state succession was pursued in full awareness of the parallel development of cultural heritage law and the post-colonial restitution debate. The regime under the 1983 Vienna Convention covered only those aspects of cultural property and historical archives which constituted the state property of the predecessor state according to its internal law at the time of state succession. Moreover, the two main criteria for the passing of state property under the 1983 Vienna Convention—the territorial location of property at the date of succession, and the connection with the activity of the predecessor state in the territory subject to state succession—hardly reflect the nature of cultural heritage disputes in cases of state succession. Accordingly, such controversies usually entail the issue of territorial provenance and significance for national cultural heritage. These principles were not reflected in the text of the 1983 Vienna Convention. Thus, it could be argued that its regime is of limited application to cultural property disputes. In fact, the most complex issues related to removal from dependent territories prior to their independence have been deliberatively left to the system of international cultural cooperation created by UNESCO, favouring bilateral agreements rather than comprehensive solutions. However, it appears that, in practice, the principle of cultural cooperation strongly promoted by many international bodies provided a convenient basis for dealing with such controversies, arising from different instances of state succession.

PART THREE

BUILDING A NEW CONSENSUS ON CULTURAL HERITAGE

State Succession After 1989

The essence of a country's long cultural continuity is represented by the universal synthesis of life phenomena: the bridge and its fortress—with the rich archaeological layers from pre-Ottoman period, religious edifices, residential zones—mahalas, arable lands, houses, bazaar, its public life in the streets and water. Architecture here presented a symbol of tolerance: a common life of Muslims, Christians and Jews. Mosques, churches, and synagogues existed side-by-side indicating that in Bosnia, the Roman Catholic Croats with their Western European culture, the eastern Orthodox Serbs with their elements of Byzantine culture, and the Sephardic Jews continued to live together with the Bosniak-Muslims for more than four centuries.

Bosnia and Herzegovina '*Nomination Dossier "The Old City of Mostar"*', January 2005, <http://whc.unesco.org/en/list/946/documents>, at 5.

1. The Contracting Parties shall cooperate in the preservation and nurture of the European cultural heritage. They shall support the preservation of monuments.
2. The Contracting Parties shall take special care of the places and cultural assets in their respective territories that bear witness to historical events and cultural and scientific achievements of the other side, and shall provide free and unhindered access to them, or endeavour to see that such access is provided, where the state does not have authority to guarantee it. Such places and cultural assets shall be placed under the protection of the laws of the respective Contracting Parties. The Contracting Parties shall take joint initiatives in this area, in a spirit of understanding and reconciliation.
3. The Contracting Parties shall endeavour, in the same spirit, to solve problems relating to cultural assets and archives, beginning with individual cases.

Article 28 of the Treaty between Federal Republic of Germany and Poland on Good Neighbourly Relations and Friendly Cooperation, signed at Bonn on 17 June 1991, 1708 UNTS 502.

5

State Succession in State Property and Tangible Cultural Heritage in the Post-Cold War Context

During the Kosovo War, just before the NATO military intervention against the Federal Republic of Yugoslavia (FRY) in spring 1999, the Serbian administration ordered the transfer of the most precious archaeological objects (around 1200 exhibits) from the Kosovo Museum in Pristina to a temporary exhibition to Belgrade. After the war, the newly established UN administration of Kosovo promptly initiated the campaign for the return of the 'kidnapped' artefacts. The crux of this controversy centred on the 6000-year-old Neolithic terracotta figurine known as the *Goddess on the Throne*. It was discovered in 1956 near Pristina, and since then has been considered one of the most significant of Kosovo's art treasures, evidence of the venerable cultural legacy and ancient history of the country.[1]

The return of the figurine was demanded in particular by the UN Special Representative of the Secretary-General for Kosovo, Michael Steiner. In 2002, he successfully recovered it from Belgrade on the occasion of the UN–FRY talks on the restoration of property displaced in the event of military conflict in Kosovo.[2] This return was not seen as a mere reversal of war displacement and removal. Indeed, the UN administration and Kosovo's museum officials explicitly linked the restitution of the *Goddess on the Throne* to the process of stabilization within the country, as the figurine came to be viewed as a representation of the cultural wealth of the whole of Kosovo.[3] With regard to this, Steiner said:

> What is truly remarkable is that she is not the expression of any ethnic group, but represents something that transcends ethnicity or politics—she represents the culture and richness of the whole region.[4]

[1] Robert Elsie, *Historical Dictionary of Kosova* (2nd edn, Scarecrow Press, 2004), 18.

[2] 'SRSG Michael Steiner Brings Goddess Home to Kosovo', Friday 31 May 2002, UN MIK/PR/746.

[3] Ibid.

[4] UNMIK *Focus Kosovo*, 2 June 2002, <http://www.unmikonline.org/pub/focuskos/june02/focuskchron.htm>, last retrieved on 15 March 2010, currently not available online.

Furthermore, when Kosovo declared independence in 2008, the *Goddess on the Throne* became central in the search for commonly acceptable symbols for a new state. Accordingly, it has been seriously considered as part of the new state emblem of Kosovo, 'a symbol of the heritage and cultural identity of Kosovo … acceptable for all the communities in Kosova because it does not have an ethnic background'.[5] The significance of this artefact was also enforced by including its image in the coat of arms of the capital city, Pristina, and the foundation of Kosovo's new state order of the *Goddess on the Throne.*

Today, the figurine is displayed in the recently re-opened Kosovo Museum in a setting dedicated to the prehistoric art of the country.[6] None of the other archaeological objects displaced by the Serbian administration has been returned, though Kosovo's authorities have constantly raised demands for their return. Importantly, in 2007, the Special Envoy of the UN Secretary-General, Martii Athisaari, recommended to the UN Security Council (2007) that for the future peaceful status of Kosovo, it was necessary for the Serbian authorities to return the archaeological and ethnological exhibits which were taken on loan from the museums of Kosovo in 1998–99. This requirement was subsequently incorporated into the 2007 UN Comprehensive Proposal for the Kosovo Status Settlement.[7]

The case of the *Goddess on the Throne* can be simply classified as a typical situation of restitution of cultural property removed in the event of armed conflict, which does not relate to the question of state succession, however, this is only partially true. Apart from the contested international status of Kosovo as a sovereign independent state and the question regarding the legitimacy of the 1999 NATO military intervention, this case actually constitutes an example of the allocation of state cultural property in the situation of separation of part of a state. Accordingly, during the process of emancipation, Kosovo claimed its sovereign rights to state art collections created in its territory prior to separation and removed during violent secession from the predecessor state. Moreover, the role assigned to the *Goddess on the Throne* is emblematic for the broader discourse on the contribution of cultural heritage to the stability of states and their boundaries.[8] In fact, it has been a general tendency of many new multi-ethnic states to search for common cultural symbols acceptable to all members of society in their past, since the possession of iconic cultural objects constitutes one of the major elements of state building and state stability. In this light, the return of the *Goddess on the Throne* to Pristina needs to be seen as a tool used to form common cultural ground between different groups within a new state, essential for its statehood.

[5] See David Charter, 'Wanted: New Flag and Anthem for Kosovo. The Symbols Are Being Sought for When the Province Declares Independence as the Republic of Kosova', *The Times*, 11 February 2008; also see Nick Thorpe, 'Kosovo Contest for State Symbols', BBC News, Pristina, Kosovo, 4 June 2007, <http://news.bbc.co.uk/2/hi/europe/6718105.stm>, accessed on 13 February 2015.

[6] Gail Warrander and Verena Knaus, *Kosovo* (2nd edn, Brandt Travel Guides 2008), 125.

[7] The Comprehensive Proposal for Kosovo Status Settlement, UN Doc. S/2007/168/Add.1, at 38.

[8] Cfr Kerstin Odendahl and Mayte Peters, 'The Significance of Cultural Heritage for State Stability and Its Protection by International Law', in Julia Raue and Patrick Sutter (eds), *Facets and Practices of State Building* (Nijhoff, 2009), 263–79.

It appears that international recognition of the value of cultural heritage for both human communities inhabiting the territory of a new state and for the cultural identity of such a state as a whole has finally accommodated the postulates raised at the time of the codification of the law on state succession. In addition, the case of the *Goddess on the Throne* has also demonstrated the increasing impact of the principles of international law for the protection of cultural heritage on the processes of dismemberment and creation of states. In particular, it reaffirmed both the obligation to restore cultural property removed in violent (military conflict) circumstances and emphasized the importance of such objects for the collective local cultural identity and its cultural development.

This chapter deals with the recent wave of state succession processes that occurred after the fall of the Iron Curtain in 1989. The dissolution of the post-Yalta structure in Europe launched a series of political and territorial changes in Eastern-bloc countries. With the dissolution of the Soviet Union, Yugoslavia, and Czechoslovakia, and with the unification of Germany, several issues with regard to the succession of states need to be addressed.[9] These include issues of continuity or discontinuity of states, state identity, accession to international treaties and obligations, distribution of state property and debts, and rights of individuals and minorities, etc.[10] Many of these are extremely contentious and cause lively debates among scholars. It appears that the post-Cold War process of state succession is not yet over and that some developments in this regard are anticipated, such as the international status of Kosovo, the secessionist movements in Georgia, Moldova, Ukraine, and Russia, etc. In particular, the case of Russian unilateral annexation of Crimea in 2014 will take centre stage for some years to come. Moreover, a number of questions arise not only from the current territorial and political reconfigurations, but also from the previous post-Second World War arrangements and agreements, which steep the issue in uncertainty.

[9] For a general overview of the issues of the post-Cold War state succession, see *inter alia* Matthew Craven, *The Decolonization of International Law: State Succession and the Law of Treaties* (OUP, 2007); Hélène Hamant, *Démembrement de l'URSS et problèmes de succession d'États* (Bruylant, 2007), Pierre Michel Eisemann and Martti Koskenniemi (eds), *La Succession d'États: la codification à l'épreuve des faits/State Succession: Codification Tested against the Facts* (Nijhoff, 2000); Mojmir Mrak (ed), *Succession of States* (Nijhoff, 1999); Vladimir D. Degan, 'Création et disparition de l'État (à la lumière du démembrement de trois fédérations multiethniques en Europe)', *RCADI* 279(1999), 195–375; Sir Arthur Watts, 'State Succession—Some Recent Practical Legal Problems', in Peter Selmer and Rüdiger Wolfrum (eds), *Liber amicorum Günther Jaenicke* (Springer, 1998), 405–26; Brigitte Stern, 'La Succession d'États', *RCADI* 262(1996), 176–424, Hélène Ruiz Fabri and Pascal Boniface (eds), *Succession d'États en Europe de l'Est et avenir de la sécurité en Europe: actes du colloque du 6 avril 1995 organisé à l'Institut International d'Administration Publique par le Cedin Paris XIII et l'IRIS,* (L.G.D.J., 1995); Geneviève Burdeau and Brigitte Stern (eds), *Dissolution, continuation et succession en Europe de l'Est* (Montchrestien, 1994); Rein Müllerson, *International Law, Rights and Politics: Developments in Eastern Europe and the CIS* (Routledge, 1994); Rein Müllerson, 'The Continuity and Succession of States, by Reference to the Former USSR and Yugoslavia', *ICLQ* 42(1993)3, 473–93; Michael Bothe and Christian Schmidt, 'Sur quelques questions de succession posées par la dissolution de l'URSS et celle de la Yougoslavie', *RGDIP* 96(1992)4, 811–42.

[10] Hanna Bokor-Szegő, 'Questions of State Identity and State Succession in Eastern and Central Europe', in Mojmir Mrak (ed), *Succession of States* (Nijhoff, 1999), 95–108.

This chapter considers the dissolution of three multinational states of the former Eastern bloc: Czechoslovakia, the Soviet Union, and Yugoslavia. It focuses on the approaches taken within the broader problem of succession to state movable property and their relationship to the allocation and distribution of cultural objects. It discusses the nature and principles driving international agreements on this matter and their subsequent implementation in state practice. It explains that such settlements broadly applied the terminology adopted by the international instruments on the protection of cultural heritage, and usually treated the question of cultural property as a certain exemption from the general regime on succession to state property. This chapter argues that the post-Cold War state practice often confused state succession with other problems related to the restitution and return of cultural property, causing politically sensitive historical debates. The nature of such a discourse on historical rights and wrongs has hindered the settlement of the majority of pending problems and claims.

5.1 State succession revisited

In a memorable article published in the 1995 volume of the *Finnish Yearbook of International Law*,[11] Malcolm Shaw argued that 'the rules of State succession are marked either by their absence or their inconsistency'.[12] Moreover, 'the claims made by the States themselves particularly concerned plus the reactions thereto by third States and by the international community in institutional form constitute the basic framework of the subject area and practice demonstrates a range of possible solutions to the problems of succession invariably posed'.[13] Thus, 'as long as the international community is founded upon States, the difficulties of State succession will be with us and the interests of stability will require an agreed framework for their resolution'.[14]

Drafted in the light of the ongoing processes of dissolution of the Soviet Union, Czechoslovakia, and Yugoslavia, Shaw pinpointed the weakness of doctrinal responses to the reality of the creation and extinction of states and their legal consequences. In this regard, the core issue at stake referred to the categorization/typology of such situations as well as the issues of reciprocal concepts of succession, identity, and continuity of states and their relevance for actual state practice.

5.1.1 Continuity, identity, and state succession

The core question relating to the processes of state succession is whether states involved in such transformations actually form completely new international legal persons or whether these processes do not affect their legal personality and identity. In principle, an answer to this question may have a tremendous impact on the

[11] Malcolm N. Shaw, 'State Succession Revisited', *Finnish Yearbook of International Law* 6(1995), 34–98, at 34.

[12] Ibid. at 97.

[13] Ibid. at 98.

[14] Ibid.

continuity of rights, obligations, international responsibilities, and the actual role of these states on the international stage.

To a certain extent, international legal theory seems to favour the concept of 'personification' of states as fixed organic entities, 'isolated both in time and space',[15] remaining stable, unaffected by political, legal, and territorial changes that they may experience.[16] In this context, the key question concerns the distinction between the concepts of 'identity' and 'continuity' of states. The first relates to the comparison of the pre- and post-succession states in order to determine whether the latter is identical with the former (pre-existing) one.[17] This concept has usually been debated through the lens of state sovereignty.[18] Such a perspective has allowed some authors to determine the factors which may or may not affect the identity of a state, and which usually overlap with the basic criteria of statehood.[19] A different approach recalls the identity of international rights and obligations rather than criteria of statehood.[20] Thus, identity serves to define whether or not the state concerned retains its legal identity, that is, whether or not it continues its personality as a state.[21] In this way, it 'provides the key to determining the proper set of norms that are to be applied in a given case'.[22] Conversely, 'continuity' functions as one of the fundamental assumptions of public international law.[23] The continuity of states is assumed notwithstanding the changes of their governments, constitutions, ideological foundations, populations, and territories.[24] Accordingly, the state exists as long as its final and undoubted extinction will be ultimately determined in the light of objective, achieved facts. Thus, the identity of the state is not questioned if its continuity is accepted. Once the continuity is ruptured, its identity generally falls.[25] Yet this formula poses certain difficulties particularly in the case of a resurrection of a state following belligerent occupation.

International law makes a fundamental distinction between state continuity and state succession.[26] The first refers to a situation when one state continues to exist regardless of sometimes drastic transformations of its political system, government, territory, and population, whereas state succession concerns the replacement of one state by another in respect of a given territory and people living therein.[27] This distinction does not, however, seem to be based on clear-cut

[15] Craven, *The Decolonization of International Law* (n 9) 52.

[16] Compare Mathew Craven, 'The Problem of State Succession and the Identity of States under International Law', *EJIL* 9(1998)1, 142–62, at 152–53.

[17] Josef L. Kunz, 'Identity of States under International Law', *AJIL* 49 (1955) 1, 68–76, at 68.

[18] See Craven, *The Decolonization of International Law* (n 9), 23 ff. and the literature quoted therein.

[19] James Crawford, *The Creation of States in International Law* (2nd edn, OUP, 2011), 669; Craven 'The Problem of State Succession' (n 16) 142, 147; Pekka T. Talari, 'State Succession in Respect of Debts: The Effect of State Succession in the 1990's on the Rules of Law', *Finnish Yearbook of International Law* 7 (1996), 134–79, at 144–45; Stern, 'La Succession d'États' (n 9) 80.

[20] Krystyna Marek, *Identity and Continuity of States in Public International Law* (2nd edn, Librairie Droz, 1968), at 68–76.

[21] Craven, 'The Problem of State Succession' (n 16) 152.

[22] Ibid. at 153.

[23] Crawford, *The Creation of States in International Law* (n 19) 667.

[24] Ibid.

[25] Cf Marek, *Identity and Continuity of States* (n 20) 7–9.

[26] Crawford, *The Creation of States in International Law* (n 19) 668.

[27] Ibid.

criteria. In particular, the determination of whether a certain factual situation gives rise to state succession or constitutes a case of continuity of the 'same' state depends on actual claims addressed by states involved and their international recognition. Indeed, 'in practice the recognition of claims to continuity or discontinuity plays a major role, even though the position taken by particular states is not constitutive'.[28]

5.1.2 Categorization of the post-1989 cases of succession and continuity

The question of identity and continuity of states was not greatly debated at the time of decolonization and subsequent codification of the law of state succession. The situation changed after 1989 with the profound political and territorial transformations in Central and Eastern Europe. These events prompted the international community to reconsider the existing legal regime on this matter. Clearly, the political and territorial changes in the former Eastern bloc had the potential to endanger the international order and the stability of interstate relations. Initially, problems arose with regard to the succession to state boundaries and the participation of the states involved in the already existing international order, including membership of international organizations and bodies, continuity of obligations under disarmament and human rights treaties, and the grave problem of what to do with existing nuclear weapons.

In this regard, the determination of whether the post-1989 events of transformation would lead to the construction of a completely new legal order based on new successor states, such as the earlier experience of decolonization, or whether some of the states involved would continue their legal personality and pre-transformation identity, was perceived as fundamental. Moreover, some of the cases involved the problem of resurrection of *de facto* extinguished states, which lost their independence in result of the forceful annexation during the Second World War.

a) Continuator states

The practice of the post-Cold War wave of state succession fully acknowledged the continuation of international legal personality and state identity of two pre-existing state organisms.[29] Clearly, this was the case of the Federal Republic of Germany (FRG) after the absorption of the territories of the former German Democratic Republic (GDR). Indeed, the Unification Treaty of 31 August 1990[30]

[28] Ibid. 670.

[29] See a systematic typological classification in: ILA, *Aspects of the Law of State Succession, Draft Final Report*, Rio de Janeiro Conference (2008), available at: <http://www.ila-hq.org/en/committees/index.cfm/cid/11>, accessed on 30 January 2015.

[30] Treaty between the Federal Republic of Germany and the German Democratic Republic on the establishment of German unity (Unification Treaty), signed on 31 August 1990, entered into

provided for the accession of the GDR to the FGR, therefore the unification process cannot be conceived as a merger of two sovereign states; rather it was an incorporation or accession of the GDR to the FRG.[31] Thus, from two former German states one became extinct and the second continued its legal personality and identity.

This case has been perceived as distinct from cases of unification such as the parallel post-colonial process of merging two Yemeni states—Yemen Arab Republic (North Yemen) and People's Democratic Republic of Yemen (South Yemen)—which in 1990 became extinguished and formed a new unitary state, the Republic of Yemen.[32] Thus, the FRG has been generally accepted as a continuator state, whereas the Republic of Yemen is a new successor state. The case of Germany has also shown that the regime adopted by the ILC and two Vienna Conventions—that is, the equalization of two categories of states succession, unification and incorporation (absorption)—does not correspond to actual state practice and, moreover, does not reflect customary international law.

A much more complex situation referred to the international status of the Russian Federation after the fall of the Soviet Union. One of the possible solution would be to classify the USSR's break-up as a case of dissolution of a multinational state. This would entail its extinction and the creation of a number of new successor states. The second option postulated by the leaders of the Russian Soviet Federative Socialist Republic (Russian SFSR) advanced the view that the dissolution of the Soviet Union took a form of devolution—separation (secession) of a number of territories from Russia, the 'core' or nucleus of the former Union.[33] Thus, the USSR was not extinguished[34] and Russia would continue to pursue its international personality.[35] Such a solution was agreed between the Russian SFRS and other post-Soviet republics at the time of formal dissolution of the USSR on 8 December 1991, pursuant to the Belavezha Accords[36] and subsequent Alma-Ata Declaration signed on 21 December 1991.[37] Thus, Russia became the sole continuator of the USSR on the grounds that it contained most of the population of the USSR and a larger majority of its territory. During the summit in Alma-Ata, the leaders of the former Soviet republics supported Russia's claim to be recognized

force on 3 October 1990, in *The Unification of Germany in 1990* (Press and Information Office of the Federal Government, 1991), 71–91.

[31] Kay Hailbronner, 'Legal Aspects of the Unification of the Two German States', *EJIL* 2(1991)1, 18–44, at 32–34.

[32] Raymond Goy, 'La réunification du Yémen', *AFDI* 36(1991), 249–65, at 263.

[33] Cf Crawford, *The Creation of States in International Law* (n 19) 705. [34] Ibid.

[35] See further Hamant, *Démembrement de l'URSS* (n 9), 323–26; Rein Müllerson, 'Law and Politics in Succession of States: International Law on Succession of States', in Brigitte Stern (ed), *Dissolution, Continuation, and Succession in Eastern Europe* (The Nijhoff, 1998), 5–32, at 8–14; Müllerson, *International Law, Rights and Politics* (n 9) 139–45.

[36] The Minsk (Belovezh Forest) Agreement on Creation of the Commonwealth signed on 8 December 1991, in Zbigniew Brzeziński and Paige Sullivan, *Russia and the Commonwealth of Independent States: Documents, Data, and Analysis* (Center for Strategic and International Studies), 43 ff.

[37] Brzeziński and Sullivan, *Russia and the Commonwealth of Independent States* (n 36) 47–8.

as the successor state of the Soviet Union for the purposes of membership of the United Nations.[38] On 24 December 1991, Boris Yeltsin, President of the Russian Federation, informed the UN Secretary General that the Soviet Union had been dissolved and that Russia would continue the Soviet Union's membership in the United Nations.[39] He confirmed the credentials of the representatives of the Soviet Union as the credentials of Russia, and requested that the name 'Soviet Union' be changed to 'Russian Federation' in all records and entries. At the beginning of 1992, Russia took both the USSR's place in the UN and its seat in the Security Council.[40] It has been recognized that the Russian Federation continues the state identity of the Soviet Union.[41] Moreover, there is a direct continuity of statehood between the Russian Empire, Soviet Russia after 1917, the Soviet Union, and the Russian Federation.[42]

b) Resurrected states—the theory of postliminium

The fall of the Eastern bloc also addressed the problem of the resurrection of states which had, in fact, become extinct. This was the case of the three Baltic States—Latvia, Lithuania, and Estonia.[43] They lost their independence as a result of forced Soviet annexation, pursuant to the secret protocols to the Non-Aggression Pact of 23 August 1939 signed by the Third Reich and the USSR (the Molotov–Ribbentrop Pact),[44] which divided the territories of Romania, Poland, Lithuania, Latvia, Estonia, and Finland into German and Soviet 'spheres of influence'. Estonia, Latvia, and a larger part of Lithuania were assigned to the USSR and subsequently annexed by it in 1940.[45] Although a number of states did not recognize *de jure* this annexation, they remained under the Soviet control after the Second World War. In fact, in later years the extinction of the Baltic states was recognized *de facto* or *per facta concludentia* by the members of the international community.[46] This attitude changed after 1991. In fact, on 6 September 1991 the

[38] See Konrad G. Bühler, *State Succession and Membership in International Organizations: Legal Theories Versus Political Pragmatism* (Kluwer Law International, 2001), 153 ff.

[39] Letter to the Secretary-General of the United Nations from the President of the Russian Federation, Moscow, 24 December 1991, UN Doc. S/RUSSIA.

[40] For the particular situation of Ukraine and Belarus, which were both UN members in their own right prior to the USSR's dissolution, see Bühler, *State Succession and Membership* (n 38) 171–76.

[41] Crawford, *The Creation of States in International Law* (n 19) 705.

[42] See for a synthesis on the international status of Russia over the centuries Tarja Långström, *Transformation in Russia and International Law* (Nijhoff, 2003).

[43] Lauri Mälksoo, *Illegal Annexation and State Continuity: the Case of the Incorporation of the Baltic States by the USSR: A Study of the Tension between Normativity and Power in International Law* (Nijhoff, 2003).

[44] The text of the Molotov–Ribbentrop Pact as well as the texts of supplementary protocols of 23 August 1939 and of 28 September 1939, available at: <http://avalon.law.yale.edu/subject_menus/nazsov.asp>, accessed on 25 January 2015.

[45] See Vilenas Vadapalas and Vytautas Žalys, 'Secret Protocols to the Soviet-German Treaties of 1939 and the Problem of Prescription in International Law', *Eesti Teaduste Akadeemia Toimetised* 39(1990)2, 131–39.

[46] See further Oliver Dörr, *Die Inkorporation als Tatbestand der Staatensukzession* (D&H, 1995), 348–49.

USSR recognized the secession of the Baltic states and this was followed by recognition of other post-Soviet republics. Shortly afterwards, on 17 September 1991, these three states became members of the UN.[47]

The nature of the independence of Lithuania, Latvia, Estonia, was, however, problematic.[48] Importantly, these claimed that they continued the legal personality of pre-Second World War independent states and viewed their histories of existence within the boundaries of the USSR as war occupation. Thus, they recalled the theory of *postliminium*;[49] that is, they were only temporarily suppressed by the USSR and subsequently regained effective freedom and control over their state territories. This thesis was generally accepted by the international community as the Baltic States were recognized as parties to a number of the pre-Second World War treaties. Thus, they were not treated as new states, successors of the Soviet Union, but the continuators of the independent states of Latvia, Estonia and Lithuania which had been suppressed in 1940. Such a solution allowed them to reject pre-existing USSR's international obligations and liabilities as well as sever any political and military ties with the Russian Federation. In fact, the Baltic states immediately oriented their politics towards Atlantic and European structures, adjusting their legal and social standards to those of Western countries, and in 2004 they joined the European Union and NATO. Yet the adoption of the *postliminium* doctrine caused certain problems concerning the questions of citizenship (especially for the large Russian minority living within their borders),[50] territory (the post-Cold War boundaries of Estonia and Lithuania differed from those existing prior to 1940), state property of the USSR, such as military structures, and state responsibility as well as the protection of cultural and memory sites.[51]

[47] Roger O'Keefe, 'The Admission to the United Nations of the ex-Soviet and ex-Yugoslav States', *Baltic Yearbook of International Law* 1(2001), 167–89.

[48] Cf a series of studies 'International Legal Status of the Baltic States', *Baltic Yearbook of International Law* 1(2001), 1–166.

[49] Crawford, *The Creation of States in International Law* (n 19) 689–90, 695–99.

[50] For a detailed analysis of the case of the Baltic States *vis-à-vis* the Russian Federation, see Ineta Ziemele, *State Continuity and Nationality: the Baltic States and Russia* (Nijhoff, 2005).

[51] The most noted example between the Baltic States, Russian minority living therein, supported by the Russian Federation, was the case of the Bronze Soldier (the Monument to the Liberators of Tallinn), a Soviet memorial erected in 1947 in the centre of Estonian capital depicting a victorious soldier of the Red Army and commemorating a place of burial of unknown number of Soviet soldiers. The Bronze Soldier had a symbolic value to Estonia's Russians, symbolizing not only Soviet victory over the Third Reich in the Second World War but also their rights to that territory. Most Estonians considered the monument as a symbol of Soviet occupation, suppression of their independence and following Stalinist repressions. Accordingly, in 2007, in a very tense atmosphere, the memorial was dismantled, human remains removed, and all the site relocated to the military cemetery of Tallinn. See further Karsten Brüggemann and Adres Kasekamp, 'Identity Politics and Contested Histories in Divided Societies: The Case of Estonian War Monuments', in Eiki Berg and Piret Ehin (eds), *Identity and Foreign Policy: Baltic-Russian Relations and European Integration* (Ashgate, 2009), 51–64, at 54 ff.

c) Successor states

As has been already discussed, only the Federal Republic of Germany and the Russian Federation were fully accepted as identical to the states existing prior to the post-Cold War wave of state succession in Central and Eastern Europe.[52] Accordingly, the Czech and Slovak Federal Republic (CSFR) ceased to exist by voluntary dissolution pursuant to the Constitutional Act of 25 November 1992.[53] This formally ended the existence of Czechoslovakia as of 31 December 1992. The dissolution of the CSFR took effect on 1 January 1993 and the Czech and Slovak Republics became new states—successors of the CSFR.[54] The former Soviet republics which came to independence in early 1990s were also treated as new states, except Russia (recognized as continuing the legal personality of the USSR) and the Baltic States (claiming the continuation of their legal personality, only temporarily suppressed by the USSR in 1940).

Finally, the case of Yugoslavia demonstrated the most complex issues relating to the continuity and succession of states. Unlike the dissolution of the CSSR and the USSR, the breakup of the Socialist Republic of Yugoslavia (SFRY) was very violent and the final settlement was coloured by international mediation and military intervention.[55] As a consequence of these events, the dissolution of the SFRY resulted in the extinction of that state and the creation of a group of new successor states. Nonetheless, one of the states emerged from the SFRY—the Federal Republic of Yugoslavia (FRY)—claimed to continue the legal personality of the former one, but the international community rejected this. Thus, in the first wave of the dismemberment of the SFRY five new states emerged: Bosnia–Herzegovina, Croatia, FRY (since 2003 the State Union of Serbia and Montenegro), Macedonia, and Slovenia. Then, in 2006, the 'new' Yugoslavia was dissolved into two states: Serbia and Montenegro. And, in 2008 through the mean of secession the Republic of Kosovo separated from Serbia.[56] Thus it is clear that the transformations of the FRY produced certain peculiarities in terms of succession and continuity. The State Union of Serbia and Montenegro was recognized as the continuing state of the FRY. Moreover, pursuant to Article 60 of the Constitutional Charter of the State Union of Serbia and Montenegro,[57]

[52] Compare Ineta Ziemele, 'Is the Distinction between State Continuity and State Succession Reality or Fiction? The Russian Federation, the Federal Republic of Yugoslavia and Germany', *Baltic Yearbook of International Law* 1(2001), 191–222.

[53] Constitutional Act No. 542/1992 on the Extinction of the Czech and Slovak Federal Republic, 25 November 1992.

[54] For historical background and internal legal processes, see *inter alia* Jiri Malenovsky, 'État: création, transformation, frontières, attitude à l'égard du droit international; Problèmes juridiques liés à la partition de la Tchécoslovaquie', *AFDI* 39(1993), 305–66, at 328, 306–10, 314–26; Václav Mikulka, 'The Dissolution of Czechoslovakia and Succession in Respect of Treaties' in Mojmir Mrak (ed), *Succession of States* (Nijhoff, 1999), 109–28, at 109–11.

[55] For a detailed chronology of the progress of events since 1989, see eg Carol Rogel, *The Breakup of Yugoslavia and Its Aftermath* (Greenwood Press, 2004).

[56] See this chapter, section 5.3.3.

[57] English translation available at: <http://www.refworld.org/pdfid/43e7547d4.pdf>, accessed on 30 January 2015.

after the dissolution of the Union, Serbia would be the sole continuator of that state. In fact, after 2006, Montenegro was recognized by the international community as a new state, whereas Serbia continued the legal personality of the pre-existing one.[58]

5.1.3 Normative framework

In principle, a clear classification of post-Cold War transformations into well-defined categories of state succession could serve to determine the proper set of rules to be applied to a given case. Yet, as has been already mentioned in Chapter 4, the solutions discussed and forwarded at the time of decolonization and parallel codification of the law of state succession have not been unanimously followed or perceived as respecting legal standards at the time of the formation of new states in Africa and Asia. In particular, neither of the two Vienna Conventions[59] entered in force prior to 1990. Thus, the applicable legal regime was based on customary international law, yet its content and consistency in the area concerned remained hotly debated.

In the context of the ongoing dissolution of the Cold-War political and territorial system, different legislative and standard-setting initiatives were undertaken. Accordingly, the ILC addressed the need for the codification of international law on state succession in respect of the nationality of natural and legal persons. In 1993, this proposal was accepted by the UN General Assembly.[60] The preparatory works on this topic were conducted throughout 1990s, but they have not yet resulted in a new instrument of codification.[61]

Parallel to the legislative activity of the ILC, problems relating to state succession were the subject of efforts by another international bodies and entities. In particular, the Council of Europe (CoE) introduced this issue into its agenda with a particular reference to nationality and the protection of human rights, in the framework of the activity of the European Commission for Democracy through Law (Venice Commission)[62] and the Committee of Legal Advisers on Public International Law (CAHDI).[63] This resulted *inter alia* in the adoption of the 2006 CoE Convention on the Avoidance of Statelessness in relation to State Succession.[64] Other work on this matter was pursued by the office of the United Nations High Commissioner for

[58] See Commission of the European Communities, 'Serbia 2006 Progress Report', Brussels, 8 November 2006, SEC (2006)1389, at 5–6.

[59] 1978 Vienna Convention on Succession of States in Respect of Treaties (1978 Vienna Convention), adopted on 23 August 1978, entered into force on 6 November 1996, 1946 UNTS 3; 1983 Vienna Convention on Succession of states in Respect of state Property, Archives and Debts (1983 Vienna Convention) adopted on 8 April 1983, not in force, UN Doc. A/CONF.117/14 (1983).

[60] UN Doc.A/RES/48/31.

[61] UN Doc.A/RES/66/92.

[62] Series of documents available on the website of the Venice Commission, see: <http://www.venice.coe.int>, accessed on 30 January 2015.

[63] See Jan Klabbers, Martti Koskenniemi, and Olivier Ribbelink, *State Practice Regarding State Succession and Issues of Recognition* (Kluwer Law International, 1999).

[64] Convention on the Avoidance of Statelessness in Relation to State Succession, signed on 19 May 2006, entered into force on 1 May 2009, ETS No. 200.

Refugees (UNHCR).[65] Special attention to general aspects of state succession was also paid by the Council of Ministers of the European Economic Community in respect of the dissolution of Yugoslavia in the framework of the Arbitration Commission of the Conference on Yugoslavia (Badinter Commission) set up in 1991.[66] Additional assistance was also provided by the International Law Association (ILA)[67] and the Institute of International Law (IIL).[68]

As regards the international legal scholarship, this has primarily dealt with the issue of state succession to treaties. This is fully understandable since the relevant state practice on this matter was widely available.[69] Moreover, the 1978 Vienna Convention entered into force in 1996 when the requirement, under Article 49, of the deposit of 15 instruments of ratification or accession, was met. In fact, a number of successor states that emerged after 1989 acceded to this international instrument.[70] Conversely, the question of succession to state property, archives, and debts remained barely examined, as state practice on this matter is not consistent and many relevant documents are not accessible. Nonetheless the 1983 Vienna Convention did not enter into force, due to the extremely privileged position of the newly independent states and the ambiguity of the provisions on the passing of state property in 'equitable proportion', its regime generally followed by the states involved.[71] In fact, it seems that the major consideration in regard to the issues of state succession in matters of state property and debts was essentially based on the concept of 'equity', which *inter alia* involves the achievement of equitable and just solutions through the negotiation of conflicting interests between states involved in processes of state succession.[72]

Some major developments also concerned the issue of state succession to international responsibility. Generally speaking, international legal scholarship differentiates the situation of continuator states and that of new states. Accordingly, the states continuing legal personality of the pre-existing states shall own all their international obligations, including those arising from wrongful acts. Conversely,

[65] See Reports on State Succession and Its Impact on the Nationality of Natural and Legal Persons, available at: <http://www.unhcr.org>, accessed on 30 January 2015.

[66] See EPC Extraordinary Ministerial Meeting, Declaration on Yugoslavia, Brussels, 27 August 1991, EPC Press Release, P.82/91; EPC Extraordinary Ministerial Meeting, Declaration on Yugoslavia, The Hague, 3 September 1991, EPC Press Release, P.84/91.

[67] ILA Committee on the Aspects of the Law of State Succession, available at: <http://www.ila-hq.org/en/committees/index.cfm/cid/11>, accessed on 30 January 2015.

[68] Two resolutions of 1995 and 2001, see <http://www.idi-iil.org>, accessed on 30 January 2015.

[69] See Gerhard Hafner and Gregor Novak, 'State Succession in Respect of Treaties', in Duncan B. Hollis (ed), *The Oxford Guide to Treaties* (OUP, 2012), 396–427.

[70] See <http://treaties.un.org/Pages/ViewDetails.aspx?src=TREATY&mtdsg_no=XXIII-2&chapter=23&lang=en>, accessed on 31 January 2015.

[71] ILA, Aspects of the Law of State Succession, Provisional Report, Berlin Conference 2004, at 11–12.

[72] See *inter alia* Władysław Czapliński, 'Equity and Equitable Principles in the Law of State Succession', in Mojmir Mrak (ed), *Succession of States* (Nijhoff, 1999), 61–73; Stefan Oeter, 'State Succession and the Struggle over Equity: Some Observations on the Laws of State Succession with Respect to State Property and Debts in Cases of Separation and Dissolution of States', *GYIL* 38(1995), 73–102.

the succession of new states to the responsibility for international delicts committed by their predecessor(s) remains much more problematic. This is founded on the widely shared opinion that the 'personal' character of delicts excluded attribution of the act to the successor state and therefore responsibility does not pass from the predecessor to the successor state.[73] There have been only few doctrinal attempts to challenge the non-succession theory.[74] Thus, the question of state succession to international responsibility remained neglected in the works of the ILC also in the area of state responsibility, as there was 'a widely held view that a new state does not, in general, succeed to any state responsibility of the predecessor State with respect to its territory'.[75] In this regard the outcome of these two parallel codification initiatives is, indeed, completely silent.

In view of the ongoing post-Cold War events, both state practice and legal doctrine gradually evolved.[76] This was noted by the ILC in its official 2001 Commentaries to the *Articles on Responsibility of States for Internationally Wrongful Acts*, in which the Special Rapporteur, James Crawford, indicated that it was 'unclear whether a new state succeeds to any state responsibility of the predecessor state with respect to its territory'.[77] The changing perspective in the matter of state succession to international responsibility was particularly due to more pragmatic approaches to the legal effects and consequences of transformations of states in order to maintain the geopolitical equilibrium of the international legal order.[78] It was argued that such equilibrium can be achieved by the analysis of different cases within their factual and legal contexts in order to search for the effective means for their solution.[79] Interestingly, the ICJ in *Gabčikovo-Nagymaros Project*

[73] Patrick Dumberry, *State Succession to International Responsibility* (Nijhoff, 2007), 35 ff. and the literature cited therein.

[74] Ibid. 52–58.

[75] James Crawford, Special Rapporteur, First Report on State Responsibility (addendum no. 5), 22 July 1998, UN Doc. A/CN.4/490/Add.5, at para. 282.

[76] Cf *inter alia* James Crawford, *State Responsibility: The General Part* (CUP, 2013), 435–55; Tai-Heng Cheng, 'Why New States Accept Old Obligations?', *University of Illinois Law Review* (2011)1, 1–52; Václav Mikulka, 'State Succession and Responsibility', in James Crawford, Alain Pellet, and Simon Olleson (eds), *The Law of International Responsibility* (OUP, 2010), 291–96; Brigitte Stern, 'Responsibilité internationale et succession d'États', in Laurence Boisson de Chazournes and Vera Gowlland-Debbas (eds), *The International Legal System in Quest of Equity and Universality/L'ordre juridique international, un système en quête d'équité et d'universalité. Liber Amicorum Georges Abi-Saab* (Nijhoff, 2001), 327–56; Dumberry, *State Succession to International Responsibility* (n 73); Patrick Dumberry, 'The Controversial Issue of State Succession to International Responsibility in Light of Recent State Practice', *GYIL* 49(2006), 413–48; Michael J. Volkovitsch, 'Righting Wrongs: Toward a New Theory of State Succession to Responsibility for International Delicts', *Columbia Law Review* 92(1992)8, 2162–214; Władysław Czaplinski, 'State Succession and State Responsibility', *CanYIL* 28(1990), 339–59.

[77] *Commentaries to the Draft Articles on Responsibility of States for Internationally Wrongful Acts Adopted by the International Law Commission at its Fifty-Third Session (2001), November 2001*, Report of the ILC on the work of its Fifty-third Session, Official Records of the General Assembly, Fifty-sixth Session, Suppl. No. 10, UN Doc. A/56/10, ch. IV.E.2, at 119, para. 3.

[78] See Stern, 'Responsibilité internationale et succession d'États' (n 76) 329 ff.

[79] For instance, Oscar Schachter, 'State Succession: The Once and Future Law', *Vanderbilt Journal of Transnational Law* 33(1993)2, 253–60;

between Slovakia and Hungary,[80] which *inter alia* involved the problem of succession by the first one to international responsibility for the wrongful acts committed by its predecessor—Czechoslovakia—against the latter, failed to pronounce explicitly on the transfer of obligations from the predecessor state to the successor state. However, it needs to be stressed that nonetheless, both parties to the litigation made reference to the principle of non-succession to obligations arising from the commission of internationally wrongful acts, the ICJ did not reject such a possibility.[81] Apparently, similar reasoning also referred to the opposite situation, that is, the succession of Slovakia in respect of secondary rights of Czechoslovakia, its predecessor, stemming from a wrongful act of Hungary.[82] The court focused its analysis on the actual provisions of contractual relations between both states and held that both Slovakia and Hungary were entitled to compensation.[83]

A major step towards a broader investigation of this topic was undertaken by Patrick Dumberry who in his extensive monograph pursued a very detailed analysis of international practice, advocating a development of new customary rules in this area of international law. These provide for both succession and non-succession to state responsibility depending on the types of succession of states and the 'specific situations and circumstances'.[84] The topic has been also put on the agenda of the IIL, within the works of the 14th Commission.[85] In fact, Marcelo G. Kohen, nominated a Rapporteur to this commission, advocated the need for the codification and/or progressive development of 'concrete guidelines to address situations in which rights and obligations emanating from the commission of an international wrongful act are involved in cases of states succession.'[86] A first attempt has been already undertaken. During the meeting of the IIL in September 2013, both the Provisional Report[87] and Draft Resolution[88] were discussed. The latter

[80] *Gabčikovo-Nagymaros Project (Hungary v. Slovakia),* Judgment of 25 September 1997, ICJ Reports 1997, 3.

[81] Ibid. at para. 151; cf Václav Mikulka: 'Succession of States in Respect of Rights of an Injured State', in James Crawford, Alain Pellet, and Simon Olleson (eds), *The Law of International Responsibility* (OUP, 2010), 965–67; Dumberry, *State Succession to International Responsibility* (n 73) 116.

[82] See Václav Mikulka: 'Succession of States in Respect of Rights of an Injured State', in James Crawford, Alain Pellet, and Simon Olleson (eds), *The Law of International Responsibility* (OUP, 2010), 965–67.

[83] *Gabčikovo-Nagymaros Project* (n 80) 78, para. 152.

[84] Dumberry, *State Succession to International Responsibility* (n 73) 420–30.

[85] Marcelo G. Kohen, Rapporteur, 'State Succession in Matters of State Responsibility Preliminary Statement (Exposé préliminaire)', in IIL, 14th Commission, 2011, unpublished.

[86] Marcelo G. Kohen, 'Succession of States in the Field of International Responsibility: the Case for Codification', in Mercelo G. Kohen, Robert Kolb, Djacoba Liva Tehindrazanarivelo (eds), *Perspectives of International Law in the 21st Century: Liber Amicorum Professor Christian Dominicé in Honour of his 80th Birthday/Perspectives du droit international au 21e siècle* (Brill, 2012), 161–74, at 174.

[87] Marcelo G. Kohen, Rapporteur, 'State Succession in Matters of State Responsibility. Provisional Report', 9 August 2013, IIL, 14th Commission, Tokyo Session, 2013, available at: <http://www.idi-iil.org/idiE/navig_ann_2013.html>, accessed on 30 January 2015.

[88] Marcelo G. Kohen, State Succession in Matters of State Responsibility. Draft Resolution, IIL, 9 August 2013, 14th Commission, Tokyo Session, 2013, available at: <http://www.idi-iil.org/idiE/navig_ann_2013.html>, accessed on 30 January 2015.

provided for a clear distinction between the cases of continuity and succession and elaborated the guiding principles applicable to distinct categories of state succession.[89] Indeed, the works of the IIL have given an important doctrinal impetus since they explicitly rejected non-succession as the major rule applicable to state succession to international responsibility. However, the existence of positive law in this area remains still debatable.[90]

5.2 The post-Cold War state succession and cultural heritage: doctrinal approaches

As already suggested, the processes initiated after 1989 included the question of the status of cultural material in state succession. However, it appears that all the cited international legislative and standard-setting initiatives have not led to a comprehensive reconsideration of the legal regimes in such matters. Arguably, the reasons of such an omission were generally based on similar foundations as the exclusion of this topic from the codification works led by Mohamed Bedjaoui. On the one hand, it appears that the problems involving the status of cultural property were not seen as being substantially different from those addressed by the general regime on succession in state property and state archives. On the other hand, the potential complexity of historical and emotional disputes was perceived to be better addressed within the already existing legal frameworks, such those of UNESCO.

5.2.1 State succession in matters of state cultural property and archives

Apparently, the only attempts in this regard were undertaken by the IIL. In its recommendation entitled *State Succession in Matters of Property and Debts* and issued at Vancouver on 26 August 2001 (2001 Vancouver Recommendation)[91] it addressed the issue of state property of major importance to the cultural heritage of a successor state, in terms of a certain exemption from general rules. Thus, under Article 16 'Allocation of Property in Accordance with the Principle of Territoriality', it reaffirmed the principle of territoriality applicable to the allocation of state property, based on the criteria of close connection and equitable apportionment. It also introduced a special regime for the movable property of major importance to the cultural heritage of a successor state (Article 16.5). Accordingly, the 'property that is of major importance to the cultural heritage of

[89] See further Chapter 6, section 6.1.2.

[90] Crawford, *State Responsibility: The General Part* (n 76) 455.

[91] IIL, Resolution 'La succession d'états en materie de biens et de dettes' (State Succession in Matters of Property and Debts), available at: <http://www.idi-iil.org/idif/resolutionsf/2001_van_01_fr.pdf>, accessed on 30 January 2015. See also Erik Jayme, 'Institut de Droit International: Tagung in Vancouver', *Praxis des Internationalen Privat- und Verfahrensrechts* 22(2002), 149–51.

a successor state from whose territory it originates shall pass to that state'. This category of property also included state archives of major importance to the cultural heritage of a successor state (Article 16.6). The IIL also recommended that 'such goods shall be identified by that state within a reasonable period of time following the succession'.

It is clear that the 2001 Vancouver Recommendation applied two general principles: 1) territoriality, and 2) major importance for the cultural heritage of a successor state. However, it did not provide any time limits as to the date of removal/dispersal or other restrictions, that is, protection of the universally ranked collections, etc. Apparently, it left the determination of the exact criteria to the discretion of the parties to a succession agreement. It is particularly ambiguous as to how the evidence of major importance to cultural heritage could be demonstrated in cases concerning objects of universal cultural value. This therefore raises the question as to whether in such situations only the principle of territoriality—that is, where the state-owned collection was created—would be decisive, or whether other criteria need to be fulfilled. Similarly, the lack of time limitations with reference to the date of displacement of properties of major importance to the cultural heritage of a successor state is very problematic. What it very striking is that the 2001 Vancouver Recommendation clearly opted for subsidiary rules, privileging agreements amongst the concerned states. This is obviously in line with the provisions of the 1983 Vienna Convention. However, as already explained, the Convention provided for an exemption from such a regime in respect of newly independent states. In such cases, the agreements cannot overrule the principle of permanent sovereignty of every people over its wealth and natural resources. Thus, the provisions of the 1983 Vienna Convention under Article 15 would allegedly have a compulsory nature. Accordingly, the newly independent states should receive not only all the property of the former colonial power situated in the territory of the new state, but also property located abroad that belonged to that territory and became property of the predecessor state. It seems that the IIL fully acknowledged the fact that such favourable treatment accorded to these states did not correspond to the international practice and led to the rejection of the 1983 Vienna Convention by many states. Consequently, the IIL did not refer to these controversial provisions on newly independent states, although the emancipation of many states, and in particular the Asiatic republics of the former USSR, had much in common with the experiences of decolonization.

An important section of Article 16 of the 2001 Vancouver Recommendation concerned a procedural principle which governs state succession to movable cultural property. One needs to assess the postulated principle of a 'reasonable' period of time in which the claims for the allocation of cultural material can be brought. Such a principle would definitely facilitate the interstate negotiations if one of the parties intentionally deterred the final settlement.

Interestingly, the 2001 Vancouver Recommendation referred to cases of cession, secession, and dissolution. The problems related to the unification or incorporation were not addressed. This approach may seem fully understandable because such transformations of states do not usually create particular problem in terms of apportionment of cultural property, however they may cause certain difficulties in terms of its allocation, protection, and management. Arguably, the IIL did not perceive such consequences to be covered by the law of state succession, but rather believed them to be regulated under municipal law of the state concerned. In fact, the only case of incorporation concerned the re-unification of Germany. This also occurred in the context of formerly divided public art collections, libraries, and archives. The Unification Treaty of 31 August 1990 did not contain any provisions on succession to state property and archives, but it was clearly recognized that all state property of the GDR would pass to the FDR.[92] Such a logical solution did not cause any particular controversies over the situation of state cultural property. One of the most commented cases related to the museum collections of East Berlin, which before unification were taken to the western part of the city. After 1990, German authorities decided to reconstruct the original distribution of museum exhibits. Accordingly, in 2005 the world-famous Egyptian collection (the Egyptian Museum of Berlin), including the Nefertiti bust, was moved from Castle Charlottenburg in former West Berlin to Museum Island, in the former East Berlin, and temporarily placed in Altes Museum. Then, in 2009 it was re-installed in the newly reconstructed Neues Museum where the collection had originally been displayed since 1850.[93]

In sum, the post-Cold War international initiatives in the matter of state succession and legal doctrine generally followed the reasoning of the ILC during the 1970s and 1980s. The codified rules of state succession to state property and archives apply to the allocation and distribution of cultural property where such property was owned by the predecessor state. The definition of cultural importance and time limitations as to the date of the removal from the territory of a successor state needs to be settled on the basis of succession arrangements between the states concerned. The question of non-state cultural property displaced under foreign domination prior to the independence of a new state has been excluded from the regime on state succession.

5.2.2 State succession in matters of international responsibility for wrongful acts against cultural heritage

As already suggested, the Post-Cold War state practice of state succession has produced a number of situations in which the states involved have had to deal with the consequences of pre-existing international wrongful acts against cultural heritage. In the vast majority of cases, these referred to the past pillages of cultural material and its intentional destruction which occurred mainly in the event of an armed conflict. In principle, the situation of continuator states seemed different

[92] Hailbronner, 'Legal Aspects' (n 31) 36.

[93] Catherine Hickley, 'Queen Nefertiti's Home, a Ruin for 70 Years, Opens in Berlin', *Bloomberg*, 16 October 2009, available at: <http://www.bloomberg.com/apps/news?pid=newsarchive&sid=aymZF9XfTIBQ>, accessed on 30 January 2015.

from that of new states, as the first logically continues the enjoyment of rights and the assumption of obligations arising from the international wrongful acts in which they were involved before the date of state succession.The rules of succession applicable to new states, however, appear more obscure.

The first problem concerned the Federal Republic of Germany. Regardless of post-Second World War positions claiming the extinction of the Third Reich as a result of *debellatio*,[94] the creation of two new German states and the unification of Berlin, the state doctrine of the FRG has claimed continuity of pre-1945 statehood. This was generally accepted. Thus, the complex international situation of Germany in 1945–90 was usually described as the existence of three separate German states (FRG, DDR, and Berlin) none of which were identical with the pre-existing defeated state.[95] The perspectives changed in result of the re-unification process. Thus, the FRG became more often recognized as continuing the identity of pre-1945 Germany in respect of international rights and obligations.[96] Arguably, it is in this light that one may interpret the series of judgements concerning the lawsuits brought by the victims and their relatives against the FRG concerning war crimes committed by the Third Reich during the Second World War. Accordingly, in the years 1997–2011[97] different civil tribunals in Greece and Italy ruled in favour of the claimants against FRG and ordered compensation to be paid to the victims of crimes committed by Germany during the Second World War—that is, prior to the birth of the FRG. The objections raised by the FGR on the basis of the rules on sovereign immunity in respect of acts committed *de jure imperii* were recognized by the European Court of Human Rights in 2002[98] and by the ICJ in 2012.[99] The courts held that under customary international law the FRG was entitled to effectively invoke state immunity even in cases concerning alleged violations of *jus cogens.* Yet the government of the FRG and both international tribunals did not question the existence of the obligations arising from the wrongful acts committed prior to 1945, which are owned by the FRG. Furthermore, the ICJ explained that the means of the realization of international responsibility in such cases should be settled through intergovernmental negotiations.[100]

Similarly, there were no doubts as to the legitimacy of claims addressed to the FGR in respect of German cultural assets removed or displaced in the event of the

[94] See Chapter 3, section 3.2.2.

[95] Crawford, *The Creation of States in International Law* (n 19) 465.

[96] Cf. Crawford, *State Responsibility: The General Part* (n 76) 449–51.

[97] In particular, see the 2000 judgment of the the Hellenic Supreme Court (*Areios Pagos*) in the *Distomo* case, *Prefecture of Voiotia v. Federal Republic of Germany*, Judgment of the Hellenic Supreme Court (Areios Pagos) of 4 May 2000, 129 ILR 514 and the 2005 decision of the Italian Court of Cassation in the *Ferrini v. Federal Republic of Germany, Corte di Cassazione (Sez. Unite)*, No. 5044, 11 March 2004, 126 ILR 658.

[98] *Kalogeropoulou and others v. Greece and Germany*, Application No. 59021/00, Decision of 12 December 2002, 2002-X ECHR Reports 417.

[99] *Jurisdictional Immunities of the State (Germany v. Italy: Greece intervening)*, Judgment of 3 February 2012, ICJ Reports 2012, 99.

[100] Ibid. para. 102.

Second World War as to its responsibility for the crimes against cultural property of other states committed by the Third Reich. However, the actual solutions were hindered by the effects of the Cold War international legal relations (such as the effects of the pre-1990 reparation arrangements adopted separately in relation to the FRG or to the GDR),[101] and obstacles arising from the rules of private law, such as prescription of claims, and good faith acquisition. In fact, after the fall of the Berlin Wall, the question of the restitution of cultural material looted and displaced in 1939–45 was raised in various international forums and led to the adoption of a set of different non-binding principles and declarations.[102] These widely recognized that practice in this matter was unsatisfactory and encouraged states to undertake every reasonable effort to achieve the restitution of cultural property looted during the Second World War under discriminatory Nazi policies. In the following years, many states and cultural institutions moved to settle these issues with former owners of cultural objects from which they were deprived in relation to the Second World War.

In the 1990s, UNESCO undertook an initiative to adopt a broader comprehensive legal framework for dealing with problems related to the displacement of cultural material during the Second World War.[103] The work was, however, hindered by the ongoing controversy between Germany and the Russian Federation over the restitution of cultural property seized by the Red Army in 1945.[104]

As already discussed, the claims of the Russian Federation in respect of the continuity of the USSR's legal personality were generally accepted by the international community. In such a view, Russia should be also held responsible for the wrongful acts against cultural property committed in particular during the Second World

[101] See Chapter 6, section 6.3.1.

[102] See in particular Washington Conference Principles on Nazi-Confiscated Art of 3 December 1998, in James D. Bindenagel (ed) *Washington Conference on Holocaust-Era Assets, November 30–December 3, 1998* (United States Government Printing Office, 1999), available at: <http://www.lootedartcommission.com/Washington-principles>, accessed on 30 January 2015; ICOM Recommendations Concerning the Return of Works of Art Belonging to Jewish Owners of 14 January 1999, <http://www.lootedartcommission.com/OXSHQE36019>, accessed on 30 January 2015; CoE Resolution 1205 (1999) Looted Jewish Cultural Property, available at: <http://assembly.coe.int/Main.asp?link=/Documents/AdoptedText/ta99/ERES1205.htm>; Vilnius International Forum on Holocaust-Era Looted Cultural Assets Declaration, 5 October 2000, available at: <http://www.lootedart.com/MFV7A818610>, accessed on 30 January 2015.

[103] Lyndell V. Prott, 'Principles for the Resolution of Disputes Concerning Cultural Heritage Displaced During the Second World War', in Elisabeth Simpson (ed), *The Spoils of War. World War II and Its Aftermath: The Loss, Reappearance, and Recovery of Cultural Property* (Harry N. Abrams, 1997), 225–30.

[104] See further *inter alia* Patrick Dumberry, 'The Controversial Issue of State Succession to International Responsibility in Light of Recent State Practice', *GYIL* 49(2006), 413–48, at 438–39; Patrick Dumberry, *State Succession to International Responsibility* (n 73), 192–94; Alexander Blankenagel, 'Eyes Wide Shut: Displaced Cultural Objects in Russian Law and Adjudication', *East European Constitutional Review* 8(1999)4, 75–80; Stephan Wilske, 'International Law and the Spoils of War: To the Victor the Right of Spoils?: The Claims for Repatriation of Art Removed from Germany by the Soviet Army During or as a Result of World War II', *UCLA Journal of International Law & Foreign Affairs* 3(1998)1, 223–82; Andrea Gattini, 'Restitution by Russia of Works of Art Removed from German Territory at the End of the Second World War', *EJIL* 7(1996)1, 67–88.

War.[105] It seems that in the years preceding the dissolution of the USSR and in the first months after the split there was a favourable climate among Soviet and then Russian political elites with regard to the restitution of displaced cultural objects. Such an attitude was expressed in the Treaty on Good-Neighborliness, Partnership and Cooperation concluded between the Russian Federation and the Federal Republic of Germany on 9 November 1990.[106] Under Article 16, this provided that both states would 'advocate the preservation of cultural treasures of the other side in their territory'. They also agreed that 'lost or unlawfully removed art treasures which are located in their territory will be returned to the owners or their legal successors'. Notwithstanding these formal arrangements, Russia refused to return German art treasures captured in 1945, arguing that they were acquired as a legitimate compensation for the Russian cultural loss caused by the German invasion at the time of the Second World War. Moreover, the Russian Federal Law of 13 May 1997[107] explicitly provided that all cultural property of the Third Reich preserved in Russian cultural institutions constituted the unalienable state property of the Federation.[108] Thus, subsequent restitutions to Germany were pursued only in terms of *ex gratia* gestures.[109] Nonetheless, Russia initiated an important programme of restoration of historical archival materials displaced due to the Second World War to other countries, in particular to the Netherlands and to Hungary.[110]

A seemingly different situation regarded state succession to responsibility for internationally wrongful acts against cultural property. This question particularly concerned the case of the former Yugoslavia. As the break-up of this multinational state was extremely violent and resulted in a great many crimes against cultural heritage committed by various parties to the conflict, the issue of international responsibility for such acts was widely addressed. As the SFRY no longer existed, the actual attribution of those crimes had to be attributed to the newly established

[105] For a comprehensive analysis of the transformation of the Russian foreign policy in these matters, see Långström, *Transformation in Russia and International Law* (n 42) 126–34; Patricia Kennedy Grimsted, 'Legalizing "Compensation" and the Spoils of War: the Russain Law on the Displaced Cultural Valuables and the Manipulation of Historic Memory, *ICJP* 17(2010)2, 217–55.

[106] Treaty between the Federal Republic of Germany and the Union of Soviet Socialist Republics on Good-Neighborliness, Partnership and Cooperation, signed on 9 November 1990, 30 ILM 505.

[107] Federal Law on Cultural Valuables Displaced to the U.S.S.R. as a Result of World War II and Located on the Territory of the Russian Federation, Federal Law N 64-FZ of 15 April 1998, adopted by the State Duma on 5 February 1997, approved by the Federation Council on 5 March 1997, available at: <http://docproj.loyola.edu/rlaw/R3.html>, accessed on 12 February 2015.

[108] For the list of post-1991 Russian legal instruments relating to cultural valuables of foreign provenance seized and transported to the Soviet Union from Germany and Eastern Europe at the end of the Second World War, or in the immediate postwar period see Patricia Kennedy Grimsted (ed), 'Russian Legal Instruments Relating to Cultural Valuables Displaced as a Result of the Second World War, 1990–2009', *ICJP* 17(2010)2, 427–91.

[109] Cf Wolfgang Eichwede, 'Trophy Art as Ambassadors: Reflections Beyond Diplomatic Deadlock in the German-Russian Dialogue Wolfgang Eichwede', *ICJP* 17(2010)2, 387–412.

[110] Patricia Kennedy Grimsted, F.J. Hoogewoud, and Eric Ketelaar (eds), *Returned from Russia. Nazi Archival Plunder in Western Europe and Recent Restitution Issues* (Institute of Art and Law, 2007), József Gehér, 'Le destin juridique des oeuvres d'art hongroises enlevées en Russie', *Miskolc Journal of International Law* 1(2004)2, 290–305.

successor states. The most important issue referred to the responsibility of the FRY, which as a result of the subsequent processes of separation of Montenegro and Kosovo became limited to its political and territorial nucleus, Serbia. Nonetheless, the Republic of Serbia continued the identity and international legal personality of the FRY and assumed its obligations arising from the breach of the rules of humanitarian law prohibiting the plunder and destruction of cultural property in armed conflict, in particular with relation to the war with Croatia.[111]

Accordingly, even in this case the question of the succession to international responsibility for wrongful acts against cultural heritage was not particularly addressed since both Croatia and Serbia were responsible for their 'own', not inherited, obligations in this regard. Thus, it remained debatable whether any specific customary norms had been already formulated, according to which succession or non-succession rules apply in cases of such crimes. In relation to this, another issue was discussed, that is, whether the successor states shall be held responsible for internationally wrongful acts against cultural heritage committed by their predecessor states during the Second World War. For instance, shall the new states, the successors of the USSR, be held responsible for art plunder and destruction of cultural heritage committed by the Red Army in the territories of the Third Reich? It appears that in practice such an unconditional obligation has not been accepted by successor states.

In fact, the negotiations undertaken by UNESCO, greatly affected by the contradictory interests of states, resulted in a fiasco. In 2007, UNESCO presented the final text of the Draft Declaration of Principles Relating to Cultural Objects Displaced in Connection with the Second World War.[112] This provided for an obligation to return cultural property to the territories from which it was taken. No time limits would apply in dealing with such cases. The final text of this document, in contrast to the initial drafts,[113] did not provide for the possibility of restitution-in-kind, and explicitly excluded the retention of cultural objects as war reparation. Moreover, it did not contain any definition of the Second World War, nor the definition of an aggressor state. These aspects of the instrument led to its firm rejection by Russia.[114] Similar objections were also raised by Poland,[115] which claimed that the exclusion of the principle of restitution-in-kind constituted an unjustified abrogation of the regime adopted by the Allied legislation after the Second World War, and therefore the Draft Declaration would be beneficial only for some states (Germany) at the expense of others. The statement of Poland went further. It argued that the Draft Declaration was of 'unjustified fragmentary

[111] See this chapter, section 5.3.3.

[112] The UNESCO Draft Declaration of Principles Relating to Cultural Objects Displaced in Relation to the Second World War, Paris, 9 March 2007, UNESCO Doc. 34C/22, Annex I; UNESCO Doc. 35C/24.

[113] Lyndell V. Prott, 'Principles for the Resolution of Disputes Concerning Cultural Heritage Displaced During the Second World War', in Elisabeth Simpson (ed), *The Spoils of War* (Harry N. Abrams Inc., 1997), at 229.

[114] UNESCO Doc. 34C/22, Annex II, at 4–5.

[115] UNESCO Doc. 34C/22, Annex II, at 2–4.

nature, and the interest of the international community calls for a more extensive regulation of the return of cultural objects'.[116] Therefore, 'it would be justified either to expand the scope of the prepared Declaration to include war conflicts and colonialism in the 19th and 20th centuries or to prepare and simultaneously adopt another declaration concerning war conflicts and colonialism in the two previous centuries which would contain corresponding instrumental solutions'.[117] In this view, Poland emphasized that the Draft Declaration did not 'constitute a source of international law' and it would serve only as 'a political act, indicating possible procedures and forms of solving a particular issue, in this case the issue of cultural objects displaced in connection with the Second World War'.[118] Finally, it opted for the continuation of *ex gratia* solutions as 'in international relations, both bilateral and multimedia, particular States may build their mutual relations on the said Declaration at their own discretion only, and not due to legal norms'.[119]

Arguably, the stormy negotiations on the text of the Draft Declaration and its final rejection have put an end to the debate on the existence of legal regime of the succession to responsibility for internationally wrongful acts against cultural heritage committed in the Second World War. As explained in Chapter 6, the actual state practice in these matters has followed *ex gratia* considerations, locating them within consensual mechanisms of cultural cooperation. It appears that similar interpretations of international law have been also applied both within the context of state succession and and that of decolonization.[120]

5.3 Cultural property and historic archives in the post-Cold War practice of state succession: select case-studies

5.3.1 Czechoslovakia

The events of the national and democratic movements in the Czechoslovak Socialist Republic (CSSR) initiated in March 1988 led to the 'Velvet Revolution' in the autumn of 1989. On 29 December a new president, Vaclav Havel, was chosen and in 1990 the first free parliamentary elections took place since 1946. In the same year the CSSR was replaced by a new federal state: Czech and Slovak Federal Republic (CSFR). However, it became obvious that the interests of the two countries were drifting in different directions. In 1992, due to political and economic tensions, the CSFR Federal Assembly decided on the dissolution of the federation. On 13 November 1992, the Constitution Act 541 on the apportionment of property of the Czech and Slovak Republics[121] was passed. Immediately, on 25 November the Federal Assembly voted the Constitution Act 542, which formally ended the existence of Czechoslovakia as of 31 December 1992.

[116] Ibid. at 4. [117] Ibid. [118] Ibid. at 3. [119] Ibid.

[120] See Chapter 6, section 6.4.

[121] Constitutional Law on the Partition of Property and Its Transfer to the Czech and Slovak Republics, 13 November 1992, Constitutional Act No. 541/1992.

a) General rules on the division of state property and the cultural exemption

The CSSR's state property comprised all immovable and movable property, including final rights, interests, and obligations of the CSSR and its organizations, situated in the state territory and abroad. Under Article 3 of the Constitutional Act 541, the division of state property was based on the principle of territoriality and generally followed the regime of Article 18 of the 1983 Vienna Convention. Accordingly, both Republics acquired the immovable property situated in their territories, and part of the movable property connected with the activities of the state in those territories. In all other questions not settled in conformity with the territorial rule, the property was divided proportionally by the populations of the two Republics (2:1 in favour of the Czech Republic).[122] Under Article 9, a special bilateral commission was established in order to implement the 1992 decision. This led to the conclusion of a number of detailed agreements adopted by the two successor states of the CSFR from 1993 onwards.

As regards the allocation of state cultural property, in the vast majority of cases this was based on territorial and institutional appurtenance. All the problematic cases were excluded from the general distribution of state property and were to be settled by a special bilateral commission established by the Czech and Slovak agreement on the reciprocal arrangement of cultural heritage issues, signed in 1993.[123] The solution to these controversial cases was finalized by 1995 and no external arbiters or experts were called.[124]

b) Czechoslovakian cultural property at the date of state succession

Following the Velvet Revolution and the democratization of political life, Czechoslovakia had to confront a number of questions on the matter of cultural heritage. It is important to mention, however, that they mainly referred to the consequences of the Second World War, in particular, the war plunder, confiscation, and post-war nationalization of private collections. In fact, there were no controversies relating to the interwar period. This was due to the fact that between the years 1918–38 there were no particular displacements of museum items between the respective territories of the Czech Republic and Slovakia. Moreover, before the creation of the dual federal republic in 1918, the history of these two countries evolved separately under Habsburg rule. Thus, as explained in Chapter 2, the interwar controversies on the rights to certain cultural treasures referred primarily to Czech and Slovak relations with former dominant powers, Austria and Hungary, respectively.

[122] See further ILA, Aspects of the Law of state Succession, Draft Final Report, Rio de Janeiro Conference (2008), at 58–59.

[123] See Andrzej Jakubowski 'National Museums in the Context of State Succession: The Negotiation of Difficult Pasts in the Post-Cold War Reality' in Dominique Poulot, José María Lanzarote Guiral, and Felicity Bodenstein (eds), *National Museums and the Negotiation of Difficult Pasts* (Linköping University Electronic Press, 2012), 19–36, at 25.

[124] Ibid.

The crucial period for the cultural patrimony of Czechoslovakia began in 1938, when the Munich Agreement was concluded. This sanctioned the annexation of the ethnically German territories of Sudetenland to the Third Reich and the transfer of other border provinces to Hungary and Poland. The partition of Czechoslovakia was concluded in 1939, which led to extensive transfers of population and the persecution of Jews under the Nazi administration. This was followed by subsequent war plunders and the post-war creation of a new political and social order. As a result of the 1945 Potsdam Agreement, German nationals had to leave the territory of Czechoslovakia. There were also extensive exchanges of minority groups with Hungary. In addition, the new socialist Czechoslovak administration issued a series of regulations, the so-called Beneš decrees,[125] which expropriated the enemy property, in particular the property of German, Austrian, and Hungarian nationals. Further Czechoslovak legislation also nationalized property of wealthy landowners. The same fate was shared by the abandoned Jewish heritage. Hence the post-war period was characterized by substantial displacement of populations and the nationalization of private art collections. As a consequence, state museums of post-war socialist Czechoslovakia acquired many displaced, looted, or confiscated cultural objects. Sometimes items taken from Slovak territory were added to Czech collections, and vice versa.

After the Velvet Revolution, democratic federal Czechoslovakia had to confront all these events, which generally focused on the restitution of cultural property. This was settled by the privatization acts passed in 1990 and 1991. Arguably, the implementation of these regulations required more complex legal solutions than the distribution of state cultural property after the 1993 dissolution. The territorial displacement of cultural objects between the two countries was not particularly frequent and was difficult to settle since during the roughly 50 years of post-war history of Czechoslovakia, both republics kept separate national collections. Therefore, all interstate controversies relating to the situation of cultural heritage were decided in the first few years after dissolution. By contrast, both states have to deal with private claims constantly.

The solutions applied to state succession to state cultural property of the former Czechoslovakia relate to two sets of issues: distribution and allocation of state cultural objects, and succession to state archives and library collections.

c) *The 1993–94 Czech–Slovak agreements on the exchange of cultural objects*

At the beginning of 1993, immediately after the official break up of Czechoslovakia, the two republics signed a bilateral agreement on the reciprocal arrangement of cultural heritage issues.[126] This appointed a special Czech and Slovak commission

[125] See Benjamin Frommer, *National Cleansing: Retribution against Nazi Collaborators in Postwar Czechoslovakia* (CUP, 2005).

[126] See Andrzej Jakubowski, 'National Museums' (n 123) 26–27.

responsible for the allocation of certain displaced cultural objects of state property. The negotiations began in 1993 and concluded in 1994.[127] On 26 September 1994 in Brno the two states signed the Agreement on the Exchange of Certain Objects of Cultural Heritage.[128] This referred to a group of medieval paintings.

The Czech Republic was obliged to hand over ten tables forming the XIV century polyptych of St Mary with Saints (Bojnicky Altar) by the famous fourteenth-centure Florentine master Nardo di Cione. The altar constitutes the only entirely preserved work by this artist. It came from the vast art collection created in the second part of the nineteenth century by a Hungarian aristocrat, Count János Pálffy (1829–1908), one of the most renowned collectors and antiquarians in Central Europe.[129] He placed his collections in several residences in Vienna, Bratislava, Budapest, and Paris as well as in his country houses situated on the present territory of Slovakia, which at that time constituted a part of the Hungarian Crown. He chose the medieval castle of Bojnice as the site for his house-museum. Among other artworks, he installed there the polyptych of Nardo di Cione. In his will, Pálffy bequeathed the core of his collection of paintings to the National Picture Gallery in Budapest, and bound his heirs to keep the residences in Bojnice, Vienna, Budapest, and Pezinok as public museums. In addition, the art collections had to be preserved in their original place and in their entirety. However, after his death and after the dissolution of Austria-Hungary, this collection was dispersed between different successors, and at the same divided by the new state borders—the majority of Pálffy's lands, including the Bojnice Castle, were situated on the territory of the newly established Republic of Czechoslovakia. In the interwar period, his heirs sold many precious pieces of art, and in 1939 the castle, its furnishing and surrounding lands were purchased by Ján Baťa, a wealth footwear manufacturer. Eventually, after the Second World War, the residence and its collections were nationalized and some artworks, including the Bojnicky Altar, sent to the National Gallery in Prague.[130]

During the negotiations after the split of the federal state, the Czech Republic agreed to transfer the altar to Slovakia provided that the latter would give an equivalent of ten paintings from the same epoch. Consequently, both republics decided to exchange the paintings whose detailed list was annexed to the 1994 Agreement. In this way, the cultural objects returned to Slovakia on the basis of territorial links with the place where the collection had been originally established. It also seems that the artistic integrity of the castle-museum was taken into consideration. However, the handing over of the property was not based on a gratuitous contractual agreement between the two successors of the CSFR. In

[127] See Kerstin Odendahl, *Kulturgüterschutz* (Mohr Siebeck, 2005), 155.

[128] Agreement between the Government of the Republic of Slovakia and the Government of Czech Republic on the Exchange of Certain Objects of Cultural Heritage, signed on 26 September 1994, (Dohoda medzi Vládou Slovenskej Republiky a Vládou Českej Republiky o výmene niektorých predmetov kultúrneho dedičstwa, podpĭsaná v Brne 26. Septembra 1994), *Official Journal of Czech Republic* 343/1994, 1547.

[129] Ingrid Ciulisová, 'Art Collecting of the Central-European Aristocracy in the Nineteenth Century: The Case of Count Pálffy', *Journal of the History of Collections* 18(2006)2, 201–9.

[130] Ibid.

fact, Slovakia had to compensate the return of the altar by the Czech Republic by supplying it with other artefacts.

Eventually, the return of the Bojnicky Altar to Slovakia took place on 15 December 1995. The official ceremony of the vesting of paintings was celebrated on 18 December and was widely commented in the mass media and perceived as a 'national' success. For the occasion, in 1997 a special Slovakian postage stamp was issued.

As regards the apportionment of state library collections, the dismemberment of Czechoslovakia did not cause any particular difficulties. Both states had separate national libraries and separate state archives. After the 'divorce' in 1993, the Czech Republic and Slovakia decided on the delimitation of certain 'federal' records, of which in the vast majority continued to be preserved on the territory of the Czech Republic. For instance, such a solution was applied with regard to the important, politically as well as historically, archive of the former socialist Ministry of the Interior. In Prague, the Czechoslovak Documentation Centre (Československé dokumentačni středisko, CSDS)[131] was established in 1999, which houses exiled Czechoslovak archival heritage produced during Soviet domination.

Thus, the division of state cultural property of the CSSR constitutes a model example of a friendly dissolution of a multinational state. Furthermore, it fits into the legal pattern worked out on the occasion of Austro–Hungarian relations in the interwar period. Moreover, in the process of amicable separation, both successor states of CSFR tended to maintain close cultural and scientific relations. Certain more precise provisions are to be found in the 1992 bilateral agreement[132] with regard to neighbour relations and the rights of minorities, which provided for the reciprocal obligations to preserve and protect the other party's cultural heritage and monuments (Article 15), reciprocal promotion of language and cultural cooperation (Article 8, 14, 16), including combating the illicit cross-border transfer of cultural material (Article 19).

5.3.2 The Soviet Union

The events of the 1989 'Autumn of Nations' in different parts of the Eastern bloc accelerated the changes already underway within the Soviet Union. The new policies of *perestroika* and *glasnost* introduced by the General Secretary of the Communist Party of the Soviet Union, Mikhail Gorbachev, in the second half of the 1980s,[133] led to the democratization of public life. Accordingly, on 7 February 1990, the Central Committee of the Communist Party of the USSR gave up its monopoly on power. In the following weeks, the 15 constituent republics of the USSR held their first competitive elections, in which political reformers and

[131] <http://csds.cz/en/csds.html>, accessed on 4 February 2015.

[132] Czech Republic and Slovakia Agreement on Good-Neighbourliness, Friendly Relations and Cooperation on 23 November 1992, 1900 UNTS 95.

[133] See Edward A. Hewett and Victor H. Winston (eds), *Milestones in Glasnost and Perestroika: Politics and People* (The Brookings Institution, 1991).

national leaders took many votes. The process of disintegration of the union was initiated.

The first to leave the Soviet Union was Lithuania, followed by two other Baltic republics, Estonia and Latvia. Subsequently, in March 1991, in a USSR-wide referendum, the majority of voters opted for the retention of the Union. Yet the Baltic States, Armenia, Georgia, and Moldova boycotted the referendum. The remaining nine republics (Russian SFSR, Ukrainian SSR, Byelorussian SSR, Kazakh SSR, Azerbaijan SSR, Uzbek SSR, Kyrgyz SSR, Turkmen SSR, and Tajik SSR) and the USSR central government agreed to continue the federal union (Agreement 9+1). On 23 April 1991, the final text of the New Union Treaty which would replace the 1922 Treaty on the Creation of the USSR was drafted.[134] This would create a new federation of sovereign states under the name the Union of Soviet Sovereign Republics, with a common president, foreign policy, and army. However, in the following months, several other republics (Armenia, Georgia, and Moldova) officially proclaimed their independence,[135] and the process of dissolution accelerated. Under these circumstances, the leaders of three Slavic republics—Belarus, Russia, and Ukraine—signed the Belavezha Accords on 8 December 1991, which formally dissolved the Soviet Union, and established the Commonwealth of Independent States (CIS). This was confirmed in the subsequent Alma-Ata Declaration signed on 21 December 1991 by 11 of the 15 post-Soviet new states: Armenia, Azerbaijan, Belarus, Kazakhstan, Kyrgyzstan, Moldova, Russian Federation, Tajikistan, Turkmenistan, Ukraine, and Uzbekistan. Two years later, in 1993, the Republic of Georgia also joined the CIS. Thus, the CIS was formed out of all the post-Soviet republics, except of the three Baltic States.

In accordance with the 1991 agreements, the CIS did not constitute a successor of the USSR. It was created as a confederation of independent states, a regional organization whose participating states were the former Soviet Republics. In the Alma-Ata declaration, the post-Soviet state leaders recognized the equal rights of CIS members. In the preamble, they declared they were:

> seeking to build democratic law-governed states, the relations between which will develop on the basis of mutual recognition and respect for state sovereignty and sovereign equality, the inalienable right to self-determination, principles of equality and noninterference in the internal affairs, the rejection of the use of force, the threat of force and economic and any other methods of pressure, a peaceful settlement of disputes, respect for human rights and freedoms, including the rights of national minorities, a conscientious fulfillment of commitments and other generally recognized principles and standards of international law.

They also stressed the importance of the reciprocal recognition of territorial integrity and the inviolability of existing borders, and they stressed the importance of mutual cooperation, and 'preservation of civilian peace and inter-ethnic accord'.

[134] Långström, *Transformation in Russia and International Law* (n 42) 180 ff.

[135] Ibid. 210; Brzeziński and Sullivan, *Russia and the Commonwealth of Independent States* (n 36) 13–21.

As already explained, in the creation of the CIS, special status was granted to the Russian Federation. It was agreed that Russia would continue to pursue the international personality of the USSR. In this context, one may associate the disintegration of the USSR and the creation of the CIS with some post-colonial mechanisms such as the British Commonwealth.[136]

The constitutional framework of the CIS was eventually established by the adoption of the 1993 CIS Charter,[137] regulating *inter alia* the main competences of common organs, dispute settlement, and collective security and military-political cooperation. After this date, the CIS passed several modifications. Some states decided on closer collaboration (ie the creation of a Union state of Russia and Belarus in December 1999);[138] another practically withdrew from the CIS structures (eg Georgia). Moreover, the territorial integrity of the post-Soviet republics has not been respected. Although the Russian Federation invoked this principle during the bloody pacification of the national uprising in Chechnya, at the same time, it openly supported the secessionist republics of Transnistria in the territory of Moldova, Abkhazia, and South Ossetia in Georgia, maintaining its military forces there. Moreover, the 2014 unlawful annexation of Crimea by Russia as well as the ongoing conflict in eastern Ukraine have seriously threatened the stability of post-Soviet state boundaries.

a) General principles on the division of state property

The division of the state property of the USSR caused serious complications due to the structure of property in the Soviet Union, and the different status of the former Soviet republics at the date of succession.

As regards the structure of the USSR's state property, this reflected the doctrine of centralized economy. According to the 1977 USSR Constitution,[139] state property was defined as 'the common wealth of all the Soviet people' (Article 10). In practice, it meant that there was no clear distinction between state property of the USSR, property of republics, communal property, etc. This caused a number of controversies over the status of certain state assets between the Russian Federation and other post-Soviet republics.

The Baltic States restored their sovereignty, lost as a result of the 1940 Soviet annexation. They were therefore not USSR successor states and generally did not claim the USSR's assets, nor did they participate in the payment of the USSR's external debt. However, they advanced claims in respect of the immovable state property situated in their territories as well as certain property abroad, as

[136] Sergei A. Voitovich, 'The Commonwealth of Independent States: An Emerging Institutional Model', *EJIL* 4(1993)3, 403–17, at 407–8.

[137] See the documentation and the analysis of the process of ratification, Brzezinski and Sullivan, *Russia and the Commonwealth of Independent States* (n 36) 414 ff.

[138] Relevant information available at: <http://eng.soyuz.by/>, accessed on 4 February 2015.

[139] Constitutional (Fundamental) Law of the Union of Soviet Socialist Republics of 7 October 1977; for English translation, see <http://www.departments.bucknell.edu/russian/const/1977toc.html>, accessed on 5 February 2015.

diplomatic and consular properties owned by them before their incorporation into the USSR.[140] Moreover, they reserved the right to retain Soviet military property situated on their territory without compensation.

During the sequence of CIS summits following the Alma-Ata Declaration of 21 December 1991, the issue of the apportionment of USSR state assets and liabilities was repeatedly addressed. Finally, at a meeting of the Council of the CIS Head of state in Moscow on 6 July 1992, three documents were signed on the issues of legal succession concerning the USSR state property abroad, state archives, debts, and assets. As regards the apportionment of state property and liabilities, the agreement of 6 July 1992 applied in accordance with the provisions of the 1991 USSR Treaty on Foreign Debt a proportional division of assets and shares in debts. In order to settle potential controversies, a special multilateral commission was established.[141] In practice, however, the final decisions were taken in a number of bilateral agreements concluded between the post-USSR states. In particular, these referred to military state property, including nuclear weapons and the Black Sea Fleet, as well as gold and diamond reserves and USSR property in space.[142]

In the following years, the post-Soviet republics did not manage to adopt uniform standards regulating succession to USSR state property. In a number of cases, certain solutions were adopted on a *de facto* basis, sometimes resulting from bilateral negotiations and agreements between the republics concerned.[143]

b) The allocation and distribution of cultural property

Importantly, the disintegration of the USSR involved at least two different scenarios. As already mentioned it primarily comprised the separation of parts of a state, as provided by both of Vienna Conventions. However, the initial stages of the process could be also classified as dissolution of a multinational state. In addition, the disintegration of the USSR also led to the creation of newly independent (post-colonial) states. For instance, some of the post-Soviet republics in Central Asia, such as Uzbekistan or Tajikistan, have never existed as separate sovereign states, although Uzbeks and Tajiks had a lengthy independent national history prior to their nineteenth century colonization by the Russian Empire. Thus in terms of state succession in cultural property, the case of the USSR referred to the European models of the allocation of cultural items, on the one hand, and the decolonization of the cultural heritage, on the other. Moreover, the situation of

[140] Rein Müllerson, 'New Developments in the Former USSR and Yugoslavia', *Virginia Journal of International Law* 33(1992–93)2, 299–322, at 311.

[141] Natalia Dronova, 'The Division of State Property in the Case of State Succession in the Former Soviet Union', in Pierre Michel Eisemann and Martti Koskenniemi (eds), *La succession d'États: la codification à l'épreuve des faits/State Succession: Codification Tested against the Facts* (Brill, 2000), 781–826, at 798, ILA, Aspects of the Law of State Succession. Economic Aspects of State Succession. Final Report, Toronto, 1996, at 8, available at: <http://www.ila-hq.org/html/layout_committee.htm>, accessed on 30 January 2015.

[142] Dronova, 'The Division of State Property' (n 141) 796 ff.

[143] Ibid. 824.

the Baltic States was completely different from other republics because the mechanisms of state succession competed with the principles concerning the protection of the cultural heritage during enemy occupation. The situation is also complicated by the fact that many cultural objects originated from more than one territory and are considered as cultural patrimony by many states and ethnic groups. Thus, for methodological purposes, it is crucial to analyse the regulations adopted in respect of the allocation of cultural property following the dismemberment of the former Soviet Union in two main contexts: the general legal frameworks applied within the states of the CIS,[144] and their implementation; and the settlements of cultural property-related disputes between the Russian Federation and the Baltic States.

With reference to the first issue, the representatives of the 11 states of the CIS signed the Agreement on the Return of Cultural and Historic Treasures to Their Country of Origin (the 1992 CIS Agreement on Cultural and Historic Treasures) in Minsk on 14 February 1992.[145] The preamble of this agreement underlined that 'the return of works of art, monuments, exhibits, archival manuscripts, documents and other cultural and artistic objects to their nations and their respective origin, shall contribute to the rival of national cultures, protection and future development of common cultural objects and shall promote better co-operation between the independent states.' It then recalled 'regulations included in the 1991 Resolution of the UN General Assembly concerning the return of the cultural property to its country of origin',[146] as well as the 1970 UNESCO Convention.[147] In order to comply with these objectives, the states parties to the 1992 CIS Agreement on Cultural and Historic Treasures undertook to 'cooperate in returning the cultural and historic treasures to their countries of origin'. This would be achieved by establishing 'on equal footing, the international commission whose responsibility shall be the design and practical implementation of the repatriation of cultural and historical property of the states-members of the Commonwealth, and the decision which categories of the said property are subject of repatriation' (Article 2).

Each state was also responsible for establishing its own commission to prepare relevant documentation concerning cultural property kept in its territory as well as in foreign territories (Article 3), and to secure 'mutual cognizance of the state museum, library and archival collections' to experts of foreign commissions (Article 4), and to safeguard in their respective territories the cultural property of nations (Article 5).

[144] For an extensive normative, theoretical, and empirical analysis of the protection and management of historical and cultural heritage in the CIS, see Igor Martynenko, *Legal Protection of Historical and Cultural Heritage in the Countries of the Customs Union within the Eurasian Economic Community* (RIOR, 2014).

[145] Agreement on the Return of Cultural and Historic Treasures to Their Country of Origin Signed by the Member States of the CIS on February 14, 1992, *Rossiskaia Gazieta*, 24 February 1992, 1–2, English translation after Wojciech Kowalski, 'Restitution of Works of Art Pursuant to Private and Public International Law', *RCADI* 288(2001), 9–244, at 88–90.

[146] UN Doc.A/RES/46/10.

[147] UNESCO Convention on the Means of Prohibiting and Preventing the Illicit Import, Export and Transfer of Ownership of Cultural Property, adopted on 14 November 1970, entered in force on 24 April 1972, 823 UNTS 231.

For the purposes of the implantation of these regulations, the same 11 states concluded a subsequent agreement on the cooperation between the CIS on 15 May 1992.[148] Under Article 3, paragraph 3, it underlined:

the need of creation of the interstate commission of experts from plenipotentiaries of the Parties for consideration of questions and preparation of recommendations about the restitution of cultural and art values on the basis of two or multilateral agreements according to the legislation and regulations of international law.

Undoubtedly, the provisions of the 1992 CIS Agreement on Cultural and Historic Treasures were very far-reaching, as they invoked extensively the right to cultural heritage and the importance of the return of cultural property for the cultural development consistently promoted by UNESCO and the United Nations. However, such an approach became the subject of vivid criticism from the very beginning. It was argued that the Agreement, recalling the 1970 UNESCO Convention, disregarded its Article 13 according to which this Convention was applicable only to the extent that it was 'consistent with the laws of each state'.[149] The point was also raised that it did not respect the principle of state sovereignty,[150] as provided under Article 6.1 of the 1972 World Heritage Convention.[151]

According to Mark Boguslavkij, a renowned Russian expert in international law, the 1992 CIS Agreement on Cultural and Historic Treasures did not provide clear criteria for determining the state of origin, time limits, procedures, or other requirements for the return. What is more, the restitution of cultural objects under this Agreement, based on measures applied in international law with reference to the liquidation of the consequences of wars and decolonization, would be inadequate in the case of the USSR disintegration.[152] Mr Boguslavkij noticed:

we cannot ignore the circumstance of the member states of the CIS not having previously any international personality as sovereign states or, even if it was the case, the fact the former state boundaries were basically different from the present ones. Hence, the country of origin can hardly be defined from historical premises (a dramatic example being the case of the Scythian gold).[153]

He then argued:

International law does not stipulate the redistribution of the cultural heritage of single multi-national states. The articles of international law assume the territorial principle

[148] Agreement on the Co-Operation in the Field of Culture Signed in Tashkent on 15 May 1992 by the Prime Ministers of Eleven States-Members of the CIS, available at: <http://cis-legislation.com/document.fwx?rgn=25693#>, accessed on 10 February 2015.

[149] Dronova, 'The Division of State Property' (n 141) 818.

[150] UNESCO Convention Concerning the Protection of World Natural and Cultural Heritage, adopted on 16 November 1972, entered into force on 17 December 1975, 1037 UNTS 151.

[151] Dronova, 'The Division of Sate Property' (n 141) 818.

[152] Mark Boguslavskij, 'Contemporary Legal Problems of Return of Cultural Property to Its Country of Origin in Russia and the Conference of Independent States', *IJCP* 3(1994)2, 243–56, at 253–54.

[153] This refers to the collections of Scythian antiquities excavated in the present-day territory of Ukraine, and preserved in the Russian collections, namely in the Hermitage. As another example, Boguslavskij recalled the paintings of Ivan Aivazoskij (1817–1900), from Armenian origin, whose paintings, created in Russia, are mostly kept in the Theodosian Museum in Crimea, Ukraine. Ibid. 253.

and agree that the cultural heritage of every country, such as the museum collections, include a variety of objects, no matter what their country of origin is. This implies that international law does not stipulate an unconditional return of any historical or cultural property to its country of origin. For this reason, the Agreement of February 14, 1992 is unprecedented in international law and putting it into practice might have far-reaching consequences, bringing about serious losses to the whole of the cultural heritage of the nations of the CIS. This does not, however, restrain the member states of the CIS from holding bilateral talks on the problem of the return of particular objects.[154]

It is clear that Boguslavkij contested the existence of the rule of international law which would provide for the unconditional return of cultural property to its place of origin, following state succession. In fact, post-colonial state practice with regard to the distribution of cultural material corresponded to this view. He also invoked the principle of priority of contractual arrangements between the states concerned, which was fully consistent with the provisions of the 1983 Vienna Convention, as well as with the practice of the UNESCO Intergovernmental Committee for Promoting the Return of Cultural Property to its Countries of Origin or its Restitution in case of Illicit Appropriation. On the other hand, the position taken by Boguslavkij also reflected the traditional reluctance of former colonial or imperial powers to conclude complex settlements on the return of cultural objects. In this context, one may read Boguslaviskij's suggestions as to the restriction of the restitution process to bilateral negotiations only, and to certain clearly identified cultural items. In this way, the position of the requesting states would obviously be much weaker *vis-à-vis* the Russian Federation, a holder of the vast majority of imperial collections. Yet, it needs to be acknowledged that such views were also driven by the objective of the protection of cultural heritage in the difficult and uncertain political situation in early 1990s.

In this context, it is worth recollecting the much more emotional attitudes adopted by some Russian museums officials, who argued that the 1992 CIS Agreement on Cultural and Historic Treasures would empty all the most important Russian collections. They claimed that the unconditional restoration of cultural objects to their countries of origin was impossible in practice. Furthermore, it would lead to the dramatic fragmentation of collections preserved for centuries and to the partition of culture.[155] It was recalled that after the signature of the CIS Agreement on Cultural and Historic Treasures, Georgia, Uzbekistan, Turkmenistan, Armenia, and Ukraine immediately asked for the return of cultural property preserved in different state museums. According to Nikolay Gubyenko, a former Soviet Minister of Culture, the already issued and potential claims would refer to more than 3 million works of art.[156] In addition, some requests, such as that of Ukraine for the return of

[154] Ibid. 254.

[155] Olga Rumyantseva, 'Who Gets What in the Post-Soviet Fall-Out', *The Art Newspaper*, 1 May 1992.

[156] Ibid.

the Monomakh's Cap (also called the Golden Cap (*Shapka Zolotaya*)), the oldest of the crowns preserved exhibited at the Kremlin Armoury in Moscow, heightened existing controversies and illustrated the complexity of issues related to post-Soviet state succession. The crown was part of the regalia of Tsarist Russia, probably of Tatar origin but traditionally attributed to Vladimir Monomakh, Velikiy Kniaz (Grand Prince) of Kievan Rus, who himself allegedly received the cap from his grandfather, the Byzantine Emperor Constantine IX Monomachus. During the rise of Tsarist Russia, it was used as a symbol of the succession from the Roman Empire to the sovereign rulers in Moscow, and served as one of the elements of political and religious doctrine of 'Moscow as the Third Rome', claiming the hegemony of the Tsars in Eastern and South-eastern Europe.[157] At the same time, however, the patrimony of the Kievan Rus constitutes an inherent component of state tradition and identity of modern Ukraine.

In the press, Russian museum officials questioned the viability of identifying the country of origin of many cultural treasures. Nikolay Gubyenko ironically suggested how some cultural property could be returned on the basis of the object's nationality. For instance, according to him, in its claim for the return of archaeological Scythian treasures, Ukraine not only had to declare its citizens as the direct descendants of the ancient Scythians but also to provide evidence that the items displayed in the Hermitage collection had been created by natives and not by Greek masters.[158]

Protests were voiced by all the major Russian cultural institutions whose directors issued a special letter to the President of the Russian Federation asking him to consider the extreme seriousness of the situation. The indignation of Russian museum leaders is reflected in the words of Dmitriy Likhachev, the Chairman of the Russian International Cultural Fund:

> If such a policy towards culture continues, I will have to apply for citizenship in a foreign country, because it is not worth living in a country whose government has an attitude to culture like ours. I will make my views known to the world community and to UNESCO.[159]

As one might have expected, in this atmosphere Russian authorities began to stall the implementation of the 1992 CIS Agreement on Cultural and Historic Treasures. The main obstacle for the execution of the 1992 CIS Agreement was whether it was conformed with the legislation in force in the Russian Federation. This related in particular to two Acts: the 1978 bill of the Russian Socialist Federal Soviet Republic (RSFSR) on the protection and utilization of historic and cultural property,[160] and the 1990 bill on urgent measures for the protection of national, cultural, and natural heritage of the nations of the RSFSR.[161] In fact,

[157] For instance, see Donald Ostrowski, *Muscovy and the Mongols: Cross-Cultural Influences on the Steppe Frontier, 1304–1589* (CUP, 1998), 173 ff.

[158] Rumyantseva, 'Who Gets What' (n 155).

[159] Ibid.

[160] Boguslavskij, 'Contemporary Legal Problems' (n 152) 255.

[161] Ibid.

these two Acts prohibited the exportation of cultural objects of state, social, or religious organizations. Such a transfer was only possible on the basis of special strictly regulated permissions. Thus, as quickly as 20 May 1992, both chambers of the Supreme Council of the Russian Federation voted an opinion concerning the 1992 CIS Agreement on Cultural and Historic Treasures.[162] Under Clause 1 of this opinion, the Supreme Council stated that the 1992 CIS Agreement 'does not conform to the legislation of the Russian Federation and the International Law concerning the cultural heritage and natural heritage of the world.' As the 1992 CIS Agreement did not impose the ratification of any specified international documents, under clause 2 the opinion stated that 'it has to be recommended to the Constitutional Commission of the Congress of People's Deputies of the Russian Federation that the draft of the Bill on international agreements of the Russian Federation should include a clause requiring an obligatory ratification of all international agreements concerning the protection of national, cultural and natural heritage of nations of Russia.'[163]

Moreover, the competent Russian authorities recommended that the repatriation negotiations be conducted in bilateral commissions rather than in any kind of multilateral body.[164] The possibility of decisively settling complex post-Soviet cultural property-related disputes was subsequently obstructed by a special decree of the President of the Russian Federation on 'particularly valuable cultural heritage objects of the nations of Russia'.[165] This, among other provisions, introduced a list of 16 main cultural institutions and museums whose integrity and intact preservation was legally guaranteed 'in the interest of the present and future Russian generations'.

Notwithstanding these obstacles, other states of the CIS took the initiative of solving the issues in the following years. During the meeting held in Minsk (11–13 January 1993), representatives of six states: Azerbaijan, Belarus, Kazakhstan, Moldavia, Turkmenistan, Ukraine, and Armenia as an observer, discussed the format of the future multilateral commissions and drafted its basic responsibilities

[162] Postanovleniye Verkhovnogo Soveta Rossiskoi Federatsii O soglashenii gosudarstv—uchastnikov Sodruzhestva Nezavisimikh Gosudarstv O vozvrashchenii kul'turnikh I istoricheskikh tsennostei gosudarstvam ih proiskhozhdeniya (Enactment of the Supreme Soviet of Russia on the Agreement on the Return of Cultural and Historical Objects to the States of Their Origin), *Vedomosti s'ezda narodnikh deputatov Rossiskoi Federatsii i Verkhovnogo Soveta Rossiskoi Federatsii* (1992) No. 23, item 1228, translation after Boguslavskij, 'Contemporary Legal Problems' (n 152) 255.

[163] Boguslavskij, 'Contemporary Legal Problems' (n 152) 255.

[164] Letter by T. Nikita, Deputy Minister of Culture and Tourism of the Russian Federation, to the Belarus Government Dated on 10 August, unpublished, after: Wojciech Kowalski, 'Repatriation of Cultural Property Following a Cession of Territory or Dissolution of Multinational States', *AAL* 6(2001)2, 139–66, at 161.

[165] Decree of the President of the Russian Federation on the Most Valuable Objects of Cultural Heritage of the Peoples of Russia, No 1487, 30 November 1992; this amended the previous Act: Decree of the President of Russian Soviet Federative Socialist Republic on the Most Valuable Objects of National Heritage of Russia, No. 294, 18 December 1991, after: Kowalski, 'Repatriation of Cultural Property' (n 164) 161.

and procedures.[166] It was suggested that the commission would not only decide on the questions concerning the allocation of cultural property, but also on the distribution of art collections transferred from Germany at the end of the Second World War, stored primarily in Moscow and St Petersburg. These would be treated as reparation of the property destroyed or lost as result of the war in each of the states of the CIS. In addition, the inclusion of other states that were part of the USSR in the 1992 CIS Agreement was also discussed.[167] The resistance of the Russian Federation left these projects uncompleted.

In the mid 1990s, the lack of Russian political will to resolve the questions of the former USSR's collections was widely criticized in Europe. Claims against Russia were made by Germany and other countries, from which the Red Army had removed art collections at the end of the Second World War, as well as by the former USSR republics. At the beginning, the interests of both groups of states diverged since the post-Soviet republics hoped for a share in such displaced properties. However, the positions of the majority of states deeply affected by Soviet domination began to converge.

All these issues emerged at the time of the admission of the Russian Federation to the CoE. While some of the former Soviet republics were accepted as members of the CoE without any obligations imposed (ie Ukraine in November 1995), Russia's acceptance was delayed. Among other issues, Russia's reluctance to help solve the question of the return of cultural objects and archives was discussed at the hearings before the CoE in 1995.[168] As a result of this, it was agreed that in the statement of intent that Russia was to sign as a requirement of its admission to the CoE, there would be commitments to the settlement of cultural heritage controversies. Accordingly, the intent of Russia, apart from the duties as to the observance of human rights, included the commitment of the Russian government

> to negotiate claims for the return of cultural property to other European countries on an ad hoc basis that differentiates between types of property (archives, works of art, buildings, etc.) and of ownership (public, private or institutional) …
>
> to settle rapidly all issues related to the return of property claimed by Council of Europe member states, in particular the archives transferred to Moscow in 1945.[169]

Arguably, the state members of the CoE attempted to force Russia to concede the return of cultural objects displaced primarily as a result of the Second World War, and during the Russian/Soviet domination in Central and Eastern Europe. The intent to adopt international standards in respect of state properties was

166 Protocol of the Sittings Devoted to the Issues of the Property of Works of Art, Minsk, 11–13 January 1993, unpublished; after Kowalski, 'Repatriation of Cultural Property' (n 164) 161.

167 Kowalski, 'Repatriation of Cultural Property' (n 164) 161.

168 After Patricia Kennedy Grimsted, *Trophies of War and Empire: The Archival Heritage of Ukraine, World War II and International Politics of Restitution* (Ukrainian Research Institute of Harvard University, 2004), 390.

169 CoE Parliamentary Assembly, Opinion No. 193(1996) on Russia's Request for Membership of the Council of Europe, 25 January 1996, para. 10, xi, xiv, available at: <http://assembly.coe.int/Main.asp?link=/Documents/AdoptedText/ta96/EOPI193.htm>, accessed on 30 January 2015.

considered as being important as the observance of human rights. Consequently, the commitment to comply with such obligations was treated as a requirement for admission to the community of democratic, civilized European nations.

In Russia, however, the resistance against any restitution from public collections was growing. In April 1995, the Russian Parliament (Duma) voted for a moratorium on restitution until a new Russian law could be adopted.[170] In 1997, in response to Russia's position, the summit of the Ministers of Culture of the CIS states inserted into a joint resolution a clause on the importance of multilateral cooperation in respect of the repatriation of cultural property.[171] However, in the same year, the Russian Duma passed the Federal Law on Cultural Valuables Displaced to the U.S.S.R. as a Result of World War II and Located on the Territory of the Russian Federation (the 1997 Russian Law on Cultural Valuables). This law, which reaffirmed state ownership of Russia over the entirety of cultural properties taken to the territory of Russia as reparation for war losses, was driven by the Cold-War concept that all removals and appropriation of cultural property made by the Red Army served as rightful reparation for cultural loss during war. Consequently, Russia does not have any legal obligation to return any of the items taken during the Second World War from the territories of states aggressors,[172] and such objects constitute the alienable property of the Russian Federation.

However, the law introduced an exemption for cultural objects of the former USSR republics. They could be returned to these states, who would bear all the expenses of such repatriation (Article 18). Accordingly, Article 7 'On the Guarantees of the Rights of Ownership of the Republic of Belarus, the Latvian Republic, the Lithuanian Republic, the Republic of Moldova, Ukraine, and the Estonian Republic to Displaced Cultural Valuables', set out the provisions on the inalienability of the Russian federal property:

> shall not apply to the rights of property of the Republic of Belorussia, the Latvian Republic, the Lithuanian Republic, the Republic of Moldova, Ukraine and the Estonian Republic to cultural objects which could find themselves among the displaced cultural values but which were plundered and taken away during World War II by Germany and/or her war allies from the territories of the Belorussian Soviet Socialist Republic, the Latvian Soviet Socialist Republic, the Lithuanian Soviet Socialist Republic, the Moldavian Soviet Socialist Republic, the Ukrainian Soviet Socialist Republic and the Estonian Soviet Socialist Republic rather than that of the Russian Soviet Federative Socialist Republic, and which were the national property of the said Union Republics rather than that of the other Union Republics which formed part of the U.S.S.R. within its boundaries as of 1 February 1950.
>
> Cultural objects referred to in section I of this Article may be turned over to whomever is their rightful owner in the Republic of Belorussia, the Latvian Republic, the Lithuanian

[170] Grimsted, *Trophies of War and Empire* (n 168) 397.

[171] Kowalski, 'Repatriation of Cultural Property' (n 164) 161.

[172] Shawn S. Stephens, 'The Hermitage and Pushkin Exhibits: An Analysis of the Ownership Rights to Cultural Properties Removed from Occupied Germany', *Houston Journal of International Law* 18(1995–96)1, 59–112.

Republic, the Republic of Moldova, Ukraine and the Estonian Republic subject to their compliance with section 4 of Article 18 of this Federal Law and their agreement to take the same approach, based on the principle of mutuality, to the cultural values of the Russian Federation to be presently found in their territory that have been displaced to the U.S.S.R. from former enemy states.

The problem with the allocation and repatriation of cultural property of the post-Soviet states was raised during an international conference which took place 19–20 June 1997 in Minsk, at the Francisk Skorina National Scientific and Educational Centre.[173] Organized under the auspices of UNESCO, the event was attended by delegates from Belarus, Germany, the UK, Poland, Russia, Ukraine, and the Czech Republic. The vast majority of speakers criticized the position of the Russian Federation both for ignoring the 1992 CIS Agreement and for the enactment of the 1997 Federal Law on Cultural Valuables.[174] They also stressed the need for closer international cooperation for the repatriation of cultural objects. At the end of the conference, all the participants issued the Final Document,[175] which noted the following postulates:

Call on the governing bodies of CIS countries to make multilateral and bilateral agreements on the issues of exposure, return and joint use of cultural values.

Appeal to the governments of CIS countries and to the Russian Federation government in particular, to:

— resume the activities of the Intergovernmental Advisory Committee on the issues of restitution of cultural values, which was stipulated by Tashkent Agreement on cooperation in the sphere of culture (1992).

— create necessary favourable conditions for experts' work, so they could study the migration of cultural values and scientifically process that massive part of cultural heritage which was concealed or excepted from the scientific use.

Appeal to the statesmen and intelligentsia of CIS countries where many museum collections are of very intricate origin and of great value for several states, to pay special attention to the search for moral ways of settlements of conflict situations and to display good will and good-neighbourly initiative on different levels....

Ask the governments of the Republic of Belarus and the Russian Federation to create states bides and scientific institutions (or departments in already existing institutions) which would deal with the issues of the exposure, return and joint use of cultural values of their own countries, which are staying abroad.

Call on for the integration of efforts to expose, return and use jointly the debatable cultural values. ***Attach*** special importance to creating of the Information bank in this

[173] Adam Mal'dzis, *The Restitution of Cultural Treasures: Problems of Repatriation and Common Usage (Legal, Scholarly and Ethical Aspects). Materials of the International Scientific Conference Held in Minsk, 19–20 June 1997*, (Nacyjanal'ny Navukova-Asvetny Cėntr Imja Francyska Skaryny, 1997).

[174] Alexander Fedoruk, 'Conference "The Restitution of Cultural Treasures: Problems of Repatriation and Common Usage" In Minsk', *Spoils of War: International Newsletter*, 4 August 1998.

[175] Final Document of the International Scientific Conference on Restitution of Cultural Values: The Problems of Return and Joint Usage (Legal, Scholarly and Moral Aspects), Minsk, 19–20 June 1997, in Mal'dzis, *The Restitution of Cultural Treasures* (n 173) 260–62.

sphere, the beginning of which is being laid at Francisk Skarina National Scientific and Educational Centre and at scientific institutions of the other post-socialist countries.[176]

Clearly, this document was only postulatory in nature, and it does not appear to have resulted in a more comprehensive approach to the question of the allocation of cultural property in the CIS territory. Arguably, the enactment of the 1997 Russian Law on Valuables constituted the climax of the tensions in the Russian Federation over the restitution of cultural property and the symbolic return to Cold War dialectics.[177] Subsequent events relating to the veto of the President of Russia, its overriding by the Duma, and the 1998 and 1999 decisions of the Russian Constitutional Court, showed how difficult it was for Russia to cope with the question of restitution.[178]

As regards the subsequent relations between the post-Soviet states, after 1997 no special multilateral bodies have been founded to resolve the problems concerning the allocation and distribution of the cultural property in the territory of the former USSR. These questions were directed to bilateral commissions which primarily focused on the displacement of property as a result of the Second World War or the objects removed for exhibitions between the Soviet republics and never returned. Moreover, it seems that during those talks, the question of the allocation of cultural property in the case of succession of states merged with other more burning issues such as post-war restitution. Thus, one may arguably claim that removal at the time of war is considered by Russia as the only undeniably illegal displacement of cultural property. In case of such removal, restitution might be granted. The Russian authorities do not intend to discuss any possible distribution of collections on the basis of country of origin, nor do they intend to settle the status of past acquisitions. Questions such as the repatriation of archives and cultural items confiscated by Tsarist or Soviet means of oppression directed against national movements can only be settled in bilateral negotiations on a case-by-case basis.

Another substantial difficulty in the post-Soviet reality is the fact that the determination of country of origin—the place where a given cultural object shall be returned—rests on the fact that the cultural and national circumstances *in situ* were drastically modified. This was due to the Stalinist policy of cultural and ethnic eradication of entire populations and communities who were brutally displaced to distant provinces of the Soviet Union. For instance, the nearly entire population of the Crimean Tatars was expelled *en masse* from the peninsula in 1944 and resettled in Uzbekistan and other Central Asian republics. As a result of this, the link between territory, people, and cultural heritage was dramatically broken. After 1991, many Tatars returned to their homeland, but others stayed. Such situations are highly characteristic for the post-Soviet ethnic and cultural fabric.

One of the best-known cases of amicably solved questions of cultural heritage between the CIS members concerned the return of medieval frescoes and mosaics to

[176] Emphasis added.
[177] Grimsted, *Trophies of War and Empire* (n 168) 397 ff.
[178] Ibid. 398 ff.

Kyiv.[179] The artworks came from the twelfth-century St Mikhail (Saint Michael's) Zlatoverkh Cathedral and Monastery in Kyiv, destroyed during the Stalinist period in the mid-1930s. Most precious frescoes and mosaics were sent to Russian museums. The remaining fragments were kept in Kyiv. In 1943, these items were looted by the Nazis and taken to Höchstädt an der Donau, Bavaria. In 1945, the American administration handed them to the authorities of the Soviet occupation zone of Germany. Only a small number of the masterpieces were returned to Kyiv in 1948, while others were sent to Russia. After the dissolution of the Soviet Union, Ukraine took a decision to reconstruct the Cathedral. The works were initiated in 1997 and concluded in 2000. In 2001, Russia agreed to hand over to Kyiv four frescoes recovered from Germany. This was based on the 1997 Russian Law on Cultural Valuables, which defines Ukraine as a victim of Nazi aggression.[180] The other returns were made in the following years.[181] However, it appears that the frescoes, which had been removed by the Soviet administration in the 1930s, remained in Russian museums. Indeed, the last example perfectly illustrates the outcome of the 1992 CIS Agreement on Cultural and Historic Treasures. The fact that this instrument was not ratified by the Russian Federation resulted in a general fiasco in establishing a proper legal framework for settling the disputes in matters of dispersed cultural property, following the dissolution of the former USSR.

Similar problems regarded the question of the allocation of cultural material in the relations between the Russian Federation and the Baltic States, which did not join the CIS and were not covered by its agreements. Thus, each of them established its own separate relations with the Russian Federation and other post-Soviet republics. The negotiations were largely conducted via special bilateral commissions on the restitution of cultural objects removed in the past (also prior to the 1920–22 peace treaties, such as the Tartu University collections),[182] with particular attention given to the events of the Second World War. The actual handing over of cultural material was rather rare and was driven by political interests rather than any legal considerations.

In fact, there were only a few returns of cultural material which can be classified as being based on the principles of the law on state succession. One of the most well-known instances concerned the transfer of the library of the Petchory Uspenski

[179] Serhij Kot, 'Kiever Knoten. Restitution zwischen der Ukraine, Deutschland, Rußland und Polen', *OstEuropa* 56(2006)1–2 (*Kunst im Konflikt Kriegsfolgen und Kooperationsfelder in Europa*), 287–300; for more on the cooperation between the Russian Federation and Ukraine, see Svetlena Nekrasova, 'Kooperation und ihre Grenzen Restitution zwischen Rußland und der Ukraine', *OstEuropa* 56(2006)1–2 (*Kunst im Konflikt Kriegsfolgen und Kooperationsfelder in Europa*), 301–10.

[180] John Varoli, 'Russia Returns Medieval Frescos to Ukraine', *The Art Newspaper*, 1 October 2004, at 10.

[181] <http://www.encyclopediaofukraine.com/display.asp?AddButton=pages\S\A\SaintMichaelsGolden6DomedMonastery.htm>, accessed on 12 February 2015.

[182] See Carl Morgenstern (ed), *Estonian–Russian Cooperation in Museology: The History and the Disposition of an Art Collection Establishment by Professor Morgenstern at Tartu University in 1803: International Restitution Conference. 15 and 16 September 2000, Tartu, Estonia (Tartu, 2001)* (Tartu University Press, 2001).

Monastery by Estonia to Russia in 1991.[183] The monastery situated near the city of Pskov was established in the fifteenth century by Orthodox hermits.[184] For centuries it has played an important cultural and political role. In the period 1920–40 it belonged to the territory of Estonia. After the Soviet annexation of this country, the borders of the new Estonian Socialist Republic were modified and the area of the Petchory Monastery passed to Russia. Following the conclusion of the Second World War, the monastery remained open although its library was nationalized and transferred to the Tartu University. Upon independence, Estonia decided to hand it over to the Petchory Monastery, possibly expecting a similar gesture from Russia.

A separate question, which has already been addressed, refers to the status of cultural property from public institutions in Crimea—archaeological objects mostly excavated in this region. Prior to the internationally unrecognized annexation of this territory by Russia in March 2014, a number of exhibits from four Crimean institutions were loaned to the Allard Pierson Museum of Amsterdam for the exhibition 'The Crimea Gold and Secrets of the Black Sea'. After the annexation of Crimea, the issue arose as to whom and to where the loaned objects shall be returned. In fact, Ukraine and Russia presented their claims, both voicing their legal and territorial rights, supported by the arguments of the preservation of the integrity of collections and of protection of cultural rights of local populations.[185] Eventually the museum decided not to return the exhibits and to 'abide by a ruling by a qualified judge or arbitrator, or further agreement between parties' as 'museums must stay out of politics'.[186] In fact, in November 2014, the Russian-controlled Crimean museums initiated legal proceedings before an Amsterdam court. Clearly, this case does not directly refer to state succession as such, because the territorial cession has neither been agreed by the states concerned nor recognized by the international community. A more complex issue concerns the right of Crimea to secede from Ukraine and to establish their own state. Yet also in the latter context, the situation of Crimea can hardly be framed in terms of state succession.[187] Therefore, alongside most difficult issues relating to the interpretation of contractual relations between the Ukraine, museums in Crimea, and the Allard Pierson Museum of Amsterdam, it needs to be stressed that for the time being 'the territory of the Crimea continues to belong to Ukraine',[188] and thus the claims

[183] <http://estonia.eu/about-estonia/culture-a-science/estonian-cultural-treasures-outside-estonia.html>, accessed on 4 February 2015.

[184] <http://www.pskovo-pechersky-monastery.ru/english/introduction>, accessed on 4 February 2015.

[185] See eg Sophia Kishkovsky, 'Ancient Crimean Gold Caught in Legal Limbo', *The Art Newspaper*, 27 March 2014, available at: <http://www.theartnewspaper.com/articles/Ancient-Crimean-gold-caught-in-legal-limbo/32122>, accessed on 4 February 2015.

[186] 'Netherlands refuses to return Crimean Scythian gold to Russia or Ukraine', *Russia Beyond the Headlines*, 22 August 2014, <http://rbth.co.uk/international/2014/08/22/netherlands_refuses_to_return_crimean_scythian_gold_to_russia_o_39237.html>, accessed on 4 February 2015.

[187] Christian Walter, 'Postscript. Self-Determination, Secession, and the Crimean Crisis 2014' in Christian Walter, Antje von Ungern-Sternberg, and Kavus Abushov (eds), *Self-Determination and Secession in International Law* (OUP, 2014), 293–312, at 305 ff.

[188] Ibid, 304.

by Russian government are not that a sovereign therein. On the other hand, the territorial and cultural origin and institutional appurtenance of the objects shall be seen as a paramount criterion in settling the dispute, irrespective of the current political crisis.

c) State archives

In Moscow on 6 July 1992, the states members of the CIS signed the Agreement on Succession with Respect to state Archives of the Former USSR (the 1992 CIS Agreement on State Archives).[189] This referred to 'the archival fonds that were created as a result of the activity of the highest governmental agencies of the former Russian Empire and the Union of Soviet Socialist Republics' (Article 1). It thus related to the whole imperial legacy of documents created by the central authorities in the period from the proclamation of the Empire in 1721 to the dissolution of the USSR in 1991.[190] The CIS states agreed that they would not demand possession of such materials deposited beyond their territories (Article 1), and they reciprocally recognized the transfer of the USSR's archives situated in their territories (Article 2). On the basis of the principle of territoriality, the CIS states were entitled to the return of those fonds which originated from their territory (Article 3). However, 'in such cases when it is impossible to physically divide a complex of documents', the principle would prevail and each of the CIS states would have 'the right to access to said documents and the receipt of any necessary copies' (Article 4). Concrete settlements as to the return of the archival material or exchange of copies were to be solved in bilateral agreements (Article 9). State archival services were supposed to 'conduct regular consultations on a multilateral and bilateral basis for the discussion of questions of collaboration in this field' (Article 5). The CIS states also agreed to facilitate access to researchers (Article 6).

To sum up, it seems that the 1992 CIS Agreement on State Archives followed the regime of succession to state archives under the 1983 Vienna Convention. It confirmed on the one hand the principle of territoriality, on the other, the principle of the protection of the integrity of archives. The priority was clearly given to the latter. Consequently, it sanctioned *a status quo* solution. It appears, however, that the Agreement only partially covered the issue of the archives of important cultural or historic values, in particular those related to the pre-Soviet history of Russia and other states of the region.[191]

The complex nature of questions relating to historic archives is illustrated by the example of the archival patrimony of the former Great Duchy of Lithuania.

[189] Agreement on Succession with Respect to State Archives of the Former USSR, Moscow, 6 July 1992, published in 'Soglashenie o pravopreemstve v otnoshenii gosudarstvennykh arkhivov byshevo Soiuza SSR', *Vestnik arkhivista* 10(1992)4, 3–5, an unofficial English translation in Grimsted, *Trophies of War and Empire* (n 168) 552–54, appendix V.

[190] Grimsted, *Trophies of War and Empire* (n 168) 41.

[191] More on the types of archival claims in the post-Cold War context, see Leopold Auer, *Disputed Archival Claims. Analysis of an International Survey: a RAMP Study* (UNESCO, 1998).

This refers primarily to the so-called Lithuanian Metrica, which represents the official register books for copies of the outgoing Grand Duke's and Sejm's (parliamentary) chancery documents concerning the period between the end of the fourteenth and eighteenth centuries. The Metrica concerns the territory of the Grand Duchy of Lithuania (considerably reduced in 1569), which corresponds to the present territories of Lithuania, Belarus, and to some extent they are also pertinent to the territories of Ukraine, Latvia, and Poland. The documents written in the official languages of the Commonwealth, old-Belarussian, Latin, and Polish were preserved until 1740 in the Royal Castle in Vilnius, from where they were transported to Warsaw. After the third partition of Poland in 1795 they were seized and taken by order of the Russian Empress Catharine II to St Petersburg and in 1888 moved to Moscow, where they have been kept until the present day. On the basis of the 1921 Treaty of Riga[192] some of the Polish parts were restored to Warsaw. During the Soviet period, selected microfilms were furnished to the requesting USSR republics.[193] After the dissolution of the Soviet Union, both Lithuania and Belarus considered themselves successors of the Great Duchy of Lithuania and claimed their rights to these priceless historic records, which are preserved in Moscow.

Other similar examples comprise the Ruthenian Metrica (1569–1673) as part of the Polish Crown Metrica, records of the Tatar Crimean Khanate (until 1783), or documents of the Cossack Hetmanate (until 1775) referring to the present territory of Ukraine, all kept in the former imperial archives of Russia.[194]

5.3.3 Yugoslavia

In 1989, it became evident that the system of government in the SFRY was ineffective and the national leaders could not agree on the rotating federal presidency. The weakness of the communist regime also ignited national and economic tensions between the SFRY republics (Bosnia–Herzegovina, Croatia, Macedonia, Montenegro, Serbia, and Slovenia). In the same year, secessionist movements began within the existing boundaries of the SFRY republics. After the formal proclamation of independence by Slovenia and Croatia in June 1991, the violent process of dissolution started. The central Yugoslav government sought to withhold the separation of other republics of the federation. In fact, out of all the SFRY republics only Serbia and Montenegro, with an overwhelming Serbian majority, decided to continue within the federation. In April 1992 both republics established a new Yugoslavia, the Federal Republic of Yugoslavia (FRY), which lasted until February 2003 when it changed to the State Union of Serbia and Montenegro before eventually dissolving in 2006. Slovenia, Croatia, and Macedonia opted for full independence. This was followed by violent secessionist movements of

[192] Peace Treaty between Poland, Russia, and the Ukraine, signed in Riga on 18 March 1921, in force upon signature, 6 LNTS 51

[193] Grimsted, *Trophies of War and Empire* (n 168) 45.

[194] Ibid. 45–46.

ethnic minorities in Croatia, Bosnia–Herzegovina, Macedonia, and Serbia. In particular, the self-determination of Serbian and Croatian minorities was strongly supported by the governments in Belgrade and Zagreb, respectively, seeking the revision of existing territorial and ethnic divisions in light of the ongoing break up of the federation. These tensions resulted in a series of military conflicts, followed by ethnic and cultural cleansing. The international community was appalled by this cruel war, the exodus of refugees, and images of destroyed cultural sites, including the internationally protected World Heritage Site of the Old City of Dubrovnik.

The most difficult case in the process of disintegration of the SFRY was that of the Republic of Bosnia and Herzegovina. In 1991, its population comprised three main ethnicities: Bosniaks (Muslims), Serbs, and Croats. From the elections in 1990, the Republic of Bosnia and Herzegovina was ruled by three ethnically based parties. The declaration of independence by Slovenia and Croatia and the subsequent reaction of Serbian minorities and of the central Yugoslav government in Belgrade ignited internal controversies over the future status of the country. This led to the break up of the tripartite ethnic coalition in October 1991, since Serbs opted for the continuation of the federation, while Bosniaks and some Croats were in favour of a definitive separation from the SFRY. Bosnia and Herzegovina declared independence from Yugoslavia in March 1992 after a national referendum, boycotted primarily by the Serbian minority. In the end of 1991, Croatian and Serbian nationals also started organizing their own autonomous communities within the territory of Bosnia–Herzegovina. This resulted in the creation of the Croatian Republic of Herzeg–Bosnia and the Serbian Republic of Herzeg–Bosnia (Republica Srpska), dividing the territory of the multi-ethnic country. The war began in April 1992 with the intervention of external armed forces from Croatia and Yugoslavia who, during the meeting in March 1991 (the Karadjordjevo meeting), agreed to divide the territory of Bosnia and Herzegovina between them.[195] The war in Bosnia–Herzegovina ended in 1995 as a result of the open military intervention of NATO (1993–95), replacing the UN Protection Force. According to the 1994 Washington[196] and 1995 Dayton Agreements,[197] the three ethnicities of Bosnia and Herzegovina, with the participation of international arbitration, decided on the structure of a new common state. The territory of Bosnia and Herzegovina was officially divided into ten cantons distributed

[195] See Ivo Banac, 'The Politics of National Homogeneity', in Brad Blitz (ed) *War and Change in the Balkans* (CUP, 2006), 30–43, at 34; Viktor Meier, *Yugoslavia: a History of its Demise* (Routledge, 1999), at 207.

[196] Confederation Agreement between the Bosnian Government and Bosnian Croats, signed on 1 March 1994, hereinafter Washington Agreement, available at: <http://www.usip.org/sites/default/files/file/resources/collections/peace_agreements/washagree_03011994.pdf>, accessed on 4 February 2015.

[197] The General Framework Agreement for Peace in Bosnia and Herzegovina, signed on 14 December 1995, hereinafter Dayton Peace Agreement, available at: <http://www.ohr.int/dpa/default.asp?content_id=3805>, accessed on 4 February 2015.

between two political entities: the Federation of Bosnia and Herzegovina, populated mainly by Croats and Bosniaks, and Republika Srpska, inhabited by Serbs.

On the date of the signing of the 1995 Dayton Peace Agreement, there were five internationally recognized successor states of the former SFRY: Slovenia, Croatia, Bosnia and Herzegovina, Macedonia, and the Federal Republic of Yugoslavia, comprising Montenegro and Serbia. However, another violent conflict was about to explode in the former Socialist Autonomous Province of Kosovo, within the Socialist Republic of Serbia. Between 1974 and 1990 Kosovo, populated by Serbs and Albanians, enjoyed a high degree of autonomy. With the 1990 constitutional reform of Serbia, Kosovo lost its freedoms which in turn led to the indirect and direct discrimination of Albanians. Hundreds of thousands of people fled to Albania and Macedonia, causing further ethnic tensions. Similar to secessionist movements in the territory of the SFRY, Kosovar Albanians proclaimed the independence of the Republic of Kosova on 22 September 1991. This, however, was not recognized by the post-SFRY states or by the European leaders, who opted for the maintenance of the territorial integrity of Serbia, and postulated adequate minority protections.

The ethnic and political tensions culminated in the open war between Yugoslav police forces, Yugoslav paramilitaries, and the Kosovar Albanian paramilitaries between 1998 and 1999. The draft of the peace agreement, granting a broad autonomy to Kosovo proposed by the NATO leaders during the conference in Rambouillet (January–March 1999), was rejected by the Serbian government. On the heels of even more violent conflicts, NATO initiated a bombing campaign against the Yugoslav army (March–June 1999). As a result of this, the international forces of NATO and the Kosovo Force (KFOR) took military control over the province. The civil administration was given to the United Nations Interim Administration Mission in Kosovo (UNMIK), formed on the basis of the 1999 United Nations Security Council Resolution 1244,[198] which was also responsible for drafting the Kosovo constitutional system. The withdrawal of the Yugoslav units was however followed by the mass flight of Serbian and Roma nationals, and by the destruction of many sites important for Serbian cultural heritage. In 1999, UNMIK established the Joint Interim Administrative Structure (JIAS), responsible for administration in the province and based on the representatives of the UNMIK and the major ethnic groups. Among other issues, the JIAS and subsequently established Provisional Institutions of Self-Government (PISG) had to settle the questions concerning the protection of cultural heritage in Kosovo,[199] which even under international administration was still subjected to brutal attacks and destruction.[200]

[198] UN Security Council Res. 1244, adopted on 10 June 1999, UN Doc. S/RES/1244 (1999).

[199] See Art. 4.3 of the Constitutional Framework for Provisional Self-Government, UNMIK/REG/2001/9, 9, available at: <http://www.unmikonline.org/regulations/2001/reg09-01.htm>, accessed on 4 February 2015.

[200] See Chapter 6, section 6.2.2.

In 2008, the internal tensions led to the declaration of Kosovo proclaimed by the Kosovar Albanians. This has not been recognized by Kosovo's Serbian population nor by the government in Belgrade. Between 2008 and 2013, the Serbian government constantly refused to maintain any direct official contact with the Republic of Kosovo, but permitted only indirect contact via the third international intermediaries UNMIK and European Union Rule of Law Mission in Kosovo (EULEX Kosovo), a European Union (EU) Common Security and Defense Policy mission providing civil international presence in Kosovo operating under the umbrella of the UNMIK.[201] Moreover, the international community remains divided as regards the legality of the unilateral declaration of independence.[202] However, in 2013, due to the EU-facilitated dialogue, chaired by the High Representative of the Union for Foreign Affairs and Security Policy, Catherine Ashton, Serbia and Kosovo reached an agreement on their future relations.[203] Accordingly, on 19 April 2013, both parties signed the First Agreement of Principles Governing the Normalization of Relations,[204] including the Implementation Plan.[205] The agreement was intended to facilitate the future relations of both countries within international and European structures,[206] but it does not amount to a recognition of Kosovo's independence by Serbia. Importantly, amongst other measures it establishes a special police commander (who will be appointed by the central authorities in Pristina from a list submitted by Serbs) and appeal court (under Kosovo's laws and procedures) for the Serbian minority in northern Kosovo. The agreement does not, however, tackle the issue of the status of the archaeological and ethnological exhibits which were taken on loan from Pristina's museums in 1998–99, although the government of Kosovo constantly claimed their repatriation.[207]

As a consequence of these developments, the entire break up of the SFRY resulted in the emergence of seven independent states: Bosnia–Herzegovina, Croatia, Kosovo, Macedonia, Montenegro, Serbia, and Slovenia.

[201] <http://www.eulex-kosovo.eu/en/front>, accessed on 4 February 20157.

[202] See *Accordance with International Law of the Unilateral Declaration of Independence in Respect of Kosovo*, Advisory Opinion of 22 July 2010, ICJ Reports 2010, 403. The Court held that international law does not contain prohibition on declarations of independence. Thus, while the declaration may not have been illegal, the issue of recognition was a political one. Kosovo's status is declared as independent under UN supervision, paras 218 ff, Compare Christian Walter, 'The Kosovo Advisory Opinion. What It Says and What It Does Not Say', in Christian Walter, Antje von Ungern-Sternberg, and Kavus Abushov (eds), *Self-Determination and Secession in International Law* (OUP, 2014), 13–26; Andrea Goia, 'Kosovo's Statehood and the Role of Recognition', *IYIL* 18(2008), 3–35, Pavel Šturma, 'The Case of Kosovo and International Law', *PYIL* 29(2009), 51–64.

[203] State of the EU Council President Herman Van Rompuy, 19 April 2013, reference CL13-032EN.

[204] Text available at: <http://www.rts.rs/upload/storyBoxFileData/2013/04/20/3224318/Originalni%20tekst%20Predloga%20sporazuma.pdf>, accessed on 4 February 2015.

[205] Text available at: <http://euobserver.com/media/src/0807580ad8281aefa2a89e38c49689f9.pdf>, accessed on 4 February 2015.

[206] See 'Serbia and Kosovo reach EU-brokered landmark accord', *BBC*. 19 April 2013, available at: <http://www.bbc.co.uk/news/world-europe-22222624>, accessed on 7 February 2015.

[207] <http://www.mfa-ks.net/?page=2,120>, accessed on 7 February 2015.

a) The Badinter Commission: principles of state succession of the SFRY

The role played by external international intervention in the process of the SFRY's dissolution has obviously been much more far-reaching. In the summer of 1991, European leaders launched a conference on Yugoslavia with the aim of assisting political changes in the territory of the SFRY. On 27 August 1991, the Council of Ministers of the EEC set up a special commission, the Arbitration Commission of the Conference on Yugoslavia (Badinter Commission), which would provide legal advice and consisted of five members headed by Robert Badinter. In the following months, the Badinter Commission issued 15 opinions on different issues that arose from the disintegration of the SFRY.[208]

In the first three opinions of 1991, the Commission expressed its views on these issues: 1) the dissolution of the SFRY; 2) the right to self-determination of ethnic minorities inside the SFRY republics; 3) the status of borders between the SFRY republics. Accordingly, it confirmed that although the SFRY 'retained its international personality, notably inside international organizations, the Republics have expressed their desire for independence', and the SFRY was 'in the process of dissolution' (Opinion no. 1). However, the territorial divisions between the SFRY republics were to be maintained on the basis of the principle *uti possidetis*: 'the boundaries between Croatia and Serbia, between Bosnia and Herzegovina and Serbia, and possibly other adjacent independent states may not be altered… except where otherwise agreed, the former boundaries become frontiers protected by international law' (Opinion no. 3).[209] In accordance with this, the Serbian population in Croatia and Bosnia and Herzegovina did not have rights to self-determination but were 'entitled to all the rights concerned to minorities and ethnic groups.' The republics concerned were bound to provide such rights and freedoms (Opinion no. 2).

In the next 12 Opinions (1992–93), the Badinter Commission dealt with the international recognition of the post-SFRY states, the settlements of problems of state succession, and the completion of the process of the dissolution of the SFRY. In Opinion no. 8, having analysed all the events in the territory of the SFRY, the Commission argued that the process of disintegration was concluded in mid-1992: 'the SFRY no longer exists'. Consequently, the FRY (Serbia and Montenegro) had to be perceived as 'a new state' and could not be 'considered the sole successor of the SFRY' (Opinion no. 10). Therefore, the FRY should not be automatically recognized by the European Communities, but its recognition

[208] Opinions nos. 1–10, see 'Text of Opinions. Documents Regarding the Situation in the Former Yugoslavia (September 25, 1991-November 16, 1992): Conference on Yugoslavia Arbitration Commission: Opinions on Questions Arising from the Dissolution of Yugoslavia', *ILM* 31(1992), 1494–526, opinions nos. 11–15, see 'Text of Advisory Opinions Judicial and Similar Proceedings: International Conference on the Former Yugoslavia Documentation on the Arbitration Commission under the Un/EC (Geneva) Conference: Advisory Opinions Nos. 11–15 of the Arbitration Commission', *ILM* 32(1993), 1587–98.

[209] See further Enver Hasani, 'Uti Possidetis Juris: from Rome to Kosovo', *Fletcher Forum of World Affairs* Summer Fall (2003), 85–97; Suzanne Lalonde, *Boundaries in a Conflicted World. The Role of* Uti Possidetis (McGill–Queen's University Press, 2002), 176 ff.

would be subject to its compliance with the conditions applied to other post-SFRY states—for instance, the incorporation of minority protection. None of the republics of the former Yugoslavia would continue the international personality of the SFRY; all the succession issues had to be resolved by a mutual agreement between new states being equally sovereign to the SFRY successor states. This should apply an equitable division of assets and obligations of the former SFRY. Similarly, membership of the SFRY in international organizations could not be continued by any of the successor states. On the basis of 'the principle of rights and duties between states in respect of international law', each new state had to 'claim for itself alone the membership rights previously enjoyed by the former SFRY' (Opinion no. 9).[210]

b) The 2001 SFRY Agreement on Succession Issues—the question of cultural property

The first proposal with regard to the apportionment of state property of the former Yugoslavia was made by the International Conference for the Former Yugoslavia (ICFY), the Badinter Committee, and the Working Group for the Succession of States, established jointly by the EEC and the United Nations, within the framework of the ICFY. The fundamental difficulty arose, however, from the fact that the dissolution of the SFRY was not made by way of a constitutional act or a succession agreement, but instead it took the form of a gradual secession of new republics, first from the SFRY and ultimately from Serbia. Thus, for a long time, there have been different interpretations and opinions as to the international status of successor states that emerged after 1991. In Opinions nos. 13–15, the Badinter Commission addressed the issues of succession to SFRY state property. These may arguably be summarized as follows: 1) the division of state property should follow the principles applied by the 1984 Vienna Convention; 2) the division should be based on the principle of equity; 3) the 'war damages have no direct impact on the division of state property, archives, or debts for purposes of state succession'; 4) the settlement of disputes between the successor states should be exercised through the 'arbitration or some other mode of peaceful settlements of their disputes'. The Badinter Commission, however, did not at any point raise the question of state succession to cultural property in the territory of the SFRY, although the first postulates as to the distribution of such materials between the successor states to the SFRY were issued as early as 1991.[211]

[210] See Alain Pellet, 'The Opinions of the Badinter Arbitration Committee. A Second Breath for the Self-Determination of Peoples', *EJIL* 3(1992)1, 178–85; Danilo Turk, 'Recognition of States: A Comment Symposium: Recent Developments in the Practice of State Recognition', *EJIL* 4(1993)1, 66–91; Peter Radan, 'The Badinter Commission. Secession, Self-Determination and Uti Possidetis', in Peter Radan (ed), *The Break-up of Yugoslavia and International Law* (Routledge, 2002), 204–43.

[211] Branka Sulć, 'Restitution and Succession of Cultural Property from Croatian Museums and Galleries', *Informatica Museologica* 23(1992)1–4, 6–17.

According to these opinions, the state property situated in the territories of the respective republics passed to the new states without any formalities. In addition, all successor states should have a proportional share in former federal assets and debts. It was argued that all pending questions would be settled in the general agreement between the successor states. Until the final settlement was reached, each successor state was responsible for the state property of the SFRY. However, for a long time such a scenario of succession to state property was shared by all the republics of the former SFRY. The 'new' Yugoslavia—the Federal Republic of Yugoslavia—considered all secessions which took place after 1991 as illegal. Therefore, the FRY did not recognize their sovereignty and rights to a proportional share in federal property. Accordingly, the FRY argued that it was the unique owner of the former SFRY but it did not exclude the possibility of offering a share in the state property of the SFRY on an *ex gratia* basis. Such an interpretation was, however, rejected by the Badinter Commission. In 1992, formal negotiations with the parties concerning further settlements of the succession issues of the former SFRY began within the framework of the ICFY and later continued under the auspices of the High Representative in Bosnia–Herzegovina.[212] Finally, after nine years of talks, the four former Yugoslav republics (Croatia, Slovenia, Bosnia and Herzegovina, and Macedonia) and the Federal Republic of Yugoslavia (the republics of Serbia and Montenegro) signed the Agreement on Succession Issues (the 2001 SFRY Agreement).[213] Clearly, this instrument did not cover the subsequent process of the dissolution of the FRY with regard to the separation of Montenegro in 2006 and Kosovo in 2008. It seems that in respect of these two cases no comprehensive succession agreements have been concluded.

Following the views of the Badinter Commission, the 2001 SFRY Agreement separated the questions concerning the armed conflict in the territory of the former SFRY from the succession issues. All issues relating to war damages and reparation were not covered. Thus, the agreement regulated the apportionment of state assets and debts according to the date of state succession, 1991, in respect of seven main groups of issues: 1) movable and immovable property; 2) diplomatic and consular properties; 3) financial assets and liabilities; 4) archives; 5) pensions; 6) other rights, interests, and liabilities; 7) private property and acquired rights.

Under this instrument, the allocation and distribution of state cultural property between the successor states to the SFRY was settled within the framework of the division of SFRY state property (Annex A). Generally speaking, the agreement followed the principles of the 1983 Vienna Convention and strictly separated the controversies that had arisen over war damages and plunder from those relating to state succession. As a general rule, the immovable as well as the tangible movable property of the SFRY located within the territory of the former SFRY shall pass

[212] See Carsten Stahn, 'The Agreement on Succession Issues of the Former Socialist Federal Republic of Yugoslavia', *AJIL* 96(2002)2, 379–97, at 379–80.

[213] Agreement on Succession Issues of the Former SFRY, Vienna, 29 June 2001, in force 2 June 2004, 2262 UNTS 251; see Arthur Watts, 'Introductory Note to Agreement on Succession Issues between the Five Successor States of the Former State of Yugoslavia', *ILM* 41(2002)1.

to the successor state 'on whose territory that property was situated on the date on which it proclaimed independence' (Article 2 (1) and Article 3 (1)). Moreover, the property (except military property) removed without authorization by another successor state was to be restored or fully compensated for by the latter (Article 3(3)). These rules, however, were derogated in respect of 'tangible movable state property of great importance to the cultural heritage of one of the successor state and which originated from the territory of that state, such as works of art, manuscripts, books and other objects of artistic, historical or archaeological interest to that state; and scientific collections and important collections of books or archives' (Article 3(2)). These objects and collections shall pass to the state concerned provided that it would identify them 'as soon as possible, but no later than 2 years after the entry into force of this Agreement' (Article 3(2)). An exemption from the general rules on the tangible movable property of the SFRY was also introduced in respect of Yugoslav property abroad. Under Annex B, 'Diplomatic and Consular Properties', such property had to be distributed proportionally between five successor states, based on the valuation in the 'Report dated 31 December 1992 on the valuation of the assets and liabilities of the former Socialist Federal Republic of Yugoslavia as at 31 December 1990' (Article 4 (3)). However, the movables forming part of SFRY diplomatic and consular properties, which were 'of great importance to the cultural heritage of one of the successor states', should pass to that state (Article 4 (5)).

In both cases, the controversies between the successor states would be settled by special joint committees (Article 5 of Annex A; Article 5 of Annex B). Importantly, the SFRY acknowledged the principle of protection of SFRY state property at the time of the negotiations. Accordingly, the successor states were required to 'take the necessary measures to prevent loss, damage or destruction to State archives, State property and assets of the SFRY in which, in accordance with the provisions of this Agreement, one or more of the other successor States have an interest' (Article 2 of the 2001 SFRY Agreement).

Clearly, the 2001 SFRY Agreement applied two fundamental principles of allocation and distribution of cultural property in state succession: the principle of territoriality and the principle of major significance to the cultural heritage of a successor state. No time limitations as to the date of the removal of the objects were specified, nor were any guidelines as to the identification of objects and the methods for their allocation provided. In addition, the 2001 SFRY Agreement did not apply the principle of the preservation of the integrity of collections. The territorial origin and cultural and historical interests of the successor states were paramount. With reference to these, some general observations can be made.

First, the lack of time limitations may arguably imply the admissibility of claims for the return of cultural treasures removed from the territory of a successor state also in the remote past. Thus, it may also relate to the cultural property displaced prior to the creation of the Yugoslav state after the First World War, namely during the Habsburg or even Ottoman rule.

Second, the passage of state property of great importance to the cultural heritage of one of the successor states, which originated from its territory, was not limited by the principle of the protection of the integrity of collections. Consequently, it seems that under the 2001 SFRY Agreement even library collections and historic archival records, whose integrity had usually been protected in international practice, should be repatriated on the basis of cultural and territorial connection.

Third, the 2001 SFRY Agreement did not provide any indication regarding the identification of state cultural property of the former SFRY. It thus remains ambiguous as to what, exactly, constitutes the state property of the SFRY with reference to cultural heritage.[214] Does it refer to the objects acquired during the Second World War or to other items illegally expropriated and displaced during the post-war communist era? May it also relate to ecclesiastic property or to municipal property preserved in the state institutions?

c) The 2001 SFRY Agreement on Succession Issues— the question of state archives

The 2001 Agreement also regulated the situation of the SFRY's state archives.[215] Basically, the provisions of Annex D concern the archival material of an administrative and judicial nature. Generally, they do not refer to the situation of the archival records of great importance to the cultural heritage of one of the successor states. However, one cannot exclude that certain archives of a cultural nature can also be apportioned on the basis of the general provision applied in Annex D. Moreover, a very broad definition of state archives of the former SFRY is applied under Article 1 of Annex D which includes, among other categories, audiovisual records and other documents which constitute cultural property (Article 1 (c)).

The 2001 SFRY Agreement applied the principles of territorial provenance and functional pertinence. Accordingly, under Article 2 of Annex D, the displaced state archives of one of the successor states or the SFRY archives should be returned to the state to which they belonged or to their proper location 'in accordance with international principles of provenance'. Under Article 3, 'the part of the SFRY state archives (administrative, current and archival records) necessary for the normal administration of the territory of one or more of the states shall, in accordance with the principle of functional pertinence, pass to those states, irrespective of where those archives are actually located'. In the same way, certain official documents on the border agreement should pass to those successor states to whose territories they refer (Article 4 (b)). In cases where the state archives should pass to more than one successor state, those states have to agree as to which state would receive the original and enable the remaining states to make copies (Article 5). As regards the state succession to international obligations arising

[214] Ibid. 186.

[215] For the negations undertaken prior to 2001, see Marija Oblack-Černi and Borut Bohte, 'Succession to the Archives of the Former Yugoslavia', in Mojmir Mrak (ed), *Succession of States* (Nijhoff, 1999), 178–85.

from bilateral agreements of the SFRY in respect of restitution of archives, they shall pass to the successor states having 'an interest in those archives' (Article 10).

Annex D to the 2001 SFRY Agreement also stated that in certain situations the state archives of the former SFRY would constitute a common heritage of the successor states, to which they all would have a 'free and unhindered access' (Article 6 (a)). In such a case, the successor state should observe 'the principle of respect for the integrity of groups of SFRY state archives so as to facilitate full access to and research in those groups of archives' (Article 6 (b)). It remains open as to whether such a solution could be applied to the archives of great importance to the cultural heritage of the one of the SFRY successor states.

As in the case of the objects constituting the cultural heritage of the successor states regulated under Article 3 (2) of Annex A to the 2001 SFRY Agreement, Annex D provides for a short time period in which the final agreement and settlements shall be concluded: a maximum of 24 months from the date on which the 2001 Agreement enters into force. Until such settlements are achieved, the successor states are responsible for the preservation of archives and shall provide an 'immediate and unhindered access' to the representatives of the interested successor states to records 'dated on or before 30 June 1991' (Article 7).

To some extent, the 2001 SFRY Agreement also refers to the allocation of private archives. Under Article 9 of Annex D, such records, which were taken from their owners after 1 December 1918 (the date of the creation of the Yugoslav state the Kingdom of Serbs, Croatians and Slovenians) shall be returned to 'where they had been produced or to their owners, according to international principles of provenance, without any compensation or other conditions'.

To sum up, the 2001 SFRY Agreement introduced a general framework for the allocation and apportionment of the tangible cultural heritage between the SFRY successor states. This was based on the principle of territorial and cultural connection. It applied an exemption from the general principles referring to state property. Accordingly, the state property of great importance to the cultural heritage of one of the successor states and which originated from its territory, passed to that state. No time limitations as to the date of their removal were applied. However, the 2001 SFRY Agreement did not provide any guideline as to the identification of objects and the proceedings of their allocation. One may expect that these would be established by the interstate commissions. It also seems that the rights to cultural property removed outside SFRY territory passed to the state from which it had been taken.

d) The execution of the 2001 SFRY Agreement

The 2001 SFRY Agreement entered into force in June 2004 after all five successor states finally signed the document. Its implementation was performed by the Standing Joint Committee comprising a senior representative of each successor state. According to Article 4 (2), as its principal task the Committee has to undertake monitoring of the effective implementation of the 2001 SFRY Agreement and serve 'as a forum in which issues arising in the course of its implementation may be discussed'. The first formal meeting had to take place within two months of the entry into force of the 2001 SFRY Agreement 'at the initiative of the Government of the Republic of Macedonia' (Article 4 (3)).

According to the information provided by Professor Miha Pogacnik, the Slovenian High Representative for Succession to the Former Yugoslavia,[216] by the end of 2008, two meetings of the Standing Joint Committee had been organized. The first took place in June 2006 and was hosted by the Republic of Macedonia in Skopje. During this, only procedural issues were addressed. Accordingly, representatives of the five SFRY successor states exchanged views regarding the implementation of the Agreement on Succession Issues and set the priorities of the Committee and discussed its draft rules of procedure.

Some crucial arrangements were made prior to the 2006 meeting. Certain issues were decided by special sub-commissions constituted by groups of experts. Some of them started working before the entry into force of the 2001 SFRY Agreement. Of the greatest importance are the Joint Committee on Succession to Movable and Immovable Property and the Committee on the Distribution of Financial Assets and Liabilities of the Former SFRY Referred to in Annex C to the Agreement on Succession Issues.[217]

The second meeting of the Standing Joint Committee was held in 2007 in the Brdo Castle near Ljubljana, hosted by the Republic of Slovenia.[218] At this stage, the procedural issues were finally settled and the subsequent arrangements were to be taken in September 2007 in Belgrade, Serbia. This did not take place, however, since the head of Serbian experts, Professor Mitrović, resigned. The major difficulties came from the lack of political will, especially in Serbia, to proceed with the negotiations. After years of delays, the meetings of the Committees were re-established. For instance, on 19 May 2011 the Joint Committee for the Succession of Diplomatic and Consular Properties of the Former SFRY gathered. The following month, the successor states managed to reach an agreement on the division of diplomatic and consular missions.[219]

Importantly, it seems that within the two-year period under Article 3 (2) of Annex A to the 2001 SFRY Agreement, the only state who delivered the list of claims to cultural heritage and archives was Slovenia. Furthermore, most of the parties to the 2001 SFRY Agreement met with serious difficulties in preparing a complete list of claims. Negotiators and scientists had hindered access to museum inventories and records kept in federal archives and depositories of the former

[216] Report on the author's telephone interview of 25 November 2008 with Prof. Miha Pogačnik, High Representative for Succession Issues of the Republic of Slovenia (since 2005).

[217] The latter reached an agreement on the distribution of the monetary gold of the National Bank of Yugoslavia of the Former SFRY deposited abroad. Some other negotiations followed the 2006 meeting, as the Joint Committee for the Succession of Diplomatic-Consular Property of ex-SFRY, ibid.

[218] Ibid.

[219] <http://www.mvep.hr/custompages/static/hrv/files/godisnjak2011/en/bilateral02.html>, accessed on 7 February 2015.

SFRY.[220] This was most likely to have been caused by the fact that the majority of them were still in the possession of the biggest successor state, Serbia, which for long did not seem interested in providing such access. It so happened that other successor states did not have enough knowledge as to where certain art-works were preserved, etc. Despite the ongoing negotiations conducted in the sub-commissions, in practice not much was really been settled. In addition, another problem arose from the provisions of the 2001 SFRY Agreement as to the maximum term for the presentation of a complete list of requested objects. Accordingly, Serbian representatives claimed that all terms had already expired since, except for Slovenia, successor states did not present their list of claimed archives and cultural objects. Therefore it was too late for any further negotiations. Such an interpretation is, however, rejected by other successor states.[221]

The 2001 SFRY Agreement clearly constituted an important and difficult compromise, but nowadays each successor state of the SFRY finds some aspects or issues unsuitable or inconvenient to its internal problems. Since a number of property issues of state succession is still pending, the question of cultural heritage is arguably perceived as a key problem within the larger framework of succession to assets and archives. In addition, it became clear that the fair apportionment and allocation of cultural property will not be possible without proper access to the archival materials of the former SFRY. In this context, the full implementation of the regulations on succession to archives seems crucial.

Apparently, the only documented settlements on the allocation of cultural property concluded after 2001 were made exclusively within the framework of post-war restitution. These refer to the series of arrangements concerning the issues of refugees and property concluded between the FRY and later by Serbia with other SFRY's successor states. The best known example regards the post-conflict Croatia–Serbia relations, particularly with reference to cultural items removed from museums in Vukovar (Croatia) by Yugoslav forces during war operations, and the cited cases of the archaeological collections from Pristina (Kosovo).

As already mentioned, the question of war plunder and destruction of the material cultural heritage in the territory of the former SFRY was not subject to the 2001 SFRY Agreement. This solution seems correct since the legal principles in respect of state succession to cultural property aim at the just allocation and apportionment of cultural material. Conversely, the core objective of the international instruments on the protection of cultural heritage during armed conflict is to provide for the preservation of such property and its restitution to the place of origin. However, a proper division of these two legal regimes in individual factual cases is often virtually impossible.

Situations such as these have been very common with regard to the events in the SFRY after 1991. Art treasures, both immovable and movable, that are part

[220] Report on the author's telephone interview of 25 November 2008 with Prof. Miha Pogačnik (n 216).

[221] Ibid.

of the Yugoslav ethnic fabric have been particularly subjected to violent reprisals based on national and ethnic tensions. Property considered as being of great cultural importance for one successor state was often situated and originated in the territory of another. Moreover, in many cases, certain treasures have been considered as part of the cultural heritage of more than one successor state, since they had been created by the mixed multi-ethnic communities. Hence, during the Yugoslav wars the cultural heritage in the territory of the former SFRY was subjected not only to intentional destruction as part of ethnic cleansing but also to forced displacement.

One of the best examples of the forced evacuation and partial destruction of cultural treasures took place in 1991 in the city of Vukovar on the Serbo–Croatian border.[222] Before 1991, the city was one of the most important cultural heritage sites in the north of the former Yugoslavia. At that time the town had four museums: the Bauer Collection, the Vukovar Municipal Museum, the History Museum, and the Ruzicka Memorial Museum. Their treasures included archaeological finds dating to 3000 and 2200 BC from the nearby Vučedol site, and a vast collection of mainly nineteenth century oil paintings. There were also private collections of paintings, as well as the ecclesiastical artefacts in the Franciscan monastery and the Serbian Orthodox Church of St Nicholas. In addition, the city protected beautiful Baroque architecture, including a well-preserved aristocratic residence (the Elz Manor).

Vukovar owed its cultural richness to the multi-ethnic history of its society. Prior to the First World War, the population of Vukovar comprised four major ethnic groups: Croats, Germans, Serbs, and Hungarians. In 1991, the population of the city comprised only two major populations, Serbs and Croats, who did not share the same view as to the future state adherence. Following Croatia's declaration of independence from Yugoslavia, the city was invaded by Serbian forces. During the siege, many items from the city's museums were stored in the basement of the Franciscan monastery. When the city was taken by Yugoslav forces at the battle of Vukovar (August–November 1991), the hidden treasures together with other property were evacuated to the territory of Serbia and stored in the basement of the city museum in Novi Sad. According to the Serbian authorities, the objective was their protection. From the beginning, Serbian officials argued that the removed collections would be restored to the Vukovar museum. By contrast, Croats perceived this removal as brutal war plunder. Moreover, they claimed that the methods of transportation as well as the conditions of storage were inadequate. In fact, the Serbian administration did not provide proper care

[222] Branka Šulc, 'The Protection of Croatia's Cultural Heritage During the War 1991–95', in Robert Layton, Peter G. Stone, and Julian Thomas (eds), *Destruction and Conservation of Cultural Property* (Routledge, 2001), 157–67, at 162; Ivana Erceg, 'Vukovar Cultural Treasure Returned', *AIM Zagreb*, (15 December 2001), <http://www.aimpress.ch/dyn/trae/archive/data/200112/11221-002-trae-zag.htm>, accessed on 10 February 2015; Nick Thorpe, 'Vukovar Treasures Gather Dust in Serb Basement. War Crimes in the Former Yugoslavia: Special Report', *The Guardian*, Friday 12 May 2000.

and surveillance to the Vukovar collections. During the forced evacuation, certain objects were stolen and some of them appeared on sale in Hungary and Germany. Others were kept hidden in humid storage spaces. Thus, one may argue that the core reason for the removal of the priceless cultural items was to keep them as war 'hostages' for the prospective political negotiations rather than due to any cultural and historical considerations.

The situation of the Vukovar treasures immediately became of international interest.[223] In October 1993, the International Council of Museums (ICOM) conducted a mission to the Republic of Croatia in order to survey the damage to Croatian museums, galleries, and collections caused by the war of 1991–93 and to identify the major areas which required international assistance. In 1994, the ICOM Advisory Board Committee recommended that the Council of Europe and ICOM conduct a joint mission to Croatia and Yugoslavia to discuss the fate of the Vukovar collections.[224] Also in the same year, the objects evacuated from Vukovar were taken to Paris for an exhibition. This was cancelled, however, and the objects were sent back to Yugoslavia. The withdrawal was due to the official motion issued by the government of Croatia to the French authorities asking for seizure of exhibited cultural objects on the basis of the First Protocol to the 1954 Hague Convention, to which both states were parties.[225] Under Article 2 of the Protocol, each state party 'undertakes to take into its custody cultural property imported into its territory either directly or indirectly from any occupied territory. This shall either be effected automatically upon the importation of the property or, failing this, at the request of the authorities of that territory.' Thus, as Lyndell Prott noticed, it was difficult to see how the French authorities 'could have refused to seize the objects in compliance with the obligation under this article.'[226] Moreover, they were also bound by the obligations, under Article 3, 'to return, at the close of hostilities, to the competent authorities of the territory previously occupied, cultural property which is in its territory, if such property has been exported in contravention of the principle laid down in the first paragraph. Such property shall never be retained as war reparations'.

In these circumstances, the first negotiations between Croatian and Yugoslav foreign ministries started in the late 1990s. In 1998, both states agreed that a future bilateral agreement on cultural cooperation needed to be based on the registration and return to Croatia of cultural property.[227] In November 2001, Croatia, and the FRY reached a consensus, and on 7 December 2001, the protocol on the return of the cultural treasures was signed in Belgrade.[228] A Joint

[223] Barbara Roberts, 'Destruction and Loss: A Report on Croatia', *Newsletter of the Getty Conservation Institute*, 9/3 (Fall 1994), available at: <http://www.getty.edu/conservation/publications/newsletters/9_3/croatia.html>, accessed on 12 February 2015.

[224] Šulc, 'The Protection of Croatia's Cultural' (n 222) 164.

[225] Lyndell V. Prott, 'Repatriation of Cultural Property', *University of British Columbia Law Review* (1995) special issue, 229–40, at 236.

[226] Ibid. at 236.

[227] Šulc, 'The Protection of Croatia's Cultural' (n 222) 164.

[228] Protocol on the Transport of Objects of Art, Cultural Assets and Other Exhibits from the Museum of Vojvodina and the Novi Sad City Museum (in Yugoslavia) to the Vukovar City Museum, Signed on 7 December 2001 in Belgrade, *Yearbook of International Humanitarian Law* 4(2001), 482.

Serbian–Croatian Commission for the Return of Cultural Property was established. Thanks to the works of this body a great majority of the items from Vukovar have been returned.[229]

A definitive settlement of the allocation of cultural items from the Vukovar collections also contributed to the conclusion of other bilateral political agreements. As has been rightly pointed out by the Croatian Minister of Culture, 'the return of the works and treasures of art of the City Museum of Vukovar is an act that will mark a new life in Vukovar and greatly contribute to the development of relations between two states and peoples.'[230] For instance, at the same time, both states concluded an agreement on the avoidance of double taxation and accelerated some other negotiations.

The return of the Vukovar treasures did not, however, come within reach of other more sensitive questions related to the allocation of cultural property in Serbo–Croatian relations. These relate primarily to the property of the Serbian Orthodox Church (SOC) in the territory of Croatia and historical archives referring to the persecution and extermination of Serbian nationals by the fascist Independent state of Croatia (the Ustaše regime) during the Second World War. From 1991 to 1993, many cultural properties and archives were removed from the Croatian territory, both by Serbian and Yugoslav troops as well as civil refugees and preserved in the territory of Serbia. For example, this was the fate of the treasures of the SOC in Vukovar, which were returned on the basis of the 2001 agreement. The view that such objects, being of great importance to Serbia, should be kept in Croatia on the basis of the territorial and historical links is obviously not shared by the Serbian representatives. As some authors suggest, more serious negotiations might start if Croatia undertook to restore, at its own expenses, the reconstruction of the Orthodox churches destroyed by its units during the war, and provide for a fair and just system of minority protection.[231]

As regards the historical archives, it is necessary to recall the case of the records of the Memorial Museum and Park in Jasenovac, situated in the territory of Croatia.[232] Their situation is particularly difficult, since the museum commemorates the largest concentration camp established by the pro-Nazi Croat regime during the Second World War. In Jasenovac, the largest numbers of victims were ethnic Serbs, considered as the main racial enemy of the Independent State of Croatia. With the independence of Croatia, the Jasenovac camp underwent severe damage. At the end of September 1991, the Croatian Army entered the Jasenovac memorial park by force. On 8 October 1991 it was was captured by the secessionist Serbian Republic of Krajina (Kniska Krajina). During the withdrawal

[229] Alix Kroeger, 'Croatia's precious artwork returned', BBC NEWS, 12 December 2001, <http://news.bbc.co.uk/2/hi/europe/1706658.stm>; 'Serbia Returns 31 Icons to Croatia', *Croatian Times*, 29 October 2010, <http:// croatiantimes.com/?id=14801>, accessed on 10 February 2015.

[230] Erceg, 'Vukovar Cultural Treasure Returned' (n 222).

[231] Ibid.

[232] <http://www.ushmm.org/information/press/press-releases/croatian-wwii-concentration-camp-records-made-available-for-first-time-by-u>, accessed on 31 January 2015.

the Croatian Army allegedly committed serious damages to the site.[233] At the later stage many documental records were removed by Serbs, stored in Banja Luca (in Serbian Krajina) in the territory of Bosnia–Herzegovina and eventually taken for safe-keeping to the United States Holocaust Memorial Museum (USHMM). Croatia and the FRY separately asked for the impartial assistance of the USHMM. Croatia aimed to recover the records to the Memorial Museum on the basis of territorial links. Conversely, Serbia—afraid of potential forgeries of the history of this concentration camp—preferred their preservation in the USA. Finally, the records returned to Jasenovac where since 2006 these are accessible in the newly reopened memorial institution.[234]Overall, it needs to be stressed that Serbia and Croatia recognized their responsibility for internationally wrongful acts against cultural property committed during the armed conflicts in 1990s. In fact, pursuant to the 2001 agreement they have undertaken the restitution of a number of items plundered or removed from their respective territories. For instance, from 2001 to 2010, Serbia returned more than 20,000 items to Croatia.[235] Moreover, on 23 March 2012, both states signed a protocol on the restitution of Croatian cultural assets from Serbia to Croatia. According to its provisions more than 1000 works of art taken during the 1990s would be returned from Serbia to Croatia.[236] The signing of this document has been widely perceived as concluding this 'outstanding bilateral issue'.[237] Some restitution has already found place.[238] In April 2014, this issue gained public attention: at the forum of the European Parliament a Croatian deputy claimed that a full restitution of cultural assets from Serbia shall constitute as condition for EU accession negotiation of Serbia. While there was no official response by Serbian authorities, the Association of Refugee and Other Associations of Serbs from Croatia voiced the rights of Serbian communities forced out of Croatia (Serbian war refugees) including the right to enjoy such heritage.[239] They also reminded the number of works of arts, churches, and houses destroyed by Croats. They argued that the cultural objects not be returned to Croatia before the conditions

[233] See <http://www.jasenovac.org/whatwasjasenovac.php>, accessed on 8 December 2014.

[234] <http://www.jusp-jasenovac.hr/Default.aspx?sid=6559>, accessed on 31 January 2015.

[235] 'Serbia Returns 31 Icons' (n 229).

[236] 'Protocol on restitution of cultural assets from Serbia to Croatia signed', 23 March 2012, available at: <http://www.culturenet.hr/default.aspx?id=44206>, accessed on 7 February 2015; the text of the protocol has not been published in English.

[237] European Commission, 'Comprehensive Monitoring Report on Croatia's State of Preparedness for EU Membership', SWD (2012) 338 final, Brussels, 10 October 2012, at 9.

[238] See information at: <http://www.min-kulture.hr/default.aspx?id=9899>, accessed on 7 February 2015. On the legal framework for cultural heritage protection in Croatia, see Igor Gliha and Tatjana Josipovic, *Croatia*, in Toshiyuki Kono and Stefan Wrbka (eds) *The Impact of Uniform Laws on the Protection of Cultural Heritage and the Preservation of Cultural Heritage in the 21st Century*, (Brill, 2010), 247–80.

[239] <http://inserbia.info/today/2014/04/return-of-cultural-treasures-to-croatia-must-not-precede-that-of-serbs>, accessed on 7 February 2015.

have been created for normal life, the reconstruction of demolished houses and churches, and a return of expelled Serbs. They also said that Croatia disregards its own legislation under which the rights of Serbs must be protected, comprising the right to use the Cyrillic alphabet, and warned that those who make the decision to return the cultural treasures will take the responsibility for their further deterioration and demise.[240]

The implementation of the SFRY Agreement has been criticized. For instance, the Conclusions from the International Scientific Conference "Settlement of Open Issues between Successor States of SFR Yugoslavia",[241] held in Belgrade on 29–30 November 2012, stated that 'in spite of the declared intentions of the parties to the Agreement to cooperate in its implementation and to finally and efficiently settle all disputed matters concerning the succession of SFRY, the hitherto results of its implementation have been modest'. It argued that 'the reasons partly lay in imprecise provisions of the Agreement' concerning bilateral agreements, and 'partly in the absence of political willingness of the governments of the successor states to start with its implementation'. Moreover, 'in the Republic of Serbia, little attention is devoted to the issues of succession and this occurs only when other successor states of SFRY present their demands' and 'no effort has been made in defining the national strategy in this field'.[242]

It also appears that due to the long-lasting political tensions and further territorial changes (the separation of Montenegro and of Kosovo from Serbia), the question of allocation and apportionment of cultural property and archives have not been properly settled. In particular, access to the necessary documentation as well as the meeting of intergovernmental talks were both repeatedly hindered. Thus, identification of cultural property by the respective successor states during the two-year period, as established by the 2001 SFRY Agreement, was generally impossible. Moreover, it seems that the effective implementation of the agreement might, in any case, lead to serious controversies between successor states, as territorial provenance and cultural interest are interpreted differently in either. In response to this it was, however, possible to observe a certain 'beyond succession' practice. As the dissolution of the SFRY escalated into armed conflict, the provisions on state succession to cultural assets were often challenged by those regulating the protection of cultural property in the event of armed conflict. In particular, preference was given to the rule of general international law ordering the unconditional restitution of cultural property removed from an occupied territory. As the principles on state succession under the 2001 SFRY Agreement may seem disputable or hardly enforceable, the result of legal actions pursued by a successor state aimed at recovering cultural properties often resulted more predictable when the removal took place under the violent circumstances of a military conflict.

[240] Ibid.

[241] See Institute for International Politics and Economics in Belgrade; available at: <http://www.diplomacy.bg.ac.rs/conferences/20121129_Settlement.htm>, accessed on 7 February 2015.

[242] Ibid. para. 9.

5.4 Conclusion

The practice of post-Cold War state succession in respect of the allocation and distribution of tangible cultural heritage in the cases of the dissolution of Czechoslovakia, the Soviet Union, and Yugoslavia manifested certain common characteristics.

First, all three cases confirmed the general principle of *uti possidetis*.[243] Thus, the formation of successor states followed or were obliged to respect (in the case of Yugoslavia) the existing administrative boundaries, although such a solution rarely corresponded with ethnic, national, and cultural divisions. Thus, it often occurred that certain important sites and properties of major importance for the cultural heritage of one successor state remained in the territory of another.

Second, as provided under Article 18 of the Vienna Convention, successor states were automatically entitled to the state property of the predecessor situated in their respective territories. With regard to state property of the predecessor located outside the territories of the successor states, the state practice also usually followed the regime of the 1983 Vienna Convention, that is, the pre-eminence of succession agreements between the states concerned and equitable distribution. However, these general rules proved inadequate for the purposes of state succession to cultural property. Therefore, in all three cases states applied certain cultural exemptions from the regime on the allocation of state property. Yet in dealing with such issues, in each of the cases concerned different strategies and considerations were adopted.

Generally speaking, the Czech Republic and Slovakia followed the model of distribution developed on the occasion of the 1932 Austro–Hungarian Agreement.[244] Accordingly, in the official negotiations, they decided on the reciprocal exchange of determined groups of cultural objects which originated from their respective territories. In the cases of important collections of documents relating to the history and culture of both states, privileged access was provided. It seems that all these arrangements have been fully implemented.

The 1992 CIS Agreement on Cultural and Historic Treasures adopted a very broad concept of return and restitution of cultural objects to their countries of origin formulated at the time of decolonization. Each of the states members of the CIS was required to establish its own commission to prepare the relevant documentation concerning cultural property kept in its territory, as well as in foreign territories. It appears that such inventories would cover not only the properties displaced prior to the dissolution of the USSR but also the objects removed as a result of illicit trafficking. The claims of states would then be examined by a special CIS multilateral commission. Such a solution largely reflected the legal framework of the 1970 UNESCO Convention and the statutes of the UNESCO

[243] Cfr Giuseppe Nesi, 'LUti Possidetis hors du contexte de la décolonisation: le cas de l'Europe', *AFDI* 44(1998), 1–143.

[244] Agreement between Austria and Hungary Concerning Certain Objects from Museum and Library Collections, with Three Protocols and Three Annexes, signed in Venice on 27 November 1932, 162 LNTS 395.

Intergovernmental Committee. Consequently, this broad objective of the 1992 CIS Agreement on Cultural and Historic Treasures coupled with the fact that it arguably privileged smaller republics against Russia—the major political actor of the CIS and former imperial power—led to the rejection of the agreement by the latter. As the vast majority of displaced cultural property was preserved in the museums, libraries, and archives of Moscow and St Petersburg, the withdrawal of Russia from the 1992 CIS Agreement on Cultural and Historic Treasures rendered the entire system ineffective. This was reinforced by further Russian legislation which vested ownership of cultural property preserved in its museums to the Russian state. Thus, the returns were allowed only on the basis of special bilateral agreements with a claimant state, always executed on an *ex gratia* basis. The unique exemption from the principle of voluntariness related to the objects displaced by the Nazi occupiers and concerned only states victims of the 1941 German aggression.

Thus, the final position between the majority of states members of the CIS in respect of Russia can be perceived as analogous to that of post-colonial relations. Indeed, Russia's rejection of the 1992 CIS Agreement on Cultural and Historic Treasures resembles the attitude of these former colonial powers, which have postponed ratification of the major international instruments on the return of cultural property and the codified rules on state succession in dread of the flood of claims issued by their former dependent territories. Therefore, they opted for bilateral solutions in which the actual transfers of cultural objects are always pursued on an *ex gratia* basis.

Finally, the 2001 SFRY Agreement included provisions on the allocation of cultural property within the broader framework of the regulation on succession to state property and archives. Accordingly, it set up the exemption from the general regime based on the 1983 Vienna Convention, stating that tangible movable state property of great importance to the cultural heritage of one of the successor states and which originated from the territory of that state shall pass to that state. Importantly, it contained non-enumerative categories of such property, including books and archives. The 2001 SFRY Agreement also provided that the successor state shall determine the catalogue as soon as possible, but no later than two years after the entry into force of the agreement. This is clearly in line with the standards promoted by legal scholarship, in particular the Institute of International Law. The execution of the 2001 SFRY Agreement has not, however, been successful due to political tensions. Moreover, similar regulations have not been adopted with reference to the separation of Montenegro and Kosovo. The only cases of actual allocation of cultural property following the dissolution of the SFRY concerned the objects removed during war operations and were based on the Hague regime for the protection of cultural property in armed conflict.

Thus, from all these developments a more general view can be put forward. Accordingly, it seems rather improbable that a regime on the allocation of state cultural property based on the principles of territorial provenance and major significance to the cultural heritage of a successor state would ever evolve into a binding rule of international law. Notwithstanding the fact that states include such principles in their succession agreements, they are very reluctant to put them into practice. Moreover, their implementation is usually hindered by different interpretations of historic and cultural ties. The actual arrangements on the allocation of cultural property is therefore more often settled in the framework of international cultural heritage law, particularly that of the 1970 UNESCO Convention. Consequently, the principles on state succession to cultural property continue as a mere non-binding set of rules, applicable only in cases where favourable 'political will' is at stake.

6

New Horizons of State Succession

Reconciliation and Cultural Cooperation

> Grinus (they say), the son of Aesanius, a descendent of Theras, and king of the island of Thera, went to Delphi to offer a hecatomb on behalf of his native city. He was accompanied by a large number of the citizens, and among the rest by Buttus ... who belonged to the Minyan family of the Euphemidae. On Grinus consulting the oracle about sundry matters, the Pythoness gave him for answer, 'that he should found a city in Libya.' Grinus replied to this: 'I, O king! Am too far advanced in years, and too inactive, for such a work. Bid one of these youngsters undertake it.' As he spoke, he pointed towards Battus ... Seven years passed from the utterance of the oracle, and not a drop of rain fell in Thera: all the trees in the island ... were killed with drought. After a while, everything began to go wrong. Ignorant of the cause of their sufferings, they again sent to Delphi to inquire for what reason they were afflicted. The Pythoness in reply reminded them reproachfully that if they and Battus would make a settlement at Cyrene in Libya, things would go better with them.[1]

With these words, Herodotus began his story on the origins of the Greek colony of Cyrene on the north-eastern coast of what is known today as Libya. The small polis, settled in *c.*630 BC, soon became one of the major commercial and cultural centres of the Mediterranean, experiencing the peak of its splendour at the beginning of the Common Era as the capital of the rich Roman province of Cyrenaica. Devastating earthquakes followed by profound economic decline influenced the decline of the city, which at the end of the fourth century AD lay completely deserted. Interest in its history and culture was resuscitated in the eighteenth century and the first systematic archaeological excavations began in the nineteenth.[2]

[1] Herodotus, *The Histories*, trans. George Rawlinson (Dutton & Co., 1862), Book IV; Fred Morrow Fling (ed), *A Source Book of Greek History*, (D. C. Heath, 1907), 38–39; online source: *Ancient History Sourcebook*, available at: <http://www.fordham.edu/halsall/ancient/630cyrene.asp>, accessed on 5 February 2015.

[2] See Dorothy M. Thorn, *The Four Seasons of Cyrene: the Excavation and explorations in 1861 of Lieutenants R. Murdoch Smith, R.E. and Edwin A. Porcher, R.N.* (L'Erma Di Bretschneider, 2007).

However, the discovery of the most famous art treasure of this ancient city—the *Venus of Cyrene*—was completely by chance during a military campaign.

In the last decades of the nineteenth century, Italy decided to stake its claim in the ongoing 'Scramble for Africa'. After the conquest of Somaliland and Eritrea and initial failures to colonize Ethiopia, Italian interests focused on the Ottoman provinces on the northern coast of Africa. As a result of the Italian–Turkish War (1911–12), Italy gained control over the territories of Tripolitania and Cyrenaica (Libya).[3] In 1912 the Treaty of Ouchy-Lausanne was signed,[4] which provided for the immediate withdrawal of the Turkish military and civil administration from these lands. Thus, Libya *de facto* became an Italian colony. On 28 December 1913, Italian soldiers made an important discovery, when torrential rains washed away the topsoil at Trajan's Baths in the Sanctuary of Apollo, in the area of the ancient Cyrene, revealing the headless marble statue of Venus.[5] The sculpture was excavated and after closer examination was recognized as a second-century Roman marble copy of a Hellenistic original representing *Aphrodite Anadyomene* (Venus Rising From the Sea). Subsequently, the statue was taken to the city of Benghazi (in Cyrenaica), where it was intended for display in a new local museum.[6] However, in 1915, it was transported to Rome and exhibited in the newly opened National Roman Museum at the Baths of Diocletian.

After the First World War Italy finally formalized its sovereign rights to Libya under the 1923 Peace Treaty of Lausanne.[7] In the interwar period, the excavations in the site of Cyrene were continued by Italian archaeologists up until 1942, when the British occupied Cyrenaica.[8] In 1951 Libya proclaimed its independence. The ruins of the ancient city attracted many foreign archaeological missions and their discoveries gained international attention. Thus, in 1982 the Archaeological Site of Cyrene was inscribed on the World Heritage List (WHL)[9] Its outstanding universal value was derived from the fact that the site preserved 'a necropolis complex which is numbered among the most extensive and varied of the ancient world'.[10] Moreover, the current 'knowledge of Hellenic sculpture is tightly linked to the finds made on the site of Cyrene during the course of 20th century excavations by American, Italian, French and Libyan archaeological teams.'[11]

[3] After the unification of Tripolitania and Cyrenaica in 1934, the name of this Italian colony was changed to Libya.

[4] Peace Treaty Ouchy-Lausanne of 18 October 1912, 217 Parry's CTS 160.

[5] Ernest A. Gardner, 'The Aphrodite from Cyrene', *The Journal of Hellenic Studies* 40(1920)2, 203–205; Gilbert Bagnani, 'Hellenistic Sculpture from Cyrene', *The Journal of Hellenic Studies* 41(1921)2, 232–46.

[6] Thorn, *The Four Seasons of Cyrene* (n 2) 220–21.

[7] Treaty of Peace with Turkey, signed at Lausanne, on 24 July 1923, 28 LNTS 11.

[8] Enzo Catani, 'L'attività archeologica di Luigi Pernier a Cirene dal 1925 al 1936', *Quaderni di Archeologia della Libya* (2002)18, 235–55.

[9] UNESCO Doc. CLT-82/CH/CONF.015/8.

[10] International Council on Monuments and Sites (ICOMOS), World Heritage List, No. 190, May 1982, at 3, available at: <http://whc.unesco.org/archive/advisory_body_evaluation/190.pdf> accessed on 29 January 2015.

[11] Ibid.

Initially, Libya did not demand the return of the artefacts removed under Italian rule. In 1956, both states signed an agreement covering various economic and financial matters arising from the succession of one sovereign state to the other in the territory of Libya, in particular, the passing of state property.[12] The agreement did not regulate the issue of the allocation of cultural property although it encouraged both states to sign an additional cultural agreement. The position of Libya changed in 1989, when it formally requested the restitution of the *Venus of Cyrene*.[13] Subsequent political and economic tensions between Libya and the Western world meant that the negotiations moved very slowly.

Eventually, on the occasion of the conclusion of the 1998 Joint Declaration between Italy and Libya constituting the premise for a future agreement covering broad political and economic scope,[14] both states discussed the question of the restitution of cultural property removed by Italy from its colony in accordance with the 1970 UNESCO Convention.[15] In 2000 the final agreement was signed,[16] and two years later, the Italian Ministry of Cultural Heritage and Activities passed a decree on the deaccession of the item from state patrimony and authorized its transfer to Libya.[17] The decision was made in favourable political circumstances since Libya initiated the process of normalization of its ties with the US and the European Union. This new approach towards political and commercial relations was also pursued through a new campaign of foreign archaeological missions and international cooperation for the preservation of the site of Cyrene,[18] in which Italian institutions played an important role. The actual restitution was, however, hindered by lawsuits brought before Italian administrative courts by Italia Nostra, an Italian non-governmental organization. This sought the annulment of the 2002 decree, arguing that the statue constituted a component of Italian cultural heritage since it had been discovered in territory subject to Italian sovereignty, therefore its transfer to a foreign state was possible, provided that a specific law was passed by the parliament. The lawsuit was rejected by the courts in two instances, both of which held that Italy was bound by the obligation under customary international law to return the cultural property to the people subject to colonial domination.[19]

[12] Agreement between the Republic of Italy and the United Kingdom of Libya on Economic Cooperation and Settlement of Issues Arising from Resolution 388(V) of 15 December 1950 of the General Assembly of the United Nations (with Exchanges of Notes and Annexes), signed on 2 October 1956, entered into force on 7 December 1957, 2328 UNTS 89.

[13] After Alessandro Chechi, 'The Return of Cultural Objects Removed in Times of Colonial Domination and International Law: The Case of the Venus of Cyrene', *IYIL* 18(2008), 159–81, at 160.

[14] Natalino Ronzitti, 'The Treaty on Friendship, Partnership and Cooperation between Italy and Libya: New Prospects for Cooperation in the Mediterranean?', *Bulletin of Italian Politics* 1(2009)1, 125–33, at 125.

[15] Convention on the Means of Prohibiting and Preventing the Illicit Import, Export and Transfer of Ownership of Cultural Property, signed on14 November 1970, entered into force 24 April 1972, 832 UNTS 231; see Chechi, 'The Return of Cultural Objects' (n 13) 160–61.

[16] Chechi, 'The Return of Cultural Objects' (n 13) 161.

[17] Ibid. 161.

[18] <http://globalheritagefund.org/what_we_do/overview/current_projects/cyrene_libya>, accessed on 5 February 2015.

[19] The decision of Italian administrative courts will be subject to further detailed analysis in this chapter, section 6.4.3.

Finally, after a wait of nearly 100 years, on 30 August 2008 the Prime Minister of Italy, Silvio Berlusconi handed over the statute to Libya's leader, Muammar al-Gaddafi. The same day, both states also concluded the Treaty on Friendship, Partnership and Cooperation,[20] which together with a group of cultural agreements signed in 2000–08 was designed to put an end to the dispute between the two countries and to Libya's claims relating to Italian colonialism. The spirit of reconciliation was paramount. As regards cultural heritage matters, both states, under Article 16 (2), agreed to cooperate in the matter of archaeology, including the question of restitution to Libya of archaeological objects and manuscripts. In addition, they undertook to cooperate with the objective of facilitating the restitution to Libya of the cultural material from other countries, removed during colonialism.

Thus, the handing over of the *Venus of Cyrene* constituted a symbolic conclusion of the previous controversies, and the promise of future productive cooperation in the retrieval of the dispersed cultural patrimony of the former Italian colony, today an important regional partner.[21]

As explained in Chapter 5, the post-Cold War succession agreements on the allocation and distribution of cultural property have generally resulted in failure. This does not mean, however, that states do not search for alternative solutions. In fact, they are often motivated by the concept of reconciliation, extensively used in recent international and domestic political discourse.[22] This chapter argues that such efforts are essentially based, in legal terms, on the procedural principle of cooperation.[23] Accordingly, it analyses the impact of international cultural heritage law on state practice with regard to the fate of tangible cultural heritage in cases of state succession. In particular, it deals with the content, sources, and status of cultural heritage obligations in state succession. It then cites the relevant international practice concerning the impact of international law for the protection of cultural heritage on state succession arrangements. First, it explores the links between the protection of human rights and preservation of tangible cultural heritage with regard to the post-dissolution legal framework for Bosnia–Herzegovina and Kosovo. Second, it deals with the principle of cultural cooperation in respect of the resolution of long-lasting cultural property disputes related to the Second World War territorial changes and population transfers, and in respect of the post-colonial context. Third, it analyses the reciprocal impact of

[20] Trattato di amicizia, partenariato e cooperazione tra la Repubblica italiana e la Grande Giamahiria araba libica popolare socialista, fatto a Bengasi il 30 agosto 2008. The treaty entered into force on 2 March 2009, GU No. 89 of 18 February 2009.

[21] In 2011, the implementation of the cultural arrangements between both states has been interrupted by the violent military conflict in Libya.

[22] Siri Gloppen, 'Roads to Reconciliation: A Conceptual Framework', in Elin Skaar, Siri Gloppen, and Astri Suhrke (eds), *Roads to Reconciliation* (Lexington Books, 2005), 17–50.

[23] See Alessandro Chechi, 'Multi-Level Cooperation to Safeguard the Human Heritage and to Secure the Return of Wrongfully Removed Cultural Objects', in Silvia Borelli and Federico Lenzerini (eds), *Cultural Heritage, Cultural Rights, Cultural Diversity. New Developments in International Law* (Nijhoff, 2012), 347–68; Alessandro Chechi, *The Settlements of International Cultural Heritage Disputes* (OUP, 2014), 296 ff.

international obligations with regard to the cultural heritage of mankind, including underwater heritage, on the practice of state succession.

6.1 Cultural heritage obligations in state succession

In the context of the new wave of territorial and political changes after 1989, successor states had to face the complexity of international cultural heritage obligations. Indeed, their sheer volume and expanding terms are due to the continuous development of international law for the protection of cultural heritage since the 1943 London Declaration.[24] The existence of clear-cut criteria of succession or non-succession in such obligations, under positive rules of international law remains, however, rather obscure. Some conclusions may arguably be forwarded regarding the formation of certain rules under general international.

6.1.1 The content and sources of cultural heritage obligations

The period 1943–89 was characterized by the progressive evolution of international cultural heritage law *vis à vis* the continuing post-colonial restitution debate and the codification of the law on state succession. After 1989, developments in the area of the international law on the protection of tangible cultural heritage accelerated. In part, this has been due to the violent events in the territory of the former Yugoslavia, followed by intentional destruction and plunder of cultural property there.

Not only did changes in the area of the international protection of cultural heritage occur at the level of international treaties—in particular multilateral conventions—but they also occurred at the level of UN ad hoc instruments of non-binding declarations and principles of soft law, state practice, and jurisprudence of international and domestic tribunals.[25] Some authors—in particular Francesco Francioni and Tullio Scovazzi—have noticed that this progress needs to be acknowledged as a consequence of the common awareness that the protection of cultural heritage in all its manifestations constitutes part of the general interest of humanity as a whole.[26] Francioni also argues that such complex

[24] The Inter-Allied Declaration against Acts of Dispossession Committed in Territories under Enemy Occupation or Control adopted in London on 5 January 1943 (the 1943 Declaration of London). The text of the London Declaration is available at: <http://www.lootedartcommission.com/inter-allied-declaration>, accessed on 31 January 2015.

[25] For a conceptual overview, see *inter alia* Francesco Francioni, 'Plurality and Interaction of Legal Orders in the Enforcement of Cultural Heritage Law', in Francesco Francioni and James Gordley (eds), *Enforcing International Cultural Heritage* (OUP, 2013), 9–19; see also Francesco Francioni 'Evolving Framework for the Protection of Cultural Heritage in International Law', in Silvia Borelli and Federico Lenzerini (eds), *Cultural Heritage, Cultural Rights, Cultural Diversity. New Developments in International Law* (Nijhoff, 2012), 3–28; Guido Carducci, 'Growing Complexity of International Art Law: Conflicts of Law, Mandatory Rules, UNSC Resolutions and EU Regulations', in Barbara T. Hoffman (ed), *Art and Cultural Heritage. Law, Policy and Practice* (CUP, 2006), 68–86.

[26] Tullio Scovazzi, 'La notion de patrimoine culturel de l'humanité dans le instruments internationaux—Rapport du Directeur d'études de la section de langue française du Centre', in

developments of international practice are evidence that today certain general principles have formed or are in the process of forming at the level of customary international law concerning the protection and enjoyment of cultural heritage.[27] He explains that because the origin of such principles arises from the general interest of the international community, it may be argued that respect for cultural heritage constitutes the object of an *erga omnes* obligation.[28] In other words, all states are bound by such an obligation even if they did not accede to international treaties on the protection of cultural heritage.

Because the international regime for the protection of material cultural heritage is fast becoming so complex, it seems necessary to analyse recent developments in six main distinctive areas:[29] 1) the protection of cultural property in the event of armed conflict and occupation; 2) the obligation to restore the material appropriated and transferred from militarily occupied territories; 3) the prevention and prohibition of the illicit traffic of movable cultural property in times of peace; 4) the protection of the common heritage of mankind; 5) the protection of underwater cultural heritage; 6) the preservation of cultural heritage as an element of protection and promotion of human rights, particularly in their collective dimension.

a) *The protection and prohibition of destruction of tangible cultural heritage*

Following the Second World War, the rules governing the situation of cultural property in the event of an international armed conflict were codified at the universal level by the 1954 Hague Convention.[30] This, for the first time, formalized the concept of 'cultural property' as an autonomous legal category requiring international protection due to the inherent value of cultural heritage for every people. The Convention also recognizes that such protection is of universal concern, because each people makes its contribution to the culture of the world. To this end, it provides a list of measures to be applied with reference to cultural property. Finally, it implicitly recalls the jurisprudence of the Nuremburg Tribunal with regard to individual criminal responsibility for acts committed against cultural property in the occupied territories. Accordingly, the 1954 Hague Convention obliges parties to undertake 'within the framework of their ordinary criminal jurisdiction, all necessary steps to prosecute and impose penal or disciplinary sanctions upon those persons, of whatever nationality, who commit or order to be committed a breach of the present Convention' (Article 28).[31]

Tullio Scovazzi and James A. R. Nafziger (eds), *Le patrimoine culturel de l'humanité/the Cultural Heritage of Mankind* (Nijhoff 2008), 3–144, at 142–44, Francesco Francioni, 'Au-delà des traités: l'émergence d'un noveau droit coutimier pour la protection du patrimoine culturel', *RGDIP* 111(2007)1, 19–42.

[27] Francioni, 'Au-delà des traités' (n 26) 41. [28] Ibid. 41. [29] Ibid.

[30] Convention for the Protection of Cultural Property in the Event of Armed Conflict, signed on 14 May 1955, entered into force on 7 August 1956, 249 UNTS 240.

[31] These provisions were subsequently reinforced under Art. 85(4)(d) of the 1977 Protocol I to the 1949 Geneva Conventions, which established the prosecution of offences against 'the clearly-recognized historic monuments, works of art or places of worship which constitute the

In response to a number of criminal acts committed against cultural property in the course of the conflicts that took place at the end of the 1980s and the beginning of the 1990s (in particular, during the Balkan wars), the Hague regime was extended to cover non-international conflicts.[32] Article 22 of the Second Protocol to the Hague Convention of 1954 for the Protection of Cultural Property in the Event of Armed Conflict (the Second Hague Protocol)[33] provides that the international regime of protection shall also 'apply in the event of an armed conflict not of an international character, occurring within the territory of one of the Parties'. This, however, does not refer to situations of 'internal disturbances and tensions, such as riots, isolated and sporadic acts of violence and other acts of a similar nature'. Moreover, the Second Hague Protocol elaborates the provisions of the 1954 Hague Convention relating to the safeguarding of and respect for cultural property and the conduct of hostilities. In particular, it established a new category of enhanced protection for tangible cultural heritage that is of greatest importance for humanity (Article 10).[34] The Protocol also provides for the most advanced and detailed regime of individual criminal responsibility for offences against cultural heritage. It introduces the principle of universal jurisdiction over the most 'serious violations' of the norms on the protection of cultural heritage, and obliges the parties to prosecute or extradite the offender regardless of his or her nationality or the location of the violation committed. Such offences not only comprise the destruction of cultural heritage, but also theft, pillage, or misappropriation of cultural material.[35]

Apart from the Hague regime of UNESCO, the principle of individual criminal responsibility for severe acts against tangible cultural heritage in the event of armed conflict has been developed in the recently drafted statutes of international criminal tribunals. This is essentially linked to the shocking examples of destruction of cultural sites in the territory of the former Yugoslavia—for example, the Old City of Dubrovnik and the ancient mosques in Bosnia. Accordingly, Article

cultural or spiritual heritage of peoples and to which special protection has been given by special arrangement, for example, within the framework of a competent international organization.' Protocol Additional to the Geneva Conventions of 12 August 1949, and relating to the Protection of Victims of International Armed Conflicts (Protocol I), signed on 8 June 1977, entered into force on 7 December 1978, 1125 UNTS 3.

[32] Jiří Toman, 'The Road to the 1999 Second Protocol', in Nout van Woudenberg and Liesbeth Lijnzaad (eds), *Protecting Cultural Property in Armed Conflict: An Insight into the 1999 Second Protocol to the Hague Convention of 1954 for the Protection of Cultural Property in the Event of Armed Conflict* (Nijhoff, 2010), 1–20.

[33] Second Protocol to the Hague Convention of 1954 for the Protection of Cultural Property in the Event of Armed Conflict, signed on 26 March 1999, entered into force on 9 March 2004, 2253 UNTS 21.

[34] See further Nout van Woundenberg, 'Enhanced Protection: A New Form of Protection under the 1999 Second Protocol', in Nout van Woudenberg and Liesbeth Lijnzaad (eds), *Protecting Cultural Property in Armed Conflict* (Nijhoff, 2010), 51–58.

[35] Mireille Hector, 'Enhancing Individual Criminal Responsibility for Offences Involving Cultural Property—the Road to the Rome Statute and the 1999 Second Protocol', in Nout van Woudenberg and Liesbeth Lijnzaad (eds), *Protecting Cultural Property in Armed Conflict* (Nijhoff, 2010), 69–76; Roger O'Keefe, *The Protection of Cultural Property in Armed Conflict* (CUP, 2006), 236.

3(d) of the Statute of the International Criminal Tribunal for ex-Yugoslavia (ICTY)[36] defines the 'seizure of, destruction or wilful damage done to institutions dedicated to religion, charity and education, the arts and sciences, historic monuments and works of art and science' as violations of the laws or customs of war. The Rome Statute of the International Criminal Court (ICC)[37] includes similar provisions. Accordingly, it criminalizes as serious violations of the laws and customs applicable in international armed conflict the intentional attacks directed 'against buildings dedicated to religion, education, art, science or charitable purposes, historic monuments, hospitals and places where the sick and wounded are collected, provided they are not military objectives' (Articles 8(2)(b)(ix) and 8(2)(e)(iv)).

The ICTY, in its jurisprudence, has already interpreted and applied the provision of Article 3(d) in a series of cases regarding the attacks against historical monuments in Croatia and Bosnia–Herzegovina. In particular, in *Kordic & Cerkez* which dealt with acts of destruction and damage of religious or educational institutions (the ancient mosques in Bosnia) the court held that the destruction of such institutions constituted 'a violation of the laws or customs of war enumerated under Article 3(d) of the Statute'. Moreover, such acts were criminalized under customary international law.[38]

Similar conclusions were also reached by the Claims Commission, established by the peace accords concluded in Algiers on 12 December 2000,[39] in order to settle the disputes between Ethiopia and Eritrea which took place during the war of 1998–2000.[40] These referred to the brief military presence of Ethiopia on the archaeological site of Matara in Eritrea, during which time significant monuments were damaged. Matara was one of the most important cities of the ancient Aksum Kingdom and preserved a vast archaeological patrimony comprising the Hawulti, an Aksumite-era obelisk (perhaps 2500 years old), considered the oldest known example of the old Ge'ez script (also known as 'Old Ethiopic').[41] This monument, of great historical and cultural significance to both Ethiopia and Eritrea, was toppled and damaged in May 2000. Eritrea accused Ethiopian troops of setting an explosive under the *Stela* before the Claims Commission. On 28 April 2004,[42] the

[36] Statute of the International Tribunal for the Prosecution of Persons Responsible for Serious Violations of International Humanitarian Law Committed in the Territory of the Former Yugoslavia since 1991, adopted on 25 May 1993, U.N. Doc. S/RES/827 (1992).

[37] Statute of the International Criminal Court (Statute of Rome), adopted on 17 July 1998, entered into force on 1 July 2002, U.N. Doc. A/CONF.183/9, 2187 UNTS 90.

[38] *Prosecutor v. Kordić and Čerkez*, Case No. IT-95-14/2-T, Judgment of 26 February 2001, para. 206.

[39] Agreement Between the Governments of the State of Eritrea and the Federal Democratic Republic of Ethiopia, signed in Algiers on 12 December 2000, entered into force on the date of signature, UN Doc. A/55/686-S/2000/1183, Annex; available at: <http://www.pca-cpa.org/upload/files/Algiers%20Agreement.pdf> accessed on 15 February 2015.

[40] See Natalie Klein, 'State Responsibility for International Humanitarian Law Violations and the Work of the Eritrea–Ethiopia Claims Commission So Far', *GYIL* 47(2004), 214–66.

[41] Edward Ullendorff, 'The Obelisk of Matara', *Journal of the Royal Asiatic Society of Great Britain and Ireland* 83(1951)1–2, 26–32.

[42] Partial Award—Central Front—Eritrea's Claims 2, 4, 6, 7, 8, and 22; available at: <http://www.pca-cpa.org/showpage.asp?pag_id=1151>, accessed on 9 February 2015.

commission, having examined the evidences provided, concluded that Ethiopia was responsible, as the occupying power in the Matara area, 'even though there is no evidence that the decision to explode the stela was anything other than a decision by one or several soldiers'.[43] It also held that 'the felling of the stela was a violation of customary international humanitarian law',[44] nonetheless the 1954 Hague Convention was not applicable, as neither Eritrea nor Ethiopia was a party to it. Thus, Ethiopia was held liable for the unlawful damage inflicted upon the *Stela* of Matara in May 2000 and was obliged to apologize Eritrea. Moreover, monetary compensation was to be paid.[45]

The next step in the development of the international regime on the protection of cultural property against serious offences against the cultural heritage occurred in response to the destruction of the sixth-century Buddhas of Bamiyan in Afghanistan.[46] In 2001, the Taliban carried out the destruction of these monumental statues, considering them as idolatrous and un-Islamic.[47] As a consequence, in 2003 UNESCO's General Conference adopted the Declaration Concerning the Intentional Destruction of Cultural Heritage.[48] This explicitly recognized that the tragic destruction of the Buddhas affected the international community as a whole. It also recalled that 'the development of rules of customary international law has also affirmed by the relevant case-law, related to the protection of cultural heritage in peacetime as well as in the event of armed conflict' (Preamble). Moreover, it provided, under Article VI, that 'a state that intentionally destroys or intentionally fails to take appropriate measures to prohibit, prevent, stop, and punish any intentional destruction of cultural heritage of great importance for humanity, whether or not it is inscribed on a list maintained by UNESCO or another international organization, bears the responsibility for such destruction, to the extent provided for by international law.'

Arguably, the 2003 UNESCO Declaration, as well as developments in the international jurisprudence, justify the conclusion that the deliberate destruction

[43] Ibid. para. 112. [44] Ibid. para. 113.

[45] Ibid. para. 114. By contrast, it is necessary to add that Eritrea's claims, founded on the rules of state succession, to recover its historical, cultural, and artistic legacy, preserved in Ethiopia, were not even considered by the latter. In fact, during the period of federation between these two states (1961–1993), the number of archaeological objects excavated in the territories of the present Eritrea were moved to major cultural institutions of Ethiopia. These particularly refer to the artefacts excavated from 1960 to 1965 by French archaeologist Francis Anfray and since then preserved in Addis Ababa. Followed Eritrea's independence, the newly founded National Museum of Eritrea in Asmara has petitioned the Ethiopian government to return artefacts. These claims have remained unanswered. See 'Eritrea wants artefacts back', News24, 10 February 2005, available at: <http://www.news24.com/Africa/News/Eritrea-wants-artefacts-back-20050210>, accessed on 31 January 2015.

[46] O'Keefe, *The Protection of Cultural Property* (n 35) 356–57.

[47] Francesco Francioni and Federico Lenzerini, 'The Obligation to Prevent and Avoid Destruction of Cultural Heritage: From Bamiyam to Iraq', in Barbara T. Hoffman (ed), *Art and Cultural Heritage: Law Policy and Practice* (CUP, 2006), 28–40, at 28–30.

[48] UNESCO Declaration concerning the Intentional Destruction of Cultural Heritage, adopted on 17 October 2003, UNESCO Doc. 32 C/Res. 33 (2003), see Federico Lenzerini, 'The UNESCO Declaration Concerning the Intentional Destruction of Cultural Heritage: One Step Forward and Two Steps Back', *IYIL* 13(2003), 131–45.

of cultural heritage in the event of armed conflict is prohibited not only under treaty law but also by customary international law. In particular, it is also argued that the obligation to respect and protect cultural property of great importance for every people and/or for the international humanity as a whole constitutes a general principle of international law of an *erga omnes* nature.[49]

b) The restitution of cultural property removed from an occupied territory and the concept of 'safe havens'

As explained in previous chapters, the question of restitution of cultural property looted or otherwise removed from the territory subject to foreign military occupation has been continually addressed in international legal discourse since at least 1815.[50] The Allied legislation, in particular the 1945 London Declaration enacted in the course of and just after the Second World War, recognized the obligation binding on all members of the international community to return cultural property appropriated and/or removed from occupied territories by the use of force and under duress. This changed as a result of the outbreak of the Cold War and the subsequent *de facto* rejection of this duty in respect of the property of the aggressors by states of Eastern bloc.

Subsequently, the issue became subject to the Hague codification on the protection of cultural property in the event of armed conflict. The 1954 Hague Protocol specifically dealt with movables, prohibiting the export of cultural property from an occupied territory and requiring the return of such property to the territory of the state from which it was removed. It also expressly forbade the appropriation of cultural property as war reparation. However, its provisions were not unanimously acknowledged as the codification of customary international law. The controversy surrounding the nature and extent of the obligation of restitution was also reflected by the initially low number of ratifications of this instrument. Moreover, the adoption of the 1954 Hague Protocol occurred at the time of decolonization, when the former dependent territories attempted to settle their claims for the return of cultural property captured and removed during colonial domination within the framework of the post-war restitution of cultural material. Such argumentation was clearly contested by the former colonial powers. Nonetheless, it seems that when the 1970 UNESCO Convention concerning the illicit traffic in cultural objects in time of peace was drafted, the duty to abstain from appropriation and transfer of such items under duress in militarily occupied territories constituted a widely recognized norm of international law. Accordingly, Article 11 of the 1970 UNESCO Convention states that 'the export and transfer of ownership of cultural property under compulsion arising directly or indirectly

[49] Francioni and Lenzerini, 'The Obligation to Prevent and Avoid Destruction' (n 47) 38–39.

[50] Compare Guido Carducci, 'L'Obligation de restitution des biens culturels et des objets d'art en cas de conflit armé: droit coutumier et droit conventionnel avant et après la Convention de La Haye de 1954; l'importance du facteur temporel dans les rapports entre les traités et la coutume', *RGDIP* 104(2000)1–2, 289–357.

from the occupation of a country by a foreign power shall be regarded as illicit.' Yet the question of restitution was much more complex as it very often involved the domestic rules on the protection of a *bona fide* purchaser and time limitations. Moreover, this issue was constantly linked to the restitution debate initiated by former colonial countries. The position of ICOM expressed in 1978, arguing that the duty of restitution would become an element of *jus cogens* of international relations, has not been confirmed by state practice and was criticized in the international legal scholarship.[51]

The situation changed after 1989, when a new wave of ratifications of the 1954 Hague Protocol occurred. Now, with 126 states parties,[52] the Protocol is one of the most important international instruments for the protection of cultural heritage. Moreover, the obligation to restore cultural material removed from the occupied territories has been fully recognized by the ad hoc legislation of the UN Security Council. In particular, the most important provisions are to be found in respect of the cultural institutions of Iraq and Kuwait.[53] According to Resolution 686 (1991),[54] the Security Council demanded that Iraq 'immediately begin to return all Kuwaiti property seized by Iraq, to be completed in the shortest possible period' (paragraph 2 (d)). Resolution 1483 of 2003[55] has been even more significant. In this instance, the Security Council decided that all member states of the United Nations 'shall take appropriate steps to facilitate the safe return to Iraqi institutions of Iraqi cultural property and other items of archaeological, historical, cultural, rare scientific, and religious importance illegally removed from the Iraq National Museum, the National Library, and other locations in Iraq' (paragraph 7). Thus, the resolution—as a binding international instrument—provided the obligation *erga omnes* to ensure that cultural property illicitly transferred from occupied territories would be returned.[56]

Despite these controversies, it seems that today the obligation to restore cultural property removed from territories under military occupation has evolved into a binding rule under customary international law.[57] This refers in particular to situations where the removal occurred in relation to genocidal or discriminatory practices, yet the technical questions related to the actual act of restitution are primarily linked to different interpretations of historic events and political circumstances.

Importantly, the obligations to protect cultural property in the event of armed conflict and to return such displaced material need to be also read in the light of the concept and current state practice of 'safe havens'. These relate to situations when movable cultural property endangered in territories of armed conflicts or other turmoil is temporarily relocated for safekeeping. In this regard, the

[51] See Chapter 4, section 4.4.2(b).

[52] See <http://portal.unesco.org/la/convention.asp?KO=15391&language=E&order=alpha>, accessed on 5 February 2015.

[53] See Carducci, 'Growing Complexity of International Art Law' (n 25) 80–81.

[54] UN Doc. S/RES/686 (1991).

[55] UN Doc. S/RES/1483 (2003).

[56] Francioni, 'Au-delà des traités' (n 26).

[57] Ibid.

examination of the international practice unearths a number of cases. As already mentioned in Chapter 3, this was the case with regard to Polish and Hungarian treasures preserved in Canada and the US, respectively. Most recent examples *inter alia* regard the evacuation of the collection of the National Library of Lebanon to Verdun in France (1979) during the first years of the Civil War (1975–90) and the preservation of different collections from Iraq in the US, Syria, Kuwait, and Saudi Arabia at different times during the recent armed conflicts in that country.[58] Yet perhaps the most extensive programme of safekeeping evacuation of cultural material was undertaken in Afghanistan. During the Taliban regime (1996–2001), the curators of the National Museum of Afghanistan of Kabul asked the Guimet Museum in Paris to take temporary charge of a number of collection pieces,[59] retrieved from the market by a non-governmental body, the Society for the Preservation of Afghanistan's Cultural Heritage (SPACH).[60] Following the consent of the French authorities these arrangements were concluded. In addition, in 1999, an 'Afghan Museum in Exile' was set up at the Swiss Afghanistan Institute in Bubendorf[61] to house the confiscated objects from the illicit art and antiquities trade until the situation in Afghanistan became stable. This activity was supported by UNESCO in its capacity as an intergovernmental organization.[62]

The last case caused the doctrine of international law to conceptualize and institutionalize 'safe havens' for endangered cultural property.[63] Indeed, the ILA Cultural Heritage Law Committee, at a conference held on 17–21 August 2008 in Rio de Janeiro, adopted the resolution entitled 'Guidelines for the Establishment and Conduct of Safe Havens'.[64] According to the definition provided by this document, 'safe havens are facilities created in order to care for cultural material that has been endangered by armed conflict, natural disasters, illegal excavation, or other insecurity and has therefore been removed for safekeeping and preservation from the territory of the source state to the territory of another state or to a place of safety in the

[58] See René Teijgeler, 'Preserving Cultural Heritage in Times of Conflict', in Gary E. Gorman and Sydney J. Shep (eds), *Preservation Management for Libraries, Archives and Museums* (Facet Publishing, 2006), 133–65, and sources quoted therein.

[59] Pierre Cambon, 'The Role of the Guimet Museum in the Study and the Preservation of Afghan Heritage', *Museum International* 55(2003)3–4, 54–61.

[60] For further information on the activities of the SPACH in that period, see Brendan Cassar and Ana Rosa Rodríguez García, 'The Society for the Preservation of Afghanistan's Cultural Heritage: an Overview of Activities since 1994', in Juliette van Krieken-Pieters (ed), *Art and Archaeology of Afghanistan: Its Fall and Survival; a Multi-Disciplinary Approach* (Brill, 2006), 15–38.

[61] <http://www.afghanistan-institut.ch>, accessed on 5 February 2015.

[62] See further Lyndell V. Prott, 'The Protection of Cultural Movables from Afghanistan: Developments in International Management', in Juliette van Krieken-Pieters (ed), *Art and Archaeology of Afghanistan: Its Fall and Survival; A Multi-Disciplinary Approach* (Brill, 2006), 189–200.

[63] Kurt Siehr, '"Safe Havens" for Endangered Cultural Objects', in Juliette van Krieken-Pieters (ed), *Art and Archaeology of Afghanistan: Its Fall and Survival; a Multi-Disciplinary Approach* (Brill, 2006), 189–200.

[64] Resolution No 2/2008, Cultural Heritage Law, the 73rd Conference of the International Law Association, held in Rio de Janeiro, Brazil, 17–21 August, 2008, available at: <http://www.ila-hq.org/en/committees/index.cfm/cid/13>, accessed on 5 February 2015.

source state'.[65] Such 'facilities' are bound to 'return cultural material items as soon as the established owner or other established source of the material so requests, provided that the safe haven is satisfied with the conditions for safekeeping and preserving the material by the requesting state or entity.'[66]

The guidelines, though of non-binding nature, demonstrate an increasing awareness of the international scholarship and practice both in rescuing cultural material threatened particularly by an armed conflict and returning such properties to the places of origin. Yet the institution of 'safe havens' may be also applied to 'other insecurity'.[67] Arguably, this could be a handful of instruments applied to violent cases of state succession, prior to final agreement on the apportionment and allocation of cultural property.[68]

c) *The prevention and prohibition of the illicit traffic of movable cultural property in times of peace*

As discussed in Chapter 4, the problem of the prohibition and prevention of illicit traffic in cultural objects has been regulated at the international level by the 1970 UNESCO Convention,[69] to date ratified by 125 states parties.[70] Important efforts have also been undertaken by the United Nations General Assembly in several resolutions concerning the return of cultural properties to their countries of origin.[71] The fundamental concepts in this matter concern the value of preserving the cultural property *in situ* as opposed to the freedom of cross-border trafficking in such objects, and the importance of the procedural principle of cooperation. Indeed, international practice shows that states tend more often to conclude special cultural cooperation agreements in which they reciprocally undertake to remediate the illicit or unauthorized circulation of cultural property originating from their respective territories, than engage in international treaties.[72] Technical and operational assistance is provided by different international bodies monitoring the

[65] Ibid. point 2; the resolution also provides a model contract between a Source State or Entity and Safe Haven.

[66] Ibid. point 4(j).

[67] Ibid. preamble.

[68] The concept of 'safe havens' has also influenced some museums' policy in respect of 'orphaned' or 'dormant' cultural assets in the possession of such entities for which no owner has been determined. In fact, certain measures have been recently undertaken to establish the standards of their custody, exposition, and search for the provenance, especially in cases of the objects that may come from occupied territories. See an extensive analysis by Sophie Engelhardt, *Nachrichtenlose Kulturgüter* (De Gruyter, 2013).

[69] See Chapter 4, section 4.4.

[70] <http://portal.unesco.org/la/convention.asp?KO=13039&language=E>, accessed on 10 October 2014.

[71] See the series of the UNGA Resolutions on the return or restitution of cultural property to the countries of origin, adopted in the years 1972–2009.

[72] Compare Frédérique Coulée, 'Quelques remarques sur la restitution interétatique des biens culturels sous l'angle du droit international public', *RGDIP* 104(2000)2, 359–92.

illicit movement of cultural objects, which draft inventories of stolen and endangered tangible cultural heritage (eg the ICOM Red List).[73]

At the regional level, the most important regulations concerning the return of unlawfully exported cultural property have been introduced in the European Union. Directive 93/7/EEC of 1993[74] sets out an obligations on all member states to cooperate with the aim of returning objects removed from one member state to another in violation of domestic rules on the protection of cultural heritage. It applies to items classified as 'national treasures' which fall into one of the categories listed in the Annex to the Directive. Directive 93/7/EEC had the potential to make a significant impact on international practice in relation to claims for the return of illicitly traded cultural objects. During the first few years following its adoption, however, it was applied to a very small number of cases.[75] This tendency continues today, although the administrative cooperation and the exchange of information on the Directive has improved both within and between the member states.[76] Moreover, many returns of unlawfully exported cultural objects have been executed following negotiations between the national authorities without recourse to the courts.[77] For these reasons a new EU directive is currently being implemented.[78]

Finally, international efforts in the area of illicit trafficking in cultural objects led to the adoption of the 1995 Unidroit Convention on Stolen and Illegally Exported Cultural Objects (the 1995 Unidroit Convention),[79] complementing the regime under the 1970 UNESCO Convention[80] in respect of private law aspects of restitution (good faith acquisition, duty of care, indemnity, etc). The 1995 Unidroit Convention deals with two situations: the restitution of stolen cultural objects (Articles 3 and 4), which can be claimed by the owners, and the return of illegally exported and removed cultural objects (Articles 5–8), which can be claimed only by the states parties to the Convention. The first embodies all stolen and unlawfully excavated objects. The second refers to objects exported or removed from the territory of the requesting state party in violation of its

[73] <http://icom.museum/what-we-do/programmes/fighting-illicit-traffic/red-list.html>, accessed on 5 February 2015.

[74] Council Directive 93/7/EEC of 15 March 1993 on the return of cultural objects unlawfully removed from the territory of a Member State, *Official Journal* L 074, 27.03.1993, 74–79, as amended.

[75] Second Report on the application of Council Directive 93/7/EEC on the return of cultural objects unlawfully removed from the territory of a Member State, COM Docs. 2005/0675 final, 5.2.2.

[76] Third Report on the application of Council Directive 93/7/EEC on the return of cultural objects unlawfully removed from the territory of a Member State, COM Docs. 2009/0408 final, 5.

[77] Ibid. 4.2, and Annex. Compare the Fourth Report on the application of Council Directive 93/7/EEC on the return of cultural objects unlawfully removed from the territory of a Member State, COM Docs. 2013/0310 final.

[78] Directive 2014/60/EU of the European Parliament and of the Council of 15 May 2014 on the return of cultural objects unlawfully removed from the territory of a Member State and amending Regulation (EU) No 1024/2012 (Recast), *Official Journal* L 159, 28.5.2014, 1–10.

[79] Adopted on 24 June 1995, entered into force on 1 July 1998, (1995) 34 *ILM* 1322; See <http://www.unidroit.org/instruments/cultural-property/1995-convention>, accessed on 5 February 2015.

[80] See further Guido Carducci, *La restitution internationale des biens culturels et des objets d'art: droit commun, Directive CEE, Conventions de l'UNESCO et d'Unidroit* (L.G.D.J, 1997); Lyndel V. Prott, 'UNESCO and Unidroit: A Partnership against Trafficking in Cultural Objects', *Uniform Law Review* 1(1996), 59–71.

domestic rules on the protection of the cultural heritage (in particular export prohibitions). In respect of stolen cultural objects, the 1995 Unidroit Convention clearly provides for the recognition of the so-called foreign patrimony laws vesting ownership title to certain cultural objects—unlawfully excavated and traded items. As regards illegally exported cultural objects, the Convention provides for the physical return of the object to the requesting state only if it proves that the removal of the object in question from its territory 'significantly' impairs its evident cultural interests. Thus, the 1995 Unidroit Convention provides for extensive cooperation and harmonization between different legal systems on the grounds of uniform law, yet its practical application is difficult to measure. To date, the 1995 Unidroit Convention has been contracted by 36 states, none of which is a market country.[81] There is no relevant case law reported. Nonetheless, the principles of the Convention on the recognition of foreign laws on protection have an important indirect impact on domestic legislation and jurisprudence, modifying the existing rules of private international law even in states which are not the parties to this instrument.[82] Moreover, one can also observe an increasing comity and cooperation between domestic judicial bodies of different states in the area of restitution and return of stolen and illegally exported cultural objects.[83]

d) The protection of world heritage

The 1972 World Heritage Convention[84] is undoubtedly the most successful international treaty in the area of cultural heritage protection. To date, 191 states have ratified or acceded to this instrument,[85] and 1007 sites have been inscribed on the WHL: 779 cultural, 197 natural, and 31 mixed properties, in 161 states parties.[86] In fact, what makes the concept of World Heritage exceptional is its universal application. Thus, it is fully recognized that certain cultural heritage sites constitute manifestations of the genius of mankind, belonging to all the peoples of the world, irrespective of the territory on which they are located. This entails a common duty to cooperate in order to safeguard and conserve world heritage in the general interest of the international community as a whole.[87] Moreover, acts against sites inscribed on the WHL are perceived as a violation of such interest

[81] <http://www.unidroit.org/status-cp>, accessed on 11 February 2015.

[82] See Andrzej Jakubowski, 'Return of Illicitly Trafficked Cultural Objects Pursuant to Private International Law: Current Developments', in Ana Filipa Vrdoljak and Francesco Francioni (eds), *Illicit Traffic of Cultural Objects in the Mediterranean*, 2009/09 *EUI Working Paper AEL*, 137–48, at 142–48.

[83] Marie Cornu and Marc-André Renold, 'New Developments in the Restitution of Cultural Property: Alternative Means of Dispute Resolution', *ICJP* 17 (2010) 1, 1–31.

[84] UNESCO Convention Concerning the Protection of World Natural and Cultural Heritage, adopted on 16 November 1972, entered into force on 17 December 1975, 1037 UNTS 151.

[85] <http://portal.unesco.org/la/convention.asp?KO=13055&language=E&order=alpha>, accessed on 8 February 2015.

[86] <http://whc.unesco.org/en/list>, accessed on 8 February 2015.

[87] Compare Roger O'Keefe, 'World Cultural Heritage: Obligations to the International Community as a Whole?', *ICLQ* 53(2004)1, 189–209.

and of commonly shared values. Importantly, in the *Strugar* case[88] concerning military attacks on the Old City of Dubrovnik—inscribed on the WHL in 1979—the ICTY found that a critical factor in imposing criminal liability on the military leaders who ordered bombardments of the city arose from the fact that its historical substance enjoyed international protection.[89] In other words, the acts against this cultural site of outstanding universal value constituted a violation of its protected status, deriving from the interest of all humanity.

e) *The protection of underwater cultural heritage*

In addition to the World Heritage regime, UNESCO adopted another major international instrument concerning material cultural heritage of all mankind. This refers to the 2001 UNESCO Convention on the Protection of the Underwater Cultural Heritage (the 2001 UNESCO Convention)[90] which promotes the concept that the archaeological heritage situated at the bottom of the sea should be used for the benefit of the international community. The treaty aimed to complete the regime of the law of the sea, which was perceived inadequate to the development of technologies enabling an uncontrolled exploration of previously inaccessible seabed.[91] In particular, these concerns referred to the contemporary usage of the traditional rules in maritime law, such as the law of salvage, entitling a person who recovers another person's ship or cargo after peril or loss at sea to a reward commensurate with the value of the property so saved, for the purposes of legitimate commercialization of excavated (recovered) underwater cultural heritage.[92]

In fact, the issues of the use, exploration, and access to the underwater cultural heritage are regulated by the range of different, often inconsistent, legal instruments under national legislation. As regards the rules of international law referring to such heritage prior to the adoption of the 2001 UNESCO Convention, the only substantive provisions were to be found under the UN Convention on the Law of the Sea (UNCLOS).[93] Article 149 states that 'all objects of an archaeological and historical nature found in the Area shall be preserved or disposed for the benefit of mankind as a whole, particular regard being paid to the preferential

88 *Prosecutor v. Strugar*, Case No. IT-01-42-T, Judgment of 31 January 2005, affirmed by the Appellate Chamber, 17 July 2008.

89 Ibid. judgment of the Trial Chamber, paras 327–329 and 461.

90 UNESCO Convention on the Protection of the Underwater Cultural Heritage, adopted on 2 November 2001, entered into force 2 January 2009, UNESCO Doc.31C/RES.24, (2002) 41 ILM 37.

91 For a general overview on the international regimes on the protection of underwater cultural heritage, see Sarah Dromgoole, *Underwater Cultural Heritage and International Law* (CUP, 2013); Patrick J. O'Keefe, *A Commentary on the UNESCO Convention on Underwater Cultural Heritage* (2nd edn, Institute of Art and Law, 2014).

92 James A. R. Nafziger, 'Historic Salvage Law Revisited', *Ocean Development & International Law* 31(2000)1–2, 81–96.

93 United Nations Convention on the Law of the Sea, adopted on 10 December 1982, entered into force 16 November 1994, 1833 UNTS 3; see Anastasia Strati, *The Protection of the Underwater Cultural Heritage: An Emerging Objective of the Contemporary Law of the Sea* (Nijhoff, 1995).

rights of the state or country of origin, or the state of cultural origin, or the state of historical and archaeological origin.' However, UNCLOS does not specify how this preservation shall be pursued. Furthermore, the wording 'preferential rights' may be interpreted in a number of ways. The distinction between different states entailed to such preferential rights may be virtually impossible,[94] including situations in which a 'country of origin' refers to a state which became extinct, thus raising the question of state succession.[95] Similarly, the provisions under Article 303 of UNCLOS concerning *inter alia* 'the rights of identifiable owners, the law of salvage or other rules of admiralty, or laws and practices with respect to cultural exchanges' are rather enigmatic, sometimes even defined as 'incomplete' and 'counterproductive', since it 'undermines the very objective of protecting the underwater cultural heritage',[96] that is, preservation in the original location.

To overcome such difficulties, the 2001 UNESCO Convention has been driven by the consideration that underwater cultural heritage shall not be subjected to commercialization but rather it shall be considered as key to the study of the history of man and civilizations. Therefore, such heritage shall enjoy special status under the international protection *in situ*. To this end, the 2001 UNESCO Convention encourages states parties to effect close cooperation within the framework of bilateral, regional, or other multilateral agreements (Article 6). It also provides, under the Annex to the Convention, for a list of standards concerning activities directed at underwater cultural heritage.[97] Overall, the UNESCO regime in this regard has been built on four major principles: 1) obligation to preserve underwater cultural heritage; 2) preservation *in situ* as the first option—the recovery of objects can be considered if it serves to their protection or knowledge about the underwater cultural heritage; 3) underwater cultural heritage should not be commercially exploited for trade or speculation, and it should not be irretrievably dispersed; 4) training and information sharing between the states in respect of underwater cultural heritage.

The 2001 UNESCO Convention has, however, been criticized by most major maritime states, particularly over the exercise of jurisdiction in respect of recovery of underwater archaeological objects, and thus was not adopted by consensus. In

[94] Vincent P. Cogliati-Bantz and Craig J. S. Forrest, 'Consistent: the Convention on the Protection of the Underwater Cultural Heritage and the United Nations Convention on the Law of the Sea', *Cambridge Journal of International and Comparative Law* 2(2013)3, 536–61, at 539; Dromgoole, *Underwater Cultural Heritage* (n 91) 122–25.

[95] See this chapter, section 6.6.

[96] Tullio Scovazzi, 'A Contradictory and Counterproductive Regime', in Roberta Garabello and Tullio Scovazzi (eds), *The Protection of the Underwater Cultural Heritage before and after the 2001 UNESCO Convention* (Nijhoff, 2003), 3–17; compare Nicola Ferri, 'The Right to Recovered Underwater Cultural Heritage: The Neglected Importance of Article 149 of the UN Law of the Sea Convention', in Silvia Borelli and Federico Lenzerini (eds), *Cultural Heritage, Cultural Rights, Cultural Diversity. New Developments in International Law* (Nijhoff, 2012), 269–73.

[97] Tullio Scovazzi, 'The Merits of the UNESCO Convention on the Protection of the Underwater Cultural Heritage', in Silvia Borelli and Federico Lenzerini (eds), *Cultural Heritage, Cultural Rights, Cultural Diversity. New Developments in International Law* (Nijhoff, 2012), 267–78.

fact, to date it has only been ratified by 49 states.[98] Thus, in international practice the objective of protecting the underwater cultural heritage often has to compete with different interests and rights—private property rights and state sovereign powers. The actual outcome of this competition has not been often favourable for the principles enshrined in the 2001 UNESCO Convention.[99] Notwithstanding these obstacles, the said treaty reaffirmed a growing trend in international law based on the assumption that the protection of cultural heritage of great importance to the history of mankind requires the joint effort of all states. Moreover, it recognized the paramount value of the procedural principle of cooperation as the most important tool to enforce the general interest of humanity as a whole in safeguarding the cultural heritage.

f) The preservation of cultural heritage as an element of the protection of human rights

The last set of international obligations discussed in this section concerns the preservation and enjoyment of cultural heritage in relation to the protection of human of rights,[100] particularly in their collective dimension.[101] In other words, it refers to the obligations of states towards the cultural heritage of minorities, groups, and indigenous peoples within their territorial sovereignty.

As already explained, in the period 1945–89 the minority question was tied to the broader human rights regime. The rights of self-determination of peoples was in practice reserved to the entire population of a given state. This changed at the end of the Cold War when new political and territorial transformations, in particular the dissolution of the USSR and the Socialist Federal Republic of Yugoslavia (SFRY), reopened the question of minority protection and self-determination in its internal dimension.[102] Similarly to post-First World War minority guarantees,

[98] <http://portal.unesco.org/la/convention.asp?KO=13520&language=E&order=alpha>, accessed on 8 February 2015.

[99] See *inter alia* Dromgoole, *Underwater Cultural Heritage* (n 91) 167 ff.; Patrizia Vigni, 'The Enforcement of Underwater Cultural Heritage by Courts', in Francesco Francioni and James Gordley (eds), *Enforcing International Cultural Heritage* (OUP, 2013), 125–49; Alessandra Lanciotti, 'The Dilemma of the Right to Ownership of Underwater Cultural Heritage: The Case of the "Getty Bronze"', in Silvia Borelli and Federico Lenzerini (eds), *Cultural Heritage, Cultural Rights, Cultural Diversity. New Developments in International Law* (Nijhoff, 2012), 301–26.

[100] For a general overview of the problems involved, see Ana Filipa Vrdoljak, 'Human Rights and Cultural Heritage in International Law', in Federico Lenzerini, Ana Filipa Vrdoljak (eds), *International Law for Common Goods, Normative Perspectives on Human Rights, Culture and Nature* (Hart, 2014), 139–74; Ana Filipa Vrdoljak, 'Liberty, Equality, Diversity: States, Cultures and International Law', in Ana Filipa Vrdoljak (ed), *The Cultural Dimension of Human Rights* (OUP, 2013), 26–70; Janet Blake, 'Taking a Human Rights Approach to Cultural Heritage Protection', *Heritage & Society* 4(2011)2, 199–238.

[101] For the extensive analysis of the impact of cultural concerns on international human rights law-making and judicial practice, see Federico Lenzerini, *The Culturalization of Human Rights Law* (OUP, 2014).

[102] Ana Filipa Vrdoljak, 'Self-Determination and Cultural Rights', in Francesco Francioni and Martin Scheinin (eds), *Cultural Human Rights* (Nijhoff, 2008), 41–78, at 63–64.

the fulfilment of minority standards formed one of the requirements of the conditional recognition of new states. After 1989, this question became part of the broader human and cultural criteria established by the European Community.[103] It is important to recall the 1989 Vienna Concluding Document issued by the Organization for Security and Co-operation in Europe (OSCE).[104] According to this the participating states 'will ensure that persons belonging to national minorities or regional cultures on their territories can maintain and develop their own culture in all its aspects, including language, literature and religion; and that they can preserve their cultural and historical monuments and objects'.[105] Moreover, the ethnic conflicts in the territory of Yugoslavia and the great losses in material cultural heritage also accelerated work on the universal and European instruments for the protection of minorities: the UN 1992 Declaration on the Rights of Persons Belonging to National or Ethnic, Religious and Linguistic Minorities,[106] and the CoE 1995 Framework Convention for the Protection of National Minorities (CoE Framework Convention).[107] The first instrument often mentions 'culture' as one of the fundamental spheres of minority protection; however, it never uses the phrase 'cultural heritage'. Inversely, the CoE Framework Convention explicitly included the preservation of cultural heritage in the list of minority rights. Accordingly, it stated that the parties to the Convention shall undertake 'to preserve the essential elements of their identity, namely their religion, language, traditions and cultural heritage' (Article 5.1).

The violent dismemberment of the SFRY played a fundamental role in the international recognition of this important relationship. The intentional destruction of monuments, temples, and libraries in different parts of the Balkans following the breakup of Yugoslavia provide terrifying evidence of the close links 'between the cleansing of cultural heritage and egregious human rights violations.'[108] This was particularly investigated in the jurisprudence of the ICTY which established individual criminal responsibility for intentional acts of destruction to cultural property. Particularly, in the *Krstić* case,[109] the ICTY found that the deliberate and systematic destruction of the cultural heritage of an ethnic group may provide evidence of the intent (*mens rea*) requirement for the commission of the crime

[103] Declaration on 'Guidelines on the Recognition of New States in Eastern Europe and in the Soviet Union', Brussels, 16 December 1991, 31 (1992) ILM 1486.

[104] Formerly the Conference on Security and Co-operation in Europe (CSCE), Concluding Document of the Third Follow-up Meeting, Vienna, 4 November 1986–19 January 1989, available at: <http://www.osce.org/mc/40881>, accessed on 10 February 2015.

[105] Ibid. para. 59.

[106] UN Declaration on the Rights of Persons Belonging to National or Ethnic, Religious and Linguistic Minorities, adopted on 18 December 1992, UN Doc. A/RES/47/135.

[107] CoE Framework Convention for the Protection of National Minorities, signed on 1 February 1995, entered into force on 1 February 1998, 2151 UNTS 243.

[108] Francesco Francioni, 'Culture, Heritage and Human Rights: An Introduction', in Francesco Francioni and Martin Scheinin (eds), *Cultural Human Rights* (Nijhoff, 2008), 3–16, at 9.

[109] *Prosecutor v. Krstić*, Case No. IT-98-33-T, Judgment of 2 August 2001, affirmed by the Appellate Chamber, 19 April 2004.

of genocide under the 1948 Genocide Convention.[110] It held that the destroying of a group may be conceived not only through its biological extermination but also 'through purposeful eradication of its culture and identity resulting in the eventual extinction of the group as an entity distinct from the remainder of the community.'[111] Moreover, the court pointed out that 'where there is physical or biological destruction there are often simultaneous attacks on the cultural and religious property and symbols of the targeted group as well, attacks which may legitimately be considered as evidence of an intent to physically destroy the group'.[112] Therefore, the ICTY took into account 'as evidence of intent to destroy the group the deliberate destruction of mosques and houses belonging to members of the group'.[113]

Importantly, the crimes against cultural heritage have been also addressed in two genocide cases before the ICJ. In the judgment concerning the *Case Concerning Application of the Convention o the Prevention and Punishment of the Crime of Genocide (Bosnia and Herzegovina v. Serbia and Montenegro)*,[114] the court noted that 'there is a conclusive evidence of the deliberate destruction of the historical, cultural and religious heritage of the protected group during the period in question'.[115] According to the Court, such acts 'cannot be considered to constitute the deliberate infliction of conditions of life calculated to bring about the physical destruction of the group',[116] and thus do not fall within the categories of acts of genocide as stated by Article II of the 1948 Genocide Convention. Yet the destruction of a group's cultural property may be considered as 'contrary to other legal norms' and 'may be highly significant inasmuch as it is directed to the elimination of all traces of the cultural or religious presence of a group'.[117] In this it recalled *inter alia* the previous ICTY judgment in *Krstić*.

The ICJ has also dealt with the destruction and plunder of cultural property committed by the Federal Republic of Yugoslavia in the *Case Concerning Application of the Convention on the Prevention and Punishment of the Crime of Genocide (Croatia v. Serbia)*.[118] Croatia asked the court to order Serbia to return any items of cultural property within its jurisdiction or control which had been seized in the course of the genocidal acts for which Serbia is responsible, as the destruction and plunder of cultural property constituted a 'part of a broader plan or pattern of activities aimed at the extinction of an ethnic group'.[119] Serbia challenged these submissions, claiming that the vast majority of the claimed property had been already returned and recalled the court's judgment the case *Bosnia and Herzegovina v. Serbia and Montenegro*. Thus, according to Serbia, the claim of Croatia was not admissible,[120] yet the ICJ rejected these objections and explained

[110] Convention on the Prevention and Punishment of the Crime of Genocide, UNGA Resolution 260 A (III) of 9 December 1948, entered into force on 12 January 1951, 78 UNTS 277.

[111] *Krstić* (n 109) judgment of the Trial Chamber, para. 574.

[112] Ibid. para. 580.

[113] Ibid.

[114] Judgment of 26 February 2007, ICJ Reports 2007, 43.

[115] Ibid. para. 344.

[116] Ibid.

[117] *Bosnia and Herzegovina v. Serbia and Montenegro*, judgment (n 114) para. 344.

[118] Judgment of 18 November 2008 (preliminary objections), ICJ Reports 2008, 412.

[119] Ibid. para. 142.

[120] Ibid. paras 140–41.

that 'the question what remedies might appropriately be ordered by the Court is one which is necessarily dependent upon the findings that the Court may in due course make of breaches of the Genocide Convention by the Respondent'.[121] Deciding on the merits,[122] the Court sustained its former view, expressed in *Bosnia and Herzegovina v. Serbia and Montenegro*, that the destruction of cultural heritage does not constitute a punishable act under the 1948 Genocide Convention[123] and confirmed that 'attacks on cultural and religious property' may be taken into account 'in order to establish an intent to destroy the group physically'.[124] The court did not elaborate more on this issue, considering that 'that there is no compelling reason in the present case for it to depart from that approach.'[125] Thus, the ICJ did not proceed with a broader discussion on the notion of 'cultural genocide' within the regime of the 1948 Genocide Convention.[126] Nonetheless, there are no doubts that the paramount role of cultural heritage in determining the existence of a national, ethnical, racial or religious group has been fully acknowledged in the international jurisprudence in relation to the conflict in the former Yugoslavia.

Parallel to international efforts in the realm of cultural rights of minorities, a separate regime has emerged in respect of indigenous peoples and their cultural heritage. They have been treated as distinctive groups due to their differing historical circumstances, linked to colonialism and foreign domination.[127] Moreover, the representatives of indigenous communities have claimed that their suppression did not cease with the emancipation of former colonies. The first efforts to accommodate the rights of these groups were undertaken by the International Labour Organization (ILO) and led to the adoption of the 1957 Indigenous and Tribal Populations Convention (No. 107),[128] applicable to members of tribal or semi-tribal populations in independent countries. The Convention *inter alia* required states parties to respect the cultural differences of such communities and to promote their cultural development.

In 1989, the ILO revised the 1957 Convention.[129] The new adopted instrument (No. 169) acknowledged the collective rights of indigenous peoples to preserve

[121] Ibid. para. 143.

[122] *Case Concerning Application of the Convention on the Prevention and Punishment of the Crime of Genocide (Croatia v. Serbia)*, Judgment of 3 February 2015, available at: <http://www.icj-cij.org/docket/files/118/18422.pdf>, accessed on 14 February 2015.

[123] Ibid. para. 388. [124] Ibid. para. 390. [125] Ibid. para. 389.

[126] See the critics of such an approach by Judge Antônio Augusto Cançado Trindade in its Dissenting opinion to the judgment of 3 February 2015, <http://www.icj-cij.org/docket/files/118/18432.pdf> accessed on 14 February 2015, paras. 227–36, 418, 421–22, and 539.

[127] See further Siegfried Wiessner, 'Culture and the Rights of Indigenous Peoples,' in Ana Filipa Vrdoljak, *The Cultural Dimension of Human Rights* (OUP, 2013), 117–57; Federico Lenzerini, 'The Trail of Broken Dreams: The Status of Indigenous Peoples in International Law', in Federico Lenzerini (ed), *Reparations for Indigenous Peoples: International and Comparative Perspectives* (OUP, 2009), 73–116.

[128] ILO Convention (No. 107) concerning the Protection and Integration of Indigenous and Other Tribal and Semi-Tribal Populations in Independent Countries, adopted on 26 June 1957, entered into force 2 June 1959, 328 UNTS 247.

[129] ILO Convention (No 169) concerning Indigenous and Tribal Peoples in Independent Countries, adopted on 27 June 1989, entered into force on 5 September 1991, 1650 UNTS 383.

and develop their own cultural identity. Although the 1989 ILO Convention did not make clear reference to the right to cultural heritage, the issue was subsequently developed by the UN Working Group on Indigenous Populations.The 1993 UN Draft Universal Declaration on the Rights of Indigenous Peoples[130] recognized that indigenous peoples have the right to practice and revitalize their cultural traditions and customs. This also included 'the right to maintain, protect and develop the past, present and future manifestations of their cultures, such as archaeological and historical sites, artefacts, designs, ceremonies, technologies and visual and performing arts and literature, as well as the right to the restitution of cultural, intellectual, religious and spiritual property taken without their free and informed consent or in violation of their laws, traditions and customs'.[131] Moreover, they had the right to the use and control of ceremonial objects and the right to the repatriation of human remains. States were required to 'take effective measures to ensure that indigenous sacred places, including burial sites, be preserved, respected and protected.'[132] Since the 1990s, a number of states with considerable communities of indigenous peoples (eg Canada) have introduced special legislative and technical measures to accommodate these principles.[133]

Subsequent UN initiatives led to the adoption by the General Assembly of the 2007 UN Declaration on the Rights of Indigenous Peoples,[134] reaffirming the principle of value of the contribution of each people to the diversity and richness of civilizations and cultures which constitute the common heritage of humankind. Thus, it provided that 'indigenous peoples have the right to maintain, control, protect and develop their cultural heritage' (Article 31(1)). They also have 'the right to practice and revitalize their cultural traditions and customs', including 'the right to maintain, protect and develop the past, present and future manifestations of their cultures, such as archaeological and historical sites, artefacts, designs, ceremonies, technologies and visual and performing arts and literature' (Article 11(1)). The 2007 Declaration also places upon states positive obligations to 'take effective measures to recognize and protect the exercise of these rights' (Article 31(2)), and to 'provide redress through effective mechanisms, which may include restitution, developed in conjunction with indigenous peoples, with respect to their cultural, intellectual, religious and spiritual property taken without their free, prior and informed consent or in violation of their laws, traditions and customs' (Article 11(2)).

Alongside the protection of minority and indigenous peoples' rights to the tangible cultural heritage, one can observe a more general interplay between cultural

[130] Adopted on 23 August 1993, UN Doc. E/CN.4/Sub.2/1993/29; E/CN.4/Sub.2/1994/2/Add.1.

[131] Ibid. Art. 12. [132] Ibid. Art. 13.

[133] See James A. R. Nafziger and Robert Kirkwood Paterson (eds), *Cultural Law: International, Comparative and Indigenous* (CUP, 2010), 425–73.

[134] Adopted on 13 September 2007, UN Doc.A/RES/61/295.

heritage and human rights in current international law and practice. In fact, the protection and preservation of cultural heritage is more often perceived 'as a part of the safeguarding of human dignity',[135] and 'an important component of the promotion and protection of all human rights, including the full realization of cultural rights.'[136] Importantly, the 2005 UNESCO Convention on the Protection and Promotion of the Diversity of Cultural Expressions[137] recognizes cultural diversity as the common concern of humanity, and reaffirms its importance for the full realization of human rights and fundamental freedoms. Thus, 'the defence and promotion of cultural diversity cannot be divorced from the commitment to the fulfilment of human rights and fundamental freedoms of minorities, groups and indigenous peoples.'[138]

The concept of a human right to cultural heritage has also been explicitly included in the text of the 2005 CoE Framework Convention on the Value of Cultural Heritage for Society (Faro Convention).[139] While other regional and international instruments in the area of cultural heritage refer to the means of protection and conservation of cultural goods, the Faro Convention addresses the questions as to why and for whom the heritage is transmitted. This is founded on the idea that knowledge and use of cultural heritage form part of rights vested in everyone, alone or collectively, to participate in cultural life as defined in the Universal Declaration of Human Rights (UDHR)[140] and guaranteed by the International Covenant on Economic, Social and Cultural Rights (ICESCR).[141] The Faro Convention employs an expanded and interdisciplinary concept of cultural heritage, the core of which are rooted peoples and human values. Thus, cultural heritage is presented as a resource for human development, for the enhancement of cultural diversity, and for the promotion of intercultural dialogue. Within this framework, the Faro Convention sets out positive obligations upon the parties which are *inter alia* required: to protect cultural heritage situated under their respective jurisdictions, regardless of its origin; to promote cultural diversity; and to establish a processes for conciliation to deal equitably with situations where contradictory values are placed on the same cultural heritage by different communities.

[135] Francioni, 'Culture, Heritage and Human Rights' (n 108) 8.

[136] Eighth recital of the UN Human Rights Council Resolution 6/11, Protection of Cultural Heritage as an Important Component of the Promotion and Protection of Cultural Rights, adopted on 28 September 2007, UN Doc. A/HRC/RES/6/11

[137] Convention on the Protection and Promotion of the Diversity of Cultural Expressions,,signed on 20 October 2005, entered into force 18 March 2007, 2440 UNTS 311.

[138] Francioni, 'Culture, Heritage and Human Rights' (n 108) 16.

[139] CoE Framework Convention on the Value of Cultural Heritage for Society adopted on 27 October 2005, entered into force on 1 June 2011, 2758 UNTS 21.

[140] Adopted in Paris on 10 December 1948, UNGA Res. 217A(III), UN Doc.A/810, 71.

[141] Adopted on 16 December 1966, entered into force on 3 January 1976, 993 UNTS 3, see Ugo Misfud Bonnici, 'The Human Right to Cultural Heritage—the Faro Convention's Contribution to the Recognition and Safeguarding of This Human Right', in Council of Europe (ed), *Heritage and Beyond* (Council of Europe Publ, 2009), 53–58, at 57–58, Patrice Mayer-Bisch, 'On the "Right to Heritage"—the Innovative Approach of Articles 1 and 2 of the Faro Convention', in Council of Europe (ed), *Heritage and Beyond* (Council of Europe Publ, 2009), 59–65.

6.1.2 The status of cultural heritage obligations in state succession

The development of international cultural heritage law in recent years has created a complex legal framework which imposes upon states substantive and procedural obligations of a binding and non-binding nature. The question arises, however, as to the status of such obligations in state succession. Accordingly, this section discusses the issue on two basic levels: 1) state succession to cultural heritage obligations in force by virtue of the pre-existing treaty commitments of the processor state; 2) succession to cultural heritage obligations binding under customary international law.

a) Treaty law

International cultural heritage obligations are established first and foremost by multilateral treaties and to a certain extent by bilateral treaties and agreements in the matter of protection of cultural heritage. The succession of states to rights and obligations arising from such legal instruments needs to be seen in the light of two opposite theories: 'continuity' and 'clean slate' (*tabula rasa*). The first provides that a successor state is bound by the international obligations undertaken by a predecessor state in respect of the territory subject to state succession. The second applies a non-succession rule which enables the successor state to decide which international engagements to continue.[142] The application of one of these doctrines is, however, conditioned by the category of territorial succession. Accordingly, it is widely accepted that in a case of cession, the treaties of the predecessor state expire with regard to the ceded territory, while the treaties of successor automatically take effect (the principle of mobility of treaty borders). Arguably, the incorporation of a state may have similar effects on the treaty engagements of the predecessor. Inversely, there is common recognition of the continuity of non-political international treaties of the predecessor state in cases where states merge. In respect of secession and dissolution of a multinational state, the 'clean slate' rule has often been taken into consideration, though not consistently.

In this respect, the 1978 Vienna Convention[143] provides for the general continuity of obligations in respect of all treaties binding on the predecessor state. The only exemption in this matter regards newly independent (post-colonial) states to which the principle of 'clean slate' is to be applied (Article 16).[144] However, post-Cold War practice has shown different approaches of successor states in respect of treaties in cases of secession and dissolution.[145] The International Law

[142] See Matthew Craven, 'The Problem of State Succession and the Identity of States under International Law', *EJIL* 9(1998)1, 142–62, at 146–51.

[143] Vienna Convention on Succession of States in Respect of Treaties, adopted on 23 August 1978, entered into force on 6 November 1996, 1946 UNTS 3.

[144] See Chapter 4.

[145] ILA, Aspects of the Law of State Succession, Draft Final Report (2008), at 70, para. 5, <http://www.ila-hq.org/en/committees/index.cfm/cid/11>, accessed on 5 February 2015.

Association (ILA) found that while successor states generally 'considered themselves as successor to the multilateral treaties, some of them adopted the clean slate rule, rendering that succession merely optional.'[146] As regards succession to bilateral treaties concluded by the predecessor state, it has also been concluded that their fate 'is generally decided through negotiation between the successor State and the other party, no matter the category of State succession involved.'[147] In fact, it appears that the continuity theory is consistently followed only in respect of succession to boundaries and other territorial regimes established by a treaty.[148]

In this context, the succession to cultural heritage obligations established by multilateral treaties at the universal and regional levels may raise some controversies. Since they do not regulate state boundaries or other territorial regimes, it appears that a successor state has the option to decide whether it will accede to a cultural heritage treaty to which a predecessor state was a party. Such an approach may be disputable, however, with regard to the obligations towards tangible cultural heritage whose preservation is of general interest to the international community; for example, the protection of cultural sites inscribed on the WHL, by a motion of the predecessor state.

As regards the post-Cold War practice of succession to multilateral treaties on the protection of cultural heritage, this has overall confirmed the regime under Article 22 and Article 23 of the 1978 Vienna Convention concerning the notification of succession by newly independent states to multilateral treaties. Such a solution corresponds with the general approach of the UN and other depositaries, either states or international organizations. In particular, the UN Secretary-General has requested to every successor state—irrespective of the type of state succession concerned—to provide specific declarations of succession to each multilateral treaty.[149]

Major controversies in this regard refer to the theory of so-called automatic succession to human rights treaties.[150] In the doctrine of international law, there is strong support for the concept claiming that human rights treaties continue to apply within the territory of a predecessor state, irrespective of the succession of states.[151] This is driven by the reasoning that the inhabitants of a given territory cannot be deprived of the rights granted to them by a human rights treaty as a result of state succession. It has also been argued that since human rights

[146] Ibid. [147] Ibid. 71, para. 8.

[148] Read Jerzy Tyranowski, 'Boundaries and Boundary Treaties in the Law of State Succession', *Thesaurus Acroasium* 14(1985), 462–540.

[149] ILA, Aspects of the Law of State Succession (n 145) 71, para. 6.

[150] For general observations, see Shabtai Rosenne 'Automatic Treaty Succession', in Jan Klabbers and Rene Lefeber (eds), *Essays on the Law of Treaties: A Collection of Essays in Honour of Bert Vierdag* (Nijhoff, 1998), 97–106.

[151] Malcolm N. Shaw, 'State Succession Revisited', *Finnish Yearbook of International Law* 6(1995), 34–98, at 84; Menno T. Kamminga, 'State Succession of Human Rights Treaties', *EJIL* 7(1996)4, 469–84; Photini Pazartzis, 'State Succession to Multilateral Treaties: Recent Developments', *Austrian Review of International and European Law* 3(1998)3, 397–415, at 414; Florentino Ruiz Ruiz, 'The Succession of States in Universal Treaties on the Protection of Human Rights and Humanitarian Law', *IJHR* 7(2003)2, 42–96, at 69.

treaties do not contain termination clauses, the cessation of obligations under such instruments is prohibited.[152] Moreover, the special character of human rights treaties is also reflected in Article 60(5) of the 1969 Vienna Convention on the Law Treaties,[153] which declares that no provision 'relating to the protection of the human person contained in treaties of a humanitarian character, in particular to provisions prohibiting any form of reprisals against persons protected by such treaties' may be terminated or suspended in response to a material breach by another party.

During the Balkan conflict, the problem of state succession became particularly relevant in the already mentioned ICJ case *Bosnia and Herzegovina v. Serbia–Montenegro*, concerning the application of the 1948 Genocide Convention in respect of ethnic cleansings and massacres of Bosniak Muslims and committed war. The Federal Republic of Yugoslavia (FRY; later Serbia and Montenegro) claimed that the court had no jurisdiction as the FRY was a new state not bound by the previous treaty commitments of the SFRY. Thus, the question arose as to whether the obligations under the UN 1948 Convention would continue, after the dissolution of a multinational state. The ICJ rejected the FRY's objections and confirmed its jurisdiction in the case without pronouncing on the automatic succession of this human rights treaty. Of special importance, however, is the separate opinion of Judge Weeramantry to the preliminary objections judgment in 1996.[154] He argued that human rights and humanitarian treaties do not represent an exchange of interests but are designed to protect the international community as a whole, rather than the interests of particular states. Furthermore, human rights treaties transcend concepts of state sovereignty. In other words, such treaties are far beyond the boundaries of state sovereignty as they are of universal concern. Moreover, human rights are not granted by the state but are the entitlement of every human being. Thus, states only confirm human rights in treaties. Last but not least, the rules protecting human rights which are part of customary international law (such as the prohibition of genocide) remain valid irrespective of state succession.

In legal doctrine the issue of automatic succession to human rights treaties has been broadly researched; however, international practice has not been uniform. In fact, some successor states opted for accession to those treaties.[155] Thus, the existence of such a customary rule of international law does not seem to be confirmed by consistent international practice and *opinio juris*. It is usually accepted that a new customary rule of international law with regard to automatic succession of

152 Kamminga, 'State Succession' (n 151) 473.

153 Concluded on 23 May 1969, entered into force on 27 January 1980, 1155 UNTS 331.

154 *Bosnia and Herzegovina v. Serbia and Montenegro*, (n 114), Separate Opinion of Judge Weeramantry, Judgment of 11 July 1996 (preliminary objections), ICJ Reports 1996, 645.

155 ILA, Aspects of the Law of State Succession (n 145) 71 para. 11, Akbar Rasulov, 'Revisiting State Succession to Humanitarian Treaties: Is There a Case for Automaticity?', *EJIL* 14(2003)1, at 141–70.

human rights treaties is *in statu nascendi*, though for the time being, general rules on state succession with regard to treaties also remain applicable in this area.[156]

It seems that international obligations on the protection of the cultural heritage of human communities inhabiting territory subject to state succession may be perceived as parallel to those providing the protection of human rights. Furthermore, it may be argued that certain obligations under international cultural heritage treaties should be treated in the same way as those arising from human rights regimes. This may apply to the prohibition of the destruction and plunder of cultural property, as provided by the 1954 Hague Convention and the 1999 Second Hague Protocol. It seems that it also concerns the obligations to protect the cultural heritage of mankind under the World Heritage Convention, as it does not constitute the concern of only domestic jurisdiction. The major consideration supporting such a thesis would consist in the intersection of the value of cultural heritage for every people and for the international community as a whole. In fact, this reasoning may arguably be associated with the position expressed by the ICJ regarding the existence of certain obligations *erga omnes* in respect of values protected by the international community as a whole.[157] In the *Barcelona Traction* case, the court held that the 'principles and rules concerning the basic rights of the human person' are applicable to all states.[158] Moreover, the ICJ earlier recognized the special status of the so-called 'universal treaties' or 'law-making treaties' which do not enshrine a balance of reciprocal interests of the state parties, but 'a common interest, namely, the accomplishment of those high purposes which are the *raison d'être* of the convention'.[159] Undoubtedly, the general interest of all humanity in the protection of cultural heritage fits perfectly within the notion of such universally recognized values.

b) Customary international law

These observations with regard to the status of human rights and humanitarian treaties in state succession lead to the issue of the continuity of international cultural heritage obligations arising from sources other than a treaty. In fact, successor states are bound not only by the obligations to which they have expressly contracted themselves or to which they have succeeded but also by customary rules of international law from the moment of their emergence.[160] Therefore, the fact of state succession

[156] ILA, Aspects of the Law of State Succession (n 145) 71 33; Marcelo Kohen, 'La codification du droit des traités: quelques éléments pour un bilan global', *RGDIP* 106(2000)3, 577–613, at 591–93.

[157] For a detailed reconstruction of the concept, see Maurizio Ragazzi, *The Concept of International Obligations Erga Omnes* (OUP, 2000).

[158] *Barcelona Traction, Light and Power Company, Limited (Belgium v. Spain)*, Judgment of 5 February 1970, ICJ Reports 1970, 3, paras 33–34.

[159] *Reservations to the Convention on the Prevention and Punishment of the Crime of Genocide*, Advisory Opinion of 28 May 1951, ICJ Reports 1951, 15, at 23; see Ruiz Ruiz, 'The Succession of States' (n 151) 42–96.

[160] See Martti Koskenniemi, 'Report of the Director of Studies of the English-Speaking Section of the Centre', in Pierre Michel Eisemann and Martti Koskenniemi (eds), *La Succession d'États: la*

does not cease the binding obligations under general principles of international law. In such cases, the continuity of such obligations does not concern the matter of state succession, as they bind all states irrespective of the date of their emergence. Clearly, this would also refer to the obligations towards tangible cultural heritage at the level of customary international law, which bind all successor states irrespective of the type of state succession concerned. As already mentioned, such obligations would regard: the prohibition of intentional destruction and plunder of cultural property in the event of armed conflict; the restitution of cultural material removed from militarily occupied territories; the protection of cultural heritage of great importance to the international community as a whole. In addition, the protection of cultural heritage of minorities, groups, and indigenous peoples as a part of human rights and minority protection standards may also be perceived as international obligations *erga omnes* or as obligations under peremptory rules of international law. It seems that the long-lasting state practice on the internationalization of minority protection may legitimate such a conviction. In fact, the Badinter Commission, in its First Opinion on state succession in the former Yugoslavia,[161] held that: 'the peremptory norms of general international law and, in particular, respect of the fundamental rights of the individual and the rights of the people and minorities, are binding on all the parties to the succession.'[162]

c) *State succession to international responsibility*

State succession to international responsibility has long been considered one of the most obscure and neglected areas of international law. Yet, as already mentioned in Chapter 5, the recent developments in the international legal scholarship shed new light on this topic. In particular, the work undertaken within the framework of the 14th Commission of the Institute of International Law (IIL) (Marcelo G. Kohen, as Rapporteur) has led to the formulation of the catalogue of guiding principles applicable to state succession in matters of state responsibility.[163] These are founded on a very strong argument that 'situations involving succession of States should not constitute a reason not to implement the consequences stemming from international wrongful acts.'[164] In other words, the principle of

codification à l'épreuve des faits/State Succession: Codification Tested against the Facts (Nijhoff, 2000), 65–132, at 108.

[161] Opinions nos. 1-10, see Text of Opinions. Documents Regarding the Situation in the Former Yugoslavia (September 25, 1991–November 16, 1992): Conference on Yugoslavia Arbitration Commission: Opinions on Questions Arising from the Dissolution of Yugoslavia, 31 (1992) *ILM* 1494.

[162] Compare the objections raised by Martii Koskenniemi as to the peremptory nature of such norms. Koskenniemi, 'Report of the Director of Studies' (n 160) 111.

[163] Marcelo G. Kohen, Rapporteur, 'State Succession in Matters of State Responsibility. Provisional Report' and 'State Succession in Matters of State Responsibility. Draft Resolution', 9 August 2013, IIL, 14th Commission, Tokyo Session, 2013, available at: <http://www.idi-iil.org/idiE/annuaireE/2013/IDI_14_Kohen.pdf>, and <http://www.idi-iil.org/idiE/annuaireE/2013/Draft_Resolution_14_Commission_2013.pdf>, accessed on 5 February 2015. Further quoted as Kohen Report and 2013 IIL Draft Resolution.

[164] 2013 IIL Draft Resolution (n 163) preamble.

international justice as well as the stability and security of international legal relations shall not be hindered due to state succession.

The major consideration of the 2013 IIL Draft Resolution State Succession in Matters of State Responsibility (2013 IIL Draft Resolution) consists in the distinction between cases of continuity and succession of states.[165] Accordingly, 'the general, though not absolute, rule proposed is that in cases in which the predecessor State continues to exist, it is this State that continues the enjoyment of rights and the assumption of obligations arising from the international wrongful acts in which it was involved before the date of State succession'.[166] This is founded on the observation that 'the same subject that has been the victim or the author of an international wrongful act holds the rights or obligations arising from this act, no matter whether its territory and population have diminished'.[167] Therefore, such a general rule has been proposed in relation to all the cases of state succession in which the predecessor state continues to exist, that is, territorial cession, secession, and creation of a newly independent state.[168] However, certain exemption from this general rule are forwarded: 1) 'intrinsically direct link of the consequences of the wrongful act with the territory or the population concerned';[169] 'wrongful act committed by an entity of the predecessor State that later becomes the successor State';[170] 'acceptance by the successor State of fulfilling the obligations'.[171]

The following fundamental consideration advanced by the 2013 IIL Draft Resolution refers to the regime applicable to distinct categories of state succession. Interestingly, the proposal distinguishes between the cases of unification and incorporation of states,[172] modifying the broadly criticized uniform regime adopted in both Vienna Conventions. On the other hand, it provides for a specific regime for newly independent states,[173] regardless of the rejection in the international practice of the solutions introduced by the 1983 Vienna Convention[174] with regard to property and archives. Moreover, the 2013 IIL Draft Resolution substantiated the relevance of the territorial factor to resolve issues of succession to responsibility. Indeed, 'the question of where the wrongful act took place is not, in the rapporteur's view, necessarily decisive'.[175] As already mentioned, the proposal provides for the principle of 'intrinsically direct link of the consequences of the wrongful act with the territory or the population concerned'. This is consistently applied in the provisions concerning specific categories of succession of states, except regarding unification and incorporation. The principle is corrective

[165] Ibid. Art. 8. [166] Kohen Report (n 163) 21, para. 50. [167] Ibid.

[168] 2013 IIL Draft Resolution (n 163) Arts 9, 10–5, and 14.

[169] Kohen Report (n 163) 21–23, paras 51–56. [170] Ibid. 23–24, paras 57.9.

[171] Ibid 24–26, paras. 60–63.

[172] 2013 IIL Draft Resolution (n 163) Arts 11–12.

[173] 2013 IIL Draft Resolution (n 163) Art. 14, see Kohen Report (n 163) 33–38, paras 88–98.

[174] 1983 Vienna Convention on Succession of states in Respect of state Property, Archives and Debts (1983 Vienna Convention), adopted on 8 April 1983, not in force, UN Doc. A/CONF.117/14 (1983).

[175] Kohen Report (n 163) 21, para. 51; Patrick Dumberry, *State Succession to International Responsibility* (Nijhoff, 2007), at 285–88 and the literature cited therein.

in nature because alongside territorial considerations it invokes a human link that may exist between the wrongful act and the population concerned. In fact, 'this is particularly relevant in cases of violations of human or minority rights', that is, when the wrongful act 'has as a direct victim a specific population.'[176] Accordingly, the continuity of obligations and rights arising from such a serious breach of international law shall be provided, irrespective of any non-succession or discontinuity claims of the states concerned. Arguably, this equitable approach appears to be one of the key achievements of the initiative undertaken by the IIL 14th Commission.

Clearly, the guidelines discussed constitute doctrinal postulates of certain solutions for future instances of state succession rather than the reflection of the evolving processes of formation of new customary rules of international law. However, a few important lessons can be learnt in respect of state succession to international responsibility for breaches of international cultural heritage obligations. First, the principle according to which continuator states enjoy rights as well as assume obligations arising from internationally wrongful acts against cultural heritage in which they were involved before the date of state succession shall be fully considered as correct and confirmed by the international practice. In fact, as discussed in Chapter 5, the cases of Germany, Russia, and Serbia have demonstrated that continuing states are recognized as holders of rights and obligations arising from the pre-succession wrongful acts against cultural heritage.

Second, in cases of succession, the status of such obligations is distinct from that of rights stemming from internationally wrongful acts committed against the predecessor state or the population concerned. As already explained, the protection and enjoyment of cultural heritage are nowadays considered as part of the human rights system, comprising its individual and collective dimension. Hence, the right to redress internationally wrongful acts against cultural heritage may be arguably treated in parallel to that of stemming from violations of human and minority rights, thus it shall continue to be enforceable irrespective of the fact of state succession. This is particularly relevant for peoples which did not constitute independent states when wrongful acts were committed. To this end, the 2013 IIL Draft Resolution provides that 'the rights stemming from an international wrongful act committed by the predecessor State or any other State against a people entitled to self-determination before the date of the State succession may be exercised by the newly independent State created by that people after that date'.[177] As the Rapporteur stated, this principle has been already recognized by both international jurisprudence and state practice.[178] Arguably, it may give to a newly independent state, which has emerged in violent circumstances, a strong judiciable argument against its predecessor and/or another state, to whom a wrongful act can be attributed, the right to claim reparation for the violation of cultural

176 Kohen Report (n 163) 23, para. 56.
177 2013 IIL Draft Resolution (n 163) Art. 14(4).
178 Kohen Report (n 163) 35–36, paras 95–98.

heritage obligations, in particular those established by humanitarian rules for the protection of cultural property. On the other hand, the newly independent state shall be held responsible for the conduct, prior to the date of state succession, of a national liberation movement which succeeded in establishing this newly independent state. Thus, the responsibility for internationally wrongful acts against cultural heritage committed by the national liberation movement shall, in principle, pass to the successor state.[179]

Apart from the specific situation of newly independent states, the consolidation of the principle on succession in secondary rights of the predecessor state arising from a wrongful act of another state would also give to successor states better legal foundations to protect their cultural heritage. In other words, a state responsible for the breach of cultural heritage obligation would still have the duty to repair, notwithstanding the replacement of an injured state by its successor.

Third, the succession to responsibility for internationally wrongful acts against cultural heritage obligations committed by the predecessor state entailing succession to the obligation to repair poses some important questions. In fact, the violations of cultural heritage obligations could be committed in different circumstances and could have distinct legal implications. Accordingly, it seems that the vast majority of wrongful acts committed by the predecessor state in matters of cultural heritage may be considered by its successor as 'odious' acts.[180] For instance, the question may be raised whether all the successor states of the SFRY shall be held responsible for the commission of war crimes, including those against cultural heritage, committed by the SFRY forces in Croatia, or whether Montenegro shall assume the obligations to repair arising for such wrongful acts committed by the Federal Republic of Yugoslavia (FRY)? In this regard, the concept of 'odiousness' derives from the theory 'odious' debts,[181] that is, debts incurred by the predecessor for purposes that served to finance war efforts against the successor state or the 'enslavement' or 'subjugation' debts contracted with objective of the colonization or other aggression against the territory and people of the successor state.[182] Since these served against the vital interests of the successor state, they

[179] 2013 IIL Draft Resolution (n 163) Art. 14(3); see Art. 10(2) of the Articles on Responsibility of States for Internationally Wrongful Acts, adopted by the International Law Commission at its Fifty-Third Session (2001), November 2001, UN Doc. A/56/83 (2001), Annex; 'The conduct of a movement, insurrectional or other, which succeeds in establishing a new State in part of the territory of a pre-existing State or in a territory under its administration shall be considered an act of the new State under international law.'

[180] See Dumberry, *State Succession to International Responsibility* (n 175) 294–97; Brigitte Stern, 'Responsibilité internationale et succession d'États', in Laurence Boisson de Chazournes and Vera Gowlland-Debbas (eds), *The International Legal System in Quest of Equity and Universality/L'ordre juridique international, un système en quête d'équité et d'universalité. Liber Amicorum Georges Abi-Saab* (Nijhoff, 2001), 327–56, at 341–43; Daniel P. O'Connell, 'Recent Problems of State Succession in Relation to New States', *RCADI* 130(1970)2, 95–206, at 165.

[181] For the first formulated in 1927 by Alexander Nahun Sack. See Alexander Nahun Sack, *Les effets de transformations des États sur leur dettes publiques et autres obligations financières* (Recueil Sirey, 1927), 146 ff.

[182] For an overview of the problem, see Robert Howse, 'The Concept of Odious Debt in Public International Law', United Nations Conference on Trade and Development, July 2007, UNCTAD/

were usually considered non-transmissible and non-enforceable under customary international law.[183] However, it seems that this is no longer supported by state practice and international legal scholarship. Even if there are strong arguments for repudiation of certain debts based on considerations of odiousness, with regard to their external policies and considering the principles of equity and fairness, states tend to prefer to renegotiate the obligations and to continue to repay the debt.[184] This matches more general trends towards greater security in international legal relations. Similar considerations shall also apply to state succession arising from 'odious' acts, as the application of an automatic non-succession rule could lead to situations when grave violations of international law 'would go simply unpunished'.[185] Clearly, it does not mean that the concept of an 'odious' act shall be completely abandoned. Arguably, the equitable principle of 'intrinsically direct link of the consequences of the wrongful act with the territory or the population concerned', as provided by the 2013 IIL Draft Resolution, may be very helpful since it conditions the actual solution on the circumstances of a given case. This arises from the necessity of an effective attribution of the commitment of an internationally wrongful act to the perpetuator state. Hence, it seems correct to determine whether the population of the successor state participated or benefited from such 'odious' acts. In light of the principles of global justice, such a determination would be arguably crucial. For instance, according to these equitable considerations, the succession of Montenegro to international responsibility of the FRY for the wrongful acts against cultural property committed in Croatia and Bosnia–Herzegovina could be better examined. In this context, the question may arise whether the same considerations would apply to succession in obligations arising from the breach of *jus cogens*, the peremptory norms of international law. Indeed, some acts of the predecessor state may involve the breach of cultural heritage obligations of *erga omnes* nature (eg the destruction of world heritage sites) or even may amount to the violations of *jus cogens* (genocidal practices). Such violations give rise to obligations being owed to the international community as a whole. Therefore, even if 'there is, indeed, no support in State practice and international case law for the proposition in support of the automatic transferability of the obligation to repair to the successor State in case of violations of *jus cogens* norms',[186] the succession in such obligations is strongly advocated.[187] This comes from the very nature of *jus cogens*, since 'each successor state is bound by such norms as an implicit condition of its entry into international society and

OSG/DP/2007/4, available at: <http://unctad.org/en/docs/osgdp20074_en.pdf>, accessed on 8 February 2015.

[183] Stern, 'Responsibilité internationale et succession d'États' (n 180) 341.

[184] Howse, 'The Concept of Odious Debt' (n 182) 22; Tai-Heng Cheng, 'Negotiating The Odious Debt Doctrine', *Law and Contemporary Problems* 70(2007)3, 7–32, at 29–31.

[185] Dumberry, *State Succession to International Responsibility* (n 175) 297.

[186] Ibid. 298.

[187] Ibid. Stern, 'Responsibilité internationale et succession d'états' (n 180) 349; Michael J. Volkovitsch, 'Righting Wrongs: Toward a New Theory of State Succession to Responsibility for International Delicts', *Columbia Law Review* 92(1992)8, 2162–214, at 2200.

accepts with them the obligation to enforce them and provide remedy for their violation'.[188] Moreover, 'the maintenance of such norms is essential to the health of the international system and cannot depend on the vagaries of history that sometimes determine the circumstances of state succession'.[189]

In sum, the zeal for standardization of the IIL in the area of state succession regarding state responsibility may appear superfluous and doctrinally formalistic in detecting customary rule of international law *in statu nascendi*. This appears especially true in respect of cultural heritage obligations. Indeed, the nature of such obligations, often involving extremely complex historical and politically sensitive aspects, may call for more flexible solutions. These can follow 'pragmatic' approaches to state succession[190] based on fairness and equity,[191] or those calling for a policy approach, which in case of lack of positive norms provides a multifaceted analysis of various interlocking factors affecting succession outcomes.[192] As has been already explained, the actual arrangements adopted by successor states in matters of responsibility for the breach of such obligations are usually based on non-succession *ex gratia* considerations. Therefore, it may be argued that the core principle applicable in such cases, expect rare instances of the violation of *jus cogens*, would be an obligation to negotiate to achieve fair and equitable solutions in the subjective relationship emerging from the commission of an internationally wrongful act against cultural heritage.

6.2 The human and cultural heritage framework for Bosnia–Herzegovina and Kosovo

The dissolution of the SFRY has indeed unveiled certain new tendencies in the practice of the protection of the tangible cultural heritage of ethnic and national minorities, which do not fit easily into the general regime on state succession. First and foremost, the obligation to protect cultural heritage constitutes part of broader human rights standards considered as requirements for the conditional recognition of new states, in particular Bosnia–Herzegovina and Kosovo as they accepted a complex set of cultural heritage obligations. However, it seems that this was not exactly a case of automatic succession of pre-existing international engagements contracted by the predecessor state. It is also disputable as to whether adherence

[188] Volkovitsch, 'Righting Wrongs' (n 187) 2200. [189] Ibid.

[190] Compare Oscar Schachter, 'State Succession: The Once and Future Law', *Vanderbilt Journal of Transnational Law* 33(1993)2, 253–60.

[191] See *inter alia* WłSadysław Czapliński, 'Equity and Equitable Principles in the Law of State Succession', in Mojmir Mrak (eds), *Succession of States* (Nijhoff 1999), 61–73; Stefan Oeter, 'State Succession and the Struggle over Equity: Some Observations on the Laws of State Succession with Respect to State Property and Debts in Cases of Separation and Dissolution of States', *GYIL* 38(1995), 73–102.

[192] See Tai-Heng Cheng, *State Succession to Commercial Obligations* (Transnational Publishers, 2006), 382–99; Tai-Heng Cheng, 'Why New States Accept Old Obligations?', *University of Illinois Law Review* 1(2011), 1–52, at 13–19.

to this cultural heritage framework could be treated in terms of the enforcement of binding principles of general international law since the volume of such obligations would exceed widely recognized international standards.

Obviously, the international legal status of the two territories was not identical. Bosnia–Herzegovina was widely recognized as a successor state to the SFRY and all international legal efforts were aimed at assisting the stabilization of boundaries and government and social relations within this state during the transition period following the violent dissolution of the predecessor state. Inversely, the status of Kosovo was extremely controversial since the regime on the dismemberment of the SFRY, based on the principle of *uti possidetis*, did not grant the right to secede to this Serbian province. Accordingly, the international framework for Kosovo was initially perceived only as humanitarian assistance, with the aim of securing peaceful coexistence between the conflicting communities of Serbs and Albanians inhabiting this region. However, in the process of Kosovo's independence, the adoption of human rights and cultural heritage obligations constituted the fundamental basis for the constitutional framework of this new state.

The frameworks for the protection of human rights and cultural heritage for Bosnia–Herzegovina and Kosovo are without a doubt the most ambitious initiatives of this sort ever undertaken by the international community. They innovatively applied the experiences arising from long-lasting international practice of minority protection as well as those referring to contemporary theories, including the protection of tangible cultural heritage within the human rights framework. Moreover, the effective implementation of the cultural heritage regime was supported by the financial and professional engagement of the international community, in particular with regard to the preservation of historic monuments.

6.2.1 Dayton and its aftermath

The breakup of the SFRY was determined by a sequence of violent humanitarian conflicts initiated in 1992 with the Balkan War (1992–95), and continued in the Kosovo war and brief skirmishes in Macedonia. These events led to a series of international dispute settlement proposals and projects on the constitutional transformation of the states emerged from the SFRY. In June 1991, just before the dissolution of Yugoslavia began, the European Community (EC) decided to include minority protection in its actions.[193] The EC Peace Conference on Yugoslavia convened in the same year in September with the intention to maintain the SFRY by democratizing its laws. To this end, it elaborated a text entitled 'Treaty Provisions for the Convention' (known also as the Carrington Draft after the name of the Chair to the Conference),[194] which served as a model for

[193] European Council in Luxemburg, 28–29 June 1991, Presidency Conclusions, SN/151/2/91, Annex V.

[194] The EC Conference (1991-1992), Draft Convention. Treaty Provision of 4 November 1991, in: Bertrand G Ramcharan (ed), *The International Conference on the Former Yugoslavia. Official Papers*, vol. 1 (Kluwer Law International, 1997), 13–23.

the subsequent proposals.[195] The Carrington Draft dealt extensively with human rights and rights of national or ethnic groups. First, it referred to already existing human rights instruments; second, it provided additional standards which the SFRY would respect. These included collective cultural rights of minorities (Article 3), but there was no explicit mention of the right to cultural heritage.

The ferocious conflict between the three ethnicities of Bosnia and Herzegovina (Serbs, Croats, and Muslim Bosniaks), supported by neighbouring states, concluded in 1995 as a result of international military intervention. The various peace plans were drafted with US involvement and resulted in the 1995 peace agreement (the Dayton Agreement),[196] which set out minority standards in accordance with the international human rights conventions in force. Following the principles of internal self-determination and *uti possidetis* already confirmed by the Badinter Commission, ethnic groups within the territory of the former Yugoslav republic of Bosnia and Herzegovina did not have the right to secede but were 'entitled to all the rights concerned to minorities and ethnic groups.'[197] Thus, they were bound to coexist in one state and reciprocally respect each others' rights. Accordingly, Annexes 6 to 8 of the Dayton Agreement regulated the situation of human communities within the country: Annex 6 concerned Human Rights, Annex 7 regulated the situation of refugees and displaced peoples, and Annex 8 established the Commission to Preserve National Monuments (CPNM). Thus, the post-dissolution legal regime not only provided for the preservation of human persons and their rights but also sanctioned the restoration of their culture, history, and identity.[198]

The CPNM was set up for a five-year transition period preceding full independence. Subsequently, in 2000, its competences would be transferred to the sovereign Government of Bosnia and Herzegovina. The mandate of the Commission was to 'receive and decide on petitions for the designation of property having cultural, historic, religious or ethnic importance as National Monuments' (Article IV). This could be classified: 'movable or immovable property of great importance to a group of people with common cultural, historic, religious or ethnic heritage, such as monuments of architecture, art or history; archaeological sites; groups of buildings; as well as cemeteries' (Article VI). The Commission was

[195] Paul C. Szasz, 'Protecting Human and Minority Rights in Bosnia: A Documentary Survey of International Proposals', *California Western International Law Journal* 25(1994), 259–88. Antal Berkes, *State Succession and Minority Rights—a Case Study of the Dissolution of the Former Yugoslavia* (LLM thesis, Central European University, 2009), 66–72.

[196] General Framework Agreement for Peace in Bosnia and Herzegovina, Initiated in Dayton, Ohio, 21 November 1995, signed in Paris on 14 December 1995, 35 ILM 89.

[197] Opinion No 2, see Text of Opinions. Documents Regarding the Situation in the Former Yugoslavia (n 161) 1497.

[198] Compare Susanne Malmstrom, 'The Relevance of International Human Rights Law for the Development of Economic, Social, and Cultural Policy in Bosnia and Herzegovina', in Michael O'Flaherty and Gregory Gisvold (eds), *Post-War Protection of Human Rights in Bosnia and Herzegovina* (Nijhoff, 1998), 157–72.

to have a mixed composition: members of ethnicities and members appointed by the Director-General of UNESCO (Article II.1).

During the first five years, the CPNM worked primarily on the construction of the list of the most valuable monuments, which in the vast majority of cases concerned religious sites.[199] It also proposed several drafts of new cultural heritage legislation for Bosnia–Herzegovina, implementing best-practice international standards. After the end of the transition period, in 2002 Bosnia–Herzegovina passed a law on the implementation of the Commission's decisions.[200] In this way, the legislation enacted by this internationally based body as to the designation of the sites under special protection, became part of the domestic legal system. The guarantee to reconstruct, rehabilitate, and protect national cultural heritage became one of the key tools for the stabilization of this successor state.

6.2.2 Cultural heritage in the constitutional framework for Kosovo

Similar measures were adopted in the case of Kosovo.[201] The draft peace agreement granting broad autonomy to Kosovo, proposed by the NATO leaders during the conference in Rambouillet (January–March 1999),[202] was however rejected by the Serbian government. After NATO military intervention and UN Security Council Resolution 1244,[203] the civil administration was passed over to the United Nations Interim Administration Mission in Kosovo (UNMIK), which was also responsible for drafting the Kosovo constitutional system. Among other issues, the provisional institutions of Kosovo had to settle questions concerning the protection of cultural heritage,[204] which even under international administration was still subject to brutal attacks and destruction. This primarily concerned the medieval monasteries of the Serbian Orthodox Church.

The Rambouillet Agreement[205] introduced certain provisions in respect of the status of cultural heritage. In the preamble to the proposed draft constitution

199 Valery Perry, 'Revering Ethnic and Cultural Cleansing: The Role of Annex 8 in Reclaiming History, Promoting Post-War Reconciliation and Preserving the Unique Cultural Heritage of Bosnia and Herzegovina', *European Yearbook of Minority Issues* 2(2002–03), 197–225, at 210–11.

200 Law on the Implementation of Decisions of the Commission to Preserve National Monuments Established Pursuant to Annex 8 of the General Framework Agreement for Peace in Bosnia and Herzegovina, 9 February 2002, available at: <http://kons.gov.ba/main.php?id_struct=83&lang=4>, accessed on 8 February 2015.

201 For the synopsis of the political and legal developments in Serbia and Kosovo after 2000, see Enver Hasani, 'The Evolution of the Succession Process in Former Yugoslavia', *Miskolc Journal of International Law* 4(2007)2, 12–37.

202 See Marc Weller, 'The Rambouillet Conference on Kosovo', *International Affairs* 75(1999)2, 211–51.

203 UN Doc. S/RES/1244 (1999)

204 See Art. 4.3 of the Constitutional Framework for Provisional Self-Government, UNMIK/REG/2001/9, with further amendments; available at: <http://www.unmikonline.org/regulations/2001/reg09-01.htm>, accessed on 4 February 2015.

205 Interim Agreement for Peace and Self-Government in Kosovo, Chateau Rambouillet, France, 23 February 1999, available at: <http://www.usip.org/sites/default/files/file/resources/collections/peace_agreements/kosovo_ramb.pdf>, accessed on 8 February 2015.

for the Self-Government of Kosovo (still an autonomous province of Serbia), it was stressed that the importance of the 'preservation and promotion of the national, cultural, and linguistic identity of each national community in Kosovo are necessary for the harmonious development of a peaceful society.' Article VII on national communities provided for additional rights for such communities 'in order to preserve and express their cultural and religious identities in accordance with international standards.' These would also be protected by 'the preservation of sites of religious, historical, or cultural importance to the national community.'

Despite the rejection of the agreement by Serbia, its principles in respect of cultural heritage were developed in subsequent international plans for Kosovo, first, in 2001 by the Constitutional Framework for Provisional Self-Government and later by the 2003 'Standards for Kosovo', which contained a set of provisions on the protection of cultural heritage. Accordingly, Kosovo's cultural heritage would be respected 'as the common patrimony of all of Kosovo's ethnic, religious and linguistic communities'. All groups were entitled to its protection on a non-discriminatory basis. However, the provisional administration did not effectively protect Serbian cultural heritage against repeated attacks in 2004. Therefore, the 2004 Kosovo Standard Implementation Plan (KSIP)[206] provided for priority actions. The protection of cultural heritage 'was given added emphasis and separate treatment as an "extra" standard'.[207] In implementing the Standards, in 2006 the Assembly of Kosova adopted the Cultural Heritage Law (CHL),[208] which regulated the internal organization of legal infrastructure covering 'the protection, preservation and promotion of the cultural heritage of Kosova.' This introduced a very broad definition of cultural heritage under protection, including tangible as well as intangible manifestations (Article 2).

In 2007, the UN Comprehensive Proposal for the Kosovo Status Settlement[209] indicated the issue of cultural heritage as one of the criteria for full self-governance of the territory. Accordingly, it postulated a special framework for the protection of Serbian patrimony in the case of a definite separation from Serbia (Annex V Religious and Cultural Heritage). In this way, the process of gaining independence was strictly conditioned by the acceptance of cultural heritage obligations in respect of sites of major importance for both the Serbian minority living in Kosovo and the Republic of Serbia, the predecessor state.

It seems that these postulates listed by the 2007 UN Comprehensive Proposal for Kosovo were not introduced before the proclamation of independence in 2008.

[206] Kosovo Standards Implementation Plan, 31 March 2004, available at: <http://www.unmikonline.org/pub/misc/ksip_eng.pdf>, accessed on 31 January 2015.

[207] The Kosovo Standards Process 2003-2007, UN MIK/StratCo 070420, available at: <http://www.unmikonline.org/standards/docs/KSP2003-2007.pdf>, accessed on 31 January 2015.

[208] Assembly of Kosovo, Cultural Heritage Law. Law No. 02/L-88, 9 October 2006, available at: <http://skupstinakosova.org/common/docs/ligjet/2006_02-L88_en.pdf>, accessed on 31 January 2015.

[209] Comprehensive Proposal for the Kosovo Status Settlement. 26 March 2007, UN Doc. S/2007/168/Add.1.

However, these efforts bore fruit at the constitutional level.[210] The adopted text of the Constitution of independent Kosovo set out extensive obligations with regard to the multi-ethnic cultural heritage of that state. Accordingly, 'the Republic of Kosovo ensures the preservation and protection of its cultural and religious heritage' (Article 9) and promotes 'the preservation of the cultural and religious heritage of all communities as an integral part of the heritage of Kosovo.' Furthermore, it 'shall have a special duty to ensure an effective protection of the entirety of sites and monuments of cultural and religious significance to the communities' (Article 58.5). Arguably, the actual framework for the protection of Serbian cultural heritage located in Kosovo can be implemented thanks to the agreement between Serbia and Kosovo on their future relations.[211] In fact, this establishes a special legal framework for the self-governance of Serbian minority in northern Kosovo. In future, this may potentially lead to the formulation of better technical and financial measures for the protection of cultural sites of great cultural importance for Serbia and communities in Kosovo.

6.3 Past territorial and population transfers—solutions based on the procedural principle of international cultural cooperation

Not only did the end of the Cold War address the issue of state succession to tangible cultural heritage in cases of dissolution and secession but it also addressed the status of such properties in respect of the unification of states and territorial cession. The major controversies on state succession to cultural property in the post-Cold War context referred to the issue of territorial transfers occurred at the end of the Second World War. This section deals with three cases: 1) Germany–Poland, 2) Poland–Ukraine, 3) Slovenia–Italy. It argues that the basic formula with which the concerned states have attempted to settle past disputes essentially consists in the application of the procedural principle of cultural cooperation.

6.3.1 Germany–Poland

The democratic transformations launched in 1989 enabled the final settlement between unified Germany and Poland in relation to the common border and other issues arising from the 1945 Potsdam Agreement.[212] The crux of legal

[210] Read Marc Weller, 'The Kosovo Constitution and Provisions for the Protection of Minorities in Europe', *European Yearbook of Minority Issues* 6(2006)7, 485–527.

[211] Statement of the EU Council President Herman Van Rompuy on agreement within facilitated dialogue on normalisation of relations between Serbia and Kosovo, 19 April 2013, reference CL13-032EN, <http://eu-un.europa.eu/articles/en/article_13414_en.htm>, accessed on 10 February 2015.

[212] See Protocol of Proceedings of the Berlin Conference, 2 August 1945, British Parliamentary Paper Miscellaneous No. 6 (1947) Cmd. 7087.

controversies between these two states consisted in different interpretations of the territorial and population transfers decided by the Allies, not confirmed by a peace treaty.[213]

As discussed in Chapter 3, as a result of the 1945 Potsdam Agreement, Poland lost nearly half of its territory to the USSR and obtained 'in return' vast territories at the expense of Germany. This was decided on the basis of Chapter VIII.B paragraph 2 of the Potsdam Agreement, which held that 'pending the final determination of Poland's western frontier', the former German territories situated on the east of the Oder-Neisse line, including the portion of East Prussia not placed under the administration of the USSR would pass to the administration of the Polish state. At the same time, pursuant to Chapter XII of the 1945 Potsdam Agreement, the transfer of the German population was ordered. Under the circumstances of the Cold War, the final settlement of these transfers was not possible. Thus, the course of border was not confirmed until the 1950 Treaty of Zgorzelec (Görlitz) with the German Democratic Republic.[214] In 1970, Poland and the Federal Republic of Germany normalized their relations under the Treaty of Warsaw,[215] in which both sides committed themselves to non-violence and accepted the existing border—the Oder-Neisse line (Article 1), imposed on Germany by the Allied powers at the 1945 Potsdam Conference.

However, the effects of the Potsdam Agreements as well as of the 1970 Treaty of Warsaw were subject to opposite interpretations by the concerned states and legal scholarship.[216] In brief, the jurisprudence of the Federal Constitutional Court and the prevailing German legal doctrine sustained that the Allied Powers did not transfer the Eastern Territories of the Third Reich to Poland, which was only granted their administration and therefore it was not authorized to act as sovereign. The last argument was particularly critical in respect of the right of Poland to dispose the property situated in these territories. Consequently, it was argued that all acts of disposal and appropriation made by Poland with reference to state and private property, including tangible cultural property situated in the former German Eastern Territories, were unlawful.[217] Furthermore, it was upheld that the 1970 Treaty of Warsaw did not solve the issue of the transfer of territory, as such a settlement could only be made by a definitive treaty signed by unified

[213] Andrzej Jakubowski, 'Territoriality and State Succession in Cultural Heritage', *IJCP* 21(2014)4, 375–96, at 386–88.

[214] The Agreement between Poland and the German Democratic Republic Concerning the Demarcation of the Established and the Existing Polish–German State Frontier, signed on 6 July 1950, 319 UNTS 93.

[215] Treaty between Poland and the Federal Republic of Germany Concerning the Basis for Normalization of Their Mutual Relations, signed on 7 December 1970, 830 UNTS 327.

[216] See *inter alia* Georg Ress, 'Die abschließende Regelung in bezug auf Deutschland', in Ulrich Beyerlin et al. (ed), *Recht zwischen Umbruch und Bewahrung* (Springer, 1995), 833–35, Ludwik Geldberg, 'The Warsaw Treaty of 1970 and the Western Boundary of Poland', *AJIL* 76(1982)1, 119–29.

[217] Stefan Turner, 'Das internationale Kulturgüterrecht und die Zerstreuung des deutschen Kulturbesitzes nach dem Zweiten Weltrieg', in Wilfried Fiedler (ed), *Internationaler Kulturgüterschutz und deutsche Frage* (Gebr. Mann, 1991), 154–82, at 180–82.

Germany.[218] On the contrary, Poland perceived the decisions of the Potsdam Agreement as constitutive and further provisions of the 1970 Warsaw Treaty as merely declaratory.[219] This interpretation also emphasized the sovereign rights of Poland to cultural property situated in the territories annexed in 1945.[220] In addition, both states represented different positions in respect of compensation due to the expelled German population, on the one hand, and war reparations to Poland, on the other.

The major controversies between the concerned states referred to four groups of cultural property: 1) movable and immovable cultural property preserved in the territories concerned; 2) property evacuated by the German administration from eastern lands to 'mainland' Germany, and *vice versa*—cultural objects transported from the western provinces to the territories which entered under the Polish control; 3) movable cultural property originated from the territories concerned and displaced from Polish or German control; these refer primarily to items removed by the Soviet troops;[221] 4) cultural heritage destroyed or plundered as a result of Nazi cultural policy and military operations. However, during the Cold War, no definitive regulations in respect of the allocation of cultural property were concluded between Poland and the German states, and after the short period of post-war restitutions, no other general settlement on cultural heritage issues was achieved.

After the unification of Germany, all these issues were immediately addressed in bilateral relations. In November 1990, both states concluded a border treaty and in 1991 the Treaty on Good Neighbourly Relations and Friendly Cooperation,[222] whose objective was 'to close the painful chapters of the past, and determined to pick up the thread of the good traditions and friendly coexistence over the centuries-long history of Germany and Poland' (preamble). Accordingly, both states undertook to 'shape their relations in a spirit of good neighbourliness and friendship ... strive for a close, peaceful cooperation, based on principles of partnership, in all spheres' and they would 'endeavour to realize the wish of their peoples for lasting understanding and reconciliation' (Article 1(1)).

The same language of collaboration and historical and European responsibility was employed with regard to the issue of cultural heritage. Under Article 28, both states decided that they would 'co-operate in the preservation and nurture

[218] Kay Hailbronner, 'Legal Aspects of the Unification of the Two German States', *EJIL* 2(1991)1, 18–41, at 18–19, 26–27 and literature quoted therein.

[219] See *inter alia* Władysław Czapliński, 'Reunification of Germany—International Legal Issues', *Co-Existence* 27(1990)4, 225–32, at 225; Krzysztof Skubiszewski, 'Administration of Territory and Sovereignty: A Comment on the Potsdam Agreement', *AVR* 23(1985)1, 31–41.

[220] See for instance Jan Pruszyński, 'Das Recht auf Kulturgüter in den westlichen und nördlichen Gebieten Polens', *PYIL* 22(1995/1996), 187–200.

[221] See further Wojciech Kowalski, 'Tytuł prawny Polski do zabytków wywiezionych z Wrocławia pod koniec i po zakończeniu II wojny światowej', *Acta Universitatis Wratislaviensis* 88 (2012), 57–80.

[222] Treaty between Federal Republic of Germany and Poland on Good Neighbourly Relations and Friendly Cooperation, signed on 17 June 1991, entered into force on 16 January 1992, 1708 UNTS 463.

of the European cultural heritage'. Arguably, this inclusion of the cultural heritage of both states within a larger European framework was very far-reaching, since many of the cultural sites situated on the Polish and German border are of a multi-ethnic and universal character (for instance, the historic cities of Wroclaw (Breslau) and Gdansk (Danizg)). Thus, many actions and projects concerning historic monuments may be conducted on a joint, multilateral, or European basis, without prejudice to national sentiments. Moreover, both states also obliged themselves to:

> take special care of the places and cultural assets in their respective territories that bear witness to historical events and cultural and scientific achievements of the other side, and shall provide free and unhindered access to them, or endeavour to see that such access is provided, where the state does not have authority to guarantee it. Such places and cultural assets shall be placed under the protection of the laws of the respective Contracting Parties. The Contracting Parties shall take joint initiatives in this area, in a spirit of understanding and reconciliation.

Subsequently, the 1991 Polish–German treaty stated that both states in 'the same spirit' would seek 'to solve problems relating to cultural assets and archives, beginning with individual cases.' The last provision was particularly important for the pending controversies over the lists of cultural items requested by both sides. Since the solution of such disputes was greatly conditioned by the contradictory interpretations of the international effects of the 1945 Potsdam Agreement, Poland and Germany decided that their settlement would be negotiated on a *case-by-case* basis, in the spirit of reconciliation.

After very promising beginnings in 1992–95, the whole process of negotiations was interrupted. The main controversy related to the collections of the Prussian State Library evacuated at the end of the Second World War by the German administration to the territories which in 1945 passed under Polish rule.[223] Germany claimed their return on the basis of Article 56 of the regulations annexed to the 1907 Hague Convention, to which Poland and Germany were the parties prior to the Second World War and which provided that at the time of war all seizure of historic monuments, works of art and science was forbidden. Moreover, the collections of the Prussian State Library constitute symbols of German culture and history and are linked to the Germans, not the Poles. In addition, state sovereignty of Poland over the concerned territories was questionable. Conversely, Poland argued that it rightfully acquired the title to collections on two bases. First, Poland acquired all the state property situated in the territories assigned to it by the 1945 Potsdam Agreement, including cultural property. Second, the collection of the Prussian State Library has to be treated as restitution-in-kind, or reparation for the immense losses of Polish national patrimony caused by the Nazis and never recompensed in the Cold War circumstances. In this context,

[223] See Antonius Jammers (ed), *Die Beziehungen der Berliner Staatsbibliothek nach Polen: Reflexionen zur Zeit- und Bestandsgeschichte* (Staatsbibliothek zu Berlin—Preußisher Kulturbesitz, 1997).

Poland recalled the Nazi's intentional destruction of the public and private libraries of Warsaw in 1944, including the precious collections of the Polish National Library. It also claimed for compensation, invoking Article 247 of the 1919 Treaty of Versailles concerning the case of the University Library of Leuven. However, Poland did not exclude the possibility of restoring the Prussian State Library to Berlin,[224] but would consider this only if Germany compensated Polish losses suffered in its library heritage. Thus, this argumentation touches upon the question of rectifying justice in international law and policy.[225]

Clearly, the first Polish argument cannot be arguably sustained because both territorial and national features of the cultural property at stake indicate Germany as the state and community of origin. The second argument is more convincing in light of the international practice prior to 1945 in respect of reparation for war damages in cultural heritage. However, the form of reparation must never be subject to a unilateral decision. In response to Poland's claims, Germany stopped the restitution of Polish objects plundered or displaced in connection with the Second World War. Up until 2013, both states have not managed to find any solution to this problem, although a number based on various forms of joint management have been discussed. It seems that any compromise would be unacceptable since both states are involved in a number of other negotiations on displaced cultural objects and are not interested in creating any 'inconvenient' precedents. Yet the climate around the negotiations has recently changed due to the important shift in German museum restitution policy affected by the so-called Gurlitt affair,[226] the discovery in 2010 of an immense collection of artworks gathered by Hildebrand Gurlitt, a Nazi art dealer. This matter has placed the topic of Nazi art plunder in view of international public opinion once again. In light of this affair, some Polish claims have also found a better response in Germany. In fact, in 2014 a long-claimed painting by Francesco Guardi, *Palace Stairs*,[227] stolen from the National Museum in Warsaw during the Second World War and then discovered in the Staatsgalerie in Stuttgart, was eventually handed over to Poland. It is, however, too early to assess how these new developments will affect the entire Polish German dispute on the fate of cultural material displaced in relation to the Second World War and state succession.

In other sectors of cultural relations, such as the promotion and protection of cultural heritage, the applied solutions between Poland and Germany seem very effective. Both states launched a number of joint cultural projects, some through a special bilateral commission established on the basis of the 1997 cultural agreement.[228] It needs to be fully acknowledged that many joint projects in the

[224] In fact, in the period 1990–2001, some precious books were handed over to Germany.

[225] See further Michał Żółtowski, *Zbiory Biblioteki Pruskiej w Polsce. Studium przypadku* (Wydawnictwa Uniwersytetu Warszawskiego, 2012).

[226] See <http://www.gurlitt.info/en>, accessed on 8 February 2015.

[227] <http://culture.pl/en/article/francesco-guardis-palace-stairs-returns-to-poland>, accessed on 8 February 2015.

[228] Agreement between the Government of the Federal Republic of Germany and the Government of the Republic of Poland Concerning Cultural Cooperation, signed on 14 July 1997, entered into force on 27 October 1999, 2060 UNTS 221.

sphere of conservation of cultural property have been financed by both public and private German funds. Moreover, as a result of interstate and inter-regional collaboration, the medieval Castle of the Teutonic Order in Malbork and the Medieval Town of Torun were inscribed on the WHL in 1997. Similarly, in 2005 a jointly administered cultural site was also inscribed on the list: Muskauer Park/Park Mużakowski astride the Neisse/Nysa River on the border between Poland and Germany. The park, created in the nineteenth century by Prince von Pückler-Muskau, a Saxon aristocrat, is a vast cultural and natural landscape which has been preserved in its entirety. In addition, in 2006 and supported by Germany, Poland managed to inscribe on the WHL another site located in territories succeeded in 1945: the Centennial Hall in Wrocław. This monument, erected in 1911–13, constitutes a 'key position in the evolution of methods of reinforcement in architecture, and one of the climax points in the history of the use of metal in structural consolidation'.[229] At the same time it is profoundly related to German and Polish history: from the initial cultural events and manifestations organized by the German city of Breslau, through the Nazi rallies headed by Adolf Hitler, to the ecumenical ceremonies celebrated there by Pope John Paul II in the 1990s.

Both states also undertook a number of programs in the spheres of conservation, research, and restoration of cultural patrimony as well as museum exchange. The latter not only applies to short-term art loans but also occasionally provides for long-term deposits; the aim being to reconstruct the original historical or artistic context when the effective restitution of an objects is virtually impossible due to the long-lasting impasse of diplomatic negotiations.

6.3.2 Ukraine–Poland

Similar problems as those described with reference to German–Polish relations also mark the controversies between Poland and its eastern neighbours.[230] These are especially relevant with reference to Ukraine, where in the multi-ethnic city of Lviv (Lwów), important Polish art and library collections have been located since the beginning of the nineteenth century. The most important cultural and scientific institution was the Ossolineum, an entity founded for the community of Lviv by private donators. As a consequence of the Soviet invasion in 1939, the city and its treasures where captured and annexed to the Ukrainian Soviet Socialist Republic (Ukrainian SSR). Under the post-Second World War arrangements, Poland had to accept the cession of its territories to the Soviet republics, on the one hand, and the transfer of nearly the entire Polish, on the other. Moreover, a large number of Ukrainian communities were also resettled from newly established eastern borderlines of Poland to ex-German territories or directly to Ukrainian SSR.

[229] Centennial Hall in Wroclaw, available at: <http://whc.unesco.org/en/list/1165>, accessed on 5 February 2015.

[230] See See Andrzej Jakubowski, 'Territoriality and State Succession' (213) 388–90.

The question of the allocation of Polish cultural property on the East was not settled under Soviet rule. In 1944–46, only a small part of the cultural material was transported to the West. This was the case for some sections of the Ossolineum, which was institutionally re-established at Wrocław in 1946. The rest of the collections was divided by the Soviet authorities between different entities in the territory of the Ukrainian SSR. Immediately after the collapse of the USSR, Poland formulated claims on the repatriation of cultural treasures from Ukraine, especially in the cases of private and institutional succession. However, there was no agreement as to the just extension of such claims. Some governmental experts claimed a 'total repatriation' of Polish cultural property; some took a much more moderate view, arguing that 'the large scale repatriation of cultural objects, as laid down in the post-war plans, would lead to a cultural cleansing and gross misrepresentation of the history of the Former Eastern Territories of the Polish Republic'.[231] Thus, the potential claims ought only to refer to the collections of great public interest, namely the Ossolineum and the Library of the last king of Poland, Stanisław August Poniatowski,[232] removed by Tsarist Russia to Kiev.

On the other hand, the rights of resettled Ukrainian communities to their cultural and religious heritage in Eastern Poland was not broached after the Second World War. Many wooden churches and their furnishings were in decay, destroyed, or given to use by the Polish population.

In 1992, both states signed a treaty on good neighbourliness, friendly relations, and cooperation.[233] In this treaty, they reciprocally confirmed the existing state boundaries and undertook to cooperate in the spirit of reconciliation and understanding to 'overwhelm prejudices and negative stereotypes in relations between both nations' (Article 12), recalling international standards expressed by the UNESCO conventions, the 1953 European Cultural Convention,[234] documents of the Commission on Security and Cooperation in Europe (CSCE), especially the Document of the Cracow Symposium on the Cultural Heritage of the CSCE Participating States[235] (Article 13.1). Ukraine and Poland committed themselves to provide adequate protection and accessibility of tangible and intangible cultural heritage ('values, monuments and objects') in their respective territories (Article 13.4). Both states would also act to ensure the discovery, preservation, unification, and accessibility of the cultural heritage. Moreover, they would seek, in accordance with the norms of international law, bilateral agreements, and other international standards, to unearth and return cultural and historic objects lost,

[231] Wojciech Kowalski, *Liquidation of the Effects of World War I in the Area of Culture* (Institute of Culture, 1994), at 101.

[232] Ibid. 100.

[233] Treaty between Ukraine and the Republic of Poland on Good Neighbourliness, Friendly Relations and Cooperation, signed on 18 May 1992, entered into force on 30 December 1992, *Journal of Laws of the Republic of Poland* (1993)125, item 573.

[234] Signed on 19 December 1954, entered into force on 5 May 1955, 218 UNTS 139.

[235] Adopted on 6 June 1991, available at: <http://www.osce.org/library/24396?download=true>, accessed on 8 February 2015.

illegally removed, or in any other way displaced in the territory of the other Side (Article 13.4).

The idea of reunification of the dispersed collections was also expressed in an additional preliminary agreement for cultural cooperation (Article 5.1):[236]

> The Side on whose territories are found objects and historical treasures of cultural, history and learning as well as archival material and library collections of the other country . . . will act to disclose, inventory, bring together, preserve, restore (those objects) and give access to them. The Side will cooperate in this area, especially in bringing together collections of art, libraries and archives that had been scattered due to historical events.

In 1996, an intergovernmental agreement on cooperation regarding the protection and return of cultural items which had been lost or illegally moved during the Second World War was signed.[237] On this basis, in mid-May 1997, a Joint Commission was established. Poland presented a very broad list of requested cultural items owned prior 1939 by the Polish state and private institutions as well as private individuals.[238] In the same month, both states signed a general agreement on cultural cooperation,[239] which under Article 17 confirmed that illegally removed objects would be returned. The second meeting of the Joint Commission took place in mid-February, and in March Ukraine issued an official response to the Polish claims, arguing that all the requested collections constituting the state domain of Ukraine were legally acquired, and could not be repatriated.

The subsequent talks concerning the exchange of certain groups of items did not bring about any positive result, however, both states successfully collaborated in the areas of conservation of cultural sites in a number of joint projects. In addition, in 1998 the historic centre of Lviv was inscribed on the WHL[240] on the basis of its multi-ethnic and multicultural character.[241] Many places of religious worship on

[236] Preliminary Agreement between Ukraine and the Republic of Poland for Cultural and Scientific Cooperation (1992), English text available in Kowalski, *Liquidation of the Effects* (n 231) 100.

[237] Agreement between Government of the Republic of Poland and Government of Ukraine on Co-operation in Protection and Restitution of Objects of Cultural Interest Lost and Illegally Removed during World War II, signed on 25 June 1996, available at: <http://www.traktaty.msz.gov.pl/fd.aspx?f=P0000007979.pdf>, accessed on 8 February 2015.

[238] Jan Pruszyński, *Wnioski rewindykacyjne księgozbioru Ossolineum oraz dzieł sztuki i zabytków ze zbiorów lwoskich [Revindication Claims Regarding the Library of Ossolineum and Works of Art and Cultural Items from the Collections of Lviv]* (MKiS Biuro Pełnomocnika Rządu do spraw Polskiego Dziedzictwa Kulturalnego za Granicą, 1998).

[239] Agreement between the Government of the Republic of Poland and the Government of Ukraine on Cooperation in the Realm of Culture, Science and Education, signed on 20 May 1997, *Journal of Laws of the Republic of Poland* (2000)3, item 29.

[240] L'viv—the Ensemble of the Historic Centre, available at: <http://whc.unesco.org/en/list/865>, accessed on 8 February 2015.

[241] Ibid. 'Justification for Inscription:

> Criterion (ii): In its urban fabric and its architecture, L'viv is an outstanding example of the fusion of the architectural and artistic traditions of eastern Europe with those of Italy and Germany. Criterion (v): The political and commercial role of L'viv attracted to it a number of ethnic groups with different cultural and religious traditions, who established separate yet interdependent communities within the city, evidence for which is still discernible in the modern townscape.'

both sites of the border were also returned to communities who had been deprived of their use and enjoyment for decades. Importantly, in 2013 Poland and Ukraine succeeded in inscribing a group of wooden *tserkvas* (Orthodox churches) of the Carpathian Region, situated in the territories of both Poland and Ukraine,[242] which according to the nomination file submitted by both governments 'are immensely important spiritual centres for local communities, who continue to participate in religious activities contributing significantly to the survival of this unique diversity of religious rites and adding an intangible, emotional context to the significance of these sites'.[243]

6.3.3 Italy–Slovenia

The last case study in this section concerns the controversy between Slovenia and Italy with regard to state succession to the so-called Istria's jewels.[244] This involved almost 100 works of art from the fourteenth to the eighteenth centuries by the most prominent artists of the Republic of Venice such as: Benedetto and Vittorio Carpaccio, Cima da Conegliano, Alvise Vivarini, Jacopo Palma il Giovane, and Giambattista Tiepolo.[245] Until 1940–41, these treasures had been preserved in three coastline municipalities of Italian Istria: Koper (Capodistria), Piran (Pirano), and Izola (Isola), known now as the Slovenian Littoral or Primorska. In 1940, before the war with Yugoslavia, Italian authorities decided to evacuate the most valuable works of art from their eastern borders, including objects from the churches and museums of Istria. The removal, ordered for preservation reasons, was done in conformity with domestic Italian legislation and was approved by local and church administrations.[246]

In the beginning, the objects were gathered at a collection point in the province of Udine. In 1943, some were returned to the owners, for example, a priceless group of paintings from Saint Anne's Church and Monastery in Koper.[247] The majority of the works of art evacuated from the Slovenian Littoral were, however,

[242] Wooden *Tserkvas* of the Carpathian Region in Poland and Ukraine, UNESCO Doc. WHC-13/37.COM/20, Paris, 5 July 2013, available at: <http://whc.unesco.org/en/list/1424>, accessed on 8 February 2015.

[243] Ibid.

[244] For a detailed analysis of the case, see Andrzej Jakubowski, 'The Legacy of Serenissima. State Succession to Istria's Jewels', in Kerstin Odendahl and Peter J. Weber (eds), *Kulturgüterschutz-Kunstrecht—Kulturrecht. Festschrift für Kurt Siehr zum 75. Geburstag aus dem Kreise des Doktoranden- und Habilitandenseminars 'Kunst und Recht'* (Nomos, 2010), 227–50.

[245] See Sonja A. Hoyer, 'List of Works of Art Removed from Koper, Izola and Piran', in Sonja A. Hoyer, Jože Hočevar, Sergio Settomini, et al. (eds), *Art Works from Koper, Izola, Piran Retained in Italy* (Ministrstvo za kulturo, 2005), 67–75.

[246] Fabrizio Magani, '1940–1946. La Soprintendenza ai Monumenti e alle Gallerie della Venezia Giulia e del Friuli e la protezione delle opere d'arte in Istria', in Francesca Castellani and Paolo Casadio (eds), *Histria. Opere d'arte restaurate: da Paolo Veneziano a Tiepolo*. Catalogo della mostra: Trieste, 23 giugno 2005–6 gennaio 2006 (Electa, 2005), 31–39.

[247] Giuliana Algeri, Stefano L'Occaso, 'Le opere d'arte della chiesa di Sant'Anna di Capodistria', in Francesca Castellani and Paolo Casadio (eds), *Histria. Opere d'arte restaurate: da Paolo Veneziano a Tiepolo*. Catalogo della mostra: Trieste, 23 giugno 2005–6 gennaio 2006 (Electa, 2005), 87–98.

sent to Rome where they remained sealed in wooden crates for the next 6- years. In 2005–06, some of these objects were exhibited at the Revoltella Museum in Trieste.

As a result of post-Second World War decisions, the Istrian peninsula became part of the territory of the SFRY. However, the allocation of Istria's jewels has never been settled. After the dissolution of Yugoslavia, Slovenia—one of the SFRY successors states—asked for the return of the evacuated objects to the places where they had been commissioned and from which they had been taken.

a) Historical background

For 400 years until the end of the eighteenth century, the municipalities of Piran, Koper, and Izola had been under the rule of the Republic of Venice. After the fall of the Republic in 1797, sovereignty over the multi-ethnic territory of Istria passed several times between the various Napoleonic states and Austria. Eventually, the 1815 Congress of Vienna granted the entire territory of Venice with its Istrian and Dalmatian settlements to Austria, which already controlled the important commercial cities of Trieste and Fiume (Rijeka) on the Adriatic cost. In 1866, Austria ceded Venice and Veneto in favour of Italy, whereas the Istrian peninsula and the city of Trieste remained under Austrian sovereignty. After the First World War and the dissolution of Austria–Hungary, the 1919 Treaty of St Germain assigned Istria to Italy. In this way, Italy gained control over a great part of the territory of the Republic of Venice and managed to recover a number of artworks of Venetian provenance.

The situation completely changed as a result of the war against Yugoslavia and the final defeat of Italy in the Second World War. On the basis of the 1947 Paris Peace Treaty, Italy ceded its Adriatic islands, the city of Rijeka, and a large part of Istria to the SFRY. The eastern coast of the Istrian peninsula (including the municipalities of Koper, Piran, and Izola) and the area of the city of Trieste formed the separate Free Territory of Trieste (FTT), which was not however considered as ceded territory in the meaning defined in the treaty (Article 21.4). The FTT remained divided between Allied military control and Yugoslavia according to the post-war demarcation line, although the 1947 Treaty established it as a neutral unitary entity with its own civil administration. The northern part of the FTT including the city of Trieste (Zone A) was controlled by the Allies and the southern part with Primorska (Zone B) by Yugoslavia. In 1952, Italy obtained administrative powers in Zone A, and in 1954 (London Memorandum)[248] the division of the FTT between Italy and the SFRY was agreed. The part of the coast,

[248] Free Territory of Trieste: Administration of Zones A and B by Italian and Yugoslav Governments. Understanding, with Annexes, between the United States of America, the United Kingdom, Italy, and Yugoslavia, signed at London on 5 October 1954, entered into force on 5 October 1954 (United States Government Printing Office, 1955); see also Glenda Sluga, *Trieste and the Italo–Yugoslav Border: Difference, Identity, and Sovereignty in Twentieth-Century Europe* (State University of New York Press, 2001).

comprising the municipalities of Koper, Piran, and Izola, was transferred to the Socialist Republic of Slovenia. Subsequently, under the 1975 Treaty of Osimo,[249] Zones A and B of the FTT were definitively divided and incorporated into the administrating states.

The 1947 Treaty obliged Italy to restore to Yugoslavia an extensive array of cultural material relating to the ceded lands, based on the rudimentary criterion of territoriality. In the execution of this treaty, in 1961 Italy and Yugoslavia signed an agreement on the regulation of restitution of cultural property. This did not, however, regulate the allocation of art objects evacuated from Zone B of the FTT. In the following years, Italy and Yugoslavia did not manage to solve the issue. In fact, the 1975 Treaty of Osimo did not contain any provisions on the allocation of artworks from Zone B, although certain attempts to address the question were made during the treaty negotiations at Osimo. Accordingly, the representatives of both states exchanged diplomatic notes in which they agreed that the 'issues relating to cultural property, works of art, archives' pertaining to the Free Territory of Trieste would be considered after the entry into force of the 1975 Osimo Treaty.[250]

Subsequently, the delegations of both states met a few times to discuss the issues. At the intergovernmental level, the talks between the SFRY and Italy ceased in 1988.[251] Separate negotiations were undertaken by Slovenian church authorities. These were possible thanks to the formal division of the diocese of Trieste and the diocese of Koper ordered by the Holy See in 1977.[252] Some talks also took place between art historians from Slovenia and Italy.[253]

The controversy over the allocation of Istria's art treasures is profoundly linked to the multinational nature of this region.[254] The tensions between different ethnic groups arose particularly at the time of the dismemberment of Austria–Hungary and the subsequent delimitation of borders between Italy and Yugoslavia. In particular, Italian Fascist assimilationist policies towards all national and ethnic minorities before the Second World War fed hostile attitudes amongst the Slavic and Italian inhabitants of Istria. The subsequent Italian invasion of Yugoslavia,

[249] Italy and Yugoslavia Treaty on the Delimitation of the Frontier for the Part Not Indicated as such in the Peace Treaty of 10 February 1947 (with Annexes, Exchange of Letters and Final Act), signed on 10 November 1975, entered into force on 11 October 1977, 1466 UNTS 25.

[250] Exchange of Letters between Mr. Milos Minic, Vice-President of the Federal Executive Council and Federal Secretary for Foreign Affairs of the Socialist Federal Republic of Yugoslavia, and Mr. Mariano Rumor, Minister for Foreign Affairs of the Italian Republic, on 10 November 1975, Osimo, Ancona, 1466 UNTS 142, letters Ib and IIb.

[251] Salvator Žitko, 'Efforts of the Authorities to Retrieve Cultural Heritage Still in Italy', in Sonja A. Hoyer, Jože Hočevar Sergio Settomini, et al. (eds), *Art Works from Koper, Izola, Piran Retained in Italy* (Ministrstvo za kulturo, 2005), 76–81, at 79.

[252] Bolla Prioribus saeculi. Dioecesis Iustinopolitana a Tergestina seiungitur et utriusque necnon quarundam aliarum dioecesium fines mutantur, 17.10.1977, 69 (1977) AAS 689.

[253] Sonja A. Hoyer, 'Art Works from Koper, Izola and Piran Still in Italy' in Sonja A. Hoyer, Jože Hočevar, Sergio Settomini, et al. (eds), *Art Works from Koper, Izola, Piran Retained in Italy* (Ministrstvo za kulturo, 2005), 62–65.

[254] For more on this topic, see Pamela Ballinger, *History in Exile: Memory and Identity at the Borders of the Balkans* (Princeton University Press, 2003).

and the cruelty and crimes of war only strengthened anti-Fascist and anti-Italian sentiment. The escalation of the conflict led to ethnic cleansing pursued by Yugoslav troops, especially in Istria in 1943–49, completed by the expulsion of practically the entire Italian population from Istria and Dalmatia. Importantly, Yugoslav action consisted in the planned erasing of Italian cultural traces in the concerned territories and their forceful policy of 'Slavization'. Thus, the removal of Venetian works of art was perceived by the Italian exiles as a rightful act of preservation of their collective identity and historical memory.

b) Legal positions after the Cold War

Following the dissolution of Yugoslavia, Slovenia was the only SFRY successor state which brought a claim against Italy for the repatriation of cultural objects. The first exchange of notes took place as early as 1992 and both states agreed to find a solution in respect of the implementation of the 1975 Osimo Treaty, including the issue of cultural property.[255] The question became public in 2002, when Italy decided to open the sealed wooden boxes containing the Istrian masterpieces which had been stored in Rome. On opening it was apparent that Italy had not provided adequate conditions for the preservation of the objects. The paintings were in urgent need of restoration.[256] That same year, Slovenia proposed to set up a commission in order to discuss the future of the artworks. In 2004, the questions concerning the repatriation of cultural property to the Slovenian Littoral were submitted at the session of the Slovenian–Italian commission for adopting the program of cultural cooperation between both states.[257]

The legal argumentation for the claims of Slovenia against Italy was prepared before the dismemberment of the SFRY. At the conferences in 1987–88, Croat and Slovene experts held that the list of demanded cultural property would be based on four criteria: territory, date of removal, category of property, and available documentation of the removal.[258] Accordingly, the claims referred to the artworks originating from the territories ceded in 1947 and those of Zone B of the FTT, removed in the period 1918–54 (from the end of the First World War until the disintegration of the FTT). The objects being claimed not only concerned state-owned cultural items but also other categories of public property. Apparently, the latter would also comprise ecclesiastic property. Relevant proof of removal was provided. The basis for the repatriation of the objects was based on the provisions of the 1947 Paris Peace Treaty and on the exchange of notes at the Osimo negotiations.[259]

[255] Žitko, 'Efforts of the Authorities' (n 251) 81.

[256] Slovenia wants return of 'Istria's jewels', BBC News, 24 May 2002, available at: <http://news.bbc.co.uk/2/hi/not_in_website/syndication/monitoring/media_reports/2002652.stm>, accessed on 31 January 2015.

[257] Žitko, 'Efforts of the Authorities' (n 251) 81.

[258] Ibid. 78.

[259] Ibid. 80.

In 2005, Slovenia issued a formal request to Italy,[260] and presented an official motion to the ICOM Legal Affairs and Properties Committee, asking for assistance in the settlement of the dispute.[261] Basically, Slovenia argued that under the 1947 Peace Treaty, Italy was obliged to hand over all cultural material removed from the territories ceded to Yugoslavia, comprising the territory of the Republic of Slovenia. Moreover, as Slovenia succeeded to the 1975 Osimo Treaty, the 1975 exchanges of notes on the allocation of cultural material removed from Zone B of the FTT were also binding.

Italy, for its part, carried out careful restoration of the disputed artworks, and on 23 June 2005 an exhibition of 21 objects (paintings, bronzes, and wooden sculptures) was opened in Trieste. The majority of items came from the churches of Koper, Piran, and from the Regional Museum of Koper. As stated in the exhibition catalogue, the objects would be permanently transferred to the National Gallery of Art in Trieste (Galleria Nazionale d'Arte Antica di Trieste).[262] The choice of the city was not accidental. Trieste was the formal administrative capital of the entire FTT, which also included the three municipalities in Zone B. Thus, it may seem that by placing the removed objects in this city all Italy complied with all its obligations under the 1947 Peace Treaty—in other words, the objects of this act were returned to the territory of the FTT.

A formal statement by the Italian government in response to Slovenia's request of 2005 has not been officially published but it can arguably be reconstructed on the basis of the few opinions expressed by the representatives of the Italian government. Accordingly, it is argued that there was no obligation to return the artworks to Slovenia, since Italy had a right and duty to evacuate and displace its cultural treasures endangered by war operations. The items requested by Slovenia came from Zone B of the FTT, which formally passed to the SFRY only in 1975 on the basis the 1975 Osimo Treaty. Thus, the objects removed from Zone B do not enter into the categories of cultural items that are to be returned to Yugoslavia under the 1947 Paris Peace Treaty. Furthermore, the 1975 Osimo Treaty did not contain any restitution clauses.

Apart from this, it has been stressed that the legal status of the evacuated cultural property was not equal since it comprised objects of state, private, and ecclesiastic property. After the Second World War, many private owners fled to Italy. Similarly, the property of Italian church parishes was transferred together with the local communities. For instance, a convent, from which artworks were taken in 1940, was subsequently closed and relocated to Italy by the communist

[260] Kurt Siehr, 'Chronicles 2005 (January 1, 2005–December 31, 2005)', *ICJP* 13(2006)4, 467–524, at 507.

[261] Legal Affairs and Properties Committee, Approach from ICOM Slovenia About the Dispute between Slovenia and Italy on Collections Removed from the Territory of What Is Now Slovenia To 'Mainland' Italy in World War II, Minutes of meeting of 22 October 2005, Paris, ICOM 2005/LEG.05, 4–5.

[262] See an introductory note by Rocco Buttiglione (Italian Ministry of Culture), in Francesca Castellani and Paolo Casadio (eds), *Histria. Opere d'arte restaurate: da Paolo Veneziano a Tiepolo.* Catalogo della mostra: Trieste, 23 giugno 2005–6 gennaio 2006 (Electa, 2005).

government of the SFRY. Thus, the rightful owners of the paintings were no longer domiciled in the ceded territory. Finally, some Italian politicians argued that the artworks in question are monuments of Italian culture and were created by Italian communities illegally expatriated from the ceded territories. Thus, the exposition of the Italian artworks in Trieste should be the only acceptable solution.

In this context, the response given by Famiano Crucianelli, Under-Secretary in the Italian Ministry of Foreign Affairs, to the parliamentary interpellation of 19 February 2007 is noteworthy.[263] Referring to the ongoing talks with Slovenia and to the possibility of formal negotiations on the status of the Istrian treasures, as agreed in 1975, the Under-Secretary argued that Italy was under no international obligation imposing the restitution of the objects concerned since they had been transported within the territory of Italy. Consequently, Italy was free to change the place of their preservation on the basis of the domestic regime for the protection of national patrimony. Moreover, the evacuation had been concluded prior to war operations. Therefore, the question of the removal of the Istrian treasures could not be examined in light of the international regime on the protection of cultural property in the event of war, in particular the UNESCO Draft Principles Relating to Cultural Objects Displaced in Connection to the Second World War. Finally, the question of the Istrian treasures could not, in any case, be discussed in terms of due restitution. It could, however, be seen in the broader framework of bilateral collaboration in matters of cultural relations, enjoyment and access to the objects in question, their conservation, study, and research.

A much more emotional response was given by the Under-Secretary in the Italian Ministry of Culture, Vittorio Sgarbi, who on various occasions expressed the view that the disputed artworks were 'completely Italian'. Therefore, they should belong to their cultural heirs—Italian exiles from the ceded territories. In this regard, Sgarbi recalled the cases of repatriation of cultural items to the indigenous communities who created them.[264] Accordingly, he invoked the significance of the links between art treasures and the memory of displaced human communities. For these reasons, the return of the evacuated art treasures to Istria would be against the dignity of exiles and such a sacrifice cannot be demanded by the Italians, Slavs, or the entire international community.[265]

c) The principle of cultural cooperation

The controversy between Italy and Slovenia illustrates just how emotionally and politically charged the issue of the allocation of cultural property in state

[263] Risposta Governo, Famiano Crucianelli, Sottosegretario di Stato Affari Esteri, Atto Camera, interrogazione a risposta scritta 4-02634 presentata da Roberto Menia, 19 February 2007, available at: <http://dati.camera.it/ocd/aic.rdf/aic4_02634_15>, accessed on 8 February 2015.

[264] Vittorio Sgarbi, 'Arte d'Istria, arte degli istriani', in Francesca Castellani and Paolo Casadio (eds), *Histria. Opere d'arte restaurate: da Paolo Veneziano a Tiepolo*. Catalogo della mostra: Trieste, 23 giugno 2005–6 gennaio 2006 (Electa, 2005), 40–42, at 40–41.

[265] Ibid. 41.

succession can be. Undoubtedly, the disputed artworks removed from public institutions and museums are territorially linked to the Istrian municipalities under the sovereignty of Slovenia. Therefore, the legal argumentation of Italy is not entirely convincing. Even if one accepts the argument that the obligation to return the cultural objects under Article 12 of the 1947 Peace Treaty does not apply to the artworks removed by Italy from Zone B of the FTT, it does not, however, exclude the right of Slovenia to the state cultural property of these territories. In such cases, the successor state would be entitled to claim for the reintegration of its cultural treasures, based on the rudimentary principle of territoriality. In addition, Yugoslavia and Italy, during the bilateral negations at Osimo in 1975, agreed that the issues relating to cultural property, works of art, and archives pertaining to the FTT needed to be considered. As mentioned, such negotiations have never produced any effect and the evacuated objects remained carefully hidden for more than 60 years in wooden crates. Nowadays, Slovenia can invoke both treaties as well as an exchange of letters between the SFRY and Italy.

However, it must be stressed that the art treasures from Istria can by no means be treated as property looted or unlawfully displaced during war. The majority of objects were evacuated by the Italian administration in 1940 from the territories under Italian sovereignty for preservation reasons and in conformity with the law applicable at the time of removal. In this regard, the Italian position needs to be fully supported. In addition, the collective rights of the exiles to control their cultural heritage need to be taken into account.

It appears that in respect of issues such as the status of Istria's jewels, the best way of settling the claims is through close international cultural cooperation. From the legal positions of Italy and Slovenia cited above, it appears that both states consider this solution as a compromise, perhaps within the broader framework of the protection of European heritage. Indeed, the cultural legacy of Venice is of great importance to all Western civilization and beyond national considerations. Thus, it seems crucial to enable the study of these masterpieces *in situ*, taking as a point of reference the totality of artistic and symbolic programmes whose essential nature constitutes the artworks in question. This would lead to the recovery of the historical and artistic context of Venetian art. Such an approach would also be in line with UNESCO standards, postulating the preservation of cultural property in its places of origin. In technical terms, both states could apply the policies of long-term deposits and loan exchanges.

However, it needs to be stressed that the receiving state shall be obliged to provide adequate measures of protection and conservation. Moreover, it seems crucial that Italy, representing the communities who created the artworks, and Slovenia, the country of origin (historical context), would jointly decide on the display, management, and common narrative of the history of the Venetian municipalities in Istria. If such requirements were to be fulfilled, the case of Istria's jewels would contribute to a sincere intercultural dialogue and a final post-Second World War reconciliation in this part of Europe.

6.4 Post-colonial reconciliation and international cultural cooperation

Alongside the post-Cold War practice of state succession in Europe, certain new developments have recently occurred with regard to the allocation of cultural property in post-colonial territories. These are largely driven by the non-legal principle of reconciliation. In legal terms, it appears that states eagerly apply the principles of cultural cooperation settled by the UN and UNESCO at the time of decolonization, in particular the UNGA Friendly Relations Declaration of 24 October 1970,[266] the 1966 UNESCO Declaration of Principles of International Cultural Co-operation, and the 1976 UNESCO Recommendation concerning the International Exchange of Cultural Property. On the other hand, these recent, international pro-cultural exchange and cooperation efforts are often hindered by the recurring debate on the principles of restitution of cultural property to its country of origin *versus* the importance of universally renowned museum and library collections.

The number of claims on the return of cultural property raised in recent years has brought about a revival of the dichotomy between cultural nationalism and internationalism, defined by John Merryman in 1986.[267] In particular, such controversies have been sparked by the debate on the future status of the Elgin Marbles, the classic Greek sculptures removed in 1801–1813 from the Parthenon and other buildings on the Acropolis of Athens and preserved in the British Museum of London.[268] The entire discourse on the repatriation of cultural treasures to their countries of origin has become known as 'elginism'.[269] In opposition to the claims raised by source and post-colonial countries, the directors of the main museums in Europe signed the 2003 Declaration on the Importance and Value of Universal Museums.[270] They claimed that while it was true that the cultural objects installed decades and even centuries ago 'in museums throughout Europe and America were acquired under conditions that are not comparable with current ones,' these objects 'over time… have become part of the museums that have cared for them, and by extension part of the heritage of the nations which house them.' Moreover, they argued that it should be acknowledged that 'museums serve not just the citizens of one nation but the people of every nation'

[266] UNGA Declaration on Principles of International Law concerning Friendly Relations and Co-operation among States in accordance with the Charter of the United Nations, adopted on 24 October 1970, UN Doc. A/RES/2625 (XXV).

[267] John H. Merryman, 'Two Ways of Thinking of Cultural Property', *AJIL* 80(1986)4, 831–53.

[268] John H. Merryman and Albert E. Elsen, *Law, Ethics and the Visual Arts* (5th edn, Kluwer Law International, 2007), 346 ff.

[269] Elginism—the origins of a word, see: <http://www.elginism.com/20080622/1151>, accessed on 31 January 2015.

[270] Declaration on the Importance and Value of Universal Museum, *ICOM News* 57(2004)1, at 4, available at: <http://icom.museum/fileadmin/user_upload/pdf/ICOM_News/2004-1/ENG/p4_2004-1.pdf>, accessed on 31 January 2015.

because such institutions 'are agents in the development of culture, whose mission is to foster knowledge by a continuous process of reinterpretation'. Therefore, the 'calls to repatriate objects that have belonged to museum collections for many years... have to be judged individually.'

With regard to the principles governing the allocation of cultural property in state succession, the theses of the 2004 Declaration essentially reaffirmed the arguments applied in succession agreements since the nineteenth century. In other words, the cultural, historical, and scientific values of universally renowned art collections shall always be weighted up against the nation- and/or territory-oriented claims of successor states. The eventual claims regarding the return of cultural objects must always be examined on a case-by-case basis.

This section of the book does not, however, deal with the problem of the restitution debate. It discusses two recent cases of the allocation of cultural property, following decolonization, settled within the framework of international cooperation in the spirit of reconciliation. First, it analyses the process of cultural reconciliation between Japan and the Korean states. Second, it recalls the reasoning of the Italian administrative courts in respect of the already quoted case of the *Venus of Cyrene*.[271]

6.4.1 The withdrawal from colonial territories: cultural reconciliation between Japan and Korea

The origins of this case stem from the long and turbulent history of these two countries, in particular with respect to the devastating plunder of Korean cultural treasures during Japanese colonial rule in the first part of the twentieth century. This example illustrates the difficulties which arise from the theory of legality of colonial appropriation of cultural material and contemporary moral and ethical considerations. Furthermore, it demonstrates that the moral responsibility to redress historic wrongs does not only lie with state actors but can also be attributed to private owners of cultural objects originating from war and colonial plunder.

a) Historical background

For centuries Korean patrimony was subjected to destruction, plunder, and illegal removal under enemy occupation during the wars with Japan. The first substantial removal of artistic objects took place during two Japanese invasions of Korea (1592–98). These short annexations of Korea served in Japanese state ideology as justification for subsequent military occupations on the basis that the Korean peninsula had always been part of the Japanese Empire. For Korea, the date of the sixteenth-century invasions constitutes a time limitation for claims against Japan for the return of national treasures.

[271] See section 6.4.2.

At the end of the nineteenth century Japan started the process of colonization of Korea concluded by the 1910 Annexation Treaty,[272] which formally transferred sovereignty over the already occupied Korean territory to Japan. The validity of this annexation was subsequently recognized by the European powers.

During Japanese colonial rule, Korean culture suffered great losses. The language and traditional surnames were suppressed. At the same time, material cultural heritage was subjected to a brutal policy. Many sites were destroyed and plundered and precious items were transported to Japan. Among other activities, the Japanese administration conducted regular exhumation of ancient tombs, including royal necropolises. Many objects ended up in private collections and over time they emerged on the international art market.[273]

Following the Second World War, the territory of Korea was divided into the northern part entrusted to the Soviet Union and the southern part occupied by the United States. After the Korean War (1950–53), the *de facto* division of the country was confirmed. During the Cold War only South Korea signed a peace treaty with Japan. However, it took place two decades after the end of Japanese colonial rule. For years South Korea was reluctant to consider any reconciliation with Japan, and the issue of destroyed and looted cultural property was one of the main obstacles for mutual peaceful relations.[274] This was also due to the failure of the post-Second World War restitution programme in East Asia which was firmly opposed by Japan.[275]

b) The Treaty on Basic Relations between Japan and South Korea

Finally, on 22 June 1965 South Korea and Japan, under pressure from the US government, signed the Treaty on Basic Relations.[276] Under Article II, it stated that 'all the treaties or agreements concluded between the Empire of Japan and the Empire of Korea on or before August 22, 1910 are already null and void'. Generally speaking, it provided the basis for peaceful mutual relations and did not address the questions of war and cultural heritage restitution and reparation. The main aim of these settlements was to provide economic assistance to Korea. Certain 'difficult' questions were not included in the treaty text. However, a separate agreement on cultural property[277] addressed the question of the repatriation of certain cultural objects removed during Japanese rule. Accordingly, under

[272] Treaty of Annexation between Korea and Japan, signed on 22 August 1910, entered into force on 29 August 1910, 212 Parry's CTS 43.

[273] For the history of looting and restitution of Korean cultural property, see Geoffrey R. Scott, 'Spoliation, Cultural Property, and Japan', *University of Pennsylvania Journal of International Law* 29(2007–08)4, 803–902.

[274] Ibid. 854.

[275] See Chapter 3, section 3.1.1.

[276] Treaty between Japan and Republic of Korea on Basic Relations, signed on 22 June 1965, 583 UNTS 33.

[277] The Agreement between the Republic of Korea and Japan Concerning Cultural Property and Exchange, signed on 22 June 1965, for the English translation of the agreement, see Scott, 'Spoliation, Cultural Property, and Japan' (n 273) 889–91.

Article II, Japan agreed to 'within six months after the validation of this Treaty, pursuant to the approved procedures, deliver the cultural properties listed in the enclosed document.' In fact, Japanese authorities handed over about 1400 cultural items to Korea, including celadon porcelain and old documents.[278]

Yet the number of repatriated objects was minuscule in light of the estimations conducted by South Korean historians, who identified tens of thousands of looted cultural items still retained in Japan. For South Korea, that set of returned cultural objects constituted only the first step in a broader restoration of lost cultural patrimony. Conversely, Japan, although agreeing to partial repatriation, considered all the appropriations and removals made after 1910 as lawful and consistent with the principles of international law. Consequently, the return of the negotiated objects closed any further negotiations and was treated as *ex gratia* gesture.[279] In the following years several returns were made to Korea by public and private persons from Japan, but always in the form of voluntary donations. For a long time, Japan was also extremely reluctant to ratify both the 1954 Hague Convention and the 1970 UNESCO Convention as it was afraid of potential claims from the former colonies and occupied territories.

c) The engagement of Japan in UNESCO activities

Changes in the official position of Japan, also with regard to the cultural heritage situated in the territory of North Korea—the Democratic People's Republic of Korea (DPRK)—began in the late 1980s. [280] In 1989 Japan created the Japanese Funds in Trust Program for the Preservation of the World Cultural Heritage, under the auspices of UNESCO.[281] In 2000, in collaboration with South Korea, Japan financially assisted the government of North Korea for the purposes of including the Complex of Koguryo Tombs situated near Pyongynang on the WHL.[282] The site was successfully inscribed on the WHL in 2004.

On 17 September 2002, Japan and North Korea signed the Pyongynang Declaration,[283] initiating peaceful collaboration between these states. North Korea claimed for the restitution and compensation for cultural losses during colonial rule (1910–45). By contrast, Japan argued that all Korean artefacts in Japanese collections had been acquired legally.[284] Finally, both states agreed that 'that establishing a fruitful political, economic and cultural relationship between

[278] Scott, 'Spoliation, Cultural Property, and Japan' (n 273) 857. [279] Ibid. 857.

[280] James Sterngold, 'South Korea Seeks Return of Its Artworks from Japan', *The New York Times*, 11 July 1991.

[281] The Japanese Funds-in-Trust for the Preservation of World Cultural Heritage, see: <http://www.unesco.emb-japan.go.jp/htm/mofaworld.htm>, accessed on 8 February 2015.

[282] Complex of Koguryo Tombs, available at: <http://whc.unesco.org/en/list/1091>, accessed on 8 February 2015.

[283] Available at: <http://www.mofa.go.jp/region/asia-paci/n_korea/pmv0209/pyongyang.html>, accessed on 8 February 2015.

[284] Eiji Yamamori, 'Smuggler's Blues: Japan Will Sign a Convention to Return Stolen Artifacts, but Cultural Affairs Officials Are Skeptical', *The Asahi Shimbum*, 22 November 2002.

Japan and the DPRK through the settlement of unfortunate past between them and the outstanding issues of concern would be consistent with the fundamental interests of both sides, and would greatly contribute to the peace and stability of the region'.[285] Moreover, they decided that 'they would sincerely discuss . . . the issue of cultural property'.[286] In the same year Japan also became to the 1970 UNESCO Convention and in 2007 to the 1954 Hague Convention.

The restoration of cultural heritage also enabled a more dynamic collaboration between both Korean states. In 2004, historians from the North and South Koreas issued a joint declaration in which they asked Japan to restore the cultural and historical treasures. At the same time, South Korea accelerated negotiations for the restitution of certain treasures removed by Japan from the present North Korean territory. This refers to the return of the Bukgwandaecheopbi monument, a stone pillar erected in 1707 in memory of a Korean admiral who had fought against the Japanese troops during the invasion at the end of sixteenth century. At the time of the Russo–Japan War of 1904–05, the monument was taken by the Japanese army. In the late 1970s it was rediscovered at the Yasukuni Shrine in Tokyo, a memorial dedicated to soldiers and other persons who died fighting on behalf of the Emperor of Japan, including the officers convicted for the commission of war crimes during the Second World War. An agreement was reached by South Korea and Japan that the monument would be returned on the occasion of the 60th anniversary of the end of the war.[287] It was shipped to South Korea in October 2005, where it was held for six months before being sent to North Korea. It is important to underline that the monument was not state property, therefore, the consent of the Yasukuni leaders was needed. On the basis of moral obligations they agreed to its restoration to the place of origin. The return of the Bukgwandaecheopbi monument cemented the cultural cooperation of both Korean states. This led to joint cultural programmes and museum art loans.[288]

In November 2010, Japan agreed to return to South Korea some 1200 royal documents Uigwa, protocols of the over 500-year-long Joseon Dynasty (1392–1910), depicting through prose and illustration the major ceremonies and rites of the royal family.[289] The decision was announced in the occasion of the Group of 20 summit in Seoul, when also France agreed to return, by a mean of renewable loan, nearly 300 Uigwe books and royal protocols, preserved in the National Library of France, which had been looted by French troops from Korea in 1866.[290] The actual handing over of the collection from Japan took place on 6 December 2011 during a special ceremony. It was reported that Japan perceived as a fulfilment of

[285] Japan–DPRK Pyongyang Declaration (n 283). [286] Ibid.

[287] Prabjat K. Mukherjee, 'Koh-I-Noor: The Mountain of Lights', *The Korea Times*, 15 December 2005.

[288] Scott, 'Spoliation, Cultural Property, and Japan' (n 273) 887.

[289] See, for example, Yoon Soyoung, 'Japan to return 1,205 Joseon books', Korea.Net, 10 November 2010, <http://www.korea.net/NewsFocus/Policies/view?articleId=83841>, accessed on 10 February 2015.

[290] Lee Kyong-hee. 'Joseon Royal Books Return Home after 145 Years in France' *Koreana*, Autumn 2011, 42–7.

its binding obligations under the 1965 agreement.[291] Yet as a matter of fact, the return appears rather an *ex gratia* gesture within the framework of bilateral cooperation and reconciliation between these two states in the light of the symbolic 100th anniversary of the 1910 Annexation Treaty.

The case of Japanese–Korean settlements demonstrated that the allocation of cultural property on the basis of general rules of international law is not satisfactory. According to the Japanese legal position, the 1910–45 annexation of Korea was lawful under the rules of international law in force at that time. Consequently, Japan was rightfully entitled to dispose the cultural property, by virtue of its sovereign capacity. On the other hand, both Korean states view the same period as a military occupation when territorial sovereignty was not transferred. Thus, all the removals and forced appropriations of cultural items were illegal. At this level, it seems that there is little place for a compromise solutions. However, in recent years, Japan has become involved in several UNESCO initiatives, and has started recognizing moral obligations towards colonized and occupied territories. In this way, some satisfactory solutions have been made without any change to the legal position of Japan towards the interpretation of past territorial transfers.

6.4.2 The case of the *Venus of Cyrene*

The return of the statue of the *Venus of Cyrene* was agreed by Italy and Libya pursuant to the 1998 Joint Declaration and the 2000 accords, followed by the deaccession decree of the Italian Ministry of Cultural Heritage and Activities of 2002. In November of the same year, an action for the annulment of this ministerial decree was brought before the Regional Administrative Tribunal of Lazio by Italia Nostra,[292] a non-governmental organization whose statutory objective is to advocate the protection of the artistic and historical heritage of the Italian nation. In its lawsuit, Italia Nostra claimed that the 2002 Decree was unlawful on the basis of three main arguments. First, the *Venus of Cyrene* was discovered on Italian territory, since in 1911 the Kingdom of Italy effectively established sovereignty over the territory concerned. Therefore, it constituted a part of Italian national heritage which could not be alienated by a mere administrative act but only through a special law. Second, the content of the 2002 Decree was contradictory: by claiming

[291] Yoshihiro Makino, 'Japan returns Korean royal archives after a century', *The Asahi Shinbun*, 8 December 2011, <http://ajw.asahi.com/article/asia/korean_peninsula/AJ201112080019a>, accessed on 7 February 2015.

[292] *Associazione Nazionale Italia Nostra Onlus v. Ministero per i Beni le Attività Culturali et al., Consiglio di Stato,* No. 3154, 23 June 2008, reproduced in *Guida al diritto-Il Sole 24 Ore* (2007)21, 91–99. Commented in: Alessandro Chechi, 'Customary Obligation to Return Cultural Property—Conventions on the Laws and Customs of War—Vienna Convention on Succession of States in Respect of State Property, Archives and Debts. Tribunale Amministrativo Regionale Del Lazio (Sez. II-Quarter), 28 February 2007, No. 3518 Associazione Nazionale Italia Nostra Onlus v. Ministero per i Beni e le Attività Culturali et al', *IYIL* 17(2007), 277–80.

a need to restore the statue to its original context it did not take into consideration that the statue of Roman and Hellenistic origin was more relevant to the Italian (European) artistic heritage, than to the Islamic one (the universality of the Cyrene UNESCO World Heritage site was not mentioned). Finally, the repatriation of the *Venus of Cyrene* would establish a precedent for further potential claims for the return of cultural objects brought against Italy.[293]

In 2007–08, the Italian administrative courts rejected this argumentation and the statue was finally shipped to Libya, and its return accompanied the conclusion of the Treaty between Italy and Libya on Friendship, Partnership and Cooperation. In this context, the reasoning of the Italian judicial bodies requires further comment.

a) The decision of 2007

In its decision of 28 February 2007, the Regional Administrative Tribunal of Lazio (TAR), rejected the claim of Italia Nostra and upheld the 2002 Decree. It explained that the *Venus of Cyrene* had been found and removed from the territory which in 1915 was not yet under Italian sovereignty. This was only transferred in 1923, on the basis of the 1923 Peace Treaty of Lausanne with Turkey. The removal of the statue was made for preservation purposes and Italy did not acquire its ownership. Such an appropriation during a military occupation was in violation of the Regulation annexed to the 1899 Hague Convention on Laws and Customs of War on Land,[294] confirmed by the Regulation annexed to the IV Hague Convention of 1907.[295] In fact, in 1915 both Italy and Turkey were parties to the 1899 Hague Convention,[296] which under Article 56 stated that 'all seizure of, and destruction, or intentional damage done to such institutions, to historical monuments, works of art or science, is prohibited, and should be made the subject of proceedings.' Therefore, Italy was obliged to return the statue.

The tribunal also held that the obligation of restitution derived from the bilateral agreements concluded with Libya in 1998 and 2000, and from two customary rules of international law: 1) the obligation to return to newly independent states the movable property removed from their territory before independence, as provided under Article 15 of the 1983 Vienna Convention; and 2) the obligation to restore the cultural property seized in time of war, as stated in both already mentioned conventions, several peace treaties and the 1954 Hague Convention. As the legal system of Italy conforms to the generally recognized principles of

[293] *Associazione Nazionale Italia Nostra* (n 292) 92–98.

[294] Hague Convention (II) with Respect to the Laws and Customs of War on Land with Annex, signed on 29 July 1899, entered into force 4 September 1900, UKTS 1 (1901).

[295] Hague Convention (IV) Respecting the Laws and Customs of War on Land, and Annex, signed on18 October 1907, entered in force 26 January 1910, UKTS 9 (1910).

[296] Tullio Scovazzi, *Diviser c'est d'étruire. Ethical Principles and Legal Rules in the Field of Return of Cultural Properties* (UNESCO, 2009), unpublished, at 16.

international law, under Article 10.1 of the Italian Constitution, such an obligation is self-executing.

The TAR then referred to the question of original context and the alleged lack of cultural links with an Islamic cultural environment. It stressed the importance of the territory of Libya in the history of the Roman Empire. Accordingly, it recalled the fact that several important Roman settlements are located in the territory of Libya (ie Sabrata, Leptis Magna), from which the Roman Emperor Septimus Severus also came. Moreover, it claimed that 'from the artistic point of view, the Alexandrian period (Hellenistic) was notoriously characterized by strong "internationalism", and by stylistic exchange between the elements of the oriental and western art, subsequently developed exactly by the Islamic art'.[297]

Finally, the tribunal pinpointed that the policy of restitution of cultural objects unlawfully seized in time of war would not lead to the impoverishment of Italian national patrimony. On the contrary, the case of the *Venus of Cyrene* could constitute an important precedent to strengthen the position of Italy in recovering cultural items illegally removed from its national territory.

The decision of the TAR met, however, with certain criticism in the Italian legal doctrine. First, the assertion that the *Venues of Cyrene* did not belong to the Italian cultural patrimony was found to be erroneous. This consisted in the argument that Italy had effectively established territorial sovereignty in Libya not on the basis of the 1923 Treaty of Lausanne, as asserted by the TAR, but on the basis of the 1912 Treaty of Ouchy. Such a conclusion was drawn from a systematic analysis of the treaties, the 1912 preliminary agreements, and the legal doctrine valid at the time.[298] Libya was not an occupied territory and the statue entered into state domain and could be rightfully removed. Consequently, there is no legal obligation for its restitution. Moreover, even if one accepted that Libya was under war occupation, this would provide an obligation for restitution with regard to Ottoman Turkey, but not in respect of Libya, who did not exist at the time of removal.[299] In addition, the TAR's ruling in this matter is contradictory since it affirms that the statue does not belong to the state, on the one hand, and confirms the 2002 Decree declassifying it from the state domain, on the other.[300] Second, the 1998 and 2000 agreements are 'mere "minute agreements" articulating the political and diplomatic commitments undertaken by the two states in order to disentangle the issues that were not settled after the end of the Italian colonization in 1943.'[301] Therefore, they could not produce any legally binding obligation on Italy analogous to those created in respect of Ethiopia under the 1947 Peace Treaty.[302] Moreover, the 2002 Decree did not produce any effects as to the alienation of the statue. Third, the TAR was wrong in recalling the 1954

297 *Associazione Nazionale Italia Nostra* (n 292) 99.

298 Natalino Ronzitti, 'Sugli obblighi di restituzione dell'Italia la sentenza amministrativa non convince', *Guida al diritto il Sole-24 Ore*, 26 May 2007, at 100.

299 Ibid. 103. 300 Ibid. 100.

301 Chechi, 'Customary Obligation to Return Cultural Property' (n 292) 279.

302 Ronzitti, 'Sugli obblighi di restituzione dell'Italia' (n 298) 103.

Hague Convention since, on the one hand, this deals with armed conflicts but not with colonial domination, and on the other, it cannot be retroactively applied.[303] Similarly, the 1983 Vienna Convention is applicable to this case because of two main considerations: 1) it does not deal with the issue of state succession to cultural property, and 2) there is a substantial difference between European practice of restitution of cultural items in cases of post-war peace treaties and territorial reconfigurations, and those concerning postcolonial processes.[304] However, the tribunal was right on the identification of the international legal custom progressively developed in the past 200 years, which consists in the return of cultural items seized and removed as a result of violent relations (war, occupation, colonization, etc).[305]

b) The decision of 2008

The TAR's decision of 2007 was appealed by Italia Nostra before the Italian Council of State (ICS). It maintained its previous argument that the art object in question had been found in Italian territory and was removed to Rome on the basis of the 1914 Royal Decree, vesting the title of all antiquities discovered in the colonies to the state. Next, it argued that the 1998 and 2000 agreements could not have legal effect on the alienation of state cultural property since they had not been properly ratified (ie not been passed by the parliament), and their implementation could not be conducted by a mere administrative decree. Finally, it questioned the TAR's decision in the part concerning the obligation of restitution on the basis of the application of the 1983 Vienna Convention (to which Italy is not party), and customary international law.

In the judgment of 23 June 2008,[306] the ICS confirmed the 2007 TAR ruling, stating that Italy was obliged to return the statue to Libya. As a result of this judgment the statue of the *Venus of Cyrene* was returned to Libya on 31 August 2008. The ICS held that the statue had not been found on the territory subject to Italian sovereignty, and expressed its view that the 1914 Royal Decree did not find application in this case. Moreover, it stated that the 2002 Decree was legitimate since it served as implementation of the already existing international obligations of Italy concerning the return of the *Venus of Cyrene*. Responding to Italia Nostra's arguments as to the applicability of the 1983 Vienna Convention and the relevance of the international regime of cultural property in time of war, the ICS held that 1) the ratification of the 1983 Vienna Convention is irrelevant as regards the customary international rule which sets forth the duty of the restitution of cultural property; and 2) similarly, the application of such a customary rule is not essentially conditioned by military occupation.

[303] Ibid. 103.

[304] Chechi, 'Customary Obligation to Return Cultural Property' (n 292) 280.

[305] Ibid. 280.

[306] *Associazione Nazionale Italia Nostra Onlus v. Ministero per i Beni le Attività Culturali et al., Consiglio di Stato*, No. 3154, 23 June 2008.

The ICS, however, went even further by stating that the customary rule sanctioning the restitution of cultural property did not merely derive from the treaty and conventional law on state succession to cultural property and the regime of laws of war. Accordingly, these were only the 'signs of the progressive formation of a general principle, abided by states in a continuous and ubiquitous manner, due to its binding character, autonomous from the implementation, ratification or adhesion to a treaty.' Moreover, the ICS continued that the obligation of restitution of cultural objects removed as a result of war or colonial domination was a 'corollary' of two general principles of international law: the prohibition of the use of force and the principle of self-determination of peoples. It explained that the principle of self-determination included identity and cultural patrimony linked to the territory of every sovereign state and linked, at the same time, to people subjected to foreign government. Consequently, from this principle derived the protection of cultural and territorial identity, which involved the obligation to return all cultural items removed by acts of war and the use of force.

The last part of the decision of the ICS is particularly interesting. The judgment clearly gave priority to international cultural heritage obligations over the provisions of domestic legislation.[307] Generally speaking, the existence of the customary rule of international law sanctioning the restitution of cultural material seized during war does not stimulate any particular controversies. However, the ICS's finding as to the existence of a customary rule imposing a duty to restore cultural items, derived from the principle of self-determination, left some perplexities. Although the application of such a principle can allegedly be discussed with reference to the post-First World War settlements in Europe, it does not seem to be proved in the post-colonial context. In fact, the right of formerly colonized peoples to the restoration of their lost cultural patrimony was confirmed on many occasions, but the international practice in this regard is very limited. By contrast, the legality of acquisitions of cultural treasures is constantly claimed by former colonial powers which do not intend to empty their national collections. Furthermore, the existence of a customary rule of international law ordering the restitution of cultural property appropriated and removed during the colonial period has been rejected by a considerable part of legal scholarship. Yet this does not mean that Libya, as the successor state, would not be entitled to the reintegration of its cultural treasures based on the rudimentary principle of territoriality. According to Article 1 of the Italo–Libyan agreement of 1956, both states expressed the intention to conclude a separate cultural agreement. Presumably, it would also cover the question of dispersed cultural property in a similar way as was regulated in parallel accords with Ethiopia.

It seems therefore that the 2008 ICS decision did not enforce an existing customary rule of international law as regards the allocation of cultural property following decolonization. Inversely, it was destined to support the foreign policy considerations of the Italian government. Arguably, it referred to the process of

[307] Scovazzi, *Diviser c'est d'étruire* (n 296) 17.

normalization of relations with Libya in the broader framework of economic and cultural cooperation. It also aimed to reinforce the position of Italy in parallel negotiations with other states and foreign museums in respect of the restoration of illicitly trafficked Italian cultural objects.

Nonetheless, the case of the *Venus of Cyrene* arguably embodies a number of current international tendencies in the settling of cultural heritage-related disputes following state succession, including decolonization. In the first place, the case largely concerns the concept of cultural reconciliation, comprising the broader recognition of the rights of formerly colonized peoples to their cultural heritage dispersed in the past. Accordingly, certain gestures of good will need to be expressed in order to put an end to a difficult past and to right historic wrongs. On the basis of such a turning point in mutual relations, states can initiate new friendly relations. The handing over of certain objects important for the cultural heritage of the other party is usually pursued in terms of a voluntary gift. However, in the case of the *Venus of Cyrene*, Italian administrative tribunals went much further, by invoking the obligation of restitution under customary international law. Second, the legal instruments concluded between Italy and Libya emphasized the procedural principle of international cooperation, including cultural cooperation. Indeed, this corresponds with current international practice, in which states tend to settle all potential disputes arising from past transfers and removals of cultural property within the framework of interstate accords on cultural cooperation rather than in succession agreements *sensu stricto*.[308] The objective of such arrangements lies in the accommodation of the various interests of states, including those of a scientific and cultural nature.

6.4.3 Post-colonial cultural cooperation: the case of the Netherlands–Indonesia shared heritage project

As discussed in Chapter 3, at the time of decolonization, the Netherlands and Indonesia had already begun the process of settlement of problems arising from the long history of the Dutch presence in East Indies. In fact, the outcome of these early bilateral negotiations between the Netherlands and Indonesia followed the principles of succession to state cultural property. However, the actual apportionment as well as the cooperation between cultural institutions proceeded very slowly. A new era began at the end of twentieth century within a series of shared-heritage initiatives, formally based on the provisions of the 1968 agreement on cultural cooperation.[309] In the early 2000s, Indonesia asked the Netherlands to exhibit collections which came from the former colonies of the East Indies. It argued that as they were 'stored in a foreign country', a wider Indonesian public

[308] Compare Chechi, 'The Return of Cultural Objects Removed' (n 13), 179–80.

[309] Agreement between the Netherlands and Indonesia on Cultural Co-Operation, signed on 7 July 1968, 739 UNTS 3.

did not have access them.[310] Apparently, this claim was perceived by Dutch officials as a first step undertaken towards a new round of difficult negotiations on the return of cultural property.[311] However, the usual mixed diplomatic commissions of experts was displaced by a joint project, the 'Shared Cultural Heritage' (SCH),[312] which considered matters beyond restitution and repatriation.

Launched (2004–07) by the National Museum of Ethnology (Rijksmuseum voor Volkenkunde) in Leiden (RVV) and the National Museum of Indonesia (Museum Nasional) in Jakarta,[313] this project had three main objectives.[314] The first consisted in capacity building and job training for staff at the National Museum of Indonesia. RVV staff helped in the planning of the new building, an extension of the National Museum in Jakarta, as well as in matters concerning conservation of artefacts. The second objective was the study of the history of the collections preserved in both museums. Accordingly, the collections were mostly formed and documented by the Batavian Society for Arts and Sciences (Bataviaasch Genootschap van Kunsten en Wetenschappen), a Dutch colonial learned society established in 1778 in Batavia (the former colonial name for Jakarta). Since 1868 the collections were stored in a new museum and library building in the centre of Jakarta (Het museum van het Koninklijk Bataviaasch Genootschap van Kunsten en Wetenschappen). Over time, many objects were transferred to the Netherlands and stored in the RVV in Leiden. Others remained in Jakarta in the former museum. Hence, the project sought to reconstruct the history of collecting in the region, and study the division of artefacts between the different museums. The Batavian Society for Arts and Sciences provided a rich archive of historical material. Finally, the third objective of the project was to exhibit newly 'reunified' collections in both countries.

In fact, as a result of the initiatives undertaken within the framework of the SCH a new modern wing, the Gedung Arca (Statue Building) of the National Museum in Jakarta, was opened in 2007. A number of research projects was also begun.[315] Perhaps most importantly, two large joint exhibitions of the Indonesian

[310] Endang Sri Hardiati and Pieter ter Keurs (eds), *Indonesia: the Discovery of the Past* (Kit Publischers, 2005), 7.

[311] Cynthia Scott, 'Sharing the Divisions of the Colonial Past: an Assessment of the Netherlands–Indonesia Shared Cultural Project, 2003–2006', *International Journal of Heritage Studies* 18(2012)1, 1–15, at 1.

[312] <http://www.culturalheritageconnections.org/wiki/Shared_Cultural_Heritage>, accessed on 15 January 2015.

[313] The project 'Shared Cultural Heritage' was funded by the Netherlands Culture Fund, the National Museum of Ethnology in Leiden, and the Indonesian Ministry for Culture and Tourism and by private sponsor, KLM Cargo. A follow-up project, under the name 'The New Museum', referring to the new building of the Museum National in Jakarta was launched in 2007 and lasted until mid-2010. After Pieter ter Keurs, 'Collecting in the Colony: Hybridity, Power and Prestige in the Netherlands East Indies', *Indonesia and the Malay World* 37(2009)108, 147–61, at 148.

[314] Pieter ter Keurs, 'A Tale of Two Museums Indonesia: The Discovery of the Past', *The Newsletter of the International Institute for Asian Studies* (2005)39, 35, available at: <http://www.iias.nl/nl/39/IIAS_NL39_35.pdf> accessed on 15 January 2015.

[315] See *inter alia* Pieter ter Keurs (eds), *Colonial Collections Revisited* (Research School CNWS, 2007).

artefacts took place at the National Museum in Jakarta (15 August–13 November 2005) and in the New Church (Nieuwe Kerk) in Amsterdam (15 December 2005–17 April 2006). In fact, the RVV and the National Museum in Jakarta preserved the largest collections of Indonesian artefacts, and thanks to the SCH project, the most significant pieces from both institutions were exhibited together to Dutch and Indonesian public. Cooperation between museums in the Netherlands and Indonesia, initiated by the SCH project, continues to this day.[316]

The outcomes of the project have been widely esteemed for overcoming 'the usual duality of heritage not only by acknowledging the material objects as the heritage of both countries, but by deeming the historical understandings that arose in relation to the objects as more meaningful than bare material possession'.[317] Furthermore, this was achieved 'by the sharing of not only the material objects, but of how to narrate the past as well'.[318] However, it needs to be stressed that such a novel model for overcoming the colonial past in the area of cultural heritage cannot replace or hinder the rights of formerly colonized peoples, deprived of their most important objects of cultural heritage, to claim their effective permanent enjoyment and access to them.

6.5 State succession and world heritage

This chapter now turns to the status of international obligations towards mankind's cultural heritage following state succession. These obligations call for the respect, safeguarding, and conservation of cultural heritage as part of the general interest of the international community and its joint commitment towards future generations.[319] The application of this principle within the framework of state succession lies in three different areas: 1) the obligation to protect world heritage sites during the violent state succession process; 2) the obligation to conserve world heritage overriding national interests in disputes relating to cultural property following state succession; 3) the joint concern and duty of successor states to cooperate to preserve and manage their common heritage within the framework of the World Heritage Convention.

As regards the first concern, recent international practice has shown that acts committed against cultural sites of great importance to humanity are fully prohibited under customary law. The ICTY decision in *Strugar* concerning the intentional bombardments of the Old City of Dubrovnik[320] has been paramount. The protected status of world heritage sites has also been applied with reference to the medieval monasteries of the Serbian Orthodox Church in Kosovo endangered by

[316] <http://www.heritage-activities.nl/themes/mutual-cultural-heritage/resource-centre/indonesia/theme-museum-cooperation>, accessed on 12 January 2015.

[317] Scott, 'Sharing the Divisions' (n 311) 11.

[318] Ibid.

[319] Scovazzi, 'La notion de patrimoine culturel de l'humanité' (n 26) 140–44.

[320] *Prosecutor v. Strugar*, Case No. IT-01-42-T, Judgment of 31 January 2005, affirmed by the Appellate Chamber, 17 July 2008.

ethnic fighting there. Accordingly, in 2004, at the behest of Serbia–Montenegro, the UNESCO WHC inscribed the fourteenth-century Dečani Monastery, representing an exceptional synthesis of Byzantine and Western medieval traditions, on the WHL.[321] In 2006, the WHC extended the properties inscribed on the WHL[322] by adding two other monasteries and one church.[323] In doing this, the Committee requested that Serbia and the provisional international administration of Kosovo undertake adequate legislative and technical measures to protect and conserve the properties in question. In the same decision and in light of the ongoing acts against these monuments, the WCH decided to inscribe the Medieval Monuments in Kosovo on the List of World Heritage in Danger, on which they still remain to date.

A significant application of the world heritage regime can be observed in respect of the Old Bridge of Mostar in Bosnia—Herzegovina.[324] The bridge was erected in the mid-sixteenth century by the order of the Ottoman Sultan, Suleiman the Magnificent, and because of its beauty and the extraordinary technical skills harnessed in its construction, it was for a long time considered as the greatest architectural work of the epoch. Moreover, as the bridge connected the banks of the Neretva river, uniting different parts of the city, it also symbolized the peaceful coexistence of the multi-ethnic and multi-religious society of Mostar.[325] During the military conflict in this country following the breakup of Yugoslavia in 1993, the historical centre of the city of Mostar was heavily damaged, and the bridge destroyed. This profoundly disrupted the local communities and was widely criticized as 'an attack against the values cherished by the international community'.[326] Thus, after the 1995 Dayton Agreement, extensive works on the reconstruction of the city and the Old Bridge were initiated under the auspices of the European Union Administration of Mostar (EUAM),[327] perceived as essential for peace to be restored in Bosnia–Herzegovina. Several international organizations, including UNESCO, formed a coalition to oversee the reconstruction of the Old Bridge and the historic city centre of Mostar.[328] This ambitious international project was initiated in 1999 and mostly completed by spring of 2004.[329] After the official reopening of the reconstructed Old Bridge in 2004, the government of Bosnia–Herzegovina presented to the UNESCO WHC a motion to inscribe the Old Bridge Area of the Old City of Mostar on the WHL. In the Nomination

[321] UNESCO Doc. WHC-04/28 COM/26, 43–44.

[322] UNESCO Doc. WHC-06/30.COM/19, 155–58.

[323] Patriarchate of Peć Monastery, Gračanica Monastery, and the Church of the Virgin of Ljeviša.

[324] For the extensive analysis of the case, see Jadranka Petrovic, *The Old Bridge of Mostar and Increasing Respect for Cultural Property in Armed Conflict* (Nijhoff, 2013).

[325] Kaia Kathryn Nordtvedt, *Old Bridge in Mostar: A Bridge between Muslims and Croats?* (McGill University, 2006), 10.

[326] Petrovic, *The Old Bridge of Mostar* (n 324) 86.

[327] See John R. Yarwood (eds), *Rebuilding Mostar: Urban Reconstruction in a War Zone* (Liverpool University Press, 1999), at 1.

[328] Maha Armaly, Carlo Blasi, and Lawrence Hannah, 'Stari Most: Rebuilding More Than a Historic Bridge in Mostar', *Museum International* 56(2004)4, 6–17.

[329] Ibid.

Dossier, it argued that the proposed cultural site constitutes the 'essence of country's long cultural continuity is represented by the universal synthesis of life phenomena: the bridge and its fortress—with the rich archaeological layers from pre-Ottoman period, religious edifices, residential zones—mahalas, arable lands, houses, bazaar, its public life in the streets and water.' Moreover, the 'architecture here presented a symbol of tolerance... mosques, churches, and synagogues existed side-by-side indicating that in Bosnia, the Roman Catholic Croats with their Western European culture, the eastern Orthodox Serbs with their elements of Byzantine culture, and the Sephardic Jews continued to live together with the Bosniak-Muslims for more than four centuries'.[330]

The UNESCO WHC recognized this and decided to inscribe the Old Bridge Area of the Old City of Mostar on the WHL.[331] It held that 'with the "renaissance" of the Old Bridge and its surroundings, the symbolic power and meaning of the City of Mostar—as an exceptional and universal symbol of coexistence of communities from diverse cultural, ethnic and religious backgrounds—has been reinforced and strengthened, underlining the unlimited efforts of human solidarity for peace and powerful co-operation in the face of overwhelming catastrophes.' Thus, it appears that the general interest of the international community in preserving world heritage has also been extended to include the common concern in reconstructing destroyed monuments for the benefit of local communities and humanity as a whole. Sadly, the high expectations of the international community that this would cement the peace have not yet been met. Many Bosnian Croats see the bridge as an imposed (artificial) symbol, glorifying Muslim domination over the central parts of the city, rather than expressing the multicultural identity of modern-day Bosnia.[332]

After the failure of the UN plan for the internationalization of the City of Jerusalem and its Holy Places, the question of these sites of great importance to humanity as a whole returned in the framework of the activity of the UNESCO WHC. In 1981 Jordan, which oversaw Muslim sites in Jerusalem since 1967, issued a proposal to inscribe the Old City of Jerusalem on the WHL. It was agreed, however, that this motion could not be taken into consideration since it could be treated as registering political or sovereign claims to the city. Thus in 1982, the World Heritage Committee inscribed the Old City of Jerusalem and its Walls on the List of World Heritage in Danger because of the deteriorating situation of the religious monuments[333] in the light of the ongoing Israeli–Palestinian conflict, as well as extensive excavations conducted by Israel at the Temple Mount, one of the most important religious sites in the Old City of Jerusalem.[334]

[330] Bosnia and Herzegovina, Nomination Dossier 'The Old City of Mostar', January 2005, at 5, <http://whc.unesco.org/en/list/946/documents>, accessed on 31 January 2015.

[331] UNESCO Doc. WHC-05/29.COM/22, AT 140–41.

[332] Scott A. Bollens, *Cities, Nationalism and Democratization* (Routledge, 2007), 188–89.

[333] UNESCO Doc. CLT-82/CH/CONF.015/8.

[334] See Anwar Abu Eisheh, 'The Protection of Heritage and Holy Sites in International Law: A Palestinian Perspective', in Marshal J. Breger, Yitzhak Reiter, and Leonard Hammer (eds), *Sacred Space in Israel and Palestine* (Routledge, 2012), 66–81, at 78–79.

In 2001, the UNESCO Director General announced the drafting of a comprehensive plan of action to safeguard the cultural heritage of the Old City of Jerusalem.[335] At its 32nd Session, following the decisions of the WHC in respect of the Plan of Action for the protection of the Palestinian heritage,[336] the General Conference invited the Director General 'as soon as possible' to set up the guidelines for this plan and the proposals for its implementation.[337] In subsequent years, a number of projects on the conservation of cultural heritage have been pursued in Eastern Jerusalem, supported by Italian and Spanish state funds.

In this context, one should recall the 'Holy Sites Project' launched in 2002 by the International Human Rights Institute of the DePaul University College of Law. This led to the formulation of the 'Principles Respecting the Holy Sites' (HSP).[338] The major concern of the HSP was to provide for peaceful relations based on the freedom of worship and cooperation between 'Jews, Christians, and Muslims throughout the region and the world.'[339] Accordingly, the proposed legal regime governing the situation in the Old City was that of the 'Common Heritage of Mankind',[340] notwithstanding the fact that the legal framework under the 1972 World Heritage Convention 'is not comprehensive and remains subject to further negotiation.'[341] It was suggested that this regime would, however, provide 'some legal guidance and suggestions on how to proceed, including, for example, the possibility of providing financial support to site maintenance that may provide incentives for the parties to participate'.[342]

Notwithstanding various initiatives undertaken by religious communities in Jerusalem and beyond,[343] the Holy Places are located at the very centre of the regional political conflict, and never more so since the declaration of independence of the State of Palestine in 2011. Moreover, after its admission to UNESCO, Palestine begin using this forum to address political issues in its relations with Israel. The status of the Holy Places thus continues to be politicized and their protection are subject to the fluctuations of the conflict between Palestine and Israel. The WHC has decided to retain the Old City of Jerusalem and its Walls on the List of World Heritage in Danger on many occasions. In addition, in 2012, Palestine succeeded in inscribing the birthplace of Jesus, the Church of the Nativity, and Bethlehem's pilgrimage route on the WHL.[344] These are also on the List of World Heritage in Danger due to the years of neglect and damage suffered in result of fights between Palestinian and Israeli forces. It needs to be stressed, however, that there is no doubt that both Israel and the new State of Palestine have obligations towards

[335] UNESCO Doc. 31C/24, para. 8.25.

[336] UNESCO Doc. WHC-03/27.COM/INF.5. [337] UNESCO Doc. 31 C/Res. 31.

[338] David E. Guinn, *Protecting Jerusalem's Holy Sites. A Strategy for Negotiating a Sacred Peace* (CUP, 2006), at 191–95, appendix 1.

[339] Ibid. 191. [340] Ibid. 194. [341] Ibid. 104–105. [342] Ibid.

[343] Sharon Rosen, 'The Importance of Interfaith Cooperation for the Protection of Jerusalem's Holy Sites, in Marshal J. Breger, Yitzhak Reiter, and Leonard Hammer (eds), *Sacred Space in Israel and Palestine* (Routledge, 2012), 251–83.

[344] <http://whc.unesco.org/en/list/1433>, accessed on 31 January 2015.

the international community to protect and safeguard these extraordinary world heritage sites.

The second application of the world heritage regime in state succession concerns the obligation to conserve such cultural sites, which overrides national interests in disputes over cultural property. In this regard, it is worth mentioning two cases where Italy solved the question of the allocation of cultural property displaced during its colonial rule in Africa. The first refers to the already discussed case of the *Venus of Cyrene*. Arguably, the return of this artefact ought to be associated with the application of the principle of the protection of the integrity of the cultural heritage of outstanding universal value. The fact that the archaeological site of Cyrene forms part of world heritage has been key for interstate negotiations regarding the allocation of cultural material excavated in this area. Indeed, the return of the artefact to its place of origin can be seen as a contribution of Italy, the former colonial power, to the safeguarding and conservation of the sites of great importance to all humanity.

The other case concerns Italy's return and erection of the Axum obelisk to Ethiopia. As mentioned in Chapter 3, the question of the return of the Axum monument has been a significant factor in the relations between Italy and Ethiopia since the conclusion of the 1947 Peace Treaty. In the meantime, the ruins of the city of Axum, including monolithic obelisks, giant stelae, royal tombs, and the ruins of ancient castles, dating from between the first and thirteenth centuries AD, were inscribed on the WHL (1980).[345] Finally, on the basis of the 1997 and 2004 agreements Italy agreed to transport and erect the obelisk in its place of origin. With UNESCO participation and financed by Italy, works were conducted in 2007–2008,[346] and on 4 September 2008 the ceremony of inauguration was held. It is important to note that the restoration of the monument enhanced its condition since at the date of the removal in 1937 the obelisk was broken into five pieces. The reconstruction can arguably be perceived as 'a sort of reparation for the delayed return.'[347]

Although the case of the Axum obelisk mainly refers to the question of restitution of cultural material removed as a result of war plunder, it also represents an attempt to compensate the cultural losses caused to former colonial territories by an imperial power. Even more important is the full application of the principle of international cooperation, with the additional engagement of UNESCO, in the matter of conserving the integrity of a world heritage site, driven by the general interest of the international community as a whole.

The last issue in this section refers to the joint concern and duty of successor states to cooperate to preserve and manage their common heritage within the framework of the World Heritage Convention. As already noted, the post-Cold War practice of state succession in respect of tangible cultural heritage also considered the situation of immovable cultural property of great importance to more

[345] Aksum World Heritage Site, <http://whc.unesco.org/en/list/15>, accessed on 5 February 2015.
[346] Scovazzi, *Diviser c'est d'étruire* (n 296) 13. [347] Ibid. 14.

than one successor state. For instance, Poland, Germany, Ukraine, and Belarus now cooperate in order to inscribe such cultural sites on the WHL. To a certain extent, they also apply different forms of joint management in cases of borderline sites, and joint research and conservation programs in respect of other cultural heritage sites.

This tendency is also followed in the post-colonial context. As mentioned in Chapter 3, in 1950 the newly independent state of Cambodia had to take on neighbouring Kingdom of Thailand in the matter of the Khmer temple of Preah Vihear which had great emotional and national value for both states. As one of the successor states of French Indochina, Cambodia acquired sovereignty over the territory of the temple. Following the 1962 ICJ judgment, the claims of Thailand were rejected and the Temple remained in the territory of Cambodia. However, it appears that the cultural objects removed by the Thai troops after Cambodia's independence were not surrendered, notwithstanding a reconciliation of sorts between both states.[348] Moreover, the dispute over the area around the Temple continued during the civil war and during the Khmer Rouge regime in Cambodia.

Following international peace efforts in Cambodia, the cultural site of Preah Vihear was eventually opened from the Thai side in 1998, and from the Cambodian side in 2003. But what was the status of the site and who would look after its conservation?[349] Cambodia proposed listing the Temple on the WHL. Thailand opposed, claiming that the nomination should have been presented by both states concerned. Finally, at the 31st WHC meeting in 2007,[350] Cambodia and Thailand were 'in full agreement that the Sacred Site of the Temple of Preah Vihear' had 'outstanding universal value' and 'must be inscribed on the World Heritage List as soon as possible.' They agreed that at the 32nd WHC session in 2008, Cambodia, fully supported by Thailand, would propose the inscription of the site. Furthermore they committed themselves to cooperate and to provide adequate measures for its protection.[351] In these circumstances, the WHC recommended the site for inscription.[352]

It seemed that the joint action of both states concerned, coupled with the universal World Heritage regime, would lead to the access, protection, and study of the sacred cultural site. However, Thailand viewed the delimitation of the protected area as controversial and it withdrew its support for inscription on the WHL. Nevertheless, the WHC inscribed the Temple in 2008, encouraging 'Cambodia to collaborate with Thailand for safeguarding the value of the property, in view of the fact that peoples of the surrounding region have long treasured the Temple of Preah Vihear.'[353]

[348] Peaceful Overture Led in Cambodia at Disputed Shrine; Reconciliation Invited, *New York Times*, 8 January 1963.

[349] Peter Cuasay, 'Borders on the Fantastic: Mimesis, Violence, and Landscape at the Temple of Preah Vihear', *Modern Asian Studies* 32(1998)4, 887–88.

[350] UNESCO Doc. WHC-07/31.COM/24, at 154.

[351] Ibid.

[352] WHC Decision 31COM 8b.24—Nomination of Natural, Mixed and Cultural Properties to the World Heritage List—the Temple of Preah Vihear, UNESCO Doc. WHC-07/31. COM/8B, at 16.

[353] WHC Decision 32 COM 8b102—Examination of Nominations—Sacred Site of the Temple of Preah Vihear (Cambodia), UNESCO Doc. Whc-08/32.Com/24, at 220–21.

Inscription on the WHL led to further tensions between both states, preventing access and the application of proper protection measures. In this context, international law experts claimed that Cambodia and Thailand shall agree on an 'international peace park', managed by a joint commission. This would 'provide security in the disputed area, and, in close cooperation with the World Heritage Committee, provide overall administration for a larger area reasonably related to the temple compound. In this way both countries could immediately begin to benefit from a site which, historically, has been considered sacred to the people on both sides and one without borders'.[354] The nature of world heritage obligations has been recently recalled by the ICJ in the judgment of the case concerning the *Request for Interpretation of the Judgment of 15 June 1962 in the Case concerning the Temple of Preah Vihear*, rendered on 11 November 2013.[355] The court held that the 1962 Judgment decided that Cambodia had sovereignty over the whole territory of the promontory of Preah Vihear and thus Thailand was required 'to withdraw from that territory the Thai military or police forces, or other guards or keepers, that were stationed there'.[356] However, it emphasized that 'the Temple of Preah Vihear is a site of religious and cultural significance for the peoples of the region and is now listed by UNESCO as a world heritage site'.[357] In this respect, the Court recalled that 'under Article 6 of the World Heritage Convention, to which both States are parties, Cambodia and Thailand must co-operate between themselves and with the international community in the protection of the site as a world heritage'.[358] The ICJ also remained that 'each State is under an obligation not to "take any deliberate measures which might damage directly or indirectly" such heritage'. In the context of these obligations, the Court emphasized 'the importance of ensuring access to the Temple from the Cambodian plain'.[359]

6.6 State succession to underwater cultural heritage

The protection of underwater cultural heritage affects a variety of interests and rights, but under international law, the notion of underwater cultural heritage remains very broad. Article 1(a) of the 2001 UNESCO Convention, defines it as 'all traces of human existence having a cultural, historical or archaeological character which have been partially or totally under water, periodically or continuously, for at least 100 years such as: (i) sites, structures, buildings, artefacts and human remains, together with their archaeological and natural context; (ii) vessels, aircraft, other vehicles or any part thereof, their cargo or other contents, together with their archaeological and natural context; and (iii) objects of prehistoric character'. According to this notion 'pipelines and cables' and 'installations

[354] William Roth, 'Temple Dispute: A Way out of the Impasse. Preah Vihear', *Bangkok Post*, 22 July 2008.

[355] *Request for Interpretation of the Judgment of 15 June 1962 in the Case Concerning the Temple of Preah Vihear (Cambodia v. Thailand)*, Judgment of 11 November 2013, ICJ Reports 2013, 281.

[356] Ibid. at 36, para. 107. [357] Ibid. at para. 106. [358] Ibid. [359] Ibid.

other than pipelines and cables' which are 'placed on the seabed shall not be considered as underwater cultural heritage' (Article 1 (b)(c)). Similarly, the European Convention on the Protection of the Archaeological Heritage[360] defines such heritage as 'structures, constructions, groups of buildings, developed sites, moveable objects, monuments of other kinds as well as their context' (Article 1(3)). Finally, the UN Convention on the Law of the Sea (UNCLOS) refers to 'objects of an archaeological and historical nature' (Articles 149 and 303(1)).

Arguably, the most controversial category concerns vessels and aircrafts comprising their cargo or other contents since the status of such material raises a number of questions as to their ownership, allocation, and protection. The balancing of these interests and rights has been solved differently under national legislation, UNCLOS, and the 2001 UNESCO Convention. However, the recent practice of domestic courts has shown that the principles of international law with regard to such heritage are being gradually enforced.[361]

For the purposes of the analysis undertaken in this book, the fundamental question concerns the application of the rules on state succession with regard to underwater state cultural property, such as sunken wrecks of military and other government-owned (or operated) vessels as well as their contents, in light of the rules concerning the protection of underwater cultural heritage. In fact, new methods of exploration of the sea and seabed reveal the importance of the issue to whom such properties belong. On the one hand, such wrecks may contain materials and information of a highly sensitive political nature. On the other, the wrecks themselves as well as their contents may constitute objects of historical, archaeological, and often material (monetary) significance. Moreover, they are usually the burial sites of human beings. Accordingly, the following issues are to be discussed: 1) the status of sunken state vessels under international law; 2) the rights of flag states and their successors *vis-à-vis* the rights of other states (or countries) having a cultural, historical, and archaeological interest in the cargo or other content; 3) the determination of the title to sunken state vessels and enforcement of the interest of all humanity in protecting underwater cultural heritage.

6.6.1 Special status and title to sunken military or other government-owned vessels

Military and other vessels, used for governmental non-commercial purposes, enjoy a special status in international law, both conventional and customary. In fact, as long as they are used for state governmental non-commercial purposes they and their cargo are protected under the regime of sovereign immunity. This is confirmed by a number of treaties on the international law of the sea.[362] Furthermore, such status

[360] European Convention on the Protection of the Archaeological Heritage (Revised), concluded at Valletta on 16 January 1992, entered into force 25 May 1995, 1966 UNTS 305.

[361] See Vigni, 'The Enforcement of Underwater Cultural Heritage' (n 99) 125–49.

[362] See *inter alia* Arts 8(1) and 9 of the Geneva Convention on the High Seas, done on 29 April 1958, entered in force on 30 September 1962, 450 UNTS 82; Art. 22 of the Geneva Convention on the Territorial Sea and Contiguous Zone, done on 29 April 1958, entered into force on 10

is also granted to state vessels under the law of state immunity. For instance, the 2004 United Nations Convention on Jurisdictional Immunities of States and Their Property[363] under Article 16 confirms the immunity from jurisdiction of a foreign state in relation to its 'warships, or naval auxiliaries' or 'other vessels owned or operated by a state and used, for the time being, only on government non-commercial service'. The same also applies to the cargo on the board of such ships.[364] Moreover, such vessels are excluded from the scope of other maritime law treaties, comprising the 1989 International Maritime Organization Convention on Salvage.[365]

Although there is no doubt that under general international law state vessels used for government non-commercial purposes are fully protected by sovereign immunity—that is, are exempted from jurisdiction and enforcement measures of other states—the issue becomes more complex when it comes to sunken state vessels.[366] In this regard, the question arises as to whether such wrecks can be still classified as state vessels and thus are protected under the rules of international law.[367] Accordingly, both the regime on the law of the sea and that on sovereign immunity do not explicitly grant immunity to sunken warships and other state-owned vessels operated for non-commercial purposes. This legal vacuum relates to the fact that sunken vessels are clearly no longer navigable and thus cannot perform their inherent functions.[368] The state practice in respect of granting sovereign immunity to such wrecks for the governmental purposes they exercise is marked by inconsistency.[369] However, if even a government-owned sunken vessel 'loses its immunity' in this regard, 'it does not mean that the flag State loses its ownership.'[370] In fact, 'the flag State retains the ownership unless the title to a sunken vessel has been lost in other circumstances, such as abandonment'.[371]

September 1964, 516 UNTS 205; Art. 32 of UNCLOS; Art. 3 of the International Convention for the Unification of Certain Rules concerning the Immunity of State-Owned Vessels, signed on 10 April 1926, entered into force on 8 January 1937, 176 LNTS 199.

363 Adopted on 2 December 2004, not in force, UN Doc. A/59/508; 44 *ILM* 803.

364 See further Douglas Guilfoyle, 'Article 16', in Roger O'Keefe and Christian J. Tams (eds), *The United Nations Convention on Jurisdictional Immunities of States and Their Property: A Commentary* (OUP, 2013), 259–76.

365 International Convention on Salvage, concluded on 28 April 1989, entered into force 14 July 1996, 1953 UNTS 165; see Art. 4(1).

366 See a comprehensive analysis by Natalino Ronzitti, Rapporteur, 'The Legal Regime of Wrecks of Warships and Other State-owned Ships in International Law', ILL, 9th Commission, Rhodes Session, 2011, *Yearbook of Institute of International Law* 74(2011), 131–77; available at: <http://www.idi-iil.org/idiE/navig_ann_2011.html>, accessed on 5 February 2015.

367 Ibid. at 142 ff., Dromgoole, *Underwater Cultural Heritage* (n 91) 135–38; Valentina Vadi, 'International Law and the Uncertain Fate of Military Sunken Vessels', *IYIL* 19(2009), 253–77, at 261.

368 Djamchid Momtaz, 'La Convention sur la protection du patrimoine culturel subaquatique', in Tafsir M. Ndiaye and Rüdiger Wolfrum (eds), *Law of the Sea, Environmental Law and Settlement of Disputes: Liber Amicorum Judge Thomas A. Mersah* (Nijhoff, 2007), 443–46, at 460; Jean Pierre Beurier, 'Pour un droit international de l'archéologie sous-marine', *RGDIP* 93(1989)1, 45–68, at 60.

369 See Dromgoole, *Underwater Cultural Heritage* (n 91) 139–46; compare Vigni, 'The Enforcement of Underwater Cultural Heritage' (n 99) 129–30, 152–53.

370 Ronzitti, 'The Legal Regime of Wrecks of Warships' (n 366) 143–44.

371 Ibid. 144.

Moreover, under the regime of sovereign immunity, state-owned property used for non-commercial governmental purposes enjoys protection both from jurisdiction and any measures of constraint.[372] Apart from that, certain objects transported on the board of warship could serve for diplomatic purposes of the flag state (diplomatic bags), as defined by Article 27 of the Vienna Convention on Diplomatic Relations.[373] Arguably, they may still enjoy the same status of inviolability after sinking.[374]

Clearly, the problems just cited as well as the location of a sunken vessel may raise a number of complex questions as to the jurisdiction over this wreck and its contents. Regardless of jurisdictional considerations, it needs to be stressed that in practice maritime powers[375] generally assert their property rights to their sunken warships and other government-owned vessels wherever they are found. Importantly, 'the very concept' of such rights 'is not limited in time, but tends to perpetuity'.[376] Thus, as long as the flag state exists, its title to sunken state vessels is not extinguished. Consequently, it is also argued that 'in case of the flag State extinction the rules on State succession on moveable public property apply for determining to whom the wreck belongs'.[377] In fact, this interpretation of succession rules in respect of sunken warships finds its confirmation in domestic jurisprudence. For instance, in 1991 in the judgment concerning the title to a bell from the *C.S.S. ALABAMA*, a Confederate cruiser sunk in 1864 off the coast of Normandy by a warship of the Union, the US District Court for the District of New Jersey held that this item was the property of the United States by capture of an enemy property, on the one hand, and by succession, on the other.[378] The US Court of Appeals for the Third Circuit upheld this judgment. Moreover, it ruled that the US government had a valid claim of ownership based on the doctrine of succession and that, as it had never abandoned its title to the warship in question.[379] Accordingly, since the USA was the sole successor of the Confederate States of America, it was entitled to the governmental property of the latter recovered from the sunken military vessel.

[372] Ibid. 144–45.

[373] Signed on 18 April 1961, entered into force on 24 April 1964, 500 UNTS 95.

[374] Ronzitti, 'The Legal Regime of Wrecks of Warships' (n 366) 144–45.

[375] For the overview of the state practice in question, see ibid. 145–52, Dromgoole, *Underwater Cultural Heritage* (n 91) 146–52; Sarah Dromgoole (ed), *The Protection of Underwater Cultural Heritage: National Perspectives in Light of the Unesco Convention 2001* (2nd edn, Nijhoff, 2006); Vadi, 'International Law and the Uncertain Fate' (n 367) 261–69; Jerry E. Walker, ą Contemporary Standard for Determining Title to Sunken Warships: A Tale of Two Vessels and Two Nations', *University of San Francisco Maritime Law Journal* 12(1999–2000)2, 311–58.

[376] Vadi, 'International Law and the Uncertain Fate' (n 367) 261.

[377] Ronzitti, 'The Legal Regime of Wrecks of Warships' (n 366) 144.

[378] *United States v. Steinmetz*, 763 F. Supp. 1293, 1297, 1991 AMC 2099, 2105 (D.N.J. 1991); see further William, J. Pallas, 'Doctrine of State Succession and the Law of Historic Shipwrecks, the Bell of the Alabama: United States v. Steinmetz', *Tulane Maritime Law Journal* 17(1992–93), 343–52.

[379] 973 F.2d 212, 1992 AMC 2879 (3d Cir. 1992).

6.6.2 Rights of other states (or countries) having a cultural, historical, and archaeological interest in the cargo or other content

The argument that the general regime on state succession to state moveable property shall determine the title to sunken warships or other state vessels constitutes a logical consequence of the retention of property rights to such material by state sovereigns, despite the event of sinking. However, the determination of the title to these objects by mere state continuity or succession of property rights does not fully settle the issues related to such material, that is, its cultural nature and significance.[380]

For centuries state ships have been used to transport a variety of goods, including cultural objects, which may have cultural, historic, or archaeological links with other states, countries, or human communities. Indeed, such objects constituted very often war booty or were otherwise displaced from the human communities who had created and/or enjoyed them. Thus, the question of the enforcement of such rights and interests has been constantly raised. In fact, as already mentioned, Article 149 of UNCLOS provides for 'preferential rights' of 'the state or country of origin, or the state of cultural origin, or the state of historical and archaeological origin' of 'all objects of an archaeological and historical nature found in the Area', that is, beyond the limits of national jurisdiction. However, the determination of cultural, historical, and archaeological origin of the vast majority of objects of underwater cultural heritage may give raise to inextricable contradictions. In this regard, the above-cited provisions do not clarify which state or countries shall be preferred, nor how such preference shall be implemented.[381]

The issue of the determination of such conflicting rights have been already subject to a number of international disputes and judicial litigations.[382] In this regard, the best known and arguably most emblematic case concerned the rights to the wreck and the content of the *Nuestra Señora de las Mercedes*, a Spanish vessel that sank at the beginning of the nineteenth century. The discovery of the wreck was announced in 2007 by a private salvage company, Odyssey Marine Exploration, Inc. (Odyssey). The wreck, initially nicknamed *Black Swan*, contained 17 tonnes of gold and silver coins (with an estimated value of US$600 million) and a number of artefacts.[383] The treasures were recovered and transported to the US. There,

[380] Patrizia Vigni, 'Historic Shipwrecks and the Limits of the Flag State Exclusive Rights', in Silvia Borelli and Federico Lenzerini (eds), *Cultural Heritage, Cultural Rights, Cultural Diversity. New Developments in International Law* (Nijhoff, 2012), 279–300.

[381] See further Dromgoole, *Underwater Cultural Heritage* (n 91) 123–25; Cogliati-Bantz and Forrest, 'Consistent: the Convention on the Protection of the Underwater Cultural Heritage' (n 94) 539.

[382] See Vigni, 'The Enforcement of Underwater Cultural Heritage' (n 99) 125–49.

[383] For a detailed description of the circumstances, see Mariano J. Aznar-Gomez, 'Trasures Hunters, Sunken State Vessels and the 2001 UNESCO Convention on the Protection of Underwater Cultural Heritage' *International Journal of Marine and Coastal Law*, 25(2010)2, 209–36, at 214 ff.

Vadi, 'International Law and the Uncertain Fate' (n 367) 253–77; Amy Strecker, 'Pirates of the Mediterranean? The Case of the "Black Swan" and its Implications for the Protection of Underwater Cultural Heritage in the Mediterranean Region', in Ana Filipa Vrdoljak and Francesco Francioni

under US admiralty law, the company filed the suit *in rem* before the US Florida Middle District Court in Tampa, claiming the seizure of the abandoned wreck and its contents.[384] Although Odyssey Marine Exploration did not disclose the location of the sunken vessel nor its identity, Spain immediately suspected that the wreck in question regarded its former warship *Nuestra Señora de las Mercedes* (hereinafter *Mercedes*), loaded with coinage from American colonies and sunk in 1804, during the Napoleonic wars. Furthermore, it alleged that the wreck must have been discovered in its territorial waters. Thus, Spain also filed its claim to the vessel and its contents in the court in Tampa,[385] asserting that the property undoubtedly constituted the wreck of *the Mercedes*, Spain's military property, over which it had not abandoned its sovereign rights. Consequently, it argued that the court in Florida lacked subject-matter jurisdiction over this property under the US Foreign Sovereign Immunity Act of 1976.[386]

The contents of the wreck raised media attention and moved other stakeholders to present their claims. Accordingly, Peru also reclaimed ownership of the content of the vessel, as the *Nuestra Señora de las Mercedes* sank on its cruise from Lima in the Spanish Viceroyality of Peru, and the treasure allegedly originated from that territory and formed its cultural patrimony. In addition, 25 descendants of Spanish sailors who died on board of the vessel filed claims against the wreck. Finally, the Bolivian Government expressed its interest in identifying the origin of the recovered treasure.[387]

The argument of Peru was particularly interesting as it *inter alia* claimed to be the legitimate owner of the Spanish Crown's property according to the rules on state succession. First, it claimed its sovereign rights 'in property that originated in its territory or was produced by its people'.[388] Moreover, it asserted that the property in question shall enjoyed state immunity.[389] Second, Peru claimed that the court should apply the rule set forth in Article 149 of UNCLOS, which grants preferential rights to the state of origin.[390] It argued that it 'is manifestly the

(eds), *Illicit Traffic of Cultural Objects in the Mediterranean* (EUI Working Paper AEL 2009/09), 59–74, at 60–63.

[384] *Odyssey Marine Exploration Inc. v. the Unidentified, Shipwrecked Vessel*, 675 F. Supp. 2d 1126 (M.D. Fla. 2009); 657 F.3d 1159 (11th Cir. 2011); 132 S. Ct. 2379 (US, 14 May 2010). For the litigation before US Florida Middle District Court in Tampa, see *Odyssey Marine Exploration Inc. v. Unidentified, Shipwrecked Vessel*, Case No: 8:07-cv-614-T-23MAP. All the documentation available at: <http://dockets.justia.com/docket/florida/flmdce/8:2007cv00614/197978>, accessed on 8 February 2015; hereinafter these documents will be quoted as '*Mercedes* Doc.'

[385] See Claimant Kingdom of Spain's Motion to Dismiss or for Summary Judgment, 22 September 2008, *Mercedes* Doc. 131.

[386] 28 U.S.C. §1602 ff.

[387] See 'Peru and Bolivia also Want Their Share of the Gold Found in Spanish Galleon', MercoPress South Atlantic News Agency, 29 December 2009, available at: <http://en.mercopress.com/2009/12/28/peru-and-bolivia-also-want-their-share-of-the-gold-found-in-spanish-galleon>, accessed on 8 February 2015.

[388] Claim to contents, artefacts, and cargo by Republic of Peru, 19 August 2008, *Mercedes* Doc. 120, at 2, para. 5.

[389] Ibid. para. 6; The Republic of Peru's Response to the Kingdom of Spain's Motion to Dismiss or for Summary Judgment, 17 November 2008, *Mercedes* Doc. 141, at 11–16.

[390] *Mercedes* Doc. 141, at 17–16.

"State or country of origin," "cultural origin," and "historical and archaeological origin" of the coins and other artifacts that were made within its territory by its people'.[391] Importantly, they were extracted from the territory of Peru during the colonial domination by '(generally the forced labour of) Peruvians'.[392] Thus, the case was not 'about sovereign rights over wrecks', but rather the dispute 'between Peru and Spain in this case is about future custody of property physically, culturally and historically originating in Peru'.[393] Moreover, this is 'the crucial linkage for recognizing sovereign interest.'[394] It also argued that this provision shall apply, notwithstanding the fact that only Spain ratified UNCLOS, whereas the US only signed but did not ratify, and Peru neither signed nor ratified it, since it reflected the rules of customary international law.[395]

Next, Peru claimed to be the legitimate owner of the Spanish Crown's cargo, arguing the law of state succession as Peru had been part of Spain in 1804.[396] It recalled the regime of the 1983 Vienna Convention as well as the development of relevant international practice in the occasion of dissolution of the USSR, Czechoslovakia, and Yugoslavia, arguing that the principle of equitable proportion constituted one of the 'most important categories of legal norms and regimes' under the modern international law on the rights and duties of successor states.[397] Accordingly, in the case of dissolution of a state, all its successors are entitled to equitable shares of the state property, with preference given to the historical and archaeological origin. Thus, Peru claimed that it was entitled to 'an equitable proportion of the treasure'.[398] Therefore, the court should apply the principles of equity in deciding on the division of that property[399] since 'general equitable principles comprise part of international law'.[400] In the light of the all arguments submitted, Peru argued that 'as a sovereign nation, is entitled to all or a substantial portion of the culturally sensitive artifacts which physically and historically originated in Peru, and which are now before this court, on multiple grounds which include the law of the sea, the law of state succession, and considerations of equity and international policy concerning condemnation of colonialism, protection of permanent sovereignty over natural wealth and resources, the protection of cultural heritage and the prohibition against pillage of occupied countries'.[401]

In its reply to Peru's submissions, Spain not only opposed Peru's legal bases to its rights to the wreck and its contents, but also opposed with justification the court's authority to adjudicate Spain's and Peru's competing claims. First, Spain acknowledged that Peru remained a part of Spain until 1824 until the Capitulation of Ayacucho, which 'specifically defines the terms of Spain's cession

[391] Ibid. 17. [392] Ibid. 2.
[393] Case No: 8:07-cv-614-T-23MAP, order of 22 December 2009, *Mercedes* Doc. 270, at 3.
[394] Ibid. [395] *Mercedes* Doc. 141, at 18–24. [396] Ibid. 26–31. [397] Ibid.
[398] Ibid. [399] Ibid. 32–34. [400] Ibid. 33.
[401] Peru's Sur-Reply in Opposition to Spain's Motion to Dismiss, 4 May 2009, *Mercedes* Doc. 206, at 11.

and the post-conflict rights of Peru vis-à-vis Spain.'[402] Accordingly, this granted Peru rights to state property 'within the territory' ceded by Spain. The Spanish military and merchant vessels were not surrendered. On the contrary, they had a six-month period to freely leave the ports of Peru. Moreover, the issue was perceived as completely settled when both states normalized their bilateral relations in 1879.[403] Spain also contested Peru's claims under Article 149 of UNCLOS. It *inter alia* argued that in 1804 Peru was part of Spain, so the place of origin of the property on board the *Mercedes* 'originated' from Spain.[404] Second, it claimed that Article 149 was not applicable in the case concerned since this provision refers only to objects found in the area beyond the limits of national jurisdiction,[405] and Peru is not a party to UNCLOS.[406] Moreover, the convention 'does not contemplate, let alone confer, jurisdiction for a U.S. court over a dispute between two independent states'.[407]

As regards Peru's claims based on international law on state succession, Spain claimed that these raised 'a nonjusticiable political question'.[408] Spain recalled that he 1983 Vienna Convention did not enter into force due to the very low number of ratifications, and its regime, especially with regard to newly independent states, was opposed as 'not representative of customary international law'.[409] Moreover, even if it was in force or 'recognized as indicative of international law, it does not apply here in any event'.[410] According to Article 4 it is not retroactive, except as may exceptionally be agreed. Thus, it cannot be applied to the situations of succession of states which occurred nearly two hundred years ago.[411] The regime of the 1983 Vienna Convention would also govern succession issues, in the absence of interstate agreements. In this case, Spain and Peru adopted such arrangements. Finally, the convention does not confer jurisdiction on a US court in terms of the division of the properties in question.[412]

Peru's claims that Spain's sovereign rights needed to be counterbalanced by its (Peru's) patrimonial interests was also deemed as 'inconsistent' by the court's Magistrate.[413] Accordingly, he held that Peru's argument was 'an equitable one grounded on claims of exploitation by its former colonial ruler'.[414] In fact, Peru assumed that 'all the specie minted in Lima came from ore mined within the boundaries of present day Peru'.[415] There are, however, serious doubts that 'given the early date of some of the coins Odyssey recovered, it is reasonable to conclude that these could have been struck from ore mined in Upper Peru (later part of the Viceroyalty of Rio de la Plata)',[416] thus beyond current territorial

[402] Kingdom of Spain Reply to the Claimant Republic of Peru Response to Spain's Motion to Dismiss or for Summary Judgment, 26 January 2009, *Mercedes* Doc. 161, at 4.

[403] Ibid. 5. [404] Ibid. 8. [405] Ibid. [406] Ibid. 10. [407] Ibid.

[408] Ibid. 11. [409] Ibid. 13. [410] Ibid. 14–15. [411] Ibid.

[412] Ibid. 15–21.

[413] Report and Recommendation. Signed by Magistrate Judge Mark A. Pizzo, 3 June 2009, *Mercedes* Doc. 209, at 29.

[414] Ibid. [415] Ibid. [416] Ibid.

boundaries of the Republic of Peru. Moreover, the court did not have jurisdiction to settle the claims based on Article 149 UNCLOS, and even if it had, Peru's argument was not 'persuasive', since 'for disputes between competing sovereigns over underwater cultural heritage discovered in international waters, there is no customary international law'.[417] The Magistrate held that 'Peru and Spain's dispute is intertwined with centuries of mutual history. Addressing their differences in this forum…would undermine the traditional notions of international comity' and constitute an 'unreasonable exercise of jurisdiction'.[418] In summary, he concluded that 'Spain and Peru's dispute over the specie is best resolved through direct negotiations between the two and not in this forum'.[419] Therefore, the sovereign immunity of Spain shall be recognized and 'all claims against the *res* be denied without prejudice'.[420] The District Judge agreed with the Magistrate's recommendations and held that 'the ineffable truth of this case is that the *Mercedes* is a naval vessel of Spain and that the wreck of this naval vessel, the vessel's cargo, and any human remains are the natural and legal patrimony of Spain and are entitled in good conscience and in law today undisturbed in perpetuity absent the consent of Spain and despite any man's aspiration to the contrary'.[421] Moreover, the principles articulated by Peru 'may govern in another forum on another day in resolving Peru's challenge to Spain's retention of the disputed items'.[422]

Thus, the District Judge validated the Magistrate's report and recommendations, but stayed the order to turn over the treasure to Spain until the Appeals process was completed. In September 2011, the 11th Circuit Court of Appeals agreed with the lower court's findings and held that Odyssey had to release the recovered *res* (the treasure) to the custody of Spain.[423] This decision was founded mainly on the interpretation of the rules of the FSIA and principle of comity between states. Interestingly, the court explained that it 'do[es] not hold the recovered *res* is ultimately Spanish property'. It merely held that 'the sovereign immunity owed the shipwreck of the *Mercedes* also applies to any cargo the *Mercedes* was carrying when it sank'.[424] Odyssey attempted to challenge the order to return the treasure to Spain before the US Supreme Court, yet its application to stay the Court of Appeals' decision was denied.[425] Thus, in February 2012, two Spanish military aircraft lifted the treasure in Florida and transported it to Spain.

[417] Ibid. 31. [418] Ibid. 32. [419] Ibid. 33. [420] Ibid. 34.

[421] *Mercedes* Doc. 270, at 4. [422] Ibid.

[423] *Odyssey Marine Exploration Inc. v. Unidentified, Shipwrecked Vessel*, 657 F.3d 1159 (11th Cir. 2011).

[424] Ibid. App. 47, footnote 16.

[425] *Odyssey Marine Exploration Inc. v. Kingdom of Spain et al.*, Sup. Ct. Decision No. 11A745, 9 February 2012, available at: <http://www.supremecourt.gov/Search.aspx?FileName=/docketfiles/11a745.htm>, accessed on 8 February 2015.

6.6.3 Title to sunken state vessels and the enforcement of the interest of all humanity in protecting underwater cultural heritage

The *Mercedes* case perfectly illustrated the clash of potential conflicting claims of states having an interest in state underwater cultural property. As the proceedings before US tribunals demonstrated, the provisions of Article 149 UNCLOS, granting 'preferential rights' to 'the state or country of origin, or the state of cultural origin, or the state of historical and archaeological origin' are hardly applicable in practice. Moreover, the enforcement of cultural rights of newly independent states to recover their cultural heritage displaced by former sovereigns and subsequently lost at sea are treated as a political issue, not regulated under customary international law.

In this light, the 2001 UNESCO Convention adopts different solutions. The Convention does not contain any provisions governing the property regime to underwater cultural heritage, 'leaving ownership as a matter to be determined by national laws'.[426] Instead, it introduces a novel concept of the interest of states with 'a verifiable link, especially a cultural, historical or archaeological link, to the underwater cultural heritage' (Article 6(2)). This solution goes beyond individual interests of state or country of origin, as provided by Article 149 of UNCLOS, thus encompassing the interests of 'all those states that feel a strong sense of identification with a particular site or recovered artifact'.[427] The 2001 UNESCO Convention refers to states with a verifiable link in a few specific contexts. Accordingly, such states may be invited to join bilateral, regional, or other multilateral agreements for the preservation of underwater cultural heritage, or to be informed or consulted in cases of the discovery or seizure of unlawfully recovered objects of underwater cultural heritage to which they may have a verifiable link.[428] For this purpose the system of the 2001 UNESCO Convention contains operational guidelines on interstate cooperation.[429] Arguably, such a framework is also consistent with a general obligation, under Article 303(1) of UNCLOS, which provides that 'states have the duty to protect objects of an archaeological and historical nature found at sea' and they 'shall cooperate for this purpose'.

Importantly, recognition of state interests needs to be applied in line with the general principle of the regime introduced by the 2001 UNESCO Convention, that is, the protection and preservation of underwater cultural heritage for the benefit of all humanity. According to the Rule 1 of the Annex to the Convention, 'the protection of underwater cultural heritage through in situ preservation shall be considered as the first option'. Therefore all the 'activities directed at underwater

[426] Dromgoole, *Underwater Cultural Heritage* (n 91) 117. [427] Ibid. 128.

[428] Ibid. 129. See Arts 6(2), 7(3), 9(5), 10(3), 11(4), 12(2), 18(3), 18(4) of the 2001 UNESCO Convention.

[429] Operational Guidelines for the Convention on the Protection of the Underwater Cultural Heritage, 29 May 2013, rules 26–28; UNESCO Doc. CLT/CEH/CHP/2013/OG/H/1, available at: <http://unesdoc.unesco.org/images/0022/002226/222670E.pdf>, accessed on 8 February 2015.

cultural heritage shall be authorized in a manner consistent with the protection of that heritage, and subject to that requirement may be authorized for the purpose of making a significant contribution to protection or knowledge or enhancement of underwater cultural heritage'.

In sum, it appears that under the evolving regime for the protection of underwater cultural heritage, the core obligation is to safeguard such heritage for the benefit of the humanity as a whole, and neither state nor private interests and rights 'can be considered as exclusive'.[430] Thus, states have the duty to cooperate for this purpose, rather than litigate in respect of their individual competing claims.

6.7 Conclusion

This chapter dealt with state succession to cultural heritage obligations. It explored their content arising from current international cultural heritage law and human rights regimes. It also examined the sources of such obligations and recalled the legal doctrine claiming that alongside treaty law, certain developments occurred at the level of customary international law. In particular, these consist in: the prohibition of the intentional destruction and plunder of cultural property in the event armed conflict; the obligation to return cultural property removed from occupied territories; the respect and safeguarding of cultural heritage of major importance to all mankind. In addition, it appears that the procedural principle of cooperation at the local, regional, and international levels gradually becomes one of the major standards in dealing with cultural heritage issues.

The status of international cultural heritage obligations in state succession depends on their sources. It seems that in recent state practice there has been no development with regard to the status of such obligations arising from treaties. In fact, these are usually seen as analogous to other treaty commitments, whose continuity is, generally speaking, conditioned by the will of a successor state. Another question refers to the status of cultural heritage obligations arising from customary international law since they do not cease simply because of state succession. In particular, new states cannot reject or disregard international obligations *erga omnes*. Similar concerns have been also addressed in relation to state succession in obligations and rights arising from the commitment of an internationally wrongful act against cultural heritage. In this regard, the system of protection of human rights and cultural heritage implemented in Bosnia–Herzegovina and Kosovo is of special importance, since the introduction of this complex set of cultural heritage obligations was designed in terms of the enforcement of universally accepted standards. Because of the volume and content of these obligations, it remains, however, highly controversial as to whether they can be treated as those arising

[430] Vigni, 'Historic Shipwrecks' (n 380) 299.

from binding non-treaty norms of general international law. Moreover, it also appears that the cultural heritage framework for Bosnia–Herzegovina and Kosovo constituted a *sui generis* initiative undertaken by the international community, which can hardly be perceived as a new formula consistently applicable in all cases of violent dissolution of a multinational state.

Finally, it has also been possible to observe a more general, operational impact of international cultural heritage law on the recent practice of state succession to state cultural property. It appears that particular priority has been given to the different multilateral and bilateral arrangements on cultural cooperation which have virtually replaced the previous practice based on succession agreements or peace treaty settlements. States tend to settle all the claims which may arise from past transfers and removals of cultural property within the framework of interstate accords on cultural cooperation and reciprocal protection of cultural heritage, rather than in succession agreements *sensu stricto*. The objective of such arrangements lies in the accommodation of different economic, cultural, or scientific interests of the states concerned (eg licit cross-border circulation of works of art and other cultural products, access to archaeological sites situated in the territory of one state by the scientists of the other, etc). Actual negotiations on the fate of the disputed cultural treasures are perceived as secondary issues. It is also a commonly accepted standard that such cultural cooperation agreements invoke the 1970 UNESCO Convention, which is arguably treated as a basis for both the resolution of current disputes relating to the illicit traffic in cultural material, and the settlement of passed situations, including those arising from state succession. The question of common rights and interests to immovable property and cultural heritage sites essentially recalls or, in particular cases, adopts the regime of the World Heritage Convention.

Solutions in respect of movable cultural property are also promoted and facilitated at different regional and non-governmental levels. In particular, the practice of long-term loans of cultural objects is regarded as one of the most efficient tools of international cultural exchange.[431] Such long-term loans provide a very convenient solution as they do not deal with the question of title. Accordingly, one state maintains the ownership of the item and the other gains its possession. It seems that these could also be fully applied as a definitive or transitory solution to complex international disputes in cases of state succession.

From the methodological perspective, the recent practice of state succession in cultural property and cultural heritage obligations does not evidence elements of a profound evolution of positive law in this area. It seems that states tend to use various, often inconsistent, techniques to handle concrete problems in actual circumstances, rather to follow precise principles or patterns. These can follow 'pragmatic' approaches to state succession, based on the principles of fairness and

[431] See eg Action Plan for the EU Promotion of Museum Collection Mobility and Loan Standards, available at: <http://www.lending-for-europe.eu/fileadmin/CM/public/documents/policy/Action_Plan_for_the_EU_Promotion.pdf>, accessed on 30 January 2015.

equity as well as those calling for a policy-oriented approach. However, it has been clearly shown that the objective of protection of cultural heritage, as an already well-established principle under general international law, constitutes one of the major interlocking factors affecting succession outcomes in matters of cultural property today.

7
Conclusion

> Visions of a heritage transcending our own domain are age-old. They reflect diverse aims: to convert to our faith, to improve the common lot by sharing our superior bequest, to reunify a fractious world. The missionary zeal of Catholic orders was universal in focus. And the secular legacies of science, capitalism, and communism have been as ardently avowed as the sacred.
>
> In the main, heritage inevitably voices private, even selfish, interests but is no longer just parochial and self-concerned. Global agencies lead the way in conserving and celebrating national and local legacies.... Major powers concede the heritage rights of small states and nonsovereign minorities. We begin to appreciate that our global village requires a unified and cultural legacy.[1]

The aim of this book was to explore to what extent the principles and practice of state succession correspond to the evolution of the concept of cultural heritage in international law. With this objective, it has provided an extensive analysis of the alterations of the international practice and legal doctrine of state succession in cultural property, since the nineteenth century to the present day. This book has shown that these changes have consisted in the gradual internationalization of the protection of tangible cultural heritage as a consequence of the growing common awareness that the preservation and enjoyment of cultural heritage in all its various manifestations form a constituent part of the general interest of humanity. The outcome of this process has been observed within three distinctive aspects of succession of states: succession to immovable and movable state cultural property, comprising state archives of major cultural importance; state succession to international cultural heritage obligations and rights, including those arising from an internationally wrongful act against cultural heritage; and the resolution of disputes relating to state succession in cultural property. Finally, the analysed state practice and the relevant legal doctrine have demonstrated some promising tendencies, which this book advocates as a list of best

[1] David Lowenthal, *The Heritage Crusade and the Spoils of History* (7th edn, CUP, 2009), 247.

standards/guidelines for ongoing and future developments in the area of state succession (Annex).

7.1 Passing of state cultural property

In regard to the principles on the passing of state cultural property, the fundamental question concerns the concept of territoriality (or territorial provenance), understood as the special link between people, land, and cultural heritage. This emerged in the nineteenth century from two major sources. Its first origin referred to the principle of territoriality governing the restitution of movables on the occasion of peace settlements concluding wars in the European continent. The second related to the matter of the allocation of state archives in cases of territorial transfers. Subsequently, the principle of territoriality concerning the passing of archives was extrapolated to state property forming part of the intellectual patrimony of a state. Yet such a link was defined differently in respect of ordinary state archives and works of art, libraries, or other property of cultural or historical significance. Accordingly, the allocation of state archives was based on territorial pertinence, while the principle of territorial provenance applied to cultural patrimony (eg Article XVIII of the 1866 Vienna Treaty of Peace between Italy and Austria–Hungary).

At the end of the First World War, the distinction between the legal regime of restitution applicable to cultural property seized in the event of war and that of state succession became fully recognized. Despite the fact that both regimes were founded on the paramount principle of territoriality binding cultural property to a given territory, their objectives were different. Accordingly, the norms of international law on restitution of cultural property to the territory from which it was removed in the event of war constituted the corollary of the prohibition of acts against property and buildings dedicated to religion, education, art, and science. Importantly, the destruction and pillage of such property was prohibited under binding international instruments on war conduct since the Peace Conferences of 1899 and 1907. Inversely, the principle of territoriality in cases of state succession provided that territorial transfers not only entailed the passing of cultural property located in the lands in question, but also the repatriation of property removed from the territory subject to state succession, prior to the date of succession (eg Article 11 of the 1921 Treaty of Riga between Poland, Russia, and Ukraine). This principle thus safeguarded the economic and cultural integrity of the territory. The difference between these two regimes did not, however, mean that in settling determined cases they could not be jointly taken into consideration, especially when state succession escalated into armed conflict, as usually happened.

The immense losses in tangible cultural heritage in many countries as a consequence of the Second World War forced the international community to adopt more efficient mechanisms for the protection of such material in the event of armed conflict. The Allied restitution programme, proclaimed by the 1943 London Declaration, fully reaffirmed the paramount nature of the principle of territoriality, which governed both the restoration of cultural property removed by the use of force or under duress in the event of war, and the allocation of such materials in state succession. Indeed, some of the post-Second World War peace treaties (eg Article 1 of Annex XIV to the 1947 Paris Peace Treaty with Italy) provided for the unconditional restoration of such properties originating from the ceded territories. Yet the profound changes of territorial boundaries in Europe, followed by the displacements of entire national and/or ethnic groups also led to the tacit recognition of the priority of collective cultural rights of a group over the general principle of territoriality. In fact, cultural property often followed the destiny of displaced communities, although such a principle for allocation was not explicitly formulated by interstate arrangements. Moreover, the process of decolonization initiated after the Second World War displayed a common and firm disagreement of predecessor states (former colonial powers) to share the cultural resources acquired during colonialism with newly independent post-colonial states. There were only a few cases which regulated the allocation of cultural property in accordance with the principle of territorial links.

Alongside this contradictory interstate practice, the subsequent codification of international law for the protection of cultural property reaffirmed the rudimentary nature of territorial provenance. It has been widely recognized that each culture deserves equal treatment and protection. Furthermore, it has been affirmed that the impoverishment of cultural heritage of one country constitutes not only an internal issue but is also part of the common concern of all humanity, as 'damage to cultural property belonging to any people whatsoever means damage to the cultural heritage of all mankind, since each people makes its contribution to the culture of the world'. This occurred in two discrete areas: protection of cultural property in the event of an armed conflict, comprising the obligation to return such items removed from militarily occupied territories, regulated under the 1954 Hague Convention and the 1954 Hague Protocol, and the prohibition and prevention of international transfer of cultural property illicitly removed from a national territory in times of peace, through the means of the procedural principle of cooperation as provided by the 1970 UNESCO Convention. Arguably, these two regimes fully affirmed that the protection of cultural property in its original historical, geographical, and cultural contexts constitutes one of the major fundaments of the current international cultural order. Thus, it appears that international cultural heritage legislation reinforced the principle of territoriality also in respect of the allocation of cultural property in state succession. This particularly refers to the property removed from the territory subject to succession in the event of armed conflict or in violation of national law on the protection of cultural heritage.

Since the mid-1960s, the experience of newly (post-colonial) independent states with regard to the lack of restoration of their tangible cultural heritage has fostered the restitution debate in various international forums. These states argued that they were entitled to the cultural property, irrespective of its current legal status, removed from their respective territories as a result of violent colonial exploitation and discriminatory policies of foreign occupants. While such claims were in line with the international legal norms ordering the restitution of cultural property displaced from the territories subject to military occupation, they went far beyond the existing application of the principle of territoriality in cases of state succession. In fact, the codified rules on succession of states to state property under the 1983 Vienna Convention did not include any special regime concerning the passing of cultural property. Moreover, the two main criteria for the passing of state property established by this treaty—the territorial location of property at the date of succession and the connection with the activity of the predecessor state in the territory subject to state succession—hardly reflect the nature of cultural heritage disputes following the changes of territorial sovereignty. Importantly, the most complex issues related to the removals from dependent territories prior to their independence have been deliberately left to the system of international cultural cooperation created by UNESCO, favouring bilateral agreements over any automatic solutions based on the principle of territorial provenance.

The new wave of state succession that occurred after 1989 has once again addressed the issue of the allocation and distribution of state cultural property in accordance with the territorial origin of an object. In fact, the rudimentary nature of such a principle has extensively been applied in the succession agreements (eg the 1994 Agreement between the Czech Republic and Slovakia, the 1992 CIS Agreement, the 2001 SFRY Agreement) on the allocation of state cultural property in the event of the recent wave of state succession. However, actual state practice has been rather disappointing as only the Czech Republic and Slovakia have managed to finalize the division of state cultural property in accordance with this principle.

The second fundamental principle on the allocation of state cultural property is usually defined on the basis of its major importance to the cultural heritage of a successor state. In other words, it concerns the cultural or historical linkage between a given property and the state from whose territory it originated. Contrary to territorial provenance, there are no clear-cut criteria defining such connections or interests. In the nineteenth century and in the first part of the twentieth century, the principle of cultural ties referred both to cultural property as an extension of national culture and to items or their collections of universally recognized cultural and scientific values which formed public collections of the predecessor state. This was due to the fact that the identity and international position of a European nation-state was built, on the one hand, on its intellectual patrimony distinctive from other nation-states, and on the other, by the possession of a considerable number of public collections of a commonly recognized universal value.

Post-First World War peace treaty practice in the matter of allocation of cultural property, extensively elaborated the principle of major significance for the cultural heritage of a successor state, supplementing the paramount principle of territorial links. In the interwar period it was essentially understood in terms of nationality of cultural treasures, although the actual criteria making concrete such cultural ties were never comprehensively formulated. In practice, they referred to the nationality or birthplace of the artist, the link between the work and the nation's history, the artistic tradition inspiring it, or even its allocation to a certain place or for a given use.

Nonetheless, the adoption of the principle of nationality, as decisive in inter-state settlements, recognized for the first time in international practice the existence of collective rights to enjoy and control material manifestations of culture and a group's (national) identity. Arguably, such an affirmation of national collective rights was profoundly linked to the emerging principle of self-determination of nations. The principle of major importance for national heritage and identity also gained particular importance after the Second World War. As already mentioned, the post-war practice in Central and Eastern Europe tacitly recognized the right of displaced populations to migrate with their most venerated cultural properties. Thus, the priority was given *de facto* to collective rights of transferred human communities over any potential interests of successor states. The relevance of this trend for the more profound changes in the law of state succession was, however, undermined by the subsequent prohibition of involuntary population transfers under Article 49 of the Fourth Geneva Convention.

During the process of decolonization, the principle of major importance to the cultural heritage of a successor state was closely tied to the principle of self-determination of peoples subject to foreign domination. Representatives of these states argued that the restoration of their dispersed cultural property was essential to (re)construct their historical memories and national identities suppressed by discriminatory policies of former colonial powers. Thus, they argued that the right to self-determination entitled them to claim the return of cultural treasures essential for their peaceful and harmonious social and cultural development. In practice, however, these allegations were rejected by the former colonial powers, arguing that their legal and cultural rights to the cultural material were acquired during their colonial rule.

After 1989, the principle of major cultural significance was also addressed in international practice, but difficulties in its interpretation have hindered its application. This has been particularly due to mutually exclusive perceptions of the content of national cultures and contradictory historical discourses.

Finally, two other principles on the allocation of state cultural property have been identified. In cases of session and dissolution, the examined state practice demonstrated that the distribution of such property could be achieved by equitable apportionment. This has usually referred to groups of cultural objects which cannot be attributed exclusively to one of the successor states in accordance with the principles of territoriality and major importance to the national cultural heritage. Such distribution of cultural properties has, however, been weighed up against the protection of the integrity of universally ranked collections. As a form of compensation for preserving such integrity, some succession agreements were set up for the transfer of certain objects to which another state might have a public interest; for instance, the exhibits completing the public collections of that state (eg 1932 Austro-Hungarian Agreement, Article 11 of the 1921 Treaty of Riga). It arguably appears that nowadays the principle of universally ranked art collections finds its full realization in the non-binding 2004 Declaration on the Importance and Value of Universal Museums, which gives priority to the interest of all peoples in enjoying and studying public art collections over the principle of territorial provenance and major cultural significance rights of the states concerned. It appears that such considerations correspond with considerable state practice, particularly with regard to the negotiation policies of the former colonial powers.

Generally speaking, it seems rather improbable that the principles on the allocation of state cultural property based on territorial provenance and major cultural interest would ever evolve into a binding set of rules of international law. Notwithstanding the fact that states include such principles in their succession agreements, they are very reluctant to put them into practice. Moreover, their implementation and enforcement is usually hindered by different interpretations of historic and cultural ties. Consequently, the principles on the passing of cultural property in the event of state succession will continue as a mere non-binding set of rules, applicable only to cases where favourable 'political will' is at stake.

7.2 Succession to international cultural heritage obligations

This book has also dealt with state succession in respect of international obligations towards tangible cultural heritage, stressing that their content arises from current international cultural heritage law and human rights regimes. The developments in the area of the international protection of cultural heritage not only regard the level of international treaties, in particular multilateral conventions, but also include UN ad hoc instruments, non-binding declarations, and principles of soft law, state practice, and jurisprudence of international and domestic tribunals. With regard to the complexity of the international regime for the protection of tangible cultural heritage, five main distinctive areas have been identified: the protection of cultural property in the event of armed conflict and occupation; the obligation to restore the cultural material appropriated and transferred from militarily occupied territories; the prevention and prohibition of the illicit traffic of movable cultural property in times of peace; the protection of the common heritage of mankind; the preservation of cultural heritage as an element of the protection and promotion of human rights, especially in their collective dimension.

Clearly, international cultural heritage obligations are established first and foremost by multilateral treaties and to a certain extent by bilateral treaties and agreements on the matter of cultural heritage protection. However, the international practice, supported by an amount of legal scholarship, has offered evidence that certain developments have occurred at the level of customary international law.

In addition, it seems that the procedural principle of cooperation at the local, regional, and global levels is in the process of becoming of one of the major standards in dealing with cultural heritage issues.

The status of cultural heritage obligations in state succession is determined by their sources. It appears that treaty obligations in matters of cultural heritage are usually seen analogous to other contractual commitments of the predecessor state. Thus, their continuity generally depends on the will of a successor state. In this context, special attention needs to be paid to the question of the theory of automatic succession of human rights and humanitarian treaties. This claims that such treaties shall continue to be binding irrespective of the fact of state succession. Such an argument is supported by the fact that human rights and humanitarian treaties do not represent an exchange of interests but are instead designed to protect the international community as a whole. Thus, such treaties lie far beyond the boundaries of state sovereignty as they address matters of universal concern. Moreover, it is argued that the fact of state succession does not put an end to the fundamental rights inherent to every human being, individually or collectively. However, the existence of such a customary rule of international law does not seem to be confirmed by consistent international practice and *opinio juris*, yet it is generally accepted that a customary rule of international law with regard to automatic succession of human rights treaties is currently *in statu nascendi*.

It appears that the international obligations on the protection of the cultural heritage of human communities inhabiting the territory subject to state succession may be perceived as running parallel to those providing the protection of human rights. In particular, the dramatic events and subsequent work of international bodies with regard to the former Yugoslavia led to the reconsideration of the relationship between tangible cultural heritage and the protection of human rights in their individual and collective capacity. Thus, the theory of automatic succession requires a more profound revision in light of cultural heritage obligations. Arguably, this may apply to the obligation to respect and protect the cultural property against destruction and plunder, as provided by the 1954 Hague Convention and the 1999 Second Hague Protocol. It seems that automatic succession shall also concern the obligations to protect the cultural heritage of mankind under the World Heritage Convention, as they do not constitute the mere concern of domestic jurisdiction. The major consideration supporting such a thesis consists in the dual value of cultural heritage for every people and for the international community as a whole. In fact, this reasoning may arguably be associated with the position expressed by the ICJ as to the existence of certain obligations *erga omnes* in respect of values protected by the international community as a whole. In the *Barcelona Traction* case, the court held that the 'principles and rules concerning the basic rights of the human person' are applicable to all states. Undoubtedly, the general interest of humanity in the protection of cultural heritage perfectly fits within the notion of such universally recognized values.

The concept that certain cultural heritage obligations *erga omnes* have emerged or are *in statu nascendi* at the level of customary international law requires a separate comment in relation to the succession of states. In principle, international obligations under customary international law do not cease in the case of state succession, since they bind all states regardless of the date of their emergence. In this sense, the continuity of such obligations does not constitute a matter of succession, as it does not involve the succession by one state to the obligations contracted by the predecessor state in its sovereign capacity.[2] Such obligations constrain all states by virtue of their status as such.

It appears that these considerations shall refer in particular to the obligation to ensure the protection of fundamental human rights. In the area of tangible cultural heritage, this shall entail the obligation of the territorial state to respect material cultural manifestations as an element of the broader legal framework for the protection and promotion of human rights. Indeed, the situation of minorities, groups, and indigenous peoples and the peaceful coexistence between them constituted one of the major concerns at the time of state succession, at least since the 1878 Treaty of Berlin. Following the First World War, this was confirmed by the League of Nations minority system founded on the principles of equality and non-discrimination. In addition, it also appears that apart from political rights, the recognition of minority rights was also manifested in the sphere of cultural matters. In other words, the minority guarantees provided for the 'recognition of the right to internal self-determination with regard to certain cultural matters, for such groups'.[3]

After the Second World War, the minority question was tied to the broader human rights regime. In this new vision, the cultural rights of minorities were embodied in human cultural rights. Under Article 27 of the International Covenant on Civil and Political Rights, the protection of minorities gained a universal application. This provided for the individual rights of persons belonging to ethnic, religious, or linguistic minorities 'to enjoy their own culture, to profess and practice their own religion, or to use their own language.' It also imposed on states obligations that were collective in nature, as members of a minority exercise their rights in community with the other members of their group.[4] These provisions have an important impact on cultural heritage as they entail both negative obligations on states to refrain from acts against cultural heritage, as well as positive obligations to provide measures of protection with regard to minority communities and their material cultural heritage.

The dissolution of the USSR and SFRY has once again opened up the question of minority protection in state succession. In a similar way to post-First World War minority guarantees, the fulfilment of minority standards has formed one

[2] Martti Koskenniemi, 'Report of the Director of Studies of the English-Speaking Section of the Centre', in Pierre Michel Eisemann and Martti Koskenniemi (eds), *La succession d'États: la codification à l'épreuve des faits/State Succession: Codification Tested against the Facts* (Nijhoff, 2000), 108.

[3] Ana Filipa Vrdoljak, *Self-determination and Cultural* Rights, in Francesco Francioni and Martin Scheinin (eds), *Cultural Human Rights* (Nijhoff, 2008), 41–78, at 77.

[4] UNHRC, General Comment No. 23, UN Doc. HRC/GEN/1/Rev.1, 38(1994), para. 6(2).

of the requirements of the conditional recognition of new states. After 1989, this question entered into the broader human and cultural criteria established by the European Community and the United Nations. Moreover, the ethnic conflicts in the territory of Yugoslavia and the great losses in material cultural heritage also accelerated work on universal and European instruments for the protection of minorities, which included 'culture' and 'cultural heritage' as core values for their protection. Apart from this, one can observe a more general interplay between cultural heritage and human rights in current international law and practice. In fact, the protection of cultural heritage is more often perceived as an important component of the promotion and protection of all human rights.

The violent dismemberment of the SFRY played a fundamental role in the international recognition of this important relationship. The acts of intentional destruction of monuments, temples, and libraries in different parts of the Balkans following the break-up of Yugoslavia provide terrible evidence of the close links between the intentional destruction of cultural heritage and severe human rights violations. This was particularly investigated in the jurisprudence of the ICTY, which established individual criminal responsibility for intentional acts of destruction to cultural property. In the *Krstić* case, the ICTY found that the deliberate and systematic destruction of the cultural heritage of an ethnic group may provide evidence of the intent (*mens rea*) requirement for the commission of the crime of genocide under the 1948 Genocide Convention. It held that the destruction of a group may be conceived not only through its biological extermination, but also 'through purposeful eradication of its culture and identity resulting in the eventual extinction of the group as an entity distinct from the remainder of the community'.

Furthermore the Badinter Commission, in its First Opinion on state succession in former Yugoslavia, held that 'the peremptory norms of general international law and, in particular, respect of the fundamental rights of the individual and the rights of the people and minorities, are binding on all the parties to the succession'. It seems that such norms shall also include the protection of tangible cultural heritage of such groups, inhabiting the territory subject to state succession. With regard to this issue, the complex set of human rights and cultural heritage obligations introduced by the international community in Bosnia–Herzegovina and Kosovo is of particular relevance. However, the volume and content of these obligations, which *inter alia* provided for the reconstruction of destroyed cultural property, raises serious doubts as to whether they can be treated as those stemming from binding norms of general international law. Thus, it can hardly be perceived as a new formula consistently applicable in all cases of violent dissolution of a multinational state.

The state practice examined in this book has not demonstrated the emergence of special rules on succession to cultural heritage treaties, yet the progressive development of the customary norm of international law with regard to the continuity of human rights and humanitarian treaties supports the legitimate expectation that cultural heritage obligations set by international treaties in this area shall also be considered as automatically binding. Such a view seems justified by the *raison d'être* of such obligations, consisting in the protection of all human rights, on the hand, and in the realization of the general interest of the international community as a whole, on the other.

As regards cultural heritage obligations under customary international law, these can be invoked against all states, irrespective of the date of their emergence, by virtue of their peremptory status as such. To date, their content remains disputable. Nonetheless, it must be stressed that the formation of such rules of general international law has been confirmed in at least three distinctive areas: the prohibition of the intentional destruction and plunder of cultural property in the event of an armed conflict; the obligation of restitution of cultural property removed from the occupied territories; and the respect and safeguarding of cultural heritage of major importance to all mankind. These shall bind all states involved in the process of state succession.

To conclude, it clearly appears that today, the preservation and enjoyment of cultural heritage do not constitute the exclusive concern of state sovereignty. Importantly, such values are of general interest to international community as a whole. Thus, the international obligations towards tangible cultural heritage developed at the level of general international law restrict the contractual freedom of states in the area of state succession with regard to cultural property. In other words, interstate succession agreements shall not infringe the international obligations *erga omnes* towards such materials and sites, since the protection of all cultural manifestations, irrespective of any political considerations and territorial reconfigurations, lies in the general interest of all mankind.

7.3 State succession and international responsibility

As regards the topic of state succession to consequences of internationally wrongful acts against cultural heritage, the Post-Cold War state practice confirmed the fundamental distinction between the cases of continuity and succession. In principle, the continuator states shall logically continue the enjoyment of rights as well as the assumption of obligations arising from the international wrongful acts committed prior to the date of state succession. In fact, the cases of Germany, Russia, and Serbia have shown that continuator states are recognized as holders of rights and obligations arising from the pre-succession wrongful acts against cultural heritage.

Conversely, the rules of succession in such obligations and rights applicable to new states have long been considered as more obscure. Yet, the state succession to international responsibility is distinct from that in rights stemming from internationally wrongful act committed against the predecessor state or the population concerned. In regard to the first issue, the recent developments of international practice and legal scholarship have shown that traditional concepts on non-transferability of obligations arising from internationally wrongful act do not correspond with state practice nor with the general principles of justice and equity. However, the existence of precise rules of succession in such obligations under general international law remains debatable. This particularly relates to obligations arising from the pre-succession wrongful acts against cultural heritage. Indeed, the nature of such obligations, often involving extremely complex historical and politically sensitive aspects may call for more flexible solutions by resort to the notions of 'fairness' and 'equity'. In fact, the actual arrangements adopted by successor states in matters of responsibility for the breach of such obligations are usually followed non-succession *ex gratia* considerations. Thus, it appears that the core principle applicable in such cases, expect of rare instances of the violation of *jus cogens*, would be an obligation to negotiate to achieve fair and equitable solutions in the subjective relationship emerging from the commission of an international wrongful act against cultural heritage. In this regard, the 2013 Draft Resolution State Succession in Matters of State Responsibility by the Institute of International Law provides an important indication. Accordingly, the obligations arising from internationally wrongful acts committed by the predecessor state shall pass to the successor state if the 'intrinsically direct link of the consequences of the wrongful act with the territory or the population concerned' can be determined.

In regard to the problem of state succession in rights arising from internationally wrongful acts against cultural heritage committed prior to the date of succession, the principle of 'intrinsically direct link' is also correct as it departs from the narrow notion of injured state towards a more equitable human solution. Indeed, wrongful acts committed against cultural heritage primarily affect collective cultural rights of human communities in a given territory. Thus, the secondary obligations shall be owed by the successor state if the wrongful act has consequences in respect of its population, and in cases of grave violations of international law such obligations shall also be owned by the international community as a whole.

7.4 Procedural principles of dispute settlements

Since the time of the formation of the nation-states of Germany and Italy in the second half of the nineteenth century, the resolution of disputes on succession to state cultural property has been perceived as an exemption from the general settlement of other succession issues. In fact, the controversies between the concerned states were settled through consensual bilateral commissions of experts (eg Italy and Austria–Hungary) or on the basis of decisions made by a special impartial arbiter (eg Hesse-Darmstadt and Prussia). These dealt with the implementation and elaboration of criteria referring to territorial links and major cultural interest of the property in question. Such a system of dispute settlement was also applied in the following waves of state succession in the twentieth and twenty-first centuries. However, since the mid 1960s, it has been possible to observe a more general, operational impact of international cultural heritage law on the recent practice of state succession to state cultural property. The state practice analysed in this book has demonstrated the pre-eminence of different multi- and bilateral arrangements on cultural cooperation. These have virtually all but completely replaced previous practice based on succession agreements or peace-treaty settlements. Indeed, states have tended to settle all the claims which may arise from the past transfers and removals of cultural property within the framework of interstate accords on cultural cooperation and reciprocal protection of cultural heritage, rather than in succession agreements *sensu stricto*. The objective of such arrangements lies in the accommodation of different economic, cultural, or scientific interests of the states concerned, in which the question of succession to state cultural property plays a secondary role. Moreover, it also appears that these cultural cooperation agreements invoke the 1970 UNESCO Convention, which is arguably treated as a basis for both: resolution of current disputes relating to the illicit traffic in cultural material and the settlement of passed situations, including those arising from the fact of state succession. Yet the question of common rights and interests to immovable property and cultural heritage sites essentially recalls or, in particular cases adopts, the regime of the World Heritage Convention. These consist in interstate cooperation in the conservation of cultural heritage sites that may be of joint interest to the states concerned, or may be of great cultural importance to one of them, but the states decide to protect their respective cultural properties reciprocally.

The principle of cooperation in settling the controversies with regard to state succession in cultural property is also linked to the concept of cultural reconciliation. Accordingly, certain gestures of good will need to be expressed in order to put an end to a difficult past and to right historic wrongs. On the basis of such a turning point in mutual relations, the concerned states can foster new friendly relations. The handing over of certain objects important for the cultural heritage of the other party is usually pursued in terms of a voluntary gift, which accompanies other settlements and interstate cultural commitments. In addition, the solutions in respect of cultural objects are also promoted and facilitated at the different regional and non-governmental levels.[5] In particular, the practice of long-term loans of cultural objects is regarded as one of the most efficient tools of international cultural exchange.

7.5 Best practices and guiding principles

On the basis of the analysis provided, this book advocates the Draft Proposal of Guiding Principles Relating to the Succession of States in respect of Tangible Cultural Heritage (the Draft Proposal) under the enclosed Annex. It is intended

[5] See *inter alia* Alessandro Chechi, 'Plurality and Coordination of Dispute Settlement Methods in the Field of Cultural Heritage', in Francesco Francioni and James Gordley (eds), *Enforcing International Cultural Heritage* (OUP, 2013), 177–205, at 186 ff. Marie Cornu and Marc-André Renold, 'New Developments in the Restitution of Cultural Property: Alternative Means of Dispute Resolution' *International Journal of Cultural Property* 17(2010)1, 1–31.

to provide general guidance for bilateral or multilateral interstate negotiations in order to facilitate the conclusion of agreements related to movable and immovable cultural property, following the succession of states. It applies to immovable and movable state cultural property, including state archives being of major cultural or historical importance to one of the states involved in succession. The Draft Proposal applies to such property situated in the territory to which the succession of states relates, or having originated from this territory, was displaced in a different location by the predecessor state (Article 1).

The principle on the passing of state property follows the provisions of the 1983 Vienna Convention, bearing in mind recent international practice and the 2001 Recommendation of the Institute of International Law. As regards the types (categories) of state succession covered by the Draft Proposal, these concern five major situations: the transfer of a part of the territory of a state to another state (cession); the separation of part or parts of the territory of a state (secession); the dissolution of a state; the unification of two or more states; incorporation of one or more states by another (Article 2). The regime on newly independent states, as provided by the 1983 Vienna Convention, has deliberately been omitted since the privileged status of post-colonial territories constituted one of the major reasons for the failure of the Convention. Moreover, it is also driven by the observation that the process of decolonization has already been concluded.

The Draft Proposal reinforces the customary principle of the protection of state property in respect of cultural property during the transition period, prior to the final attribution of property to one of the states concerned. In addition, it encourages those states to apply the principles of international cultural cooperation and exchange of cultural property providing that the arrangements concluded in this matter would not impair the rights of the states concerned and the rights of third parties. Moreover, it provides that the states involved in succession shall cooperate in cases where the cultural property located in their respective territories may be of great importance to the cultural heritage of another state or states. In particular, such measures of cooperation shall concern free, unhindered, or privileged access to such property for the citizens or scientists of that state which has an important cultural interest in this property; international cultural exchange through short-term loans and deposits under medium- or long-term arrangements; establishment of safe havens in order to safeguard most endangered cultural property (Article 5).

Next, the Draft Proposal reaffirms that the attribution of cultural property shall be governed by the principle of territorial provenance and major importance to the cultural heritage of one of the states concerned. In this regard, it provides for the guidelines of conduct applicable to the process of final attribution arrangements. It encourages the states concerned to undertake joint projects with regard to the conservation and management of immovable and movable cultural property of common cultural interest (Article 7(2) and 9(3)). It also requires the states involved in succession to protect their respective tangible cultural heritage reciprocally (Article 7(1), Article 10(4)). Moreover, it asks them to ensure reciprocal access to the relevant documentation concerning state archives and state cultural property which passes, or may pass to another state, in order to facilitate the final settlement. In particular, such access shall be granted to museum inventories, catalogues of public libraries, and archives (Article 10(2)).

Finally, the Draft Proposal encourages the states involved in succession to settle the disputes that may arise in respect of the attribution of cultural property on the basis of consensual agreements. In cases of major difficulties in achieving the final arrangements, UNESCO expert assistance shall be considered.

Thus, the crux of the guidelines provided by the Draft Proposal consists in the procedural principle of cooperation, and the mutual respect of all cultural manifestations, recognizing that tangible cultural heritage constitutes one of the basic elements of the culture of every people, and in the understanding that a variety of cultures contributes to the cultural heritage of mankind, whose protection and enjoyment is of general interest to the international community as a whole.

ANNEX

Draft Proposal of Guiding Principles Relating to the Succession of States in respect of Tangible Cultural Heritage

Considering the development of State practice in recent years, notably following the disintegration of the Union of Soviet Socialist Republics, the dismemberment of the Socialist Federal Republic of Yugoslavia and the separation of the Czech and Slovak Federal Republic as well as the unification of Germany;

Acknowledging the Convention on Succession of States in respect of State Property, Archives and Debts, adopted on 8 April 1983 by the United Nations Conference in Vienna;

Recalling the conventions adopted by the General Conferences of the United Nations Educational, Scientific and Cultural Organization: the Hague Convention for the Protection of Cultural Property in the Event of Armed Conflict of 14 May 1954, and its additional Protocols; the Convention on the Means of Prohibiting and Preventing the Illicit Import, Export and Transfer of Ownership of Cultural Property of 14 November 1970; the Convention concerning the Protection of the World Cultural and Natural Heritage 1972 of 16 November 1972; the Convention on the Protection of the Underwater Cultural Heritage of 2 November 2001;

Recognizing the importance of the Resolution on State Succession in Matters of Property and Debts, adopted on 26 August 2001 by the Institute of International Law in its session in Vancouver;

Taking into consideration the Declaration of Principles of International Cultural Co-operation adopted on 6 November 1966 by the General Conferences of the United Nations Educational, Scientific and Cultural Organization;

Considering that tangible cultural heritage constitutes one of the basic elements of civilization and of the culture of every people;

Considering that the culture of each people makes its contribution to the cultural heritage of all mankind, whose protection and enjoyment is of general interest to the international community as a whole;

Recognizing that the protection of cultural heritage constitutes an important component of the promotion and protection of all human rights, including the full realization of cultural rights;

Recognizing that international cooperation constitutes one of the most efficient means of resolution of cultural heritage-related disputes and one of the major tools for safeguarding and protecting cultural heritage for the benefit of future generations;

This Draft Proposal *urges* States concerned to resolve disputes on the allocation and protection of cultural property taking into account, as appropriate, the following principles:

A. Scope of application

Article 1

This Draft Proposal is intended to provide general guidance for bilateral or multilateral interstate negotiations in order to facilitate the conclusion of agreements related to movable and immovable cultural property, following succession of States. Under this Draft Proposal 'Cultural Property' means the property, which:

a) is listed under Article 1 of the 1970 UNESCO Convention on the Means of Prohibiting and Preventing the Illicit Import, Export and Transfer of Ownership of Cultural Property;
b) is listed under Article 1 of the 1972 UNESCO Convention concerning the Protection of the World Cultural and Natural Heritage;
c) was at the date of the succession of States owned by the predecessor State, according to the internal law of that State and in conformity with international law;
d) is situated in the territory to which the succession of States relates, or having originated from said territory, was displaced to a different location by the predecessor State.

Article 2

This Draft Proposal applies to situations of the replacement of one State by another in the domains of government, administration, and international relations of the territory (succession of States), which include the following categories: transfer of a part of the territory of a State to another State (cession); separation of part or parts of the territory of a State (secession); dissolution of a State; unification of two or more States; incorporation of one or more States by another.

B. Obligations of States prior to final attribution of cultural property

Article 3

Prior to a final arrangement on the attribution of cultural property to one of the States concerned, to the extent possible, the interests of those States and the requirements of good faith shall be taken into account.

Article 4

The States concerned are required to take, at all times, the necessary measures to prevent the loss, damage or destruction to State archives, and State cultural property that may be of major importance to the cultural heritage of another State. Before being attributed to one of the States concerned, such property shall be protected in accordance with the law of the State on whose territory it is located. The rights of third parties shall be respected.

Article 5

1. In the transition period, preceding the attribution of cultural property to one of the States concerned, the principles of international cultural cooperation and exchange

of cultural property shall apply. The arrangements in this matter concluded between those States shall not impair the rights of those States and the rights of third parties.

2. Prior to a final arrangement on the attribution of cultural property, the States concerned shall cooperate in cases where the cultural property located in their respective territories may be of great importance to the cultural heritage of another State or States. In particular, they are encouraged:
   a) to provide free, unhindered or privileged access to such property to the citizens or scientists of that State, which has an important cultural interest in this property;
   b) to cooperate in order to facilitate international cultural exchange through means of short-term loans and deposits under medium or long-term arrangements;
   c) to establish safe havens in order to safeguard most endangered cultural property.

C. Passing of State cultural property

Article 6

Immovable cultural property of the predecessor State situated within the territory subject to succession passes to that successor State on whose territory it is located.

Article 7

1. The States concerned shall closely cooperate in cases where the immovable cultural property located in their respective territories may be of great importance to the cultural heritage of another State or States. In particular, they are required to respect such property and to take the necessary measures to prevent its loss, damage or destruction. The States concerned may also provide free, unhindered, or privileged access to such property to the citizens or scientists of that State, which has an important cultural interest in this property.
2. In relation to the immovable cultural property of major importance to the cultural heritage of more than one State, this may be managed and conserved jointly by the States concerned. The conditions and duties of such a joint venture shall be regulated by the States concerned, in the spirit of mutual understanding and respect for cultural values and historical interpretations attached to the immovable cultural property in question.

Article 8

The passing of the immovable cultural property of the predecessor State situated outside its territory, such as scientific and cultural institutions, State museums, libraries, and historical archives situated abroad, shall occur in accordance with the following principles:

a) In the event of incorporation and unification of two or more States, the immovable cultural property situated outside their territories passes to the successor State.
b) In the case of dissolution of a State, the immovable cultural property of the predecessor State situated outside its territory shall pass to that successor State whose cultural heritage it forms. If such an important cultural linkage cannot be established, it passes to the successor States in equitable proportions. The successor States shall reach an

agreement as to its apportionment in an equitable manner, or, if not possible, apply the principle of compensation.

c) In the event of cession and separation of part or parts of a territory of a State (secession), the immovable cultural property of the predecessor State situated outside its territory remains, in principle, the property of the predecessor State. Nevertheless, successor States have the right to an equitable apportionment of the property of the predecessor State situated outside its territory.

Article 9

1. The movable cultural property of the predecessor State that is of major importance to the cultural heritage of a successor State from whose territory it originates, shall pass to that State. Such objects shall be identified by that State as soon as possible, but within a reasonable period of time following the succession. The passing of movable cultural property shall be regulated by the States concerned.
2. In the event of dissolution or separation of part or parts of the territory of a State (secession), the movable cultural property, which cannot be attributed to any of the States concerned on the basis of the criteria listed in paragraph 1, passes to the successor State or to the successor States, in equitable proportions.
3. When it is justified by a particular value attached to determined collections of universal cultural or scientific importance, the States concerned may jointly decide to preserve the integrity of such ensembles and maintain them as their common heritage. The States concerned shall, by an agreement to be reached as soon as possible, determine the retention of such groups of movable cultural property as their common heritage, to which they shall have free and unhindered access. The common heritage shall be financed by proportional cost sharing and jointly managed by a special body established for this purpose. The competences of such a body shall be regulated by the States concerned, and may include: the control on the general utilization of the collections, methods of their conservations and policy of exhibitions and loans, etc. Nothing in this paragraph shall be interpreted so as to abrogate the principles listed in paragraph 1.

Article 10

1. The States concerned shall cooperate and consult amongst each other in order to reach an agreement on an inventory of movable cultural property and its apportionment.
2. The States concerned shall reciprocally provide access to the relevant documentation concerning State archives and State cultural property which passes, or may pass to another State. In particular, such access shall be granted to museum and archive inventories, catalogues of public libraries.
3. The procedural principle of cooperation and the principle of good faith shall govern the conduct of States concerned in drafting the criteria of major importance to their respective cultural heritage interests. In case of disagreement, they may ask the Director General of UNESCO to provide expert assistance.
4. In any case, the States concerned shall provide, in their respective territories, adequate means of protection to movable cultural property that is of major importance to the cultural heritage, regardless of its origin.

Article 11

The rules contained in Article 8 of this Draft Proposal on the immovable cultural property of the predecessor State situated outside its territory apply *mutatis mutandis* also to movable cultural property.

Article 12

The rules contained in Articles 9–10 of this Draft Proposal on movable cultural property shall also apply to State archival records of major importance to the cultural heritage of States involved in the succession.

D. Settlement of disputes

Article 13

In case of disagreement, the States concerned shall have recourse to adequate means for the settlement of disputes. They are encouraged to bring their disputes before impartial arbitration or mediation commissions. The expert assistance of UNESCO is strongly recommended.

Select Bibliography

Adler, Philip J. 'Serbs, Magyars, and Staatsinteresse in Eighteenth Century Austria: A Study in the History of Habsburg Administration', *Austrian History Yearbook* 12(1976)1, 116–47.

Agarval, Hari Om. *State Succession. A Study of Indian Cases* (Allahabad Law Agency, 1980).

Akinsha, Konstantin, Kozlov, Grigorii̇̈, and Hochfield, Sylvia. *Beautiful Loot: The Soviet Plunder of Europe's Art Treasures* (Random House, 1995).

Akinsha, Konstantin. 'Stalin's Decrees and Soviet Trophy Brigades: Compensation, Restitution in Kind, or "Trophies" of War?', *International Journal of Cultural Property* 17(2010)2, 195–216.

Alcock, Anthony Evelyn. *A History of the Protection of Regional Cultural Minorities in Europe: from the Edict of Nantes to the Present Day* (MacMillan, 2000).

Alings, Reinhard. *Monument und Nation: das Bild vom Nationalstaat im Medium Denkmal—zum Verhältnis von Nation und Staat im deutschen Kaiserreich, 1871–1918* (De Gruyter, 1996).

Anton, Michael, *Internationales Kulturgüterprivat- und Zivilverfahrensrecht* (De Gruyter, 2010).

Arai-Takahashi, Yutaka. *The Law of Occupation Continuity and Change of International Humanitarian Law, and its Interaction with International Human Rights Law* (Brill, 2009).

Armaly, Maha, Blasi, Carlo, and Hannah, Lawrence. 'Stari Most: Rebuilding More than a Historic Bridge in Mostar', *Museum International* 56(2004)4, 6–17.

D'Arnoux de Fleury de l'Hermite, Henri. *Objects et monuments d'art devant le droit des gens* (L. Clercx, 1934).

Auer, Leopold, *Disputed Archival Claims. Analysis of an International Survey: a RAMP Study* (UNESCO, 1998).

Auer, Leopold, and Thomas, Christiane. 'The Austro-Yugoslavian Convention on Archives: A Case Study in State Succession', *Information Development* 1(1985)3, 169–75.

Aznar-Gomez, Mariano J. 'Treasure Hunters, Sunken State Vessels and the 2001 UNESCO Convention on the Protection of Underwater Cultural Heritage', *International Journal of Marine and Coastal Law* 25(2010)2, 209–36.

Banac, Ivo. 'The Politics of National Homogeneity', in Brad Blitz (ed), *War and Change in the Balkans* (CUP, 2006), 30–43.

Bedjaoui, Mohammed. 'Eighth Report on Succession of States in respect of Matters other than Treaties', UN Doc. A/CN.4/292.

Bedjaoui, Mohammed. 'Eleventh Report on the Succession of States in Respect of Matters Other Than Treaties', UN Doc. A/CN.4/322 and Corr. 1 and Add.1 and 2.

Bedjaoui, Mohammed. 'Problèmes récentes de succession d'etats dans les etats noveaux', *RCADI* 130(1970)2, 455–585.

Bedjaoui, Mohammed. 'Third Report on the Succession of States in Respect of Matters Other Than Treaties', UN Doc. A/CN.4/226.

Bedjaoui, Mohammed. *Towards a New International Economic Order Paris* (UNESCO, 1979).

Bell, Christine. *On the Law of Peace: Peace Agreements and the Lex Pacificatoria* (OUP, 2008).

Benveniśtî, Eyāl. *The International Law of Occupation*, 2nd edn. (Princeton University Press, 2004).

Bergvelt, Ellinoor, Meijers, Debora, J., Tibbe, Lieskie, et al. (eds), *Napoleon's Legacy: The Rise of National Museums in Europe 1794–1830* (GH Verlag, 2009),

Berman, Nathaniel. 'Beyond Colonialism and Nationalism? Ethiopia. Czechoslavakia and Peaceful Change', *Nordic Journal of International Law* 65(1996)3/4, 421–79.

Bethlehem, Daniel, L., and Weller, Marc (eds), *The 'Yugoslav' Crisis in International Law* (CUP, 1997).

Beurier, Jean-Pierre. 'Pour un droit international de l'archéologie sous-marine', *RGDIP* 93(1989)1, 45–68.

Blake, Janet. 'On Defining the Cultural Heritage', *ICLQ* 49(2000)1, 61–85.

Blake, Janet. 'Taking a Human Rights Approach to Cultural Heritage Protection', *Heritage & Society* 4(2011)2, 199–238.

Blankenagel, Alexander. 'Eyes Wide Shut: Displaced Cultural Objects in Russian Law and Adjudication', *East European Constitutional Review* 8(1999)4, 75–80.

Blower, Jonathan. 'Max Dvořák and Austrian Denkmalpflege at War', *Journal of Art Historiography* (2009)1, 1–19.

Blumenwitz, Dieter. *What is Germany? Exploring Germany's Status after World War II* (Kulturstiftung d. Dt. Vertriebenen, 1989).

Boguslavskij, Mark. 'Contemporary Legal Problems of Return of Cultural Property to its Country of Origin in Russia and the Conference of Independent States', *IJCP* 3(1994)2, 243–56.

Bokor-Szegő, Hanna. 'Questions of State Identity and State Succession in Eastern and Central Europe', in Mojmir Mrak (ed), *Succession of States* (Nijhoff, 1999), 95–108.

Bonnici, Ugo Misfud. 'The Human Right to Cultural Heritage—The Faro Convention's Contribution to the Recognition and Safeguarding of This Human Right', in Council of Europe (ed), *Heritage and Beyond* (Council of Europe Publ, 2009), 57–58.

Borzęcki, Jerzy. *The Soviet–Polish Peace of 1921 and the Creation of Interwar Europe* (Yale University Press, 2008).

Bothe, Michael, and Schmidt, Christian. 'Sur quelques questions de succession posées par la dissolution de l'URSS et celle de la Yougoslavie', *RGDIP* 96(1992)4, 811–42.

Bouaïta, Nabil. 'La restitution des archives nationales et biens culturels à leurs pays d'origine dans le cadre du nouvel ordre culturel', *Revue de droit international, de sciences diplomatiques et politiques* 61(1983)1, 27–48.

Brüggeman, Karsten, and Kasekamp, Andres. 'Identity Politics and Contested Histories in Divided Societies: The Case of Estonian War Monuments', in Eiki Berg and Piret Ehin (eds), *Identity and Foreign Policy: Baltic–Russian Relations and European Integration* (Ashgate, 2009), 51–64.

Brzeziński, Zbigniew, and Sullivan, Paige. *Russia and the Commonwealth of Independent States: Documents, Data, and Analysis* (M.E. Sharpe, Inc., 1997).

Buhler, Konrad G. *State Succession and Membership in International Organizations: Legal Theories versus Political Pragmatism* (Kluwer Law International, 2001).

Burdeau, Geneviève. 'Droit International Public: Rapport Français', in *La protection des biens culturels. Journées polonaises de 1989, Travaux de l'Association Henri Capitant des amis de la culture juridique française* 40(1989), 59–70.

Burdeau, Geneviève, and Stern, Brigitte (eds). *Dissolution, continuation et succession en Europe de l'Est* (Montchrestien, 1994).

Burnett, Philip. *Reparations at the Paris Peace Conference from Standpoint of the American Delegation* (Vol. I; Octagon Books, 1940).

Buzzini, Gionata P., and Condorelli, Luigi. 'Article 11: List of World Heritage in Danger and Deletion of a Property from the World Heritage List', in Francesco Francioni and Federico Lenzerini (eds), *The 1972 World Heritage Convention: A Commentary* (OUP, 2007), 175–200.

Carducci, Guido. 'Growing Complexity of international Art Law: Conflicts of Law, Mandatory Rules, UNSC Resolutions and EU Regulations', in Barbara T. Hoffman (ed), *Art and Cultural Heritage. Law, Policy and Practice* (CUP, 2006), 68–86.

Carducci, Guido. *La restitution internationale des biens culturels et des objets d'art: droit commun, Directive CEE, Conventions de l'UNESCO et d'Unidroit* (L.G.D.J, 1997).

Carducci, Guido. 'L'Obligation de restitution des biens culturels et des objets d'art en cas de conflit armé: droit coutumier et droit conventionnel avant et après la Convention de La Haye de 1954; l'importance du facteur temporel dans les rapports entre les traités et la coutume', *RGDIP* 104(2000)1–2, 289–357.

Casanova, Eugenio. 'Gli archivi nei trattati internazionali', *Gli Archivi Italiani* 5(1918), 179–201.

Cassar, Brendan, and Rodríguez García, Ana Rosa. 'The Society for the Preservation of Afghanistan's Cultural Heritage: an Overview of Activities since 1994', in Juliette van Krieken-Pieters (ed), *Art and Archaeology of Afghanistan: Its Fall and Survival; a Multi-Disciplinary Approach* (Brill, 2006), 15–38.

Cassese, Antonio. *Self-determination of Peoples. A Legal Reappraisal* (CUP, 1995).

Castellani, Francesca, and Casadio, Paolo, (eds), *Histria. Opere d'arte restaurate: da Paolo Veneziano a Tiepolo.* Catalogo della mostra: Trieste, 23 giugno 2005–6 gennaio 2006 (Electa, 2005).

Chechi, Alessandro. 'Customary obligation to return cultural property—Conventions on the Laws and Customs of War—Vienna Convention on Succession of States in respect of State Property, Archives and Debts. Tribunale Amministrativo Regionale del Lazio (Sez. II-quarter), 28 February 2007, No. 3518 Associazione Nazionale Italia Nostra Onlus v. Ministero per i Beni e le Attività Culturali et al.', *IYIL* 17(2007), 277–80.

Chechi, Alessandro. 'Multi-Level Cooperation to Safeguard the Human Heritage and to Secure the Return of Wrongfully Removed Cultural Objects', in Silvia Borelli and Federico Lenzerini (eds), *Cultural Heritage, Cultural Rights, Cultural Diversity. New Developments in International Law* (Nijhoff, 2012), 347–68.

Chechi, Alessandro. 'Plurality and Coordination of Dispute Settlement Methods in the Field of Cultural Heritage', in Francesco Francioni and James Gordley (eds), *Enforcing International Cultural Heritage* (OUP, 2013), 177–205.

Chechi, Alessandro. 'The Return of Cultural Objects Removed in Times of Colonial Domination and International Law: the Case of the Venus of Cyrene', *IYIL* 18(2008), 159–81.

Chechi, Alessandro, *The Settlements of International Cultural Heritage Disputes* (OUP, 2014).

Cheng, Tai-Heng. 'Renegotiating the Odious Debt Doctrine', *Law and Contemporary Problems* 70(2007)3, 7–32.

Cheng, Tai-Heng. *State Succession to Commercial Obligations* (Transnational Publishers, 2006).

Cheng, Tai-Heng. 'Why New States Accept Old Obligations?', *University of Illinois Law Review* (2011)1, 1–52.

Cholewinski, Ryszard. 'State Duty Towards Ethnic Minorities: Positive or Negative?', *Human Rights Quarterly* 10(1988)3, 344–71.

Ciulisová, Ingrid. 'Art Collecting of the Central-European Aristocracy in the Nineteenth Century: The Case of Count Pálffy', *Journal of the History of Collections* 18(2006)2, 201–09.

Cogliati–Bantz, Vincent, and Forrest, Craig. 'Consistent: the Convention on the Protection of the Underwater Cultural Heritage and the United Nations Convention on the Law of the Sea', *Cambridge Journal of International and Comparative Law* 2(2013)3, 536–61.

Coombes, Annie E. *Reinventing Africa: Museums, Material Culture and Popular Imagination in Late Victorian and Edwardian England* (Yale University Press, 1997).

Cornu, Marie. *Le droit culturel des biens. L'intérêt culturel juridiquement protégé* (Bruylant, 1996).

Cornu, Marie, and Renold, Marc-André. 'New Developments in the Restitution of Cultural Property: Alternative Means of Dispute Resolution', *IJCP* 17(2010)1, 1–31.

Coulée, Frédérique. 'Quelques remarques sur la restitution interétatique des biens culturels sous l'angle du droit international public', *RGDIP* 104(2000)2, 359–92.

Craven, Matthew. *The Decolonization of International Law State Succession and the Law of Treaties* (OUP, 2007).

Craven, Matthew. 'The Genocide Case, the Law of Treaties and State Succession', *BYIL* 68(1997), 127–63.

Craven, Matthew. 'The Problem of State Succession and the Identity of States under International Law', *EJIL* 9(1998)1, 142–62.

Critescu, Aureliu. *The Right to Self-determination Historical and Current Development on the Basis of United Nations Instruments*, U.N. Doc. E/CN.4/Sub.2/404/Rev. 1, (1981).

Crawford, James. *State Responsibility: The General Part* (CUP, 2013).

Crawford, James. *The Creation of States in International Law*, 2nd edn. (OUP, 2007).

Crawford, James, Pellet, Alain, and Olleson, Simon (eds), *The Law of International Responsibility*, (OUP, 2010).

Cuasay, Peter. 'Borders on the Fantastic: Mimesis, Violence, and Landscape at the Temple of Preah Vihear', *Modern Asian Studies* 32(1998)4, 849–90.

Czapliński, Władysław. 'Equity and Equitable Principles in the Law of State Succession', in Mojmir Mrak (ed), *Succession of States* (Nijhoff 1999), 61–73.

Czapliński, Władysław. 'Reunification of Germany—International Legal Issues', *Co-existence* 27(1990)4, 225–32.

Czapliński, Władysław. 'State Succession and State Responsibility', *CanYIL* 28(1990), 339–59.

Czapliński, Władysław. *Zmiany terytorialne w Europie Środkowej i Wschodniej i ich skutki międzynarodowo prawne* (Scholar, 1998).

Czubek, Grażyna, and Kosiewski, Piotr (eds). *Cultural Assets and the Problem of Property. The Case of Central Europe after 1989* (The Batory Foundation Trio, 2005).

Danilenko, Gennadii Mikhailovich. *Law-making in the International Community* (Nijhoff, 1993).

D'Aspremont, Jean. 'Decolonization and the International Law of Succession: Between Regime Exhaustion and Paradigmatic Inconclusiveness', *Chinese Journal of International Law* 12(2013)2, 321–37.

D'Aspremont, Jean. *Formalism and the Sources of International Law: A Theory of the Ascertainment of Legal Rules* (OUP, 2011).

D'Aspremont, Jean (ed). *Participants in the International Legal System. Multiple Perspectives on Non-State Actors in International Law* (Routledge, 2011).

Degan, Vladimir D. 'Création et disparition de l'État à la lumière du démembrement de trois fédérations multiethniques en Europe', *RCADI* 279(1999), 195–375.

Dimitrijevic, Vojin. 'The Construction of States: Nationalism and the Definition of Nation-States in Post-communist European Countries', in Brigitte Stern (ed), *Dissolution, Continuation, and Succession in Eastern Europe* (Nijhoff, 1998), 147–70.

Dromgoole, Sarah. *Underwater Cultural Heritage and International Law* (CUP, 2013).

Dromgoole, Sarah (ed). *The Protection of Underwater Cultural Heritage: National Perspectives in Light of the UNESCO Convention 2001*, 2nd edn. (Nijhoff: 2006).

Dronova, Natalia. 'The Division of State Property in the Case of State Succession in the Former Soviet Union', in Pierre Michel Eisemann and Martti Koskenniemi (eds), *La succession d'États: la codification à l'épreuve des faits/State Succession: Codification Tested Against the Facts* (Nijhoff, 2000), 781–826.

Dumberry, Patrick. *State Succession to International Responsibility* (Nijhoff, 2007).

Dumberry, Patrick, and Turp, Daniel. 'State Succession with Respect to Multilateral Treaties in the Context of Secession: from the Principle of Tabula Rasa to the Emergence of a Presumption of Continuity of Treaties', *Baltic Yearbook of International Law* 13(2013), 27–65.

Dumberry, Patrick. 'The Consequences of Turkey Being the "Continuing" State of the Ottoman Empire in Terms of International Responsibility for Internationally Wrongful Acts', *International Criminal Law Review* 14(2014)2, 261–73.

Dumberry, Patrick. 'The Controversial Issue of State Succession to International Responsibility in Light of Recent State Practice', *GYIL* 49(2006), 413–48.

Dupuy, Pierre-Marie, 'Some Reflections on Contemporary International Law and the Appeal to Universal Values', *EJIL* 16(2005)1, 131–37.

Dupuy, Pierre-Marie. 'The Impact of Legal Instruments Adopted by UNESCO on General International Law', in Abdulqawi A. Yusuf (ed), *Standard-setting in UNESCO. Normative Action in Education, Science and Culture: Essays in Commemoration of the Sixtieth Anniversary of UNESCO* (Vol. 1; UNESCO, 2007), 351–63.

Ehlert, Caroline. *Prosecuting the Destruction of Cultural Property in International Criminal Law: with a Case Study on the Khmer Rouge's Destruction of Cambodia's Heritage* (Nijhoff, 2013).

Eichwede, Wolfgang, 'Trophy Art as Ambassadors: Reflections Beyond Diplomatic Deadlock in the German–Russian Dialogue Wolfgang Eichwede', *ICJP* 17(2010)2, 387–412.

Eisheh, Anwar Abu. 'The Protection of Heritage and Holy Sites in International Law: A Palestinian Perspective', in Marshal J. Breger, Yitzhak Reiter, and Leonard Hammer (eds), *Sacred Space in Israel and Palestine* (Routledge, 2012), 66–81.

Eisemann, Pierre Michel. 'L' indépendance du Kosovo', in Société Française pour le Droit International, *Droit international et relations internationales* (Pedone, 2010), 107–119.

Eisemann, Pierre Michel, and Koskenniemi, Martti (eds), *La succession d'États: la codification à l' épreuve des faits/State Succession: Codification Tested Against the Facts* (Nijhoff, 2000).

Emiliani, Andrea. *Leggi, bandi e provvedimenti per la tutela dei beni artistici e culturali negli antichi stati italiani, 1571–1860* (Nouva Alfa, 1996).

Engelhardt, Sophie. *Nachrichtenlose Kulturgüter* (De Gruyter, 2013).

Engstler, Ludwig. *Die territoriale Bindung von Kulturgütern im Rahmen des Völkerrechts* (C. Heymann, 1964).

Fabri, Hélène Ruiz, and Boniface, Pascal (eds), *Succession d'États en Europe de l'Est et avenir de la sécurité en Europe: actes du colloque du 6 avril 1995 organisé à l'Institut international d'administration publique par le CEDIN Paris XIII et l'IRIS* (L.G.D.J., 1995).

Fastenrath, Ulrlich, Schweisfurth, Theodor, and Ebenroth, Carsten, Th. (eds), *Das Recht der Staatensukzession* (Müller, 1996).

Fechner, Frank G. 'The Fundamental Aims of Cultural Property Law', *IJCP* 7(1998)2, 376–94.

Ferri, Nicola. 'The Right to Recovered Underwater Cultural Heritage: The Neglected Importance of Article 149 of the UN Law of the Sea Convention', in Silvia Borelli and Federico Lenzerini (eds), *Cultural Heritage, Cultural Rights, Cultural Diversity. New Developments in International Law* (Nijhoff, 2012), 253–66.

Fiedler, Wilfried. 'Die Allierte (Londoner) Erklärung vom 5.I.1943', in Jürgen Basedow (ed), *Privatrecht in der internationalen Arena, Liber Amicorum Kurt Siehr* (T.M.C. Asser Instituut 2000), 197–218.

Fiedler, Wilfried. *Kulturgüter als Kriegsbeute? Rechtliche Probleme der Rückführung deutscher Kulturgüter aus Rußland* (Müller, 1995).

Fiedler, Wilfried (ed). *Internationaler Kulturgüterschutz und deutsche Frage* (Gebr. Mann, 1991).

Fink, Carole. *Defending the Rights of Others. The Great Powers, the Jews, and International Minority Protection 1878–1938* (CUP, 2004).

Fouilloux, Gérard. 'La succession aux biens publics français dans les États nouveaux d'Afrique', *AFDI* 11(1965), 885–915.

Francioni, Francesco. 'A Dynamic Evolution of Concept and Scope: From Cultural Property to Cultural Heritage', in Abdulqawi A. Yusuf (ed), *Standard-setting in UNESCO. Normative Action in Education, Science and Culture: Essays in Commemoration of the Sixtieth Anniversary of UNESCO* (Vol. 1; UNESCO, 2007), 221–36.

Francioni, Francesco. 'Au-delà des traités: l'émergence d'un noveau droit coutimier pour la protection du patrimoine culturel', *RGDIP* 111(2007)1, 19–42.

Francioni, Francesco. 'Evolving Framework for the Protection of Cultural Heritage in International Law', in Silvia Borelli and Federico Lenzerini (eds), *Cultural Heritage, Cultural Rights, Cultural Diversity. New Developments in International Law* (Nijhoff, 2012), 3–28.

Francioni, Francesco. 'Plurality and Interaction of Legal Orders in the Enforcement of Cultural Heritage Law', in Francesco Francioni and James Gordley (eds), *Enforcing International Cultural Heritage* (OUP, 2013), 9–19.

Francioni, Francesco. 'Reparation for Indigenous Peoples: Is International Law Ready to Ensure Redress for Historical Injustices?', in Federico Lenzerini (ed), *Reparations for Indigenous Peoples: International and Comparative Perspectives* (OUP, 2009), 27–46.

Francioni, Francesco and Federico Lenzerini (eds), *The 1972 World Heritage Convention: A Commentary* (OUP, 2008).

Francioni, Francesco and Lenzerini, Federico. 'The Obligation to Prevent and Avoid Destruction of Cultural Heritage: From Bamiyam to Iraq', in Barbara T. Hoffman (ed), *Art and Cultural Heritage: Law Policy and Practice* (CUP, 2006), 28–40.

Francioni, Francesco, and Scheinin, Martin (eds), *Cultural Human Rights* (Nijhoff, 2008).

Frommer, Benjamin, *National Cleansing: Retribution against Nazi Collaborators in Postwar Czechoslovakia* (CUP, 2005).

Frowein, Jochen, Abr. 'The Reunification of Germany', *AJIL* 85(1992)1, 152–63.

Gaddis, John Lewis. *The Cold War: A New History* (Penguin Press, 2005).

Gattini, Andrea. 'Restitution by Russia of Works of Art Removed from German Territory at the End of the Second World War', *EJIL* 7(1996)1, 67–88.

Gautier, Philippe. 'Droit International Public: Rapport Belge', *La protection des biens culturels. Journées polonaises de 1989. Travaux de l'Association Henri Capitant des amis de la culture juridique française* 40(1989), 35–48.

Gautron, Jean-Claude. 'Sur quelques aspects de la succession d'Etats au Sénégal', *AFDI* 8(1962), 836–64.

Gehér, József. 'Le destin juridique des oeuvres d'art hongroises enlevées en Russie', *Miskolc Journal of International Law* 1(2004)2, 290–305.

Geluwe van, Huguette. 'Belgium's Contribution to the Zairian Cultural Heritage', *Museum* 31(1979)1, 32–37.

Ghoshray, Saby. 'Repatriation of the Kohinoor Diamond: Expanding the Legal Paradigm for Cultural Heritage', *Fordham International Law Journal* 31(2007–08)3, 741–80.

Gillman, Derek. *The Idea of Cultural Heritage*, 2nd edn. (CUP, 2010).

Glahn, von Gerhard. *The Occupation of Enemy Territory: A Commentary on the Law and Practice of Belligerent Occupation* (University of Minnesota Press, 1957).

Goia, Andrea. 'Kosovo's Statehood and the Role of Recognition', *IYIL* 18(2008), 3–35.

Goldmann, Klaus. 'The Trojan Treasures in Berlin: The Disappearance and Search for the Objects after World War II', in Elisabeth Simpson (ed), *The Spoils of War. World War II and Its Aftermath: The Loss, Reappearance and Recovery of Cultural Property* (Harry N. Abrams, Inc., Publishers, 1997), 200–03.

Gould, Cecil. *Trophy of Conquest: The Museé Napoleón and the creation of the Louvre* (Faber & Faber, 1965).

Goy, Raymond. 'Le régime international de l'importation, de l'exportation et du transfert de propriété des biens culturels', *AFDI* 16(1970), 605–24.

Goy, Raymond, 'La réunification du Yémen', *AFDI* 36(1991), 249–65.

Greenfield, Jeanette. *The Return of Cultural Treasures*, 3rd edn. (Cambridge, 2007).

Grimsted Kennedy, Patricia, 'Legalizing "Compensation" and the Spoils of War: the Russian Law on the Displaced Cultural Valuables and the Manipulation of Historic Memory, *ICJP* 17(2010)2, 217–55.

Grimsted Kennedy, Patricia (ed), 'Russian Legal Instruments Relating to Cultural Valuables Displaced as a Result of the Second World War, 1990–2009, *ICJP* 17(2010)2, 427–491.

Grimsted Kennedy, Patricia. *Trophies of War and Empire: The Archival Heritage of Ukraine, World War II and International Politics of Restitution* (Ukrainian Research Institute of Harvard University, 2004).

Grimsted Kennedy, Patricia, Hoogewoud, F.J., and Ketelaar, Eric (eds), *Returned from Russia. Nazi Archival Plunder in Western Europe and Recent Restitution Issues* (Institute of Art and Law, 2007).

Grotius, Hugo. *The Rights of War and Peace, Including the Law of Nature and of Nations. Translation of De Jure Belli Ac Pacis* (Amstelaedami 1680), trans. Archibald Colin Campbell (M. Walter Dunne, 1901 (reprint edition 1979)).

Gruber, Annie. *Le droit international de la succession d'États* (Bruylant, 1986).

Guilfoyle, Douglas. 'Article 16', in Roger O'Keefe and Christian J. Tams (eds), *The United Nations Convention on Jurisdictional Immunities of States and Their Property: A Commentary* (OUP, 2013), 259–76.

Guinn, David. *Protecting Jerusalem's Holy Sites. A Strategy for Negotiating a Sacred Peace* (CUP, 2006).

Hafner, Gerhard, and Kornfeind, Elisabeth. 'The Recent Austrian Practice of State Succession: Does the Clean Slate Rule Still Exist?', *Austrian Review of International and European Law* 1(1996)1, 1–49.

Hafner, Gerhard, and Novak Gregor. 'State Succession in Respect of Treaties', in Duncan B. Hollis (ed), *The Oxford Guide to Treaties* (OUP, 2012), 396–427.

Hailbronner, Kay. 'Legal Aspects of the Unification of the Two German States', *EJIL* 2(1991)1, 18–41.

Hall, William, Edward. *Treatise of International Law*, 4th edn. (Clarendon Press, 1909).

Hamant, Hélène, *Démembrement de l'URSS et problèmes de succession d'États* (Bruylant, 2007).

Hardiati, Endang Sri, and Keurs, Pieter Ter (eds). *Indonesia: the Discovery of the Past* (Kit Publishers, 2005).

Hasani, Enver. 'The Evolution of the Succession Process in Former Yugoslavia', *Miskolc Journal of International Law* 4(2007)2, 12–37.

Hasani, Enver. 'Uti Possidetis Juris: from Rome to Kosovo', *Fletcher Forum of World Affairs* Summer/Fall (2003), 85–97.

Hatti, Vivek K. 'India's Right to Reclaim Cultural and Art Treasures from Britain under International Law', *The George Washington Journal of International Law and Economics* 32(2000)3, 465–95.

Hobsbawn, Eric. *Nations and Nationalism since 1780: Programme, Myth, Reality* (CUP, 1997).

Hollander, Barnett. *The International Law of Art for Lawyers, Collectors and Artists* (Bowes & Bowes, 1959).

Howard, John B. *The Paris Agreement on Reparations from Germany* (United States Government Printing Office, 1946).

Hoyer, Sonja, A., Hočevar, Jože, Settomini, Sergio, et al. (eds). *Art Works from Koper, Izola, Piran Retained in Italy* (Ministrstvo za kulturo, 2005).

Huber, Max. *Die Staatensuccession. Völkerrechtliche und staatsrechtliche Praxis im XIX. Jahrhundert.* (D&H, 1898).

Hudson, Robert. *After Yugoslavia: Identities and Politics within the Successor States* (Palgrave Macmillan, 2012).

Huguenin-Bergenat, Yves. *Kulturgüter bei Staatensukzession: Die internationalen Verträge Österreichs nach dem Zerfall der österreichisch-ungarischen Monarchie im Spiegel des aktuellen Völkerrechts* (De Gruyter, 2010).

Jacob, Luis. *La clause de livraison des archives publiques dans les traités d'annexion* (M. Giard et E. Briere, 1915).

Jakubowski, Andrzej. 'National Museums in the Context of State Succession: The Negotiation of Difficult Pasts in the Post-Cold War Reality' in Dominique Poulot, José María Lanzarote Guiral and Felicity Bodenstein (eds), *National Museums and the Negotiation of Difficult Pasts* (Linköping University Electronic Press, 2012), 19–36.

Jakubowski, Andrzej, 'Territoriality and State Succession in Cultural Heritage', *ICJP* 21(2014)4, 375–396.

Jakubowski, Andrzej. 'The Human Dimension of State Succession to Cultural Property: the Balkan Lesson', in Silvia Borelli and Federico Lenzerini (eds), *Cultural*

Heritage, Cultural Rights, Cultural Diversity. New Developments in International Law (Nijhoff, 2012), 369–90.

Jakubowski, Andrzej. 'The Legacy of Serenissima. State Succession to Istria's Jewels', in Kerstin Odendahl and Peter J. Weber (eds), *Kulturgüterschutz- Kunstrecht—Kulturrecht. Festschrift für Kurt Siehr zum 75. Geburstag aus dem Kreise des Doktoranden- und Habilitandenseminars 'Kunst und Recht'* (Nomos, 2010), 227–50.

Jayme, Erik. 'Die Nationalität des Kunstwerkes als Rechtsfrage', in Reinhard Mußgnug (ed), *Aktuelle Fragen des Kulturgüterschutzes: Beiträge zur Reform des deutschen Kulturgutschutzgesetzes 1955 und seiner Angleichung an den europäischen Kulturgüterschutz* (Müller, 1998), 7–29.

Jayme, Erik. 'Institut de Droit International: Tagung in Vancouver', *Praxis des Internationalen Privat- und Verfahrensrechts* 22(2002), 149–51.

Kamminga, Menno T. 'Human Rights Treaties and State Succession', in CoE European Commission for Democracy through Law (Venice Commission) (ed), *The Status of International Treaties on Human Rights* (Council of Europe, 2006), 31–42.

Kamminga, Menno T. 'Impact on State Succession in Respect of Treaties', in Menno T. Kamminga and Martin Scheinin (eds), *The Impact of Human Rights Law on General International Law* (OUP, 2009), 99–110.

Kamminga, Menno T. 'State Succession of Human Rights Treaties', *EJIL* 7(1996)4, 469–84.

Keith, Arthur B. *The Theory of State Succession with Special Reference to English and Colonial Law* (Waterlow and Sons, 1907).

Kellermann, Alfred E., Siehr, Kurt, and Einhorn, Talia (eds), *Israel among the Nations—International and Comparative Law Perspectives on Israel's 50th Anniversary.* (Kluwer Law International, 1998),

Keurs, Pieter Ter. 'Collecting in the Colony: Hybridity, Power and Prestige in the Netherlands East Indies', *Indonesia and the Malay World* 37(2009)108, 147–61.

Keurs, Pieter Ter, (eds), *Colonial Collections Revisited* (Research School CNWS, 2007).

Klein, Natalie. 'State Responsibility for International Humanitarian Law Violations and the Work of the Eritrea–Ethiopia Claims Commission So Far', *GYIL* 47(2004), 214–66.

Knop, Karen. *Self-determination and Diversity* (CUP, 2002).

Kohen, Marcelo, Gustavo, 'Le problème des frontières en cas de dissolution et de séparation d'États', *RBDI* 31(1998)1, 129–60.

Kohen, Marcelo, Gustavo. *Possession contestée et souveraineté territoriale* (Pr. Univ. de France, 1997).

Kohen, Marcelo, Gustavo (ed). *Secession. International Law Perspectives* (CUP, 2006).

Kohen, Marcelo Gustavo. 'Succession of States in the Field of International Responsibility: the Case for Codification', in Marcelo G. Kohen, Robert Kolb, and Djacoba Liva Tehindrazanarivelo (eds), *Perspectives of International Law in the 21st Century: liber amicorum Professor Christian Dominicé in Honour of his 80th Birthday/Perspectives du droit international au 21e siècle* (Brill, 2012), 161–74.

Koskenniemi, Martti. 'Report of the Director of Studies of the English-Speaking Section of the Centre', in Pierre Michel Eisemann and Martti Koskenniemi (eds), *La succession d'États: la codification à l'épreuve des faits/State Succession: Codification Tested Against the Facts* (Nijhoff, 2000), 65–132.

Kowalski, Wojciech. *Liquidation of the Effects of World War II in the Area of Culture* (Institute of Culture, 1994).

Kowalski, Wojciech. *Art Treasures & War. A Study on the Restitution of Looted Cultural Property, Pursuant to Public International Law* (Institute of Art & Law, 1998).

Kowalski, Wojciech. 'Repatriation of Cultural Property Following a Cession of Territory or Dissolution of Multinational States', *AAL* 6(2001)2, 139–66.

Kowalski, Wojciech. 'Restitution of Works of Art Pursuant to Private and Public International Law', *RCADI* 288(2001), 9–244.

Kuntz, Josef, L. 'Identity of States Under International Law', *AJIL* 49(1995)1, 68–76.

Kurtz, Michael J. *America and the Return of Nazi Contraband: The Recovery of Europe's Cultural Treasures* (CUP, 2006).

Lalonde, Suzanne. *Boundaries in a Conflicted World. The Role of* Uti Possidetis (McGill–Queen's University Press, 2002).

Lambourne, Nicola. 'Production versus Destruction: Art, World War I and Art History', *Art History* 22(1999)3, 347–63.

Långström, Tarja. *Transformation in Russia and International Law* (Nijhoff, 2003).

Lauterpacht, Elihu. *Jerusalem and the Holy Places* (Anglo–Israel Association, 1968).

Lauterpacht, Hersch. 'Succession of States with respect to Private Law Obligations', in Elihu Lauterpacht (ed), *International Law Collected Papers of Hersch Lauterpacht,* (Vol. I; CUP, 1977), 121–39.

Layton, Robert, Stone, Peter, G., and Thomas, Julian (eds). *Destruction and Conservation of Cultural Property* (Routledge, 2001).

Lemkin, Raphael. *Axis Rule in Occupied Europe: Laws of Occupation—Analysis of Government—Proposals for Redress* (Carnegie Endowment for International Peace, 1944).

Lenin, Vladimir. *The Right of Nations to Self-determination. Selected Writings* (International Publishers, 1951).

Lenzerini, Federico. *Culturalization of Human Rights Law* (OUP, 2014).

Lenzerini, Federico. 'The UNESCO Declaration Concerning the Intentional Destruction of Cultural Heritage: One Step forward and Two Steps Back', *IYIL* 13(2003), 131–45.

Lenzerini, Federico (ed). *Reparations for Indigenous Peoples: International and Comparative Perspectives* (OUP, 2009).

Lowenthal, David. *The Heritage Crusade and the Spoils of History*, 7th edn. (CUP 2009).

Ludwik Geldberg. 'The Warsaw Treaty of 1970 and the Western Boundary of Poland', *AJIL* 76(1982)1, 119–29.

Luzio, Alessandro. *Gli arazzi dei Gonzaga restituiti dall'Austria* (Arti Grafiche, 1919).

M'Bow, Amadou-Mahtar. 'A Plea for the Return of an Irreplaceable Cultural Heritage to Those Who Created It, 7 June 1978', *Museum* 31(1979)1, 58.

Maclellan, Andrew. 'For and against the Universal Museum in and after the Age of Napoleon', in Ellinoor Bergvelt, Debora J. Meijers, Lieske Tibbe, et al. (eds), *Napoleon's Legacy: The Rise of National Museums in Europe 1794–1830* (GH Verlag, 2009), 91–100.

McTurnan, Kahin George. *The Asian–African Conference: Bandung, Indonesia, April 1955* (Cornell University Press, 1956).

Maget, Antoinette. *Collectionnisme public et conscience patrimoniale* (Harmattan, 2009).

Makonnen, Yilma. 'State Successsion in Africa: Selected Problems', *RCADI* 200(1986-V), 93–234.

Mal'dzìs, Adam (ed). *The Restitution of Cultural Treasures: Problems of Repatriation and Common Usage (Legal, Scholary, and Ethical Aspects)* (Nacyjanal'ny navukova-asvetny centr imja F. Skaryny, 1997).

Malenovsky, Jiri. 'État: création, transformation, frontières, attitude à l'égard du droit international; Problèmes juridiques liés à la partition de la Tchécoslovaquie', *AFDI* 39 (1993), 305–36.

Malmstrom, Susanne. 'The Relevance of International Human Rights Law for the Development of Economic, Social, and Cultural Policy in Bosnia and Herzegovina', in Michael O'Flaherty and Gregory Gisvold (eds), *Post-War Protection of Human Rights in Bosnia and Herzegovina* (Nijhoff, 1998), 157–72.

Mancini, Susanna. 'Rethinking the Boundaries of Democratic Secession. Liberalism, Nationalism, and the Rights of Minorities to Self-determination', *International Journal of Constitutional Law* 6(2008)3–4, 553–84.

Markx-Veldhuijzen, Francisca (ed). *State Succession: Codification Tested against the Facts; Selective bibliography* (Hague Academy of International Law. Center for Studies and Research, 1996).

Martynenko, Igor. *Legal Protection of Historical and Cultural Heritage in the Countries of the Customs Union within the Eurasian Economic Community* (RIOR, 2013).

Mastroberardino, Margaret M. 'The Last Prisoners of World War II', *Pace International Law Review* 9(1997), 315–56.

May, Gaston. 'La saisie des archives du Départment de la Meurthe pendant la guerre de 1870–1871', *RGDIP* 18(1911)1, 22–36.

Mayer-Bisch, Patrice. 'On the "Right to Heritage"—The Innovative approach of Articles 1 and 2 of the Faro Convention', in Council of Europe (ed), *Heritage and Beyond* (Council of Europe Publ, 2009), 59–65.

Mälksoo, Lauri. *Illegal Annexation and State Continuity: the Case of the Incorporation of the Baltic States by the USSR: A Study of the Tension between Normativity and Power in International Law* (Nijhoff, 2003).

Menon, P. K. *The Succession of States in respect to Treaties, State Property, Archives, and Debts* (E. Mellen Press, 1991).

Meriboute, Zidane. *La codification de la succession d'États aux traités: décolonisation, sécession, unification* (Presses Universitaires de France, 1984).

Merryman, John. 'Two Ways of Thinking of Cultural Property', *AJIL* 80(1986)4, 831–53.

Merryman, John. 'The Public Interest in Cultural Property', *California Law Review*, 77(1989)2, 339–64.

Merryman, John, H., and Elsen, Albert E. *Law, Ethics and the Visual Arts*, 5th edn. (Kluwer Law International, 2007).

Mikulka, Václav. 'State Succession and Responsibility', in James Crawford, Alain Pellet, and Simon Olleson. (eds), *The Law of International Responsibility* (OUP, 2010), 291–96.

Mikulka, Václav. 'Succession of States in Respect of Rights of an Injured State', in James Crawford, Alain Pellet, and Simon Olleson (eds), *The Law of International Responsibility* (OUP, 2010), 965–67.

Mikulka, Václav. 'The Dissolution of Czechoslovakia and Succession in Respect of Treaties' in Mojmir Mrak (ed), *Succession of States* (NIjhoff, 1999), 109–28.

Miles, Margaret, M., *Art as Plunder* (CUP, 2008).

Mireille, Hector. 'Enhancing Individual Criminal Responsibility for Offences Involving Cultural Property—the Road to the Rome Statute and the 1999 Second Protocol', in Nout van Woudenberg and Liesbeth Lijnzaad (eds), *Protecting Cultural Property in Armed Conflict: An Insight into the 1999 Second Protocol to the Hague Convention of 1954 for the Protection of Cultural Property in the Event of Armed Conflict* (Nijhoff, 2010), 69–76.

Momtaz, Djamchid. 'La Convention sur la protection du patrimoine culturel subaquatique', in Tafsir M. Ndiaye and Rüdiger Wolfrum (eds), *Law of the Sea, Environmental Law and Settlement of Disputes: Liber Amicorum Judge Thomas A. Mersah* (Nijhoff, 2007), 443–61.

Morgenstern, Carl (ed). *Estonian–Russian Cooperation in Museology: The History and the Disposition of an Art Collection Establishment by Professor Morgenstern at Tartu University in 1803: International Restitution Conference. 15 and 16 September 2000, Tartu, Estonia (Tartu, 2001)* (Tartu University Press, 2001).

Mrak, Mojmir (ed). *Succession of States* (Nijhoff, 1999).

Müllerson, Rein. *International Law, Rights and Politics: Developments in Eastern Europe and the CIS* (Routledge, 1994).

Müllerson, Rein. 'Law and Politics in Succession of States: International Law on Succession of States', in Brigitte Stern (ed), *Dissolution, Continuation, and Succession in Eastern Europe* (Nijhoff, 1998), 5–32.

Müllerson, Rein. 'New Developments in the Former USSR and Yugoslavia', *Virginia Journal of International Law* 33(1992–93)2, 299–22.

Müllerson, Rein. 'The Continuity and Succession of States, by Reference to the Former USSR and Yugoslavia', *ICLQ* 42(1993)3, 473–93.

Müntz, Eugène. 'Les annexions de collections d'art ou de bibliothèque et leur rôle dans les relations internationales,' *Revue d'Histoire Diplomatique* 8(1894), 481–97, 9(1895), 375–93, 10(1896), 481–508.

Müntz, Eugène. 'Les invasions de 1814–1815 et la spolation de nos musées. Episodes d'histoire diplomatique', *La Nouvelle Revue* (1897), 193–207, 703–16.

Musgrave, Thomas D., *Self-Determination and National Minorities* (OUP, 2000),

Mussgnug, Reinhard. *Wem gehört Nofretete?* (De Gruyter, 1977).

Nafziger, James, A.R. 'Historic Salvage Law Revisited', *Ocean Development & International Law* 31(2000)1–2, 81–96.

Nafziger, James, A.R. 'The New International Framework for the Return, Restitution, or Forfeiture of Cultural Property', *N.Y.U. Journal of International Law and Politics* 15(1983)4, 789–812.

Nafziger, James A.R., and Paterson, Robert Kirkwood (eds), *Cultural Law: International, Comparative and Indigenous* (CUP 2010).

Nahlik, Stanisław, E. *Grabież dzieł sztuki: rodowód zbrodni międzynarodowej/La pillage des œuvres d'art historique: d'un crime international* (Ossolineum, 1958).

Nahlik, Stanisław, E. 'La protection internationale des biens culturels en cas de conflit armé', *RCADI* 120(1967)1, 64–163.

Nahlik, Stanisław, E. 'The Case of the Displaced Art Treasures. History and Appreciation of a Polish–Canadian Strife', *GYIL* 23(1980), 255–95.

Nekrasova, Svetlena. 'Kooperation und ihre Grenzen Restitution zwischen Rußland und der Ukraine', *OstEuropa,* 56(2006)1–2 *(Kunst im Konflikt Kriegsfolgen und Kooperationsfelder in Europa),* 301–10.

Nesi, Giuseppe. 'L'Uti possidetis hors du contexte de la décolonisation: le cas de l'Europe', *AFDI* 44(1998), 1–143.

Nieć, Halina (ed). *Cultural Rights and Wrongs* (UNESCO, 1998).

Nieć, Halina. 'Sovereign Rights to Cultural Property', *PYIL* 4(1971), 239–53.

Nowlan, Jacqueline. '*Cultural Property and the Nuremberg War Crimes Trial*', *Humanitäres Völkerrecht* 6(1993)4, 221–23.

'O'. 'International Arbitration under the Treaty of St. Germain', *BYIL* 4(1923/24), 124–30.

Oblak-Černi, Marija, and Bohte, Borut. 'Succession to the Archives of the Former Yugoslavia', in Mojmir Mrak (ed), *Succession of States* (Nijhoff, 1999), 171–85.

O'Connell, Daniel Patrick. *State Succession in Municipal Law and International Law* (Vols I and II; CUP, 1967).

O'Connell, Daniel Patrick. 'Recent Problems of State Succession in Relation to New States', *RCADI* 130(1970)2, 95–206.

O'Connell, Daniel Patrick. *The Law of State Succession* (CUP, 1956).

Odendahl, Kerstin. *Kulturgüterschutz* (Mohr Siebeck, 2005).

Odendahl, Kerstin, and Peters, Mayte. 'The Significance of Cultural Heritage for State Stability and its Protection by International Law', in Julia Raue and Patrick Sutter (eds), *Facets and Practices of State Building* (Nijhoff 2009), 263–79.

Oeter, Stefan. 'State Succession and the Struggle over Equity: Some Observations on the Laws of State Succession with Respect to State Property and Debts in Cases of Separation and Dissolution of States', *GYIL* 38(1995), 73–102.

O'Keefe, Patrick J. *A Commentary on the UNESCO Convention on Underwater Cultural Heritage*, 2nd edn. (Institute of Art and Law, 2014).

O'Keefe, Roger. 'The admission to the United Nations of the ex-Soviet and ex-Yugoslav States', *Baltic Yearbook of International Law* 1(2001), 167–89.

O'Keefe, Roger. 'The Meaning of "Cultural Property" under the 1954 Hague Convention', *NILR* 46(1999), 26–56.

O'Keefe, Roger. *The Protection of Cultural Property in Armed Conflict* (CUP, 2006).

O'Keefe, Roger. 'World Cultural Heritage: Obligations To The International Community As A Whole?', *ICLQ* 53(2004)1, 189–209.

Opocensky, Jan. 'La remise des archives à la Tchécoslovaquie par l'Autriche', in François Louis Ganshof and Guillaume Des Marez (eds), *Compte Rendu Du Ve Congrès International Des Sciences Historique* (Weissenbruch, 1923), 450–52.

Orakhelashvili, Alexander. *Peremptory Norms in International Law* (OUP, 2008).

Paczkowski, Joseph. 'Les principes de la remise des actes en connexion avec les changements de frontière entre les États', in Guillaume Des Marez and François Louis Ganshof (eds), *Compte rendu du Ve Congrès international des sciences historique* (Weissenbruch, 1923), 457–60.

Paenson, Isaac. *Les Conséquences financières de la succession des états (1932–1953)* (Domat-Montchrestien, 1954).

Pallas, William, J. 'Doctrine of State Succession and the Law of Historic Shipwrecks, the Bell of the Alabama: United States v. Steinmetz', *Tulane Maritime Law Journal* 17(1992–93), 343–52.

Pankhurst, Richard. 'Ethiopia, the Aksum Obelisk, and the Return of Africa's Cultural Heritage', *African Affairs* 98(1999)391, 229–39.

Papenfuβ, Dieter. 'The Fate of the International Treaties of the GDR within the Framework of German Unification', *AJIL* 92(1998)3, 469–88.

Pazartzis, Photini. 'Secession and International Law: the European Dimension', Marcelo G. Kohen (ed), *Secession. International Law Perspectives* (CUP, 2006), 355–73.

Pazartzis, Photini. 'State Succession to Multilateral Treaties: Recent Developments, Austrian Review of International and European Law', *Austrian Review of International and European Law* 3(1998)3, 397–415.

Pellet, Alain. 'The Opinions of the Badinter Arbitration Committee. A Second Breath for the Self-Determination of Peoples', *EJIL* 3(1992)1, 178–85.

Perrot, Xavier. *De la restitution internationale des biens culturels aux XIXe et XXe siècles: vers une autnomie juridique. These pour obternir le grade de docteur de l'Université de Limoges* (Université de Limoges, 2005).

Perry, Valery. 'Revering Ethnic and Cultural Cleansing: The Role of Annex 8 in Reclaiming History, Promoting Post-War Reconciliation and Preserving the Unique Cultural Heritage of Bosnia and Herzegovina', *European Yearbook of Minority Issues* 2(2002–03), 197–225.

Peters, Robert. '"Remedying Historical Injustice": Ethical and Historical Considerations in Returning Cultural Materials', in Silvia Borelli and Federico Lenzerini (eds), *Cultural Heritage, Cultural Rights, Cultural Diversity. New Developments in International Law* (Nijhoff, 2012), 141–56.

Petersman, Ernst-Ulrich. 'From State Sovereignty to the "Sovereignty of Citizens" in the International Relations Law of the EU?' in Neil Walker (ed), *Sovereignty in Transition* (Hart, 2003), 145–65.

Petrović, Jadranka. *Old Bridge of Mostar and Increasing Respect for Cultural Property in Armed Conflict* (Nijhoff, 2013).

Piotrowski, Tadeusz. *Poland's Holocaust: Ethnic Strife, Collaboration with Occupying Forces and Genocide in the Second Republic (1918–*1947) (McFarland & Company Inc., 1998).

Posner, Ernest. 'Effects of Changes of Sovereignty on Archives', in Ken Munden (ed), *Archives and the Public Interest: Selected Essays by Ernst Posner* (Public Affairs Press, 1967), 168–81.

Pott, Peter H., and Sutaarga, M. Amir. 'Arrangements Concluded or in Progress for the Return of Objects: the Netherlands–Indonesia', *Museum* 31(1979)1, 38–42.

Poupart, Isabelle. 'Succession aux traités et droits de l'homme: vers la reconnaissance d'une protection ininterrompue des individus', in Pierre Michel Eisemann and Martti Koskenniemi (eds), *La succession d'états: la codification á l'épreuve des faits/State Succession: Codification Tested against the Facts* (Nijhoff, 2000), 465–90.

Powell, Nicolas. 'Notes on German Art Collections Since 1945', *The Burlington Magazine* 96(1954)620, 338–44.

Pradier-Fodéré, Paul. *Traité de droit international public européen et americain suivant les progrés de la science et de la pratique contemporaines* (Vol. 7; Pedone, 1897).

Preece, Jennifer Jackson, 'Minority Rights in Europe: from Westphalia to Helsinki', *Review of International Studies* 23(1997)1, 1–18.

Prott, Lyndel V. 'Problems of Private International Law for the Protection of the Cultural Heritage', *RCADI* 217(1989)5, 215–318.

Prott, Lyndel V. 'Principles for the Resolution of Disputes Concerning Cultural Heritage Displaced during the Second World War', in Elisabeth Simpson (ed), *The Spoils of War, World War II and Its Aftermath: The Loss, Reappearance, and Recovery of Cultural Property* (Harry N. Abrams, Inc., 1997), 225–30.

Prott, Lyndel V. 'Repatriation of Cultural Property', *University of British Columbia Law Review,* (1995) special issue, 229–40.

Prott, Lyndel V. 'The Protection of Cultural Movables from Afghanistan: Developments in International Management', in Juliette van Krieken-Pieters (ed), *Art and Archaeology of Afghanistan: Its Fall and Survival; a Multi-Disciplinary Approach* (Brill, 2006), 189–200.

Prott, Lyndel V. 'UNESCO and Unidroit: a Partnership against Trafficking in Cultural Objects', *Uniform Law Review* 1(1996), 59–71.

Prott, Lyndel V., and O'Keefe, Patrick J. 'Cultural Heritage or Cultural Property?', *IJCP* 1(1992)2, 307–20.

Prott, Lyndel V., and O'Keefe, Patrick J. *Law and the Cultural Heritage* (Vol. I, Discovery and Excavations. OUP, 1984).

Prott, Lyndel V., and O'Keefe, Patrick J. *Law and the Cultural Heritage* (Vol. III, Movement. Butterworths, 1989).

Pruszyński, Jan. 'Das Recht auf Kulturgüter in den westlichen und nördlichen Gebieten Polens', *PYIL* 22(1995/1996), 187–200.

Pruszyński, Jan. *Wnioski rewindykacyjne księgozbioru Ossolineum oraz dzieł sztuki i zabytków ze zbiorów lwoskich [Revindication Claims Regarding the Library of Ossolineum and Works of Art and Cultural Items from the Collections of Lviv]* (Ministerstwo Kultury i Sztuki, Biuro Pełnomocnika Rządu do spraw Polskiego Dziedzictwa Kulturalnego za Granicą, 1998).

Quatremère de Quincy, Antoine-Chrysostome. *Canova et ses ouvrages, ou mémoires historiques sur la vie et les travaux de ce célèbre artiste* (A. Le Clerc, 1836).

Rachmaran, Bertrand, G. (ed). *The International Conference on the Former Yugoslavia. Official Papers* (Vol. I; Kluwer Law International, 1997).

Radan, Peter. 'The Badinter Commission. Secession, self-determination and uti possidetis', in Peter Radan (ed), *The Break-up of Yugoslavia and International Law* (Routledge, 2002), 204–43.

Ragazzi, Maurizio, *The Concept of International Obligations Erga Omnes* (OUP, 2000).

Rainer, Johann. 'Die italienische Militärmission in Wien 1918–1920', in Alexander Novotny and Othmar Pickl (eds), *Festschrift Hermann Wiesflecker zum 60. Geburtstag* (Hist. Institut der Univ., 1973), 267–80.

Rasulov, Akbar. 'Revisiting State Succession to Humanitarian Treaties: Is There a Case for Automaticity?', *EJIL* 14(2003)1, 141–70.

Reichle, Natasha. 'Ideas of Portraiture: Prajñāpāramitā in Java and Sumatra', in Natasha Reichle (ed), *Violence and Serenity: Late Buddhist Sculpture from Indonesia* (University of Hawai'i Press, 2007), 51–84.

Rigby, Douglas. 'Cultural Reparations and a New Western Tradition', *American Scholar* (Summer 1944)273, 278–84.

Rogel, Carol. *The Breakup of Yugoslavia and Its Aftermath* (Greenwood Press, 2004).

Ronzitti, Natalino. *La successione internazionale tra Stati* (Vol. 1; Giuffrè, 1970).

Ronzitti, Natalino. 'Sugli obblighi di restituzione dell'Italia la sentenza amministrativa non convince', *Guida al diritto il Sole-24 Ore*, 26 May 2007, 100–03.

Ronzitti, Natalino. 'The Treaty on Friendship, Partnership and Cooperation between Italy and Libya: New Prospects for Cooperation in the Mediterranean?', 1(2009)1, *Bulletin of Italian Politics*, 125–33.

Ronzitti, Natalino, Calamia, Antonio, and Mengozzi, Paolo (eds), *I rapporti di vicinato tra Italia e Jugoslavia* (Giuffrè, 1984).

Rosen, Sharon. 'The Importance of Interfaith Cooperation for the Protection of Jerusalem's Holy Sites, in Marshal J. Breger, Yitzhak Reiter, and Leonard Hammer (eds), *Sacred Space in Israel and Palestine* (Routledge, 2012), 251–83.

Rosenne, Shabtai. 'Automatic Treaty Succession', in Jan Klabbers and Rene Lefeber (eds), *Essays on the Law of Treaties: A Collection of Essays in Honour of Bert Vierdag* (Nijhoff, 1998), 97–106.

Rosenne, Shabtai. 'Israel: Some Legal Aspects of the Transition from Mandate to Independence: December 1947–15 May 1948', in Alfred E. Kellermann, Kurt Siehr, Talia Einhorn (eds), *Israel among the Nations—International and Comparative Law Perspectives on Israel's 50th Anniversary* (Kluwer Law International, 1998), 311–42.

Rothfels, Hans. 'Nationalität und Grenze im späten 19. und frühen 20. Jahrhundert', *Vierteljahrshefte für Zeitgeschichte* 9(1961)3, 225–33.

Rousseau, Charles. 'États-Uni et Hongrie: Remise de la couronne de Saint Etienne à la Hongrie par les États-Unis', *RGDIP* 82(1978)3, 883–85.

Rousseau, Charles. 'Refus de la Grande-Bretagne de restituer le Koh-i-Noor au Pakistan', *RGDIP* 81(1977)2, 545–47.

Ruiz Ruiz, Florentino. 'The Succession of States in Universal Treaties on the Protection of Human Rights and Humanitarian Law', *IJHR* 7(2003)2, 42–96.

Rumyantseva, Olga. 'Who gets what in the Post-Soviet fall-out', *The Art Newspaper*, 1 May 1992.

Sack, Alexander Nahun. *Les effets de transformations des États sur leur dettes publiques et autres obligations financières* (Recueil Sirey, 1927).

Sandholtz, Wayne. *Prohibiting. Plunder: How Norms Change* (OUP, 2007).

Savoy, Bénédicte. 'The Looting of Art: The Museum as a Place of Legitimization', in Ellinoor Bergvelt, Debora J. Meijers, Lieske Tibbe, et al. (eds), *Napoleon's Legacy: The Rise of National Museums in Europe 1794–1830* (GH Verlag, 2009), 29–40.

Savoy, Bénédicte. *Patrimoine annexé: Les siasies de bien culturels pratiqués par la France en Allemagne autour de 1800* (Vols 1–2; Editions de la Maison des Sciences de l'Homme, 2003).

Sax, Joseph. 'Heritage Preservation as a Public Duty: The Abbé Grégoire and Origins of an Idea', *Michigan Law Review* 88(1990)5, 1142–69.

Schachter, Oscar. 'State Succession: The Once and Future Law', *Vanderbilt Journal of Transnational Law* 33(1993)2, 253–60.

Schairer, Suzanne, L. 'The Intersection f Human Rights and Cultural Property Issues under International Law', *IYIL* 11(2001), 59–99.

Schorlemer, von, Sabine, *Internationaler Kulturgüterschutz* (D&H, 1992).

Scott, Cynthia, 'Sharing the Divisions of the Colonial Past: an Assessment of the Netherlands–Indonesia Shared Cultural Project, 2003–2006', *International Journal of Heritage Studies* 18(2012)1, 1–15.

Scott, Geoffrey R. 'Spoliation, Cultural Property, and Japan', *University of Pennsylvania Journal of International Law* 29(2007–08)4, 803–902.

Scovazzi, Tullio. 'A Contradictory and Counterproductive Regime', in Roberta Garabello and Tullio Scovazzi (eds), *The Protection of the Underwater Cultural Heritage Before and After the 2001 UNESCO Convention* (Nijhoff 2003), 3–18.

Scovazzi, Tullio. *Diviser c'est d'étruire. Ethical Principles and Legal Rules in the Field of Return of Cultural Properties* (UNESCO, May 2009), unpublished.

Scovazzi, Tullio. 'La notion de patrimoine culturel de l'humanité dans le instruments internationaux—Rapport du directeur d'études de la section de langue française du centre', in Tullio Scovazzi and James A. R. Nafziger (eds), *Le patrimoine culturel de l'humanité/The Cultural Heritage of Mankind* (Nijhoff, 2008), 3–144.

Scovazzi, Tullio. 'The Merits of the UNESCO Convention on the Protection of the Underwater Cultural Heritage', in Silvia Borelli and Federico Lenzerini (eds), *Cultural Heritage, Cultural Rights, Cultural Diversity. New Developments in International Law* (Nijhoff, 2012), 267–78.

Scovazzi, Tullio, and Nafziger, James, A.R. (eds), *Le patrimoine culturel de l'humanité/The Cultural Heritage of Mankind* (Nijhoff, 2008).

Sharma, Surya P. *Territorial Acquisition, Disputes, and International Law* (Kluwer Law International, 1997).

Shaw, Malcolm N. 'Peoples, Territorialism and Boundaries', *EJIL* 8(1997)3, 478–507.

Shaw, Malcolm N. 'State Succession Revisited', *Finish Yearbook of International Law* 5(1994), 34–98.

Siehr, Kurt. 'Globalization and National Culture', *Vanderbilt Journal of Transnational Law* 38(2005)4, 1067–96.

Siehr, Kurt. 'International Art Trade and Law', *RCADI* 243(1993)6, 9–292.

Siehr, Kurt. '"Safe Havens" for Endangered Cultural Objects', in Juliette van Krieken-Pieters (ed), *Art and Archaeology of Afghanistan: Its Fall and Survival; a Multi-Disciplinary Approach* (Brill, 2006), 189–200.

Siehr, Kurt. 'The Protection of Cultural Heritage and International Commerce', *IJCP* 6(1997)2, 304–25.

Skaar, Elin, Gloppen, Siri, and Suhrke, Astri (eds). *Roads to Reconciliation* (Lexington Books, 2005).

Skubiszewski, Krzysztof. 'Administration of Territory and Sovereignty: A Comment on the Potsdam Agreement', *AVR* 23(1985)1, 31–41.

Speroni, Mario. *La tutela dei beni culturali negli stati italiani preunitari* (Giuffrè, 1988).

Stahn, Carsten. 'The Agreement on Succession Issues of the Former Socialist Federal Republic of Yugoslavia', *AJIL* 96(2002)2, 379–97.

Stahn, Carsten. *The Law and Practice of International Territorial Administration: Versailles to Iraq and Beyond* (CUP, 2008).

Stara, Alexandra. *The Museum of French Monuments 1795–1816* (Ashgate, 2013).

Stephens, S. Shawn. 'The Hermitage and Pushkin Exhibits: An Analysis of the Ownership Rights to Cultural Properties Removed From Occupied Germany', *Houston Journal of International Law* 18(1995–96)1, 59–112.

Stern, Brigitte. 'La succession d'États', *RCADI* 262(1996), 176–424.

Stern, Brigitte (ed). *Dissolution, Continuation, and Succession in Eastern Europe* (Nijhoff, 1998).

Stern, Brigitte. 'Responsibilité internationale et succession d'États', in Laurence Boisson de Chazournes and Vera Gowlland-Debbas (eds), *The International Legal System in Quest of Equity and Universality/L'ordre juridique international, un système en quête d'équité et d'universalité. Liber Amicorum Georges Abi-Saab* (Nijhoff, 2001), 327–56.

Sterngold, James. 'South Korea Seeks Return of its Artworks From Japan', *The New York Times*, 23 September 2008.

Strati, Anastasia. *The Protection of the Underwater Cultural Heritage: An Emerging Objective of the Contemporary Law of the Sea* (Nijhoff, 1995).

Strecker, Amy. 'Pirates of the Mediterranean? The Case of the "Black Swan" and its Implications for the Protection of Underwater Cultural Heritage in the Mediterranean Region', in Ana Filipa Vrdoljak and Francesco Francioni (eds), *Illicit Traffic of Cultural Objects in the Mediterranean* (EUI Working Paper AEL 2009/09), 59–74.

Šturma, Pavel. 'The Case of Kosovo and International Law', *PYIL* 29(2009), 51–64.

Šulc, Branka. 'Restitution and Succession of Cultural Property from Croatian Museums and Galleries', *Informatica Museologica* 23(1992)1–4, 6–17.

Šulc, Branka. 'The Protection of Croatia's cultural heritage during the war 1991–95', in Robert Layton, Peter G. Stone, and Julian Thomas (eds), *Destruction and Conservation of Cultural Property* (Routledge, 2001), 157–67.

Suny, Ronald D. Grigor. '"Don't Paint Nationalism Red!": National Revolution and Socialist Anti-imperialism', in Prasenjut Duara (ed), *Decolonization: Perspectives from Now and Then Rewriting Histories* (Routledge, 2004), 176–98.

Szasz, Paul C. 'Protecting Human and Minority Rights in Bosnia: A Documentary Survey of International Proposals', *California Western International Law Journal* 25(1995).

Talari, Pekka, T. 'State Succession in Respect of Debts: The Effect of State Succession in the 1990's on the Rules of Law' *Finnish Yearbook of International Law* 7(1996), 134–79.

Tauss, Susanne. '"Robbery is the Most Noble Occupation": The Looting of Art during the Thirty Years' War', in Klaus Bussmann and Heinz Schilling (eds), *1648 War and Peace in Europe. Catalog of the Council of Europe Exposition; Münster, Osnabrück 1998/99* (Vol. 2; S.N. Publishing Company, 1998), 281–88.

Taylor, Francis Henry. *The Taste of Angels. A History of Art Collecting from Ramses to Napoleon* (Little, Brown & Co., 1948).

Taylor, Myron C. (ed). *Wartime Correspondence Between President Roosevelt and Pope Pius XII* (Macmillan, 1947).

Teijgeler, René. 'Preserving Cultural Heritage in Times of Conflict', in Gary E. Gorman and Sydney J. Shep, *Preservation Management for Libraries, Archives and Museums* (Facet Publishing, 2006), 133–65.

Thiele, Just, M. *The Life of Thorvaldsen*, trans. Mordaunt, Roger Barnard (Chapman and Hall, 1865).

Thornberry, Patrick, Martín Estébanez, María Amor (eds). *Minority Rights in Europe* (Council of Europe, 2004).

Tietze, Hans. *Die Entführung von wiener Kunstwerken nach Italien: eine Darlegung unseres Rechtsstandpunktes; mit einem offenen Brief an die italienischen Fachgenossen von Max Dvorák* (Schroll, 1919).

Tietze, Hans. 'L'accord austro-hongrois sur la répartition des collections de la maison des Habsbourg', *Mouseion* (1933)23–24, 92–97.

Toman, Jiří. 'The Road to the 1999 Second Protocol', in Nout van Woudenberg and Liesbeth Lijnzaad (eds), *Protecting Cultural Property in Armed Conflict: An Insight into the 1999 Second Protocol to the Hague Convention of 1954 for the Protection of Cultural Property in the Event of Armed Conflict*, (Nijhoff, 2010), 1–20.

Tomuschat, Christian. 'Secession and Self-determination', in Marcelo G. Kohen (ed), *Secession. International Law Perspectives* (CUP, 2006), 23–45.

Treves, Tullio. *Diritto internazionale: problemi fondamentali* (Giuffrè, 2005).

Trevor-Roper, Hugh. *Plunder of the Arts in the Seventeenth Century* (Thames and Hudson, 1970).

Trial of the Major War Criminals before the International Military Tribunal, Nuremberg 14 November 1945–1 October 1946, Vol. 22 (International Military Tribunal, 1948),

True, Wilhelm. *Art Plunder: the Fate of Works of Art in War, Revolution, and Unrest*, trans. Basil Creighton (The John Day Company, 1961).

Tshiluila, Shaje. 'Inventorying Movable Cultural Property: National Museum of Zaire', *Museum* 39(1987)1, 50–51.

Turk, Danilo. 'Recognition of States: A Comment Symposium: Recent Developments in the Practice of State Recognition', *EJIL* 4(1993)1, 66–91.

Turner, Stefan. 'Das Internationale Kulturgüterrecht und die Zerstreuung des deutschen Kulturbesitzes nach dem Zweiten Weltrieg', in Wilfried Fiedler (ed), *Internationaler Kulturgüterschutz und deutsche Frage* (Gebr. Mann Verlag, 1991), 154–82.

Turner, Stefan. 'Die Zuornung beweglicher Kulturgüter im Völkerrecht', in Wilfried Fiedler (ed), *Internationaler Kulturgüterschutz und deutsche Frage* (Gebr. Mann Verlag, 1991), 19–108.

Tyranowski, Jerzy. 'Boundaries and Boundary Treaties in the Law of State Succession', *Thesaurus Acroasium* 14(1985), 462–540.

Unger, Aryeh L. *Constitutional Development in the USSR: a Guide to the Soviet Constitutions* (Methuen & Co. Ltd, 1981).

Vadapalas, Vlenas, and Żalys Vytautas. 'Secret Protocols to the Soviet-German Treaties of 1939 and the Problem of Prescription in International Law', *Eesti Teaduste Akadeemia Toimetised* 39(1990)2, 131–39.

Vadi, Valentina. 'International Law and the Uncertain Fate of Military Sunken Vessels', *IYIL* 19(2009), 253–77.

Varoli, John. 'Russia Returns Medieval Frescos to Ukraine', *The Art Newspaper*, 1 October 2004.

Vásárhelyi, István. *Restitution in international law* (Akad. Kiadó, 1964).

Vattel, de Emer. *The Law of Nations or Principles of the Law of Nature, Applied to the Conduct and Affairs of Nations and Sovereigns* (G.G. and J. Robinson, 1797).

Verzijl, Jan H.W. *State Succession* (Sijthoff, 1974).

Visscher, Charles de. 'La protection des patimoines artistiques et historiques nationaux: nécessité d'une réglamentation internationale', *Mouseion* (1938)43–44, 7–34.

Vigni, Patrizia. 'Historic Shipwrecks and the Limits of the Flag State Exclusive Rights', in Silvia Borelli and Federico Lenzerini (eds), *Cultural Heritage, Cultural Rights, Cultural Diversity. New Developments in International Law* (Nijhoff, 2012), 279–300.

Vigni, Patrizia. 'The Enforcement of Underwater Cultural Heritage by Courts', in Francesco Francioni and James Gordley (eds), *Enforcing International Cultural Heritage* (OUP, 2013), 125–49.

Visscher, Charles de. *International Protection of Works of Art and Historic Monuments* (The Department of State Publications, 1949).

Visscher, Charles de. 'Les monuments historique et les ouevres d'art en temps de guerre et dans les traités de paix', *La protection des monuments et ouevres d'art en tempes de guerre. Manuel technique et juridique* (Office International des Musées, 1939).

Voitovich, Sergei, A. 'The Commonwealth of Independent States: An Emerging. Institutional Model', *EJIL* 4(1993)3, 403–7.

Volkovitsch, Michael, J. 'Righting Wrongs: Toward a New Theory of State Succession to Responsibility for International Delicts', *Columbia Law Review* 92(1992)8, 2162–214.

Vrdoljak, Ana Filipa. 'Enforcement of Restitution of Cultural Heritage through Peace Agreements', in Francesco Francioni and James Gordley (eds), *Enforcing International Cultural Heritage* (OUP, 2013), 22–39.

Vrdoljak, Ana Filipa. 'Human Rights and Cultural Heritage in International Law', in Federico Lenzerini, Ana Filipa Vrdoljak (eds), *International Law for Common Goods, Normative Perspectives on Human Rights, Culture and Nature* (Hart, 2014), 139–74.

Vrdoljak, Ana Filipa. *International Law, Museums and the Return of Cultural Objects* (CUP, 2006).

Vrdoljak, Ana Filipa. 'Liberty, Equality, Diversity: States, Cultures and International Law', in Ana Filipa Vrdoljak (ed), *The Cultural Dimension of Human Rights* (OUP, 2013), 26–70.

Vrdoljak, Ana Filipa. 'Reparations for Cultural Loss', in Federico Lenzerini (ed), *Reparations for Indigenous Peoples: International and Comparative Perspectives* (OUP, 2009), 197–228.

Vrdoljak, Ana Filipa. 'Self-Determination and Cultural Rights', in Francesco Francioni and Martin Scheinin (eds), *Cultural Human Rights* (Nijhoff, 2008), 41–78.

Vrdoljak, Ana Filipa (ed). *The Cultural Dimension of Human Rights* (OUP, 2013).

Wagner, Peter. From Monuments to Human Rights: Redefining "Heritage" in the Work of the Council of Europe', in *Forward Planning: the Function of Cultural Heritage in Changing Europe* (Council of Europe Publ, 2001), 9–28.

Wallot, Jean-Pierre. 'Les grands principes internationale concernant la migration des archives', *Archives* 28(1996–1997), 3–18.

Walter, Christian, 'Postscript. Self-Determination, Secession, and the Crimean Crisis 2014' in Christian Walter, Antje von Ungern-Sternberg, and Kavus Abushov (eds), *Self-Determination and Secession in International Law* (OUP, 2014), 293–312.

Walter, Christian, 'The Kosovo Advisory Opinion. What It Says and What It Does Not Say', in Christian Walter, Antje von Ungern-Sternberg, and Kavus Abushov (eds), *Self-Determination and Secession in International Law* (OUP, 2014), 13–26.

Warrander, Gail, and Knaus, Veren, *Kosovo*, 2nd edn (Brandt Travel Guides, 2010),

Watts, Arthur. 'Introductory Note to Agreement on Succession Issues between the Five Successor States of the Former State of Yugoslavia', 41(2002) *ILM* 1.

Watts, Arthur. 'State Succession—Some Recent Practical Legal Problems', in Peter Selmer, and Rüdiger Wolfrum (eds), *Liber amicorum Günther Jaenicke* (Springer, 1998), 405–26.

Weller, Marc. 'The Kosovo Constitution and Provisions for the Protection of Minorities in Europe', *European Yearbook of Minority Issues* 6(2006)7, 485–527.

Weller, Marc. 'The Rambouillet Conference on Kosovo', *International Affairs* 75(1999)2, 211–51.

Wescher, Paul. *Kunstraub unter Napoleon* (Mann, 1976).

Williams, Sharon A. *The International and National Protection of Movable Cultural Property: A Comparative Study* (Oceana Publications, 1978).

Williams, Sharon. 'The Polish Art Treasures in Canada, 1940–1960', *CanYIL* 15(1977), 146–72.

Wiessner, Siegfried. 'Culture and the Rights of Indigenous Peoples', in Ana Filipa Vrdoljak, *The Cultural Dimension of Human Rights* (OUP, 2013), 117–57.

Wilske, Stephan. 'International Law and the Spoils of War: To the Victor the Right of Spoils?: The Claims for Repatriation of Art Removed from Germany by the Soviet Army During or as a Result of World War II', *UCLA Journal of International Law & Foreign Affairs* 3(1998)1, 223–82.

Woundeberg van, Nout. 'Enhanced Protection: A New Form of Protection under the 1999 Second Protocol', in Nout van Woudenberg and Liesbeth Lijnzaad (eds), *Protecting Cultural Property in Armed Conflict: An Insight into the 1999 Second Protocol to the Hague Convention of 1954 for the Protection of Cultural Property in the Event of Armed Conflict*, (Nijhoff, 2010), 51–58.

Yarwood, John R (eds). *Rebuilding Mostar: Urban Reconstruction in a War Zone* (Liverpool University Press 1999).

Zašova, Svetlana. 'État successeur ou continuateur?: la République fédérale de Yougoslavie (Serbie-Monténégro) et les Nations Unies: annexe V', in Evelyne Lagrange, and Jean-Marc Sorel (eds), *Droit des organisations internationales* (L.G.D.J./Lextenso éditions, 2013), 317–25.

Zayas de, Alfred, M. *A Terrible Revenge. The Ethnic Cleansing of the East European Germans, 1944–1950* (St. Martin's Press, 1994).

Zayas de, Alfred, M. 'International Law and Mass Population Transfers', *HILJ* 16(1975), 207–58.

Zayas de, Alfred, M. *Nemesis at Potsdam: the Anglo-Americans and the Expulsion of the Germans; Background, Execution, Consequences* (London: Routledge & Kegan Paul, 1979).

Zemanek, Karl. 'State Succession after Decolonization', *RCADI* 116(1965)3, 188–300.

Ziemele, Ineta. 'Is the Distinction between State Continuity and Sate Succession Reality or Fiction?', *Baltic Yearbook of International Law* 1(2001), 191–222.

Ziemele, Ineta. *State Continuity and Nationality: the Baltic States and Russia* (Nijhoff, 2005).

Ziemele, Ineta. 'The State Border between Latvia and Russia and the Doctrine of Continuity of the Republic of Latvia', *Baltic Yearbook of International Law* 9(2009), 95–132.

Zimmermann, Andreas. 'Secession and the Law of State Succession', in Marcelo G. Kohen (ed), *Secession. International Law Perspectives* (CUP, 2006), 209–30.

Zimmermann, Andreas. 'The International Court of Justice and State Succession to Treaties: Avoiding Principled Answers to Questions of Principle', in Christian J. Tams and James Sloan (eds), *The Development of International Law by the International Court of Justice* (OUP, 2013), 53–68.

Index

The manufacturer's authorised representative in the EU for product safety is Oxford University Press España S.A. of el Parque Empresarial San Fernando de Henares, Avenida de Castilla, 2 – 28830 Madrid (www.oup.es/en or product.safety@oup.com). OUP España S.A. also acts as importer into Spain of products made by the manufacturer.

www.ingramcontent.com/pod-product-compliance
Lightning Source LLC
LaVergne TN
LVHW011906200926
848484LV00002B/546
* 9 7 8 0 1 9 8 7 3 8 0 6 0 *